FOAL

SURPRISE ATTACK

Library of Congress Cataloging-in-Publication Data
Hancock, Larry J., author.
 Surprise attack : from Pearl Harbor to 9/11 to Benghazi / Larry Hancock.
    pages cm
  ISBN 978-1-61902-566-0
1. Intelligence service--United States--History--20th century. 2. Intelligence service--United States--History--21st century. I. Title.

  JK468.I6H365 2015
  327.1273--dc23
                                    2015018085

Cover design by Charles Brock, Faceout Studio
Interior design by Tabitha Lahr

COUNTERPOINT
2560 Ninth Street, Suite 318
Berkeley, CA 94710
www.counterpointpress.com

Printed in the United States of America
Distributed by Publishers Group West

10 9 8 7 6 5 4 3 2 1

SURPRISE ATTACK

FROM PEARL HARBOR TO 9/11 TO BENGHAZI

LARRY HANCOCK

COUNTERPOINT
BERKELEY

CONTENTS

....

"Warning does not exist until it has been conveyed to the policymaker and he must know that he has been warned . . . policymakers must realize that warning cannot be issued with absolute certainty, even under the best of circumstances. . . . [N]o matter how brilliant the intelligence performance, the nation will have failed if no action is taken."

—Cynthia Grabo, *Anticipating Surprise: Analysis for Strategic Warning*, 13-14

....

Chapter 1

·························

WARNINGS

here are always warnings!

In January 1941, Admiral Isoroku Yamamoto prepared and transmitted a paper titled "Views on Preparations for War" to the Japanese Minister of the Navy. Yamamoto's paper addressed the likelihood that Japan would enter into war with America if the United States continued to oppose Japan's efforts to expand its territorial influence in pursuit of desperately needed natural resources. Japan had based its effort at becoming a world power on militarization and industrialization. It had invaded and annexed Manchuria (Korea) in 1931 and begun an invasion of China in 1937. Years of military action had dramatically increased its demand for natural resources, in particular oil, iron and aviation gas. In response to the Japanese invasion of China, in 1938 American economic sanctions had embargoed shipments of war materials other than petroleum. When Japan invaded the Vietnam territories of French Indochina in 1940, the Roosevelt administration moved to embargo American sales of scrap iron and steel—extending federal licensing and controls that had already been placed on sales of aviation fuel and high-grade scrap iron.

As of January 1941, Japan had been locked up in years of warfare and was becoming desperate for the natural resources to sustain its military effort as well as the overall growth of Japanese industry. American embargos were hurting the Japanese, but beyond that, the

American Navy represented the only major obstacle to their seizure of the strategic fuel and mineral resources held by the European colonial regimes in Southeast Asia and Malaya. To enable such an effort and remove the American strategic threat, Yamamoto's paper called for a surprise attack on the first day of the war, striking the American fleet at Pearl Harbor in Hawaii.

The strategic threat of Japanese surprise attacks conducted in conjunction with its further military moves south was not something the American military missed. In an almost simultaneous communication of January 1941, Chief of American Naval Operations Admiral Harold R. Stark expressed his concerns of such a Japanese action to the American Secretary of the Navy. In his message, Stark stated his opinion that "[i]f war eventuates with Japan it is believed easily possible that hostilities would be eventuated by a surprise attack upon the fleet [the American Pacific Fleet] or the naval base at Pearl Harbor."[1] Stark identified the most likely threats as being an "air bombing attack" and "air torpedo attack." Secretary of the Navy Frank Knox concurred with Stark's views and referred them to Major General Walter Short, the commander of the U.S. Army's Hawaiian Department.

Admiral Yamamoto's proposal evolved into a detailed tactical plan of attack on the American Pacific Fleet and its port facilities at Pearl Harbor. It was based in his strategic assessment that a Japanese military move through the South China Sea against British and Dutch territories would immediately be threatened by a westward surge of the American fleet—past Midway Island and Guam and on through the Japanese-mandated islands in Micronesia to the Philippines. An early version of the U.S. War Plan Orange (war with Japan) had indeed called for just such a fleet surge, referred to as a "Through Ticket to Manila," but that concept had been refined in 1934 to a more complex set of intermediate fleet movements.[2]

At that time the plan for the American Asiatic Fleet was also changed from a defense of the Philippines to a retreat from the region at the onset of any Japanese attack. As of January 1941, Yamamoto's strategic understanding of America's war plan was outdated—but that had little impact on his continued planning to significantly weaken America's Pacific Fleet before it could move west. And his plan was not based on the need for absolute surprise; the task force that ultimately sailed against Hawaii was briefed and fully prepared to fight its way forward—even under attack—to carry out its mission against Pearl Harbor.[3]

Threat observations and assessments such as Admiral Stark's are a routine and ongoing outcome of strategic intelligence, the assessment of international political and military trends. Strategic warnings are critical to both international policy development and high-level military planning. Stark's views were based on several discrete elements, including the Japanese incursions into Indochina in 1940. Japanese military success had forced the French into an accord allowing a major Japanese troop presence there, as well as granting transit rights for even larger forces. Stark was also persuaded of the threat by other factors, such as the firm stance by Japan that it absolutely had to have increased access to natural resources in Southeast Asia, the continuing diplomatic confrontation between Japan and the United States and a long history of American military exercises that had shown Pearl Harbor to be vulnerable to surprise air attack. In 1932, during a joint Army–Navy exercise the commander of the "attacking" Navy force had raced his carriers to Hawaii, catching the Army defenders totally by surprise. His air attack, at dawn on February 7, had caught defending aircraft on the ground and established full air superiority, exposing the base's facilities to a devastating attack.

Ironically, Stark's strategic assessment was almost immediately joined by a second warning, communicated in January 1941. Edward Crocker, the first secretary to the American embassy in Tokyo, sent a dispatch to the State Department. His warning was based on information from a diplomatic source in Tokyo. Crocker's dispatch related that he had been informed by a Peruvian diplomatic colleague that in the event of "trouble with the United States," Japan would attempt a surprise mass attack on Pearl Harbor. The Peruvian ambassador did not name his specific sources but stated that one of them was Japanese. After considerable inquiry, it was determined that the Peruvian diplomat was most likely passing on comments picked up by his secretary-translator.[4] The ultimate source was unclear, and the timing may have been coincidental, but apparently a range of individuals were discussing and speculating on the possibility of such an attack.

The State Department advised the U.S. Navy of the diplomatic intelligence from Tokyo; however, the official Navy assessment was that with the known disposition of the Japanese naval force at that particular point, no such attack was considered to be imminent. The Navy's short-term assessment was accurate, but it would be much less so when "trouble" seriously escalated in November of that same year—at a point when the entire Navy intelligence network was losing track of several of Japan's airplane carrier groups.

Strategic warnings such as Admiral Stark's are certainly important in the overall study of surprise attacks, but in reality they are only part of the story. The full story involves threat intelligence, more specific warnings, actual alerts and ultimately the command-and-control responses that occur in response to the attacks themselves. All are part of the surprise attack story, and all contribute to understanding the history of America's response to such attacks, on the nation and on Americans and American assets overseas. If we are to fully understand that history, and more importantly learn something from its terrible lessons, it is necessary to become familiar with all the elements, from intelligence collection and strategic warning to the practices and protocols of attack preparedness and response.

Of course it's obvious that the basic elements related to dealing with potential surprise attacks would evolve and become almost agonizingly more complicated as the conventional threats of the 1940s were replaced by several decades of Cold War—with the ongoing threat of preemptive nuclear strikes. The complexity of warnings intelligence and threat response only increased in the 21st century, under a much broader range of threats ranging from global terror attacks from non-state actors to deniable cyber attacks by independents or rogue nations to coordinated military/cyber/space attacks. At the time of this writing, all of those elements remain in the total threat "matrix," exacerbated and magnified by seemingly never-ending military confrontations and tensions among regional powers.

Before venturing into such a complex environment, it is necessary first to explore the basics of surprise attacks in a simpler context, specifically in regard to the Japanese attacks in the Pacific in 1941. While the strike on Pearl Harbor immediately comes to mind, the Japanese actually opened the war against America with a dual attack—two strikes originally intended to occur virtually simultaneously but with that plan going astray in its earliest hours. While the attack on America in Hawaii was indeed largely a surprise attack, with local warnings and alerts over only a few hours, the Japanese moves against the Philippines were delayed by weather. That allowed a substantial, full-fledged state-of-combat warning to be communicated to the military command there.

The attacks in Hawaii and the Philippines provide a virtually unique comparison not only of the warning systems but also the tactical responses that followed, the alerts, the military reaction and the performance of the overall chain of military command and control as seen in two virtually concurrent attacks. Comparison of the American responses to these two "surprise attacks" proves revealing—and more than a little disconcerting. It also provides a series of benchmarks that can be used to determine the extent to which lessons were learned and carried into future decades.

As the months passed during 1941, there were continually increasing indications that Japan was preparing its military to move south, into the region of British Malaya and the Dutch East Indies. Its strategic intentions were clear and openly stated; there were only two real questions: first, whether some sort of diplomatic accommodation would prevent military action, and second, if diplomacy failed, exactly where the Japanese would strike first. From the military perspective, the only viable answer to the question of Japanese attack plans was tactical intelligence, the real-time monitoring of Japanese naval unit movements via radio signal interception and, when possible, aerial reconnaissance. In January 1941, American naval intelligence had determined that the Japanese Navy was in no position to immediately threaten Pearl Harbor. That situation was much less clear by the fall of that year.

American radio tracking of Japanese naval units—signals intelligence (SIGINT)—was being conducted by some sixteen Pacific monitoring stations and an even more extensive network of monitors operated by the Federal Communications Commission inside the United States. That network used direction-finding equipment to track the location of ship broadcasts and was supported by an intense effort at code breaking, to actually translate the coded radio messages being sent by both military and diplomatic personnel. That code-breaking effort had been in play since 1921 when American code breakers had become able to read enough of the Japanese diplomatic codes to provide critical information to the negotiators in the international naval-arms treaty talks of that year. The story of American and Japanese code-breaking efforts prior to and during WWII is far beyond our scope and focus here; readers are referred to John Prados's groundbreaking work on the subject, *Combined Fleet Decoded: The Secret History of American Intelligence and the Japanese Navy in World War II.*

Our first point of focus in the Japanese strikes of December 1941 is on the strategic warnings that were provided to the commands that would come under attack. Threat indications and indications analysis are the key practices in what was to become a highly developed strategic intelligence specialty, "Warnings Intelligence," formalized during the Cold War. Warnings intelligence involves the constant search for developments, indicating that a hostile state or group is preparing an action that could affect American national security. To quote Cynthia Grabo, an intelligence service authority on the practice, "An indication can be a development of any kind. Specifically it may be a confirmed fact, a possible fact or an absence of something, a fragment of information, a photograph, a propaganda broadcast, a diplomatic note, a call-up of reservists, a deployment of forces, a military alert, an agent report or anything else."[5] Some of most significant indicators relate to the steps, including the marshaling and movement of military forces, that the adversary would need to take in order to initiate hostilities.

General indications of imminent Japanese military action began to escalate significantly in the early fall of 1941. In October the commander in chief of the Pacific Fleet (CINCPAC) alerted six American submarines to prepare for departure to Japan on short notice, submarines at Midway Island were directed to assume a war patrol in a ten-mile radius around the island, two submarines were sent to Wake Island to begin a similar patrol and orders were given to dispatch a squadron of reconnaissance planes for daily patrols in a hundred-mile radius around

Midway. In addition, all Army and Navy troop transports, ammunition ships and others with military-related cargo were to be given military escort when sailing to or from Honolulu and Manila.[6]

During late November 1941, primary-attack warning indicators began to be "tripped." False and diversionary Japanese radio messages, obscuring naval movements, became apparent. American tracking station operators noted in their reports that signals traffic had suddenly become very complex, with the same message being repeated numerous times, a characteristic of communications deception and of units going to "receive only" radio silence.[7] By November 24, American naval intelligence was increasingly in the dark about the locations of a number of Japanese aircraft carriers. The ships had gone to total radio silence—just as the Japanese ships had that turned up off Indochina supporting Japanese landings there a year earlier. While they didn't fully realize it at the time, in reality naval combat intelligence had lost track of Japan's First, Second and Fifth Carrier Divisions. It would not locate them again until after hostilities had begun.

While the location of several Japanese carriers had become problematic, signals intelligence was able to track the movement of a number of heavy cruisers and battleships proceeding toward the South China Sea. The implications of those movements were not lost on the naval command, and Pacific Fleet Commander Husband Kimmel advised Naval Operations and the Navy command in the Philippines that the Japanese were engaged in an active military operation, involving two task forces. It appeared that Japanese military action was imminent.

The implications were also fully understood in the highest circles of military command in Washington, D.C. On November 24, Chief of Naval Operations Stark dispatched a top-secret estimate of the situation to the senior Navy commanders in the Pacific, CINCPAC Kimmel in Hawaii and Admiral Thomas Hart in the Philippines:

> *Chances of favorable outcome of negotiations with Japan very doubtful. This situation coupled with statements of Japanese Government and movements of their naval and military forces indicate that a surprise*

*aggressive movement in any direction including attack
on the Philippines and Guam is a possibility. Chief of
Staff has seen this dispatch concurs and requests ad-
dressees to inform senior Army officers in their areas.
Utmost secrecy necessary not to complicate an already
tense situation or precipitate Japanese action.*[8]

It would be hard to visualize a situation involving a broader range of strategic warnings. CINCPAC had advised Washington and the Philippines
that Japanese military action appeared to be imminent. The chief of Naval
Operations had advised CINCPAC and the Philippines' Navy commander
to expect surprise attacks on American installations in conjunction with
Japanese military action. Within days, Washington made the situation
clearer by specifically issuing a "war warning" message to all Pacific military commands, including not only Hawaii and the Philippines but those
responsible for the West Coast and the Panama Canal. The wording in the
message to Admiral Kimmel in Hawaii was especially specific:

*Chances of favorable outcome of negotiations with
Japan very doubtful. This situation coupled with statements of Japanese Government and movements of
their naval and military forces indicate that a surprise
aggressive movement in any direction including attack
on the Philippines and Guam is a possibility. Chief of
Staff has seen this dispatch concurs and requests ad-
dressees to inform senior Army officers in their areas.
Utmost secrecy necessary not to complicate an already
tense situation or precipitate Japanese action. This dispatch is to be considered a war warning. Negotiations
with Japan looking towards stabilization of relations
with Japan in the Pacific have ceased and an aggressive move by Japan is expected within the next few
days. The number and equipment of Japanese troops
and the organization of the naval task forces indicates*

an amphibious operation against the Philippines, Thai
or Kra peninsula or possibly Borneo . . . [9]

For our focus, certain points need to be noted about these messages. First, in terms of strategic/threat warning, the general threat of surprise attack was seemingly as evident as we will find in virtually any of the instances of the following decades, including that of a terror strike inside the United States in the fall of 2001. Second, while the commanders at Pearl Harbor would receive the most criticism and actual disciplinary action following the initial Japanese attacks, it was the Philippines command, in particular General MacArthur, who had been most specifically warned that the imminent Japanese military action would involve a surprise attack on his forces. Finally, the last sentence of the message sent to Kimmel and Hart, with its order to conduct defensive preparations in secrecy, brings up a subject to devote considerable discussion to as this work proceeds—the concept and effectiveness of "deterrence."

In its classic usage, deterrence is a simple concept, involving the availability and use of sufficient power to preclude an attack through the threat of immediate and overwhelming reprisal. In future chapters, we will see atomic deterrence emerge as a major military strategy, initially for America and later for the Soviet Union. The practice of Cold War atomic deterrence involved—and continues to involve even in the 21st century—highly visible retaliatory forces. However, in the days before the Japanese attacks, America's military preparations were being taken in great secrecy, with the great concern over "provoking" the Japanese. The quandary of effective deterrence versus the risk of provocation is a subject that we will also consistently revisit as we proceed.

By the end of November 1941, strategic warnings with regard to imminent Japanese military action, including surprise attacks on American forces, were in place. The next step in defending against attack rested with the theater military commands. In particular it rested on two different elements of defense. The first element involved preparations for detecting and intercepting any incoming attack, well beyond striking range of the attack's target. The second was a realistic assessment of the minimum time available given detection of an incoming attack and the preparation of a defense based on no more than that amount of warning.

On December 1, the Japanese changed all naval call signs, seriously escalating their overall tracking disruption efforts. Increased uncertainty for the American signals intelligence network translated to effective disguise for the Japanese naval commanders. As of December 3, combat intelligence in Hawaii was reporting to CINCPAC that no information on carriers or submarines was being developed. CINCPAC staff were also receiving information from various sources including Naval Operations that a broad range of Japanese embassies were burning code books and classified material—the list of embassies included those in Hong Kong, Singapore, Batavia, Manila, Washington and London. Several of the embassies had even been ordered to totally destroy their own diplomatic code translation machines. Both Admiral Kimmel in Hawaii and Admiral Hart in the Philippines were advised of the actions of the Japanese embassies. Washington felt it was a key short-term "indicator"—clearly war was going to break out within a matter of hours or at most a few days.[10]

While many Japanese carriers and submarines had "gone missing," signals tracking did indicate a concentration of naval forces in the vicinity of both Taiwan and Indochina; large numbers of ships had formed into convoys. That very large flotilla was designated the "South Expeditionary Force" and appeared to be in the process of moving. British reconnaissance aircraft confirmed the southern movement of a convoy on December 5. On December 6, London advised Washington that the two convoys had been observed sailing toward Malaya; the two parties included eight cruisers, twenty destroyers and at least thirty-five transport ships. Estimates had been made that the force could contain up to twenty-five thousand troops.[11]

Clearly the Japanese were moving as predicted and in a force composition that suggested not only attack but invasion. The only Japanese carriers being tracked were those in the area of the southern force, where they had been monitored for some time. The locations and movements of all other major carrier groups remained unknown. And in the first days of December, the Army's newly established air warning system (AWS) reported Japanese aircraft flying reconnaissance missions over the Philippines.[12] Strategically only one question remained: Would the Japanese engage in a major military offensive while leaving their flanks open to attack from American forces in the Philippines?

In terms of warning indicators, virtually all types had been "tripped"—dramatic changes in diplomatic staff activities, the creation and actual deployment of very large war fleets headed toward publicly stated Japanese resource objectives, extensive diversionary measures to conceal the movements of key naval assets such as aircraft carrier groups. There seemed to be little doubt that the Japanese would strike against the British and Dutch colonial territories, and in that event the United States would honor its mutual defense commitments and implement its war plans against Japan. The United States was preparing for war, with the limited resources it could siphon off from its ongoing support of Britain and convoy protection activities in the Atlantic. The Pacific commands were reacting, under orders to maintain an extremely low profile, accelerating training, readying ships and aircraft and preparing for combat in the western Pacific.

On December 5, the U.S. aircraft carrier *Lexington* and an escort of cruisers were dispatched from Hawaii with a cargo of fighter aircraft for the reinforcement of Midway Island. A scouting force led by the cruiser *Indianapolis*—consisting of five older destroyers converted to mine sweepers—was sent to the area of Johnston Island. Another group, led by the carrier *Enterprise*, was near Wake Island, having earlier been sent with reinforcement aircraft for the base there. In addition, Washington had decided to break a long-standing rule and had sent two specially equipped photo reconnaissance B-24 bombers to Hawaii. CINCPAC Kimmel was advised that the planes were to overfly and covertly photograph Japanese bases in the Mandates (islands in the central Pacific earlier assigned to Japanese governance by the League of Nations) during a trans-Pacific flight to the Philippines.

Beyond that, dramatic moves had already been made to build up the Army Air Forces in the Philippines. Hawaii had been stripped of its own B-17s, which were sent on to the Philippines. The American war plan for conflict with Japan (War Plan Orange) specified not only the defense of the Philippines but offensive air raids against all Japanese forces and bases within range of air operations. Specifically Secretary of War Marshall had designated attacks from the Philippines as being of "great strategic importance" in establishing a threat to the flank of any Japanese advance to the south. If the Japanese moved, General MacArthur was expected to engage the Japanese as quickly as possible in support of the war plan.[13] The newly created Army Air Forces in the Far East, with MacArthur in command, had been with the mission not only of supporting the war plan but of developing a "strategic defense in Asia."

As of December 1941, American military forces in the Philippines, Hawaii, the Panama Canal and even the west coast of the United States had been alerted with a war warning, a warning of imminent hostilities. In terms of command and control, the Pacific commands had received the highest possible warning, and there were very specific expectations within senior command levels as to what the field commanders would be doing in terms not only of anticipated offensive and defensive preparations but in providing for their own tactical intelligence. The Navy's signals intelligence and code-breaking teams had been and would continue to be aggressive in their attempts to locate Japanese naval forces, but Japan's tightly controlled radio practices and extensive signals diversionary transmissions were proving effective. In retrospect, all the indications of pending attacks by the Japanese were in place—along with the historical knowledge that the Japanese military inevitably "protected its flanks" and engaged in surprise attacks. Yet while the data was there, the coherent practices of preparing for the onset of combat were lacking.

During one of the many official inquiries following the surprise attacks of December 7 and 8, 1941, the observation was made that there was "no doctrine on how to identify the symptoms," nothing had been laid out on how to analyze and evaluate indicators, and the military lacked "any idea that intelligence should give warning of a surprise attack before a declaration of war." The threat indications were being registered, but there was "no thought of lining them all up and trying to put two and two together, otherwise than by haphazard memory. . . . There was no pretense of a considered assembly of the bits and pieces of military intelligence. There were only able but much too busy top executive officials trying to do the job of intelligence off the cuff."[14] The commanders in both the Philippines and Hawaii appear to have focused on the injunction to prepare their defense while maintaining a low profile; however, not "provoking" the Japanese offered little opportunity to deter them. The result was that both commands effectively lost the option of long-range detection and interdiction of incoming attacks. The only option left on the table was that of detecting any actual attack and employing an extremely quick defensive response.

For both commands, detection was going to have to rely on two basic tools: Aerial reconnaissance and radar and air warning systems were available to the commanders in the Philippines and Hawaii. Yet as several inquiries and a number of excellent books have revealed, those commanders seem to have focused their primary attention not on those assets but rather on preparations for going on the offensive in the western Pacific. Tracing the actual measures taken by both commands will lead us into the details of alerts, reconnaissance and air defense in both Hawaii and the Philippines.

The results of those measures—and their total failure—served as extremely bitter lessons for the nation's military. The American defeats in Hawaii and the Philippines were burned into the minds of virtually all the senior American military commanders who went on to fight the Second World War. The casualties they suffered, fighting back from a series of defeats in the first two years of the war, the narrow margin between victory and defeat—all of it helped burn the thought of surprise attack into their memories.

The experience would drive a generation of officers to focus on defending the nation against surprise attack—and produce an ongoing postwar demand for threat intelligence regardless of cost or risk. Beyond that, the attacks in both Hawaii and the Philippines allow a unique historical comparison not only of warning systems but of military reaction, alert practices and the performance of the military command-and-control system. Comparison of the responses by both commands is revealing—and more than a little disconcerting, foreshadowing certain patterns that continue to reappear. Most importantly, it provides a series of benchmarks that we will reference when exploring similar warnings and attacks over future decades.

Chapter 2

....

INTERDICT OR INTERCEPT

A s of late November 1941, there was virtual certainty that a Japanese military advance into the British and Dutch territories in Southeast Asia and Malaya was imminent. That certainty was confirmed in early December with United States detection and tracking of large flotillas advancing south toward those areas. Given the ongoing mutual defense planning and commitments to both the British and Dutch, there was little doubt that the United States would soon be engaged in combat in the western Pacific. The only questions were exactly where and when it would begin.

The military leadership in Washington continued to follow President Franklin Roosevelt's cautions against provoking the Japanese with any overt acts. Roosevelt himself was largely focused on developing military support for the British and the implications of escalating German naval engagement in the Atlantic. With much of the nation politically still leaning toward isolationism, the initiative was largely left with the Japanese. It would be the Japanese war plans that defined the initial combat.

With the likely aggressor holding both the strategic and tactical initiatives, American commands in the Pacific were left to operate in a state of high alert and active defense. The operational context of the alert was especially complicated because of the fact that both Army and Navy commands played major offensive and defensive roles in Hawaii and the Philippines—and the anticipated missions of the two services were quite different. The commander of the Pacific Fleet, Admiral Husband Kimmel, was located in Hawaii, but his oversight and mission were for overall Pacific Fleet action. That mission left him with the command responsibility for fleet defense but with a primary focus on what appeared to be imminent combat in the South China Sea and across the waters of the western Pacific. It was assumed that American naval combat would begin around the islands known as the Malay Barrier (Malaya, Borneo, Sumatra, Java—the chain of islands between the South China Sea and Australia). Kimmel's responsibilities were broad, and his orders affected forces across the width of the Pacific. Admiral Thomas Hart, headquartered in the Philippines, operated under Kimmel's direction and carried the responsibility for coordinating naval operations with America's allies in the region.

Both Kimmel and Hart had concerns over defense of fleet bases and installations. As early as March 1941, Kimmel had urged the Army commander of the Hawaiian Department to review the status of the air warning systems on the Hawaiian Islands. Kimmel stressed that in his view, defense against aerial attack was a first priority and all means had to be taken to ensure an adequate air detection and defense for the fleet.[1] Kimmel had asked for a review of the air defense, given that the Army had actually been assigned the responsibility of defending the fleet at the Hawaiian anchorages from air attack. From a military perspective, the best possible air defense for the fleet would have been the interdiction of any carrier-launched attack. Ideally that would require detecting enemy ships at sea and attacking them before they could successfully launch strike aircraft. A less satisfactory alternative was detecting incoming aircraft formations and attacking them with interceptors before they came within firing and bombing range of the key Navy anchorages and facilities on the islands.

The Army commander, Major General Walter Short, was himself quite aware of the need for a reliable air warning system; one of his first projects upon taking the command had been to investigate the existing system, and he had been adamant about stopping the quibbling between various units and groups that had delayed work on creating an effective Aircraft Warning Service for the islands. His correspondence of the time spoke to creating a detection system that could spot incoming aircraft at a seventy-five-mile range around the islands and provide for pursuit aircraft to take to the air for interceptions within a "minimum time."[2] Accomplishing those goals and intercepting attacking planes offshore would certainly have done a great deal to blunt the air attacks that struck Pearl Harbor. However, actually interdicting an attack would have required intercepting the enemy at a much greater distance, before planes could be launched from aircraft carriers or assembled into strike forces. Interdiction was possible only if an attack was detected well out at sea, and that could be done only through long-range air reconnaissance patrols.

The lack of long-range aerial reconnaissance was the key element in the failure to intercept the Japanese carrier forces as they made their final approach to Hawaii. If enemy carriers could have been attacked at their aircraft launch ranges—some 200 to 250 miles out—American air and naval engagement could have delayed and at least disrupted Japanese operations. A series of prior naval and air exercises had prepared for just such interdiction, the most recent one being in May 1941, when a joint Army–Navy exercise had detected an attacking flotilla several hundred miles at sea and effectively attacked them.[3] Admiral Yamamoto had prepared the Japanese attack on Hawaii with that contingency well in mind; his forces were fully prepared to fight their way into striking range.

By the fall of 1941, the Navy had taken the position that it simply could not support long-range patrol flights from Hawaii—based on its own lack of planes and personnel as well as the need to conduct ongoing fleet sea operations and maintain a high state of readiness for an anticipated westward surge. In conjunction with its sea operations, the naval groups dispatched to transport interceptor aircraft to Wake and Midway islands were conducting aerial patrols, but those patrols limited long-range reconnaissance to specific corridors to the west and southwest of Hawaii.

Yet even if the Japanese Pearl Harbor attack was not detected and interdicted at sea, there was still a reasonable chance of intercepting incoming aircraft and engaging them before they could begin their bombing runs. That responsibility was totally on the Army, its Aircraft Warning Service and the modern pursuit aircraft that were to be stationed on alert on a number of island airfields. The Hawaiian Army command believed that it was able to mount successful medium-range interception. On November 14 an exercise was conducted in which "enemy" carrier plane launches were detected some eighty miles at sea. Six pursuit planes took to the air within six minutes, intercepting the incoming aircraft some thirty miles from Pearl Harbor.[4] The Army General Officers were reportedly impressed—unfortunately, the devil is always in the details, and the conditions of that exercise were far from routine on the island and, as it turned out, very far from the reality of December 7, only weeks later.

On the Navy side, its routine in-shore air patrols out of Hawaii had changed little since the previous summer of 1940; no significant changes had occurred even following the war warning of November 27. Worse yet, the relatively short-range naval air patrols were conducted in an unchanging pattern. Japanese agents on the islands reported that the Navy planes departed at breakfast, returned at lunchtime and then took off again to return before sunset. No nighttime patrols were conducted. The Navy was focused on protecting its fleet from surprise submarine attack, patrolling waters close in to the islands. Those patrols did prove effective for their limited mission, identifying and supporting attacks on Japanese submarines over several hours prior to the air strikes of Sunday, December 7, but they offered very little warning of an incoming air attack.

As of early December, the Army on Hawaii had a total of twelve B-17 bombers that could have been used for long-range reconnaissance, but half of them were out of service, having been cannibalized for parts. New B-17s were all being routed to the Philippines, to establish a true offensive threat close on the Japanese flank. Based on its lack of ability to conduct a comprehensive long-range patrol around the island, the decision was made that no long-range patrolling was viable. Instead, the Hawaiian Army defense relied largely on its air warning system, based on radar detection and a communications network between various observers and its interceptor commands.

The radar system was to have had three large, stationary transmitters; however, the towers for their antennas had not yet arrived, so they remained inactive. Six mobile radars had been deployed but were largely being used for training. In contrast, the Panama Canal had been sent two radar sets in October 1940, and by November 1941, both units were being operated twenty-four hours a day.[5] The Hawaiian mobile radar sites operated during regular weekly duty hours but had also been tasked with operating from 4:00 AM to 7:00 AM in the morning. It was one of those mobile stations that actually detected and reported the inbound Japanese air groups on the morning of Sunday, December 7.

That radar site was in the process of shutting down when a trace suggesting a large formation of aircraft was noted. The formation was "enormous," estimated to be at least fifty aircraft and at a range of 132 miles. The operators determined that they should inform the Air Warning information center, even though they were now beyond their normal duty schedule and the information center would likely have shut down as well. The center's plotting staff had indeed departed at 7 AM, the end of their special Sunday morning shift. At the point when the center's number was called, the aircraft were some 110 miles out. The call was answered by the switchboard operator, who happened to notice one of the pursuit aircraft officers who was acting as an assistant in flight control that morning. The officer was new to the job, having completed only one shift in interceptor control a few days earlier.

During normal duty hours the control center was charged with plotting aircraft reported by the various mobile radar units. Depending on the radar contacts, they would attempt to identify the aircraft—but identification was a major problem because the War Department policy of the time was that all military flight information was classified and not generally communicated. The Army identification center also had no real-time information on Navy flights. Given the number of transit aircraft moving through Hawaii, the lack of friendly aircraft information presented a very fundamental problem.

As it happened, the report of the incoming Japanese formation was disregarded because the flight control officer heard information from a pilot friend that certain music was played on a local radio station whenever a group of aircraft was coming in from the States—the aircraft would home in directionally on the commercial broadcast—and he had heard just such music on his way to work. Based on that, he assumed that the radar report had been generated by friendly aircraft coming into the islands, and no alert was forwarded to the Army pursuit aircraft commander.

At the time of that initial radar detection, an effective tactical warning of the incoming air strike would have given at least thirty minutes' warning to get pursuit fighters into the air.[6] But the reality of the situation was that such a warning was meaningless because the pursuit aircraft had been dispersed and configured to prevent a sabotage attack from the ground. Later inquiries determined that it would have taken two to three hours to arm and launch a significant aerial defense. At the time of the attack the standing order for alert aircraft was four hours, and that order had not been changed following the war alert of November 27. There had also been no further effort to coordinate "friend or foe" identification following the war alert.[7] The few planes that did manage to get off the ground during the Japanese attack acquitted themselves extremely well—but there was simply no "alert" air defense capable of responding to match the timeframe of even the best possible radar warning.

What emerged from a later inquiry into the American defenses was an obvious series of disconnects in the Hawaiian Department's air defense system. There was no long-range Navy or Army reconnaissance that would have provided the hours necessary to assemble and launch an aerial interdiction force. The tactical Army radar net and intercept control center were not operating at anything like a war alert status. Even if they had been, the actual radar detection and warning would have been fruitless, since the radar's range was totally inconsistent with the time required to put the alert pursuit fighter force into the air over the island. Such a failure to synchronize known detection capabilities with the defense in place is one we would encounter on a number of occasions through the years, including the attacks on New York City and Washington, D.C., in 2001.

Clearly the Hawaiian air defense had suffered from some very fundamental problems. Any chance of interdicting an approaching force at a distance had been forfeited by the lack of long-range aerial reconnaissance. Beyond that, the available radar and intercept control system were not staffed or operating under anything approaching true war alert conditions, a fact that would later amaze the War Department, given its war alert warning to both Hawaii and the Philippines.

In spite of the failure of the Army's aircraft warning system, the Navy's inshore air and surface patrols could have provided a final level of tactical warning. Such a warning could have at least raised an alarm in time for the fleet to fully man all the gun stations on its ships as well as the anti-aircraft gun defenses on shore—at least establishing a final alert and ready "point defense" for the fleet.

At 6:30 AM, a Navy stores and supply ship, the *Antares*, was moving toward the Pearl Harbor anchorage. At that point its crew sighted what they took to be the conning tower of an unknown submarine. It appeared that the sub was maneuvering into the harbor, and the sighting was reported to the destroyer *Ward*, on inshore waters patrol. By 6:40 the *Ward* had engaged the sub with depth charges and transmitted a radio report describing the submarine's sinking.

At that point a series of telephone calls began going up the Navy ship chain of command, slowed by a number of busy signals. At the same time, calls were going up the air patrol side of the command chain, relating the separate sighting of an unidentified submarine by a Navy patrol aircraft. While the calls were proceeding, the *Ward* established sound contact with yet another unidentified submarine at 7:03 AM. The *Ward* immediately attacked with depth charges and visually confirmed oil bubbles, indicating the sinking of the craft.

However, due to the fact that there had been a number of previous false reports of submarine encounters—or reports that had not been verified—when these submarine contact reports reached CINCPAC commander Admiral Kimmel, he did not immediately conclude that an organized attack was in progress. The entire submarine reporting process took approximately half an hour, at the end of which Kimmel was still holding on any decision to escalate the fleet alert, waiting on "further developments."[8] The first wave of Japanese torpedo bomber strikes began at approximately 7:51 AM.

Admiral Kimmel had been caught in a decision-making quandary that we will repeatedly observe in regard to ambiguous attack warnings—in both the United States and the Soviet Union. If Kimmel had immediately elevated his alert conditions—ordering ship's crew to man weapons positions, raising steam in his battleships or even beginning to unmoor and surge them out of the harbor—such measures would have become obvious to the public—and to the Japanese agents reporting on activities in the harbor. The press would have demanded an explanation, questions about an imminent Japanese attack would have been raised and Japanese spies would have been given a perfect view of what the fleet was able to do to defend itself. Kimmel had been instructed to conduct both his defensive and offensive preparations with a major concern toward not escalating international tensions, or raising fear among the local civilian population. Later inquiries determined that he had taken those cautions very seriously.

In later decades, during the Cold War, duty commanders of America's strategic nuclear forces would be placed in an even worse quandary. Increasingly advanced technology detection systems would produce a number of atomic attack alerts. At that point the Strategic Air Command senior officer faced an imminent decision either to "flush" alert bombers off their airfields or possibly lose them all within ten to fifteen minutes—if an incoming missile attack was real. If the alert indication was a mistake (a flock of geese, a meteor shower, etc.) and he chose to surge his force airborne, the Soviets might well interpret it as the first indication of an American attack. The decision was awesome in its implications; a mistake could be either a "country-breaker" or a "career-breaker."[9]

In terms of tactical warning, the American forces on Hawaii had received well over an hour's notice from the first submarine engagement and some forty-five minutes' warning from the initial radar detection of a very large incoming aircraft formation. The Army air defense system had totally failed to respond to the warning. The Navy alerting system had worked far better with Admiral Kimmel at least receiving word of multiple submarine encounters. Yet those responsible for ordering a response viewed the warnings as ambiguous and were still awaiting further information as the attack began.

The surprise attack on Pearl Harbor exposes a number of issues, including the limitations of tactical warning, the realities of communications at the beginning of an attack and the difficulties in linking attack detection to actual defense. It also raises some serious cautions in regard to the human side of the command and control, even at a purely local level. A perfectly adequate plan for the defense of Hawaii had been prepared in early 1941, but a lack of resources and global priorities had prevented its execution. The actual defense that had evolved simply was no match for the attack that had been projected—a projection that was agonizingly similar to what happened on that Sunday morning in 1941. But the commanders had not stepped back and matched their capability to what the Japanese had been expected to do; their detection systems and alert forces did not match up with even the best warning they might receive. It will not be the last time we observe such a mismatch.

Of course, it seems that defensive plans and preparations should work much more effectively in situations where an attack is preceded by conclusive advance warning. In that regard, we are able to make an extremely accurate comparison between defense against surprise attack and defense with warning—over a period of a single day in 1941. The attacks on the Philippines on December 8, 1941, were no surprise at all. There were literally hours of warning for the Philippines, and there should have been no "command quandary" for General Douglas MacArthur. He received immediate notice that the Japanese had attacked the United States in Hawaii and that American forces were in active combat with the Japanese.

In fact, the Japanese strikes against the Philippines occurred following a much more specific set of warnings than those given to Admiral Kimmel and Major General Short in Hawaii. The Washington warnings of November had specifically mentioned the threat of a Japanese surprise attack on the Philippines. Beyond that the American war planning directed MacArthur to prepare for both a defense of the Philippines and strategic attacks on Japanese bases in coordination with the British and Dutch. In the event of military action by Japan, MacArthur was to go on the offensive immediately and utilize the strategic bomber force that was being developed under his command. The war plan specifically called for the bomber force to "conduct air raids against Japanese forces within tactical range."[10]

Major General Lewis Brereton, the Army Air Forces' commander for the Philippines, was very active in preparing for improved air operations during 1941, but he faced a great number of challenges, both in the weeks before the Japanese attacks and in the hours immediately after the first Japanese air strikes. As in Hawaii, the Philippines did have operational radar units and an air warning service linked to P-40 pursuit aircraft. However, after close inspection, Brereton informed both General MacArthur and Army headquarters in Washington that his bomber force was exposed to air attack and that the Philippine air defense was "totally inadequate." Army chief of staff George Marshall replied to Brereton that he understood the issue but that the Philippines were being reinforced at as fast a rate as possible and that all involved were subject to a "calculated risk" that the Japanese would not attack prior to April 1942, when a sufficient strategic bomber force would be in place as a deterrent.[11]

A September 1941 practice exercise of the air warning system resulted in the total failure of the air defense, validating Brereton's concerns. Even with general warning of an incoming air attack exercise, the ground-controlled intercept network totally failed to put fighters in contact with a simulated attack on the major American air base at Clark Field. The failure exposed the fact that even with radar detection, extensive practice between ground controllers and interceptor pilots is necessary to bring about successful interceptions—especially when the radar does not have a height-finding capability as the early units did not. Under conditions of clouds, rain or even haze—not to mention darkness—it was not uncommon for interceptors to totally pass by attacking formations either above or below them.

Although Brereton had placed his forces on twenty-four-hour alert status following the November 27 war warning—with all groups at around-the-clock readiness and all training canceled—the Philippine air defense appears to have been no better and possibly worse than that in Hawaii. The Philippine command had fewer trained personnel and shocking shortages of combat supplies such as ammunition. Fifty-caliber ammunition for the pursuit aircraft was in such short supply that there was virtually none for pilot gunnery practice or even to live-sight the machine guns on new P-40 fighters prior to the actual Japanese attacks. Many of the fighters went into their first combat engagements only to find their guns simply did not work.[12]

The one advantage that the Philippines had, and were aggressively pursuing, was long-range reconnaissance. That capability included both Army B-17 bombers and Navy long-range PBY patrol aircraft. In July, Navy long-range patrols spotted and tracked the Japanese naval force that had completed its control over southern Vietnam. British and American air patrols proved effective in tracking the Japanese surge toward the Malay Barrier in the late fall of 1941. Beyond that, American long-range reconnaissance focused on the large Japanese-held air bases on Formosa (Taiwan). Those bases were within striking range of the Philippines and posed the major air threat to key installations such as Clark Field north of Manila; a number of major Philippine installations were within six hundred to seven hundred miles of the Japanese bases on Formosa.

Reconnaissance of Formosa was critical for two reasons: First, monitoring any major new concentration of bombing forces provided another indication that attack was imminent. Second, it was critical to developing bombing maps and navigation aids for use in attacking such a strategic Japanese target as quickly as possible in the event of hostilities. Air commander Brereton requested MacArthur's authorization for high-altitude reconnaissance over the Japanese air bases on southern Formosa immediately following the war warning of November 27—his request was denied. However, MacArthur had already been advised that the War Department was waiving prior concerns over provocation in order to fly B-24 bombers on photo reconnaissance over the Japanese-mandated islands in the central Pacific. The aircraft were to land in the Philippines after the overflights of the Japanese islands.[13] And American forces in the Philippines began to observe Japanese military reconnaissance flights over the islands beginning the first week of December 1941.

Although MacArthur failed to approve a comprehensive high-altitude reconnaissance of Formosa, both Army B-17s and Navy PBYs maintained long-range surveillance of the island and monitored the Japanese aircraft buildup as best they could. On December 5, a Japanese fighter fired on one of the Army bombers, and a day later, on December 6, the reconnaissance reported the Formosa airfields "stacked with bombers," clearly indicating an imminent air offensive.

At 3:55 AM on December 8 (December 7 in Hawaii), the War Department sent General MacArthur a cable stating that hostilities with Japan had commenced following a surprise attack on Hawaii and Pearl Harbor. By 5:15 all Philippine commands had been informed of the war condition, confirmed by Army headquarters in Washington, and were in a full state of alert. MacArthur himself had failed to respond at all to the War Department cable, and a second message directing him to reply immediately was sent at 7:37 AM.

That War Department cable also received no response, and at 7:55 AM Washington telephoned MacArthur directly; at that point Washington was advised only that two attacks on Philippine locations had already occurred. Some five hours later, at 12:55 PM, Clark Field was attacked by Japanese bomber formations, and half of the Army's strategic B-17 bomber force was destroyed on the ground—along with a third of the command's best P-40 interceptors and its major radar facility.

Clearly there were issues with command, control and communications to the Philippines, and those will be discussed in detail in the following chapter. Yet in contrast to Hawaii, the Philippines had not only received very specific strategic warnings and local tactical intelligence of an imminent attack, they had received several hours' notice that American combat with Japan was already in progress. The unfortunate result was that even with warning, its air defense performed very much as Brereton had advised Marshall it would—ineffectively.

A very early aerial attack, just after midnight, had been detected by radar, and pursuit aircraft were launched. Due to the lack of height-finding radar, the two aircraft formations totally missed each other in the dark. Radio communications both within the air defense network and with the interceptors proved very unreliable, and because the P-40s required considerable alert time to reach the height of the Japanese bombers, the P-40s were also relatively ineffective at high- versus lower-altitude combat. The long-distance radio alert networks and special tactics that the American Volunteer Group in China (the "Flying Tigers') would later develop with the P-40s were simply not available in the first air combat over the Philippines.[14]

Most significantly, the attack on the Philippines was not a surprise attack; MacArthur had immediate intelligence indication of pending air attacks, and he had hours of warning and notification of a state of combat from Washington, based on the Hawaii attacks. While his air defense may simply have been hamstrung by its inherent problems, there were no such limitations in regard to his other major mission—compliance with the strategic bombing element of the war plan.

His air commander was most definitely aware of that mission and began an immediate push to implement bombing against Formosa. At 5 AM, Brereton had requested permission to launch bomber strikes but was denied access to MacArthur by his military aide. Brereton tried again at 7 AM—by then two locations in the Philippines had been bombed—and was told not to make the first "overt act." At 8 AM Brereton pushed again, expressing strong concern about having his own bombers hit on the ground; he received no reply until 8:50. At that time he was told that he should conduct further reconnaissance of Formosa before launching attacks. It was only at 10:14 AM that MacArthur actually authorized bombing missions, but then only to be conducted in late afternoon.[15] Shortly after the noon hour, the planes Brereton had organized for the Formosa strike were destroyed on the ground at Clark Field.

Following the war, it was learned that the Japanese air strikes had been delayed by low-level fog and unfavorable weather on Formosa. If Brereton had been given permission to send off the strikes that he requested as early as 5 AM, his B-17s would very likely have caught the Japanese air attack on the ground on Formosa. The Japanese force would have been fully fueled and armed with maximum bomb loads. Such an American attack would have produced absolute carnage among the Japanese force, with potentially strategic effect. In addition it might well have left the Army's B-17 force intact, for sustained bombing of the inbound Japanese naval force.

The lessons learned from the Japanese attacks on Hawaii and the Philippines remain clear and specific. Long-range reconnaissance can detect and allow the tactical warning required for interdiction of surprise attacks. To do so it must be constant, effective and not constrained. Long-range intelligence was not available to Hawaii; it was to the Philippines—where its value was negated by delays in command decision-making.

Tactical warnings on the order of forty-five minutes to an hour were available to Hawaii, but communications problems and ambiguity of the information prevented the alerting that would have at least given the American fleet a chance for an effective point defense. The Philippines had concrete tactical warnings of several hours. Its air defense system was simply not up to the task. On the other hand, the Philippines had more than ample warning to fulfill its strategic mission. The reasons for failure in that task were clearly at a local command level; no viable explanation for MacArthur's delay in executing his war plan was ever obtained.

However, those were not the only obvious points of failure. Other areas of failure were just as identifiable but more complex—and largely due to human factors. As we shall see, major problems in command, control and communications became painfully clear as follow-on inquiries proceeded.

Chapter 3

....

ERRORS OF COMMAND

In the months and years following the attack on Pearl Harbor, numerous formal inquiries examined why the Hawaiian Army and Navy commands suffered such a devastating surprise attack, especially given that they had been operating under a clear war warning from their military superiors in Washington, D.C. For a variety of reasons, no such inquiries were made with regard to the disastrous first-day losses in the Philippines. A number of authors have dealt with the personalities and issues of the Pearl Harbor failure; those inquiries and the questions of responsibility are a story in themselves. Readers are referred to Gordon Prange, Donald Goldstein and Katherine Dillon's *Pearl Harbor: The Verdict of History* as the most detailed and objective study of those issues. For our purposes it is most important to evaluate both attacks in the strictly military issues of command, control and communications—referred to in contemporary military terminology as C3.

Command and control in Hawaii and the Philippines appears to have failed on two levels. The first level of failure was based in a series of operational disconnects within the local commands themselves; the second failure was created by a massive gap between local command execution and headquarters command expectations. Based strictly on the communications—reports, memoranda and orders—exchanged between each command and its Washington headquarters during 1941, all levels of command would seem to have been of one accord, with planning and action totally synchronized.

As early as March 1941, Pacific Fleet commander Husband Kimmel directed the preparation of a plan for joint action: to address potential surprise attacks on the main island of Oahu and fleet units within the Hawaiian waters. This planning document (the Martin-Bellinger Report) proved extremely thorough and to a very great extent foresaw exactly the attack that would strike by the end of that same year.[1] In its summary of the situation the report noted that enemy submarines or a fast-raiding force including aircraft carriers escorted by cruisers (sailing from "Orange"/Japan) might well arrive off Hawaii undetected and with no prior tactical intelligence warning.

Such an attack would likely precede any actual declaration of war and would be launched by carriers operating inside three hundred miles of the islands. The sudden appearance of submarines in Hawaiian waters was noted as strong tactical indication of pending attack, and the attack itself was most likely to occur at dawn—to take advantage of an approach during darkness to thwart Navy patrol plane detection. The report even projected the most dangerous area of attack was out of the so-called "vacant sea" waters to the north and northwest of Hawaii, a region less frequently traveled by commercial vessels and not on the normal military transportation routes to the west and southwest of Hawaii.

The report summarized both existing defense deficiencies and necessary steps to defeat any such surprise attack, with the key element being the capability for a full, ongoing long-range aerial patrol around the Hawaiian Islands. It specifically noted that at the time of its preparation—March 1941—the aircraft and personnel required for such a patrol were not available. The report was submitted to Kimmel and copied to Navy headquarters in Washington, D.C., at the end of March. Both the Navy and War departments were pleased with and endorsed the study. Hawaii and Washington were in apparent agreement on the most probable threat and defensive requirements.

The fundamental problem lay in the fact that while the Washington headquarters approved the study and defensive strategy, they did not provide the resources to fulfill the key long-range reconnaissance element of an effective defense. The problem was exacerbated by the fact that neither the Navy nor Army commanders in Hawaii pushed back vigorously enough in their communications to headquarters to ensure they forced higher command attention to the issue. Worse yet, the language in several Army and Navy communications to and from Washington contained few details on or discussion of the full range of defensive measures being implemented. Given the Martin-Bellinger plan, which Washington had endorsed, the War Department assumed that interdiction air patrols were being conducted from Hawaii. However, a November message from Washington simply affirmed that reconnaissance be conducted "as was deemed necessary." Admiral Kimmel was indeed conducting patrols, but only from islands and ships far to the southwest of Hawaii. In turn, following further warnings, Hawaii advised that it was taking appropriate measures against sabotage but made no mention that it did not have the aircraft required to conduct long-range patrols.

Yet as early as December 1940, the Navy had ceased all its long-range air patrols out of Hawaii to focus on training and fleet readiness—those patrols were never restored, even after the war warning of November 27, 1941. Admiral Kimmel never specifically raised that issue with Washington prior to the Japanese attacks, leaving the issue of defensive reconnaissance strictly to the Army, which had been left with the long-range patrol duty.[2]

In turn, there is no evidence that the Navy command or the War Department specifically followed up on the issue of long-range patrols as a critical defense element. There were no higher command inspections of the actual defense preparations and only very general communications from Washington. In later years, testimony from senior command officers made it clear that the command practice of the time was to give directives, pass on warnings and alerts and rely on the theater commands to carry them out. A more detailed involvement was simply not standard procedure and seems to have been viewed as something on the level of interference in the chain of command.

That approach was felt to be consistent with "traditional American military policy." Such a view of command protocol seems consistent with and certainly not unique to headquarters command interaction with Hawaii. The Washington headquarters commands also never made detailed follow-ups or inspections of the other theaters specifically affected by the war warning—the Philippines, Panama or Alaska.[3] Yet, as one follow-up on the congressional inquiry noted, tradition or no, the commander's job "is only half completed upon the issuance of the order; it is discharged when he determines the order has been executed."[4]

The lack of senior command involvement was also consistent between the Navy and the Army. The war warning message of November specifically referenced increased reconnaissance, but General Short's response made specific reference only to his additional actions to defend against sabotage attacks, his primary concern of the time. The War Department made no response to Short's reply message, and the War Plans Division provided no critique of his actions or conducted any further query about his actual increase of reconnaissance and patrol activities.[5] While Admiral Kimmel had focused on the readiness for the fleet and defense of the more exposed American bases to the west, General Short had deferred on any long-range patrols due to limited numbers of long-range B-17 heavy bombers and had passed on the option of using older but available B-18 medium bombers. Short had focused his efforts on training and preventing sabotage. The lack of any higher-level command follow-up left Washington literally in the dark in regard to the reality of Hawaii's true defensive posture—leading to its later shock and state of virtual disbelief following the Japanese attacks.

There is no question that it was standard practice for senior command at the War and Navy departments to "keep their hands off" operations inside the theater and local commands. What appears to be the most fundamental issue with regard to a lack of defense against the attacks on both Hawaii and the Philippines lies in the fact that as events moved into a context of imminent threat, there was no real change from the routine peacetime practices and protocols of command. In concept, all levels of command were in agreement; in execution, there were massive disconnects.

We will examine similar disconnects between Washington and the Philippines command in further detail, but with regard to Hawaii, there were also command disconnects beyond the lack of comprehensive, ongoing long-range air patrols—as called for and agreed upon in the March plan for the defense of the fleet in Hawaii. The core of that plan had been long-range detection and interdiction of an attacking cruiser/carrier force. Ideally the detection would have been within the 700-mile range of the patrol aircraft, giving Army bombers the opportunity for long-range attack and allowing the Navy the chance to surge fleet elements out of Pearl Harbor. This would lead to full-scale interdiction and engage the attackers at sea before they reached a distance of 200–250 miles, at which they could launch their own aircraft. However, if long-range detection failed, medium-range detection by radar in the range of 100-plus miles would allow alert interceptors to be launched. The P-40 pursuit planes would engage and disrupt the attack while the Army and Navy anti-aircraft installations would have dealt with those aircraft that made it through, at least blunting any effective bombing attack, if not totally preventing it.

Washington knew that the Hawaiian command had radar; it had bombers and fighters and extensive anti-aircraft defenses. But given the lack of detail in communications from Hawaii to Washington, there was no War Department appreciation for the true operational readiness of the Aircraft Warning Service or the actual intercept capabilities of the Army Air Forces in Hawaii. In reality, the radar system itself was far from complete: Three major stations had not received their antennas, there was very limited radar experience on the islands and personnel were primarily involved in system familiarization and training. Yet there were eight operational mobile sets, certainly enough to maintain a full war-alert class watch on the most dangerous approach areas—including the "vacant sea" region to the north-northwest. That was conclusively proven by the actual radar detection and tracking of the Japanese air strike on the morning of December 7, 1941. But the available mobile units were operating only during limited hours and not on anything like a full-alert condition, in contrast to the twenty-four-hour alert maintained by the warning service in the Philippines. During the follow-on inquiries, General Short was forced to admit that even if he had the material for a fully equipped network of stations, he would have operated them in the same training mode as he had done.[6]

Even more discouraging than Short's admission was testimony from individuals in the lower levels within his command. Warning and pursuit service personnel directly involved with the air defense painted a picture of senior officers' lack of understanding and basic neglect of the air defense system. Junior officers could not even get permission or personnel to develop an effective combat information control center. The list of fundamental problems was dramatic—the acceptable operational range of the radars on island was only eighty to a hundred miles. There was no reliable communications network among the radar sites, the information/intercept control center and the pursuit aircraft. Liaison command lines between the Army and Navy had not been installed, no "friend or foe" aircraft identification system was in place between the two commands and, worse yet, the War Department was not sharing information about aircraft in transit. In short, there was no "linkage" in place allowing the various pieces of the defense to work with each other, and there were no exercises that forced command attention to the weakness.

Those within the air warning service did share those problems with General Short, but he seems not to have truly understood their implications and even deferred putting an identification system into place until after a state of war existed so as not to hinder training or further complicate a crowded airspace over the main island of Oahu.[7] The final disconnect in the entire system was that Short's own concerns over sabotage resulted in the absence of any truly "alert" interceptor force. Literally it would have taken two to three hours to arm and launch a significant air defense. Given the limited state of the island's radar detection capability, the net result was no organized air defense at all— which was exactly what the Japanese attack encountered early on Sunday morning, December 7, 1941.

There have been any number of articles and books written about issues and failures in regard to the attack on Pearl Harbor, many of them focusing the lack of last-minute—twenty-four to forty-eight-hour—warning. It certainly is true that highly suggestive information was known in Washington but not shared with or communicated in a timely manner to the Hawaiian commanders immediately before the attacks. Yet an objective assessment has to conclude that Kimmel's and Short's performance with regard to executing specific defensive plans developed as early as March was lacking, as was assertiveness in communicating their limitations to higher command. Given Kimmel's caution in going to a full alert on Sunday morning, even with multiple submarines being both sighted and sunk by his patrols, it remains an open question whether he might have responded simply to more warnings from Washington. The low-profile defensive measures ordered by both Short and Kimmel—even under a full war alert—and their lack of responsiveness to ongoing issues raised within their own commands, challenges the idea that further warnings would have or could have compensated for months of lagging preparations.

If Washington had realized the true limitations of the Hawaiian defense, if it had exercised operational oversight and held Kimmel and Short to the defense plan of March 1941, there would have been numerous arguments over tradeoffs, fleet readiness versus training, allocating patrol planes and bombers to Hawaii versus sending them west to the most exposed island bases and the Philippines. There would have been even more objections to transferring ships from the Pacific Fleet to the Atlantic, demands for more equipment, personnel and above all aircraft. There would certainly have been debate about the deployment of Navy submarines, ships or even carriers for forward detection and warning. A heightened level of dialog might have forced some serious attention from the commander in chief and his senior commanders—who instead were primarily focused on the Atlantic. They were looking east, toward actual naval combat on convoy missions to Britain, to the immense needs for equipment by the British and the daunting task of growing and training the standing Army and Army Air Forces. The Hawaiian Army command and the Pacific Fleet had their orders; they were left to execute them. In the broadest terms, command authority was executed—control was not.

It is not difficult to understand why the American high command's attention might have been diverted by what seemed more immediate priorities during much of 1941. However, with the Japanese military movements and the diplomatic stalemate of October and November, its attention to details of defense should have shifted to the Pacific. Given the specific war warning of November 27, it remains difficult to fathom why the U.S. military continued using the traditional "hands-off" command protocol followed by both headquarters staff and commanders in Washington. The lag of operational dialog between Washington and its Pacific commands during the weeks in which combat in the Pacific was considered imminent constitutes an indictment of the command practices being followed in Washington. And at the highest levels, the failure in switching priorities, in breaking from fixed agendas to address other, imminent threats, is one we will consistently encounter as we review surprise attacks in later decades.

The conclusion that there were truly two levels of command-and-control failure in regard to the Hawaiian defense seems obvious, yet only the theater commanders seem to have been disciplined for their failure. Headquarters commanders and staff suffered no military disciplinary action, despite the fact that successive congressional inquiries identified and simply described their basic failure—if you give a command, you (or your staff) have the responsibility for ensuring it is followed. That did not happen in regard to the defense of Hawaii. It appears that the higher command assertion of compliance with traditional military command protocol and the realities of immediately entering World War II seem to have outweighed any disciplinary actions involving the headquarters command or staffs—that and the pressing fact that all parties had suddenly become immersed in full-scale global warfare.

However, Pearl Harbor was not the only unmitigated disaster of the first two days of combat with Japan. The attacks on the Philippines, and the destruction of America's much-vaunted heavy bomber force on Japan's flank, was also a strategic blow. The rapidly expanding Philippines-based B-17 force would have posed a singular threat to Japanese forces moving down through the South China Sea, toward the Malaya Barrier region. More importantly, it might well have put the huge Japanese air bases on Formosa at risk. The Pacific Fleet had been neutralized for a time by the Pearl Harbor attack; the threat of long-range American bombing from the Philippines was totally eliminated by Japanese air strikes.

The combined result gave Japan the time it needed to complete its southern push. It would only be after the totally unanticipated American-carrier-launched B-25B bomber raid on Japan in April 1942 (the Doolittle Mission) that the shock of an air strike against Tokyo and its home islands would force the Japanese military to move back into the mid-Pacific to expand its defensive parameter. That move exposed the Japanese Navy to attack by the only remaining American weapon, the fleet carriers that were not at Pearl Harbor on December 7. The Japanese carrier losses at the battle of Midway Island signaled the end of the Japanese Pacific expansion.

For our purposes, the basic questions are why the Japanese attack on the Philippines was so successful, and how a strategic bombing force so highly regarded in Washington could be totally lost to the American war effort. It is true that amassing a strategic bombing force in the Philippines had been considered a high-risk gambit from the time of its inception. Yet the existence of a bombing force in the Philippines had been viewed as immensely important, since it would have been one of the only immediate deterrents to Japanese territorial expansion. And as a credible deterrent, the heavy bomber force was equally at risk. The Japanese could not be expected to tolerate such a threat to their Southern advance; they would either be forced to remove it or to defer any true push toward the British and Dutch resources they coveted.[8] If and when they made the decision to actually move south, there was virtually no doubt that the Army Air Forces in the Philippines would be attacked.

The American bombing deterrence strategy was quite public and well known to the Japanese. On November 15, 1941, Army chief George Marshall had held a private press conference for several of the largest American newspaper and magazine outlets. In that meeting he specifically stated, "We are preparing for an offensive war against Japan," citing thirty-five heavy B-17 bombers then in the Philippines with more going over as quickly as they were available.[9] By December 10, the American strategic force was to be in place and ready to act; the only risk was that Japan would attack first.

That Marshall press briefing has been confirmed and acknowledged by Secretary of War Henry Stimson himself; its purpose remains unknown, but it was consistent with coverage that had already been appearing in the American press. In October, the *United States News* had run an article on strategic bombing of Japan, tracing routes from a number of potential foreign air bases. The article even noted the possibility of crippling the Japanese fleet with air attacks, triggering a repudiation from the Japanese. More specifically to the point, a similar *New York Times* article was headlined "Philippines As a Fortress—New Air Power Gives Islands Offensive Strength, Changing Strategy in Pacific."[10]

The War Department's air fleet plans were indeed ambitious, intended to place 170 heavy and 86 medium bombers in the Philippines by early 1942. Yet by October 1941, only nine B-17 heavy bombers had reached the Philippines. Those figures were made clear to President Franklin Roosevelt at the end of October, as part of his review of the disposition of B-17 aircraft production. At that point, given the lack of progress in any diplomatic settlement, Roosevelt could have challenged the entire strategy as being far too unrealistic—too little, too late—but he did not. At the same time other more practical matters were being left undiscussed—such as the lack of large amounts of fuel for bomber operations and the difficulties encountered in transporting sufficient quantities of fuel and bombs to the Philippines. The transit situation was so challenging that the B-17's flying out toward the Philippines and Hawaii had to be stripped of guns and ammunition simply to lighten the load so they could make the long-distance flights.

The record shows that General MacArthur had been fully briefed on the strategic bombing from the Philippines and had heartily endorsed it. He had also been part of several discussions in which it was made clear that if the Japanese were to actually invade the British and Dutch possessions, America would have to protect its flank with attacks. In fact, Secretary of War Stimson later remarked that the war warning of November 27 was redundant for the Philippines; MacArthur had already been well advised of the threat and of his role in the new war plans.

Yet if strategic bombing in the event of combat had become a priority goal for MacArthur, certain questions seem obvious: Were there specific bombing plans; what was the state of target reconnaissance; to what extent did the development of navigation and bombing raids and crew training support the strategic bombing mission? What did his command actually do in October, November and early December in an effort to prepare to execute the war plan? The answer is—surprisingly little. The corollary question is what the War Department was doing to monitor the Army Far East Air Force's implementation of this strategic weapon; the answer—even less.

Prior to research of the last decade, little was known about the specifics of the Philippine preparations, simply because there were no official inquiries or investigations comparable to those dealing with Pearl Harbor. Furthermore, there were no disciplinary actions. It is only in the extensive historical research of William Bartch and his books *MacArthur's Pearl Harbor* and *Doomed from the Start* (on the Philippines air defense) that we find truly significant detail.[11] [12]

It was known that MacArthur had directed increased long-range patrolling following the war alert, particularly in the vicinity of Formosa. But although those patrols reported a massive buildup of Japanese aircraft, it appears that virtually nothing was done with that intelligence. Bartch's research reveals that MacArthur was actually directed to conduct active reconnaissance "prior to a state of war"; he was left with the decision to authorize high-level flights over the Japanese targets and even to provide fighter escort for patrols around Formosa if deemed necessary. He also knew that the War Department had authorized overflights of the Japanese-mandated islands. However, he chose not to approve a request for high-level reconnaissance over the Japanese air bases, the sort of reconnaissance necessary for building detailed strike planes for his bombers.

It also appears that MacArthur was well aware that no such preparations had been carried out—we know that because following the attacks on Pearl Harbor, after being informed that a state of American combat with Japan existed, he repeatedly turned down bombing requests from his air chief, responding that air reconnaissance was required before he could authorize an actual strike. It hardly needs to be noted that if MacArthur had taken his war plan assignments seriously, that reconnaissance should have been done and a fully developed set of bombing plans for Formosa should have already existed. Indeed, there should have been a set of basic bombing plans for several Japanese targets.

It can equally be said that the War Department planning staff in Washington should have been asking to review the strategic bombing plans. After all, the secretary of war had held a press conference on exactly that subject. Yet MacArthur was never queried on details of his reconnaissance, or his bombing plans—not even as the senior staffs in Washington, D.C. were monitoring reports on the progress of the Japanese fleets going south, in what was quite obviously an invasion movement. Once again, there was a lack of "linkage," in this case between the war plan and preparation for its execution under combat conditions. And there were no "exercises" related to actually implementing strategic bombing to raise attention to the issue.

All of this leads us to the final "C" in failure in command, control and communications—communications. Disconnects in command and control were clear; in retrospect the issues with communications are equally obvious. There was a very simple and fundamental lack of real-time operational command from Washington to the Pacific theaters on both December 7 and December 8. Amazingly, with long-distance cable circuits available from Washington to both field headquarters, nobody picked up a telephone until it was far too late.

The first error in basic command communications might have been innocuous if circumstances had been different. It began with a code-breaking work against the Japanese diplomatic code, in messages transmitted to their embassy in Washington, relating to the failure of negotiations between the two countries. The upshot was that the Japanese diplomatic staff had been ordered to deliver a specific message at a very specific time and to destroy their code machines. The time would be 1:00 PM in Washington—but lower-echelon military staff were quick to realize that time would be 7:30 AM in Hawaii, the early-morning time frame often noted in regard to potential surprise air attacks.

That news, and its possible implications, began to go up the chain of command, first communicated to Admiral Harold Stark, chief of naval operations. Stark made no specific response other than to ensure the message was carried on to both the White House and the State Department. The message was also taken to the chief of staff of the War Department, George Marshall. Unfortunately, Marshall was late to work, and although his staff tried to rush him through the implications of the message, he was slow to respond. Everyone agreed the message was significant, but there was no focus on its potential timing in regard to Hawaii. Marshall got on the phone to Admiral Stark, suggesting another warning message for the Pacific—Stark demurred, saying that so many warnings had been sent that he hesitated to send any more. However, after considering the situation a bit more, Stark called back within a minute or so, agreeing to a warning message, with priority being given to the Philippines. Apparently none of those involved discussed simply calling the commands, possibly due to prior concerns over the secure scrambler system being effective.

A message was prepared for transmission by the Navy to both Navy and Army commands. Normally Navy radio communications were quite good, but that day atmospherics blocked the signals to Hawaii, and ultimately the message was sent via commercial telegraph service with no special priority. The telegraph messenger in Hawaii was on his way, by bicycle, to deliver it just as the first air attacks on Pearl Harbor began.

It's a frustrating and sad story, possibly a truly missed opportunity to spur an alert at the last minute that would have least provided an increased point defense against incoming aircraft. We have no way of knowing what would have happened even if Stark or Marshall had each picked up his scrambler phone. Marshall himself later said that he would have first called MacArthur and then the Panama Canal Zone.[13]

Yet the story of communications to the Philippines on November 8—following the attacks on Hawaii—is far more damning, including the telephone calls that were not made between Washington and General MacArthur. We will see other failures in communications as we continue—many of them—yet few will be as mind boggling.

At 3:22 AM in Manila, very early on the morning of December 8, a War Department telegram arrived. Not a telephone call, a telegram. At that point the world was aware of the Japanese attacks on Pearl Harbor. The telegram was short and to the point—hostilities with Japan had commenced, Pearl Harbor had been raided, execute your war plan. There was no response from Manila to the War Department for some hours; the War Department then sent another telegram to MacArthur, directing him to "reply immediately."

No reply was forthcoming, and hours later, at 7:55 AM in the morning Manila time, the War Department actually placed a phone call. At that time no explanation for the failure to respond was given; it was acknowledged that two Japanese attacks had already been made inside the Philippines. MacArthur had made no report to Washington for some six hours after being notified that hostilities had begun. In turn he was never questioned about his actions in execution of the war plan.[14]

It was not until 8 AM in the morning that General Marshall personally called MacArthur. The discussion appears to have been brief, with Marshall's concern that MacArthur's planes not be caught on the ground by air attack. A little more than four hours later, a major portion of the American Army Air Forces bombing and pursuit force was indeed caught on the ground and destroyed. No explanation for the lack of response or lack of action following the call from General Marshall was ever made, nor any disciplinary action taken. Communications dramatically lagged behind actual events, and in the end Marshall and others were simply left aghast that the same fate had befallen the Philippines, with more than eight hours' very specific tactical warning.

The successful Japanese attacks of December 7 and 8 had a number of long-term consequences. As noted previously, they created an ongoing military leadership obsession with knowing what potential enemies were doing. They also fostered a trend to more active operational high-command involvement in potential and actual crisis circumstances—if at all possible, they were not going to miss opportunities to interdict attacks in the future.

Beyond that, especially as the Cold War emerged and moved to nuclear confrontation, there would be a major change in command and control. Operational control, enabled by dramatic advances in communications technology, would ultimately be extended all the way to the president in the role of commander in chief. The emergence of what would come to be called "National Command Authority" is a trend that we will follow in great detail. Its goal was to ensure that with National Command Authority, there would be no future disconnects between command and control such as had occurred in Hawaii and the Philippines. Huge amounts of planning and money would be devoted to ensuring that the chain of command would be preserved and operate effectively in real time. We will trace its implementation and effectiveness in following chapters.

Chapter 4

....

A NEW THREAT

Moving beyond the attacks that brought the United States into World War II, we find that even as that global conflict ended, senior American military officers had already begun to take the view that the Soviet Union was in the process of replacing the Axis as the major threat to the security of the United States and to Western, non-Communist governments in general. The American military had received early indications that the Soviets were fundamentally unreliable allies, beginning in the summer of 1944.

In the fall of 1943, General Henry Arnold, commander of the American Army Air Forces, had proposed the idea of staging U.S. bombers through Soviet airfields to attack targets in eastern Germany and Poland. B-17s would be able to hit hard-to-reach targets and draw German air defenses from the west prior to the D-Day invasion. President Roosevelt broached the idea directly with Soviet premier Joseph Stalin, who was extremely reticent. However, after many months of negotiation, plans were accepted for a shuttle bombing operation designated "Frantic."[1]

Unfortunately, Frantic's execution came to match its codename. Although it was initially successful in its first missions, planes returning to the Soviet bases were followed by German aircraft. The Soviets would not allow American fighters to intercept the German reconnaissance aircraft, and the result was a massive 150-bomber German air raid that destroyed 43 B-17s and damaged another 26. The Russians provided virtually no air defense and refused to permit American fighters to go into action. In the end the effort exacerbated American/Soviet military differences. Stalin, then enjoying some of his first major military successes in the war, proved not at all interested in sharing the credit for further victories.

Further confirmation of the Soviet attitude continued; in July 1944 the Soviets refused to return three B-29 bombers that had diverted to a Soviet base during an air mission over Manchuria. The crews were eventually repatriated, but the Soviets kept the bombers, took them apart piece by piece and copied them—quickly providing themselves with the ability to build the long-range bombers that they had lacked. Those copies, which the Soviets designated the "T-4," would eventually be viewed as a strategic air threat to the continental United States in the earliest years of the Cold War.[2]

Concerns about the Soviets were not at all unique to the American military; senior officers in the State Department came to feel that it was simply impossible to negotiate with the Soviets. Russian representatives were empowered only to present demands; they were not even allowed to report what had been presented to them, only to restate what they had said, how well they had said it and what the effect had been.[3] The Soviet unwillingness to truly negotiate or compromise became even clearer during the Allied conference at Yalta in February of 1945.

At that point in the war, the Soviet armies had completely occupied Poland and most of Eastern Europe. Their forces in the east outnumbered those of the allies in the west of Europe by a factor of three to one. The massive development of the Soviet land army had created a reality in which the Western allies had little real choice other than accepting Soviet postwar conditions. During the conference, Russian premier Stalin unabashedly and openly asserted the Soviet position—"whoever occupies a territory imposes its own social system."[4] Events would also prove that Stalin's stated position on "reparations" was equally pragmatic; whatever German territory was occupied by the Soviet Army was quickly stripped of all manufacturing and industrial assets, which were immediately shipped to the Soviet Union.

American relations with the Soviets soured further in the spring of 1945. A dramatic note from Stalin directly to President Roosevelt carried the accusation that the Western allies were responding to peace approaches from Germany and were willing essentially to "sell out" Russia to reach a separate peace. That note was followed by accusations by Stalin that the Western military command was intentionally providing misleading intelligence to the Red Army. Such exchanges seriously swayed Roosevelt's opinions in regard to American/Soviet relations. He privately remarked, "We can't do business with Stalin," describing him as "not a man of his word."[5]

Following Roosevelt's death, ongoing concern over the activities and overwhelming strength of the Red Army in Eastern Europe led to the first American contingency planning for military conflict with the Soviet Union. In May 1945, a photomapping operation designated "Casey Jones" began over Western and South-Central Europe. Its mission was to produce comprehensive maps that would be needed for a bombing effort should the Red Army continue west.[6]

General Lauris Norstad's Army Air Forces Air Plans staff expanded on the preliminary work done in August 1945, developing a document titled "A Strategic Chart of Certain Russian and Manchurian Areas." In essence it was an early strategic targeting study, anticipating the need for long-range bombing of the Soviet Union. That line of thinking reflected a number of senior officers' beliefs, including their rapidly evolving respect for the power of aerial atomic attacks. During the same month, the commander of the U.S. Army Air Forces in the Pacific, General Carl Andrew Spaatz, had proposed that the 509th Composite Group—utilized for the atomic bombing of Japan—should be retained intact. Following his proposal, the group was designated the 509th Bomb Wing. During the immediate postwar period, the 509th flew the only B-29 aircraft configured for atomic bombing; the unit was stationed at Roswell Army Air Force Base in New Mexico.

Early planning for a preemptive attack on the Soviets proved to be fully consistent with a Joint Chiefs of Staff (JCS) planning document issued the following month, on September 20, 1945. The Joint Chiefs expressed the need for a "first strike" strategic atomic policy and directed that during a crisis, even as diplomacy proceeded, preparations to strike a "preventative" first blow should be taken.[7] By October 1945, the Joint Intelligence Committee of the JCS expanded the studies, preparing a more detailed planning draft built around a potential nuclear interdiction strike on the Soviets. In light of their experiences at the beginning of the recent global war, senior military commanders had no intention that the United States would again be placed at risk of losing a war begun by yet another enemy surprise attack on American forces.

The October attack plan called for an attack delivering between twenty and thirty atomic bombs. That was considered a realistic assessment of the number of potential atomic weapons that could be immediately constructed given currently available uranium ore and isotope production facilities. That plan was sent to General Leslie Groves, head of the supersecret Manhattan atomic project. That targeting chart designated fifteen key Russian cities; an appendix listed the number of bombs required to destroy each city—six each for Moscow and Leningrad. The plan also included B-29 staging areas and flight paths.[8]

The final draft of the expanded 1945 atomic strike plan called for the destruction of some sixty-six Soviet cities considered to have strategic importance, through military action and possible atomic attacks. The plan called for stockpiling 466 Nagasaki-class atomic bombs. Because of their general lack of knowledge of atomic bombs and their effective employment by air forces, the planners decided to add further atomic warfare studies as a priority project for the Army Air Research and Development staff.

The continued American focus on atomic weaponry was made public in the October 1945 Navy press conference, held by the commander in chief of the United States Navy Fleet, Admiral Ernest King. Admiral King provided the press with details of a planned atomic test series that was to involve eighty to a hundred surplus target ships. Both the Army Air Forces and the Navy were involved with the test, designed to determine the future survivability of Navy surface ships in the face of atomic attack. In January of 1946, President Harry Truman appointed the Deputy Chief of Naval Operations for Special Weapons, William Blandy, to head a joint Army–Navy task force to conduct the tests—

designated "Operation Crossroads." Two bombs were dropped on July 26, and the project received extensive press coverage, firmly establishing American military preeminence in the public's mind, both domestically and overseas.

American public confidence in its military superiority was buoyed by the atomic tests, while both the State Department and the military's Soviet fears were dramatically substantiated in early 1946. In a major February 1946 public address, Stalin asserted that there was no hope for a peaceful international order; forces fundamentally hostile to the Soviet system posed an ongoing threat, and the Soviets would have to maintain themselves in a state of military readiness. There would be no major downsizing of the Russian military—force reductions were being conducted at a furious pace by the American military—and consumer goods production would be sacrificed to Soviet rearmament. Stalin's speech prompted the senior American diplomat in Moscow to cable a stern and extended eight-thousand-word warning to Washington. George Kennan's lengthy letter described the Soviet view of world affairs as being "neurotic."[9]

Kennan viewed the Russians as obsessed by centuries of foreign incursion and driven to use every possible means of undermining any potential external threat. He perceived that a deeply pervasive fear of the outside world, magnified by the extensive destruction inside Russia and millions of dead in the recent war, was driving them to undermine and destabilize the Western powers. He anticipated the Soviet international policy to be one of political warfare—involving extensive activities to increase Western political uncertainties. He also anticipated that the Soviets would constantly probe and push to exacerbate fears and political chaos in nations adjacent to them. It was a strategy of psychological warfare, designed to preempt the emergence of stronger relationships with the Western powers and with America in particular. Kennan concluded there could be "no peaceful coexistence" between the West and Soviet Russia.[10] His cable produced an uproar in Washington and was circulated by Secretary of Defense James Forrestal to a variety of senior officers in all the armed services.

President Truman's senior State Department advisors were no less outspoken about the Soviet regime. Averell Harriman put the matter to Truman in no uncertain terms, describing the Soviet threat to the West: "[The western allies] were faced with a Barbarian invasion of Europe. [The Soviet Union] meant to take over its neighbors and install the Soviet system of secret police and state control." Any negotiation or agreement with the Soviets would mean abandoning "any illusion that the Soviet government was likely to soon act in accordance with the principles to which the rest of the world held in international affairs."[11]

The view that the Soviets under Joseph Stalin were initiating a state of ongoing political and psychological warfare became prevalent within the American government. Secretary of State Dean Acheson considered that the Soviets, at Stalin's direction, had already begun the run-up to an actual "offensive." The first stage in a territorial move against the West seemed confirmed by Khrushchev's "election" speech and in the Soviet political domination of Poland.

After Poland, the immediate flashpoint of confrontation shifted to Yugoslavia. Soviet military forces moved to support a newly formed Yugoslav government within the Soviet zone of occupation. It had become routine practice for American transports flying relief supplies to use a direct route between Udine in northeastern Italy and Vienna in Austria. That route crossed the far western regions of Yugoslavia, and the Yugoslavs were encouraged by the Soviets to assert their airspace rights. In July two Yugoslav pilots flying Soviet Yak-3 fighters intercepted and challenged an American C-47 transport, which escaped them by flying into cloud cover. In early August another American transport flying the same route was attacked and forced down to a landing. In addition to the four-man Army Air Forces crew, there were four passengers including Hungarians and a Turkish officer. The Turkish officer was badly wounded during the incident; the aircraft and personnel were released within a few days. Within two weeks Yak-3 fighters intercepted and downed another C-37 transport, killing all four of the American crew. In the face of protests that the flight had been forced off course by bad weather, the Yugoslavs simply cited the provocation of some 278 claimed Western unauthorized airspace violations during July and August alone.[12]

The air attacks in western Yugoslavia occurred during a time of international tension, with the Soviets encouraging political unrest in both Turkey and Greece. In particular the Soviets wanted military control over the Bosphorus (the Istanbul Strait), a key to Soviet commercial and naval transit from the Black Sea to the Mediterranean. The Russians were working with a variety of local political factions to destabilize northern Greece and certain provinces in Turkey. Earlier in April, the battleship *Missouri* had been sent to transport the remains of a Turkish ambassador to Istanbul; it remained there as an American show of force until continuing an extensive Mediterranean cruise that summer. It was joined in the Mediterranean by the new American super-carrier, the *Franklin D. Roosevelt.*

Following the aircraft attacks over Yugoslavia, the United States responded by reinforcing its air forces in northern Italy, sending more troops to the demarcation line with Yugoslavia and moving American naval forces into Greek waters. No further military confrontations occurred, but the Soviets continued to engage in political subversion and attempts to establish a Communist political presence in northern Greece, Turkey and Iran.[13]

It seemed that the Soviets and the Anglo-American allies had moved into a mode of full-scale political and military confrontation and that even neutrals would be placed under increasing pressure to declare themselves for either the "East" or the "West." Soviet psychological warfare was in full play. Given this state of affairs, what would seem like rather minor unidentified aerial sightings became a major point of interest for both British and American military intelligence—as well as the State Departments of both countries. The incidents involved a series of reports of "wingless airplanes," first from Sweden and then across other Scandinavian countries.

The first sightings of what came to be called "ghost flyers" or "ghost rockets" occurred in May 1946; the following articles from the paper *Dagens Nyheter,* the first from May 24 and the second from May 26, provide good basic descriptions of the objects being observed as well contemporary suspicions of Soviet responsibility:

> *Two night watchmen in Landskrona-Posten sight*
> *"wingless, cigar-shaped body of dimensions of a small*

airplane, which at regular intervals spurted bunches of sparks from its tail." Estimated altitude at only 100 meters and moving at "ordinary airplane speed" to southwest.

Even if reports of a wingless aircraft spurting fire over Landskrona are to be treated with a certain reserve, it is very possible that what people saw were V-1 bombs fired by the Russians from some experimental station on the Baltic Coast. This statement was made by an air expert, to whom Dagens Nyheter submitted the reports in yesterday's telegrams. The experts state that the whole of Germany has been fine-combed by the occupying powers for robot bomb material and experiments are being carried out zealously. Just as with the Germans, a number of projectiles went on courses not intended (the Bäckebo bomb belongs to these), bombs from the Continent can naturally now land in or make short-cuts over Sweden. The observations made by the inhabitants of Landskrona, namely that the sparks from the tail come at intervals, agrees with the V-1 bomb's manner of operation. It is true that the witnesses have given the length of the projectiles now seen as considerably less than the V-1 bomb's 6-7 metres but it is easy to err on such points.

As spring advanced, the Swedish newspapers began to carry additional reports of flying objects, objects that continued to be described as similar in physical characteristics to the V-1 and V-2 missiles introduced by the Germans at the end of WWII. Within weeks and with continual broad media coverage, those reports blossomed into a wave of similar sightings across the Scandinavian countries. An excellent, detailed study of this wave of sightings can be found in part four of a series of extensive, illustrated chronologies by Joel Carpenter, *Guided Missiles and UFOs: A Tangle of Fear—1937–53.*[14]

Both the British and U.S. military took an early interest in the sightings; a message from the British air attaché in Stockholm on June 1, 1946, stated that the matter had already been discussed with the Swedish Air Force—which had not yet been able to officially confirm any sightings but had agreed to pass on related information of interest. There is additional evidence that American Army Intelligence was concerned in the very beginning that the Russians had pushed ahead in exploiting German technology. On June 24, the Pentagon requested that German rocket scientist Wernher von Braun be interviewed—Washington wanted an immediate evaluation of the German technicians who had been left in the Soviet zone and an estimate of how long it might take for them to perfect an intercontinental missile.[15]

The British air attaché in Sweden began to include newspaper clippings with his reports and made a regular practice of forwarding articles to the Air Staff (Intelligence) of the British Air Ministry. The ongoing reports fueled a growing concern that the Soviets were indeed supplementing political action with psychological warfare. On June 1, 1946, the Swedish daily *Aftonbladet* published the following report:

> *Helsingfors, Saturday. Mysterious objects, considered to be some kind of peculiar "meteors" or some new V-bomb being tested, have flown over Helsingfors. The mysterious wingless projectiles, which fly on a north-east–south-west course, appear to have their "bases" somewhere north of Lake Ladoga. The objects flew over Helsingfors last week, on Friday night.*

Following the June 12 report from Eskilstuna, the Swedish Ministry of Defense issued orders to all its personnel to report such observations to its headquarters and requested that its military attachés in Norway and Denmark also collect and forward reports from those countries. At that point the descriptions in several of the "rocket" sightings certainly did appear to be similar to the German V-1 "flying bombs." A sighting of two objects in Norway—the Norwegian newspaper was referring to such objects as "Flier X's"—gives an example of the similarity:

The "Flier X's" were sighted in daylight by numbers of people. At one location four family members (Sigvart Skaug, his wife and grown son and daughter) had observed one from two separate locations. Mrs. Skaug and her daughter saw them first from the top of a high ridge at a place which is called Badstuakeren. They heard a loud noise in the air and believed at first there was a plane coming. But the sound did not resemble plane noise; it was more like a powerful whistle. Right afterwards they caught sight of two plane-like objects which came from over the edge of the woods at a tremendous speed and so low that the two women involuntarily threw themselves down on the ground. The air current was so strong that the treetops swayed.[16]

The U.S. State Department was quite interested in the unidentified aerial object reports, incorporating them into its messages discussing the recent arrival of six units of the U.S. Atlantic Fleet in Stockholm, one of a number of stops on its European tour. State Department dispatches indicated the objects were coming from the south and were thought to have been launched by the Soviets from Estonia. The State Department suspected that it was a psychological warfare effort to intimidate the Swedes in conjunction with either ongoing loan negotiations or the growing American military prestige associated with the American fleet call and the recent series of highly publicized American atomic tests in the Bikini islands. The Soviets also appeared to be significantly escalating political pressure on Sweden.

The State Department remarks underscore an emerging American view that the Soviets were actively involved in putting intense diplomatic pressure on the Scandinavian countries, in particular Sweden, in order to preserve Russian influence and encourage them to maintain a position of neutrality rather than move to the Western alliance. The remark about the visit of Admiral Henry Hewitt to Stockholm illustrates an active competition for political influence on Sweden coming from both the Americans and the Soviets.

As commander of U.S. Naval Forces in Europe, Hewitt had transferred his flag from London to the cruiser USS *Houston* for what was essentially a diplomatic mission. The cruisers USS *Houston* and *Little Rock*, accompanied by four destroyers, carried out a show of friendly American military strength to a series of ports along the Baltic and North Sea, beginning in June 1946. The flotilla visited Copenhagen, Stockholm, transited the Kiel Canal to Amsterdam, visited Antwerp, went to Plymouth and ended its tour in Lisbon, Portugal—with an average stay of a week in each location.

In Lisbon, the flotilla was joined by one of the newest American aircraft carriers, the *Franklin Roosevelt*. During its time in Lisbon some two hundred Portuguese government leaders put out to sea aboard the carrier to observe air group exercises and demonstrations.[17] As earlier noted, that summer, in response to the continued Soviet pressures against Greece and Turkey, the battleship USS *Missouri* was detached on a Mediterranean cruise following the return of the body of the deceased Turkish ambassador to the United States. The naval initiative emphasized the new American military presence in both Europe and the Mediterranean, with additional visits to Greece as well as Italy, Algiers and Morocco. The *Missouri* flotilla was also commanded by Admiral Hewitt, following his earlier cruise through Scandinavia.

The American State Department sensitivity to Soviet pressures expressed in the diplomatic summary on the "rocket-like missiles," sent by the American embassy in Sweden, provides an excellent illustration of the emerging geopolitical confrontation. The American presence in Europe was growing dramatically, and the Soviets were deeply concerned about that. The report's comments about psychological warfare as a Soviet reaction to the Bikini (Operation Crossroads) atomic tests of July 1946 are especially insightful.

There is little doubt that with intense press and media coverage, the daylight Scandinavian "rocket-like missile" sightings fueled a much broader wave of reports, many involving the sorts of mystery night lights that do little more than overwhelm intelligence groups. But beyond the conventional and the astronomical misidentifications, the Swedish Ghost Rocket committee assigned to study the reports concluded that there was a limited number of very credible close-range daylight sightings—sightings of both winged and unwinged cylinders. Some of the objects had been observed to crash into lakes with very visible impacts. Fragments had been recovered on land and from beneath the service of the lakes. Available documents show that Swedish, British and American military sources were of the same opinion and that their initial estimates were that there were a core of sightings that did indeed represent guided missiles and rockets, very likely launched by the Russians.

An American War Department message of July 16 advised that the Swedish defense staff were studying fragments but that they were small and nothing large had been recovered.[18] Reportedly some Swedish officials believed that the objects might be either test firings or some type of "war of nerves" being launched against the Western Bloc. Apparently the same officials were also concerned about supplying too much information to the British or Americans for fear that it would be used to undermine the vital Swedish position of neutrality. The July War Department report was referred to Army Air Forces generals Carl Andrew Spaatz, Lauris Norstad and Henry Aurand.

The Swedish military also came to believe that at least a few of the sightings related to German V-1–type cruise missile technology and that the objects were subject to some sort of control using narrow, high-frequency radio beams. Potential control centers were calculated, and there was also speculation that ships might be used as control points.[19]

On July 18, the British clandestinely sent a representative from the British military to Sweden, an expert in artillery and rocket intelligence. At the request of the Swedes, the specialist traveled to Stockholm for a briefing, wearing civilian clothes and concealing his military status. He reported that the Swedes had placed a demand for the "utmost secrecy" on British involvement in the matter of the "rocket missiles," previously referred to as "Flyer X"—but, as the broader wave of sightings had developed, more commonly referred to as ghost rockets. The information pertaining to his mission was to be confined solely to selected members of the British and Swedish general staffs. By the end of July, the British air attaché in Stockholm telegraphed the British Foreign Office that he had been asked by Swedish Air Staff to take all possible measures to prevent the Americans from finding out the full cooperation between the British and Swedes in investigating the mystery missiles.

Leakage of the cooperative investigation was seen as potentially embarrassing to Swedish authorities and potentially damaging to their international position of neutrality between the Soviet and Western blocs. The following week, a memorandum to the British Air Ministry reported that the Swedes had reactivated their wartime radars and immediately begun tracking unidentified objects.[20] Given the design and capabilities of the radar sites, the fact that they were able to detect and track the objects suggests the unidentified devices were in the class of either a V-1 cruise missile or some type of glide bomb, both of which traveled at aircraft-class speeds—rather than the V-2 ballistic missile, which traveled at 1,600 miles per second during its flight.

On July 16 one British legation source in Stockholm cabled the British Foreign Office to report that he had met with Swedish Chief of Combined Intelligence. The Swedes were definitely worried that the Soviets were behind the objects but that they would not make a public statement because of "the vital importance of utmost secrecy and delicacy of the position regarding other nations."[21] This view may well have influenced Swedish actions of the following month—which abruptly put a stop to a planned Swedish Air Staff cooperative project with the British, intended to pinpoint the origins of the devices.

A few days later a U.S. War Department memo was sent to the Commanding General U.S. Army Air Forces and copied to General Curtis LeMay—then heading Air Research and Development. LeMay was in the process of moving from that position to take command of Army Air Forces in Western Europe. The memo relayed information on rockets and missiles in Scandinavia that had come in from military attachés and State Department representatives. An attached map showed possible launch sites including Peenemünde, the former German missile center then in the Soviet zone of occupation.

The Swedes themselves did have a limited radar capability, and their concern about Russian involvement was such that the Swedish Air Staff attempted to track the unidentified objects. The initial equipment used was the British Ames 66—Mark II, the RAF designation for the

SCR 615 ground-control intercept set. That unit has a range of only twenty-five miles for objects at a thousand feet of altitude and thirty-five miles up to twenty-five thousand feet.[22] Reportedly in late July, the Swedes obtained a four-minute radar plot of an object approaching from northwest of Uppsala, Sweden, at approximately 3,800 meters. The plot showed the object executing a curve of something like 120 degrees and returning back in the general direction from which it had originated. Given the range limitations of the SCR 615 radar, it would have been impossible to pinpoint the object's point of origin, especially if it were outside of Sweden. The object's speed, low altitude and apparent guidance certainly seemed consistent with an enhanced V-1–class cruise missile of the type both the U.S. and Soviets were working with during that period. To obtain fully documented evidence of the device's origins, a more elaborate radar tracking network had to be established.

By late summer 1946, it appears that both the Swedish and British military were of the opinion that certain of the observed aerial objects were most likely Russian rockets of some type. This explains the decision by the British to send in an RAF technical party under a "cover" to expand radar tracking of the objects—with the obvious intention of documenting their origin. The cover story provided to conceal intelligence interest in the ghost rockets was that of an invitation from the Swedish Air Force to assist with radar and signals equipment for the new Vampire jet aircraft being obtained from the British. One of the team members made two visits to Sweden and recommended locations for the tracking radar.

The full British party was to depart on August 22, 1946, but the whole project was blocked at the last minute by order of the Swedish prime minister, based on unspecified political grounds. The mission and its cancellation did leak to the Swedish media and were reported. Within days the British prime minister demanded an explanation of the cancellation of the radar mission. No formal Swedish reply was received, leaving the British legation in Stockholm to make extensive speculation about possible motives. If an answer was actually provided to the British, it was done secretly. However, in Sweden, although it was impossible to officially document, it appears that the initial political and diplomatic concerns in regard to "secrecy and delicacy" in international relations may very well have overridden any decision to continue a more in-depth technical inquiry or to publicly name the Russians in regard to certain of the objects being reported.

The release of British military documents from this period makes it clear that the Swedish military had indeed been very aggressively investigating the unidentified objects with the help of the British while holding the U.S. military at arm's length. Classified British communications contain considerable information about joint British–Swedish investigations, while American intelligence communications on the subject are often speculative and based largely in news reports or anecdotal conversations.

British documents also reflect the Swedish policy of withholding information from the Americans in order to maintain some level of separation from being seen as a confirmed "Western Bloc" alliance member. The effectiveness of their information control can be seen in the degree of speculation in a mid-August report prepared by the American naval attaché in Sweden. That report comments on the "evasiveness" of Swedish military staff on the subject and focuses on the apparent lack of any practical Swedish response to the objects as an active military threat (no military leaves canceled, no mobilizations, no attempts to intercept the missiles with jet fighters) and as an indication that the Swedes themselves were possibly experimenting with rockets. Apparently the naval attaché was unaware of the active British–Swedish technical collaboration in investigating the mystery rockets. The American naval attaché report also raised the possibility that the objects might be Russian, launched as part of an effort to pressure the Swedes on the proposed Russian–Swedish trade agreement or as leverage to prevent Sweden from joining the Western Bloc.

In direct contrast to the naval attaché's report and speculations on a possible Swedish hoax, in mid-August an Army Air Forces memorandum presented a very different and much more concerned view. The Army intelligence estimate noted that the reports that it had received were insufficient for a conclusive finding. But its initial estimate of the situation was that from a technical perspective, the objects did indeed appear to be guided missiles—missiles with turbojet or ramjet engines, similar to an enlarged V-1.

The Army intelligence report proposed the former German missile development site of Peenemünde as the most likely launching point, although other possibilities included the Aland Islands, the Porkkala area of Finland, and the Dago Islands, Estonia. Generally the launchings appeared to come from the north German coast, aimed northward along the Baltic. A seven-hundred-mile radius of potential launch sites had been reported, and presumed flight range was definitely in excess of one hundred miles. Accuracy was not known, but long-range control of direction and propulsion, long-range homing on cities, and probable short-range homing had been reported. Demolition by explosion or burning charge seems to be indicated as a part of the flights. Although the V-1 cruise missile was mentioned, there was also speculation that the Russians might be testing an improved V-2 rocket design, which the Germans had designated "A-9."[23]

In addition to the technical estimate from Army Air Forces Headquarters, the most significant high-level American intelligence assessment of the ghost rockets is found in a top-secret memorandum from the director of the newly formed Central Intelligence Group (CIG) to President Truman.[24] CIG director Hoyt Vandenberg reported that his Central Intelligence Group had concluded that the "weight of evidence" pointed to Peenemünde as the origin of the missiles and stated that they had information that Swedish radar course-plotting had led to the conclusion that Peenemünde was indeed the launch site.[25]

CIG speculated that the missiles were extended-range developments of the V-1 being aimed for the Gulf of Bothnia for test purposes and not overflying Swedish territory specifically for intimidation. They were thought to be capable of self-destruction by a small demolition charge or burning. An even later American intelligence report, done in January 1947 by the War Department's Intelligence Division, also concluded that hard-core reports were very real devices and that they were of Russian origin. The report concluded that the Soviets were known to be working on various guided missiles. They had the ability to produce, and probably had tested, missiles of the V-1 type, and the best evidence was that there had been a limited number of real sightings of low-flying missiles of the V-1 type.

These American assessments seem to have been subtly confirmed by the Swedish Ghost Rocket committee. A draft memo from that group in December 1946 stated that nearly one hundred impacts had been reported and that thirty pieces of debris were recovered. The reports of objects seen in daylight were considered to have been "real physical objects." There was also mention of "unspecified" information obtained from radio and radar tracking as well as from "special sources."[26] A reference to radar, echo and other equipment observations had been contained in a Swedish Defense Staff statement of October 1946. It seems likely that technical intelligence had confirmed the devices themselves, if not their exact origins.

The implications of these early Western intelligence assessments are dramatic. A summary letter from General Hoyt Vandenberg, serving as Director of Central Intelligence in the newly formed United States Central Intelligence Group (CIG), directed the development of a top-secret report on the subject to President Harry Truman. The report concluded that a core group of observations had been of jet-propelled V-1–type missiles. The devices contained a small explosive charge for self-destruction, and their range had been increased by the elimination of a full-size explosive warhead. The missiles were guided and controlled not only by preset controls but likely by remote radio control. Most importantly, the consensus was that the devices had been launched not for test purposes but rather for political and "intimidation" effect.[27]

At the highest levels of American intelligence—both the War Department and the then-new Central Intelligence Group—the presumption was that the Russians not only had advanced versions of the WWII German rocket designs but that they were quite willing to launch them in areas where they could fall into neutral countries. The Swedish Ghost Rocket committee and apparently the Swedish Defense Staff appear to have concurred in that assessment yet determined to make no official charges for political reasons.

The references to "intimidation" in the CIG report extended to the assessment that the Soviets might well be attempting to influence both Scandinavian politics and Western Bloc diplomatic behavior, demonstrating to Britain that it was within range of such weapons and impressing the United States with its capabilities to quickly develop technically advanced new weapons. It was no small matter that Joseph Stalin appeared willing to introduce such advanced devices into the tense East–West power confrontation—for purposes of political and diplomatic leverage as well as a form of psychological warfare ploy to counter the vaunted American atomic advantage.

The operative question at the end of 1946 was exactly how hard the Soviets were willing to push, how far it might go. If they were willing to take the risk of using captured German weapons for intimidation purposes, for high-risk psychological warfare, did it indicate that they were truly desperate to counter the perceived political and military threat of an American atomic arsenal? Uncertainty about Soviet limits was emerging as a major fear factor. But there were other fears as well.

In point of fact, the American military and senior political leaders were much less sanguine in regard to their military superiority over the Soviets. President Truman was considerably troubled by Moscow's maintenance of a huge standing army of four and a half million men.[28] There appeared to be no doubt that the Soviets were willing to use the overwhelming size of the Red Army to back Soviet political initiatives ranging from Poland, Austria, Hungary and Romania across the continent to Manchuria. It seemed that Stalin was moving toward aggressive territorial hegemony on all the Russian borders, from Persia through the Mediterranean Balkans and potentially even into Western Europe.

Within the American government, the general perception of a potential Soviet military threat continued to be very real. During 1946 Truman had received a one-hundred-page report from two of his presidential staff. The report summarized their fact-finding with the Joint Chiefs, the Secretary of Defense, the intelligence community, the State Department and other sources at the highest levels of government. That report minced no words, calling the Soviet Union's foreign policy "a direct threat to American security . . . designed to prepare the Soviet Union for war" and calling for the United States to prepare immediately for atomic and biological warfare.[29] Truman found the report so volatile that he had the twenty copies confiscated and locked up in the White House safe.

America had pushed back diplomatically against Stalin's creation of an Eastern Bloc and against both his ongoing political aggression and apparent territorial ambitions. But by the beginning of 1947, President Truman and the American military were being forced to face how extremely unprepared the United States was for any immediate conflict. America had fewer than two Army divisions and twelve air groups in Europe. Its total armed forces numbered less than one and a half million. Intelligence assessments determined that the Soviet Army could roll across all of Europe in a matter of weeks; even saving a small beachhead on the Continent would be a major challenge.

In terms of American actual atomic capabilities, the reality of the situation was equally disturbing. During 1946, President Truman, along with the American public, had assumed that the U.S. could rely on its atomic weapons advantage. However, early in 1947, as the new Atomic Energy Commission (AEC) took over from the Manhattan Project, the president was given an atomic weapons briefing. In April 1947 the commissioners privately (and verbally only, since the news was too shocking to be put into writing) informed Truman that a detailed inventory at Los Alamos revealed that there was no atomic stockpile; in fact there was not a single operational weapon in the vault at Los Alamos.[30]

Possibly one bomb could be made operational, but there would be no more for months to come. There were lots of pieces, no weapons, just piles of pieces. There were no experienced assembly teams at Los Alamos and certainly none in the military. And on the "delivery" side, less than half the atomic-bomb-modified B-29s of the 509th Squadron were still operational. Of those, half of the aircraft were constantly out of service for maintenance.[31] If the Soviets had been able to ascertain the true status of the 509th, they would have quickly realized that the American much-touted atomic advantage was actually nonexistent.

Worse yet, the three atomic weapons reactors at Hanford, Washington, had to be shut down due to an unanticipated radioactive "disease." With the Hanford piles down, polonium (used in "charging" the weapons) production would have to cease and any weapons that could be assembled would have only a one-year life span. The production of new bomb cores would take months. The Soviet Union was aware of this reactor problem; during 1947 and 1948 the U.S. would learn just how successful Soviet espionage of the American Manhattan atomic program had truly been—the Russians knew far more about the American program than anyone would have imagined.

The one thing the Soviets seem not to have been aware of was the fact that America had not actually built an atomic weapons stockpile.[32] As it was, the U.S. strategic position was so dire that the Bikini atom bomb demonstration used two of the only three available atomic weapons. The third had been scheduled for the test but was held back specifically in the event of a potential conflict with the Soviets.[33]

A full and "unsanitized" picture of the immediate post–World War II American military position has emerged only in recent years. A 1979 book on the Strategic Air Command describes the Bikini tests as so successful that the third bomb did not need to be dropped.[34] A totally different perspective is offered by historian Richard Rhodes in *Dark Sun: The Making of the Hydrogen Bomb*, including the fact that the primary target of the Bikini atomic test—the battleship *Nevada*—was left afloat and that the B-29's bomb sight was later determined to have been miscalibrated. The reality of the testing was that Manhattan atomic project chief General Groves proposed to the Joint Chiefs that it would be best to save the single remaining weapon in inventory—and they agreed.[35]

One early book on the history of Strategic Air Command—in rather dramatic hyperbole—notes that future historians would record that the supply of American nuclear weapons in the Mariana Islands, available immediately following the atomic bombings of Hiroshima and Nagasaki, was sufficient to "effectively destroy in a single day every Japanese city with a population in excess of 30,000 people."[36] Instead, history now records that there were actually no additional atomic bombs available at all.

In reality, as of 1947, American atomic strike capability was a myth—and beyond that America itself literally had no continental air defense. If the Soviets were preparing for a military advance, or for a surprise attack on the West, the situation was dire.

Chapter 5

....

HOLLOW FORCE

By the early fall of 1945, the highest levels of the American military had begun contingency planning for air strikes on the Soviet Union. Russia's huge, battle-hardened and extremely formidable Red Army was securely emplaced in Eastern Europe. If Stalin had decided to move west from Berlin and occupied East Germany, there would have been no way to resist the Red Army on the ground. Atomic strikes against Soviet military and industrial facilities were seen as the only option for interdicting any surprise moves by Soviet forces. The Army Air Forces plans staff had begun charting targets in both Europe and the Soviet Union, and the Joint Chiefs had endorsed a policy including preemptive air attacks.

However, senior American officers and staff quickly came to realize just how much more preparation was going to be needed to create a truly credible, long-range strategic air force. Aircraft, personnel, weapons, bases, logistics and training all posed immediate challenges. At the end of 1945, a global B-29 bombing force was simply a goal, no more a reality than had been a strategic B-17 heavy bomber force in the Western Pacific in the fall of 1941.

The Strategic Air Command (SAC) was created in 1946, with a mission of conducting long-range bombing offensives anywhere on the globe as well as performing long-distance land and sea reconnaissance.[1] According to the Strategic Air Command's first chief, General George

Kenney, the command was in "sad" condition in its earliest days. Only one group was equipped with the most modern high-altitude B-29 bombers; the rest of the bomber groups existed largely on paper, at best equipped with medium-range B-25s. All of SAC's assigned fighter groups were under-strength. In addition to its lack of aircraft, SAC also lacked qualified instructors and had critical shortages in radar, power plants and even aircraft maintenance. America—and the Russians—assumed that SAC was standing at the ready as a very real strategic deterrent; in reality it was something much less.[2, 3]

In addition to its developmental challenges, SAC was going to have to meet three major goals to fulfill its mission. It had to become highly mobile, given that it was to be a global force and its initial aircraft would have to operate from bases outside the continental United States for strikes against Soviet targets. In order to become a true deterrent force, it would have to be a "force in being"; there would be no time to mobilize, arm, train, etc.—SAC would need to be on alert twenty-four hours a day, seven days a week. That would be something new in modern warfare, a supreme challenge.

Finally, SAC was going to have to be exceptionally good at its core skills—navigation and bombing. That would mean a routine of ongoing bombing exercises, primarily at night, using radar navigation.[4] The year 1947 was definitely a very challenging one for SAC, but progress was made against virtually all its goals, especially air mobility. Deployments into the Pacific went well, although Europe proved more difficult. A SAC effort based out of Gieblestadt, Germany, was greatly handicapped by territorial overflight permissions. The new governments in Europe were quite touchy about their airspaces. Polar operations initially proved exceptionally difficult, and SAC focused its efforts on bases in Iceland and the British Isles.

It was especially challenging for SAC to develop at the rate required by the new and constantly more demanding American war plans, themselves constantly evolving in light of an apparently escalating threat of Soviet military confrontation. In 1946 the MAKEFAST plan had called for six SAC groups to deploy to England and Cairo, Egypt, in the event of war; their mission would have been to destroy three fourths of Soviet petroleum production in order to stop any Red Army surge west.[5] Those attacks would have been conventional bombing; in 1947 a new war plan—EARSHOT—called for the addition of atomic bombing. It was succeeded by plan BROILER in March 1948, a much broader attack from bases in England, targeting Soviet government centers, urban industrial areas and petroleum facilities. A succession of war plans followed during 1948, FROLIC, and then HALFMOON in May. The HARROW atomic bombing annex to HALFMOON described dropping the entire American inventory of some fifty atomic bombs on twenty Soviet cities. The goal was to paralyze at least half of Soviet industry, but realistically the plan still assumed the Red Army would overrun all of Western Europe during the first phase of any conflict.

In 1948, General Curtis LeMay succeeded General Kenney as SAC commander. LeMay began to fine-tune many of the personnel, mobility and logistics initiatives that Kinney had begun, but beyond that his most significant impact was to put the command on a permanent "war footing." Deterrence based in a strategic force operating on a "war footing" can be illustrated by comparing LeMay's early SAC command actions with the actions not taken in regard to the strategic bombing mission assigned to General Douglas MacArthur's command, the mission that had been assigned as a deterrent against Japan.[6]

In his first months at SAC, LeMay had numerous concerns about his new command, but three deserve special comment—all built around the question of war readiness. The first question was the actual SAC war plan, which of course should have included not simply target lists but details of units, weapons and personnel assignments, navigation charts, transit logistics and numerous other details including actual bombing schedules. LeMay began by requesting a copy of the war plan; that simple request created a furor, with a senior staff officer hand-carrying what turned out to be a very slim folder, with only a few sheets of paper. LeMay was definitely not impressed by a war plan for the nation's only strategic atomic strike force that "could be carried in an officer's pocket."[7]

Then there was the bombing. LeMay had already been warned by an earlier headquarters review that raised questions about SAC's training. There was little question that the command was understaffed and many of its personnel overworked; the issue was whether with its growing pains its bombing ability was really as good as its training paperwork seemed to indicate. Shortly after his arrival, LeMay asked for the bombing scores—they were so good he simply didn't believe them, so he then asked for the radar photos of the bomb runs. It quickly became apparent that the scores were good because the plane commanders were not bombing from their specified combat altitudes but from much lower heights of only twelve thousand to fifteen thousand feet. When LeMay asked the obvious question, the reply was that the bombing radars weren't working accurately at combat altitude, so the crews simply lowered their attacks to an altitude where the radar was effective. Beyond that, LeMay noted that they were not even "bombing realistic targets . . . they were bombing a reflector out on the ocean . . . it was completely unrealistic."[8] As one of his staff officers put it, "everybody thought they were doing fine . . . the first thing to do was convince them otherwise."

LeMay was a very convincing commander. His no-nonsense leadership style could be abrasive, but it was also imminently objective and factual—sometimes disturbingly so. While commanding American units flying missions over Europe, LeMay reached the conclusion that the only way to improve bombing accuracy was to fly directly to the target, with none of the standard "zigzagging" then in use to avoid flak. When challenged by his pilots that such a tactic would be suicidal, he responded in a manner that became his command trademark, stating that he believed it could be done and that he would personally fly the lead bomber. He did so, proving in the tactic; LeMay then proceeded to fly lead aircraft on the most dangerous missions, the position most targeted by German air defense.

Within months of taking command of SAC, LeMay ordered the entire command into a full-scale exercise, an attack against Dayton, Ohio. It was to be totally realistic, flown at combat altitudes, using every airplane SAC could put in the air. Bombing would be from thirty thousand feet at actual industrial and military targets, not radar reflectors. The exercise proved that neither the men nor the planes had routinely been tested at actual combat altitude. Aircraft pressurization failed, oxygen didn't work, and relatively few crews even located Dayton. Those who did bombed from one to two miles off-target, distances where even the atomic bombs of the day would have had limited effect, conventional bombs none. LeMay called it SAC's darkest day: "Not one aircraft finished that mission as briefed, not one."[9]

Having made his point to SAC command staff and SAC air crews, LeMay was not hesitant to gain the attention of his unit commanders. Doing so was relatively simple, done with classic LeMay directness. LeMay personally flew to a major SAC base, MacDill AFB, in Florida. Upon arrival the general—always fearfully succinct—approached the duty officer and gave a one-sentence command: "execute your war plan."[10] What followed has been simply described as "pandemonium"; LeMay then canceled the exercise and flew back to SAC headquarters. To the amazement of all parties he directed no disciplinary action but immediately called a staff meeting and described the incident in some detail. Six months later he personally conducted the same type of surprise exercise at Hunter AFB in Georgia; the exercise went like clockwork. SAC quickly learned that its commander required nothing less than "clockwork" execution. It became SAC's standard; rigor was expected. Failure to execute or any sign of "fudging" results—in exercises, bombing or navigation—was unacceptable.

In retrospect one can only wonder what would have happened if the LeMay style of senior command had been in place in either Hawaii or the Philippines in 1941. The commanders in both those theaters, Army and Navy, conducted a number of defensive exercises that were judged largely to be satisfactory. In reality the exercises focused primarily on actual engagement/combat. Weaknesses in detection and interception were never resolved—false assumptions about both became brutally clear only months later. The exercises were simply not realistic enough and certainly not conducted under conditions of maximum difficulty for the defense—which would be an enemy's preference. It was only to be in the disastrous first days of combat that those commands learned how poorly they had prepared. SAC learned the lesson of its most fundamental weakness—equipment, navigation and bombing—at combat altitude over Dayton, Ohio, during peacetime. It was painful but not disastrous.

As with LeMay at SAC, the commanders in Hawaii had also focused heavily on training. That was one of the reasons given for not elevating their alert conditions, even after the late November 1941 war alert. In fact, training was such a priority for General Short that key elements of the Hawaiian air defense system were not made operational; his direction was to implement them only once a state of war existed. CINCPAC Kimmel placed his priorities on training and preparation to surge the Pearl Harbor fleet west—if war came. The Philippines had gone to a much higher state-of-war alert, yet there seems to be little evidence that all the Navy coordination with Dutch and British allies and all the reconnaissance flights around primary wartime targets such as the Japanese bases on Formosa had produced any sort of detailed, tactical war plans. When the Japanese attacked the Philippines, it took hours for General MacArthur to issue an order to his bomber force commander—not to launch an attack but rather proceed with further reconnaissance so that an effective strike could be planned.

The difference in command practices between LeMay's and those of the Pacific pre–WWII commanders is key to our exploration of surprise attacks. Effective preparation for attack readiness involves a mix of the commander's style of command, a demand for absolute realism and an obsession with detail in training and exercises. Beyond that it requires that a very special attitude be established in the overall command leadership. Under LeMay, the SAC "mantra" was that all its training was to be conducted under war conditions; its commanders demanded that it function as if it were already at war, not preparing for it. Absolutely nothing was to be taken for granted, and if an unknown or unanticipated issue emerged, it was worth a commander's job not to report it to higher command.

The command, not just the commander, had to share an attitude that LeMay himself described as a "frame of mind." Kimmel, Short and MacArthur were all commanders "preparing for war" in 1941. In contrast LeMay operated SAC with the attitude that it continually existed in a wartime condition. That attitude, which by all accounts existed at all levels within SAC, is clear in LeMay's own words: "We [SAC] are at war now. So that, if actually we did go to war the very next morning or even that night, we would stumble through no period in which preliminary motions would be wasted. We had to be ready to go then."[11]

LeMay's attention to detail extended to all aspects of SAC global operations, and he was unremitting in his efforts to ensure that as a unified command, it had access to all the assets and resources it needed to fight a war—regardless of the state of readiness or performance of other commands. As an example, global exercises quickly revealed that the existing Air Force communications systems were totally unable to handle SAC's needs. The Air Force did not even have its own command communications network until 1949, when the teletype systems designated "AIRCOMNET" became operational. That network was intended to carry both administrative and operational traffic, but SAC's global deployments quickly overwhelmed its capabilities. By 1950 SAC had its own integrated telephone and teletype network, the Strategic Operational Control System (SOCS). The system was quickly extended to both continental and overseas bases.[12]

In line with LeMay's philosophy of constant test and exercise, SOCS was used in a field command post exercise in 1950 and immediately proved far too slow; it took almost five hours for message transmission—the general was not pleased. By June 1952, a follow-on exercise showed average transmission time dropping to forty-eight minutes. LeMay's quest for operational command and control took SAC through many network iterations and into global high-frequency systems connecting the command to its airborne force. The general continually maintained that the Air Force's overall communication network of the 1950s (STRATCOM) still did not meet the real-time operational needs of SAC. LeMay's bottom line was that no element of the command's war fighting operation was to be left untested—and continually improved. Ultimately SAC installed its own network of overseas radio relay sites and moved to high-frequency and single-side band radio (SSB)—which extended the SAC commander's communication ability directly to the cockpit of airborne bombers around the globe. The system allowed LeMay to reach any aircraft commander literally within thirty seconds.[13]

For LeMay, his successors and for SAC as a strategic command, there was no peacetime—there was simply an ongoing period during which weapons were not actually used. SAC maintained that status for years; it was an extremely costly practice by virtually all measures, including lives. In terms of both defending against and deterring surprise attack the practices of the Strategic Air Command provide a fundamental benchmark against which other efforts can be measured.

Yet even as LeMay was dealing with SAC's internal shortcomings and problems, the command faced an external challenge beyond even his immediate control. Assuming that it met his standards for its core skills, that it was fully equipped and trained as well as highly mobile, its power was meaningless unless its bombing strikes could be effectively targeted. Targeting intelligence had to be a major priority for SAC. And along with targeting, there was also the question of exactly how difficult it was going to be to make it through the Soviet air defenses to those targets. Continually knowing the details of the Soviet air defense network was also key.

That question was critical to any American force that might be thrown against a sudden Soviet territorial expansion—from the Far East to southern Europe and the Balkans. Even at the end of the war, before SAC was created and began its development, the United States did have one force available for strategic global action. That force was the huge and largely modernized American Navy, with global air reach in the form of its new super-carrier groups. The Navy had global capability, and it was likely to receive the first call to action in theaters around the world. And it was the Navy that had moved first to test and collect detailed intelligence on Soviet defenses.

In October 1945, six weeks after the Japanese surrender, a Navy Mariner patrol bomber had flown within miles of Russian occupation forces in Port Arthur, Manchuria. As it turned for home, the Navy plane was attacked by a Russian fighter. The Mariner made it back to base safely, and four months later the Navy sent another patrol bomber over Darien, near Port Arthur—the site of a large Russian radar installation. That flight was intercepted by two Soviet fighters that again attacked the American aircraft; it also made it home, and the Navy issued the first of what was to become a long line of claims that its pilots were simply disoriented and off course.[14]

While photographic reconnaissance would later become a major element of SAC long-range targeting intelligence, electronic reconnaissance was the key to penetrating air defenses during an attack. Electronic intelligence—commonly referred to as ELINT—focuses on detecting the frequencies and pulse trains associated with active radar broadcasts, both broad-pattern search radars (early warning and tracking) as well as more tightly focused weapons-targeting systems. The goal is to locate and characterize the various radars involved in an air defense network.

With sufficient data and analysis, the different types of radar signals are categorized by frequency and signal pattern, effectively creating a series of fingerprints (signatures) for radar transmitters. That allows attacking aircraft to know when they are being scanned, when they have been detected and when they are actually being targeted for attack by radar-guided guns, missiles or aircraft. Intentionally flying so as to be detected, then performing a variety of evasive maneuvers, is the only way to force the full suite of defense radars to respond, and that practice came to be referred to as "ferreting." Of course the two sides involved in such flights have different views of them—to one side it's simply intelligence collection, while to the other side it's more commonly viewed as "provocation."

Navy "ferret" flights toward Soviet positions in the east continued following the end of World War II, targeting large radar installations on Big Diomede Island on the Soviet side of the Bering Strait between Russia and Alaska three times in 1946 and early 1947.[15] Electronic intelligence flights would later come to include signals intelligence as well. Signals intelligence (SIGINT) focuses on the defense's radio, microwave, telephone and other voice and data command-and-control communications. It's one thing to understand the potential adversaries' defense assets—radars, anti-aircraft installations, and interceptor aircraft—but it's especially valuable to monitor their actual communications to understand their warning and alert protocols, especially when they actually issue orders to engage and/or fire. Of course, the potential adversary will change and upgrade their equipment, and once they are aware of ferreting, they will routinely change their communication's protocols. Such changes become significant strategic intelligence indicators, but that means the ferreting must also continue, and that leads to actual engagement with the enemies defenses—and casualties.

The Soviets quickly evaluated the rather obvious patterns in the Navy ferret flights and those of a number of other missions conducted around the Soviet frontiers in Europe and the Mediterranean beginning in 1946. They easily tracked the ferrets by radar and quickly concluded that American and British military intelligence groups were at work—with the obvious intent of collecting information on defenses that would need to be penetrated in air attacks. That led to an ongoing series of even more aggressive intercepts of the ferret flights and attacks on American aircraft—which the U.S. military continued to explain with reference to weather or navigational difficulties.[16] As the years passed and ferret flights were joined by ongoing high-altitude photographic reconnaissance flights, meteorological research would be added to the list of "innocent" explanations. Later during the Cold War, beginning in the 1950s, the Soviets conducted their own electronic and signals intelligence, primarily with large and extremely well equipped "trawlers" operating off the American coasts and in the vicinity of American naval units. Both sides were fishing for information, the Soviets literally turning to "fishing" as a cover for their activities.

Yet even in the earliest days, the American intelligence flights encouraged the Soviets to begin a series of ferret missions of their own. Soviet aircraft flying from Vladivostok to Tokyo frequently flew outside their designated corridors to reconnoiter military installations and the U.S. 7th Fleet. The same tactics were used by the Soviets in Germany and over Sweden. Soviet aircraft routinely penetrated Swedish airspace on apparent ferret missions in both 1946 and 1947, in the same period in which the ghost flyer incidents were occurring.[17]

In fact, certain of those incursions reinforced the idea that the Soviets were involved with the unidentified aerial objects and that at least a few of them were part of a Soviet psychological warfare effort. As noted previously, the American War Department and its Central Intelligence Group (CIG) had reached the conclusion that the Russians had been behind certain of the missile sightings reported over the Scandinavian countries and the matter had simply been too politically sensitive in those nations for any official protests to the Russians.

With that ongoing concern, in July 1947, American Naval Intelligence began conducting ferret flights against the former German rocket experimental center at Peenemünde, suspected as a source for certain of the mystery rockets. During those flights, missile radio guidance and control signals were detected, at 14.5 megacycles, with durations up to fourteen minutes. Swedish officers also reported long-radio interception of long-wave, guided-missile-control signals. Intelligence assessment concluded that the signals suggested experimentation with either radio-controlled aircraft or enhanced V-1–type devices.[18] Clearly some sort of rocket/missile activity was still going on at Peenemünde, and based on the Swedish intercepts it involved the remote control of aerial devices.

A related Air Force document from August 1948 described the observation by the Swedish Armed Forces commander in chief, who had observed an aerial explosion that was felt to be due to some sort of guided missile originating from the Estonian Islands (Dago or Osel). The Swedes had proceeded to conduct their own aerial reconnaissance of the area and reported that there seemed to have been a civilian evacuation from the west coasts of the islands. The Swedes used long, focal-length cameras in that aerial reconnaissance, on loan from the U.S. Air Force Directorate of Intelligence.[19] The Swedish flights were monitored and aggressively challenged by the Soviets. Swedish aircraft came under attack by Soviet MIGs; in one incident a Swedish plane was repeatedly attacked and forced to crash land with the crew taking casualties.[20]

In 1948 and 1949, Swedish pilots began a series of reconnaissance flights over targeted Baltic islands including Estonia and Saaremaa. The flights were made with a specially equipped F-51 Mustang aircraft that carried a K-22 high-resolution camera supplied by the United States. The goal of the flights was to locate suspected Russian missile sites that were felt to have been associated with the ghost rockets, presumably V-1 type devices. Other related documents reported that the Swedes had not yet produced specific positive proof of launches, but it was noted that they were exceptionally handicapped in that effort by having had no radar capable of tracking missiles.

The Swedes also moved to use three ground radar stations and two radar-equipped destroyers in an ongoing radar watch; unfortunately, the sets were Swedish modified versions of the original short-range British radar sets and were not operated twenty-four hours a day. No unexplained sightings were reported from the use of that equipment.[21] But by that point the ghost flyer sightings had virtually ceased, and no doubt the Soviets were well aware of the Swedish reconnaissance and tracking initiatives. There were no further reports similar to the original, close-range, low-altitude sightings of V-1–type guided craft.

In the larger scheme of things, ferreting was certainly not the only high-risk activity in progress in the immediate postwar years, and SAC's attention turned to a totally new region, one that would be key to any long-range attacks between continental America and the Soviet Union. That region was the Arctic, the polar route that provided the shortest distance for bomber strikes—in either direction. In pursuit of its atomic attack planning, SAC had a great deal to learn about conducting an air strike against Russia using the most direct routes across the Arctic. It was critical for SAC to acquire information not only on the details of the geography but also on weather systems and magnetic phenomena of the airspace over Canada, Alaska and Greenland. It was also vital to learn to what extent there were Soviet air defenses on polar routes into Russia.

The pressing need for intelligence on the far north led to the 1946 formation of one of the first units in the newly created Strategic Air Command. The unit was not a bomber group but rather a reconnaissance squadron. The B-29–equipped, 46th Reconnaissance Squadron was established at Ladd Field, outside Fairbanks, Alaska, in June 1946. Project Nanook was initiated, with the objective of mapping the Alaskan, Aleutian and Siberian regions as well as northern Greenland. That would allow SAC bombers to strike into Soviet Siberian air bases and to operate out of a major strategic American base at Thule, Greenland. The 46th was expected to prepare and train SAC strike groups, beginning with the original 509th atomic bomber unit, for "war day" over the Arctic.[22] Plans were also made to take the long-range aerial reconnaissance effort much further, all the way to its actual targets. SAC began planning and preparing for what would be required to send Air Force reconnaissance flights a distance of five thousand miles—across the entire breadth of Russia.[23]

The U.S. military was planning for all types of intelligence collection, not only around Russia's borders but across its territory and airspace, focusing on key strategic targets such as air bases, ports and industrial complexes. With their own plans in mind, it was obvious that senior American officers and intelligence staff would wonder if—and when—the Soviets might begin to engage in their own reconnaissance missions, missions not only in Western Europe or in the vicinity of overseas American installations but possibly over Hawaii and Alaska or even the continental United States itself. The increase in Soviet ferret air activities in and around the politically sensitive Scandinavian countries elevated suspicions that the Soviets would soon appear elsewhere. Given the "hollow" state of the American nuclear deterrent, an effective Soviet intelligence collection effort was a serious threat. SAC and the CIA had begun preparations for continental-wide reconnaissance of the Soviet Union; but might the Soviets attempt reconnaissance over the continental United States?

American military intelligence was already receiving information pertaining to a series of British aerial object reports that had begun in late 1945 and extended into 1947. The British Air Ministry was concerned that a number of unidentified radar tracks might well be high-altitude, high-speed Russian reconnaissance. In fact, the Air Ministry was so concerned that they established an official, if secret, project—Operation Charlie—to detect and if possible to intercept the flights.[24] That project is described in considerable detail by Dr. David Clarke, and his work is available for online reference.[25]

The British sightings began before the wave of ghost flyer/rocket sightings in Scandinavia and involved the English radar and interceptor defense network that monitored their east coast and the North Sea approaches to the British Isles. The long-range British radars—designated the "Chain Home system"—picked up a number of very high-altitude tracks over the North Sea, from sources above thirty-five thousand feet and moving at speeds beyond any of the interceptors of the period. The initial concern was that they were Soviet electronic and signals monitoring flights, possibly intended to profile the limits of the British air defense radar.

By the spring of 1947, the British press had wind of the fact that there were mystery planes flying over their coasts—which the Royal Air Force could not intercept. The newspaper reports stated that the mystery craft were being tracked on penetration flights over the interior of England, with speeds in excess of four hundred miles per hour. The British Air Ministry did admit the existence of such radar tracks, designating them as "X" object tracks (X being the "unknown" in mathematical equations). Reportedly the X-tracks became so common that the unknown craft became referred to in fighter control simply as "Charlie."

By January 1947, during a British air-defense training mission, a very oddly behaving high-altitude radar track was observed in the vicinity of the exercise, and an interception was ordered. The target was then observed at lower altitudes, in the vicinity of British bombers involved in the penetration exercise. Efforts at an intercept continued during several additional radar contacts at the lower altitudes, and the affair was reported to the U.S. Army Air Forces by the British Air Ministry. The unidentified aircraft was reportedly being chased over the North Sea for a period of half an hour, apparently taking very controlled and efficient evasive action. That same day, another X object radar track had been observed and Meteor jet interceptors were directed toward it but were unable to follow it due to lack of fuel.

That incident was also linked to another "X raid" earlier that same day. Shortly after 12 noon, Meteor jets from the 74th and 245th squadrons had been involved in air-defense practice under the command of Royal Air Force ground-control intercept trackers. During the exercise an unidentified target was tracked at thirty thousand feet over Norfolk, England. The commanding officer of 74th Squadron, Squadron Leader Cooksey, was asked to divert and intercept but was unable to follow the target due to lack of fuel. Yet another observation followed within a day, and Fighter Command extended its night-watch operations, directing all stations to be on the alert for "Charlie." During the following weeks, several very good tracks were observed and plotted, some for more than thirty minutes. Interceptions were attempted, but the targets proved extremely evasive and the interceptors and targets would both be lost, disappearing below radar coverage. At the time the RAF fighter command felt that the objects were not only real but controlled and extremely capable in combat maneuvers.

Ultimately the Air Ministry took the position that at least some of the mystery radar tracks were due to the unpredictable movements of "leaking" meteorological balloons or freak weather conditions. Apparently that conclusion was made based on the known limitations of Soviet medium-range bombers of that period. Still, the series of very high-altitude (30,000 feet plus) and relatively high-speed (450 miles per hour) radar tracks were not easily explained by the leaking weather balloon scenario. The Air Ministry report also made no mention of the fact that the Germans had flown some of their very first all-jet, long-range Arado bombers over England on photo reconnaissance missions in the last months of the war. Later it became known that the Russians had captured and were working with the German Ju 287, which had a 612-mile range, ceiling of 30,000 feet and speed of more than 600 miles per hour. In addition, the Americans had captured German Arado jet bombers with a 967-mile range, a 32,000-foot ceiling and a speed of 461 miles per hour. There are no specific records of Russian seizure of Arados, but some 210 had been produced, including 14 four-jet versions.

The British and Scandinavian experiences had certainly sensitized the American War Department to the possibility of Soviet reconnaissance, and by the summer of 1947, it seemed that a highly covert Soviet effort might well be extending to overseas American military bases. Some one hundred Navy personnel at Pearl Harbor observed a silver-colored, oblong object passing over the base, zigzagging, and speeding up and slowing down. The object was at high altitude as it passed over the fleet anchorage.

That same month, a series of unidentified objects were reported over the critical Atlantic air transit base at Harmon Field in Newfoundland. Two Pan American Airways mechanics and a third individual reported an object flying at high velocity, paralleling the ground, leaving a trail and apparently "burning" a path through a cloud formation. Two other individuals also saw the object's trail, which remained in the sky for almost an hour. The trail was also photographed by another airline employee, and those photographs substantiated the observations. The men estimated the object's size as approximating that of a C-54 transport plane, and its trail was several miles in length. The sightings in Newfoundland resulted in Air Intelligence directing an urgent study by Air Technical command engineering staff and intelligence officers from Wright Field.[26] There was a serious concern that the Soviets might have begun to use captured German technology to conduct either reconnaissance or psychological warfare operations against American military facilities.

That concern was reinforced by a report out of Alaska. The crew of a cargo aircraft observed a highly maneuverable craft crossing their path and then swinging behind to trail them. The object later accelerated and left them at an airspeed calculated at five hundred miles per hour. If the objects seen in Alaska and over Newfoundland had indeed been Soviet reconnaissance flights, they were coming over exactly the same routes that SAC had identified for its own polar reconnaissance activities. Similar sightings in Alaska and Newfoundland, within days of each other, definitely fueled concerns over possible Soviet reconnaissance activity.[27]

A Wright-Patterson intelligence team was ordered to leave for Newfoundland "immediately."[28] That intelligence team's report reinforced the perception that the Soviets might not only be using captured rockets and jet bombers but pushing German research projects forward to produce even more dangerous new craft. By that point the Air Force had seen enough of captured German research materials to appreciate the highly advanced technology that the Germans had been developing as the war had ended. The Wright-Patterson team commented that the trail observed in Newfoundland suggested combustion in a turbojet, athodyd motor (ramjet) or some combination of such next-generation power plants. The absence of noise and the apparent dissolving of the clouds suggested a large airflow and considerable heat. In short, their assessment was that some advanced foreign aircraft had passed over Harmon Field.[29] The War Department was taking the matter quite seriously as well. In August it directed technical intelligence at Wright Field to send an office interrogator to Fort Bliss to interrogate German scientist Gerhard Riesig concerning a book known to be in Russian hands, *Distant Control of Rockets*, possibly written by him. He was to be interrogated "regarding contents of book and possible location other documents pertaining to Project ABSTRACT. Please inform this headquarters name of officer being sent to Fort Bliss so that Office Chief of Ordnance may be notified prior to his visit."[30]

Concern over the possible Soviet activity intensified as more objects were observed maneuvering over American bases overseas. There seemed to be particular interest in Newfoundland—three airmen with the 147 AACS Squadron observed two small crescent-shaped objects pass over them at approximately twice the speed of the jets with which they were familiar. The objects were flying a zigzag path heading west, and were relatively low (an estimated 1,200 feet). They disappeared into the clouds, and a few seconds later one of the objects emerged from the clouds and continued on west. Exactly the same sort of objects were reported on the other side of the globe, by headquarters Fourth Air Force in Guam. Three American enlisted men observed two small, crescent-shaped craft, traveling at a speed twice that of a fighter plane.

By September 1947, reports from London, Newfoundland, Alaska and Guam had been joined by reports from Japan, where area surveillance radar had picked up a target at 89 miles' distance and tracked it over a path of some 70 miles—until it suddenly faded from the screen (it was thought to have rapidly descended out of the tracking beam, a common tactic for ferret flights). The object's speed was estimated at between 800 and 900 miles per hour. More importantly, the report noted that its behavior suggested that it had carried a radar receiver that had detected the defense radar scan and allowed it to take evasive maneuvers. At the time it seemed very likely that the Soviets were indeed performing both reconnaissance and ferret flights over America's allies and its overseas bases. The next, and more threatening, questions were whether they would show up over installations in the continental United States—and, if so, what could be done about it.

As early as 1946, General Spaatz, commander of the Army Air Forces, had openly expressed his concerns about the threat of a Russian surprise air attack coming over the North Pole, with the goal of destroying the vital Hanford atomic facilities as well as military industrial centers on the American west coast—in particular the massive Boeing aircraft plants near Seattle. The Soviets were known to have long-range bombers—the TU-4s copied from interned B-29 bombers held despite protests during the war—with the range for one-way bombing missions across the polar route. Round-trip Soviet strikes placed Seattle within range and one-way missions from Siberian airfields could strike all the way to Kansas. Spaatz's concern over a Soviet strike from Siberia helped direct SAC's focus to the polar route (both over Alaska and over the North Atlantic) as a reconnaissance priority. Obviously those same routes were also a defensive priority. Unfortunately, American air defense was just as much a "hollow force" immediately following the war as was its strategic bombing force. Soviet reconnaissance, if it existed, was unlikely to be detected other than being observed directly over American military and industrial targets, and it was even more unlikely to be intercepted even if observed.

During the Second World War, America had deployed a major continental air defense network. Some ninety-five mobile and stationary radar units were set up on the east and west coasts, with detection ranges of 150 miles at altitudes up to twenty thousand feet. A ground observer corps of thousands of civilian volunteers was formed to supplement the radar detection as a continental Air Defense Command (ADC) was rushed into place. However, with progress in the war, a direct attack on America seemed unlikely, and the ADC was disbanded in 1943.[31]

Much less publically—under strict wartime security—a single air defensive unit was pushed into service during the last year of the war. During late 1944 and into 1945, ranchers, farmers and others across the western United States had begun to report very specific observations of bright, stationary objects, many at high altitudes but some descending. On a number of occasions the reports described bright, stationary fireballs. These reports were generally disregarded and even laughed at—until U.S. forces captured large, hydrogen-filled paper balloons containing a large wad of magnesium flash powder. It was then realized that the observers had indeed been witnessing unconventional (and self-destroying) Japanese stratospheric balloon devices that had crossed the entire Pacific Ocean.

The Japanese had developed and launched a unique, unconventional weapon—stratospheric balloon bombs. Some nine thousand balloon bombs had been released by a special Japanese Army Regiment beginning in 1944. Due to the small size of the payload, the project appears to have been primarily one of psychological warfare. Joel Carpenter's article "Paper Threat—The first intercontinental weapon system: Japanese Fu-Go ('Windship Weapon') balloons," provides a comprehensive study of this subject and is highly recommended. Carpenter describes the fact that the Fu-Go devices were unique in many ways. Their innovative ballast control systems made extreme long distance (trans-Pacific flight) possible. The Fu-Gos also incorporated devices for self-destruction by burning; those did sometimes fail, and both military intelligence organizations and the FBI recovered crashed balloons.

Daylight aerial sightings of the balloons had come from points as far apart as Los Angeles and Chicago. Balloon debris was discovered in Arizona, Alaska, Iowa and Nebraska. Unexploded bombs turned up in Idaho, Colorado, Michigan and Texas. One balloon dropped near the huge Boeing aircraft plant near Everett, Washington. A few balloons were intercepted and shot down by fighters. Bits of metal, fragments of paper and exploded and unexploded bombs turned up in Washington State, Montana, Idaho, British Columbia, Manitoba, Colorado, Michigan, Texas and Mexico.

A quick and effective intelligence estimate of Fu-Go balloon information resulted in the deployment of a sophisticated air defense system specifically for the Seattle area, involving three radar stations, activation of a special ground observer corps, a report filter center, designation of special interceptor aircraft and the implementation of a ground-control intercept group. This project, "Sunset," was rushed into place within two months in order to defend the vital defense installations in the Pacific Northwest.[32]

Based on fears of a preemptive Soviet strike over the pole, targeting those same key defense facilities, the American Air Defense Command (ADC) was quickly reactivated in 1946. Initially it had even fewer resources than SAC. The new Air Defense Command had no operational radars and no interceptor aircraft other than those in the National Guard. By the end of November 1946, a single P-61 night fighter squadron was in place near Tacoma, Washington.[33] It was the only interceptor group on the West Coast; the only other interceptor group was a single daylight squadron of P-47s that had been moved to Don Field in Maine. Neither group would actually become operational until the spring of 1947.[34]

Those two interceptor groups had been rushed into place based on General Spaatz's decision to prioritize continental air defense in terms of a polar focus against the perceived, immediate Soviet threat. He was determined to deploy whatever defenses could be brought into action against the Alaskan and Northern Atlantic flying routes into the continental United States.[35] Still, Spaatz was left with the hard fact that the rush to postwar demobilization had gutted all the armed services, but the Air Force in particular had only 18% of its aircraft at combat readiness, and only two of the eighteen air combat groups left were considered combat ready.[36]

Despite Spaatz's concerns and a push to put at least a strategic air defense in place on the polar air lanes, air defenses at America's most strategic sites lagged noticeably. More than a year later, in June 1947, the newly organized Atomic Energy Commission (AEC) requested that the secretary of war review military protection at its key sites—as far as they could determine no special military protection was being given to any of them.[37] As of the summer of 1947, none of the Atomic Energy Commissions production facilities, the atomic weapons assembly site in Albuquerque, New Mexico, or the Roswell, New Mexico, base of the 509th atomic bombing squadron had any active air defense.

Amazingly, and largely unknown to the American public, for the first three years following the Second World War, with the perception of a major, unpredictable Soviet threat dramatically escalating, the United States had no real strategic deterrent force in place. Worse yet, it had literally nothing in the way of an air defense in the event that the Soviets decided to preempt America's atomic advantage by attacks on the United States' most vital air bases, atomic and aircraft facilities.

Chapter 6

....

UNCERTAINTIES AT HOME

ven before the end of the Second World War, both American diplomats and senior military officers had become extremely concerned about how territorially aggressive the Soviet Union might become following the defeat of Germany and later Japan. Joseph Stalin fueled those fears with his use of the Red Army as the war in Europe came to a close—not only in occupying Eastern Europe but in leveraging force to impose Soviet-centric political regimes within his span of military influence. Stalin's actions and statements led the Joint Chiefs of Staff to take the position that the development and consolidation of Soviet power were "the greatest threat to the United States in the foreseeable future."[1]

From a military perspective, the most imminent Soviet threat seemed to be a surprise advance of the Red Army either further west into Europe or southward. The Baltic was under Soviet political pressure as were states in the Caucus and even Turkey and Iran. Other than projecting American naval forces through the Mediterranean, the only American option seemed to be strategic air power—building a long-range striking force that could deploy against a ground advance in Western Europe or through North African bases to strike into southern Russia. If any confrontation turned to true global warfare, America could only hope to stop the Red Army by striking across the Arctic, devastating the Soviet industrial base and transportation networks.

While that strategic bombing force was being developed, the immediate necessity was to begin a reconnaissance effort, mapping polar strike routes, collecting weather and navigation information and conducting electronic "ferreting" of Soviet air defense capabilities. The Soviets quickly identified the American reconnaissance activities and began their own photo and ferret flights in the Baltic, over Germany and around Japan, paying particular attention to the American 7th Fleet in the Pacific.

Concerns over Soviet reconnaissance strengthened in 1947, with incidents such as the radar tracking of an intruding aircraft by personnel at an air base near Hokkaido, Japan. A ground-control-approach (GCA) radar operator tracked a target moving at speeds in excess of 600 miles per hour. During the observation it made four different changes in heading, with one course reversal of 360 degrees immediately following a GCA radio call to the local air control tower, suggesting that the craft was performing signals intelligence. After the course reversal it departed the area, fading out of range. The incident caused considerable interest in Washington, D.C., and personnel from the Air Force air technical intelligence center at Wright-Patterson became convinced that it was significant. It was noted that the air base was within 230 miles of an operational Soviet air base on Sakhalin Island.[2] A report on the sighting commented that Soviet jet aircraft were estimated to be capable of speeds of up to 604 miles per hour. It had become known that the Soviets had captured prototypes of the German Junkers four-jet bomber and in the spring of 1947 were test-flying the advanced aircraft. The Junkers Ju 287 had a speed of more than 600 miles per hour, a range of more than 600 miles and could operate at altitudes of 30,000 feet.

Such observations escalated the concern that the Soviets might be preparing their own long-range strike plans. Perhaps they were even contemplating a preemptive strike with new long-range bombers, engineered from American B-29s that they had seized during the war. Fears of such a Soviet long-range bomber were confirmed in August 1947 when Tu-4s were flown over an Aviation Day parade in Moscow. The immediate American concern was that the Soviets would engage in a crash construction program. The Soviets were indeed rushing to copy the B-29, and the Tupolev organization was able to put a Russian version, the Tu-4, into full production in 1948.[3]

The U.S. knew that such aircraft had the capability for cross-polar attacks, round-trip to the Pacific Northwest or one-way suicide attacks as far as Kansas or possibly New Mexico. The Soviets didn't yet have the atomic bomb, but even mass conventional bombing in a surprise attack could have gutted the American nuclear capability, taking out the Hanford, Washington, atomic plants where plutonium was produced and possibly reaching all the way to the atomic weapon design-and-assembly facilities in Los Alamos and Albuquerque, New Mexico. The major American aircraft plants were also accessible targets on the West Coast, with all major factories in the northwest in Seattle and farther south in Los Angeles.

In addition to reconnaissance for its own war planning, SAC missions in 1946 and 1947 also focused on threat intelligence, searching for Siberian airfields that could be used to stage surprise attacks on the U.S. They were also scanning for signs of the anticipated Tu-4 aircraft. The missions didn't find new bases in some of the suspected areas, but they did provide solid evidence of new air-base construction in the Soviet north and along coastal areas. The airfields, along with new submarine bases, were assumed to be capable of supporting offensive missions.[4] In later years, in flying over one of the bases in Siberia, one SAC aircraft came out of a cloud to find itself among a whole group of B-29 lookalikes. By sheer coincidence they had flown into the midst of a formation of new Soviet Tu-4s. Luck was with the American crew, and they managed to slip away from the formation and depart without notice.[5]

By 1947 American photo and signals intelligence around the fringes of Soviet territory was in full swing, and electronic intelligence (ELINT) confirmed that new air defense networks were already in place in both Europe and Asia. A chain of some thirty-nine Soviet radar stations had been plotted in Europe, with another eleven stations across its eastern Soviet borders.[6] And in 1947 the United States had nothing at all comparable to that new Soviet radar network. The almost total lack of continental American surveillance radar stations meant that even if the Soviets began to conduct reconnaissance over strategic American targets, they would likely go undetected.

While the American Air Defense Command (ADC) had been reactivated in 1946, even with its best effort, there was going to be nothing on the order of a continental air defense for some time. The ADC began 1947 with no operational radars and a single P-61 night fighter squadron near Tacoma, Washington.[7] The only other interceptor group was a single daylight squadron of P-47s, based in Maine. Neither group actually became operational until the spring of 1947; even then they needed extensive practice in ground-controlled interception before they could become effective.[8] During 1947, WWII radar sets were ordered out of storage with the intention of placing them in Albuquerque, New Mexico, to monitor the airspace around the Special (Atomic) Weapons Command at Sandia Air Base. Sandia Base was to be the first of a planned series of atomic weapons storage facilities, utilizing an extensive cave system in the Manzano Mountains southeast of the city. The reactivated Air Defense Command also moved to establish radar stations at Half Moon Bay near San Francisco and Arlington in Washington State. Later, radars were deployed in New Jersey and Montauk, New York.

But it was not until April 1948 that Air Force headquarters issued an order to establish comprehensive surveillance radar networks for all the key strategic facilities in New Mexico, including the Atomic Energy Commission (AEC) research-and-development installations at Los Alamos and Walker AFB at Roswell, New Mexico. Walker AFB was the home of the 509th atomic bomb group. Both the ADC and SAC initially faced a serious lack of trained personnel. The personnel situation was so limiting that when General Carl Andrew Spaatz, commander of the Air Force, ordered radar stations in the Northwest to twenty-four-hour operation—in March of 1948—there were not enough operators and technicians to comply with his directive.[9] The initial Air Force radar deployment was also dependent on obsolescent WWII radars, some without height-finding capability. That first temporary radar network was known as "Lashup"—in some cases the radar equipment literally had to be lashed to poles and towers. Even with major headquarters pressure, that network began to become operational only in the summer of 1948.[10] Lashup was not fully in place until 1949.[11]

Limited surveillance radars, no height finding, training only just begun on ground-controlled interceptor techniques and no controlled flight zones to discriminate friend from foe—in many ways the American air defense of 1947–1948 was in much the same state as that of Hawaii and the Philippines in December 1941. Clearly there was reason to worry about Soviet aerial penetration, whether it be reconnaissance, ferreting or potentially a surprise strike. Any preemptive Soviet strike would have encountered neither effective detection nor interception.

It was not until 1949 that an integrated air defense plan began to go into place for American atomic facilities and key strategic weapons manufacturing regions. General Ennis Whitehead of the Continental Air Command reached an agreement with the Civil Aeronautics Agency to coordinate information on commercial flights into the Northwest and on the East Coast. Up to that point there simply had been no controlled American flight zones for commercial aircraft and no guidelines on interception. Whitehead issued orders to intercept and shoot down suspected hostile aircraft in the vicinity of Hanford and Oak Ridge; that order was rescinded in January 1950 but went back into place in April of that year.[12] By 1950 radar sites were set up at forty-four sites in the industrial Northeast, the Great Lakes, Washington State and California. Lashup remained in place and at least minimally operational until a new and improved integrated system started to go into place in 1952.

But as 1947 had begun, all those plans and even a rudimentary continental air defense system for key defense sites were in the future. Due to its rapid and extensive demobilization following WWII, in the spring of 1947, the United States had no air-defense radar search network,[13] extremely limited interceptor capability,[14] no ground observer corps, and no significant interceptor or ground defenses for even its most key atomic and defense industry facilities.[15] In 1947 the American military literally had no way to detect aircraft coming into its airspace and no way to be sure that the Soviets were not beginning covert reconnaissance or ferret operations around its own borders or over key facilities.

All in all, it was an environment in which uncertainty was rampant and exposure to psychological warfare was extremely high.

As previously noted, in 1947 and 1948 the Swedes, with covert American and British support, were still conducting reconnaissance flights to find out exactly what the Soviets might have been doing with advanced German rocket and missile technology—and losing aircraft and personnel to Soviet fighters in the process. As 1947 progressed, United States Air Force intelligence began to review reports suggesting that the Soviets were very possibly probing American overseas bases and perhaps even continental defense installations. Over the following two years all three American military services as well as the FBI would deal with those indications, and ultimately the concern would become serious enough to take the issue—very secretly—to the Joint Chiefs of Staff.

The intelligence collections and analysis activities of the period from 1947 to 1952 provide us with a great deal of insight into the evolution of threat and warnings intelligence in the earliest years of the Cold War. That story also reveals some fundamental problems with warnings intelligence in general. The year 1947 became historically known as the year in which "UFOs" came to America. Beginning in early summer a wave of both military and civilian sightings swept the nation—and the press—from one coast to the other. All and all it was quite similar to the sighting wave that had spread across the Scandinavian countries only a year earlier. And as in 1946, while the majority of the reports were misidentifications of natural meteorological and astronomical phenomena, aircraft and weather balloons, there was a core of "high-value" observations made by military personnel and pilots in and around key American defense facilities. As the months passed, first the Air Force, then the Navy began to investigate those core sightings and to take them quite seriously—despite very contrary public statements to the public and the media.

One of the first concerns was that, as in the Japanese radar tracking incident mentioned earlier, several of the incidents reported by military personnel described the flight behavior of the objects as reflecting not only great control but indicating military characteristics—including protective formations and evasive maneuvers. In one July 1947 daylight sighting at Hamilton Air Force Base, California, two shiny, white fifteen- to twenty-five-foot–diameter objects were observed. The first object was sighted as it headed right over a P-80 jet fighter coming in on a preliminary landing—in an approach at around six thousand feet. A second object then appeared, flying a left-to-right "protective" maneuver over the first craft until they each passed southward toward Oakland and then out over the ocean. Both the observers, a captain and a lieutenant, gave identical descriptions of the objects and their pass over the airfield. The total duration of their sighting lasted about fifteen seconds as the craft sped by in a clear sky.

The objects appeared to be traveling three to four times the apparent speed of the P-80 Shooting Star, the first operational American jet fighter. One of the objects flew straight and level while the other seemed to be weaving from side to side as if it were providing escort. Another July sighting, at the San Diego Naval Air Station, came from two Navy chief petty officers who observed a three-object, triangular formation coming into the base area from the west (off the Pacific Ocean), circling to within some twenty miles of the base and then banking to reverse course and heading out to sea. The speed of the objects was only moderate, estimated at four hundred miles per hour.

Unidentified object sightings over American military bases began in the early summer of 1947 and continued through the end of the decade. They were reported in the immediate vicinity of major military bases and aerospace development centers, not only in the United States but on a global scale—from Newfoundland to Guam, Hawaii to Alaska. Sightings were reported at low to medium altitudes over the White Sands missile/rocket test range and the Muroc high-speed aircraft test center. Other reports came from military observers at the huge San Francisco air bases of Fairfield-Suisun (the military's major Pacific transport hub) and Hamilton Field near San Francisco—a key Air Defense Command base and home to the first postwar American all-weather fighter squadrons.

One of the outstanding questions relating to the possibility of Soviet craft being involved in such incidents was how such relatively small objects could be operating at great distances from Soviet territory. One solution investigated by Air Technical Intelligence was the use of blimps or other lighter-than-air craft serving as "piggyback" carriers for long-distance flights. Given the wartime success of the Japanese "Fu-Go" balloon project, it was known that high-altitude balloons could loft payloads from Asia not only as far as the Pacific Northwest but into the midwestern and southwestern states. Major American intelligence groups had concluded that the Soviets had been willing to engage in a very high-risk psychological warfare operation in Scandinavia, possibly even over England. If they were bold enough—or desperate enough—to do that, there was certainly reason to fear that they might extend operations to the United States.

As the summer of 1947 progressed, the initial concerns over what appeared to be displays of skilled evasive maneuvers and possible ferret-type activities in certain sightings were joined by observations suggesting advanced technology. Several key reports contained elements matching advanced design and propulsion technology bearing a considerable resemblance to German work collected at the end of the war, much of that even then being examined by American aircraft firms and by technical specialists in the Air Intelligence technical divisions at Wright-Patterson Air Force Base in Ohio.

In early summer 1947, General Spaatz personally directed the 4th Air Force, responsible for West Coast Air Defense, to assign intelligence resources to an investigation of unidentified object reports. Reports were to be forwarded to the Air Materiel Command and Wright-Patterson base in Dayton, Ohio, home of the Air Technical Intelligence Division. Spaatz's concerns soon began to percolate through to the Air Force intelligence organization, and in the first half of July, General George Schulgen (Air Intelligence Requirements Division) informally contacted General Nathan Twining (Chief, Air Materiel Command/AMC) to request an assessment of the sightings that were being reported. General Schulgen also contacted the Federal Bureau of Investigation, informing them that the Army Air Forces would be actively investigating the unidentified flying objects and that the intelligence division was also using its scientific assets. The Air Materiel Command was ordered to evaluate the reports as to whether they represented some celestial phenomenon or were actually foreign, controlled mechanical devices. Schulgen personally expressed concern that the sightings might be a Communist-orchestrated effort to create fear of a Russian secret weapon.

Given the context of the times, the Air Force concern about Russian aerial devices and reconnaissance and/or psychological warfare seemed quite reasonable. Still, the Air Force faced a major problem: that of obtaining solid information on the unidentified objects. Certainly the characteristics of the reported objects could be studied, but the real specialty of the Air Intelligence teams at Wright-Patterson Air Materiel Command was technical analysis. Their mission had been and remained avoiding technological surprise, advancing Air Force technology and identifying strategic intent of potential enemies through their technology. Technical intelligence operated under the Directorate of Intelligence, and one of its primary missions was "exploitation," the acquisition of enemy technology and science.[16]

The Army Air Force Directorate of Intelligence had been in charge of the Operation Lusty field teams during the final months of World War II. That operation was responsible for the collection of as much advanced German Air Force (Luftwaffe) technology and science as humanly possible. As a result of that effort more than one thousand tons of technical papers had been brought to Air Technical Intelligence at Wright-Patterson by the spring of 1947 and approximately one hundred German scientists were in residence there—all in an effort to jump-start the American aeronautical industry in the fields of jets and rockets.[17] It was only beginning to become clear to what extent the pragmatic American focus on optimizing existing designs had caused it to lag behind the Germans in those fields, including the fundamental science and technology required for supersonic flight and weapons. Air Technical Intelligence had an immense task in front of it with the captured German technology and devices, but at least it involved practices with which it was familiar, developed for the study of actual, physical hardware.

Unfortunately, in regard to its new, unidentified object assignment, there was no hardware immediately available for analysis. In fact, there was virtually no technical intelligence at all, not even radar tracking data—and no obvious way to rectify the situation. There were very few available interceptors or even personnel with experience in ground-controlled interception. In 1948 a request was made for assistance in intercepting and investigating unidentified objects as part of the intelligence collection assignment. That request was refused; it was judged there were simply no available aircraft for such an effort. Beyond that, General Schulgen's outreach to the Federal Bureau of Investigation met with a less-than-enthusiastic response. Director Hoover's initial reply to the request was to note that the Bureau would cooperate only if given access to any objects recovered by the Air Force.[18]

For a period of less than ninety days, the FBI became actively involved with unidentified objects. A policy statement was issued that directed field offices to investigate any sighting that was brought to their attention and to ascertain whether it was a bona fide sighting, a prank, a publicity stunt or possibly a subversive act. While some leads did prove to be hoaxes, the Bureau also received and documented some good-quality sightings. One of the most significant was the observation by a United Airlines crew on July 4. While in the vicinity of Emmett, Idaho, at 6,500 feet the pilot and copilot observed two separate groups of objects—the second remaining in sight for some twelve to fifteen minutes. The objects had a flat base, a slightly rounded contour, with the apparent span of a DC-8 aircraft. The FBI did extensive interviews and background checks on the pilots.[19] That sighting, along with a number of pilot observations, would become key material for the initial Air Force intelligence assessment.

Unfortunately for the Air Force, FBI support rapidly deteriorated when the Bureau became aware of an Air Defense Command letter that Bureau personnel felt implied that the role of the FBI was viewed simply as a filter for pranks so that the Air Force could concentrate on serious reports. When this was brought to the attention of Director Hoover, he quickly advised the Air Force that he could not permit the personnel of his organization to be used in such a matter and issued a directive advising that all flying disc reports be referred to the Air Force and that no investigations be performed by the Bureau.[20] The Bureau did continue to receive reports and on certain occasions became directly involved— primarily when incidents appeared to relate to the protection of vital installations such as atomic facilities.

By late July 1947, Lieutenant Colonel George Garrett (Directorate of Intelligence/Office of Intelligence Requirements, Collections Branch) and his staff had collected and completed a preliminary study of a number of the most credible unidentified object reports, including a list of patterns and physical characteristics. The Directorate of Intelligence reported to the Air Force commanding general as a staff command, along with the service's major operating commands such as the strategic, tactical and air defense commands—SAC, TAC and ADC. The directorate had two major roles: the collection and analysis of intelligence. The Office of Intelligence Requirements directed the collections function. The Office of Air Intelligence performed analysis, prepared threat assessment and estimates and prepared defense recommendations. Overall the priority of all the directorate's offices was the Soviet threat. The Air Materiel Command (AMC) also served under the direction of the Air Force commanding general and its Technical Intelligence Division (TID), provided engineering studies and support to a number of commands, including Air Intelligence.

We do not have the actual list of field reports evaluated as part of the initial UFO intelligence collections in the summer and early fall of 1947; we also have no meeting notes, records or transcripts from the technical reviews. We do have a listing from the Air Force archives of which case files were designated as unidentified, and we have a series of preliminary reports and estimates that make it quite clear that by the fall of 1947 there was no question at all that a core of reports demonstrated that unidentified objects did exist and it was felt that the next key task was to determine their origin. The intelligence specialists seemed relatively confident that they would resolve that question within a few months, certainly in no more than a year.[21]

It appears that the sightings from Newfoundland mentioned in the previous chapter weighed heavily in the assessment. A team from the Technical Intelligence Division of AMC had rushed to Newfoundland to do field investigation of three separate sets of sightings by a number of military and airline personnel, all occurring over a few days in July. The upshot was that both the maneuvers of the objects, as well as secondary effects in the form of smoke trails and an actual path cut through a cloud (both photographed), suggested certain advanced German technology that Wright-Patterson was already in the process of cataloging.[22]

General Spaatz took the findings very seriously and directed a number of actions involving contacting and interrogating a number of German scientists both in American and overseas. And in August the Air Intelligence Requirements Division sent a memo outlining several elements common to the most reliable sightings. At that point an effort was being made to focus on further intelligence collection, effectively "profiling" the target.[23]

Beyond that, the collections memorandum offered further observations that actually defined a very specific advanced aircraft platform—one that could have represented a serious military threat if confirmed. A pair of German aircraft designers had worked on a series of "crescent" or flying wing-shaped aircraft—not unlike the later Northrup Flying Wing, which evolved into today's B-2 Spirit stealth bomber. In the last days of the war those designers (actually brothers with the family name Horten) were working on the prototype of a jet-powered craft designated the "Horten 229." The craft was powered by dual turbojet engines and had an estimated speed above six hundred miles per hour and a ceiling of fifty-two thousand feet. It would have far exceeded any aircraft flying at the end of the war. Beyond that, the Horten brothers had completed designs for a six-engine, long-range, intercontinental bomber designated the "Horten IX." The Air Intelligence memorandum of August 1947 noted reports that some four of the craft had been completed when the war ended, and a "more recent report indicates that the Russians are now planning to build a fleet of 1,800 Horten VIII (six-engine pusher)–type flying wing aircraft."[24]

Unfortunately no further information on that Soviet intelligence has ever been located, but given that it came out of the Air Intelligence headquarters staff and was placed into a collections memorandum, it must have seemed credible at the time. If the Soviets had indeed built such a fleet, it would have provided them with an immense strategic air advantage. Indeed, for the next six to eight months Air Intelligence went into a virtual frenzy attempting to track down details on the Horten aircraft and the Horten brothers, both in Europe and America. It would not be until early in 1948 that the perceived threat of a fleet of Soviet Horten-derived intercontinental bombers was largely eliminated.[25]

In the interim, the Technical Intelligence group at Air Materiel Command reported in September 1947 that in its considered opinion key sightings of the unidentified objects were "something real and not visionary or fictitious" and requested that Air Force Headquarters authorize a security-designated project for ongoing study. In response, as of December 1947, the Chief of Air Intelligence had created a new project, designated "Project Sign." The memorandum authorizing the project noted that the Directorate of Intelligence had already begun analyzing the sightings for evidence of photoreconnaissance, ferreting and psychological warfare. At that point, while numerous reports had come from the American coasts, there was no pattern of sightings near principle strategic target areas.[26] In short, the focus of the Sign project was basic "threat analysis," first and foremost the question of whether or not the objects constituted an imminent threat and, second, if at all possible, to identify their place of origin.

Given the total lack of radar resources to actually monitor or track flight paths of the unidentified objects, the study proved to be especially challenging. There were not even interceptors to be spared to pursue them for closer observations or photographs. Of course, the most obvious solution, and one that Technical Intelligence normally relied upon, was to obtain physical evidence. As it happened, some such evidence did surface during 1948—yet even advanced technical studies of such material proved just as inconclusive as with materials obtained during the ghost rocket scare in Scandinavia. Worse yet, it appears that Air Force intelligence itself was generally not even aware of that physical evidence and its extensive testing by other groups.

On July 6, 1948, in Midland, Michigan, an object was seen to disintegrate in flames near a Dow Chemical plant. Internal analysis at Dow labs determined that the recovered remains included that a "sizable amount of magnesium" had been involved and well as some thorite (the mineral most closely associated with the atomic element thorium). The material itself was determined to be moderately radioactive. The FBI performed a very basic inquiry on the incident, but the Air Force was initially not involved. In-depth research by Joel Carpenter has revealed a much more complex story involved with the Midland fireball. His work is described in an essay titled "The Midland Fireball: Dow Chemical's Early Involvement with UFOs."[27] Readers are encouraged to study the entire report; a brief summary of key points in the essay includes the fact that the senior Dow analyst, John (Hans) Grebe, performing the initial study, had been one of the key scientists responsible for many of Dow's own major chemical advances.

Grebe was considered by colleagues at Dow to be a genius; the early commercial success of his research encouraged Dow to give him broad leeway, and he established the company's Physical Research Laboratory. Grebe's labs produced an ongoing stream of valuable inventions including Styrofoam and a type of synthetic rubber highly valuable to the U.S. military during WWII. He also developed a process for extracting magnesium from seawater; it became Dow's main source for that metal. Grebe's role in advising the American military was extensive. He served as an observer at the 1946 Operation Crossroads nuclear tests and worked closely with the U.S. Army Chemical Corps on highly classified chemical warfare projects.

In 1948 Grebe was named chief technical advisor for the Army Chemical Corps. In September of that year, while working at Edgewood Arsenal, Grebe requested an update on the fireball investigation from Dow Chemical. After reviewing the material and considering the available data—including the fact that the sand from the "fall" had produced a different chemical spectrum than sand from the surrounding area—Grebe wrote a memorandum to his Army superior. He expressed his belief that the incident should be taken very seriously and that there was every indication that that object might have been a "self-consuming" missile, capable of producing considerable smoke and leaving behind only the minimum residue; that residue might suggest a battery and radio transmitter had been included with the device.

Grebe's note presented the possibility that the Midland fireball had been some sort of self-destructive device, not unlike those that had been discussed in certain of the Scandinavian reports. He seems to have reached that conclusion independently; however, Carpenter presents other information suggesting that the same sorts of conclusions were being reached in regard to other similar incidents of the period.

In the interim, Grebe had pursued his own concerns by personally visiting Colonel Holger Toftoy of Army Ordnance, the commander of Project Hermes. Hermes was the Army's comprehensive missile development program based at White Sands, involving a variety of test and development launches, including both actual German V-2 missiles and a number of derivatives based on the V-2 concept. In an October 18, 1948, conference with Toftoy and officers from the Army Chemical Corps, Grebe briefed the officers on the scientific analyses of the fragments from the Midland incident. He placed particular emphasis on that fact that soil materials recovered from the area included nuggets of "fairly pure" silver and some thorium. The residue produced detectable radioactivity some ten times that of the natural background and possibly could be attributed to thorium-coated filaments in electronic equipment (although excessive for normal use in known applications). There was also evidence of magnesium, which had been completely oxidized.

Grebe advanced the hypothesis that at least some of the unidentified aerial objects being reported might be small, magnesium-based devices capable of being propelled over several thousand miles and self-destructing. The traces of silver and thorium might have been the remains of control systems. Grebe's concept may well have been based in his WWII work for Dow Chemical, which had involved building a special, shock-resistant housing for the highly miniaturized and ruggedized vacuum tubes that were part of the proximity fuse developed by the United States, one of the most closely guarded secrets of the war. Those devices were capable of surviving acceleration of some several thousand times the force of earth's gravity, orders of magnitude beyond accelerations that would destroy standard electronic devices.

Generally speaking, Grebe envisioned something very much like a small artillery shell, but one with an aerodynamic design and internal electronics that would allow some degree of flight at the end of its trajectory. It seems significant that two years later, during a conference on "green fireballs" at the Los Alamos atomic laboratories, Dr. Edward Teller would mention the possibility that the fireballs being observed over key defense facilities in New Mexico could be generated by the final stage of a long-range artillery device, fired from the Soviet Union. In side comments, Teller mentioned that the best answer he could come up with was a multi-stage shell fired from what he referred to as a "pencil gun."[28] Either Teller had independently come to the same general conclusion as Grebe or Grebe's hypothesis had been circulated to some key people within the American scientific community.

During the meeting with Colonel Toftoy, it was agreed that the Army would generate a memo to a special Bureau of Standards group, asking them to investigate mechanisms that could propel devices of the general type envisioned by Grebe. That group, essentially hidden within the standards agency, had worked closely with the Army during the recent war, on projects including an American television-guided bomb, a passive radar homing glide bomb and a radar-guided anti-ship glide bomb. The Bureau's engineers had invented a process for "painting" electrical circuits, a forerunner to printed circuits.

Joel Carpenter reports being unable to find any details of actual follow-on meetings with that special Bureau of Standards group, but the Midland incident remained a real concern, apparently known at least at the highest levels of the American military. On December 2, 1949, General Hoyt Vandenberg, the Air Force chief of staff, communicated with the Air Force aerial object study group (as of February 1949 Grudge had succeeded Project Sign). Vandenberg requested information about Technical Intelligence's investigation of the Midland fireball. The project personnel responded that they had no details on the incident and requested copies from their chief of staff. There seems to be no indication that Grudge seriously followed up on Grebe's work on the Midland incident; however, it was not the only materials investigation that had not been actively investigated by the Air Materiel Command under either Project Sign or Project Grudge.

In July 1948 (the exact date is unknown) something very similar to the Midland incident had occurred at West Ridge, New Hampshire. Witnesses noticed a circular area of individually burning patches of grass. The spirals of smoke and flame appeared to have been caused by extremely hot debris from some object that had exploded in the air, scattering material across a circle some hundreds of feet in diameter. Samples of the slag-like debris were provided to an MIT scientist, Dr. Francis

Reintjes, who conducted a detailed analysis using MIT facilities. An FBI document dated July 29, 1948, notes in the analysis and comments that the incident was not widely known, given that only a few instructors remained on campus during the summer session.

Reintjes reported that pieces provided to him seemed to be part of a thin-walled, man-made device. Four of the fragments, when pieced together, appeared to have been part of a hollow cylinder some eight inches in diameter and with a wall thickness of three-sixteenths of an inch. The material itself was ordinary cast iron, but it had been subjected to a very high degree of heat. He stated that it closely resembled material from V-2 rocket engine linings that he had seen during an earlier assignment at White Sands.[29] Apparently the MIT/FBI report never made it to Project Sign, which was wrapping up its investigation—stating it was unable to do a true technical assessment given the lack of access to any materials related to the objects under study.

Both the Midland and West Ridge observations and studies become even more interesting when referenced to a later incident that Joel Carpenter notes in his study of the Midland fireball case. More than two years later, in 1952, the Bureau of Standards was involved with an analysis of material that had been obtained in the Washington, D.C., area during a wave of unidentified object sightings over the nation's capital. Commander Alvin Moore, of the U.S. Navy, had obtained fragments recovered after jet interceptors engaged and in one instance may have actually fired on one of the objects. The testing revealed that the fragments were from an artificially produced artifact, composed primarily of magnesium (filled with millions of microscopic iron particles). The scientists reported that the fragments appeared to have been a section of a cylinder, some 10.4 inches in diameter. Commander Moore sent the report to Captain Edward Ruppelt—at that time in charge of the newest Air Force UFO investigation (Project Blue Book)—who forwarded it to the Battelle Memorial Institute. At that point Battelle was performing a contract study of UFO reports for the Air Force. However, it appears that the fragments received only cursory study and no comment by Battelle.[30]

In isolation the Washington, D.C., fragment might have seemed uninteresting, but when combined with its similarity to the studies at

Dow Chemical and MIT, as well as certain of the analyses from the previous 1946 reports out of Scandinavia, there remains a possibility of "self-destructive" rocket devices and an ongoing Soviet psychological warfare effort. Air Force reports of the period 1948–1952 continued to note how its inquiries were hampered by the lack of actual physical materials; in retrospect it appears that the studies themselves failed to consider just such evidence. It's a mystery that will likely never be resolved; Stalin-era security was relentless and could be deadly to those involved in secret military projects.

One of the classic mistakes in threat and warnings analysis is the "rejection of evidence which does not match the hypothesis or preconceptions" of senior intelligence staff. Experts in strategic intelligence point out that the rejection of indications that either conflict with an overall assessment or—perhaps more importantly—that "might upset one's superiors" is a far more common problem than is acknowledged within the professional community. A variety of new techniques would later be developed to address exactly that problem, specifically to ensure that "unpopular scenarios were not rejected simply due to conflict with the prevailing climate of opinion." Cynthia Grabo notes how "maddening" it is for analysts to bring forth indications and then encounter a superior who simply refuses to accept them in terms of an already established position. She notes that in such instances positions quickly harden and the atmosphere becomes "emotionally charged."[31]

According to remarks from many of the participants themselves, by the official end of Project Sign, Air Force senior Pentagon intelligence staff had indeed moved into a very fixed perception. An October 1948 memo from the Air Materiel Command summarized its study of some 180 incidents and acknowledged that there remained a certain number of reports that had no reasonable explanation. However, since the AMC personnel had been unable to obtain physical evidence, there was simply insufficient data for any conclusions on the nature or origins of the objects in those incidents. The memo concluded with the opinion that it did not feel it advisable to present the press information on objects that could not be identified and upon which the Air Force could not present reasonable conclusions.[32]

Of course, such a position left the public in a state of general uncertainty in regard to unidentified objects, and if such sightings continued, or escalated to any extent, that uncertainty could only grow. The American popular press had already reported on several incidents that suggested that the Soviets might be targeting the continental United States. Photos of a smoke cloud produced by a dramatic meteor fall in Kansas had garnered national press attention. The smoke cloud had started over Nebraska and run south into Kansas, making a highly visible and unusual trail. Headlines had speculated that the spectacular exploding fireball over Kansas might have been a Russian "ranging shot" to the center of the country.[33] Dr. Lincoln LaPaz, of the University of New Mexico meteoritics institute, investigated the Kansas meteor reports and was able to plot its course and eventually recover fragments, addressing public fears over that particular incident. Later LaPaz would gain considerable attention in regard to "green fireballs" over key nuclear facilities in New Mexico, telling everyone who would listen that those were quite unnatural and potentially represented foreign technology.

The Project Sign assessment focused on the point that while it had been unable to "identify" the core sightings it found credible, it could find no evidence that the incidents represented any imminent military threat. It did leave the door open to the possibility that certain sightings represented a combination of reconnaissance, ferreting and, perhaps most importantly, psychological warfare. Of course, it took some time for the intelligence bureaucracy to process all this into an official headquarters statement, but in the interim the study project was redesignated "Project Grudge" in December 1948. In April 1949, Air Force Intelligence Chief General Cabell presented the overall findings on the unidentified aerial objects to the Joint Intelligence Committee (advisory committee to the American Joint Chiefs of Staff). The overview was in line with the earliest 1947 Sign draft report, stressing that some core sightings were credible and unexplained, that there might be new technologies involved—including atomic power—but once again the primary conclusion was that there was no indication that they represented any imminent military threat.

Yet just as the Air Force intelligence investigation was ramping down its aerial phenomena investigation, a host of new reports began to come in from some of the most key defense installations in the nation. A new pattern of sightings began to emerge, just the sort of pattern that the initial Air Force studies of 1947 had anticipated as indicating a true threat but that it had not found at that point. In some ways the situation was reminiscent of early 1941 when sources in Japan reported a Japanese war plan beginning with a surprise attack on Pearl Harbor. At that point the Navy had concluded that the available movements of Japanese ships indicated no imminent threat to Pearl Harbor. In 1949 the Air Force officially concluded that observations of unidentified aerial objects represented no strategic Soviet threat, largely because the objects did not appear to be "targeting" America's key atomic facilities—such as those in New Mexico.

New Mexico had seen a limited number of unidentified object reports during the summer wave of 1947; those were primarily from the Holloman/White Sands area, where personnel engaged in balloon and missile activities had cause to be watching the sky. The geographic focus for the 1947 sightings had been the Pacific Northwest (California, Washington, Oregon and Idaho), leaving New Mexico in fourteenth place in reports (seventeen compared to Washington State's eighty-three).[34] There was also no indication of any early 1947 sightings at the Los Alamos atomic facility—one of the most isolated and strategically important sites in America.

Yet in the last months of 1948 UFO reports out of New Mexico began to reflect a dramatic change. A series of observations began to come from Los Alamos atomic development labs. On the morning of September 23 a number of Scientific Labs personnel waiting for a plane reported seeing a glint in the sky—which upon further observation appeared to be a circular, metallic object high in the north. Its appearance was that of a dime, seen edge-on from something like fifty feet. The same day, an Atomic Energy Commission (AEC) security guard reported an oval orange object, highly luminous, crossing the sky over the facility in level flight and trailing flame. The object was seen to disappear into a cloud.

Those first September reports were the precursor to a wave of regional sightings that lasted throughout 1949 and well into 1950. The sightings consisted of two distinct types—nighttime fireballs, primarily of a relatively unique green color, many with "flat" trajectories, and daytime sightings of disc-, ball-shaped and cylindrical objects. The new wave of unidentified aerial objects extended from the atomic weapons development facilities at Los Alamos south to the Atomic Weapons Command assembly site at Sandia Base, outside Albuquerque.

Many of the weapons design, engineering and testing functions originally begun at Los Alamos had recently been relocated to a facility east of Kirtland Air Force Base (southeast of Albuquerque); by 1948 it was first called Sandia Base and later Sandia Laboratory. Sandia Base also housed the Armed Forces Special Weapons Project (formerly the Manhattan Project), and in 1949 the Department of Defense established the Armed Forces Special (Atomic) Weapons Command there. Sandia Base and Kirtland AFB respectively served as weapons assembly and deployment points for atomic weapons; SAC bombers had to make an intermediate stop at Kirtland to pick up the bombs for atomic missions. Later Sandia Base took charge of establishing and operating a limited number of other atomic weapons storage facilities located around the nation, known as Q Areas.[35] For all practical purposes, through 1949, Albuquerque/Sandia Base was the most strategic location in the country in regard to actual American atomic war fighting capability.[36]

On December 5, 1948, a meeting between Air Force Office of Special Investigations (OSI), Army Counter Intelligence Corps (CIC) and the Department of Justice (DOJ) was held at Sandia Base. The subject of the meeting was a series of observations (including one made personally by Dr. Lincoln LaPaz of the University of New Mexico along with OSI personnel) of green fireballs sighted in the vicinity of Los Alamos and Albuquerque. In the Sandia Base meeting the Los Alamos AEC chief inspector summarized elements of the fireball phenomena including remarks by Dr. LaPaz—among them LaPaz's mention of similar green fireballs in the area of the Hanford atomic works. The FBI was copied on the meeting memo, and reports were sent to respective headquarters; a follow-up conference was scheduled on Sandia Base for December 13.

A December 21 letter from the Director of Military Applications of the Atomic Energy Commission records the fact that AEC headquarters was very much aware of the numerous Los Alamos security team UFO observations and of Dr. La Paz's evaluation as well as of the OSI's intent to investigate. The AEC recommendation in the letter was limited to a call for monitoring the situation and coordinating with Military and Air Force Intelligence in Washington. On December 21, the chief inspector for AEC Security at Los Alamos advised his area manager of continuing reports by night security personnel of rapidly moving, high-intensity blue-green lights in the vicinity of the Los Alamos facility. At least one observer commented that he felt the "gaseous appearance" of the light to be the exhaust from some sort of engine. Los Alamos was not alone however; on December 6, an AEC security services employee had reported a green fireball directly over the Sandia Base nuclear weapons assembly site, about a third the apparent size of a full moon and with a flaming tail.

Separately, on January 4, 1949, Fourth Army G2 (Intelligence) reported to the Army director of intelligence that there had been some twenty reports over the prior six weeks of intense, white or greenish lights at an altitude of 5,000 to 7,200 feet (far too low to be meteors), traveling at what appeared to be supersonic speed but with no noise at all. One of the reasons that the Army was especially concerned about unidentified objects in the Southwest was that it had its own security problems—in particular with a brand-new atomic weapons site being put into place at Killeen Base, near Fort Hood and Gray Air Force Base.

Early in 1949, the ongoing Albuquerque and Los Alamos sightings prompted the Air Force OSI at Kirtland AFB to begin its own focused investigation. Over the following weeks Kirtland AFB OSI obtained numerous quality observations of fireballs over central New Mexico, including aerial observations describing the objects being sighted at extremely low levels, aircraft altitude or below, down to only a few hundred feet above the ground—and in one instance appearing to originate at ground level. OSI agents personally observed the green fireballs from aircraft, noting their flat trajectory and apparently aircraft-level altitude (estimated at seventeen thousand feet, only a couple of thousand feet above their aircraft). Headquarters Fourth Army also requested (on January 3, 1949) that a thorough investigation be conducted, reflecting the fact that Army Intelligence was fully aware of the phenomenon and its possible security implications.

As a follow-up to the January 10 inter-agency meeting at Kirtland, on February 2, the AEC security director proposed a meeting of investigators and scientists to discuss the lights/fireballs, with a tentative date of February 18 at Los Alamos. Fourth Army responded positively to the proposal, with Army Intelligence expressing its intention to participate. However, in response to a letter advising the Pentagon of its participation, a "corrective" letter was sent to Fourth Army advising them that the subject of UFOs was already under study and suggesting they were only unexplained due to lack of sufficient data. Clearly the official Pentagon position had established a major barrier to any serious security investigation of the reports coming out of the Southwest.

An "informal" meeting, permitted by the AEC, was convened at Los Alamos, on February 16; attendees included Fourth Army, AEC Security, the FBI, Dr. LaPaz and six scientists from the University of California, including Dr. Edward Teller, perhaps the leading atomic physicist of the time. Air Materiel Command had been invited but declined to send a representative. Numerous reports were discussed at length, with extended exchanges between the scientists and LaPaz. When one of the scientists inquired about National Defense Establishment interest, the Army representative stated that the general reaction was that the regional people were perceived as "crackpots" and that it would be easiest if the scientists verified that the objects were actually meteors. Toward the end of the meeting, one OSI representative expressed a lack of understanding of AMC's role and noted that without some higher-level directive, his office would be reducing its own investigative efforts. Apparently based on the AMC attendee's remarks, the Army representative left the meeting, out of frustration.

On March 13, two military police at Sandia Base reported a spherical object with a flaming tail twice its length. The object was estimated at one half the size of the full moon. Within days, on March 21, a number of witnesses at both Sandia Labs and Kirtland AFB observed multiple UFOs between 1:00 and 1:30 in the afternoon—they were described as round, silver colored and silent. And on March 24, three Sandia Labs military police reported a hovering, round, silver-colored object that departed first in level flight but then straight up at high speed. Minutes later yet another MP reported four similar objects flying at high speed several thousand feet over the base.[37] These sightings emphasize the point that although the period was famous for its "green fireballs," when a report summarizing some 150 sightings near New Mexico atomic sites was compiled in the summer of 1950, discs and round, flat-shaped objects constituted a significant proportion of the total.[38]

Beginning in March 1949, Fourth Army's own unidentified object security concerns had begun to focus on the new atomic-weapons storage site. Killeen Base was adjacent to Gray Air Force Base and was to house one of the first of the new Q Areas, storage areas to deploy atomic weapons assembled at Sandia Base in Albuquerque. They were guarded there by units of the 12th Armored Battalion, under Fourth Army Command.

On March 6, 1949, a patrol in the Killeen Base AFSWP (Armed Forces Special Weapons Project) area reported a small blue-white, oblong object traveling over the area, other Army patrols also observed unidentified lights/objects from 8:30 PM to 2 AM. The following day, at 1:30 in the afternoon, an Army private observed an orange teardrop-shaped object drop vertically in front of him. On March 17, an Army captain (assistant intelligence officer) at the nuclear weapons site was preparing to fire flares to prove that recent sightings had been misidentification of flares—but while making his preparations, he and his men observed unidentified lights that clearly were not flares. At the end of March, an Army lieutenant on patrol observed a reddish white ball of fire pass horizontally over the base airstrip and noted interference on his field telephone while he was reporting the sighting.

Sightings continued in both the Q Area and across Fort Hood. In early May at 11:30 in the morning two Army majors and a captain observed two oblong, highly reflective white discs, flying at around a thousand feet and with an estimated 200–250 miles per hour and making a shallow turn. With concerns growing due to the frequency and quality of such observations, a network of artillery observers, with their ranging and plotting equipment, was organized and put into place. In early May, sites began making measured/triangulated observations. On May 6, a brilliant light, changing from pinkish to green, was seen at 4,000 yards. It was in sight for almost an hour, descending from 1,200 feet to 440 feet. On May 7, two sites established a triangulated observation of a brilliant, white diamond-shaped object at a distance of 1,500 feet. It was tracked for fifty seconds and traveled twenty miles, reflecting a calculated speed of 1,300 miles per hour and dropping in altitude. No sound was heard. The following day, May 8, three observation posts observed a similar, brilliant diamond-shaped object at an altitude of 1,600 feet, slowly descending for some nine minutes. During these sightings a second instance of radio interference was reported.

The early May sightings led Fourth Army headquarters to approach Air Force intelligence at San Antonio for help in investigating the lights; however, the AFOSI colonel declined, stating he was still awaiting direction from headquarters in Washington. Unwilling to accept such a reply, Fourth Army convened the first of a series of weekly meetings with representatives from Army CIC, Navy Intelligence, the FBI and Armed Forces Special Weapons (Atomic) Project personnel. The Army and Navy personnel agreed that the reports were "a source of grave concern"; the AFSWP folks felt that someone would come up with a natural explanation; and the FBI and AFOSI offered no comments at all.[39]

On May 19, a daylight sighting (8:39 AM) reported a round, silver, thin object seen for some five minutes. The object was rocking, giving an edgewise file. It continued irregular motion as it traveled upward and away at a slight angle. Sightings continued into June, with another triangulated observation on the evening of June 6; the object was within four miles of one observation post; shortly after 9 PM individuals in the plotting network tracked a hovering orange object some thirty to seventy feet in diameter and one mile in altitude. After two minutes and forty seconds of observation it began moving in level flight and then appeared to explode in a shower of particles.

By July 1949, the Killeen/Hood reports had begun to diminish, and an Army report (Summary of Observations of Aerial Phenomena, Fort Hood, Texas) provides a detailed summary of incidents that began on March 6. It described an ongoing series of sightings of "fire balls," usually greenish white but sometimes orange-red in color. The lights were round, oblong and diamond shaped; some moved, but others appeared as bursts of light. They had been seen in groups of from four to fifty. The incidents were frequent and widespread—in one instance observed by more than a hundred personnel. Army artillery observers used plotting equipment to get a "fix" on them; those observations, conducted on March 7, provided specifications on at least three different appearances. Three fireballs were observed and plotted, ranging from fifteen to twenty-four yards in diameter and at a height of some 1,000 to 1,600 feet. The lights were generally stationary, although one moved some 120 yards over forty minutes. Durations were from fifty-seven seconds to forty minutes. The lights "bracketed" the restricted Killeen atomic storage Q Area. All area flights, training exercises and other military activity had been eliminated as possible sources.

Clearly many of the Killeen site observations were totally distinct from the "green fireball" observations over New Mexico, representing some activity going on at almost ground level and in some cases lasting for extended periods of time. And the activity was extremely localized, involving an exceptionally secure area. However, both the Air Force and the Army at the Pentagon seemed to have simply lumped the green fireballs together with the Killeen reports and fallen back on the accepted Air Force intelligence report to close off discussion of what would seem to have been a major national security issue. This left regional Army personnel in Texas extremely frustrated—sharing much the same emotions as those of the atomic weapons personnel at Los Alamos and Kirtland AFB in New Mexico.

Air Force Captain Edward Ruppelt, head of the Air Force UFO Project Blue Book (which followed Project Grudge), later discussed the Killeen sightings (without revealing the actual name or location of the base) and noted the total Air Force lack of interest. He discussed the response as illustrating a "new look" within the Air Force that had emerged by 1949. It was an aggressively "anti-UFO" attitude, brought about largely because it had begun to become clear that the Project Sign people assigned to identify the UFOs had failed and "people don't like to be losers," much less to be seen as incompetent. "The people on the

UFO project began to think that maybe the brass didn't consider them too sharp." The brass proved to be much happier with a snappy "it was a balloon" response—that was much better than "it might be real but we can't prove it."[40]

However, despite the position being communicated to the field from the Pentagon, we now know that there was less than unanimous intelligence agreement that the issue of the fireballs had been resolved. In his paper "The White Sands Proof," longtime researcher Bruce Maccabee relates that in 1952, during a controversy over press articles about sightings at White Sands, the Air Force Scientific Advisory Board had recommended that information on fireball studies not be declassified "for a variety of reasons." Chief among them was the fact that "no scientific explanation for any of the fireballs and other phenomena" had been revealed by a separate 1950 Air Force–sponsored study (Project Twinkle) and that "some reputable scientists still believed that the observed phenomena were man-made." A follow-on memo from the Directorate of Intelligence to the Directorate of Research and Development supported that opinion on the basis that releasing information "would cause undue speculation and give rise to unwarranted fears among the populace," resulting from release when there had been no real solution.[41]

Following the AMC memo on the results of the AMC's Project Sign effort, most of the original staff departed as Project Sign evolved into Project Grudge and essentially entered a state that could be described as "housekeeping." The final report of Project Grudge, issued in December 1949, was overwhelmingly negative, with one exception. It continued to note that the unidentified object reports be monitored for their possible psychological warfare implications.

The United States military faced a host of uncertainties as the World War II decade ended, most of them having to do with the capabilities and intentions of the Soviet Union. Joseph Stalin was viewed as intensely aggressive and equally unpredictable. It is not outside the realm of possibility that Stalin used agents inside the United States to conduct a psychological warfare operation in and around America's nuclear weapons facilities—establishing the threat that the Soviets could indeed act inside America, at the heart of its nuclear warfare complex. Such a program may have continued through the early stages of the Korean conflict, when it appeared that America might be forced to actually use its nuclear weapons again.

Maskirovka/"deception" and psychological warfare practices have long been a Russian military specialty—they were brought into play again as recently as 2014, in Ukraine and, were used extensively throughout the Cold War. In retrospect it appears that there was considerable American intelligence concern over some level of Soviet involvement with the mysterious aerial activities in and around American nuclear facilities but that it was subsumed by the broader need to counter general public fears over unidentified aerial objects that the Air Force could neither intercept nor fully explain.

In one sense it appears that there was a serious intelligence failure in the lack of thorough investigation of the unidentified object sightings at key American atomic facilities in New Mexico. In other periods of the early Cold War era, such incidents surely would have been a major intelligence priority. During the first years of the 1950s, with the advent of the Korean War and President Truman's declaration of a state of national emergency, the atomic site reports became just another element of uncertainty in a growing series of national "fear factors."

Chapter 7

....

FEAR FACTORS

I n November and December 1941, prewar intelligence had produced a solid set of indications suggesting an imminent Japanese attack; the only question had been its scope and whether it would begin with surprise attacks on the American military. The attacks on Pearl Harbor and the Philippines had answered that question and engrained the belief that any new enemy would begin future conflicts in exactly the same way: unannounced and with devastating surprise attacks. As World War II ended, the American Congress was advised by Army Air Force Commander General Carl Andrew Spaatz that the United States was vulnerable to air attack in any future war, and Spaatz warned that only the availability of atomic weapons in sufficient quantities could deter a potential aggressor.

The emergence of the Soviet Union as the dominant global threat, and total failure to engage in any successful negotiations with the Soviets, had left both America's diplomats and its military with the perception that only overwhelming, dominant military force would prevent the Soviets from territorial expansion. In 1946 a message from George Kennan, stationed at the U.S. embassy in Moscow, warned Secretary of State Marshall that the Soviets were hostile and "impervious to the logic of reason" but "highly sensitive to the logic of force."[1] The view in Washington, D.C., was that "negotiation was both futile and unnecessary"—futile because the Soviets refused to offer any proof of sincerity and unnecessary because they would back down if the calculus of force was unquestionably against them.[2]

To the surprise of many, but in at least partial confirmation of this assessment, Joseph Stalin did not immediately launch the Red Army into any further territorial aggression following the end of the war. The common belief came to be that his hesitancy was simply due to the fact that America had atomic weapons and an air arm capable of delivering them and the Soviets did not. The perception existed that once the Soviets themselves possessed atomic weapons, war would be a certainty.[3]

That view seemed further validated by the outcome of the Berlin crisis of 1948–1949, when the Soviets blockaded the city but ultimately were willing to lift the blockade, following both a dramatic airlift to supply Berlin over the winter and the deployment of SAC bombers to Europe. Even at that point, General LeMay, then Air Force theater commander in Europe, had become sufficiently confident in the power of a SAC preemptive strike to propose a test of will, with a small unit of American Army troops forcing the blockade. If the Americans were engaged by the Soviets, LeMay was prepared to hit Soviet airfields and totally interdict any support for the Red Army in Europe. That plan was submitted to the Army commander in Europe and forwarded back to Washington, where it was rejected.[4]

LeMay's proposal surfaced an issue that would become central to the command and control of atomic weapons over the course of the Cold War: interdiction through preemptive attack. The concept of preemption had first surfaced in print as early as 1946, with the publication of a book by William Borden, with the title *There Will Be No Time*. Like a great number of other World War II veterans, Borden had served in combat and felt that many of his friends and fellow servicemen would not have died "had a little more honest realism been displayed before Pearl Harbor."[5] Borden, like many others during the first years of the Cold War, would lobby the point that "no armed peace could exist indefinitely." That was to become an influential view; by 1949 Borden became the executive director of the congressional committee responsible for the development and production of the American atomic arsenal.

In a top-secret study of 1947, the American military had reached a similar conclusion, based on its own real-world testing of newer atomic weapons. The "Crossroads" series of atomic tests at the Bikini Atoll in the South Pacific had been held to evaluate the atomic bomb as a military weapon. In the final report of the Joint Chiefs Evaluation Board, among other points it noted:

> *The value of surprise in attack has increased with every increase in the potency of weapons. With the advent of the atomic bomb, surprise has achieved supreme value so that an aggressor, striking suddenly and unexpectedly with a number of atomic bombs might, in the first assault upon his vital targets, achieve such an order of advantage as would insure the ultimate defeat of an initially stronger adversary.*
>
> *There must be national recognition of the probability of surprise attack and a consequential revision of our traditional attitudes toward what constitute acts of aggression so that our armed forces may plan and operate in accordance with the realities of atomic warfare. Our policy of national defense must provide for the employment of every practical means to prevent surprise attack. Offensive measures will be the only generally effective means of defense, and the United States must be prepared to employ them before a potential enemy can inflict significant damage upon us.*
>
> *For defense against atomic weapons, chief reliance must be upon the prevention or frustration of an enemy attack, or upon immediate retaliatory measures which will overwhelm an enemy and result in the destruction of his power and ability to make war. Essential to any plan of defense will be (a) knowledge as to whether potential enemies are in possession of the means to produce weapons of nuclear fission and (b) knowledge of their readying an attack. To gain this*

*knowledge there will be required an intelligence service
with a far greater effectiveness than any such service
this country has had in peace or war.*[6]

In conclusion, the Joint Chiefs report took a definitive position on
atomic warfare policy, pointing out that traditionally the policy of the
United States had been one of nonaggression but that continuing such
a policy in an atomic weapons context would "court catastrophe, if not
national annihilation . . . it is necessary that, while adhering in the future
to our historic policy of non-aggression, we revise past definition of what
constitutes aggression." That point would evolve into an ongoing debate
over the options of "attack on threat" versus "attack on warning"—a debate that would become a fundamental controversy in regard to nuclear
warfare command and control throughout the Cold War era.

There was little doubt that Premier Joseph Stalin was perfectly capable of ordering a Soviet surprise attack at any time. That fear drove
much of the initial reconnaissance, ferreting and signals intelligence
missions previously discussed. Yet even with all the active Navy and
SAC reconnaissance from 1946 to 1949, there was limited evidence
of any massive formations of the feared Soviet Tu-4 long-range bombers. In 1948 Air Force intelligence reported sighting some forty-eight of
them, but there were no signs of the concentrations the Soviets needed
for a preemptive strike. SAC had located large numbers of Soviet fighters and medium-range bombers in Europe, but General LeMay noted
that they were sitting exposed on airfields parked "wing to wing" and
presented easy targets for SAC.

In April 1950, in conjunction with war planning exercises, Air
Force intelligence offered the first assessment of Soviet strike potential following their explosion of an atomic device in August 1949. The
estimate was staggering—Intelligence Chief Charles Cabell forecast
some 1,200 Tu-4 intercontinental bombers in place by mid-1952. Air
Force Commander General George Kenney felt that estimate to be low
and projected a Soviet force on the order of 1,500 long-range bombers. Vandenberg also felt that Cabell had also underestimated Soviet
atomic weapon production and provided his own estimate at some 300

atomic bombs by mid-1952. Kenney noted that it was safer to err on the upside, given how badly the Japanese air strength had been underestimated prior to the Second World War.

In 1950, at the time of the Air Force estimate of Soviet capabilities circa 1952, SAC itself was fielding some 520 long-range bombers, and the American atomic inventory held fewer than 200 weapons. In 1952 SAC would have fewer than 900 atomic-capable aircraft.[7] In retrospect, it is now estimated that the actual Soviet Tu-4 force deployed in 1952 was on the order of 850 aircraft, comparable to that of SAC but not configured or deployed as a strategic nuclear bombing force.

Most significantly, in his 1950 letter, Kenney characterized the then-current "Off Tackle" American war plan as simply unrealistic—the plan projected using 292 bombs against 104 Soviet targets. SAC was to conduct bombing from Europe and bases around the Mediterranean. In planning for a global war, anticipated as occurring in the summer of 1952, Kenney felt it was going to be a question of whether SAC atomic strikes could take Russia out of the war before their atomic attacks knocked out America—it was just that simple. In addition, given the still lagging state of American air defense, Vandenberg did not feel that it would be sufficient to counter any Soviet surprise air attack.[8] Kenney's air defense estimate was to prove quite sanguine. In 1953 SAC flew a series of major mock war-game strikes against U.S. cities using only ninety-nine bombers. Air Defense Command, even with its significantly improved radar deployment, large numbers of jet interceptors and an extensive network of ground observers, proved totally ineffective. Only two bombers were "killed" prior to bomb release over their targets.

In concluding his assessment—submitted to Air Force chief of staff Hoyt Vandenberg—General Kenney strongly made the point that the United States was essentially at war and every effort needed to be made to convince the public and Congress that a state of war already existed and that the United States should act preemptively to strike Russia—at least to the point of preventing any Soviet advance in Europe. He did not consider such an action to be "preventive war," since in his mind a state of war already existed.

The Air Force threat intelligence estimate of spring 1950 was followed by the first ever United States National Intelligence Estimate of Soviet Capabilities and Intentions from the Central Intelligence Agency, issued in November, 1950:

> *There is, and will continue to be, grave danger of war between the USSR and its satellites on the one hand and the US and its allies on the other . . . . The Soviet rulers may deliberately provoke such a war ['general war with the Western Powers'] at the time when, in their opinion, the relative strength of the USSR is at its maximum. It is estimated that such a period will exist from now through 1954, with the peak of Soviet strength relative to the Western Powers being reached about 1952.*[9]

American intelligence was unified in anticipating a surprise attack by the Soviets; however, military intelligence was monitoring—and initially underestimating—the size of the North Korean military buildup. By March 1950, Army intelligence was reporting that the North had assembled and staged sufficient forces to invade the South at any time (always a significant warnings indicator) yet offered the judgment that attack was not imminent. General MacArthur and his staff concurred, based largely on generalized political assessments, "diluting" the purely military indications.[10] Deference to MacArthur's political evaluation resulted in the "surprise" invasion of South Korea by the Communist North Koreans. Washington had remained focused on a Soviet Army advance, anticipated since 1946. Stalin had been expected to move the Red Army west, south or southeast, directly expanding Soviet territorial influence. SAC had been created and developed at a frantic pace, first to provide massive conventional bombing to interdict such an advance and later the atomic bombing power to destroy the Soviet industrial and transportation base. That was the threat and response embodied in the contemporary April 1950 Off Tackle war plan.

Instead, in June of that year American troops faced a massive onslaught by a different enemy—from North Koreans rolling down the

Korean peninsula to the south. By that winter the Americans would face a second massive ground assault, from the People's Republic of China. Chinese armies, advancing in literal human wave attacks, flowed down through North Korea from their own border in Manchuria. That advance resulted in one of the greatest series of combat defeats in American military history, creating an international disaster for the anti-Communist forces.[11]

The weapons actually used in the Korean conflict also demonstrated the extent to which American strategic weapons policy had crystallized totally around atomic warfare against the Soviet Union. First the decision was made not to use atomic weapons against the North Korean advance or even its logistic "tail" back to the north. Then, with the massive Chinese surge and dramatic American losses, once again the decision was made not to employ atomic weapons against either the Chinese troops or their support infrastructure—railroad marshaling yards, transportation hubs, ammunition depots and airfields. That decision was particularly controversial given the active war involvement of the Chinese air bases supporting the increasingly dangerous Russian MiG jet aircraft deployment, flown by both Chinese and Soviet pilots.

SAC was sent to combat in Korea, over General LeMay's strong objections. In the face of a presidential and Joint Chiefs decision not to employ atomic weapons, he went on record that the combat might squander SAC's aircraft and crews that needed to be constantly available for war with the Soviets. Instead, the Joint Chiefs directed SAC conventional bombing to "knock the North Koreans out of the war . . . combat crews were to be flown to exhaustion if necessary."[12] By the end of the conflict, SAC had flown more than 21,000 combat missions, dropping more than 160,000 tons of conventional bombs. It had obliterated the only eighteen strategic targets in North Korea in a little more than three months—including ten airfields on the North Korean side of the Manchurian border.[13] Although no nuclear attacks were ever ordered, SAC did maintain the nuclear option. Even as the armistice was being concluded, it conducted Operation Big Stick, focused on moving a massive bomber force to the Far East in the event that the North Koreans violated the agreement. As part of the overall operation some twenty SAC bombers carried atomic bomb casings, ready for the integration of actual nuclear explosives that had been transported early in the conflict.[14]

The Korean conflict triggered a huge buildup in overall American forces, involving a more than 300% increase in U.S. military spending. Yet it became clear that the American response had been driven not strictly by what the North Koreans and Chinese were doing in Korea but rather the view that the surprise attack in Korea was simply an early indicator of future Soviet action. Secretary of State Dean Acheson noted that President Truman had been provided with assessments from both State and Defense Departments that the Soviets had the "capability" for local action either directly or through their "satellites" not only along their own borders but in moving to a more general war. In short, the Korean conflict was interpreted as a strategic indicator of future Soviet military action. President Truman confirmed that view in his own request to Congress for the military spending surge, specifically stating that manpower and military needs were going to be significantly more than what was required solely in regard to the fighting in Korea.[15]

It would be decades before oral history interviews, including those with Nikita Khrushchev, would reveal that Premier Stalin had supported the Koreans—and Chinese—primarily as a strategic diversion.[16] By 1950–1953 America was known to hold a huge nuclear superiority as compared to the Soviets, who had only a few atomic weapons and lacked any strategic air delivery capability comparable to that of SAC. There had already been public calls from prominent Americans to deliver the Soviet Union an ultimatum on atomic disarmament; Korea represented a Soviet opportunity to both divert the American military and to turn U.S. attention toward China as an enemy. The fact that it might well have taken America into full-scale war with China was not a particular concern for Stalin. In 1950, Korea functioned as an effective strategy to deal with American strategic superiority—with the newly Communist North Koreans and Chinese doing the fighting, taking the bloodletting and testing American willingness to use atomic weapons.

Truman's call for a new, massive military development program was consistent with the advice he was receiving from virtually all his advisors. It was also consistent with the projected likelihood of a Soviet surprise atomic attack as early as the summer of 1952, an assessment jointly given by the Joint Chiefs and the CIA. Establishing a continental air defense was part of that initiative, but the heart of the program was a major move forward with both atomic and thermonuclear weapons development and production. The stockpile of American nuclear weapons expanded exponentially during the next two decades; the distribution of that weaponry resulted in a network of atomic field depots, then expanded to American Navy vessels and finally to stockpiles of strategic and tactical weapons around the globe.

At the end of 1950, America had something on the order of 280 atomic weapons; they were primarily held in one location, and there were only a handful of production and manufacturing facilities capable of producing the numbers needed for the anticipated nuclear confrontation of 1952. In his April war planning summary, General Kenney had discussed his fears of Communist sabotage, even on SAC bases. He had mentioned statements by American Communists that in the event of war with the Soviets, SAC's atomic bombers would never make it off the ground. Yet while Kenney had called for serious efforts toward increased base security, there seems to have been very little discussion of any dramatic measures to significantly elevate either ground security or air defense at the handful of critical nuclear installations. In future years, with stockpiles of thousands of weapons, that would not be a concern, but in 1950 there were no massive stockpiles, and there would not be if the key facilities didn't move to a wartime level of production. In retrospect, with the deep concern about the perceived Soviet threat and the 1948–1949 history of suspicious activity around the atomic weapons assembly and storage "Q sites," it's rather amazing that senior levels of both intelligence and military command were not more concerned about a new spike in suspicious air and ground-level incidents that began at Hanford and Oak Ridge in 1950.[17]

By 1950, those key facilities did have at least basic air defense and a level of ground-level security—search radars, interceptors on call, security patrols on the ground, and twenty-four-hour ground and air observation stations. The bad news was that those improved detection and warning measures began to produce an ongoing series of reports of both air and ground penetrations occurring around the sites. Only days after the conflict began in Korea, an F-94 jet interceptor, on nighttime patrol over the Hanford atomic reservation in Washington State, detected an incoming, unidentified object. The jet was at 26,000 feet when its gun-sight radar picked up a track approaching at high speed. A red glow was seen, outlining a very large disc-shaped object. The object approached the jet head-on, and the pilot banked sharply; at that point the object reversed its direction and headed directly for the F-94 again. The pilot felt that he was under attack and prepared to fire, but the UFO jogged aside at the last moment, again and again approaching the jet and veering off. The pilot described playing "cat and mouse" with the object for some fifteen minutes before it stopped, flashed a red light twice and then sped off at very high speed. The entire incident had every appearance of a classic "ferret" penetration, with the object intentionally engaging the interceptor to test its capabilities.

That appears to have been only the first in what became an ongoing series of observations at the Hanford plants. An Army memorandum of August 1950 reported a series of sightings of objects above fifteen thousand feet and of negative attempts by Air Force jets to intercept the unidentified objects. Alerts were issued to radar units, fighter squadrons, and anti-aircraft positions. Reports were made to both the FBI and the Atomic Energy Commission. Yet it appears that Air Force intelligence was not monitoring the situation at all—most likely because it was fully engaged in dealing with the disastrous American retreat down the Korean peninsula.

Following the Hanford incidents, a concentration of incidents began to be reported from the Oak Ridge atomic facility in Tennessee. Beginning on October 12, a cluster of sightings occurred over and around the Oak Ridge reservation. On October 12, 1950, at 1:25 PM, Air Defense command radar observers detected eleven (and possibly more) unidentified targets over the Oak Ridge restricted flight zone. An F-82 was scrambled some nine minutes later and vectored toward two radar targets. The plane closed but made no visual contact; no sightings were made from the ground.

Three days later on October 15, at 3:25 PM, three security guards and a caretaker visually observed a large object (as large as a four-room house) over the K-25 security area. It was silver in color, saucer-shaped, with a "blister" on top of the saucer as well as windows on the side.

At approximately the same time an AEC Security Service trooper and an employee of the University of Tennessee sighted an object some twelve thousand to fifteen thousand feet over the Solway security gate. An FBI report on the incident contains the following information: "This object appeared to be an aircraft which was starting to make an out-side loop, trailing smoke behind. Soon these two men realized that the formerly described smoke behind the aircraft was a tail. This object continued to descend in a controlled dive, and when it approached the ground it leveled off and flew slowly, parallel to the ground."[18]

The object came within 210 feet of the two observers and was par-alleling the ground at approximately 6 feet. Trooper Rymer attempted to approach the object, but as he did it became smaller and started mov-ing in a southeasterly direction. This object is said to have approached a nine-foot cyclone chain-link fence and made a controlled movement to clear the fence, then a willow tree, then a telephone post and wire, after which the object gained momentum and altitude and cleared a hill at approximately one mile away.

About five minutes later the object reappeared from approximately the same location from which it had disappeared, but only for a few seconds. By the time the object appeared the second time, Joe Zarzecki, captain of the Atomic Energy Commission Security Patrol, was pres-ent and also witnessed this phenomenon. During the incident Knox-ville Airport Radar reported intermittent, short "paints" on its radar displays; the returns would be brief, disappearing only to reappear at another location.

The FBI Knoxville office reported on the Oak Ridge incidents but conducted no investigation, only forwarding information. In the inter-im a wave of further reports spiked, extending through the months up to the Chinese–Korean intervention in November 1950. By October, the Pentagon had become aware of the situation, and a brief report of October 1950 noted, "There is substantial evidence that unidentified objects have been sighted over the AEC installation. It is further evident that officials of the investigative agencies are concerned over the situation and it is not viewed with levity. The possibility of radio controlled objects cannot be dismissed."[19] Yet there is no sign that the incidents were truly making any impression on the high command. No additional defensive measures were ordered, nor did the incidents produce estimates or alerts of potential Soviet preemptive actions—such as covert attacks or sabotage at the American nuclear facilities.

Eventually a series of unexplained radiation and radar incidents—some suggestive of radar penetration measures similar to the "blanketing" of air defense radar by chaff deployment—led to an inconclusive inquiry by a team from Air Technical Intelligence at Wright-Patterson.[20] On December 10, 1950, a Richmond FBI office memorandum reported that they had been confidentially advised by Army Intelligence (Counter Intelligence/CIC) that the CIC had been placed on "high alert" for any information regarding "flying saucers." Based on the content of the memo, local Air Force intelligence was not aware of any such alert. Army CIC advised the FBI that information on the alert was highly confidential and was not to be distributed. Given the significant waves of encounters and observations at both Hanford and Oak Ridge, it seems that at least for a time the Army may have taken the matter of atomic security seriously, more seriously than either the Air Force or even the Atomic Energy Commission.

An interesting point of timing is that the spikes in security incidents around Hanford and Oak Ridge coincided not just with the beginning of the Korean conflict and the initial advance by the North Koreans but extended through the route of the U.N. forces when the Chinese entered the conflict. That was the period in which President Truman had most seriously considered the use of atomic weapons and actually deployed bombs to Okinawa with SAC aircraft. While it's purely speculative, it is certainly possible that the incidents at the American atomic plants might have been security tests of a sort, possibly precursors to actual sabotage attempts to disrupt work at the facilities. Russian military practice has a long history of using both deception and "masking." A limited number of staged incidents around the atomic facilities might well have masked much more serious and low-profile sabotage preparations. It is impossible to know what might have happened in the event that the U.S. had employed atomic weapons in Asia, or directly attacked Soviet bases. In the end, the ongoing incidents produced little in the way of additional site security measures and the sightings faded away—in the same time frame that it became apparent that President Truman had turned away from American military requests for the use of atomic weapons in the Asian theater.

With our focus on the subject of surprise attacks, it's important to return to the point that the events of 1950, and thoughts of a Soviet preemptive strike by 1952, had begun to raise some very fundamental concerns about the control of nuclear weapons, and the chain of command for their use. Indeed, the control of atomic weapons was initially unlike anything known in military history. In the earliest postwar years the American military neither possessed the existing atomic weapons nor controlled their production. In June 1946, America had proposed the creation of an International Atomic Energy Commission to oversee, license and control all atomic work—hopefully leading to the U.S. disposal of all its own weaponry. Any hopes for such an effort were aborted when the Soviet Union flatly rejected any idea of an international atomic energy authority within weeks of the proposal. Still, with some hope on the long-term prospects of atomic control, in August of that year, President Truman signed legislation creating a civilian Atomic Entergy Commission (AEC). At the time, the hope for the AEC was that its primary focus would be the peaceful use of atomic energy.

From a practical standpoint, the creation of a civilian authority meant that all atomic-weapons materials production, all weapons assembly and all storage of assembled weapons remained under AEC control. Only under presidential direction would the AEC actually hand over weapons assembled at the Albuquerque Sandia Base to SAC. Those weapons had to be picked up at Kirtland Air Force Base and transported to staging areas, or carried directly on weapons exercises and tests. Clearly such a protocol placed severe limitations on responding to any type of surprise attack. At first that was not seen as a major problem, since the Soviets had no long-range striking force and it was felt that it would take them a matter of weeks to organize and stage their forces for any major ground assault—something that would be detected by American reconnaissance in time to allow for any preemption the president might order. And for practical purposes there had not been all that many bombs to be distributed in any event, nine in 1946 and only thirteen in 1947.

The issues of atomic weapons "availability" and actual use in a wartime environment began to become increasingly clear during the Korean conflict. Richard Rhodes, in *Dark Sun: The Making of the Hydrogen Bomb*, details a process that lasted for months—involving not only the decision-making itself but the practical logistics of weapons release, transport and staging for actual combat use.[21] The Korean timeline of events gives a useful benchmark for the time required (circa 1950) for an American atomic response—as well as of the complexity of the chain of command involved.

By that time something on the order of 150 weapons were available, stored at Sandia Base in Albuquerque, under control of the AEC and General Robert Montague, the base commander. When the Korean combat began in June of that year, President Truman ordered the Joint Chiefs to assess the use of atomic weapons. In July, the theater commander, General Douglas MacArthur, requested the Joint Chiefs to consider making atomic weapons available—they would be used to seal off border transit routes should either the Chinese or the Soviets intervene with forces out of Manchuria. At the end of July, SAC was requested to provide ten atomic bombing aircraft for Korea. General LeMay adamantly opposed the request, since SAC still had only one squadron (the 509th) with aircraft suitable for atomic bombing. LeMay was in a very special command position, with the ability to exercise considerable independent influence given that SAC reported directly to the Joint Chiefs as a command rather than through the normal Air Force command structure.[22] SAC remained focused on its strategic Soviet mission, and LeMay's primary concern was accelerating Soviet reconnaissance and developing the most accurate targeting information that could be developed. At that point the Soviet targets identified by SAC numbered in the thousands, catalogued in the Air Intelligence Center's Target Data Inventory and Bombing Encyclopedia.[23]

On August 1, 1950, ten atomic-capable aircraft, each carrying two unarmed atomic bombs, were sent to follow two SAC conventional bomber groups already on the way to the Far East. One of the air-craft suffered a propeller problem on takeoff and crashed on attempting to circle and land. That accident at the huge Fairfield–Suisun transit base outside San Francisco resulted in a fire and explosion and scat-tered mildly radioactive material on the airfield. The other nine bomb-ers proceeded to Guam but were recalled in mid-September; the bombs and their support maintenance team remained on Guam. At the end of August, the National Security Council had officially warned that Korea was only the first phase of a Soviet global war effort. Stalin appeared to be validating that warning, ultimately moving thirteen air divisions to the vicinity of Korea and ten armored regiments into Chinese cities to provide rear area defense and free Chinese units to move into Korea. Somewhat surprisingly, the Joint Chiefs determined that atomic weap-ons would not be effective on the Korean battlefield. Apparently there was also some concern that if atomic weapons were used and did not prove militarily decisive, their deterrent value would have been seri-ously diminished.[24]

Conventional combat and extensive SAC bombing eventually turned back the initial North Korean incursion into the South, and the U.N. forces advanced north, directly toward the Chinese border in Manchu-ria. The Chinese responded with a massive cross-border attack, which quickly overwhelmed General MacArthur's forces. MacArthur had re-sisted strategic intelligence warnings that the Chinese were poised to move, and even tactical intelligence that they were actually on the move. His response to the "surprise" Chinese attack in Korea seems agoniz-ingly reminiscent of his lack of immediate action in the Philippines when given several hours of notice following news of the Japanese attack on Pearl Harbor. By the end of November MacArthur described the situa-tion as "out of control," and President Truman issued a public statement that the theater commander would have decision-making control over atomic weapons if the executive decision to release them was made. At the highest levels, the thought seems to have been that atomic bombing would not be effective unless it was part of an overall campaign against Red China.[25]

Whether or not such a campaign was going to occur was still a subject of intense debate in 1951, especially following the Communist Chinese counteroffensive, which began in November 1950 and savaged some seven American Marine and Army divisions. A fighting retreat had resulted in the evacuation of some 105,000 American and South Korean (ROK) forces by the American Navy at the end of December 1950. The Communist offensive in Korea had the United States deeply concerned; President Truman declared a state of national emergency, and in the midst of it all, the nation suffered its first postwar surprise attack scare.

On December 6, 1950, new air-defense radar installations detected what appeared to be a number of unidentified aerial objects approaching the northeastern U.S. Virtually nothing of this event became public at the time; however, in his memoirs President Truman wrote that on that morning he had been advised that radar was showing large formations of incoming aircraft. He was also advised that interceptors had been scrambled and that the air defenses in New England were on alert. Apparently Eisenhower simply left the matter with the military, proceeding with his own agenda for the day.

Later, while still in meetings, Eisenhower was advised that the incident was a false alarm, based on false signatures from the radars.[26] Apparently the true source of the alert was never defined, at least not in available records; various individuals felt that it was either an atmospheric anomaly, possibly a flight of geese or even an Air Force transport aircraft approaching Goose Bay, Labrador. Given the context of the time and concerns over Soviet military action, the apparent lack of coordination among senior administration officials, including the president, suggests a rather surprising lack of preparation and organization—the concept of timely "national command authority" was well in the future even in the first year of American combat in Korea.

With war-heightened nerves, and concerns that the Soviets might respond militarily to American bombing of Yalu River Bridge approaches on the Manchurian border, President Truman privately assured British Prime Minister Clement Attlee that he was not prepared to use atomic weapons even to prevent "a major military disaster."[27] Truman himself pushed for a cease-fire in Korea while the military situation remained chaotic and seemingly dire. In March 1951, MacArthur again pushed for atomic capability to attack Chinese airfields in Manchuria, and the following month the Soviets moved two hundred bombers into striking range of not only Korea but American bases in Japan. They also massed a fleet of some ninety submarines, posing the threat of moving to cut American supply lines to both Korea and Japan.

The apparent staging for Soviet combat prompted the Joint Chiefs to request atomic retaliation in the event of any "major attack" on U.S. forces. That request again surfaced the question of exactly how that retaliation could happen, as the military still had no direct control over the atomic weapons. Truman, by that time having totally lost confidence in MacArthur, balked—asking how he could release atomic weapons to a commander he did not trust. The net result of considerable Pentagon dialog was that MacArthur was dismissed and nine atomic weapons were officially transferred to the military on April 11, specifically to Air Force Chief of Staff Hoyt Vandenberg.

SAC's 9th bombing group deployed to Guam, loaded atomic weapons and moved on to Okinawa for "training." Almost immediately Washington ordered them back to Guam, and ultimately it was determined that the weapons could be used only following a request from the theater commander (General Thomas Ridgeway) and approval by the Joint Chiefs. On August 28, Ridgeway did request authority—in the event of "necessity"—to use the atomic bombs with twelve hours' notice. That necessity never occurred, and by November 1951, LeMay requested that—given the lack of any imminent threat of a Communist advance—the atomic bombing group be released to return to the continental United States so that SAC could continue its strategic training and preparations. The bombers returned; however, the Air Force and SAC retained the nine atomic weapons. They were not returned to AEC control.

With the U.S. engaged in full-scale warfare in Korea, with its troops under intense pressure from human-wave Chinese attacks and with solid indications that the Soviets had massed both bombing squadrons and submarines in apparent preparation for a knockout surprise attack, it had taken political negotiation and several weeks simply to legally release atomic weapons to the Air Force, much less to fully position them for a bombing campaign. The Korean experience also illustrated the tremendous reticence to use atomic weapons against strategic Chinese or Soviet targets, even with major American ground units being overrun, exactly the use that had initially been contemplated for them. As the Korean War ended and the Truman administration was replaced by that of Dwight Eisenhower, major questions clearly existed in regard to the effectiveness of atomic retaliation in response to any major surprise attack. It was not just a matter of decision-making; it was also a very practical matter of placing the weapons where they might actually be used in a timely fashion if such an attack did occur.

As combat in Korea continued through 1952, American intelligence learned that Stalin had ordered the creation of one hundred new tactical bomber regiments; there could be no justification for such a dramatic air buildup other than to support a Red Army advance. Even worse, by spring 1952, it looked as if the elements for a Soviet surprise nuclear strike were beginning to come into place. First, radiation sampling and analysis had determined that the ongoing Soviet nuclear tests had moved to weapons rather than "test devices" and that most recent test had involved an actual weapon delivered by an atomic-bombing-capable Tu-4 aircraft.

SAC reconnaissance flights had located a string of airfields across Siberia, airfields that had been upgraded to support Tu-4 bombers.[28] Beyond that, signals intelligence had tracked a series of Tu-4 flights into those advanced fields. By 1952, the Soviets had atomic bombs, intercontinental bombers and a series of forward air bases; conceptually they had indeed developed the capability of launching one-way surprise attacks on the continental United States.[29] The threat was presumed to be real; the immediate issue was whether or not the U.S. could obtain advance warning of any attack and to what extent it could defend against it.

The fear of a surprise Soviet strike had become so substantive that the Joint Chiefs directed an urgent joint Navy and Air Force program of shallow overflights of Soviet territory.[30] On joint flights, Navy Neptune aircraft located target installations and Air Force B-50 reconnaissance planes photographed the targeted radar installations and airfields. A number of joint flights were made between April and June 1952, locating and collecting target data on the Soviet sites.

In turn, the Air Defense Command's initiative within the continental U.S. had moved significantly forward as the Korean War continued.[31] The Lashup radar installations covered the approaches to both coasts of the U.S. as well as critical installations such as Oak Ridge and the New Mexico atomic warfare sites. Better yet, a much-improved permanent radar network was coming into place to replace the Lashup facilities, and by the summer of 1952 there was radar coverage of not only the northern border but key industrial sites in the Midwest and Northeast. A 1950 SAC exercise against Seattle and the Hanford plants had illustrated how ineffective radar was against low-level attacks. To compensate for that a complementary network of ground observers had been rushed into place as a national priority, and by July 1952 some three hundred thousand volunteers shared shifts at sixteen thousand observation posts along the west coast, northern tier states and the northeastern states.[32]

The new surveillance radar capability had significantly improved capabilities for detecting a surprise air attack, but even after some six years of effort, Air Defense Command still faced the practical problems of intercepting and destroying a well-planned, strategic attack. Its interceptor force included a limited number of all-weather jet interceptors. But the jets were assigned only to the most strategic target areas in the Pacific Northwest (around Seattle and Hanford), the San Francisco Bay Area naval and air bases, the Chicago and Detroit industrial centers and the northeastern corridor from Washington, D.C., to New York City. The rest of the country had only limited coverage by daytime jet fighters and World War II–era, propeller-driven fighters. For example there were no all-weather interceptors stationed in New Mexico, around the Oak Ridge facilities, the new Savannah River nuclear complex in South Carolina (focused on plutonium and tritium production, critical to thermonuclear/hydrogen bomb production) or protecting a number of the new atomic-parts plants going into operation around the nation.

The primary all-weather interceptors (equipped with batteries of unguided rockets for bomber formation interception) were the F-94 and

F-86D. In 1952, each type was deployed in five squadrons; F-86 deployment would triple by 1954. With speeds well above six hundred miles per hour and service ceilings of more than fifty thousand feet, both the F-94 Starfire and F-86 Sabrejet were certainly capable of bringing down the Soviet Tu-4 "Bull" bombers if they could locate and intercept them. Range was an issue for both interceptors, with the Sabrejet particularly limited, having operational combat range of 330 miles and the Starfire to a bit more than eight hundred miles. The primary daytime jet interceptors were F-86s with some fourteen squadrons deployed in 1952. Practically speaking, for continental air defense, the limited ranges of these jet fighters demanded a very large number of aircraft, pilots and alert airfields. In order to maintain a full alert, pilots spent more than a hundred hours a week on base.

As of 1952, only a limited number of the defense radar sites had height-finding radar capability. Ground control of interceptor aircraft was as challenging as ever in bad weather or at night, and many interceptor units, with pilots rotating from air combat missions in Korea, were not yet well trained in GCI intercepts. The introduction of all-weather interceptors such as the F-94D and F-86D, with their own onboard radar, was a major step forward for air defense, but in many instances nighttime interception proved quite difficult without ground guidance of the interceptors to the proper altitude. SAC exercises also proved that low-level attacks could defeat even the best combination of ground and air radar interception. Given little to no experience with actual Soviet bombing tactics, Air Defense Command had to assume that it would face a combination of high- and low-altitude attacks, under the most challenging conditions for interception. LeMay and SAC consistently practiced surprise attacks that proved embarrassing to Air Defense Command. In one such exercise a flight of fifteen B-36 bombers departed an air base in Arizona. Instead of returning to land as their flight plan specified, the bombers approached their field, dropped to five hundred feet and flew south some three hundred miles into Mexico before heading out over the ocean. The "bomber stream" flew north at low altitude, no more than one thousand feet, for a full day, arriving near Vancouver Island. At that point they moved up to forty thousand feet altitude and headed southeast toward targets across the Pacific Northwest, appearing at least for a time on air defense radar. All fifteen bombers conducted successful simulated attacks, completely avoiding Air Defense Command efforts to intercept them.[33]

On April 16, 1952, the worst fears of Soviet surprise attack once again seemed to be coming true. Details of the incidents were kept secret, and it would take decades for the full story of that day to emerge. Joel Carpenter and Francis Ridge were ultimately able to describe the events in their 2002 monograph on the air-defense readiness alert of that date.[34] April 16 began with a warning from Air Force Intelligence to Air Defense Command—classified sources had produced indications of "ominous" new Soviet activities. While those sources remain classified, it seems likely that they included the signals intelligence previously mentioned, intercepts tracking the new Soviet Tu-4 bombers on flights into Siberian forward bases.

The first tactical warning of the day came from a remote observation post in the Bering Sea: What appeared to be vapor trails from four aircraft were sighted moving east–southeast toward the continental United States. The sighting went to a control center at Elmendorf AFB near Anchorage, Alaska. From Elmendorf it was routed on to McChord AFB in Tacoma, then to Hamilton AFB in California—and finally arrived at around midnight local time at Air Defense Command (located at Ent AFB in Colorado). The duty staff at ADC immediately notified the Royal Canadian Air Force and ADC sub-commands and raised an alert for perimeter radar stations.

While alerting was in progress, Ent attempted to contact Elmendorf AFB directly only to have the line go dead, producing frustration and more concern. At around 2:30 AM the Ent Combat Operations Center woke the ADC vice commander, informing him of a "hot" situation. In what we will find to be a common response, given the relatively limited information available, the vice commander hesitated to call a full alert activating interceptors and anti-aircraft units. While still discussing the situation with his staff officers, another urgent notice arrived. An Eastern Defense radar unit at Presque Isle, Maine, had just reported five unidentified objects as incoming. Given the appearance of separate attacks coming in over the two major polar routes—exactly as anticipated in Soviet attack scenarios—a nationwide Air Defense Readiness alert was ordered at 3:10 AM.

Both the Pentagon and SAC were informed; SAC moved to launch its alert bombers. Alert interceptors were manned and backup fighters brought to alert status. The Tactical Air Command and Air Reserve units both moved to hand off their fighters to Air Defense Command control. Within half an hour Army anti-aircraft sites were ordered to be manned and interceptors were streaking toward the unknown targets off the East Coast.

When the fighters did intercept the incoming aircraft, it was determined that all three were commercial airliners, all far off course and off schedule. They had reported their flight deviations to Canadian air traffic control centers, but the changes had not been passed on to Air Defense. Shortly before 6 AM, the alert was canceled. Reportedly the Pentagon Air Staff was very critical of the alert, charging that the Air Defense commander had overreacted. The media appears to have missed covering the alert; however, the Pentagon's reaction is worth noting. As we will see in numerous instances, the risk of receiving command criticism would become a major factor in slowing responses to early indications of possible attacks. While that would prove to be a saving grace in an era of intercontinental missile threats, it also speaks to one of the fundamental weaknesses of defending against any modern-day surprise attack.

In a larger sense, the events of April 16, 1952, illustrated that the American air defense was still operating on a knife edge; its ability to identify friend from foe in real time remained limited, and there were clearly issues with communications between sites and commands. The incident had also occurred during the best possible defense scenario— high-altitude detection at considerable distance from potential targets. It was very unlikely that in any real surprise attack the Soviets would be that considerate. Low-altitude approaches and short-range detection might well preclude conventional intercept tactics. Given that in any real attack the Soviet pilots would be on essentially suicidal one-way missions, there was even serious Air Force discussion of the need for interceptor pilots to ram incoming bombers.

Surprisingly, neither the attack alerts of December 1950 nor that of April 1952 received any significant press coverage. Given all the new interceptor bases, radar installations and the growth of a highly visible ground observer corps, public concerns over the nation's vulnerability to air attack were being addressed relatively successfully—at least up to the time that unidentified objects arrived over Washington, D.C., in the summer of 1952. The first known appearance (unreported at the time) involved radar tracking from a series of Army radar units some 180 miles northwest of the capital; following the first incident, orders were received for Army anti-aircraft units to engage the objects if the opportunity presented. On several occasions F-94 interceptors were scrambled and obtained radar locks, but the objects departed just as pilots prepared to fire.[35]

Later UFO appearances over the nation's capital were widely reported and have been written about extensively. Radar tracked them over the White House, the Capitol building, Andrews Air Force Base and even followed them pacing aircraft taking off from Washington National airport. The first evening, July 19, the radar tracking and visual observations began shortly before midnight; interceptors were eventually requested but did not appear over the Capitol until after 2 AM. The radar tracks disappeared just as the interceptors arrived, and they returned for an hour or more after they departed.

This time there was extensive media coverage of the incidents, and it was not coverage that reassured the public or furthered confidence in American air defense. Immediate thoughts were of the Soviets and one reporter "accosted" a Soviet embassy attaché over violations of American airspace.[36] Air Force explanations of false radar tracks being caused by weather phenomena were rejected by highly experienced civilian radar operators at the Washington airports, and the public was clearly on edge over the July 19–20 incident.

Within less than a week, on the evening of July 26–27, the unidentified objects were back over Washington, D.C., widely tracked by radar and reported visually beginning shortly before 8:30 PM in the evening. Reports continued to come in, and around 10:30 press were invited to watch the radar screens at Washington National airport. At 10:52 all returns simultaneously vanished, and Air Force officers present in the Andrews radar room asked the press to leave. Within half an hour the tracks were back, and at least seven of them were classified as "solid," definitely not weather (weather returns were visible on the screens and clearly designated as such by the radar operators). Commercial aircraft were reporting sightings as well. Jet interceptors arrived once more, and around 11 PM one of the pilots reported being surrounded by the objects; his report was confirmed by radar tracks of the objects around his jet. Before the pilot could determine what action to take, if any, the objects simultaneously moved away from him.

Given the early press participation, the whole incident led to widespread reporting, with headlines in papers across the nation. It also led to a specific request from President Truman. On July 29 he asked the National Security Council to address the unidentified objects in terms of a potential threat to United States security. That presidential request led to a number of studies and extensive new dialog within the entire intelligence community. Ultimately a panel was convened by the CIA, assigned the mission of preparing a specific response for the president.

The panel's findings and recommendations were twofold. First, they reported that no specific conclusion could be made on the nature of the objects being reported; however, it was unanimously agreed that—once again, as in the 1948 Air Force conclusions—they showed no sign of presenting an imminent military threat. The second conclusion was that such incidents did represent a clear and present danger in terms of national security, that danger being related to the public being a target of Soviet psychological warfare. The panel noted that the air defense system was exposed to being "swamped" by false reports during any actual attack and that general public panic could tie up communications and greatly hinder air defense. In order to avoid that the panel suggested several measures, including media and educational efforts—even entertainment industry programs—to desensitize the public in regard to unidentified objects. It also recommended that UFO groups should be placed under surveillance as possible sources of witting ("subversive") or unwitting ("irresponsible") involvement in further panicking the public.[37] The panel specifically named the Civilian

Flying Saucer Investigators of Los Angeles and the Aerial Phenomena Research Organization in Wisconsin to be watched and commented on their "apparent irresponsibility and the possible use of such groups for subversive purposes."[38]

As 1952 ended, the United States was still at war in Korea; it had been through significant battlefield defeats but deferred on using atomic weapons. The Air Defense Command had secretly experienced its first general continental alert and found itself to still be lacking in a number of areas. Unaware of the poor air defense performance in mock attack exercises and during the first real air defense alert, the American public had instead become concerned by repeated appearances of unidentified objects over Washington, D.C.—the Air Force's public relations response to the Washington incidents had been less than convincing for either the media or the general public.

The good news was that Stalin had not actually launched his own attacks, and the most current Air Force and National Intelligence assessments suggested that the year of maximum risk had slipped from 1952 to 1954, largely due to the apparent Soviet delay in actually assembling a sufficient intercontinental bombing force. The bad news was that the nation was obviously moving into a period of ongoing Cold War—a situation that President Eisenhower feared might cost the nation dearly in the long run. He was deeply concerned that a sustained military confrontation could ultimately begin to cost Americans their basic liberties in the interest of national security—or force them into the moral dilemma of preemptive atomic war against the Soviets.

Chapter 8

....

MIRROR IMAGING

ollowing the end of general combat in Korea, both the United States and the Soviet Union moved into a decade of dramatic military buildup, each essentially "mirroring" the actions of the other. As early as 1947, anticipating a Soviet ground attack, the Strategic Air Command had been created, with the mission of establishing such an overwhelming threat to the Soviet Union that any aggression on its part would either be deterred or neutralized by destruction of the Soviet industrial and military infrastructure. In turn, the Soviets monitored the highly visible expansion of SAC, its overseas deployments and the dramatic increase in American reconnaissance and ferret missions against Soviet military bases.

The rapid development of the SAC long-range bomber-force effort had indeed provided a deterrent against new Soviet military action, and that deterrent would become even more sophisticated through the early 1960s. During that period SAC was always several years ahead of the Soviets, not only in terms of aircraft but in terms of logistics and proven operational capability. SAC's growth occurred in the context of Soviet premier Stalin's decision to maintain the immense Red Army at the end of the Second World War—at a time when the Western powers were frenetically rushing toward a dramatic reduction in their own armed forces. In 1946 Stalin had openly stated that there could be no peace with the capitalist West; it simply presented too much of a threat to the Soviet Union.

He also refused all international efforts toward atomic weapons control and even rejected something as basic as a mutual open skies agreement to reduce fears of military preparations by either bloc. Stalin used the Red Army as a powerful force for intimidation in Eastern Europe, brutally suppressing independent political movements and establishing Soviet dominance over a territorial buffer extending far beyond the Russian borders. And he encouraged and supported the Korean conflict, very possibly hoping to generate a full-scale war between the United States and China. Any extended combat with China would have certainly bled the modest American military force, and equally important, such a war might well have consumed much of the limited American atomic stockpile.

What more Stalin might have done militarily before his sudden death in 1953 is impossible to know; however, his order for the creation of an immense medium-range jet bomber force certainly indicates he was bracing for further conflict. Even after his passing, his successors retained something of the same attitudes, which continued to be reflected in their war plans for decades. The Warsaw Pact war plan of 1964 laid out the specific details of an armored advance through Germany, across the Rhine and occupying Lyon, France. The Russians would have moved to some 230 miles southeast of Paris in a single week. The plan called for a rate of advance unexcelled in military history—and made possible by the use of some 131 atomic missiles and bombs. A surprise Soviet first strike was to use 41 atomic weapons, and a reserve of 12 atomic devices would be held for use in the event of unexpected points of opposition.[1]

The Soviets responded to the Strategic Air Command by constructing what was to become very possibly the world's largest and most capable air defense network. They also began to produce their own Long Range Aviation force, initially built around copies of the American B-29 bomber, designated the Tu-4 "Bull" by American intelligence. In turn, SAC quickly began to migrate to jet-powered strategic B-47 bombers and by 1952 was flying prototypes of an advanced, very long-range atomic bomber, the B-52. The Soviets mirrored SAC's effort, developing their own equivalent jet bomber, the M-4 Hammer, designated the "Bison" by the Western militaries.

The Bison first flew in 1953, and in what seems to have been something of an intelligence leak, the February 1954 issue of *Aviation Week* magazine carried rumors of a new Soviet bomber, capable of atomic attacks on the United States from bases deep inside Russia. The aircraft itself was first seen in public at May Day 1954 activities in Moscow. Reportedly its appearance was a complete shock to American intelligence, much as had been the appearance of the MiG-19 supersonic fighter.

In 1955, during a July flyover in Moscow, U.S. observers noted a total of twenty-eight Bison bombers flying in two separate formations. American intelligence rushed to project the mass production of a major new fleet of Soviet strategic bombers. Those projections served to drive much of the huge American military expansion during the Eisenhower administration. In reality, the Soviets had outdone themselves. In striving to impress foreign powers, they had flown ten aircraft in the first formation, circled them around to join eight more and then flown the full eighteen aircraft they possessed. That single psychological "coup" generated wide American fear of a "bomber gap" and fueled public demand not only for expanding the American nuclear deterrent but for drastically improving air defense. The fears of a bomber gap also drove President Dwight Eisenhower to approve a radically escalated series of deep reconnaissance missions over the Soviet Union, which in turn prompted the Soviets' rush to an ever increasing air defense, in particular the development of high-altitude anti-aircraft missiles.

The "surprise attack" story of the mid-1950s, up to 1962, was one of the Americans' and Soviet Bloc's "mirroring" each other's fears and actions, racing to compensate for what each viewed as its immediate weaknesses and at the same time building up atomic weapons stockpiles that were sized not to make specific threats but simply to match or exceed the other side's stockpiles—perception and assumption rather than reality became the armament drivers for both America and the Soviet Union.

Military historian B. Bruce-Briggs describes the fundamentals of "mirror imaging" in his book *The Shield of Faith: The Hidden Struggle for Strategic Defense*. In addition to providing a very objective assessment of the American struggle to develop a working air defense, Bruce-Briggs notes that the fundamental error in American estimates of Soviet capability was one of assumption. Since the Joint Chiefs of Staff had determined that strategic bombing represented the "ultimate weapon" for America, it was only natural to project the Soviets would reach the same conclusion. Long after Joseph Stalin's death, his obstinacy and aggressive behavior had become the core of American strategic planning—the assumption was that as soon as the Soviets could prepare themselves for a surprise air attack on the West, they would carry it out.

The result was that in viewing first "Bulls" (the B-29 long-range bomber copies) and then the all-jet "Bisons," American intelligence began to project its own strategic war plan onto the Soviets—producing estimates of a huge strategic Soviet bombing force. The Air Force had commissioned RAND ("research and development," a nonprofit source for Air Force technical studies initially formed by Douglas Aircraft) to perform a study of the Soviet bomber threat. That 1953 study focused on low-level attacks by Tu-4 Bull bombers carrying atomic weapons of up to one hundred kilotons. The RAND conclusion was that a surprise attack by as few as fifty of the Tu-4 Bulls could take out more than half of SAC's force on the ground. The study also postulated that it would take the Soviets some fifteen to thirty days to organize such an attack but that a low-level strike would be virtually impossible to detect without advance warning.

As we explore such projections and studies as well as their ramifications, it is important to keep in mind that such a massive, Soviet long-range bomber force was never actually built. An estimated eight hundred–plus Tu-4 Bull aircraft were produced, but the vast majority were assigned to Soviet Naval Aviation for long-range reconnaissance, primarily focusing on the American Navy. The total production of the much-feared, all-jet Bison bomber turned out to be only ninety-three aircraft. Eventually, when the Soviets did build a large bomber force, it would be a very different "animal" from the strategic attack force that was being anticipated in the early years of the 1950s.

The aircraft that the Soviets did produce in truly large numbers—close to two thousand—was the Tu-16, designated the "Badger." The two-jet turbojet Badger entered service in 1954 and was capable of carrying a very large payload over a range of some three thousand miles.

Although initially configured for air-dropped bombs, it was quickly adapted to carry early Soviet cruise missiles, with their own range of some ninety miles. The Badger, along with its Kennel and Komet cruise missiles, was deployed in support of Soviet Naval Aviation, against American and Western-Bloc naval forces, intended as a "carrier killer." It was also widely used for long-range reconnaissance, surveillance, and electronic warfare and electronic and signals intelligence. Of the total Badgers built, some 260 variants were built for the cruise missile role and 453 as bombers. Over time many of the bombers were converted for roles in reconnaissance and electronic warfare.

In his book on strategic defense, Bruce-Briggs points out that both the U.S. Air Force and Navy contended for position as the driving force setting American strategic military planning following World War II, with the Air Force taking the lead based on its atomic bombing capability. In the Soviet Union, the premier service had been and remained the artillery. During the war the artillery had boosted its image with variants of its mobile, Katyusha multiple-rocket launcher; the Katyusha had proved devastating in saturation attacks. As the Soviets adapted and expanded on captured German rocket technology, the new rocket weapons were treated first as medium- and then very long-range artillery. The Soviet equivalent of SAC was not a strategic bombing force but from the beginning was conceived and designated the "Strategic Rocket Force."[2]

Rockets became a very early key to Soviet air defense as well. Based in data available only after the end of the Cold War, it has become clear that following the Korean conflict, the Soviets put their military spending not into a massive strategic air program but rather into a huge expansion of their radar network and anti-aircraft artillery. Most significantly they moved huge resources into the development of a series of extremely capable anti-aircraft rockets and missiles. During the years when SAC and General LeMay were worrying about the Soviets preempting and "killing" the SAC bomber force on the ground, the Soviets were preparing to kill SAC in the air on the approaches to Russia.[3]

At that time, however, circa 1954, the American intelligence view of the Soviet military threat was something quite different. The roots of Soviet threat assessment were based not in concrete "indicators" but rather in assumptions of Soviet intention, and not just in "most likely" estimates but rather in "worst case" judgments.[4] The experience of World War II and an ongoing series of "fear factors" had essentially placed the American military, public and even the intelligence community in a war mentality. Memoranda from the earliest postwar years as well as a series of warnings from senior Air Force officers were adamant that the American public had to be made to understand that a state of war with the Soviets already existed. Such thoughts were strongly stated in highly classified national policy documents such as National Security Directive No. 68: "the Soviet Union, unlike previous aspirants to hegemony, is animated by a new fanatic faith, antithetical to our own, and seeks to impose its absolutely authority over the rest of the world."[5]

To fully appreciate the depth and breadth of the American public's fear of imminent Soviet surprise attack, it's useful to revisit the popular literature of the mid-1950s. Philip Wylie was one of the more successful fiction writers of the period; his books continually appeared on the national library book club reading lists. In 1954 Wyle scored a bestseller with the title *Tomorrow!*, a story of surprise atomic attack on the United States—the book was dedicated to the men and women of the Federal Civil Defense and to those patriots dedicated to "doing their best to save the sum of things."

Tomorrow! began with Air Force intelligence and a highly classified operation to deal with secret high-level Soviet air reconnaissance of the United States. Con (aircraft condensation) trails had been spotted over Alaska and Canada and were known to have been made by Soviet aircraft. As the book began, new evidence had confirmed that the Soviets had recently begun secretly flying reconnaissance missions across the breadth of the continental United States. The Soviets had been flying at very high altitude, tracked on radar, but Air Force interceptors had been unable to reach them, at best obtaining long-range gun camera photos. A new operation was to be carried out by high-altitude, armed American bombers, able to reach the Soviets and shoot them down so as to obtain positive proof of their activities. Every high-altitude American aircraft available was to be sent aloft across the country. The risk was that if the Soviets realized that all American bombers are being deployed in the special operation, rather than being on alert to attack Russia, the Soviets might take the opportunity to actually attack America. In *Tomorrow!* the Russians did recognize the opportunity and they did launch a surprise attack. On a Sunday near Christmas, a formation of Soviet bombers struck across the undefended southern U.S. border. That strike was only a diversion, shortly followed by massive streams of bombers coming over the polar routes. The result was formations of Soviet planes roaming across the United States, atomic bombing American cities at will:[6]

> *The group of men were absolutely silent . . . the flags moved towards Chicago . . . and Indianapolis, Detroit and Toledo. . . . There were scarlet flags on four of them . . . all coastal cities and big ones, San Francisco, Los Angeles, New York and Philadelphia. The scarlet flags were for H-bombs. Here and there, over the whole continent the sky was peopled with dying young Americans and their dying enemy . . . pilots of jets, after the first few quarter hours, did not bother to press their gun and rocket releases. Whenever they saw a red star on alien wings, they plunged headlong. . . . As they died they knew they had struck a target that no man, with but one life, could afford to miss.[7]*

Wyle's book was seminal, highly influential and in one sense an accurate mirror image of exactly the sort of long-range aerial reconnaissance SAC was preparing to conduct over the Soviet Union—and the atomic strike it was preparing to deliver against Russia. There were dozens of similar books—with titles such as *The Murder of the U.S.A, Fight for Life, Not This August, The Conquered Place, The Long Tomorrow, Forbidden Area* and *Alas Babylon*—which spanned the decade from 1951 to 1959. All dealt with sophisticated and cunning Soviet plans, surprise attacks and atomic bombings, and many ended with a successful Soviet occupation of America, supported by further city atomic bombing as punishment for any ongoing opposition. America's intelligence and military leadership was not alone in assuming imminent Soviet surprise attack; they were reflecting the most fundamental fear of the nation.

Such popular fears mirrored concerns at the highest level of American government. President Eisenhower was so uncertain of American intelligence on the Soviets that he created the Technological Capabilities panel—known informally as the "surprise attack" or "Killian" panel for its head, Dr. James Killian, the president of the Massachusetts Institute of Technology. The panel's extensive studies produced proposals for weapons such as sea-launched and medium-range ballistic missiles, accelerated deployment of distant radar warning networks and intelligence collection using very high-altitude aircraft and eventually earth satellites, as rocket capabilities evolved.

As of 1955, that worst-case threat anticipated in U.S. military planning was based on the perception of a rapidly developing Soviet jet bomber force, capable of striking across the United States from bases well inside Russia. An attack force comparable to SAC's own plans was projected, with up to 800 Soviet heavy bombers supported by tankers and mid-air refueling capability. Those tankers would also allow the anticipated Soviet medium-range bomber force of some 850 aircraft to attain intercontinental capability, forming a total potential threat of well over 1,600 bombers capable of a mass attack on America. In reality the Soviets never built the anticipated 350–400 tankers, limiting themselves to some 70 such aircraft, and as mentioned earlier, they built no more than 100 of the feared four jet bombers.[8]

We know that now—but only in hindsight. Given the fears at the time, it would have been fatal to leave the nation exposed. With knowledge of what a surprise atomic attack could do, there was simply no room for error. As of 1955 the challenge was to find the Soviet bombers, to find how fast the force was growing and where it was based. President Eisenhower used the July 1955 Geneva summit to propose an "Open Skies" program to the Soviets, allowing both countries to fly reconnaissance over each other to guard against surprise attacks. The Soviets flatly rejected the proposal, further feeding American fears. The only option left was to go "Bison hunting," and SAC and the CIA were going to have to penetrate Russia as never before. SAC would go in force, across the entire northern border of the Soviet Union. The CIA would go "high" across its midsection.

The military, working with Cambridge Research Laboratories and commercial firms such as General Mills, had been working on very high-altitude balloon projects for years; the first of their giant Skyhook balloons was launched in New Mexico in 1947.[9] There were several early proposals for balloon-based photography of the Soviet Union. The key was to design the balloons for constant-altitude flight. Beginning in 1950 or 1951, development turned to a very specific top-secret project—WS-119L—which used Skyhook balloons flying at altitudes from fifty thousand to one hundred thousand feet to blanket the whole of Russia. It was conducted under the cover of an atmospheric research project designated "Moby Dick." To further conceal the fundamental reconnaissance project, different names were used at various launch sites—Project Gopher at Alamogordo, New Mexico, and Gray Back, Moby Dick Hi and Grandson at other locations.[10]

The balloons were to drift across Russia on the jet stream, exit over the Pacific and respond to radio signals that would trigger the photographic equipment to detach and parachute down for recovery by specifically equipped aircraft. The project anticipated launching up to three thousand balloons from Western Europe and Turkey. Test launches of both Skyhook and Moby Dick high-altitude balloons had already been caught in the jet stream and carried across the Atlantic, so there was little doubt that the balloons could perform the overall mission.

Testing and training for the project began at Lowry AFB, outside Denver, Colorado, in May 1955. Nine launches were conducted in May, and nine failed—twenty-six balloons were sent up in June but of that number only six launches were fully successful. More testing and training were needed, and the decision was made to postpone operational launches until 1956.

The operational very high-altitude program, generally referred to as Genetrix, began launches in January 1956. For the first two weeks goodly numbers of balloons made it all the way across Russia; there were not even any Soviet protests. But by February, the Soviet air defenses had begun to take a major toll on the balloons; protests were registered, and the president ordered the program stopped. All told, some five hundred balloons had been launched, at least fifty cameras were recovered, and more than 8% of the Russian landscape had been captured in more than thirteen thousand photographs.[11]

SAC itself had previously conducted highly risky reconnaissance flights over the Soviet Union—on a very limited basis. President Eisenhower had authorized a series of flights beginning in 1954; specially configured B-47 reconnaissance aircraft and supporting tankers were assigned to photography missions over the Kola Peninsula in far northwestern Russia. On the first flight, two aircraft flew north of Murmansk and recovered from the mission at bases in England. A third plane continued deeper into Russia—some six hundred miles—before exiting to the west.

The SAC RB-47 passed over the Murmansk area, photographing airfields and observing MiG interceptors that were scrambled to intercept them. As it proceeded, the American aircraft was monitored by several different sets of interceptors, none of which attempted attacks. As the SAC flight continued and began to photograph additional airfields, MiGs began firing runs on the aircraft. Given that the MiGs were operating at their ceiling altitudes, their gunnery proved poor. The SAC crew attempted to engage the MiGs using the B-47 tail cannon but had aiming problems with the automatic controls. Eventually they were able to fire a few bursts manually, but then their guns ceased to work at all. Continued attacks by the MiGs did result in hitting the American aircraft, with at least one cannon round hitting the body of the aircraft and knocking out the plane's intercom.

The MiGs followed the plane as it continued its mission, continuing to make firing passes well beyond the Soviet borders and in airspace over Finland. One MiG even tried and failed in a ramming attempt. Despite considerable difficulties the crew made it to England, leaving behind considerable Finnish media coverage of what had appeared to be an air battle, possibly between American and Soviet planes. In 1954 all parties involved completely denied the event had occurred. In his book *Shadow Flights: America's Secret Air War Against the Soviet Union,* Curtis Peebles provides a detailed account of those early SAC penetration missions and the risks the American crews faced during the flights.[12]

Following the Genetrix balloon launches in early 1956, SAC was next in line for yet another series of Soviet probes authorized by President Eisenhower. The project was to be far more exhaustive than anything previously attempted, and a special SAC unit of twenty-one RB-47–type aircraft and two squadrons of KC-97 E tankers were assigned. The project was designated "Homerun" and operated out of Thule AFB in Greenland. It was assigned to cover the entire 3,500-mile northern coastline of Russia. Standard missions involved a pair of aircraft: one signals intelligence and one photographic. The SIGINT aircraft monitored radar and other defense-related transmissions and worked to identify target locations for photography. The majority of the flights normally flew only a few miles beyond the Soviet borders; they tested Soviet northern defenses and prospected for advanced-bomber staging bases that could be used for cross-polar strikes against the U.S.

Project Homerun was conducted over an intense six-week period; the project's final effort was considerably different from the efforts of the flights that had preceded it. On May 6, a formation of six B-47s took off from Thule, crossed the North Pole and moved down into the Soviet Union. The mass flight moved deep into and across Russia, exited across the Bering Strait and landed at Eielson AFB in Alaska. All told SAC had flown 146 missions over Russia during a seven-week period, its aircraft had been untouched and it had determined that far northern Russia contained only a small number of radar stations. There had been only a handful of attempts to intercept the SAC aircraft, and in all cases the MiGs had failed to engage. It appeared that the entire stretch of the Soviet northern border was largely undefended, much of the territory simply a frozen wasteland. There was neither any significant defense nor any sign of advance bombing bases, much less the new Bison jet aircraft.[13]

Still, the Bisons had the range and ability to operate from deep inside Russia; the Genetrix program had attempted to probe that region but had aborted early, leaving key regions uncovered. The 1956 penetrations continued, and the third round was handed off to a newcomer, the CIA's U-2 very high-altitude photo-reconnaissance aircraft.

That effort to develop what became known as the U-2 had started in 1954, with studies showing that even with all its improvements, the existing American defense network could not stop even a serious strike by the early Tu-4 propeller-driven bombers. President Eisenhower had challenged his scientific advisory panel to come up with a solution for advance reconnaissance—a solution that could deliver enough advance warning of a pending Soviet attack in time either to deter or interdict it. As a result of his initiative, a new group designated the "Surprise Attack Panel" was formed—but out of a concern for the sensitivity of the subject, it was soon redesigned as the "Technological Capabilities Panel." Its efforts were to result in a project named Aquatone, which gave birth to the U-2, designed to fly at will over the Soviet Union, at heights unreachable by then current interceptors and anti-aircraft missiles.

The intelligence target list for the U-2 included atomic facilities, missile development and test sites, naval installations and bomber manufacturing plants and bases. A new National Intelligence Estimate of mid-1955 warned of the possibility of an imminent Soviet surprise attack. That warning added to the urgency of the U-2 project, and by July 1956, the operational U-2 missions, designated "Chalice," began.

There was hope that Soviet radar might not be able to detect the U-2 at its operational altitudes of up to seventy thousand feet. That hope was rapidly dashed during the very first U-2 mission. Signals intelligence intercepted Soviet defense communications tracking the plane, and the pilot himself observed several efforts by MiG fighters to intercept and attempt "snap-up" shots, hoping for a lucky hit. Some twenty attacks were made as the U-2 cruised over an extended route involving major Soviet cities, including both Minsk and Leningrad. The second mission was equally ambitious, targeting Moscow and research-and-development facilities near the Soviet capital. There may have been suspicions that the Soviets had probed Washington, D.C., in 1952 but there was absolutely no doubt America was flying at will over the Soviets' capital in July 1956. Both sides knew it—the Soviets could track the U-2, although not continuously—but they could do nothing to bring it down.

By the end of July, eight U-2 flights had been made, covering nine major bomber bases in the western USSR. The photography did reveal nuclear-weapons loading pits, but it found absolutely none of some one hundred Bison bombers the Air Force had estimated to be operational.[14] By November 1956, extensive photo analysis had produced a new, top-secret CIA intelligence estimate, and the Eisenhower administration knew that the "bomber gap"—the subject of so much intense political exchange—simply did not exist. As in many other instances it could not reveal that information to Congress or the public for fear of compromising its sources. Doing so might also have led to questions about what all those American aircraft and crews had been doing on what amounted to combat reconnaissance missions over the Soviet Union. In retrospect it must be noted that short of actually conducting a surprise attack on the Soviets, the balloon, bomber and U-2 overflights of 1956 "mirrored" exactly the sort of fictional Soviet reconnaissance of the United States described in the 1954 publication *Tomorrow!*—but in reality the flights had been American rather than Soviet.

Surprisingly, we now know that the Soviet leadership had not viewed the 1956 flights as a precursor to an American surprise attack—they had viewed them as pure intimidation, a demonstration that SAC did indeed constitute an effective deterrent, bluntly demonstrating the weakness of the Russian homeland defense. Soviet attempts to intercept and engage the American aircraft had cost Soviet casualties as well. Russian pilots operating beyond the limits of their aircraft had lost control and crashed; interceptors had collided and even been shot down by their own anti-aircraft missiles simultaneously targeting Americans aircraft, particularly the U-2.

Nikita Khrushchev discussed the matter with his son, picturing the Americans as "laughing" at the Soviets while the flights were occurring. It was something that could not be tolerated, and while the secret penetration missions alleviated American fears of any imminent bomber attack, they pushed the Soviets into the development of advanced interceptor missiles. The Soviets knew exactly what they needed to bring down the U-2s: high-altitude interceptors and anti-aircraft missiles, and dramatically improved air defense. It would take time, but ultimately the Soviets would bring down a U-2, aborting a new peace initiative by President Eisenhower.

It should also be remembered that the development and mainte-nance of American nuclear deterrence were accomplished only with significant sacrifice and casualties. SAC as well as Navy air and sub-marine units secretly operated under what amounted to wartime con-ditions throughout the 1950s and well into the 1960s. Their losses in reconnaissance and surveillance flights were ongoing and are now well documented in works such as *The Price of Vigilance: Attacks on Ameri-can Surveillance Flights*, by Larry Tart and Robert Keefe. William Bur-rows's historical research on covert reconnaissance flights, published in *By Any Means Necessary,* developed a list of some fifteen American aircraft engaged and attacked by the Soviets. The personnel losses in each attack involved between twelve and fifteen crew members, in some instances more.[15]

No doubt the full casualty count of American personnel lost on secret missions is still incomplete, and the ongoing aircraft and casual-ties taken by SAC over the same period have still to be publicly tallied. Those losses occurred annually, as its bombers, tankers and transports carried out an extremely demanding training regimen, coupled with fre-quent overseas deployments and rotations. The level of SAC operations was nothing short of stupendous; in a random sample of sixty days in 1956, SAC had some 1,353 planes engaged in "war maneuvers."[16] Every three minutes of every day, seven days a week, a SAC aircraft was involved in midair refueling; bringing two massive aircraft together and coupling them for fuel transfer during nighttime and all-weather flying conditions certainly carried its own hazards. Reconnaissance and deterrence were only two elements of the overall American response to fears of an imminent Soviet surprise attack—the third element was defense, specifically air defense executed by the Continental Air Defense Command—succeeded by the North American Aerospace Defense Command in 1957. Operating a 24/7 air defense during all seasons and scrambling alert aircraft at night and under the most hazardous weather conditions was more than just challenging for the pilots and crews involved with the alert interceptors; it carried the same level of risk and losses that were being suffered by SAC. The interceptor com-mand operated on an equivalent wartime footing, assuming that each unknown series of radar tracks or sightings could be part of an incoming surprise attack.

Major General Roger Ramey, deputy chief of Air Force Operations, was quoted by reporters as saying that interceptors had raced aloft on hundreds of occasions in pursuit of unidentified aerial objects; that sort of defensive response was simply "standard procedure."[17] Regardless of the ultimate nature of the target, those interceptions were treated seriously. On occasion the interceptors fired on the unknowns, while on other occasions the jets scrambled into bad weather or suffered mechanical problems; planes crashed and crews died as a result of the efforts.[18] While it did not suffer the secret combat losses that the Air Force and Navy reconnaissance crews faced, the Air Defense Command compiled its own casualty list. A survey of *New York Times* articles revealed that between 1951 and 1956, the Air Force, Navy and Marine Corps lost a total of some 185 interceptor aircraft over the United States and its adjacent coastal waters. Those losses resulted in the deaths of more than 200 interceptor pilots, a number of them combat veterans of the Korean War.[19]

One of the problems that emerged as the enlarged air defense network became operational circa 1952 was that actual interceptions of unidentified targets by high-speed jet aircraft were quite challenging. The basic task of directing/"vectoring" interceptors to the correct altitude had been a problem before height-finder radar was available, and even with radar, considerable practice was required to develop the shared skills needed by ground controllers and pilots. There was a growing need to destroy incoming bombers well away from their targets. That need escalated with the development of air-launched "standoff" missiles. Both the U.S. and the Soviets developed a series of effective, air-launched missiles for bombers—with ranges of one to two hundred miles. The Soviets began testing the Raduga Kh-20 air-launched atomic weapon in 1954; its range was on the order of five hundred miles.

In the new era of jet aircraft warfare there was little time for a series of classic gun and cannon attacks on the target; incoming bombers needed to be totally destroyed as quickly and as far away from their intended targets as possible. Interception became even more challenging with the supersonic speeds of the new American Century–series jet fighters (F-100–F-106). Those interceptors came into service beginning in the early 1960s. It became clear that effective air defense control was far more complex than during the Second World War.

At jet and supersonic jet speeds, it became questionable as to whether human pilots could be effective without a technological breakthrough. Two such breakthroughs were seen as possible solutions to the problem of reducing time to "kill" enemy aircraft. Self-guided missiles were needed to accomplish the kills, whether launched from the ground or from interceptors. Such missiles were capable of destroying targets well beyond the range of the guns, cannon and short-range unguided missiles available on the early all-weather interceptors such as the F-94.

Work had begun on a series of guided air-to-air missiles as early as 1946. One of the first to go into actual testing was the AAM-A-2 Falcon, in 1949. By the time the missile entered service in 1956 it had been redesigned as the GAR-1. The GAR-1 (Falcon) ultimately went into service on several of the Century-series fighters, with both radar and heat-seeking versions. One of the major advantages of the new missile was the ability for the interceptor to "fire and forget," leaving the missile to home in on the target with its own on-board targeting electronics. The Falcon/GAR's limitation was its relatively small conventional warhead and the fact that it lacked a proximity fuse—a direct hit on the target was required. That issue was eventually addressed by providing air-to-air missiles with nuclear warheads. The first atomic-armed, air-to-air missile was the Air Force's Genie atomic (but unguided) weapon, with a range of only six miles. Its blast radius precluded the need for precision guidance since its 1.5-kiloton warhead provided a lethal blast radius of up to 1,000 feet. It would have certainly not only destroyed its individual target but would have seriously affected other enemy aircraft in the immediate area.

A prototype of another new air-to-air missile—the "Sidewinder"— was tested in 1953 and entered operational use in 1956. The Sidewinder definitely extended the kill capability of American interceptors, having an effective range of some twenty miles. The American Navy also developed its own air-to-air, radar-guided interceptor missile—the Sparrow—as early as 1946, and the Sparrow was deployed on naval aircraft in the 1950s. As with virtually all other types of both missiles and aircraft, standard practice was for each service to develop and deploy its own versions based on its own specific, perceived needs.

A brute-force alternative to the precision-guided missiles, with the capacity of destroying multiple enemy targets or disrupting entire aircraft formations, was to arm ground-based anti-aircraft missiles with large, high-explosive warheads. Weight constraints limited the range of such missiles, but that problem was resolved by creating defensive rings of missile sites around major cities and key military installations. The earliest such sites were intended to replace the Army's anti-aircraft, radar-guided gun units; the missile sites were manned and operated on a fifteen-minute alert basis by Army personnel. The deployed weapons were Nike Ajax missiles, with a range of twenty-five to thirty miles to an altitude of almost seventy thousand feet. They carried conventional high-explosive fragmentation warheads—creating a bust cloud of hardened steel cubes to create maximum destruction.

Nike Ajax began to be deployed in 1954, and missile batteries were initially placed at some sixty sites, mounting a thousand missiles. By 1962 another two hundred Nike sites were operational, with a total of more than four thousand missiles. Nike sites literally formed rings of defense around major cities and bases, with the number of sites dependent on the target being defended—as an example, Chicago was surrounded by twenty-two missile batteries, Los Angeles by sixteen sites and New York by nineteen.

Given that twenty-five miles was still a fairly limited interception range, even with sites around the perimeter of the target areas, a successor was rushed into operation as a replacement for the Ajax version. Nike Hercules had a range of more than seventy-five miles, a ceiling altitude up to one hundred thousand feet and carried an atomic warhead of twenty kilotons, larger than the atomic bombs dropped on Japan at the end of the Second World War. It was powered entirely by solid fuel rocket motors, which dramatically reduced the dangers of handling liquid fuel at the sites and significantly improved the ability to maintain them in a constant firing alert status. The Nike Hercules effort placed thousands of atomic weapons around major American cities, with the sites under control of the Army or Army National Guard.[20] The longer range of the Hercules version allowed the Army to actually reduce the total number of Nike sites during the period of 1958–1962, and additional Nike Hercules batteries were place in Alaska, Hawaii and Thule, Greenland.

Given the ongoing fears of the Soviet long-range bombers—disproven by SAC and U-2 reconnaissance but kept highly secret to preserve intelligence collection methods—the Nike systems were further supplemented by Air Force ground-launched interceptor missiles, intended to have an even longer range than the Nike, and equipped with atomic warheads. To gain that range, the first version of the Air Force interceptor—Bomarc—was essentially a large, winged, chemical-powered ramjet rocket, unlike the multistage solid/chemical rocket-launched Nikes. The Air Force anti-aircraft project had actually begun in 1946, as did many similar projects from both the Army and Navy. Inter-service missile competition was rife during the early Cold War years, with variants of almost every class of missile pursued by all three services. The Bomarc ramjet proved to be a major problem for the Air Force; the missile experienced significant delays and greatly escalating the costs.[21] Under tremendous competitive pressure from the Army Nike, the Air Force issued production contracts for it in 1957, while still encountering significant problems with the prototypes—including total flameouts of the ramjet while in flight.[22] Ultimately the Air Force switched to a solid fuel booster for the missile, resolving the problem of maintaining liquid fuel missiles on ongoing alert and also extending its range to some 440 miles. The Bomarcs did not become operational until 1959, and despite ambitious deployment plans, ultimately only eight sites in the United States and two sites in Canada were in place in the early 1960s.

There was no doubt as to the power of the new air-to-air and ground-to-air missiles, especially those with atomic warheads. The problem that remained was getting them on target and controlling them in extremely high-speed engagements. As early as 1947, various committees, panels and subpanels of the Research and Development Board (organized as part of the huge effort associated with the National Security Act of 1947) had begun to study not only dramatically enhanced radar defenses but the use of "automatic equipment to pick up and relay information to an air defense control system that would reduce the human element to a minimum."[23]

A consensus was growing that "successful interceptions of high-speed attacking airborne objects" would be possible only with fully automatic systems—human responses and reflexes were simply going to be too slow to manage high-speed, supersonic combat. That consensus was soon supported by real-world exercises with radar ground-controlled intercept. Exercises were demonstrating that it was increasingly difficult for pilots in the new jets to accurately approach targets from the rear, a classic attack strategy. The new jets were so fast that approach turns had to be made miles away and the level of coordination between ground controllers and the pilots was extremely challenging.[24]

The real-world information from the early radar-directed intercept exercises, the anticipated availability of advanced jet interceptors, air- and ground-guided interceptor missiles and the appreciation that any successful interdiction of an air attack was going to require sufficient warning to begin interception attacks hundreds of miles away from their targets were the subject of an ongoing series of meetings and studies. By 1954, the combination of fears over a potential Soviet jet bomber attack and the Soviet explosion of a hydrogen bomb had led the National Security Council to recommend two immense new air defense projects. Those projects were then proposed by the Eisenhower administration and funded by Congress.

The first, a complement to the northern American border radar "fence"—the "Pinetree Line"—became operational in 1954. The Pinenetree Line added some thirty additional search radars to America's northern border, constructed in Canada and with funding and manpower from the U.S. The Canadians also installed a northern radar fence to protect their own cities, a series of unmanned microwave sites—the Mid-Canada Line—which detected any aircraft flying over them. It was a functional solution for the Canadian north, which had virtually no routine commercial air traffic.[25] A new, very long-range radar fence would be going to the very top of the continent and would have the capability of detecting high-altitude jet aircraft. The Distant Early Warning Line (DEW Line) was a crash air defense project, an extreme challenge given the Arctic cold and both extreme construction and weather challenges. It demanded a major effort, but with an immense push the major portion of the DEW Line was declared "technically ready" in 1957.

The second, and even more demanding, air defense project established a single computer-driven, linked detection and interception control system for the entire North American continent. Initial work on such a system had begun in 1950; it evolved into a named project—Lincoln—in 1951. Its ultimate product was the SAGE system—shorthand for Semi-Automatic Ground Environment—of integrated air defense. It was felt to be so vital to American defense that as one of its managers recalled, "We had all the money we wanted for SAGE until Sputnik."[26] The SAGE effort was immense; the cost exceeded that of the Second World War Manhattan atomic bomb project. Its first regional combat battle post became operational in January of 1959, and by 1962 it was fully operational. From that point on SAGE took over tracking hostile targets, directing interceptors and actually controlling the launch of both air-to-air missiles and ground-based rockets.

The story of SAGE has been dealt with extensively elsewhere, including the ongoing questions about its true ability to withstand attack. Several SAC exercises demonstrated that its radar component continued to be vulnerable, at least at low altitudes with individual attacks by jet bombers. Low-altitude attacks had historically been a major problem in radar defense. As early as 1951–1952, SAC commander LeMay requested that the CIA use its covert Air Operations teams to conduct a series of low-level attacks against strategic targets including SAC installations. The CIA aircrews flew from Kitty Hawk, North Carolina, over Norfolk, Virginia, and right up the Potomac, successfully "attacking" their primary target—the White House. CIA teams also conducted successful low-level attacks against Andrews AFB, steel mills in Pennsylvania, research facilities in New York and Boston harbor with its planes totally undetected. The exercises had proved extremely embarrassing to the Air Defense Command and upsetting to LeMay.

In another series of exercises, ADC interceptors were alerted to missions against SAC bases, but even when anticipated "enemy" aircraft were detected it had proved virtually impossible to vector ADC jets onto them at low altitudes. In the end all of the CIA's low-level, night-time "attacks" went either undetected or, if detected, unsuccessfully intercepted.[27] Such experiences may help explain why even as SAGE was being fully deployed in the early 1960s, SAC felt confident that it could conduct successful attacks against the huge and highly capable Soviet air defense network—using extreme low-level penetration tactics.[28]

Certainly the SAGE story is relevant to our overall subject of defending against surprise attacks, but most surprising is the fact that the SAGE system—and the massively enhanced continental air defense spending—moved forward despite the classified knowledge that the feared Soviet "bomber gap" had never really existed. While not shared with the public, or even Congress, the results of the intense SAC and CIA U-2 reconnaissance efforts of 1956 had been processed and integrated into the highest-level national security intelligence studies by mid-1958. A Special National Intelligence Estimate, issued by the CIA in June of that year, contained a much more realistic evaluation of the strength and composition of the Soviet long-range bomber force.[29]

The report began by noting that the operational Soviet force was composed primarily of medium-range bombers, capable of operations in the areas over and immediately beyond Soviet borders and capable of attacking the continental United States only in one-way missions. It specifically noted that the Soviets appeared to have foregone any immediate buildup in either long-range Bear or Bison bomber forces. It was anticipated that a new medium-range bomber with limited supersonic "dash" capability might be introduced in the early 1960s. Its best estimate was that by mid-1963 the Soviets would have a long-range force of two to three hundred bomber and tanker aircraft, with a growing turn to long-range intermediate and intercontinental missiles as the strategic weapon of choice.

For reference, in 1958 America's Strategic Air Command long-range bomber force consisted of 1,945 long-range bombers and 962 tankers plus 51 transports. SAC also had three Atlas D intercontinental ballistic-missile and one Snark long-range cruise-missile squadrons. By 1963 SAC operated 1,505 all-jet strategic bombers (including 86 supersonic B-58 bombers), 613 jet tankers and 306 propeller-driven tankers. SAC missile units in 1963 included 13 Atlas ICBM squadrons, 22 Titan

ICBM squadrons and 13 Minuteman ICBM squadrons.[30] The American strategic advantage was becoming overwhelming in 1958, and by 1962–1963 there would be a major imbalance with the Soviets, in the United States' favor.

With SAGE, an entire new generation of jet interceptors (the Century Series) and the new atomic warhead ground-to-air missile battery network, by 1962 America was at the absolute peak of its defensive capability. One hundred and ninety-two primary and ninety-two gap filler surveillance radars were in place in the continental U.S., the DEW line was operational, and forty-one interceptor squadrons with eight hundred aircraft were operational as well as batteries of Nike Hercules and Bomarc atomic warhead missiles. America was prepared to at least neutralize a good portion of any air attack the Soviets might throw at it, and the Soviets knew that. As we know now, they had chosen to go a different route than the U.S., foregoing building a huge bomber force, opting instead to focus on long-range missiles.

The bomber "gap" of 1954–1955 created a fear that never materialized. However, fear alone, and the need to preserve intelligence sources and methods, was enough to trigger a major surge in American military spending. Beyond spending, another and much less visible surge had begun to occur—a tremendous surge in the production and deployment of atomic weapons. It would be decades before the American public became aware of how massive atomic weapons production had become, first by the United States—then mirrored by the Soviet Union.

The development of an immense Soviet nuclear stockpile was simple enough to explain; the Soviets felt they had to match and if possible exceed the American stockpile. In hindsight the growth of the gigantic American atomic weapons inventory is more difficult to comprehend. Initially it was simple enough to understand: Build enough atomic bombs to destroy the Soviet infrastructure and win a war in the event that Stalin launched a campaign of territorial expansion with the Red Army. Over the years it became something far more complex—a process that many of those involved in felt had assumed a life of its own, beyond any measure of rational control.

Chapter 9

....

TARGETING

One of the most fundamental factors in the military surge of the second half of the 1950s was the tremendous growth of the American atomic nuclear stockpile and the spread of atomic weapons far beyond SAC, throughout all three services. The integration of atomic warheads into a suite of weapons independently fielded not only by the Air Force but by the Navy on carriers and submarines as well as on Army battlefield missiles and artillery had dramatically broadened the American nuclear weapons inventory. Atomic warheads were being introduced virtually everywhere, from Navy depth charges to the M-65 medium-range Army battlefield cannon. By the late 1950s, the Army had developed weapons ranging from the "Atomic Annie" nuclear artillery piece to the "Davy Crockett" recoil-less gun and atomic land mines for use in Europe.

In the 1960s tripod-mounted Davy Crockett guns—firing small projectiles with 10- to 20-ton atomic warheads—and the atomic mines were deployed as part of a tactical plan to blunt any Red Army advance through the Fulda Gap into Germany. Thousands of small and large atomic warheads were being fielded with the American military around the globe. The Truman-era concept of a complex atomic-weapons-centralized control procedure, which had involved turning over individual bombs to SAC only under very special circumstances, had first become unworkable with the growth and forward deployment of SAC. Later, during the

Eisenhower administration, the services and theater commanders came to hold and target their own individual atomic inventories.

Initially it had been the SAC target list that had dramatically escalated atomic bomb production. In 1945 the initial number of Soviet targets was basically a list of sixty-five cities that represented the manufacturing and transportation core of the USSR. Destroying them was to have gutted the ability of the Soviets to move the Red Army outside their borders. By 1952 Air Force Chief of Staff Hoyt Vandenberg advised President Truman that the Air Force had identified somewhere between five thousand and six thousand Soviet targets that would need to be destroyed in the event of war.[1]

As noted in earlier chapters, during the late '40s and throughout the 1950s various Air Force and CIA intelligence estimates presented an ongoing and escalating threat of Soviet surprise attack. That threat was characterized in terms of estimated capability, rather than with discussion of any specific threat indicators. The Soviets had routinely used their military to suppress any signs of opposition within their Eastern Bloc border states; they had sponsored insurgencies around the globe (some truly Communist, some simply nationalist). Given the ongoing rise of new Communist or Communist Bloc–leaning governments, it was simply assumed that a Cold War was in progress and that it would turn "hot" with a Soviet surprise attack whenever the Soviets felt that they had achieved a strategic position that would allow large-scale military action.

In February 1955, the National Security Council issued directive NSC 5511, establishing the Net Evaluation Subcommittee. That directive, signed by President Eisenhower, tasked the Net Evaluation group with studying, evaluating and preparing an annual report dealing with any type of overt or covert attack the Soviet Union might be capable of executing. The Net Evaluation group was to consider the current and future states of American defense programs as compared to estimated Soviet capabilities. Their report was to forecast damages from such Soviet attacks—whether they be an initial surprise attack with some warning, a surprise attack with only general strategic warning or a general attack with sufficient warning to move the U.S. military to full alert and initiate retaliatory action.[2]

Evaluations were to be presented to the National Security Council in October each year and project against a date three years in the future. If circumstances indicated a situation that would significantly affect the net capabilities of the USSR to inflict injury on the continental U.S. or its installations overseas, a report was to be submitted immediately. The Net Evaluation Subcommittee membership was to be headed by the chairman of the Joint Chiefs of Staff and include members of various intelligence and security groups as well as the director of the Central Intelligence Agency.

In brief, the subcommittee was charged with projecting American strategic exposure or advantage as compared with the Soviet Union. The project was intended to provide direction for focused intelligence collection as well as guidance for U.S. military development and defensive preparations. The reports were to project changing levels of risk and characterize the Soviet threat. For reference, we now have available a Joint Chiefs memorandum on the Net Evaluation Subcommittee report for 1956, along with a lengthy appendix discussing "Strategic Surprise."[3] The estimate in that appendix focused on a Soviet surprise attack during an international crisis of some twenty days, a timeframe that allowed for American alerting and staging.

The Soviet attack was assumed to eliminate the American nuclear capability and included concurrent Soviet ground offensives in Europe and the Middle East. The projected nuclear exchange was estimated to take only fourteen hours, conducted by more than 1,700 Soviet aircraft that would deliver 6,600 megatons of atomic explosive on the U.S. and its allies. The attack was anticipated to begin with the explosion of ten megaton weapons concealed within the Soviet embassies in Washington, D.C., and New York, accompanied by short-range missile launches from Soviet submarines. The incoming air attacks were presumed to be detected by the early warning radars, providing between two and six hours of further staging of the U.S. military to alert positions.

The Soviet attack was presumed to have wiped out the United States government, to have largely destroyed the nation's transportation, power and manufacturing resources as well as its labor pool—despite huge losses to the attacking aircraft. The estimate noted that only in the case of a "full alert" and appropriate government leadership action could "continuity of government" be preserved. The effectiveness of the American retaliation assumed that the attack had begun with half of SAC's overseas force on alert, a third of its continental forces on alert and with the Tactical Air Command and Navy on one third alert. SAC was estimated to be capable of launching its aircraft within five to seven minutes, TAC and the Navy within approximately half an hour and Snark surface-to-surface missiles within half an hour.

Some of the details of the estimates, particularly of Soviet damage, are still redacted in available documents; however, the conclusion was that the American counterattack would leave the Soviets with only 10% of their available atomic weapons, the U.S. with 80% and U.S. forces in a position to "terminate" any further Soviet action—albeit with the United States government and infrastructure almost totally destroyed in the surprise attack. The strategic threat assessment concluded by projecting that by 1959, the United States and the Soviet Union would both have the capability of destroying each other in a surprise attack—in short, the two nations would have achieved a state of "mutual destruction."

Several points about this early assessment are quite important. It's clear that as early as 1956 the assumption was that a state of "mutual destruction" would exist prior to the end of the decade. If the Soviets struck first, the U.S. would essentially be destroyed but would destroy Russia in return. It was also assumed that Washington, D.C., as well as New York would be immediately destroyed—by hidden atomic devices and submarine-launched missiles—prior to any detection of incoming bombers. That assumption raised the issue of "continuity of government" as well as that of national command authority. It was only with relatively extended warning during a time of international crisis that the president or other senior government figures would survive the initial attack. In fact, continuity of government was deemed impossible in circumstances other than a full alert. The assessment gives no details but seems to imply that the president would have moved away from the capital during such a crisis alert condition.

During the following years of the Eisenhower administration, the annual Net evaluations appear to have been much the same, perhaps surprisingly so even with a dramatically escalated defensive program—the projections for success in a Soviet surprise attack remained largely the same. In fact in 1959, there was discussion that the reports were becoming so similar that without some major technological change, there might be no real use in continuing the exercise. The only area of significant uncertainty (an issue first brought up by President Eisenhower in 1958) was the discussion of the targeting of American retaliatory strikes. There was some question as to whether they should remain focused on cities and essentially total destruction of the population of the USSR or whether they should focus on Soviet military targets, with the intent of totally eliminating Soviet military capability. Eisenhower's remarks during his Net briefing also suggest that he was becoming concerned that the continuing growth of SAC's targeting list might be creating a situation of "overkill." Eisenhower noted that he recalled an initial bombing inventory of some seventy targets but that the plan in place had come to include every Soviet city of more than twenty-five thousand people.[4]

Indeed, with what we now know, the president may have been one of the few people aware of how dramatically the SAC targeting list had grown. General LeMay had withheld his Basic War Plan from the Joint Chiefs of Staff—on the grounds of security—and even held it secret from other commands within the Air Force. With regard to the atomic stockpile, the 298 bombs of 1950 had become almost 2,500 weapons by 1955 and would exceed 27,000 by 1963.[5] For reference, as of 1954, the Soviets had held something on the order of 150 atomic bombs.

By the late 1950s the number of American nuclear weapons had grown so dramatically, and various types of atomic weapons were spread so widely among the services, that there was increasing concern that in any conflict, the effects of the weapons might be influenced by the timing of their actual delivery. That included the very real possibility of American aircraft from different services or units arriving at the target at the same time and being lost to an attack already in progress. SAC's own plan was essentially to bomb its way into the Soviet Union, using atomic weapons to clear a path through defensive installations all the way to its primary targets.

As of 1952 the Navy had announced that all its future attack planes would carry atomic weapons. New Air Force fighter bombers assigned to tactical commands in the European and Far Eastern theaters were also developing atomic attack capability. There was every reason to worry that independent attacks by Air Force tactical fighter bombers (under theater command), Navy aircraft and submarines, and even the use of Army battlefield atomic weapons might conflict with SAC's attack plan. Inter-service rivalries, SAC dominance in the conduct of strategic nuclear warfare and a host of contending opinions on the subject of nuclear weapons control had resulted in years of debate but virtually no progress in resolving the overall issue of nuclear weapon delivery in the earliest hours and days of an atomic war.[6]

From 1955 to 1958 SAC hosted a series of World Wide Coordination Conferences, with attendees from all services and commands. The intent of the conferences was to coordinate atomic target assignments, during both initial strikes and post-hostilities. A history of the effort describes the challenges for that effort as "formidable" and notes that even with the new initiative, there was duplication and even triplication of planned attacks.[7] A series of joint exercises from 1958 to 1960 revealed at least two hundred "time over target" conflicts in the attack plans of the various services. It was also clear that the addition of new atomic missiles, such as the Navy's Polaris submarine-launched weapon, would only exacerbate potential conflicts. Given the individual interests of the various military services, SAC and the Joint Chiefs, the road to a fully integrated target list and attack plan was not an easy one. Vice Admiral Jerry Miller gives an insider's view of the service politics in his book *Stockpile: The Story Behind 10,000 Strategic Nuclear Weapons,* and other now-available historical studies call out additional issues.[8] Ultimately, in August 1960, Secretary of Defense Thomas Gates issued a directive, supported by President Eisenhower, that broke the deadlock and created a new entity, the Joint Strategic Target Planning Staff, located at SAC headquarters in Omaha, Nebraska.

The new joint staff was charged with developing a unified target list (National Strategic Target List/NSTL) and a Single Integrated Operational Plan (SIOP) for attacking the targets. The work of the new Joint

Strategic Planning Staff provided a major contribution to SIOP-62, the 1960 Net assessment projecting the nuclear balance circa 1962–1963. The initial target list developed to support the SIOP-62 assessment came from SAC and included some four thousand positively identified and located individual targets. SIOP-62 itself projected an American "alert force" attack by 874 weapon platforms including SAC bombers, Atlas intercontinental ballistic missiles (ICBMs), Navy carriers and both Regulus and Polaris missile-carrying submarines—delivering 1,447 atomic warheads. Follow-on forces would involve an additional 1,446 aircraft and missile strikes, including battlefield short-range and intermediate-range missiles—the follow-on strikes were to deliver 1,976 additional warheads and bombs.[9] By December 1960, a finalized target National Strategic Target List (NSTL) was reviewed by the Secretary of Defense, the Joint Chiefs and representatives from all commands.

The attack portion of SIOP-62 had evolved from a general directional statement to a very tightly focused targeting and attack plan, designed to destroy the atomic forces and major military of both Russia and China as well as sufficient of their urban/industrial complexes to paralyze their economies and destroy their ability to wage war.[10] The plan was described as being flexible; however, in those terms the "flexibility" (some sixteen iterations of target combinations) was essentially based in the amount of advance warning and preparation time given to the services as well as the extent to which various delivery systems could be deployed under "positive control." The primary example of "positive control" was the ability to launch and hold airborne SAC bombers and tankers at points from which they could be ordered forward as specific attacks were required.

The preparation of the Single Integrated Operational Plan, its evolution and its effect on drastically growing the American stockpile are discussed in great detail by Vice Admiral Miller, a longtime participant in the development of the SIOP. His insights over a period of several administrations provide an invaluable inside view of the complex relationship between intelligence estimates, stockpile growth and the philosophies of atomic warfare over the Cold War decades. The SIOP, the command-and-control protocols that were developed to actually implement it during a nuclear exchange, and the subject of "overkill" are critical to understanding the concept of nuclear "deterrence" against surprise attack.

In comparing the limited number of released memoranda, attachments and reports on several years of Net evaluations, one of the most striking points relates to discussion of American preemptive strikes against the Soviets. We know that topic was broached during both the Truman and Eisenhower administrations. Both the Joint Chiefs and various Air Force commanders repeatedly stressed the point that with nuclear weapons, the advantage in any conflict had overwhelmingly moved to the attacker.

In 1953, President Truman had rejected a confidential security study that had recommended giving the Soviets a deadline on atomic weapons and carrying out a preemptive strike if they rejected the ultimatum.[11] Another study group, working under the Joint Chiefs, had proposed "deliberately precipitating" war with the Soviets while the United States still held a significant advantage in atomic weapons. The momentum for preemption had grown so strong that by the fall of 1954 Eisenhower had been forced to issue a Basic National Policy Statement: "The United States and its allies must reject the concept of preventive war or acts intended to provoke war."[12] Given Eisenhower's directive, and the CIA's estimate that it would take the Soviets a month to assemble and deliver its weapons, the Joint Chiefs were left with the alternative tactic of delivering as many weapons as possible, should an attack begin; it was felt that SAC would be able to deliver some 750 atomic bombs within only a few hours.

It appears that Eisenhower's policy statement largely precluded further discussion of preemptive attack, at least in regard to the annual Net evaluations discussions. We do know that studies of American preemptive strikes had continued, even under Eisenhower. Following his first Net evaluation briefing in July 1961, President Kennedy asked whether or not the effects on the Soviets of an American preemptive strike were known. Kennedy was informed that such studies had been routinely conducted since 1957, and Joint Chiefs Chairman Hickey committed to briefing the president on those studies—as well as the trends in effectiveness of the planned American attacks.

In retrospect, President Kennedy's questions were extremely intuitive, not necessarily in regard to consideration of actually launching a preemptive attack but in the context of strategic military leverage. As it happened, there was indeed a strategic window developing, during the period of 1962–1964. The overall American military advantage would become so striking that it offered Kennedy the opportunity for a new peace initiative with the Soviets. However, from the Soviet perspective, the imbalance was increasingly troubling. While the Soviets themselves had been active in covert military and political action operations against Western powers, they had carried out a relatively limited number of ferret and strategic reconnaissance missions, nothing even remotely similar to SAC's Operation Homerun. They had also never conducted any of the massive and publicized military exercises that SAC used to demonstrate American strategic superiority. SAC operations such as Powerhouse and Road Block, in which more than a thousand missions were flown over North America and the Arctic throughout 1956, illustrated SAC's superiority in a most dramatic fashion.[13]

Such operations were unabashedly intended to deter any sort of Soviet military action and made it clear to Russian leadership that it would be simply fruitless to try to grow a matching bomber force of their own. It also appears that such demonstrations were key in causing the Soviet leadership to turn its attention to a strategic alternative—long-range ballistic missiles. In February 1956, Premier Nikita Khrushchev and several key Soviet leaders made a visit to the main, highly secret missile development center, NII-88. During that visit, they received their first in-depth briefing on Soviet strategic rocketry—in fact, it was the first time any of them had seen a Soviet rocket since the death of Premier Stalin in 1953.[14] The high point of their visit was the introduction of the R-5 ballistic missile. The R-5 weighed in at twenty nine tons, carried an eighty-kiloton nuclear warhead and at that time had a range of eight hundred miles. Better yet, it was operational and had recently delivered the first live nuclear warhead carried by a long-range missile.

As of 1956, the USSR actually had an operational, atomic-capable, intermediate-range ballistic missile (IRBM). The leadership committee was then shown a map of Europe, illustrating that if launched from

Soviet territory, the IRBM could strike every nation in Europe except Spain and Portugal. When asked how many launches and atomic weapons would be required to effectively destroy England and France, the answer was five for England and perhaps as many as seven for France.[15] Premier Khrushchev was reportedly not only amazed, he was struck by how "cost-effective" such a weapon would be as compared to massive bomber fleets.

Of course the obvious question to follow was what the next long-range missile the Soviets would develop would be. The group was taken further into the complex and shown a completed rocket; it was huge. The rocket was designated R-7, capable of carrying an atomic warhead more than five thousand miles; it would become the first Soviet intercontinental ballistic missile (ICBM). The dialog quickly turned to the R-7 and America.[16] The R-7 could strike the U.S. in no more than half an hour; even if it was detected by the new American DEW Line, there could be no more than half an hour's warning. SAC's bombers would be caught on the ground; there would be virtually no time for an alert before the first nuclear warheads exploded. The ICBM could change the entire strategic balance. During that same visit, the chief missile designer also put forth the idea that the R-7 could do something more; it could put a satellite vehicle into earth orbit. And it could very likely do so before the Americans, with their promised civilian satellite science program announced as part of their contribution to the International Geophysical Year (1957–1958) global science effort.

During that first visit, Khrushchev only promised to consider the satellite project, but he immediately began a major reallocation of military spending to IRBM and ICBM missile projects. During 1957, the Soviet military budget saw a decrease in spending for ground forces of 34% and an increase for the strategic/rocket mission of some 127%.[17] Funding for the Soviet long-range bomber effort was already limited; it received no significant increase at all. After considering, Khrushchev also decided that a satellite launch would dramatically embarrass the United States, and in addition, it would plainly make the point to the entire world that the USSR had intercontinental-class ballistic missiles and that they worked. At that point, there was growing public concern that America's crash ICBM program was experiencing major problems. As of December 1957, the leading U.S. ICBM candidate was the Atlas missile. At that point it had been tested in two launches from the Air Force Atlantic Missile Range at Cape Canaveral, Florida. Both launches had experienced immediate problems, and the two Atlas missiles had been destroyed in flight by range safety officers.[18]

The Atlas team did achieve a successful, highly public test that December, and the results were flashed to President Eisenhower, who was attending a NATO conference in Paris. The problem was that the Soviet R-7 had placed the world's first artificial satellite in earth's orbit two months earlier; the successful Atlas launch did little to dilute doubts about America's technical superiority. The Soviets had stolen an even more successful march with Sputnik than with their propaganda coup introducing what appeared to be the beginning of a jet bomber fleet only a couple of years earlier. The effect was once again to ignite American military fears of a Soviet first-strike capability—and concerns over Soviet international political exploitation of the new "missile gap."

Premier Khrushchev had given considerable thought to beating the United States into earth's orbit and staged a carefully orchestrated sequence of events to enhance Sputnik's impact. The October satellite launch was accompanied by the Soviet announcement of a successful intercontinental missile test along with two major hydrogen bomb detonations, then, in November, the launch of an even larger satellite. Those elements all combined not only to embarrass both America and the Eisenhower administration but to bring into question the viability of America's chief nuclear deterrent, the SAC bombing force. Khrushchev had been quick to remark to the world press that the Soviet ICBMs meant that the days of strategic bombing were coming to an end, implying that SAC would soon be outmoded. On October 9, President Eisenhower walked into what quickly became the first hostile press conference of his two terms. He was clearly unprepared for the barrage of aggressive and challenging questions he experienced, ranging from whether or not he felt SAC to be outmoded to why his former Secretary of Defense, Charles Wilson (who had left office on October 1957), had remarked on his last day that he doubted the Soviets even had an ICBM program.

As with its earlier bomber propaganda ploy, the Soviet satellite launches triggered a series of new American national intelligence estimates. In later years, one of the CIA's top Soviet military analysts described the nature of these estimates quite succinctly: "You'll never get court martialed for saying they [the Soviets] have a new type of weapon and they don't . . . but you will lose your ass if you say they don't and it turns out that they do."[19] His insight leaves us with little surprise in finding that the National Intelligence Estimate (NIE 11-10-57) of December 1957 focused heavily on Soviet missile capability, predicting some ten operational ICBMs by mid-1959[20] and projecting a target force of 500 missiles located at 50 sites. The anticipated ICBM system was expected to be highly visible, not only due the large launching and fueling facilities but due to a considerable expansion of railroad networks for delivery of the missile components.

The NIE estimated that special missile trains of more than one hundred cars would be needed for the task of servicing the five hundred launch pads, which in turn would require the construction of more than five hundred miles of new railroad sidings. The follow-on NIE of August 1958 projected a capability for one hundred Soviet ICBMs in 1960 and up to five hundred in 1960—at the latest 1962. By October 1958 the CIA began to back down a bit on its estimates of size and timing of the anticipated Soviet ICBM force. The projection anticipated an operational force of ten prototype missiles in 1958 and moved back the date for a five-hundred-missile force to 1962–1963.[21]

The detailed story of the politics and personal agendas of the "missile gap" has been fully told elsewhere; the "missile gap" itself proved not unlike the "bomber gap" in that it never actually existed, and in reality both intermediate and intercontinental missiles would lead to a huge American strategic advantage over the Soviets within only a few years. Ongoing American U-2 flights, soon followed by the super-secret Corona surveillance satellite program (which began in 1959), provided no evidence of any dramatic deployment of Soviet ICBMs. The initial Soviet choice of liquid-fueled missiles, launching from aboveground pads and requiring extensive railroad-track feeders and sidings, would have made such installations highly visible.

Once again President Eisenhower had clear evidence that a highly publicized strategic "gap" never truly existed. And once again, to protect intelligence sources and methods—most especially the new Corona satellite capability—he was forced to withhold the story from Congress and the public. The result was an immense burst in American missile development and deployment. Eisenhower was forced into a position of allowing a supplemental budget increase of more than $900 million to add six new wings of SAC B-52 bombers to allay fears of a bomber gap. Spending on multiple IRBM and ICBM systems to address the nonexistent missile gap would consume a far larger amount of money; it would also generate a truly huge American missile arsenal.

The Soviets had essentially done it to themselves again, scaring the American public and Congress into funding and delivering what would become a massive strategic advantage in both bombers and missiles by 1962–1963. By September 1961 a new National Intelligence Estimate pegged the number of Soviet ICBMs at twenty-five with no sign of additional missiles coming online in the near future. It had also become clear that the Soviets had made the wrong choice in deploying their ICBMs above ground—entirely exposed to an American preemptive strike. The United States was deploying its Atlas and Titan ICBMs in underground silos and pressing forward with a fleet of undetectable submarine-based ICBMs built around nuclear subs and Polaris missiles.

The risk of long-range missile attacks was going to bring significant new challenges to command and control of any defense against surprise attack. Yet even before that, the integration of atomic weapons into all levels of the American military had raised the issue of "pre-delegation" of the use of those weapons in defense—and the issue of full-scale retaliation with the president dead, injured or simply out of communication in the event of a major surprise attack. We now know that President Eisenhower issued a directive in 1957 authorizing commanders of American field armies, fleets and air forces to use strictly defensive atomic weapons such as air-to-air missiles and ground-launched missiles in the event of a surprise air attack on the United States, its territories and possessions. The directive also allowed the use of atomic weapons over coastal air-defense identification zones including over international waters. Use of such weapons against air attacks on friendly countries was also authorized, given consent of that country. Authority was also granted for U.S. forces in international waters to use atomic weapons during any type of attack by Sino–Soviet forces.[22] Given the increasing creep of atomic weapons into all areas of the military, such pre-delegation for defense was virtually mandatory for any effective response to surprise attack.

Eisenhower's pre-delegation directive reserved retaliatory atomic strikes to authorization from the president, except under the circumstance that communications with the president became impossible during an attack in progress. In that event the Department of Defense was directed and authorized to "expend nuclear weapons" in retaliation against the identified enemy. Retaliatory strikes were not to be made against enemy forces within friendly nations except under specific agreements and understandings. The directive also cited certain operational limitations in the use of nuclear weapons. They were not to be used, even in defense, against "minor attacks" or "upon attacks against minor U.S. forces" in which damage did not constitute a major threat to U.S. forces or the nation itself. Any use of atomic weapons was to be immediately reported to the president.

The guidelines in the directive were elaborated on in an operational document—"Instructions for the Expenditure of Nuclear Weapons in Accordance with the Presidential Authorization," dated May 27, 1957.[23] Several examples of qualifying attacks were provided as additional guidance in regard to defensive use of atomic weapons. Those examples were specific and essentially established as formal "Rules of Engagement" within which nuclear weapons could be used. They included (a) submarine or surface craft launching or controlling missiles against the United States, its territories or possessions, (b) a Sino-Soviet–bloc force engaging in any type of missile, bombing, air-to-air or strafing attack in international waters or on foreign territory, (c) a Sino-Soviet–bloc force engaging in a major ground or paratroop attack penetrating and advancing against U.S. forces in a foreign territory. Unidentified submarines or aircraft engaging in such attacks were to be assumed to be Sino-Soviet–bloc forces.

Pre-delegation was extended only to "authorizing commanders" specified as commander in chief; U.S., commander in chief; Europe, commander in chief; Alaska, commander in chief; Atlantic, commander in chief; Pacific, commander in chief; Continental Air Defense and commander in chief of Strategic Air Command. The instructions noted that commanders of numbered Army forces, fleets and air forces might be designated from time to time as authorized individuals based on recommendation by the Joint Chiefs and concurrence by the secretary of defense and the president.

Given the detailed attention to the subject by Eisenhower and his cabinet, it's not surprising that there was significant follow-on dialog on the subject of pre-delegation. Secretary of State John Foster Dulles strenuously opposed giving any military authority that was not in line with the political agreements in place with allied and friendly nations. The president hesitated to constrain American forces with regard to their own defense against attack. He was also adamant that instructions should primarily be verbal, with as little in writing as possible. The president was of the opinion that only the six or seven commanders of the unified and specified commands were to be verbally briefed on pre-delegation and its operational guidelines.[24] In a letter of November 2, 1959, President Eisenhower directed the secretary of defense to conduct such briefings, noting that the commanders were to be informed that they would be constrained in the overseas use of atomic weapons by "the limitations in accordance with international agreements."[25]

It must be stressed that clear rules of engagement, established and communicated in advance, are one of the most fundamental keys to any effective defense against surprise attack. Clearly the Eisenhower administration, with a former General and Supreme Commander of NATO as America's commander in chief, understood and established such directives, specified the rules of engagement and ensured the basic communications necessary to establish those rules within the command structure of both the unified and specified commands. As we go forward, we will return to that point—and evaluate the relative competency of later administrations in regard to defensive preparations and rules of engagement, for both military and major terror attacks.

With an understanding of pre-delegation as authorized during the Eisenhower administration, we turn to the subjects of deterrence and retaliation—and the strategic balance as it was perceived circa 1961. As the Eisenhower administration was succeeded by that of President John Kennedy, American atomic response to surprise attack was defined in the Single Integrated Operational Plan, in particular SIOP-62. As we have noted, the basic Net evaluation subcommittee assessments had become so similar over the years that even by 1959, there had been a real question as to their becoming simply redundant. The assumptions in virtually all the assessments and planning were that any conflict would begin during a period of international tension and that there would be some level of strategic warning allowing certain forces to move to higher alert levels.

Actual combat was assumed to start with a Soviet surprise attack, an attack that would begin with the destruction of Washington, D.C., and New York, either through the explosion of atomic weapons smuggled into Soviet embassies in those cities or, perhaps more realistically, by the explosion of hydrogen weapons covertly positioned in freighters in adjacent waters, or dropped into adjacent waters by passing ships. In any event, the destruction of both major cities would signal the start of the war, and unless special preparations had been taken beforehand, the national government of the United States would be decapitated in a single stroke. Events of the early 1960s made it dramatically clear that even if the basic SIOP assumptions had not changed, the requirements for national command and control were changing with the advent of the "missile age"—and for surprise attacks that would provide either no warning at all or at the most some fifteen minutes from the time of ICBM detection to nuclear warhead detonation.

The first fully integrated American attack plan—SIOP-62—provided for a massive American atomic attack in retaliation or preemptively with "unequivocal strategic warning of impending Sino-Soviet attack." That strike targeted the Sino–Soviet bloc, including the Soviet Union, China and a number of "Eastern-bloc" Soviet client states in the Warsaw Pact. Some 3,200 atomic weapons would have been aimed at a total of 1,060 targets—in a single "spasm" strike, first with alert units and as quickly as possible followed by the rest of the American and allied forces.[26] Historical studies of the total SIOP strike have estimated that it would have involved a total explosive force of some 7,847 megatons; the alert strike would have killed 175 million Russians and Chinese; the result of the full strike would have been 285 million killed and 40 million injured.[27]

In short, as of 1961–1962, in the event of a surprise atomic attack on the United States, or with unequivocal warning of imminent attack, the SIOP was to be executed. The degree of flexibility in the operational plan itself was extremely limited, largely related to how much warning was available and the mix of alert and follow-on forces at the time of the attack. Certain levels of tactical flexibility in execution were also left to field and theater commanders.[28]

In addressing our overall subject of surprise attack, it is especially important to be able to compare plans with actual events. The Kennedy administration's first major military confrontation with the Soviets did indeed involve the risk of either a limited nuclear exchange or of a Soviet surprise attack. It involved confrontation with the Soviets in Germany, specifically over the city of Berlin. In general the crisis developed very much in line with established planning Net assessments and SIOP assumptions.

The Net evaluations and even the SIOP had assumed that a conflict would emerge during a period of international confrontation and crisis. During such a period the Soviets would have time to generate forces for an attack and the United States would move through some if not all states of alert. The Kennedy administration faced exactly that scenario in 1961. In June 1961, during a meeting between President Kennedy and Premier Khrushchev, the Soviet premier threatened to sign a peace treaty with East Germany. Khrushchev further stated he would end all previous Allied access agreements regarding Berlin. The Americans, British and French responded that no such treaty would abrogate their rights of access to Berlin. In turn Khrushchev issued an ultimatum for Western-Bloc forces to withdraw from the city by the end of 1961.

With a potential crisis developing over Berlin, President Kennedy addressed the nation via television on July 25, stating that he was willing to begin new talks on Berlin, but that while the United States wanted peace, it would not surrender to the Soviets where Berlin was concerned. Kennedy requested an additional $3.25 billion in military spending and called for the addition of six new Army divisions and two new Marine divisions. He also announced plans to call up American military reserves.

Unrest over the fate of Berlin drove an increasing number of East Germans to flee to the West through the city. As the flight west escalated, East Germany secretly began preparations to close its borders. By the end of August the German border was closed and construction of an actual wall between East and West Berlin began. President Kennedy ordered 148,000 National Guard and Reserve personnel to active duty on August 30. The mobilization included eighteen tactical fighter squadrons, four tactical reconnaissance squadrons, and six tactical air transport squadrons. During November, three more Air National Guard fighter squadrons were mobilized.

From late October into November, Operation Stair Step incrementally moved eight of the tactical fighter units, with 216 aircraft, to Europe. President Kennedy's goal was to demonstrate the American commitment, without doing so in a single surge of forces that might have triggered a Soviet military response. Beyond those overt military moves, Kennedy and his staff began a detailed planning process for a series of steps that were to guide the evolving confrontation; the planning was highly secret and was conducted under the codenames Poodle Blanket and Pony Blanket.[29] Kennedy's guidance outlined a series of stages beginning with non-nuclear air action, non-nuclear ground action, worldwide maritime control and blockade—but as a very last resort, first selective "demonstration" nuclear attacks and limited tactical use of nuclear weapons.

Kennedy anticipated that the Soviets might move to the level of full-scale atomic attack during any of those stages and anticipated that a move by Western powers to use nuclear weapons would indeed provoke a full-scale Soviet surprise attack. Clearly Kennedy was focused on directing initial military action toward conventional forces. His intent was to sufficiently increase conventional Western forces to the point that the Soviets would be deterred before any combat began. One of his early problems was that for various reasons, America's European allies were much more willing to move toward early use of tactical atomic weapons than to rush into conventional-force buildups.[30]

There were incidents involving American diplomatic personnel passing into East Berlin in October 1961, but none of them led to the diplomats' being denied access. At the end of October the situation became so tense that groups of American and Soviet tanks faced each other at a Berlin border checkpoint. Both sets of tanks were fully loaded with live munitions and had orders to fire if fired upon. Eventually all the tanks withdrew, virtually simultaneously, and the confrontation slowly evaporated, leaving a divided city and the infamous Berlin Wall in place.

It can be argued that President Kennedy, with a full knowledge of American strategic nuclear superiority, had carefully leveraged that advantage in a controlled, incremental response to the Berlin crisis. He had focused on conventional options, knowing that the Soviets were well aware of their strategic weakness. Khrushchev, in turn, was fully aware of the American nuclear advantage—including the numerous tactical atomic weapons available for use in Europe. In the standard Russian calculus of force, pushing the Berlin crisis to a full nuclear exchange would have been suicidal for the Soviets given the lack of anything approaching strategic nuclear parity. In retrospect, a number of historians have concluded that Kennedy had forced Khrushchev to back down by effectively demonstrating that the "correlation of forces" in Europe demonstrated an American superiority that simply could not be denied.[31]

Oral history work, following the end of the Cold War with the USSR, has revealed that the Soviet leadership consistently held a very real fear of American nuclear superiority. It was a fear that had begun during the Eisenhower era but continued long afterward. Even when the Soviets had managed to build a land- and submarine-based missile force that provided a true state of "mutual assured destruction," they continued to suspect any American initiative that appeared capable of giving the United States anything like the option of a preemptive nuclear strike.[32]

With that fundamental fear of the United States and with his recent Berlin experience, as of the spring of 1962 Premier Khrushchev had every reason to be seriously concerned about Soviet strategic weakness. Khrushchev had also made a very serious mistake in 1957, effectively merging public perception of Soviet ICBM success with the launch of Sputnik and the explosion of large hydrogen bombs. At the time it had appeared to be a brilliant propaganda move, garnering considerable international influence for the Soviets and effectively undermining American public confidence in its superiority. But as Khrushchev bragged to the press about mass-producing ICBMs—"like sausages"—a series of poor decisions, manufacturing problems and sheer bad luck had dramatically slowed the actual deployment of a long-range Soviet missile force.

Initially the missile deployment appeared to be going well, and the Soviets were able to field several hundred medium- (MRBM) and intermediate- (IRBM) range missiles in a belt along their western border—effectively putting Western Europe under true atomic bombardment threat by 1962.[33] The success of the R-7 missile in the first Soviet long-range tests and in lofting Sputnik into orbit led to it being pursued as initial ICBM of choice. Yet despite its power, the rocket used a combination of fuels that required it to be filled only immediately before launching, and as it had to be constantly "topped off," that process took some five hours.

It was also highly risky, as the topping off created a "combustible mist" that could saturate personnel's clothing, and in its early launches there were horrible deaths when individuals actually self-ignited and burned—new safety processes further slowed preparation of the rocket.[34] Five hours from alert to launch was simply not going to be acceptable for a strategic missile. Beyond that the size of the R-7 meant it required large, aboveground launch pads and gantries—it was simply a sitting duck in any nuclear exchange. The R-7 proved to be neither a viable defensive nor offensive weapon, and in the end only seven such missiles were deployed on a total of four launch pads.

The Soviets had to start from scratch to develop a credible ICBM.[35] They accomplished that with the R-16, but that rocket's development had suffered a dramatic setback during testing. Against recommendations of his engineering staff, a military commander ordered repairs on a fully fueled prototype rocket. The resulting explosion in October 1960 killed more than a hundred people and delayed further development by months. The R-16 did become operational in 1962, but by that fall no more than twenty were deployed and available for launch.

The Soviets also carried out a crash project to put ICBMs into nuclear submarines, just as the Americans had done with Polaris missiles. While the missiles themselves had been developed, there were serious problems with the early Soviet submarine nuclear reactors. Fires had occurred in the reactors, lives had been lost, and during 1961 and most of 1962 the submarines were in port undergoing major rework and refits on the reactors. The Soviet ICBM and submarine-launched missile problems would all be resolved, and by the end of the decade, a truly credible Soviet strategic force would ultimately go into place. But as of early 1962, it seemed the Sputnik gambit actually put the USSR in an extremely exposed position. The reality of the strategic balance sheet at that point suggested a tremendous Soviet disadvantage:

> 204 American Atlas and Titan ICBMs deployed—in underground silos

> 7 Soviet R-7 missiles and 20 R-16 ICBMs available on above ground launch pads

> 90 American Jupiter and Thor IRBMs deployed in Britain and Turkey with the capability of striking major targets inside Russia with only a few minutes, flying time

> No Soviet IRBMs in range of the continental United States

> 32 Polaris ICBMs on patrol in American nuclear submarines plus 6 Regulus cruise missiles on patrol in diesel submarines

> No Soviet missile submarines on patrol; all in port with major nuclear reactor problems[36]

This window of Soviet exposure was quite obvious to American intelligence and its military planners. We also know that the window of Soviet exposure was discussed in high-level American strategy meetings. When President Kennedy himself raised the subject of Soviet exposure, he was told that there would be a window in late 1963 where additional American land- and sea-based missiles would place the USSR in a position of maximum risk to a preemptive American nuclear strike. The American advantage had been seen as decisive in 1961 during the Berlin crisis; it was going to become exponentially more so by 1963.

The concept of just such a strategic window—another type of "gap"—had been the theme of a best-selling novel, *Alas, Babylon*, written by Pat Frank and widely read in 1959. Frank's "gap" had referred to a Soviet window of opportunity in 1960–1961, based largely in the perceived Soviet missile superiority following Sputnik's launch.

> *Remember the Russian General who came over, in Berlin? An air general . . . a human being . . . he brought us their war plan in his head. . . . It won't be zero hour, it'll be Zero minute. They'll use no planes in the first wave, only missiles. They plan to kill every base and missile site in Europe and Africa and the U.K. with their T-2 and T-3 IRs. They plan to kill every base on this continent, and the Pacific, with their ICs plus missiles launched from subs. They'll use SUSAC—that's what we call their Strategic Air Force—to mop up.*
>
> *Can they get away with it? Three years ago they couldn't, three years hence when we have our own ICBM batteries emplaced, a big fleet of missile toting subs, and Nike-Zeus . . . they couldn't. But right now we're in what they call "the gap." Theoretically, they figure they can do it. I'm pretty sure they can't—we may have some surprises for them—but that's not the point. Point is, if they think they can get away with it, we have lost.*
>
> *. . . I think we lost some time ago because the last five sputniks have been reconnaissance satellites.*

They've been mapping us . . . measuring us for the Sunday punch.[37]

Frank's "gap" insight was right on the money—but the American window of exposure had not happened as he predicted due to the bad decisions and bad luck in the Soviet missile program. Instead, his projected window of American exposure had passed. By 1962 America had deployed the weapons he had projected. The Soviets had not, and had never achieved a window of preemptive advantage where the United States most certainly had. Indeed there were public statements from American defense leaders that the U.S. had achieved nuclear supremacy and there was a real fear among Soviet leaders that "hawks" within the American military were promoting using that supremacy to eliminate the Communist threat "once and for all."[38]

The American strategic advantage of 1962–1963 was about to produce a major nuclear flashpoint. In July of 1962 Premier Khrushchev reached the decision that he simply had to buy the USSR time. To do so he embarked on exactly the sort of secret Soviet generation of a strategic attack force that had been pictured in the Net assessments. Those studies assumed that if such a force generation was detected in sufficient time it would serve as the potential trigger for a preemptive American nuclear strike. During the early 1950s great efforts had been made to determine if the Soviets were massing long-range bomber formations at forward air bases. If such deployments had been detected, there was a strong possibility that SAC would have been sent on interdiction missions. In the fall of 1962, exactly that sort of secret Soviet deployment was detected—not with bombers that would have to fly thousands of miles to strike but with missiles that were within only a few minutes' flight time from the majority of the continental United States.

Chapter 10

....

CRISIS

During the early summer of 1962, several different American intelligence services began to generate indications of a major Soviet military surge into Cuba. Human intelligence provided descriptions of a huge influx of Soviet "tourists," thousands of young men of military age, dressed in similar civilian attire. When questioned, Soviet officials provided the universal answer that they were either tourists or agricultural advisors. Beyond that the National Security Agency had monitored and tracked the movement of eighty-five Soviet-Bloc merchant ships moving toward Cuba. And the Cuban government had taken considerable effort to begin sealing off areas of its docks, placing barricades and setting up security zones.

The larger crates coming off the merchant ships were clearly not agricultural implements intended for Cuban sugarcane fields. In reality they contained military equipment ranging from large patrol boats to medium-range jet bombers. Certain cargo was observed being transported and uncrated; the tarps did not conceal that there were good-size missiles arriving. By August the CIA advised President Kennedy that the Soviets were engaged in setting up an island-wide surface-to-air missile system. Queries were made to Soviet diplomats, including quite senior personnel. The consistent response was that anything the Soviets might be doing for Cuba was strictly of a defensive nature. After all, the United States had sponsored one failed invasion by Cuban exiles in

1961 and continued to stage major military exercises quite obviously modeling a full-scale invasion of the Soviets' only sworn Communist ally in the Western Hemisphere. The Soviet Union was simply acting according to its responsibility to protect Cuba from invasion.

Indeed the Soviets had made a commitment to a massive military investment in Cuba—one with highly secret elements that went far beyond pure defensive measures. In April, Khrushchev had ordered the movement of Soviet air defense units to Cuba, transferring 180 SA-2 anti-aircraft missiles as well as a number of coastal defense missiles. At the time SA-2s were the most advanced air defense missiles in the world and had brought down an American U-2 over Russia in 1959. A motorized infantry regiment of some 2,500 troops was ordered to Cuba to provide security for the missile sites; it was the first time Soviet combat troops had been sent outside the Warsaw Pact nations of Eastern Europe.[1]

In May, the Soviet premier had made the decision to pursue a much more ambitious operation, which, if successful, would reestablish Soviet strategic nuclear parity with the United States, compensate for the window of exposure caused by the delays in Soviet ICBM and nuclear missile submarine deployment—and ensure that the USSR could not be pressured as it had been during the Berlin crisis of the previous year.

According to Khrushchev himself, what was preying on his mind that May was not just the overall Soviet strategic disparity but something new and especially troubling. In 1962, the Soviets had no more than twenty six ICBM missiles capable of launching against the United States; they had no deployed submarine-based atomic missiles. Launch of any of the Soviet-based missiles against the continental United States would have been detected within some thirty minutes of detonation, providing American alert forces at least fifteen minutes to launch in retaliation. Under SIOP-62 retaliation would have included not only SAC's bombers and ICBMs, the Navy's submarine-launched Polaris missiles, but large numbers of alert fighter-bomber forces in Europe as well as some ninety Jupiter and Thor intermediate-range missiles in Turkey and Britain.

In terms of closest proximity to Russia, atomic-armed American alert aircraft had been in place in Europe for a number of years. The Air Force had maintained a strike force of atomic fighter bombers in

Europe since 1952; the operation was called Victor Alert. The early Cold War practice of deploying B-29 bombers to forward bases in England had been minimized with the advent of Soviet atomic weapons. In the American view, alert atomic fighter bombers in Europe gave the Western alliance the ability to blunt a move west by supporting a defensive line "as far east as possible." That "forward strategy" of atomic defense was intended to eliminate the Soviet ability to concentrate their conventional forces. Placing alert aircraft in position to strike any Soviet advance was officially referred to as Quick Reaction Alert—to the pilots and crews it was Victor Alert.[2]

The first aircraft to deploy for Victor Alert was the F-84G jet fighter bomber, carrying a specially designed and built Mk-7 nuclear bomb, weighing less than two thousand pounds. The bomb was only one kiloton, considered effective for battlefield use, but even then the F-84 literally had to "toss" the weapon, looping back to escape the blast.[3] Over the years Victor Alert aircraft flew out of Britain, France (for a time, until 1959) and West Germany. Quick-reaction atomic alert groups were also deployed in the Far East, in South Korea and on Okinawa. The Soviet Union responded by equipping and deploying its own frontal aviation units with atomic bombs.

Of course from the Soviet perspective, the Victor Alert aircraft would also have been perfectly capable of joining in any Western surprise attack. Still, the aircraft were hours away from major Soviet targets even at jet speed. And by 1962, the Victor Alert air bases were all bracketed by Soviet intermediate-range nuclear missiles.

In addition to Victor Alert, since 1958 the Soviets had been forced to accept the reality that a number of nuclear-armed SAC bombers were always in the air, flying routes that positioned them far forward and simply waiting for a "go signal" to continue on with strikes into the USSR. General Thomas Power had initiated a limited airborne alert program, with the intent of ensuring a SAC retaliation even in the event of a Soviet surprise attack on SAC's ground alert aircraft. As of early 1961 more than six thousand airborne alert missions had been flown.[4]

In January of that year Power publicly announced that twelve SAC bombers would be constantly in the air, fully armed with hydrogen bombs, in an operation designated "Chrome Dome." In fact Power allowed the press to write at will about the operation, and it received considerable coverage. There were two Chrome Dome "fail-safe" circuits: One track carried B-52 bombers across the Atlantic toward a southern approach to the USSR; another went north around the fringe of the Arctic Ocean. The southern route led to a fail-safe point an hour's flying time from the Soviet border but only two hours' flight from Moscow.[5] The bombers were under positive control, with a coded emergency action message required to send them past their fail-safe point and into an actual nuclear strike.

The fail-safe concept and positive control first became a subject of public question and concern in 1962, with the publication of Eugene Burdock's best-selling book *Fail-Safe*. In *Fail-Safe* a minor computer-component failure results in airborne alert aircraft accidentally being sent on attack missions into the Soviet Union. In a fascinating coincidence, one of the nation's most widely read weekly magazines, *The Saturday Evening Post*, issued the first in a three-part serialization of the book in its October 13, 1962, issue—at the very beginning of what was to become known as the Cuban Missile Crisis. The story was the lead for the *Post* cover, with the headline "Can Accident Trigger Nuclear War?"

General Power had initiated the highly demanding and expensive airborne alert operation to absolutely ensure SAC's retaliatory capability. The effort involved not only bombers but a considerable number of tanker aircraft, necessary to sustain the global operation with a series of in-air refueling operations. It was a highly demanding operation, and the Soviets had never attempted anything remotely similar to it. Its roots lay in the mid-'50s fear of a "bomber gap"—which had essentially disproved U-2 reconnaissance at the same time Power launched the effort. Still, Air Force intelligence was not happy with the CIA assessment, and SAC argued that the U-2 flights were simply missing the Soviet bomber force. The concept of a "missile gap" sustained the airborne alert, maintaining the fear that a surprise attack could destroy SAC's ground alert force. And when the missile gap continued to be challenged by the CIA, SAC maintained its position that aerial and satellite reconnaissance was simply missing the hidden Soviet ICBM force.

Chrome Dome aircraft also flew a route over the huge American radar installation at Thule, Greenland, under the assumption that Thule would be the first casualty in any true surprise attack and the Chrome Dome aircraft could provide radio alert to SAC in case of such an event. SAC's airborne alert mission was truly impressive, but in retrospect it spanned the period from 1958 to 1968 when the Soviets possessed relatively limited first-strike capability. The Chrome Dome alert was canceled in 1968, following the crash of a B-52 carrying four hydrogen bombs on the Thule alert patrol. Ironically, SAC's airborne alert ceased just at the point that the Soviet ICBM force began to surpass the United States and their ballistic submarine force became formidable. In essence, the SAC airborne alert ended just when the threat it had been created to counter became real.

Yet in 1962, even at the southern Chrome Dome fail-safe point, SAC was still two hours away from Moscow, and America's continental-based ballistic missiles were half an hour away. Khrushchev's new worry in 1962 was something that seems to have become quite personal to him while on vacation at a Black Sea resort in May. That was the proximity of a new atomic threat—posed by American Thor and Jupiter IRBMs in Britain, Italy and especially in Turkey. Khrushchev seems to have been specifically troubled not by SAC, not by the new American submarine missiles, not by the Victor Alert atomic weapons carriers or by Chrome Dome—not even by the atomic weapons on American carriers in the Mediterranean. What was preying on his mind—enough to drive him to the extremely risky Cuban missile gambit—was the installation of American medium-range missiles (MRBMs) in Turkey.

The Jupiter missiles in Turkey were just becoming operational as Khrushchev was vacationing on the Black Sea. In terms of the overall American strategic nuclear arsenal, the Jupiters going into Turkey and the IRBMs already in Italy and Britain were already obsolete. Those rockets had been developed as theater weapon extensions of early battlefield missiles such as the Redstone. The first to go into operation, some sixty Thor missiles in 1959, were based in Britain. They carried megaton-class warheads and were targeted on Eastern Europe. In 1962, the installation of Jupiter MRBMs began in Turkey. The key to Khrushchev's worries was that the Turkish Jupiter sites allowed the missiles—carrying a single 1.45-megaton-class warhead and with a range of up to 1,750 miles—to reach many of the major Soviet population centers, including the key facilities responsible for Soviet military command and control. Moscow, Leningrad, Kiev, Minsk and Gorky were all within only minutes of flying time for the Turkish Jupiter IRBMs.[6] Reportedly, during his Black Sea stay, Khrushchev was seen repeatedly looking across the waters toward Turkey and exclaiming that he could almost see the American nuclear missiles aimed at him.

The Soviet premier's concern with the Turkish missiles was actually more intuitive than is generally discussed in much of the historical writing on the Cuban Missile Crisis. While the overall American atomic arsenal represented a huge threat to the Soviet Union, the Jupiter missiles represented a very specific threat if used in a surprise attack. As true ballistic missiles, their total flight time to the most distant target within range was on the order of sixteen minutes. In reviewing the first Net evaluation studies we noted that all Soviet surprise attacks were assumed to have started with what later became referred to as "decapitation" strikes using Soviet atomic devices planted in their embassies, on ships in harbors or on missiles launched at short range from sea. Decapitation was viewed as the first step in any effective surprise attack. Decapitation strikes would destroy key military command-and-control centers such as the Pentagon, and they would remove much of the national government infrastructure and personnel including senior leadership. An effective decapitation strike might even disrupt the command-and-control network to the extent that retaliation would be become confused, limited and less than decisive.

In later years, Soviet submarine-launched ICBMs would pose just that threat to the United States, and alerts would be declared if Soviet submarines were detected moving too close to the United States within decapitation strike range. Yet while American planners fully understood the extreme threat of decapitation and its potential effect on nuclear command and control, it seems to have escaped them that the almost obsolete Jupiter MRBMs going operational in Turkey in 1962 represented exactly that type of decapitation threat to the Soviets. To the

Soviets, always concerned about American preemption, and especially so in 1962, the Jupiters represented a very real danger, one that could have enabled a successful first strike against them. To America, they were simply one more element of the strategic retaliation arsenal, one more deterrent—to Khrushchev they seem to have been the last straw.

In later years much would be written, including remarks by Premier Khrushchev himself, that his primary concern at the time had been for Cuba. He felt that it would be a terrible international blow for world Communism and the reputation of the USSR if the Americans were to destroy the Castro regime. While that might well be true to an extent, there is far more evidence to suggest that his primary concern was actually the dangerous strategic advantage held by the United States. One of his later remarks was much more revealing as to his true emotional state in April 1962: "it was high time that America learned what it feels like to have her own land and her own people threatened."[7] Of course, there might have been a bit of dissemblance even in that remark; certainly Khrushchev was well aware that America had continuously felt threatened. His own actions—ranging from his unwisely chosen "we will bury you" public remarks in 1956 to his coordinated and quite successful ICBM superiority propaganda initiative in 1957—had helped maintain a sense of Soviet threat.

More likely, Khrushchev's desire for America to feel threatened in 1962 reflected his feelings toward the American military establishment and the Kennedy administration. Of course, from an internal political standpoint, it was far better to speak passionately to the Soviet Politburo leaders about support for their revolutionary socialist ally and its efforts in Latin America than to focus on the delays and failures of his own early rocket and missile strategy. A strong emotional message about defending revolutionary comrades in Cuba was also important —and widely used by Soviet commanders—to inspire more than forty thousand Soviet troops who were committed to the Cuban operation.

What the Soviet premier really needed in 1962 was a wild card, something that would demonstrate to the Americans that there was no "window" of opportunity against the Soviets. It would be something to divert the "hawks" in the American military and policymaking community from any temptation to take advantage politically or even militarily of the window of Soviet weakness. Certainly there was some reason for Khrushchev to concern himself with just such American hawks. One of the most popular books of 1962 was Fletcher Knebel's *Seven Days in May*, the story of a military/political coup to oust an American president considered to be weak and naïve in the face of Soviet duplicity.

The book reflected the known and sometimes publicly expressed dissatisfaction within certain senior command levels of the American military community. Such views were based in the belief that President Kennedy had demonstrated an unacceptable level of weakness in not commanding full American military support for the Cuban exile landings in the spring of 1961.[8] The duplicity presented in the book involved the Soviets cheating on a nuclear disarmament treaty; its storyline reflected the fact that as a new, relatively young president, Kennedy was under constant pressure from his senior military leadership—and a good percentage of the voting public—to act assertively toward the Soviets.

The strategic wild card Khrushchev determined to put into play was a plan to place medium-range (600- to 1,800-mile) and intermediate-range (600- to 3,400-mile) ballistic missiles in Cuba. Once in place, the medium-range missiles would bring the eastern half of the United States within striking distance. That would expose American targets including New York and Washington, D.C., as well as a number of major southeastern SAC air bases. Those first-phase missiles would have also posted a decapitation threat, similar to that of the American Jupiter missiles in Turkey.

The first medium-range weapons, SS-4 missiles, were to be followed as quickly as possible by a longer-range version, the SS-5 intermediate-range missile. Those IRBMs had the range to cover any target in the continental United States and Canada, including virtually all SAC bases and the Atlas and Titan ICBM sites. Placing such missiles in Cuba would have also performed an end run on the entire American defense system, which had focused its long-range radar detection against strikes from the north or across its eastern and western coasts.

To further enhance a Cuban on-island nuclear capability, a squadron of seventeen light bombers was dispatched. The IL-28 bombers were dated, relatively slow and low flying, but they had the capability for offshore patrols and could even carry a single nuclear bomb against invading ships or landing craft. Beyond that, they had sufficient range for surprise nuclear strikes against targets in Florida, in particular the major SAC air bases located there. In that regard they held a special advantage given the relative weakness of the southern U.S. radar screen. At least four atomic mines were also delivered to Cuba.

The full extent of the Cuban operation—designated "Anadyr"— did not emerge during the actual missile crisis of 1962. When the full military details did become known, some as recently as 2008, they certainly undermined Khrushchev's position that it had all been simply in defense of Cuba.[9] The basic force structure included two anti-aircraft rocket divisions, with some 144 launchers supplied with 575 rockets. A rocket artillery force of four thousand Soviet troops operated a total of 24 missile batteries. The air defense was supplemented with a full fighter squadron of 40 MiG-21 interceptors, possibly the world's most advanced operational interceptor at that point. Both missiles and interceptors were tied into an extensive Soviet-class air defense network.

The Soviet ground-force commitment was equally impressive, including four motorized/armored infantry regiments fully equipped with their own integrated air defense, and a suite of anti-tank weapons, howitzers, self-propelled artillery and mortar units. Each regiment included its own armored personnel carriers and a tank battalion with thirty-one tanks. The Soviet troops making up the four regiments included ten thousand officers and enlisted men. Perhaps most significantly, from a defensive standpoint, the Soviet units—like their American counterparts—had integrated tactical atomic missiles. The extent of Soviet tactical atomic weaponry deployed to Cuba was extensive, and the first indications of its existence became known only late in the crisis, well after American invasion plans had been made.

Khrushchev himself ordered the dispatch of a Luna (designated "Frog" by Western militaries) short-range missile battalion, with three missile batteries and twelve missiles each. One battery was attached to three of the four motorized Army regiments. With a range of approximately twenty-five miles, the Lunas were capable of engaging American land forces or even naval forces offshore—and the Lunas were to be armed with twelve 20-kiloton atomic warheads. The Luna missile battalions were supplemented with a Soviet Navy coastal defense regiment, equipped with six mobile cruise-missile launchers with missiles. Those cruise missiles had a range up to fifteen to twenty-five miles and were deployed to interdict anticipated American amphibious landings.

The Soviet Air Force also sent two regiments equipped with FKR-1 tactical atomic cruise missiles. Each regiment had eight truck-pulled launchers with forty cruise missiles. Those missiles had a range of up to ninety miles and carried a twelve-kiloton warhead. Historian Michael Dobbs's contemporary research has revealed the details of an extremely secret movement of the tactical cruise missiles—in a plan coordinated by the Russians with Raul Castro—to target the huge American military base at Guantanamo Bay.[10] It was assumed that Guantanamo would be used as a base to stage ground attacks into Cuba's far eastern Oriente province. To preempt that, the Soviets spent weeks establishing tank units and tactical missile positions around the American base. Well-concealed launch positions for the cruise missile launchers were prepared and nuclear warheads distributed out of the first shipment to arrive on the island. If combat had broken out, the Soviets were fully prepared to send nuclear cruise missiles from positions only fifteen miles from the base. Guantanamo would have quickly ceased to exist, destroyed with far more Soviet nuclear firepower than the United States had used against Japan in World War II.

The Soviets had not only established a major air defense in Cuba; they had deployed a large Red Army ground force, one quite capable of defending the island.[11] The four motorized infantry regiments—with tank battalions—were supported by at least ninety tactical missiles, the majority equipped with nuclear warheads. The Anadyr military commanders had standing orders permitting them to use tactical weapons at their own discretion in the event of an American attack. The tactical nuclear weaponry was not unusual for the time, commonly found in both Eastern- and Western-bloc army formations in Europe. Yet in retrospect, the thought of using that amount of nuclear firepower in defense of an island nation the size of Cuba seems virtually insane.

If "defensive" nuclear weapons had been used against American forces, it is hard to conceive of anything other than a major American nuclear response against Cuba by the Strategic Air Command. Any such response would have left the island virtually uninhabitable. That leads to the second major element of the Anadyr operation: the placement of medium-range nuclear missiles throughout Cuba. In later years, much of the ground force sent to Cuba was justified as simply protection for the missiles. That actually makes little sense. Ostensibly the missiles would themselves have been used only in retaliation during an attack on Cuba, yet unless they could have been secretly placed and totally disguised, any pre-attack reconnaissance would have located them and bombers or missiles dispatched to eliminate them in advance. Such a task would not have fallen to ground troops in an invasion. In reality the existence of operational "offensive" weapons, in place and well protected, was something else entirely—a strategic Soviet nuclear deterrent. In a deterrence scenario, Cuba served simply as an attractive forward fire base for Khrushchev, much like West Germany or Turkey did for the United States. Fundamentally the missiles deployed to Cuba were intended to neutralize American strategic dominance, not defend the Cuban revolution.

The number of medium- and intermediate-range missile forces designated for Cuba was also far beyond anything that could reasonably have been considered "defensive." If matters had proceeded as planned, without detection, the Soviets would have positioned some sixty nuclear missiles in central and western Cuba for maximum coverage of major American cities and key strategic military targets. Those missiles would have carried megaton-class hydrogen warheads, putting Washington, D.C., within thirteen minutes of flight time for an H-bomb strike. The Soviets had established two key storage facilities for nuclear weapons on the island, one only twelve miles southwest of Havana. In October, at the start of the missile crisis, one Soviet transport had already carried in ninety nuclear warheads—thirty-six megaton devices for the R-4 missiles, forty-eight kiloton-class warheads for the cruise missiles and twelve nuclear bombs for the IL-28 jet bombers. Due to the accelerated pace of the project, the nuclear storage sites and transfer depots were not at all up to Soviet standards in construction or security. Because of that, none of the warhead and bomb storage locations were identified by American reconnaissance during the crisis.

The strategic threat of sixty ballistic missiles, all with atomic warheads, targeting the largest population centers and military facilities in the continental U.S. would have been immense. The missiles would have been capable of flying through the nation's weakest defensive radar screen in a matter of minutes, offering little or no warning before impact and detonation. Before the targeting frenzy of the late 1950s, America's military planners had felt that a few dozen nuclear weapons could destroy the Soviet war fighting capability. In 1962 sixty ballistic missiles in Cuba might well have done the same thing if launched in a surprise attack; they represented a massive "decapitation" threat.

Surprisingly, the decapitation advantage presented by the Cuban missiles seems largely to have escaped both President Kennedy and Defense Secretary McNamara. When first briefed on the confirmation of offensive ballistic missiles on the island, Kennedy asked, "Why does he put these in there?" "What's the advantage of that?" "It's just as if we began to put a major number of medium-range missiles into Turkey . . . " McGeorge Bundy, Kennedy's national security advisor, reminded the president that they had done just that, but his remark didn't seem to penetrate.[12] That dialog suggests that both Kennedy and McNamara seem not to have grasped the very special threat of decapitation as compared to mutual assured destruction. On the other hand, fears of decapitation and preemption would prove a constant in Russian thinking.

Of course Kennedy was thinking in terms of his own policies and intentions, not Khrushchev's fears. As the crisis continued, certain of his military advisors brought up the value of the missiles in a Soviet surprise attack. The Joint Chiefs took the position that the missiles did make a strategic difference—Secretary of Defense McNamara didn't accept that view; he felt that they didn't change the larger strategic picture. President Kennedy even remarked that "geography doesn't make much difference . . . what does it matter if you get blown up by a missile based on Cuba or an ICBM flying from the Soviet Union?"[13] While correct from a personal standpoint, that remark was made spontaneously in the earliest moments of the crisis, and the president quickly began to receive a crash course in the realities of nuclear confrontation. As matters would prove, he was to be a far quicker student than many of his senior civilian and military staff.

Pentagon staff analysts quickly developed and presented a study of the Cuban missile threat—but it was built strictly on the calculus of retaliation. At least thirty-four of the seventy-six SAC bases were within range of the initial Cuban missiles going into place; follow-on weapons with longer ranges would expose all of SAC. But the hardened American ICBM sites and the Polaris missile submarines would survive. Even with the Cuban missiles, a Soviet surprise attack would leave at least 483 American hydrogen warheads to use in retaliation, and that would be more than enough to destroy the USSR.[14] In terms of mutual assured destruction, the conclusion was that Soviet missiles in Cuba would not change the strategic balance. In reality, the two sides continued to look past each other: McNamara and Kennedy considering only the impact on retaliation to a Soviet surprise attack, the Soviets looking for an advantage that would reduce the American strategic advantage and protect them from an American surprise attack.

The full story of the Cuban Missile Crisis has been told elsewhere, with extensive detail added in recent years. Our focus in exploring the events of fall 1962 will be on crisis protocol, on what the experience revealed about the realities of nuclear command and control and on how those lessons resulted in the creation of what came to be known as National Command Authority. Beyond that, we will also discuss the weaknesses that were revealed in America's war planning, in particular in regard to the Single Integrated Operational Plan (SIOP). The Cuban Missile Crisis was the first true test for potential nuclear war fighting since the SIOP had become operational, and the missile crisis was President Kennedy's first real experience with the limits of its flexibility. The missile crisis would expose fundamental problems with the plan and the directions for its execution—correcting those weaknesses would prove extremely challenging.

In the context of the earlier Eisenhower-era war planning, the highly secret Soviet surge into Cuba had every appearance of preparation for a Soviet surprise attack. It did not match the familiar scenario of a period of international crisis during which the Western and Eastern blocs moved—in stages—toward military confrontation, allowing an increasing series of heightened alerts while senior officials engaged in dialog. Instead, it had the appearance of the surprise attack fears of the 1950s. Initially those fears had centered on long-range American reconnaissance aircraft returning with photographs of massive Soviet forward air bases—bases filled with long-range bombers, bombers sitting over loading pits for atomic weapons. Such photographs never emerged; fears of the covert generation of a Soviet bomber fleet gradually subsided.

After that it had been the fear of U-2 or Corona satellite photography producing photos of extensive new ICBM launch-site complexes. Those complexes would have been fed from new railroad networks, with large gantries and even larger intercontinental missiles installed and ready for launch. Such photographs and threats had never actually emerged, and the missile-gap fears subsided. Yet it was exactly that sort of fear that emerged again in 1962, with photos of crash construction secretly putting large numbers of offensive missile sites in place—not in Russia but in Cuba. The fear reached crisis proportions as more and more images of camouflaged missile sites poured onto executive desks and tables in Washington, D.C.

In terms of intelligence work, at the time the crisis of 1962 seemed to represent a triumph of tactical intelligence collection and an absolute failure of threat analysis. In examining the NET strategic evaluations and the SIOP planning of 1959–1962, it becomes evident that the American military, the national intelligence community and the senior Kennedy administration principals were all fully aware of the significant strategic superiority the U.S. possessed circa 1960—and the fact that it would grow even more significant through 1963. If anything, they may even have underestimated the window of Soviet exposure, not being fully aware in real time of the technical problems the Soviets were experiencing with deploying ICBMs and nuclear missile submarines.

The Berlin crisis of 1961 had demonstrated that the Soviets could be forced to back down from challenging the West. At the time there were even some random worries that the Soviets might feel themselves backed into the corner. In contrast, President Kennedy's Net briefing question about the exposure of the Soviets to preemptive attack highlights the positive perception that it might have been exactly the right time to press a peace initiative, to push for a nuclear test ban, to be more open to neutrality in international affairs rather than forcing everyone into Western and Eastern blocs—all themes of the new Kennedy administration. There simply was no strong strategic warning coming from the intelligence community that it might be a time of maximum threat rather than maximum opportunity.

That view is confirmed by the astonishment and anger that emerged when intelligence of a Soviet offensive move was brought before President Kennedy. Of course there was no surprise about Soviet activity in Cuba; there had been extensive military intelligence of a conventional military buildup. Yet on October 16, 1962, when analysts from the National Photographic Interpretations Center (one of the most secret units within the national intelligence community) briefed the president on the actual installation of medium-range missiles capable of reaching much of the United States—including the Eastern Seaboard—it came as a total shock. Up to that point, CIA director John McCone had been the only major intelligence-community voice suggesting the Soviets might go that far, but with McCone being a relative newcomer to the CIA, even his own agency had not lined up to support his warnings. When proof of the Soviet duplicity was presented, even President Kennedy's more restrained remarks conveyed the gravity of the situation: "there has been a concerted Soviet effort to mislead the U.S. government and its President on a matter of the highest importance."[15]

On October 16, the immediate questions were very basic: Were the missiles ready to fire, and were there atomic warheads with them or on them?[16] There was simply no strategic understanding of why the Soviets would take such a gamble; they had obviously moved to establish offensive missiles under a blanket of total secrecy, using their conventional military buildup as a cover. When challenged about the issue of offensive weapons in Cuba, over several months, the Soviets had repeatedly lied. And since the move appeared to make no sense from the overall strategic balance of mutual assured destruction—at least as perceived from the

American viewpoint—the fear grew that there was a very real and imminent threat of attack. Worse yet, given the realities of the missiles' flight times, it would have been an attack that could put atomic warheads on the White House and Pentagon with no warning whatsoever.

The seriousness of the situation was captured in a proposed ultimatum discussed during one of the earliest conferences on the crisis. The wording was to be intentionally blunt; Khrushchev was to be told "that we have located these offensive weapons; we're maintaining a constant surveillance over them; if there is ever any indication that they're to be launched against this country, we will respond not only against Cuba but we will respond directly against the Soviet Union. . . . "[17] It's hard to interpret that wording as anything other than a warning that any indication of Cuban-armed missile launch preparations would draw not only American military interdiction but also a general preemptive attack on both Cuba and the Soviet Bloc.

The leadership in Washington, D.C., was reacting to the possibility that the Soviets were either positioning themselves to launch a surprise attack or to hold the United States hostage in international affairs with a strategic fait accompli in Cuba. The threat of imminent attack could not be ignored; it surfaced in October 1962 just as it had in the fall of 1941. Once again a "war alert"–class warning was issued—this time with full involvement by both the White House and a well-coordinated communication through the Joint Chiefs of Staff. Unlike in 1941, there would be no chance of under-reaction by senior commanders.[18] On the other hand, circumstances would demonstrate that substantial "chain of command" issues remained. And once again, reality would demonstrate that all the planning in the world could not substitute for realistic drills and "exercises."

One of the first priorities was to immediately gather tactical intelligence on the medium-range missiles, using high-altitude U-2 photo reconnaissance. The U.S. hoped to obtain information about the missiles themselves and the state of the new Soviet air defense network being rushed into place in Cuba—given that the first option on the table was an air strike on the missiles. The huge escalation in crisis management activity was carried out under a cover of business as usual at the White House.

The president kept his scheduled appointments, the U-2s flew, NPIC analysts worked around the clock and cabinet members took extensive precautions not to fuel press impressions of a crisis in play. Within days the picture became clearer—and much more threatening. New launch sites were discovered, including sites for intermediate-range ballistic missiles. The IRBMs were game changers; with double the range of the first medium-range missiles discovered, they would be capable of putting the majority of SAC's continental bases at risk. Worse yet, at least some missiles were going operational; they could be launched within eighteen hours, and they were indeed capable of carrying hydrogen warheads.

The good news was that the advances in airborne intelligence collection had allowed an extremely quick definition of the threat. The remaining questions were how to interdict it and, in particular, how to do so without provoking an irrational and fatal "spasm" launch of operational Cuban missiles. Kennedy's military advisors were convinced that they could engineer a conventional strike without the situation going nuclear.

In response Secretary of Defense McNamara raised a number of issues related to Soviet command and control of the missiles. Where were the nuclear warheads and nuclear storage sites? None had been specifically located for targeting purposes—in fact none would be during the crisis. What orders did the local commanders have with regard to using their weapons if attacked? How good were Soviet communications on the island? And more important still, did the premier and military leadership in Moscow truly have real-time control over Soviet forces in Cuba? Would local commanders reach their own decisions about when to engage? Certainly they would be pressured to do so by the Cuban comrades. There were no answers to McNamara's questions. Nor would there be answers to similar questions in later years, during American administrations that seriously contemplated controlled nuclear war fighting.

President Kennedy had his own reasons to challenge the certainty of his military advisors in regard to their ability to control any large-scale attack on Cuba. Kennedy himself had served as a low-ranking Navy combat officer during World War II; he had personal experience with how often commands and directions could be delayed or never received during actual combat. And, like most field-level commanders, he fully appreciated that there was never enough real combat intelligence available, no matter what headquarters might believe or claim. Much later, Kennedy commented on the fact that prudence had been critical, not acting on the first intelligence, in the emotions of the moment, especially the initial anger. But that was later, in the beginning; even as he was being presented with detailed attack plans, his initial reaction was that events would simply go out of control—some poor guy was not going to get the right word in time, and things would go bad. It would take decades to understand exactly how accurate Kennedy's intuition had been.

As of October 22, Premier Khrushchev realized that the Americans had discovered the ballistic missile element of Operation Anadyr. His suspicions were confirmed in a television address by President Kennedy as well as by major moves such as the evacuation of military families from the American base at Guantanamo Bay. Khrushchev's response, as at other points during the crisis, was to exercise stronger control over the Soviet forces in Cuba. Standard doctrine called for Soviet forces to employ tactical nuclear weapons as necessary during combat. After much debate, the details of which are still not fully known, Moscow issued orders placing release of tactical nuclear weapons under direct authorization from the Kremlin. Soviet doctrine would also have placed the use of theater ballistic missiles such as the medium-range S-4s under local launch control in the event of an attack and potential destruction of the missiles. Orders were issued that removed that authority strictly to Moscow.

In addition, there was no order issued for general Soviet military action related to generating offensive forces other than taking its small number of intercontinental missiles to alert. In one instance a Mars planetary spacecraft was pulled off a booster, the scientific launch canceled and the booster armed with a nuclear warhead—demonstrating the severe lack of deployed Soviet ICBMs. However, in general, outside of Cuba itself, the Soviet military generally held back from any obvious elevation of readiness, unlike the dramatic alert and readiness escalation within the American military. There were knee-jerk reactions in Moscow, heated exchanges and damaged reputations, but in the end, Moscow leaned toward increasing prudence and control as the crisis escalated.

Still, the Soviet leadership had been caught in the act; the immediate concern was how far the American military response might extend. Had Anadyr pushed them to seriously consider a preemptive response, and if so, how far would that extend; could it go beyond Cuba? For the next two weeks the Soviet leadership looked for signs; the real danger would be whether—as President Kennedy feared—some misstep would drive a desperate act of preemption. And there were American missteps; the following is a brief survey of significant command-and-control "glitches," some potentially disastrous, that actually occurred during the missile crisis.

As early as October 22, 1962, there were plenty of visible indications of the American military deployments. The North American Aerospace Defense Command (NORAD) issued orders to arm its interceptors with Genie atomic missiles and to disperse them to secondary fields. F-106s began to surge out of their normal bases, taking their atomic missiles to fields that in many cases had limited or no security or, for that matter, alert facilities. It was not an exercise that had ever been practiced in detail, and accidents began to occur, including interceptors running off the ends of runways not really long enough for fully armed aircraft. In at least one instance, cranes had to be brought in to extract an F-106 (and its atomic missile) from the clay at the end of a runway.[19]

During the president's speech on October 22, the Strategic Air Command had moved to Defense Condition 3 (DEFCON 3) for the first time in its history. That alert status called for SAC to be able to put its entire bomber fleet airborne within fifteen minutes—fifty-four additional B-52s were immediately launched to join the dozen planes already in the Chrome Dome airborne alert force. DEFCON 3 also called for a dispersal of aircraft to a variety of secondary fields, many of them at both large and small commercial airports. As with Air Defense Command's dispersal, SAC's move also proved challenging. Even SAC had never attempted a full dispersal, and its problems ranged from weapon-loaded bombers being towed out of deep ruts made on taxi strips to pilots having to pay for fueling bombers on their personal credit cards.

The Soviets made a very prudent command decision on October 22, ordering four diesel submarines on their way to Cuba to hold back, taking position several hundred miles from the island. The Soviet Navy was well aware that the underwater choke points on the route to Cuba were monitored by American sound sensors, and detection of a force of Soviet submarines would escalate the situation, very possibly leading to an attack on the units. It was a decision of caution but far too late; the U.S. Navy was already tracking the submarines and had orders to intercept them, stopping their further movement toward Cuba. In one of his early moves toward asserting personal command, President Kennedy expressed his concern that standard Navy procedures of dropping exercise-type depth charges might provoke the Soviets; he ordered the use of smaller "noise makers."[20]

Once again Kennedy's intuition was good; what had been standard practice in the days of conventional warfare had become much more dangerous in the nuclear age. As it happened, some of the submarines dispatched to Cuba carried prototype atomic torpedoes. In one incident, even the use of noise makers against a Soviet sub—with its crew exhausted, suffering from low oxygen levels and combat stress—provoked the decision to use an atomic torpedo against the harassing American destroyer. Only the Soviet captain's last-minute order canceled the action and precluded an incident that most likely would have ignited open nuclear warfare.[21]

As of October 23, an all-out American reconnaissance effort was in progress over Cuba. Navy photo aircraft began extreme low-level passes over the island. The goal was high-quality pictures of Soviet missile sites, but the flights quickly produced additional evidence of the huge Soviet military surge onto the island. The ongoing flights fanned Cuban anger and frustrated the Soviet troops; the Soviets had orders to hold fire, and at that point they were in control of the air defense system. Castro, the most emotional figure in the confrontation, ordered his conventional anti-aircraft units to engage, but the jet reconnaissance pilots were highly skilled and operating at extremely low altitudes. Unless or until the Soviets began to actively use their radar detection and fire control units, the reconnaissance flights were going to continue to expose Soviet assets on the island. Obviously an American air attack could come at any time, and the ballistic missile units were ordered into a crash effort to bring their missiles operational—indicating an obvious disconnect in Soviet thinking, since fully operational and armed missiles were exactly what was most likely to provoke maximum American preemption. The Soviets had moved toward prudence in virtually every aspect of their military response—except the most dangerous one. They were still rushing to establish what could very well be interpreted as a nuclear decapitation strike capability.

October 23 also saw the first major issue/conflict in American command and control. At that point, with numerous Soviet ships in and around Cuba and with submarines being tracked, the U.S. Navy was in standard operating procedure mode. Neither Defense Secretary Robert McNamara nor his deputy, Roswell Gilpatric, was copied on the operations messages going out from the Commander in Chief Atlantic. Not ones to defer to military protocol, McNamara and Gilpatric personally went to the Navy plotting room at the Pentagon and began to question the duty admiral. Not happy with the answers, McNamara engaged the Chief of Naval Operations (CNO), Admiral George Anderson, with the same questions. Reportedly the admiral's view was that McNamara was meddling with the traditional chain of command; he was neither prepared for nor happy with supplying answers to detailed operational questions in matters that were properly the task of his subordinate commanders. The admiral's attitude was not unique among senior Navy commanders; during the Bay of Pigs operation senior admirals (without White House or secretary of defense knowledge) had readied units far beyond the scope of the plan, including a Marine Brigade landing team, two squadrons of destroyers and a battle group including the aircraft carrier *Independence* and the light cruiser *Galveston*.[22]

At one point in his dialog with McNamara and Gilpatric the admiral described classic practices for stopping a Soviet vessel, beginning with a shot across the bow and proceeding to fire at the ship's rudder. Firing at a Soviet ship during such a crisis without a direct order from McNamara or the president was not acceptable to McNamara, and he bluntly told the admiral that no shots would be fired without civilian command authorization. Further details of the conversation are in some doubt, but it's clear the admiral lost his temper, telling the secretary of defense to leave those who knew how to do the job to do it—McNamara departed, but only after repeating his order. The incident would be one of the early indications that things were going to be changing in regard to the operational chain of command, as well as the accepted protocols for crisis command and control.

Other issues with command and control were soon to emerge, especially in regard to crisis communications. One of the most urgent concerns was whether Soviet ships moving toward Cuba would continue onward—to be intercepted by American forces that had been ordered to establish a blockade of the island. If ships with military cargoes continued toward Cuba, the confrontation would escalate very quickly. Navy reconnaissance identified several ships that were likely missile carriers and determined at least one pair of such ships was being escorted by a submarine. There is some doubt as to whether or not the president and secretary of defense were aware that the rules of engagement issued by CNO Anderson had included instructions to destroy the ships if they did not comply with orders from the American Navy. A destroyer, supported by an aircraft carrier, was standing by to intercept and enforce the blockade. With cabinet officers including President Kennedy and Secretary McNamara in a special meeting, it quickly became clear that information on true movements of the Soviet ships was not available to them. Initially a note was received that six Soviet ships had stopped or reversed course—but the message said nothing about whether they were incoming or outgoing from Cuba.

Eventually CIA Director John McCone left the room to investigate. He returned with the word that the Office of Naval Intelligence did have good news: The ships were inbound, and it was felt they might have stopped or turned back. Given that tracking the ships was still largely dependent on the decades-old method of radio detection finding, the Navy had been uncertain of its information, which was indeed fragmented and mixed. Navy analysts argued over the issue for the better part of the day. Given that the early reports were inconclusive, they elected to keep the information to themselves.

The situation was also exacerbated by the fact that secure communications circuits were overloaded—"emergency"-class messages were taking four hours to process, and "operational/immediate" traffic was backed up for up to seven hours.[23] It took some thirty hours to determine that the Soviets had indeed ordered their ships to hold or turn back—yet another sign that real-time command and control of a nuclear confrontation was very much an illusion. That wasn't nearly as bad as it was going to get: Within a few days, at the absolute height of the crisis, operational traffic between the Pentagon and its naval forces was being delayed by six to eight hours. And as far as messages between Washington, D.C., and Moscow, with routing and translations that was taking up to twelve hours.

October 23 also saw issues of command and control emerge during the Strategic Air Command's move to advanced alert. A general order had been approved to raise all forces to Defense Condition 3; however, the president had authorized SAC to go further, executing its special command authority to move to DEFCON 2, putting its entire force to alert. In doing so, SAC commander Power seems to have gone a bit beyond expectations. SAC routinely communicated with its global forces via special radio circuits; however, those communications were normally coded and secure. On October 23 Power broadcast over the Primary Alerting System (the war alert system), sending in the clear with no code in use. He stressed the seriousness of the situation and emphasized SAC's advanced state of readiness. Soviet monitoring stations quickly picked up and passed the message back to Moscow. Although the news was never officially confirmed, Power may have gone even a step further in getting across his message. According to a retired SAC wing commander, at the height of the crisis airborne alert bombers were flown past their normal fail-safe points and into Soviet airspace. Such a move would have been immediately obvious—and more than a little threatening to the Soviet air defense network.[24]

The Pentagon itself was conscious of taking the Soviets by surprise with something that might look like the first indication of an American nuclear strike. With that concern a planned test launch of a Thor-Delta missile from Cape Canaveral was postponed on October 24. However, President Kennedy's standing concern that all levels of the military might not stay synchronized continued to be validated. Rather than being totally canceled, the Thor-Delta launch was simply rescheduled. The Thor-

Delta was indeed launched—on October 27—arguably the tensest day of the whole crisis.[25] Yet while the Pentagon was at least trying to exercise caution, on October 26, the Strategic Air Command had taken control of the ballistic missiles at the Vandenberg test facility in California and installed nuclear warheads on them. SAC was fully aware that its bases were routinely monitored by Soviet intelligence; the issue of "base watchers" had long been a security concern. However, in this instance, SAC openly armed the Vandenberg missiles and then allowed one remaining test ICBM to be launched in a ballistic trajectory over the Pacific per a pre-crisis schedule.[26] A Minuteman launch at the height of the crisis no doubt created an increased amount of Soviet tension. All in all, it seems that while the president and even the Pentagon may have been moving with great caution, General Power and SAC were taking their own initiatives to demonstrate the seriousness of the situation to the Soviets.

There were other issues of command and control and other instances of communications lagging far behind real-time actions in the field. The period of October 26–28, during the height of the crisis, was particularly difficult for communications and coordination—as President Kennedy had feared, the number of people "not getting the word" was increasing. On October 27, the rescheduled test launch of the Thor-Delta from Cape Canaveral was conducted; however, the test had not been communicated to the North American Aerospace Defense Command, and its "radar fence" detected an object suddenly appearing in space over the southern United States. No track was immediately evident, and the first thought was that it was a medium-range missile launch out of Cuba. If so, it was known that there might be no more than five minutes' detection of any such warhead before impact. Fortunately, the radar track was soon determined to be outbound rather than incoming, and no attack alert was generated.[27]

There had been no doubt that a missile threat from Cuba had negated the majority of America's air and missile detection capabilities. What followed was a rush project—"Falling Leaves"—to redirect and rework at least some radar assets to be able to deal with incoming missiles from the south. On October 28, a voice call from the New Jersey radar center to the North American Aerospace Defense Command reported a missile launch from Cuba, with imminent impact on Tampa, Florida. There was no doubt about the track, and an attack clearly seemed under way. NORAD began a frantic check, polling a nuclear detonation warning network that had sensors in the majority of major American cities. No explosion was reported from Tampa, and in time it was determined that someone had been running a test tape at the New Jersey radar facility. Still, the incident made it clear that there would truly be no effective warning of a missile attack out of Cuba.

Later that same day, the ground-based radar "fence" that detected objects at orbital altitude passing over the United States detected what at first appeared to be multiple unidentified objects—possibly in ballistic trajectories. Eventually the report was found to have been produced by a satellite reentry; however, once again NORAD came under immense pressure to immediately declare whether or not a surprise attack was developing. It was yet another warning that during a time of crisis, there were going to be real "human factor" issues in play. In later years it would become even clearer that accidents happened; false indications would be generated, and human decision-making was critical. It would also become clear that the human factor had a tendency to slow down the warnings process far beyond planned response times.

Ultimately the missile crisis was resolved, missiles in Cuba and Turkey were removed and in the end the United States simply moved a nuclear missile submarine into the Mediterranean, if anything worsening the strategic balance for the Soviets in the short term. Khrushchev's strategic gambit had failed, and that failure was to have a definite impact in shortening his own time as the chief political power in the USSR.

American intelligence came out of the crisis with a considerably enhanced reputation: Television broadcasts and several United Nations presentations had included a series of dramatic photographs, exposing the Soviet missile sites to one and all. The low-level photographs taken by amazingly skillful Navy, Marine and Air Force pilots were especially dramatic. At the end of the crisis, Navy reconnaissance overflights offered detailed information about the Soviet withdrawal. It seemed that nothing could escape American intelligence once it was unleashed on a target, even if the target was an entire island nation. The public might have been even more impressed if it had access to the full details of the electronic intelligence collection and ferret activities conducted during the crisis. That work had been extremely vital in assessing the stages by which both the Soviet air defense network and the ballistic missile sites had gone operational. Fidel Castro had pressed the Soviets to activate their radar network as quickly as possible to assist the Cubans in targeting the low-flying American reconnaissance planes—their ongoing appearance was proving both frustrating and embarrassing to Fidel and his military.

The USS *Oxford*, operating as point for the electronic intelligence collection, had cruised a slow figure-eight path just off the Cuban coast, in sight of land and continually harassed by Cuban planes and boats. It was the *Oxford* that had first identified signals from the new Soviet air surveillance radar sets, then intercepted voice traffic showing that Soviet personnel were running the Cuban air defense. Most importantly, the *Oxford* identified the point at which both surveillance and targeting radars began operation—from that point on American aircraft were exposed to immediate attack.

The *Oxford*'s work was complemented by SAC B-47 electronics intelligence (ELINT) aircraft operating around the periphery of the island. The SAC aircraft were able to determine when the most dangerous point was reached—the activation of fire control radars. That fact was reported at the time of an October 27 U-2 flight over the island. When subordinate Soviet commanders determined that the flight was likely to expose some of their key assets, including tactical nuclear missiles around Guantanamo, they took it on their own authority to bring down the American plane with a surface-to-air missile. The SAC monitoring aircraft immediately advised its headquarters that fire control radar had been activated, but there was no way to inform the U-2 pilot—he was flying under strict orders of radio silence.[28]

The photographic and electronics intelligence collection story for the Cuban Missile Crisis was indeed breathtaking. Yet with information only released at the end of the Cold War with the USSR, it is now known that American intelligence had actually failed in several potentially disastrous areas. Perhaps most striking is the fact that no information on numbers or locations of the nuclear warheads and bombs delivered to Cuba was ever developed. Beyond that, it was some days into the crisis that any indication of tactical atomic weapons emerged. That came from a single, low-level Marine photo flight on October 25; photo analysis surfaced the possibility that Luna mobile missile launchers might have been introduced—yet the CIA still reported it as only a possibility. Other tactical weapons, such as the relatively large number of truck-towed atomic cruise missiles—including those secretly targeting Guantanamo—were never discovered.

The military response to warnings of tactical atomic weapons in Cuba was limited at best. The American admiral assigned to assemble an invasion force requested the inclusion of mobile Honest John missile launchers and atomic field cannon. The Joint Chiefs allowed him to load the launchers but denied his request for the actual missiles and shells—if circumstances dictated they could be supplied as needed. Tactical nuclear warfare in a Cuban landing was given no specific attention in casualty estimates.[29] In retrospect, the American military significantly and dangerously underestimated the Soviet military capability inside Cuba.

Its proposals for early air attacks assumed accurate targeting of virtually all the ballistic missile sites—although a caveat was given that strikes might not provide 100% coverage. Michael Dobbs's contemporary oral history work with Russian and Cuban personnel has revealed extensive detail about the movement of Soviet missile units deployed in Cuba and the planning for relocation of the ballistic missile units if detected. As American planners were finalizing plans for air attacks to eliminate the launch sites that had been identified (not all had), the commander of the Soviet missile regiments was well aware that his launch sites had been overflown by the Americans. He anticipated the planned air strikes and had ordered his missiles to be relocated to pre-planned reserve positions.[30] American military estimates of Soviet rocketry doctrine seem to have considerably underestimated their capabilities.

Given Soviet tactical doctrine on the use of battlefield nuclear weapons, including medium-range missiles, early American air strikes, parachute landings, special operations insertions—all could have triggered Soviet use of nuclear weapons just as the destroyer operation against a Soviet submarine had almost resulted in a nuclear torpedo launch.

Under attack and combat stress, not to mention no real-time chain of communications/command (a major problem for Soviet forces inside Cuba), the assumptions of American headquarters military planning could have quickly become irrelevant.

In the end, with limited knowledge, the American intelligence groups felt considerable pride in their work. The military services—particularly SAC—were pleased with the extent to which the Soviets had recognized their superiority. Certain senior officers were less impressed; General LeMay had clearly wanted to completely destroy the Communist menace in Cuba—and perhaps more than just in Cuba. He felt that the U.S. had actually lost credibility in the missile confrontation.

In turn President Kennedy, Secretary of Defense McNamara and other figures in the civilian authority had been much less impressed with military command, control and communications. They would no doubt have been even more concerned if certain of the incidents mentioned above had been brought to their attention. The military was satisfied with its practices and protocols; civilian leadership had felt a loss of control and an ongoing sense that the crisis could have gone out of control at any point. We now know that there were ongoing twists and turns in the Soviet internal dialog during the crisis—Khrushchev made a number of aggressive and dangerous decisions, only to be persuaded to change his mind. In the earliest days of the crisis, standard Soviet military doctrine on local control of nuclear weapons could well have resulted in a nuclear response during any attack. Only later did Soviet leadership decisions revoke that authority and bring such decisions back to Moscow. Given President Kennedy's concerns, there were going to be a number of changes and extensions to American civilian authority during such crises. The era of treating nuclear engagement as an extension of conventional military practices was over—change was most definitely in the wind.

Chapter 11

....

CONTINUITY OF COMMAND

istorically, the American president, acting as commander in chief, had not assumed an operational role in military command. The president selected senior commanders, monitored their effectiveness, replaced them if they didn't deliver on the battlefield or if they proved to be a political liability for his administration. Examples of such actions range from President Abraham Lincoln's rotation of commanders during the Civil War to President Harry Truman's replacement of General Douglas MacArthur during the Korean conflict. It should also be noted that America's presidents have often had less than perfect relationships with their senior military commanders.

President Truman became so frustrated with inter-service rivalries and the apparent unwillingness of the service chiefs to follow orders from the secretary of defense that he considered their actions to be insubordinate. Truman responded by calling all of the Joint Chiefs into his office in a 1948 meeting; he gave them specific written directives, including reprimands for their previous actions.[1] Following Korea, disputes over military policies and spending became more and more of a public issue. President Eisenhower, in constant budget and spending conflict with his service chiefs, saw several of them retire during his administration. Certain of the retirees began to publicly lambast his decisions, in speeches and articles. Eisenhower was so offended by this behavior that he made inquiries as to whether they were legally eligible for court-martial proceedings, even in retirement. Eisenhower, whose military experience led him to strong personal views about relationships with subordinates, viewed the retired officer's actions as "legalized insubordination."[2]

While policy and priority disagreements between presidents and their senior commanders were not uncommon, up until the era of atomic warfare, they had little impact on actual war fighting—simply because presidents were not involved in real-time military decision-making. That began to change during the Truman administration as President Truman asserted civilian control over atomic weapons. We previously reviewed the extensive Truman-era debate over military possession of actual atomic weapons, something that Truman delegated to the civilian Atomic Energy Commission. That issue alone led to some of the first extensive operational dialog between Truman and the Joint Chiefs, involving a series of ongoing decisions to use or not use atomic weapons in the Korean combat. With the integration of atomic weapons into all phases of the American military, including air defense systems, President Eisenhower was forced into more of an operational command role. To some extent he addressed that with pre-delegation and with rules and guidelines for authorized commanders, governing when and how they would execute their authority for the release and use of atomic weapons.

Given that in a surprise nuclear attack a decapitation strike of some sort would have likely eliminated both the president and vice president—and likely the Joint Chief staff at the Pentagon—some type of prior authorization for the use of atomic defensive weapons as well as the initiation of the SIOP retaliation plan had become an operational reality. Eisenhower responded with a 1957 decision to "pre-delegate" the use of nuclear weapons to the senior commanders at both unified and specified commands, both at home and abroad. The unified commands were those that included multiple services and a broad mission, initially including theater commanders such as the Commander in Chief Europe, Commander in Chief Atlantic, Commander in Chief Pacific and Commander in Chief Far East. The Strategic Air Command was the primary specified command reporting to the Joint Chiefs; however, there were others, and the Chiefs had the ability to designate new, specified commands as circumstances dictated. The 1957 Eisenhower directive essentially moved atomic-weapons-release authority down into the military chain of command. A smaller set of five "Authorizing Commanders" including the Commander in Chief of SAC (CINSAC) were given the authority to initiate retaliation in the event that a nuclear attack was under way and the president could not be contacted.[3]

Pre-delegation addressed a major policy problem in war fighting during a surprise attack, but a number of very practical problems remained—including linking warning of a nuclear attack into a joint national command system, creating the opportunity for presidential notification as well as effective and timely notification of the authorized service commanders. The issue of centralized national command was actually not a new one. In 1946, while still serving as chief of staff of the Army, Eisenhower had been requested by the chairman of the Senate Banking and Finance Committee to direct the Joint Chiefs in a study that would address making the nation as invulnerable as possible to future surprise attacks. The study was intended to address "continuity of command" as well as actions to be taken to preserve the nation's industry, its financial and transportation infrastructure and its population.[4] In a process similar to the lengthy debate over operational control and targeting of nuclear weapons, that study spawned several years of a "painfully slow" effort to develop a Joint Services Command Post (JCP) command center—not to mention an effective national emergency communications network.

By 1948, little progress had been made beyond the decisions that the national command center would remain in Washington, D.C., at the seat of government, and that during an emergency the secretary of defense, the Joint Chiefs and portions of their staffs would be relocated there. In 1949 National Security Council Directive 68 called for a "hardened and sheltered command and control system to ensure communications under attack."[5] While no definition was given for such a system, it seems to have been assumed that there would be an alternative command post and Fort Ritchie, Maryland, had been suggested. The Fort Ritchie alternate site, designated the Alternative Joint Command Center, was approved in 1950; however, it was to be staffed only following an attack, and with personnel relocated from their normal duty stations.

Major Joint Command Post disagreements continued, with viewpoints differing among the services as well as by SAC; it seemed that everyone preferred his own independent command post. In 1952 the Joint Chiefs agreed that in case of war, personnel could be relocated to Fort Ritchie, and if he desired, the president could relocate as well. Somewhat surprisingly, even with the advent of Soviet thermonuclear bombs, it would not be until late in the 1950s that relocation of personnel during or after an actual attack would be recognized as unfeasible. It seems that either the Joint Chiefs were not taking the scenarios in the Net evaluation reports seriously or simply assumed that a period of worsening international relations would give them time to raise alert levels and staff the Alternative Joint Command Center.

Given the lack of progress in any inter-service agreement, plus SAC's preeminent role in strategic warfare, it's not surprising to find that SAC's own command post at the Pentagon evolved into the Kennedy-era National Military Command Center. SAC's Pentagon center was initially established in 1950, as a point for passing messages from the Far East at the beginning of the Korean conflict. Given SAC's overall mission, communications lines were established to the Air Defense Command and the National Command authorities at the Capitol. At the president's request, a line was run to the White House, and protocols were established for alerting him in the event of any attack on the United States.

By 1951, more permanent facilities were established at the Pentagon, and the SAC center began to assume a de facto role as a hub for national command and control. By 1952 the center had also established procedures for transmitting prepared emergency action alerts in the advent of a crisis; it was given the task of maintaining the "Checklist of Joint Chiefs Actions on the Imminence or Outbreak of War." By 1955 the National Security Council had designated the Air Force command post at the Pentagon as the National Air Defense Warning Center.[6] Early in the 1960s the center would be enhanced, made a key asset of the Joint Chiefs and secretary of defense and named as the National Military Command Center.

SAC's operational command-and-control needs were also seminal in driving much of both the warning and retaliation control system that came into place at the beginning of the Kennedy administration. Studies determined that it was literally impossible to "harden" ground-based control centers to "ride out" a surprise nuclear attack. The most viable option was to establish an airborne command capability, using a number of both ground- and air-alert control aircraft—with the capability of carrying on SAC battle operations in a post-attack environment. Those aircraft would have to continue communications with ground-based SAC command centers, with NORAD, with SAC's own air groups overseas and with the main or alternative Joint Command Post.

SAC began ground-alert operation of the aerial command posts in July 1960 and continuous airborne operations in February 1961. As usual SAC was driving itself and its own strategic mission, and to some extent everyone else was following along. The outstanding question was how to firmly tie SAC and the nuclear elements of the other services into national civilian authority. That authority had become more clearly defined with the Department of Defense Reorganization Act of 1958, which considerably strengthened the command authority of the secretary of defense. It also removed the civilian service chiefs from the operational chain of command. What was emerging was a definitive National Command Authority, communications from the president and secretary of defense through the Joint Chiefs to the unified and special force commanders. Ultimately it would be the president and secretary of defense who would jointly hold the authority for nuclear war-making and initiation of the SIOP.[7]

From an operational standpoint, that meant that the president and secretary of defense needed to be in constant contact with the Joint Chiefs. In turn the Joint Chiefs had to maintain communications with SAC and with the unified commanders responsible for the nuclear missile submarines and the atomic alert fighter bombers in Europe and the Pacific. The parameters for that contact, based on time of warning for any surprise attack, had also begun to change dramatically by the early 1960s.

During the 1950s the focus was on bombers. The DEW Line, Mid-Canada Line and Pinetree Line were the keys to detecting a bomber attack at long range. By the early 1960s the advent of Soviet intercontinental missiles dramatically changed that warning equation. Any surprise attacks from that point on were most likely to be first detected either by actual atomic explosions from warheads delivered by submarine-launched missiles or by new, very long-range ballistic-missile warning systems. The half-hour warning of the 1950s became the fifteen-minute warning of the missile age. SAC would be driven to that fifteen minutes— either its ground-alert bombers would "flush" off their fields within fifteen minutes or be destroyed. In turn, the Navy would be driven to locate Soviet forward-deployed missile submarines, which could carry out true decapitation launches against both the National Command Authority and SAC's ground-alert bombers.

Beginning early in the Kennedy administration, the Joint Chiefs conducted a series of studies projecting that the emerging Soviet ICBM force would achieve parity by 1969 and thereafter exceed that of the United States. The sheer number of Soviet ICBMs would allow sufficient atomic strikes on American command-and-control sites and communications facilities to effectively decapitate National Command Authority. The risk for the American command-and-control system was obvious. The military's contention was that in any full-scale attack, communication with the unified and special commands would become so compromised that retaliation would likely fail unless pre-delegation of some sort was continued. Worse yet, retaliation decisions would have to be made in a number of minutes, and it seemed improbable that the full chain of command, from the radar stations to the president, could be effectively executed in only fifteen minutes.[8]

It had become increasingly clear that any true surprise attack was going to find the president at the White House—or traveling. It would find the secretary of defense either at the Capitol, the Pentagon—or traveling. That reality led to a conclusion that the White House was going to need seriously improved communications capabilities. It was also increasingly clear that the alternative command center at Fort Ritchie was not significantly more secure than the Pentagon in the event of a true attack. One possible solution for a survivable National Command Authority—given at least some minimal warning or an advanced state of alert—was a civilian equivalent to the SAC airborne command post. Special planes were adapted for that purpose, and the NCA aircraft was designated as the "National Airborne Emergency Command Post" (NEACP). Its operational codename was "Nightwatch." Initially Nightwatch used the radio call sign "Silver Dollar"; later its call sign would be changed daily. The Nightwatch aircraft was normally maintained on ground alert at Andrews Air Force Base outside of Washington, D.C.; however, it was flown in periodic exercises, with battle management and communications staff onboard.

Given that the radio range of the aircraft was limited, it had the ability to call into signal transfer points where the radio circuit would be interfaced and calls routed as if they were regular land-line telephone calls. American Telephone and Telegraph operated a number of such hubs (Combat Ciders) for the Air Force, as part of its worldwide communications network. SAC's airborne alert command post (Looking Glass), its alternate airborne command aircraft, and other VIP aircraft (operated by the Special Air Mission at Andrews AFB outside Washington) all carried equipment for Combat Cider access. When in the air on exercises Nightwatch routinely used a Combat Cider access point designated "Waldorf," located in Maryland. For a time, during the 1960s, the Navy would also operate a floating national command post on the cruiser *Northampton*, the National Emergency Command Post Afloat (NECPA).[9]

In an additional effort to maintain National Command Authority while the president was traveling, the Air Force Special Air Mission operated a commercial transport aircraft, equipped with special communications equipment and personnel. That aircraft, designated *Air Force One* when the president was onboard, also contained secure emergency teletype circuits that could be used to authorize the SIOP. In addition, the White House Communications Agency transported and operated mobile communications equipment along with the presidential party; the goal was to ensure that the president was always within minutes of a secure voice telephone circuit.

Despite all those preparations, the realities of a surprise missile attack remained. In 1963, a time and motion study was performed, exploring presidential "extraction" during an attack. The goal was to determine if the fifteen-minute planning guideline was realistic. The study concluded that there was simply no way that the president would be able to leave the White House, be helicoptered to Andrews Air Force Base (where Nightwatch was on alert), board the aircraft and be carried out of the Washington area before being incinerated in the multiple hydrogen warhead explosions that the Soviets would target on the area of the nation's capital.[10] Acknowledging the fact that decapitation was extremely likely early in any true surprise attack, the Eisenhower pre-delegation guidelines were continued in effect by President Kennedy.

Putting the new airborne and ship-based command centers in place was a major step forward in establishing a virtually real-time global command-and-control resource for the National Command Authority, but their operation was still dependent on reliable, redundant and survivable communications. To that end, in March 1961, Secretary Robert McNamara directed the Joint Chiefs to review and study the command-and-control apparatus "particularly as it relates to strategic forces." The Chiefs were to recommend changes to ensure that the system would be continuously responsive to "duly constituted authority."[11]

After much study and debate, the final recommendation, signed off on by McNamara in April 1962, involved four major elements: a National Military Command Center at the Pentagon; an Alternative National Military Command Center at Fort Ritchie, Maryland; and the airborne and seaborne emergency command centers. The overall entity was called the National Military Command System (NMCS). The Joint Chiefs also proposed that the NMCS be integrated into global military operations through the creation of an integrated communications network, the Worldwide Military Command and Control System. McNamara also approved that proposal in July of 1962 but directed that the worldwide system needed to address the communications needs of the president, top civilian leaders and international diplomacy and intelligence.[12]

The events of the Cuban Missile Crisis emphasized the need for much-improved command, control and communications; the response was the integration of the National Military Command Center (NMCC) and with a much-improved Worldwide Military Command

and Control System. Operation of the National Military Command Center had actually begun by the time of the Cuban Missile Crisis, and the NMCC played a role in all the military crises of the 1960s, beginning with the Gulf of Tonkin incidents off Vietnam in 1964. The following years saw considerable technical enhancement to the worldwide military communications network, with a constant effort toward adding advanced and alternative technology solutions to ensure at least a minimal level of communications during and even after an atomic attack on the nation.

By 1963 considerable progress had been made in defining the national chain of command, establishing a system of joint command posts including backup airborne and seaborne facilities and linking various communications systems to establish a worldwide command-and-control network. The military side of ensuring continuity of national command had been addressed, with certain options to ensure that the president was linked into the system at all times. If time permitted, the president could even be extracted to an airborne command center.

The civilian side of the command and communications issue, however, remained to be addressed; measures were needed to provide the president not just with the intelligence and the options during a surprise attack but during any national or international crisis. And, as indicated by McNamara's guidance with regard to the development of the worldwide communications network, there was an ongoing focus on integrating civilian decision-making and control into the operational military command system in all its phases, including conventional military activities. Several elements had combined to influence that trend, which first became pronounced during the Kennedy administration.

Advances in broadcast television coverage, new undersea cables and expanded news coverage of all sorts were focusing more and more scrutiny on presidential decision-making. Reporters were becoming quite adept at sensing tension and crisis simply by monitoring changes in activity among cabinet members. The media wanted breaking news, and they wanted presidential and administration commentary on it. President Kennedy himself had set certain expectations for his own media visibility as early as the nationally broadcast debates leading up to his election. If the administration was expected to appear "in the know" and be perceived as proactively responding to global events, its own demand for information was going to increase exponentially.

The solution to this challenge entailed bringing real-time information from all the major government departments and agencies directly into the White House. It had been routine for key departments such as State Department and key agencies such as the Federal Bureau of Investigation, the Central Intelligence Agency and the National Security Administration to maintain their own "watch centers" around the clock. The State Department watch center collected news from embassies and consulates around the globe, routing information to other groups who might be interested or affected by it. Each of the military services maintained its own command centers as well as numerous centers within its various units. The unified and specified commands maintained their own centers, and in some cases, as with the Navy, certain of the regional commanders even operated alert airborne command centers. The military was working to connect those various centers into the new National Military Command Center, and the White House was going to need its own all-inconclusive watch center, with myriad military, intelligence and departmental connections.

The new watch center for the White House and the president became known as the Situation Room; it was staffed around the clock by Situation Room duty officers, with telephone and teletype connections to all the major civilian departments and agencies as well as the service watch centers, the National Military Command Center at the Pentagon and to the North American Aerospace Defense Command. When the president was traveling the Situation Room maintained links to him through the Special Air Mission at Andrews Air Force Base. The Special Air Mission operated the aircraft used by the president and vice president. Communications circuits and switching for the Situation Room as well as communications links to Andrews were installed and maintained by the White House Communications Agency (WHCA).

The WHCA was also responsible for the mobile communications equipment that was carried by separate transport aircraft on each presidential trip, ensuring constant voice access to and for the president. As time and events progressed, official information sources for the center would be supplemented by the media itself, first with wire service teletype, then with broadcast news and decades later with several twenty-four-hour news services, led first by the Cable News Network (CNN). In times of crisis, as early as 1963, some of the most current news going into the Situation Room, and being relayed on, would come from wire service bulletins and television news coverage. The history and evolution of the Situation Room provides an intimate view into the reality of civilian crisis response; one of the best sources for an inside look is Michael Bohn's *Nerve Center: Inside the White House Situation Room.*

Nothing like the Situation Room had existed before 1961; it was created largely from scratch by Kennedy's national security advisor McGeorge Bundy. Bundy's own position was itself a new creation—previously presidents had aides of various sorts, administrative and military, but nothing on the order of Bundy's responsibilities. In 1961, at the height of the Cold War, John Kennedy's relationship with the Joint Chiefs had become strained, an extension of the policy disagreements that had existed during both the Truman and Eisenhower administrations. That strain would continue with Kennedy's immediate successor, Lyndon Johnson. Kennedy's relationship with the Joint Chiefs soured early; he felt that they had not clearly warned him of the risks of the Bay of Pigs plan, which had been a disaster in the earliest days of his presidency. In turn the Chiefs maintained that they had never been fully integrated into the project by the CIA and that the new president had not clearly asked for their input—their feeling was that if Kennedy had simply called on them to sustain the exile landings with American military support, both Fidel Castro and Communism would already be gone from Cuba.[13]

There was a fundamental difference in Kennedy's worldview and that of the Joint Chiefs. Kennedy was a pragmatist; he favored controlled, incremental responses to international challenges. His preference was for low-intensity military actions, such as blockades. He was fascinated with the opportunity to use Special Forces and the option of supporting counterinsurgency through a combination of extremely localized military action—with small units—and civil developmental activities. When he asked the Joint Chiefs for a plan that would deal with a Communist insurgency in Laos, they responded that such involvement could lead to major ground warfare in Southeast Asia and that they would need to commit sixty thousand troops. They would also need to be prepared to engage the Chinese and warned that Kennedy should not act unless he was committed to use nuclear weapons to "guarantee victory."[14] That was not a viable solution from the new president's perspective. In response Kennedy moved to a combination of covert action and economic development that maintained at least a minimal level of neutrality in Laos, until full-scale warfare in Vietnam brought the North Vietnamese into the equation and overwhelmed any low-intensity solution.

Kennedy was looking for flexibility, and he wasn't getting it from his Joint Chiefs. The events of the Cuban Missile Crisis confirmed his concerns in that regard, leaving him with the impression that what his commanders really wanted of him was not to be involved and make decisions but simply to hand off military operations to them and let them take the actions a purely military solution demanded. Perhaps the most dramatic example of that sort of attitude surfaced during the missile crisis of 1962. Kennedy had expressed his concerns that an attack on Soviet sites and personnel in Cuba might provoke a "spasm" response, leading to full nuclear engagement and seventy million Americans dead.

Full-scale nuclear war was a condition that the Air Force chief, General LeMay, had lived with for a decade. LeMay offhandedly commented to the president, "You're in a pretty bad fix."[15] When the president asked him to repeat his remark, which Kennedy found highly impertinent, LeMay did so. Kennedy reminded him that LeMay was also in the same fix, "personally." Kennedy had been amazed at the blithe remark and apparent total confidence that there would be no Soviet response. Later Kennedy remarked to his friend Dave Powers that the Chiefs had a real advantage in the event that they were wrong: "If we listen to them and do what they want us to do, none of us will be alive later to tell them that they were wrong."[16]

Kennedy's concern over what he felt to be the inflexible and "unimaginative" views of the Joint Chiefs led him to bring General Maxwell Taylor as a "Military Representative to the President" and to further empower McGeorge Bundy's position of National Security Advisor. In October 1962 Kennedy officially appointed Taylor as the chairman of the Joint Chiefs of Staff. President Kennedy was determined to use Secretary of Defense McNamara, Taylor and Bundy to balance the military input to his administration's decision-making. To ensure that balance, Kennedy needed comprehensive, real-time intelligence and information. The answer to that need lay in the constitution and operation of the new Situation Room, a project driven by Bundy.

In turn, the Situation Room, with its constantly expanding access to information, produced something new in presidential command and control—something that political scientists would term the "operational presidency." There is no doubt that the disaster at the Bay of Pigs, during Kennedy's earliest months in the White House, fueled his desire for more detailed information than had been presented to previous presidents. Detail-oriented by nature, Kennedy had remained largely at a distance during the supposedly "deniable" Cuban CIA operation. He had no access to real-time operational information and continued his regular schedule of activities. For that matter CIA director Allen Dulles was overseas and apparently assumed no operational control himself; indeed he seemed more remote from the operation than even the president, who was at least taking telephone calls. Later inquiries would picture operational command and control during that period as a virtual study in how not to conduct military operations. From that point on President Kennedy began to demand the same "raw information" for the White House that had previously been retained by senior intelligence and military officers—he wanted the actual data, not a filtered version of it.

Kennedy's experience during the Cuban Missile Crisis had intensified his demand for intelligence, while highlighting how painfully slow military communications could be, and demonstrating the fact that there was no existing practice of passing information to the White House from the various command centers and watch centers. There was no doubt that when the director of the CIA had to leave a presidential meeting at the height of the crisis—to find out the status of Russian ships approaching the naval blockade—new practices and protocols were needed.

Still, President Kennedy did not want it to appear that the White House was putting a military command center into place. The name "Situation Room" was carefully selected to portray it as an intelligence center, making information available to all senior White House staff and even cabinet officers.[17] While a small conference room was added to the communications work area, the new facility was characterized as an intelligence collection operation—Situation Room duty officers collected and collated breaking news from the media and integrated it with information from military centers and agencies. The president was advised of breaking international events, generally through the National Security Advisor or his deputy.

In instances of major crises, especially those with military implications, the members of the National Security Council were informed, and several of them routinely collected in the conference area to access incoming information. Usage of the conference room, especially for meetings, varied according to presidential style and comfort. Kennedy conducted most of the Cuban missile strategy sessions in the Cabinet Room of the White House or the Oval Office. Presidents Nixon and Ford almost never used the Situation Room conference area, while Presidents Clinton and George W. Bush used it for military-related meetings. President Johnson was perhaps the most frequent user of the conference area; reportedly he used it so often for strategy and actual military planning sessions during the Vietnam War that he had the chair from his office installed in the room.[18]

The Situation Room became operational in the spring of 1963; however, following the assassination of President Kennedy, it was Lyndon Johnson rather than Kennedy who most dramatically translated the wealth of new information coming into the White House in what has been called the "operational presidency." Political scientists introduced that term to help illustrate the transition in decision-making power from governmental entities such as the State Department and the Defense Department, to the White House.[19] Prior to the advent of the Situation Room, the State Department and the military services had maintained their own global communications channels. In terms of foreign policy, the State Department served as the channel for delivering presidential

messages to foreign governments and for channeling international diplomatic communications to the White House. With the advent of the
Situation Room and its enhanced communications, President Kennedy
could simply pick up a phone and ask to be connected to a foreign leader—often a challenge for the duty officers but a task they routinely managed to carry out. In later administrations even cabinet officers took
advantage of the ability for communications "end runs." During the
Vietnam War Henry Kissinger established a secret backchannel to the
North Vietnamese using Situation Room circuits; later he would do the
same thing in highly secret discussions with the Chinese. Such actions
were done without State Department staff knowledge and reduced that
department's previous impact on foreign policy.

President Johnson carried the "operational presidency" to perhaps
unanticipated levels—especially into the realm of tactical military command. Staff described Johnson as the "all-time champ" with regards to
his demand for both detail and immediate notification of global events:
"Johnson wanted to be the first to know about an incident."[20] During the 1950s President Eisenhower had been dissatisfied with the time
it took intelligence alerts to get to the White House, and in response
the National Security Administration created the CRITICOM system,
which was able to move critical messages—designated "Critics"—from
intelligence agencies to the White House in ten minutes or less. While
most presidents had relied on their staff, in particular the Situation
Room and national security advisor, to filter what was often a considerable stream of Critic messages, Johnson wanted to see them all.

As the fighting in Southeast Asia escalated, the Joint Chiefs became
increasingly concerned that the United States would have to take aggressive action against North Vietnam if the South was to be saved.
Unable to make any progress with Secretary of Defense McNamara, the
Chiefs requested a personal meeting with the president. Johnson was
concerned about the risk of full-scale combat with China or even of Soviet intervention; he proved to be more than unreceptive to the Chiefs'
remarks. In what has been described as a singularly critical breach between the American military and civilian leadership, participants in the
meeting reported Johnson turning on the Chiefs and screaming personal

obscenities at them. He ridiculed them for coming to him with military "advice" and ensured them they could not even begin to understand the "weight on his shoulders." After several more rounds of cursing he bluntly told them he was not going to allow any military idiots to talk him into World War III and told them to get the hell out of his office.[21]

Increasingly, following his confrontation with the Joint Chiefs, Johnson turned to personal involvement in the Vietnam combat. Matters proceeded to the point where Johnson began to study military maps and authorize individual air strikes. In conjunction with Secretary of Defense McNamara, he began to micromanage combat decisions to a level never conceived of by his predecessors, including General Eisenhower. During the first two years of the "Rolling Thunder" air campaign against North Vietnam, the decisions on targets, the number of missions to be flown and in some cases even pilot tactics were made during Tuesday luncheons at the White House—attended by Johnson, the secretaries of state and defense, National Security Advisor Walt Rostow and the presidential press secretary. No military professionals were present at those planning sessions until late in 1967. Constantly seeking negotiations, Johnson would not allow bombing of critical targets, and he established extremely "elaborate and restrictive" rules of engagement for American aircraft.[22] Johnson's role as an operational president, in particular his military role in Southeast Asia, is far beyond our focus or scope; readers will find extensive details in H.R. McMaster's book *Dereliction of Duty: Lyndon Johnson, Robert McNamara, the Joint Chiefs of Staff, and the Lies That Led to Vietnam*.

The flow of information through the Situation Room allowed the emergence of a presidential crisis control across a number of venues. In a national security situation such as President Kennedy had experienced with Soviet missiles in Cuba, the power of the White House watch center could prove extremely valuable. When used for a much more direct role in actual military command and control, especially in the absence of the president and by elected or cabinet-level individuals not experienced or adequately briefed in hands-on crisis management, there was a serious downside. President Kennedy had fully realized the danger of letting the Situation Room take over the role properly held by the

National Military Command Center at the Pentagon. In our review of succeeding national security crises, we will find that certain presidential successors, and their staffs, did not demonstrate that same distinction.

The emergence of the Situation Room was one of the final steps in establishing true continuity of command, from the National Command Authority to the individual combatant commands. But continuity of command requires more than organization charts and task listings; it demands more than a well-developed, secure communications network. It requires that the individuals involved know their roles, are trained in them, participate in exercises related to crisis command and control and are equipped to perform their role under high degrees of stress. We will review a number of examples that allow us to access exactly how well continuity of command has worked under stress.

President Kennedy had taken the initiative to establish a system of national continuity of command, one adequate for potential nuclear confrontations in the age of ICBMs and submarine-launched atomic weapons. It was designed for the missile age—an era of fifteen-minute warnings or perhaps even of National Command Authority decapitation. Sadly and ironically the first real test of the system came with his own assassination. It came with both the president and vice president out of Washington, D.C.; in Texas, with most of the American cabinet in the air on an international diplomacy mission to Japan; and with the presidential airborne alert aircraft in the air on a training exercise. President Kennedy's murder was the first real-world test of the new continuity of command system—and in several key elements, the system failed miserably.

Normally United States military services perform after-action studies of major incidents, with the intention of identifying failures and learning lessons to improve their practices. We have been unable to determine that any government agency, including the Joint Chiefs or the White House itself, ever studied the Kennedy assassination—or later the attack on President Ronald Reagan—specifically to assess the performance of continuity of command practices. The following continuity of command assessment is drawn from the oral history and chronological work done by William Manchester and by the author's own research.[23]

From a technical standpoint, all of the communications systems intended to support continuity of command were in place on November 22, 1963. The White House Communications Agency, staffed by Army personnel, had established a local communications network in Dallas. Communications equipment, carried by an Air Force transport, was in place at Dallas's Love Field and along the president's motorcade route, as well as at the World Trade Center, where he was scheduled to give a noontime speech. The president's aircraft was connected into the local communications network, operated by the Secret Service.[24] At approximately 1:31 Eastern Standard Time, the aircraft's pilot heard a transmission on the Secret Service radio net, "Lancer is hurt . . . it looks bad. . . . "—Lancer was the Secret Service codename for President Kennedy.

At 1:34, a United Press flash message out of Dallas was placed on the UPI news wire. It contained news directly from the point of the shooting, based on a radio telephone call from reporter Merriman Smith. Smith was reporting from a press pool car in the motorcade through downtown Dallas. The UPI wire was the first information on the attack to arrive at the Situation Room. At 1:36 ABC radio broadcast Smith's reports of gunshots fired at the motorcade. By 1:40 CBS interrupted its highly popular television program, *As the World Turns*, to broadcast news that shots had been fired in Dallas and that President Kennedy was reported to have been seriously wounded. From that point on, several senior government officials, including the CIA director, appear to have acted based on simply following the news broadcasts from the closest possible television.

Sometime between 1:40 and 2 PM, Secret Service agent Roy Kellerman, who had been in the president's car, called from the Parkland Hospital emergency room and contacted the White House Secret Service office. One of President Kennedy's military aides on the trip, Godfrey McHugh, used the same emergency room phone to very briefly alert both the NMCC and the Pentagon; he seems to have actually been looking for information rather than providing it. Other calls were manually rerouted by White House Communications Agency specialists traveling with the president's party. Instead of using the local network available in the motorcade vehicles and linked through equipment at

Love Field, the hospital commercial circuits became the primary links back to Washington. The Secret Service's local radio telephone network was largely bypassed with the stress and circumstances of the attack.[25]

The UPI wire message had already alerted the NMCC to the attack in Dallas; a Pentagon alert buzzer was immediately triggered. However, at that point, the crisis response becomes unclear and certainly lagged at the most senior levels. We have no record of what communications occurred between the NMCC and the alternate alert centers. There should have been immediate communications checks with Fort Ritchie, the airborne alert command center/Nightwatch—most importantly there should have been an immediate check with NORAD, the SAC war room and SAC's airborne alternative command center. We don't know if those communications occurred; what we do know is that neither the Joint Chiefs nor the secretary of defense appears to have personally moved to verify the status of national command and control.

The Chiefs were in a planning meeting with senior officers from the German military. When word was passed to them, they did not leave the meeting. At approximately 2 PM Eastern Standard Time they briefly "huddled" with Secretary McNamara and returned to the meeting with the Germans. As a result of the quick meeting, at 2:15 a flash alert was sent to all American military bases that the president had been critically wounded and that the military must be alert.[26] That initial alert actually involved no overall increase in defense condition levels. It was only at 2:50 PM that the Joint Chiefs increased the national defense readiness condition from DEFCON 5 (the lowest peacetime condition) to DEFCON 4. The DEFCON 4 alert status was maintained until 12:30 on Sunday, November 24.[27]

Given that any attack on the president could very well have represented the first indication of a Soviet decapitation effort, a lag of forty-five minutes from the first message to the NMCC to the first Joint Chiefs alert to the military represented what has to be considered a slow response at best. Certainly at that point, the pace and level of the U.S. military alert lagged far behind what the plan had called for with any potential surprise attack. In retrospect, since we know there was no attack in the making, it's easy to not to be critical. However, in the context of the time, low-level bombing attacks or submarine missile launches could easily have been on their way into Washington, D.C., during the first half hour after the UPI wire from Dallas reached the NMCC. For that matter, previously smuggled and hidden atomic devices could have exploded at any time. The absence of a NORAD ICBM warning was surely no guarantee that some sort of attack was not imminent. In the context of the times, it seems amazing that the Joint Chiefs, other than General LeMay, who was away from Washington on vacation, should simply have remained in a routine planning meeting with German military officers after receiving news of an attack on the president of the United States.[28]

Based on official record, including a transcript of *Air Force One* communications, it appears that after forty-five minutes, there had been no personal communication at all between either the National Military Command Center or the Situation Room and Vice President Johnson (now legally commander in chief) or Speaker of the House John McCormack, next in the line of presidential succession after Johnson. In fact, during the whole crisis, while Johnson was in Dallas and on his flight back to Washington, the new president himself never initiated any type of military contact with the NMCC, the secretary of defense or the Joint Chiefs. While his behavior is clearly understandable from an emotional standpoint, it was far short of the demanding expectations of continuity of civilian command. Speaker of the House McCormack also displayed a highly emotional reaction; he essentially refused to step into his role in the legal chain of succession—turning Secret Service protection away from his door the afternoon of the assassination and refusing to accept protection or deal with the succession issue in the following months.[29]

By approximately 2 PM, a massive number of telephone calls inside Washington, D.C., and on trunks in and out of the city had saturated the telephone network, causing wide-scale outages. Some talk of sabotage began; whether or not the outages affected any of the command and watch centers is unknown. We do know that the head of the Joint Chiefs, General Maxwell Taylor, issued a special warning to troops in the Washington area. We have no further details on his motive or what that warning actually produced in terms of military activity. There is no record of an increased military presence at any government facilities. In the larger sense, what McNamara—as the only acting element of "national command authority"—Taylor and McGeorge Bundy were not doing is as instructive as what they did. One of President Kennedy's many motivations in sitting up the new national command structure was to ensure that in any crisis, including that of imminent or actual attack, civilian control was exercised and the U.S. military response was measured—and monitored.

While there is no evidence that the overall American defense condition was ever elevated beyond DEFCON 4, news reports and oral history interviews indicate that individual commands most definitely did elevate their alert conditions, as they were authorized to do. The Strategic Air Command moved to DEFCON 3, and some of its units appear to have gone to alert levels comparable to those of DEFCON 2. News reports talk of ICBM crews going to full alert, preparing for launch on command. The CINCPAC commander, Admiral Felt, placed the 7th Fleet on DEFCON 3, which put all crews at General Quarters and authorized preparation of "special weapons" (nuclear weapons) for use. Certain task forces in the Far East moved toward forward positions, in strike range of their designated war targets.[30] In addition, the U.S. European Army commander stationed in Bonn, Germany, reportedly alerted and mobilized his forces to deal with a Soviet-Bloc attack.

All of those actions may well have been fully prudent, even possibly short of what might have been expected. As we will discuss shortly, the unified and specified commanders' operational guidance of that date appears to have specified a far more dramatic nuclear response than what either Kennedy or McNamara had understood. However, the NMCC, the Situation Room and the newly defined structure of National Command Authority had been developed with the assumption that civilian authority would be in constant communication with and in control of the military command system. Yet there is no sign that Johnson, McNamara, Taylor or Bundy assumed any ongoing role in the operational details of the military preparedness response that did go into place on November 22, 1963. Beyond that neither McNamara,

Taylor nor Bundy appears to have taken any note of their responsibility to prepare or advise the new president of his National Command Authority role as commander in chief.

In regard to continuity of command, one of the most critical duties of president is to be in communication and available to give orders in regard to execution of the Single Integrated Operational Plan, in the event of imminent or actual attack on the nation. It is imperative that the NMCC or one of the alternate command centers be in constant contact with the president and that there be a secure emergency-action message link between the president and the various alert centers. In 1963, while traveling, the president was supposedly connected by a secure teletype circuit available in *Air Force One*.

Given the complexity of the SIOP, the plan itself is always carried by a military aide who stays in close physical proximity to the president. The president carries a card with the voice code that allows him direct implementation while in communications with the NMCC, the SAC war room or alternate command centers. Given that there may only be minutes to respond, it is obvious that the commander in chief must be familiar with the SIOP material, the communications protocols, and the passwords required; more than that, the president must be prepared to handle the process virtually by reflex while under immense stress.

In Washington, the White House Military Office is charged with ensuring those protocols are followed in the event of a warning from the NMCC. While the president is traveling, responsibility is somewhat unclear, but it seems reasonable that any military aides with the president would have to take the responsibility of ensuring that the SIOP codes were available (they are carried by a military officer traveling with the president, in what is generally referred to as the "bomb bag"). Two senior military aides and the bomb bag carrier were traveling with President Kennedy in Dallas and returned with President Johnson on *Air Force One*.

As of November 22, 1963, the bomb bag officer had never been introduced to the Secret Service detail protecting the president; he and his responsibilities had not been made a factor in their planning or response practices.[31] Yet his critical role was well known within the national command structure, from the staff in the NMCC to McNamara, Taylor and certainly to the military aides in Dallas. General Taylor told William Manchester that he had worried about the bomb bag in Dallas, and whether it was secure. But Taylor gave no order to check its status, and the bag carrier had indeed been separated from Johnson for well over an hour; in fact the Secret Service had initially refused to board him onto *Air Force One* when Johnson returned to that aircraft at Love Field. Worse yet, it appears that Johnson himself had never been briefed on the bag, the details of handling the SIOP, the command protocols or virtually anything relating to his potential command role.[32]

Equally surprisingly, the presidential military aides in Dallas apparently made no immediate attempt while at Parkland Hospital to locate the bomb bag carrier, to put Johnson in touch with the NMCC, to brief him on any matters relating to the current military alert status or to communicate on those matters to the NMCC, Taylor or McNamara. It was only after Johnson had left Parkland Hospital and boarded *Air Force One* that one aide advised him that the bomb bag was on board. Reportedly Johnson showed no special interest and continued watching broadcast news on TV sets in the plane.[33]

Johnson did make a number of calls back to Washington, D.C., although he initially had no idea what communications were available on the plane. None of the calls were of a military or command-and-control nature; beyond that it appears that the aircraft communications operators were so busy placing and receiving telephone traffic that they had little or no time to monitor the emergency action telegraph circuit. Later, Johnson is reported to have simply stared out the window while the aircraft was returning to Washington—he had been the first person to remark about a Communist conspiracy in Dallas—and comment to his young Texas media friend Bill Moyers that he "wondered if the missiles were flying?"[34] The death of President Kennedy was a national tragedy; the events immediately following did not speak well for national command and control or of the continuity of civilian command during a possible attack or national crisis.

One of the remaining mysteries of that day is the fact that the operational guidance for the SIOP of the time seems not to have been what

President Kennedy and Secretary of Defense McNamara would have assumed it to be, despite all their efforts to increase the flexibility of the SIOP itself. Recent work by historical researchers reveals that at some point, apparently in either 1963 or early 1964, an operational directive was attached to the SIOP that called for full-scale nuclear retaliation against the total Sino–Soviet bloc in response to a small-scale or even accidental nuclear attack. The same level of full American "spasm" nuclear response was to be made even to an attack involving purely conventional weapons.

Beyond that, any type of attack that resulted in the death of the president or that isolated him from the chain of command was also to trigger a full nuclear response. Such operational directions were completely counter to the guidance given for SIOP preparation during the years 1962–1964 and directly conflicted with the guidance for SIOP preparation given by President Kennedy, Secretary of Defense McNamara and the Joint Chiefs.

The Eisenhower-era SIOP documents make it clear that from the first iteration of the SIOP process, the president had authorized the SIOP and provided guidance in its execution. Under President Eisenhower, when the SIOP was completed, it was distributed and then supplemented with concrete directions for actually using nuclear weapons. We have a released version of the Eisenhower operations for the first SIOP, SIOP-62, which is titled "Instructions for the Expenditure of Nuclear Weapons in Accordance with the Presidential Authorization Dated May 27, 1957."[35] Several examples of qualifying attacks were provided as additional guidance with regard to the use of atomic weapons, and that document was used to brief the designated senior unified and specified commanders. We also know, from later documents, that the codename for the operational instructions document was "Furtherance."[36]

The pre-delegation directive of 1957 withheld atomic weaponry from use in minor attacks against American forces and even against the nation itself. It specified that retaliation be conducted only against the attacking nation. Yet it did recognize that in any major attack, the president might very quickly be removed from the chain of command, either by death, injury or simply a loss in communications during an attack. What it did not do was stipulate any protocol other than authorizing the Department of Defense (DOD) to direct retaliation in the event of an attack on the United States in which the commander in chief was dead or out of touch. In that event, given that the primary strategic forces of the period were within the Strategic Air Command, there would have been little recourse other than for DOD to issue the retaliation order to SAC. Given what we now know of SAC's targeting list, even prior to the first SIOP, with only the direction in Eisenhower's directive of 1957, it would be difficult to imagine a retaliatory strike involving anything less than a full SAC strike against the Sino–Soviet bloc.

Copies of both the historical summary of the Eisenhower-era SIOP-62 and its related "Furtherance" have been released. Those directions did not call for a full retaliatory attack against the Sino–Soviet bloc, and there is no reference to the new elements that eventually worked their way into the Furtherance instructions, which appear to have come into effect in 1963–1964. Those broader and more drastic instructions were discovered and ultimately were brought to President Johnson's attention in 1968 and immediately altered.

Historical summaries of both the SIOP-63 and SIOP-64, the Kennedy-era plans, have been released. SIOP-63 was the first plan directed by President Kennedy and Secretary of Defense Robert McNamara; it represents the President Kennedy focus on control in any use of nuclear weapons.[37] The "Background" to that document makes special mention of President Kennedy's desire for "control, flexibility and choices." It specifically expresses Kennedy's and Secretary McNamara's concerns about a "too rigidly geared massive retaliation to a surprise attack" and calls for "latitude" in a "controlled response." The presidential guidance for the SIOP demanded "options" and the ability to "withhold" portions of the SIOP to optimize flexibility. In response, SIOP-63 contained a considerable number of options, excluding one or more countries from initial attack, reduction of follow-on forces, recall of manned systems after launch, selective launch of the positive control SAC force, and the establishment of alternative targets for missiles.

During development of the actual plan, General Power of SAC opposed major objections from Commander in Chief Atlantic and Commander in Chief Pacific, maintaining that the guidance for SIOP-63 did not need to change and could be the same as SIOP-62. Ultimately, over Power's objections, the Joint Chiefs did issue a new guidance for SIOP-63 in October 1962. That guidance called for the option of withholding attacks against China as well as individual "communist satellite" countries, a significant change from SIOP-62. In addition a series of five additional options for "withholds" were included. In June 1963 the Joint Chiefs received two days of briefings; they, along with Secretary of Defense McNamara, accepted the new levels of flexibility and approved SIOP-63 as operational on August 1, 1963.

A historical discussion of SIOP-64 is also available, and it notes an emphasis on "flexibility" and "controlled response" as representing the Kennedy administration guidance and notes that SIOP-64 was also to be significantly different from SIOP-62.[38] Guidance for SIOP-64 was noted as being largely the same as for SIOP-63, with one difference being that the SIOP was no longer specified as an annual document.

The missing piece of the SIOP story is the lack of released Furtherance instructions for any of the post-Eisenhower plans. The only information we have on Furtherance during that period comes from the 1968 incident in which Secretary of Defense Clark Clifford identified what were considered to be the "dangerous" instructions in the then current Furtherance and recommended an immediate issuance of new instructions. Released documents make it clear that when the issue was brought to Johnson, his key cabinet members and the Joint Chiefs all readily agreed that the "existing operations guidelines was dangerous and needed to be changed immediately."[39] With Johnson's concurrence an agreement was reached to alter the Furtherance instructions; an immediate communication was issued to all unified and specified commanders that "alternative" operational plans for executing the SIOP and General War plan were being developed and would be communicated as soon as they were available.[40]

It remains impossible to equate the flexibility added to the Kennedy Administration SIOP-63 with the Furtherance instructions brought to the attention of President Johnson in 1968. At some point the flexibility of the Kennedy SIOP seems to have been dramatically compromised by the actual wording of the Furtherance instructions, which governed the execution of the SIOP. Those instructions would normally have been approved by both Secretary of Defense McNamara and the Joint Chiefs. Yet in 1968 Secretary of Defense Clark Clifford and the Chiefs appeared to be very surprised by the wording in the instructions and concurred they were potentially dangerous and required immediate alteration.

Even now it is unclear as to when and under whose authority the "spasm" Furtherance was initiated—yet it appears to have been in effect in 1963–1964. There is no indication of it being associated with the Eisenhower directives on pre-delegation, which were quite detailed. It also seems foreign to the Kennedy administration, which adopted the Eisenhower policy but began to push for additional flexibility in the SIOP—and was insistent about political control of any atomic weapons use. All we know for certain is that a very dangerous version of the Furtherance was put into place at some point within the Kennedy/Johnson era. That set of instructions appears to have called for an immediate escalation to nuclear combat, even in response to an accidental or conventional attack on the United States—or the death or unavailability of the president. Those instructions were immediately canceled upon being brought to the attention of President Johnson. That cancellation provided senior commanders with the appropriate flexibility to respond to accidental or conventional attacks with a non-nuclear response and removed the directions for a total spasm response to even conventional attacks on American forces. It also removed the direction automatically calling for full-scale nuclear retaliation following the death of the president.[41]

Chapter 12

....

MIND GAMES, MASKIROVKA AND ATOMIC WAR FIGHTING

I n the 21st century, the insights gained from a distance in time, from oral histories and document releases—especially from Russia following the collapse of the Soviet Union—provide a considerable advantage in evaluating the true possibilities of surprise attack in the earliest decades of the Cold War. We have also gained some ability to evaluate the possibility of preemption and the success of deterrence during those years. Beyond that, we are much better able to evaluate how the fears and posturing of both sides drove each to mirror the assumed actions of the other.

It seems fair to say that America's "first fear," that Premier Joseph Stalin would use the huge, experienced Red Army for Soviet territorial advantage, was quite justified. In several instances Soviet military might was used to install compliant Communist regimes in power in Eastern Europe; any and all revolts against such regimes were quickly and brutally suppressed. Russia, motivated by centuries of foreign incursions, was fixated on building itself a forward buffer zone. The only question is how far that buffer would have extended if Stalin had lived beyond 1953. While his intentions clearly cannot be known, his order for the creation of a huge medium-range bombing force, given only shortly before his death, suggests that further advances remained a possibility. That view is supported by the fact that Soviet War plans are now known to have existed for the occupation of much of Western Europe; those same war plans were updated and retained well after the Soviets gained nuclear weapons—and the plans showed no hesitancy to use them in a drive west.

America's nuclear weapons and the creation of SAC have to be viewed as an early deterrent to any such ground attack by Stalin. We now know that Stalin did comment to close associates about the Soviet exposure to a nuclear attack by SAC. It gave him pause and led him to seek both strategic diversions and very possibly to conduct a series of psychological warfare activities to divert the temptation for an American surprise attack. Nuclear warfare as a counter to the Soviet threat, the idea of American disarmament ultimatums to the Soviets and proposals for actual preemptive atomic strikes were indeed discussed within certain segments of the American military as well as among the nation's politicians. There was temptation toward actions that would "eliminate the Communist threat" once and for all—and there were factions pushing for just such a strike in the late 1940s and early 1950s.

While atomic deterrence very likely stopped any move by Stalin to use the Red Army for a conventional military push, we now know that in its earliest years the American nuclear strike capability was far less than Stalin most likely realized. But American presidents and generals played the strategic nuclear card consistently and well, from the earliest confrontations in Berlin onward. Stalin was not prepared to test the American global bombing capability, but he may well have covertly acted to undermine global perception of American superiority. The extent of Soviet psychological warfare—leveraging the threat of captured and enhanced German technology—to suggest Soviet secret weaponry as a counter to America's atomic bomb will never be known. Under Stalin's regime those sorts of secrets were well protected; those who knew Stalin's secrets were highly disposable, both before and immediately following his sudden death. But while we cannot know all of Stalin's secrets, released American and British documents prove without a doubt that American intelligence thought the Soviets had begun conducting psychological warfare in Western Europe immediately after the war, in 1946. The British military and British press were both diverted by what they presumed were advanced aircraft or missiles, operating over the North Sea and occasionally over England itself during 1946 and 1947. At the time American Central Intelligence secretly concluded the Soviets to be behind the unidentified object reports. Initially Air Force intelligence expressed the same assessment. In later years, sightings of mysterious objects and lights over key American defense facilities cultivated fears that the Soviets had technology—and possibly "weapons carriers"—that America lacked. Ultimately no concrete proof emerged that the Soviets were behind the mystery objects, but from 1947 through 1952 that possibility was a true concern within military intelligence. It was also a fear much discussed in the media and by the American public.

There were other and much less publicly discussed reasons for concern. Even a small force of Soviet Tu-4–class long-range bombers, facing a virtually nonexistent American continental air defense, offered Stalin the option of destroying the key American atomic production facility at Hanford, Oregon, the huge West Coast aircraft plants—and with one-way missions—the option of surprise attack on the entire American atomic combat capability, resident in various New Mexico locations in 1947–1948. Such a Soviet strike was considered possible and is mentioned in Air Force threat analyses of the period. With no American atomic stockpile in existence, with the Hanford plants gone and with no immediate opportunity to produce new atomic weapons, the Red Army would have had more than enough time to secure all of Western Europe prior to any significant American atomic response.

Ultimately Stalin chose a much lower risk option for diverting America from acting on the temptation toward a preemptive attack on the Soviet Union. At the time the 1950 North Korean invasion of the South was a serious shock to American assumptions, which had focused on the immediate Communist threat of Stalin moving either west or south across his own borders. Unwilling to give up that view, the planners and policymakers interpreted the Korean invasion as simply a warning that Stalin was preparing to launch preemptive warfare on the West.

Yet with information now available, we now know that it was the North Korean regime itself that drove the invasion, both dragging and tempting its larger Communist brethren to support it. At first Stalin was against providing support; he waffled over a period of several months. We can deduce from his remarks that he was prepared to accept an American-backed regime on his Manchurian borders—after all, what did it really matter? Ultimately he came to view the conflict more as a true opportunity to get the Americans involved in a full-scale ground war in Asia, against not just North Korea but the Chinese military.

That sort of ground combat would have been extremely expensive in terms of men and material for America, costing the Soviets nothing and very possibly minimizing the growing strength of what appeared to be an emerging competitor for leadership in the global Communist cause. Largely alone among senior American military commanders, General Curtis LeMay offered the opinion that Korea was simply a diversion. Focused solely on the Soviets, LeMay was totally unwilling to divert resources from SAC training and in a race to develop a decisive nuclear striking force. LeMay even used the need for SAC training as a justification to bring back personnel who had been sent to deploy atomic weapons for potential use in Korea. For LeMay, Korea was a distraction from developing SAC's ability to devastate the Soviet Union; for Stalin, Korea was all about diverting America from totally focusing its military on Russia. As part of that ploy, Stalin was perfectly happy with surging the limited number of Soviet long-range bombers and submarines into Far Eastern bases at the height of the Korean conflict, focusing American attention on regional combat far from the Soviet heartlands.

Overall, it appears that the growth and credibility of American strategic nuclear air power did deter Stalin from using the Red Army in any major ground efforts during the immediate postwar years. Yet it also prompted an ongoing series of Soviet moves that only generated additional American fear, uncertainty and doubt. First the Soviets turned down all proposals for international atomic control; then they rejected the idea of Eisenhower's "open skies," which would have allowed each bloc to examine the other, ensuring no secret buildup of forces for a surprise strike. To America that meant the Soviets were hiding something; to the Soviets it was vital to avoid revealing their strategic weakness. From their viewpoint open skies simply would have provided SAC a perfect targeting reconnaissance opportunity, laying the groundwork for a precision American surprise attack.

The first official American intelligence warning of a high-risk date for a Soviet surprise nuclear strike was issued in 1950, projected for the period of 1952–1954. Studies mirroring the U.S. development of a strategic bombing force estimated that by then the Soviets would have amassed a strike force comparable to that of SAC—with some 1,200 long-range bombers and up to 200 atomic weapons. It was felt that a successful strike with only 50 nuclear bombs would seriously damage the United States. The 1954 NET assessment, for the years 1957–1958, projected a Soviet attack with up to 800 atomic weapons in the 60-kiloton range as well as a quantity of megaton hydrogen weapons (still classified in released documents).[1] The Net subcommittee report for 1950 also concluded that American continental air defense was so lacking that they were not adequate to "prevent, neutralize or seriously deter the military or covert attack which the USSR is capable of launching."[2]

In reality, the Soviets never developed such an intercontinental bombing capability, focusing instead on medium-range bombers and aircraft that could be used against American naval forces off their coasts. Of course the American public didn't know that; instead they were bombarded with a series of books and media articles that made an imminent Soviet nuclear attack both very real and very threatening. As early as September 1953 a special presidential advisory panel headed by retired Air Force General James Doolittle had proposed giving the Soviets a two-year ultimatum to accept terms of nuclear control—if they demurred the United States would conduct a preemptive atomic strike.

In a similar vein, following the 1953 presentation of the Joint Chiefs Net Evaluation Committee report, President Eisenhower asked the NSC's subcommittee if they had given thought to what the Soviets must be thinking about their own strategic exposure. The chairman advised him that the Soviets knew where they stood and that "any attack on the United States during this period would be an act of desperation and not an exercise of military judgment"—Eisenhower responded that the Soviets must be "scared as hell."[3]

With no strategic force comparable to SAC's, the Soviets returned again and again to one of their most consistent military tactics—deception or, in Russian, "maskirovka." In fact deception seems to have been the Soviets' primary deterrent up until they achieved nuclear strike parity with the United States at the end of the 1960s. In 1954 it was a deception creating the impression that they had, or certainly would have as quickly as they could build them, a large, long-range jet bomber force. The deception worked brilliantly; its net result was to convince American planners that the Soviets would indeed present a true threat—if allowed enough time to deploy their growing nuclear weapons capability with a jet bomber force.

The planners assumed that Soviets were about to mirror what the U.S. was doing with SAC and that if they ever reached a position where they could effectively carry out a surprise nuclear attack on America, they would. The Soviet success with their bomber ploy produced several American responses. The first were yet more proposals from military leaders that the only way to ensure the nation's security was to attack the Soviets preemptively, before they could gain—or convince themselves they held—enough of a strategic advantage to launch their own strike.[4]

In 1954 a Joint Chiefs advisory group proposed to the president that America should "deliberately precipitate war with the USSR in the near future . . . " allowing the nation to take advantage of its nuclear warfare superiority.[5] Eisenhower was appalled by the idea of deliberately provoking war; it struck him as contrary to the most basic American principles. Still, there continued to be dialog and discussion of American preemption, enough so that President Eisenhower was himself forced to draw the line, formally rejecting preemptive nuclear warfare as an option for America.[6]

Fear of a growing Soviet jet bomber force didn't move Eisenhower to preemption, but it did result in his endorsement of yet another surge in American spending; SAC was going to grow even larger. It also led Eisenhower to direct and support a series of major, high-risk American intelligence efforts to locate the forecast bomber squadrons. That effort began with the Genetrix operation high-altitude balloon photographic overflights, increased with Navy and Air Force ferret flights and extended to the massive SAC Homerun project of extensive Soviet overflight efforts.

None of those efforts located any sign of the anticipated Soviet bomber force—but Air Force intelligence worried that they were simply missing them. Debate over a Soviet bomber threat continued, with studies presented that by 1957 the Soviets would be able to destroy American nuclear retaliatory power in a surprise attack.[7] It took a series of high-risk U-2 high-altitude missions over the heart of the Soviet Union, but after some three years Eisenhower and the CIA (if not the Air Force) were convinced there was truly no bomber gap.

The American reconnaissance campaigns had secretly assured Eisenhower, but they had also dramatically illustrated to the Soviets how vulnerable they really were. General LeMay later described how well SAC had made its point by flying a formation of reconnaissance bombers over the major Soviet city of Vladivostok at high noon. Soviet MiGs were seen but didn't even make an effort to engage the American aircraft. LeMay knew and the Soviets knew that "we could just as well have launched bombing attacks . . . just as well . . . at that point in time."[8]

In reality it was the USSR rather than America that was terribly exposed to nuclear attack during the 1950s. Certain American military and political factions were continuously tempted toward preemption regardless of Eisenhower's opposition, and Premier Nikita Khrushchev clearly felt the threat. In 1957 it led him to approve and organize yet another major campaign of Maskirovka, creating the impression of a Soviet ICBM force already in rapid deployment. The campaign involved launches of intercontinental missiles across Russia into the Pacific, continual and ever larger Soviet atomic weapons tests and ultimately the launch of the world's first man-made satellite. It was all amazingly successful, and it did indeed shake America, producing the fear of a missile gap. And in a familiar pattern, the end result was to spur America into a frenzy of multiple missile developments and a rapid deployment of both land and submarine ballistic missile deployments—as well as a move to place battlefield ballistic missiles within only minutes' flying time from most of western Russia.

Each time the Soviets succeeded with "psychological deterrence," they triggered another round of U.S. military spending and accelerated growth in America's strategic nuclear striking power, which in turn actually worsened the Soviets' true strategic position. In 1961, following

a Net subcommittee briefing, President Kennedy—like Eisenhower before him—was struck by the degree of American superiority, asking if
studies had been made of the results of an American preemptive strike.
We can only speculate that Kennedy's thoughts were similar to Eisenhower's, assuming that the Soviets must have known how exposed they
were. Given Kennedy's overall goal to move toward lower-intensity
confrontations with the Soviets, to add levels of control over the use
of nuclear weapons and to move for a ban on atomic testing, it seems
reasonable to speculate that he was thinking of how the American superiority could be leveraged diplomatically.

Of course Premier Khrushchev was very much aware of the degree
of Soviet exposure. But by the spring of 1962 he wasn't thinking of
"negotiating from weakness," but rather how to immediately address
the American strategic supremacy and deter any moves by American
war hawks to actually employ their advantage militarily. Khrushchev
viewed Kennedy as inexperienced and not in full control of a very complex American political environment. Fear of Kennedy being pressured
into military action, combined with American deployment of ballistic
missiles in Turkey—capable of a decapitation strike on the Soviet leadership—drove him into a terribly risky move. Khrushchev's Cuban missile gambit was carried out with extreme secrecy. If undetected and
successful it would not have given the Soviet Union an overall strategic
advantage, but it would have definitely changed the tactical balance,
positioning some sixty hydrogen warheads within only minutes' flight
across America's relatively undefended southern border. In 1962 a decade of Maskirovka ended with a totally different type of deception;
this time a real Soviet military deception involving real weapons worked
only too well. Indeed, it worked so well it almost triggered exactly what
the Soviets most wished to avoid: American preemption.

And all the while, as American nuclear superiority fueled Soviet
paranoia and as Soviet deceptions fueled American fears, American nuclear stockpiling and deployment had assumed a life all its own, seemingly driven only by fear and "targeting," totally disconnected from the
reality of its potential use. In 1945, Pentagon planners had identified a
list of ten key industrial targets in the Soviet Union that, if destroyed by

bombing, would enable the United States to win in any military conflict with the Soviets. By the late 1940s, the delivery by SAC of some forty to fifty atomic weapons against Soviet manufacturing, transportation and logistics hubs was considered sufficient to interdict any major advance attempted by the Red Army.[9] In 1954 studies indicated that successful delivery of fifty Soviet atomic weapons against major American cities and military targets would very likely destroy America's ability to fight and pose a dire threat to continued governance of the nation.

With those estimates in mind, the actual rate of growth in American atomic weaponry is not only shocking but obviously raises a number of questions as to both need and use. By 1955 the American nuclear stockpile contained more than three thousand nuclear weapons, while the Soviets held two hundred. The Eisenhower administration funded a huge investment in atomic-weapons development facilities, and those facilities proved highly efficient—by 1957 the American stockpile had doubled to more than six thousand weapons, exceeding by more than ten times the six hundred–plus Soviet atomic bombs. In 1959 the American strategic stockpile had grown past fifteen thousand, some fifteen times the thousand Soviet weapon inventory. By the time of the Cuban missile crisis in 1962, the American stockpile had exceeded twenty-seven thousand as compared to some three thousand–plus held by the Soviet Union.[10] Perhaps the most obvious question is that of "overkill"; if fifty to one hundred hydrogen bombs, delivered on major cities, industrial complexes and national infrastructure, could essentially "kill" a nation, not to mention eliminate its potential to conduct a war, what was the need for almost thirty thousand atomic bombs and warheads?

A large part of the answer lies in the fact that the Eisenhower administration, in an effort to cap manpower requirements and hold down the expense of building a conventional force to match the Red Army, had determined to integrate atomic weaponry as a less expensive "force multiplier." To that extent much smaller atomic warheads had been integrated into the United States Army, which prepared itself to conduct warfare on an "atomic battlefield." In 1957 the Army began organizing and deploying specialized units prepared to conduct tactical atomic combat in Europe. The formations were designated "Pentomic

Divisions."[11] For full-scale tactical atomic combat, designed to stop the long-anticipated Red Army advance west, the Army needed artillery with atomic shells, field pieces with atomic shells, atomic mines and even weapons such as the Davy Crockett, which fired what were essentially atomic hand grenades over modest distances. They also required air support from Air Force and Navy fighter bombers with appropriately sized nuclear bombs. For its own operations the Navy required atomic depth charges, atomic anti-submarine weapons and atomic torpedoes, and its own aircraft needed atomic bombs to support actions by the Marines and atomic air defense missiles and air-to-air missiles with nuclear warheads to protect its fleets.

The demand for tactical atomic weaponry in the late 1950s and 1960s was extensive; development was ongoing, and production was added to satisfy the demands from each service. Beyond that, the surge to build a viable continental air defense meant a huge growth in nuclear warheads for both air-to-air and ground-launched nuclear missiles. Of course the size of such tactical and defense-oriented weapons was much smaller than the strategic megaton-class devices carried by SAC bombers and missiles. The actual peak in nuclear explosive power—"megatonage"—was reached circa 1960, with something on the order of 19,000 million tons of atomic explosive in the American inventory. It would continually decrease from that height to only 5,000 megatons in 1980.[12]

Subtracting the tactical and defensive weapons from the total count allows a more realistic assessment of the strategic nuclear weapons—some of which contained up to twenty megatons of explosive power in a single bomb. The first formalized Single Integrated Operations Plan, which went into effect in 1961, called for delivering 3,500 thermonuclear atomic devices onto the Soviet Union and China. The war plan for 1974 would have delivered 8,000 onto not only the Soviet Union and Eastern Bloc nations but onto China as well. We noted previously that as early as 1956, President Eisenhower had questioned the escalation of targeting in the war plan; however, he made no move to restrict its growth.

Debate surrounding the issue of "overkill" would grow, especially in the 1970s, but nothing seemed to hold back the growth of the inventory or the war plans. Instead of questioning the size of the stockpile, much of the recurring debate was simply an issue of how strategic nuclear engagement might be managed. The core issue was whether the initial strike would be a full-blown assault on each targeted nation, producing maximum casualties, or an attempt to destroy the enemy's war fighting forces—in particular its missile sites. That debate would be recurring, intense, cogently phrased and with many erudite papers and studies supporting each position. Yet fundamentally it was always a question of either immediate "nation killing" or some limited strike to minimize further attacks on America while somehow controlling the escalation of atomic engagement. We will return to that subject in a following chapter, examining the idea that there could actually be "controlled" atomic warfare, with dialog and negotiation occurring in the midst of ongoing atomic exchanges.

In going back to the most basic numbers, of some 3,500 megaton-class warheads to be delivered in the war plan/SIOP of 1961, the basic question remains: Why do you need 3,000-plus if you can kill an enemy nation with some 300? The answer reflects the fundamental, hard-core pragmatism of the strategic targeting decision process.

To begin with, the war plan specifically called for delivering 3,423 atomic weapons using 2,258 weapon carriers. The carriers included not only every SAC long-range bomber but also eight types of Air Force medium bombers and Victor Alert fighter bombers. Beyond that it utilized seven types of Navy missiles and aircraft. The American strike force focused on 2,200 primary targets, 199 of which were cities and industrial centers while another 85 were centers of government or known communications-and-control centers.[13] Hydrogen bombs on some 250 largely civilian targets would destroy 90% of the Soviet Union's industrial base; its civilian population was considered collateral damage. That was the nation-killing part of the plan.

Along with those strikes, the American forces were presumed to fight their way to those targets by blasting out the Soviet air defense. Some 835 operational air defense installations and 76 major air bases would be attacked to clear the way for the nation-killing strikes. Separate counterforce strikes were targeted on known missile complexes and atomic-weapons storage facilities. Given the realities of combat, military planning had to consider the loss of a quantity of the attacking platforms. Some would be lost in fratricidal explosions even with the best possible joint planning, which meant multiple attacks on numerous primary targets, to ensure that at least the minimum number of weapons was delivered. And that destruction was evaluated strictly in terms of the blast destruction of the atomic weapon being used. Collateral damage from fires, secondary explosions and radioactivity was not part of the destruction calculus. Of course that meant the calculus also did not include the secondary effects of airborne radiation on America itself—or for that matter all the overhead atomic air bursts from the American defensive missile force.

Obviously SAC planning and the SIOP itself were developed as a brute force tool, with built-in assumptions that attacking the Soviet Union would require a huge amount of destruction simply to get past the Soviet air defense. The Soviets had put an immense effort into that defense, built from the beginning specifically to stop SAC—which was viewed not just as an American retaliatory force but as a true first-strike threat, capable of being launched not only to kill Russia but to destroy Communism itself in the process.

Based on records releases and contemporary research, we now know that the Soviet air defense capability was indeed truly awesome—far greater than that suggested by the SIOP targeting list. By 1964 American intelligence had identified 1,892 Soviet radar sites and a staggering total of 5,985 operational radars. The Soviet long-distance detection network—functionally equivalent to the American DEW Line and designated "Tall King"—contained 187 stations with a secondary line consisting of 387 deployed radars. And that was simply the detection side of their air defense. The destruction side employed an extended array of jamming sites designed to blind SAC's bombers, at least 10,000 jet interceptors and more than 1,000 ground-to-air missile sites.

It became clear by the early 1960s that the classic high-altitude SAC attack tactics were no longer viable. SAC adapted by instituting an entirely new regime of low-level, under-the-radar penetration, with pop-up weapons launch and the use of aircraft-launched standoff missiles. The Soviets were preparing for those tactics as well. By 1964 they had begun deployment of a new generation of SA-3 anti-aircraft missiles at some ninety-one sites. The SA-3s were specifically designed to shoot down low-level SAC aircraft, even those flying a few hundred feet above the ground.[14] From a purely pragmatic view, it was going to take a very large number of atomic strikes to simply clear the way for any effective attack on the Soviets.

In retrospect, the period of 1962–1965 appears to be the apex of American strategic nuclear superiority over the Soviets. It represented the peak of the SAC bomber force, combined with a major lead in deploying ICBMs in hardened silos and in Navy nuclear submarines. SAC's Chrome Dome airborne alert was at maximum, and so was the fighter bomber Victor Alert in Europe and Asia. It also represented the ultimate in deployment of a continental American air defense, with SAGE fully operational and rings of ground-to-air nuclear warhead missiles emplaced around most major metropolitan areas and key industrial/defense sites. Yet at its virtual peak in strategic nuclear power, America became focused on ground combat in Southeast Asia, and by the time it had extracted itself from that, the Soviets had fulfilled Khrushchev's initial missile and rocket strategy. The American strategic lead had evaporated. As the 1970s began, the era of nuclear strike parity had arrived.

The concept of "mutual assured destruction" had been introduced by Defense Secretary Robert McNamara in the early 1960s. Even at the height of the Cuban Missile Crisis, with ballistic missiles in place in Cuba, the Soviets were still fully exposed to total destruction in an American retaliatory strike. Conceivably America held the ability to survive as a nation while preempting with a surprise attack—but had formally chosen to avoid that strategic option. The Soviets would have simply been committing suicide in pursuing that course themselves.

As the decade of the 1960s ended, there was no doubt at all that a preemptive attack or escalation to full-scale nuclear combat would simply annihilate both countries—and beyond that, virtually all the Western and Eastern Bloc powers. Certainly that was the plan embodied in full execution of the American SIOP. Perhaps most surprisingly, even with nuclear strike parity in terms of intercontinental missiles and warheads, the stockpiles of nuclear weapons—primarily the Soviet stockpile—either continued to grow or remained near their maximum.

By 1975, the United States held 27,000 weapons, and the Soviets had advanced to almost 20,000. In 1983 the United States had actually reduced their total inventory to 23,000, while the Soviets had built a stockpile of some 35,000 weapons—a total exchange would have detonated well over 30,000 atomic weapons across the planet.

The number seems almost surreal; Presidents Truman and Eisenhower would have failed to comprehend or understand it. In truth even the leadership, at least on the American side, may not have fully appreciated the total risk or even the true size of the American inventory. Remarks from those actually involved in developing the SIOP suggest that few defense secretaries and even fewer presidents made any personal inquiry into the nature or content of the SIOP and its related targeting.[15] The only president known to have actually made any special effort to learn any of the details of the SIOP or its targeting process was Gerald Ford.

The stockpiles and SIOP remained largely driven by the cold logic of the targeting process; the numbers on the target list continued to grow, and the growing difficulty in "killing" them demanded more and more warheads. The Soviets had matched the Americans with fully hardened silos for their missile force and with submarine-launched missiles. Beyond that they were implementing a network of hardened command centers, alternative command centers and alternative command-and-control communications networks that mirrored the American system but far exceeded it in both breadth and scope.

The American atomic strike plan dealt not only with a huge air and missile defense network including radars, guns, defense missiles and fighters; it targeted a growing range of both hardened and mobile missile launchers, the Soviet industrial complex—including virtually every city of any size—and an extensive set of command-and-control targets. In the beginning the strategic goal had simply been to destroy enough key infrastructure to interdict the Red Army and bring any conventional combat to an end. Some three decades later the reality of the force in place in both blocs had evolved to something far different.

As the nuclear stockpiles had grown, a good deal of work and study was devoted to the option of a "counterforce" targeting strategy.

"Counterforce" had initially been proposed by Secretary of Defense Robert McNamara. It was to offer sufficient attack options to focus one particular series of nuclear strikes on purely military targets, in particular offensive missile and bomber assets. Its goal was to reduce American damage and casualties while allowing options for "withholding" initial strikes on major population centers and civilian casualties on the Communist nations. Moves toward a counterforce strategy certainly sounded more measured—a shift away from a focus on mass civilian deaths; however, a pure counterforce strategy against hardened sites demanded a huge number of delivery systems and a significant number of atomic warheads. It required a saturation effort against each target, improved accuracy and even special "burrowing" warheads. If anything, "counterforce" tended to increase both the cost and the operational challenge of the American nuclear strategy; it had actually fueled the need for more strategic nuclear weapons.

Following Richard Nixon's election as president, he and his national security advisor, Henry Kissinger, received an initial SIOP briefing. Kissinger personally investigated and extensively critiqued the SIOP. He took exception to the limited flexibility of the plan, proclaiming even its most basic options to be far too broad. In a review with President Nixon, Kissinger described it as a "horrific strategy," proposing that Nixon endorse a study aimed at revising it. While Nixon complained about the military bureaucracy, he refused to endorse the study.[16] The dialog and debate continued throughout his presidency, without any immediate alterations in the SIOP. A full study of Nixon/Kissinger-era nuclear strategy debates, along with released reference documents, may be found in William Burr's essay "To Have the Only Option That of Killing 80 Million People Is the Height of Immorality: The Nixon Administration, the SIOP, and the Search for Limited Nuclear Options, 1969–1974."[17]

Ultimately, Kissinger's attitude toward limitations in the then-current SIOP seems to have prevailed, and by early 1974, President Nixon signed a national security decision memorandum directing the preparation of a wide range of limited nuclear employment options that could be used to demonstrate the seriousness of the situation to an adversary as well as show a desire to exercise restraint. Overall, Nixon's guidance appears to have been one of caution, moving away from a limited set of broad options with select withdrawals and designing a new series of options more consistent with diplomatic realities of the time. Certainly the Nixon/Kissinger outreach to China would have weighed in on such thoughts; indeed, Kissinger's standard response of coupling both overt and covert military action to diplomacy was no doubt influential. It seems probable that the guidance and movement of the Nixon administration in regard to the SIOP reflected Kissinger's own approach to world affairs in general—more than any specific philosophy of President Nixon.

Ford's successor, President Jimmy Carter, also pursued a guidance of greater flexibly, but one with something of a twist added. One of his primary concerns was the development of a plan—and command protocol—with sufficient flexibility to ensure that neither side was forced into a "spasm" during the escalation of conventional combat. With nuclear parity between the two longtime adversaries, the possibility of spasm retaliation had assumed a terrible new dimension. The concern over such a reaction was itself nothing new; both Eisenhower and Kennedy had been worried about the same issue. However, that was during a time when an American spasm response translated into significant "overkill" of the Eastern Bloc, with huge collateral damage in Europe and Asia. By the Carter era, a spasm response by either side would have assured virtually total annihilation of both nations and would have had serious collateral consequences for the entire planet, an issue generally missing from the strategy dialogs throughout the Cold War.

The Carter administration's initial SIOP guidance was largely one of continuity; the United States was to maintain both conventional and nuclear parity with the Soviet Union, ensuring deterrence and in the event of attack to inflict an "appropriate retaliatory response," a sufficient retaliatory capability in the event of a Soviet first strike. Deterrence was described as maintaining the ability to "inflict an unacceptable level of damage" on the Soviet Union in the event of a first strike. Embedded in that essentially familiar language were two points that held significant implications; the mention of "appropriate" retaliatory response was coupled with a statement requiring the maintenance of adequate command-and-control capability to "execute limited strategic employment options."[18]

It had been one thing for President Kennedy to give guidance for levels of escalation and controlled steps toward limited used of nuclear weapons during the Berlin Crisis of 1961. With America's huge strategic nuclear superiority, he held the ultimate leverage to negotiate, and he did so effectively. By the Carter era, no such American strategic advantage existed; if anything the Soviets themselves held a strategic edge. Yet Carter's guidance still expressed the concept that some sort of limited and controllable nuclear exchange was a possibility and that, beyond that, even in response to a Soviet atomic first strike there was the opportunity for control to manage an "appropriate" level of retaliation.

In addition, the Carter administration's studies placed considerable focus not only on flexibility in the SIOP but the development of limited nuclear warfare plans for use in regard to China and against Soviet conventional forces in Europe. The discussions involved the ability to monitor and attack Soviet mobile forces during any nuclear exchange; there seems to have been an assumption that American intelligence was capable of delivering reliable tactical information during at least some levels of nuclear exchange and that command and control was sufficiently robust to allow effective nuclear war fighting.[19] Certainly such assumptions had been realistic in the earlier days of SAC; early nuclear war planning had envisioned ongoing attacks over some weeks. Surprisingly, with the delivery vehicles and nuclear stockpiles available to both sides by the late 1970s, the assumption of controlled nuclear exchange remained in effect. Nuclear weapons were still discussed not simply in terms of deterrence against a surprise nuclear attack but also in terms of their use in conjunction with conventional military action and as leverage in the diplomatic arena.

Available documents suggest that Carter's national security advisor, Zbigniew Brzezinski, was a prime mover in Carter administration thinking with regard to controllable nuclear combat. In one memorandum he discussed the capability of satellite intelligence to allow nuclear weapons to support general-purpose military operations in the same manner that bombers had supported the Normandy invasion of World War II. In his vision of nuclear flexibility, Brzezinski focused on the responsibility of the National Command Authority in atomic war fighting during any atomic exchange, pointing out that the SIOP did not and never could contain that requisite flexibility. He felt that such matters were also beyond the Joint Chiefs staff and called for the defense secretary to begin generating actual exercises involving the National Command Authority. In one memorandum he noted a recent exercise— Gauntlet—in which Defense Secretary Harold Brown had participated. In the course of the exercise Brown had begun "chasing general purpose forces in East Europe and Korea with strategic [atomic] weapons."[20] In the war gaming Brown had acted with no coordination with conventional force commanders in those theaters.

Brzezinski appears to have endorsed such thinking, promoting his views that it was only realistic to integrate strategic and conventional weapons in major combat. With the sort of intelligence and command-and-control capabilities then available, he felt that well-controlled use of strategic nuclear weapons could avoid prolonged exchanges or stalemates. He used the word "radical" to describe his viewpoint, and that would certainly seem accurate. Brzezinski's aggressive position on flexible targeting and the integration of conventional and strategic war fighting eventually resulted in concerns that the Carter administration had come to believe that nuclear combat could be finitely controlled.[21]

Such strategy dialogs fed on themselves to the extent that the issues became public, producing media commentary about a possible change in American nuclear strategy. The Carter administration denied such charges, but as President Ronald Reagan succeeded Carter, there was a growing Soviet concern that the United States had concluded that it could control matters during an atomic exchange—being able to engage in "flexible" atomic warfare while still maintaining communications with the Soviets and conducting negotiations to minimize the destruction. President Reagan's early remarks about the Soviet "evil empire," his administration's huge surge in military spending and even certain of his personal statements about being able to "win a nuclear war" frightened elements of the American public and, as we now know, seriously

scared the Soviet leaders. In fact, the early years of the Reagan administration's policies made the Soviets so concerned that at more than one
point, they were virtually stampeded into their own preemptive strike
in self-defense.

During the period of 1980–1983 a number of individual elements
fueled Soviet fears that the United States was once again positioning itself for preemption—or "winning" a nuclear war—even in the face of
the huge Soviet missile force and what appeared to be assured mutual
destruction in any exchange. One of the key elements involved a new generation of American weapons. Those weapons resurfaced the much earlier fear of American decapitation attacks, the same fear that had driven
Premier Khrushchev into his extremely high-risk Cuban missile strategy.

As early as the mid-1960s, the United States had deployed Pershing
I battlefield missiles (the successor to the Redstone) in Europe. Those
missiles had a range of approximately 450 miles and supported warheads
of sixty to two hundred kilotons. Over time they were deployed in
sufficient numbers to largely replace the Victor Alert fighter-bomber
quick reaction force in Western Europe. However, in the late 1970s, to
counter long-range Soviet battlefield missiles, the Army began a move
toward replacement of the Pershing I missiles with Pershing II missiles.
The Pershing II's range was extended to 1,100 miles, once again
bringing much of western Russia under exposure of ballistic missile
attack with virtually no warning. The Pershing II had a smaller warhead
(five to sixty kilotons), but there were plans to make those warheads
earth-penetrating. Beyond that the Gryphon ground-launched cruise
missile, much slower but with a longer range of up to 1,600 miles and
a two-hundred-kiloton warhead, was being developed for deployment
in Europe.

News of such weapons, especially the Pershing II, with earth-
penetrating warheads, suggested to the Soviets that America was once
again positioning itself for an effective decapitation strike. That suspicion
was further exacerbated by early news leaks of American "stealth"
aircraft technology. During the 1980 presidential race, Ronald Reagan
accused President Jimmy Carter of being weak on defense, citing his
refusal to support the B-1 bomber as a successor to the aging B-52. In

response, Carter disclosed that the Department of Defense was working on a new generation of radar-evading "stealth" aircraft. Much media speculation was devoted to stealth aircraft, and eventually the small F-117 bomber was disclosed. A wave of F-117 aircraft, operating out of German bases, could have served as an "invisible" surgical tool to conduct surprise atomic attacks on the Soviet command-and-control system as well as Soviet leadership. While the United States viewed "stealthy" aircraft as essential to penetrate the massive and still growing Soviet air defense, once again the Soviets viewed them as potential enablers for a preemptive American attack.

With information available only following the collapse of the Soviet Union, we now understand the extent to which the Soviets were extremely concerned during the early Reagan administration years. By 1983 they were in the midst of a war scare comparable to that of the American response to the discovery of Soviet missiles in Cuba in 1962. The level of Soviet fear was not at all appreciated by American intelligence or leadership, itself deeply involved in demonstrating an assertive international military and diplomatic posture in regards to the Soviet Union. From the American perspective, the deeply felt Soviet fears were unrealistic, possibly expressed for internal political purposes or for international diplomatic posturing. After all, the American leadership knew it had no intentions of attacking the Soviets.

Yet President Reagan's rhetoric in regard to the Soviets being "the focus of evil in the world" clearly seemed both real and sincere to Soviet premier Yuri Andropov—who began to refer to Reagan as irrational, accusing him of "fanning the flames of war." Reagan's March 1983 announcement of the Strategic Defense Initiative, intended to protect America from even a major missile attack, was perceived by the Soviets as establishing the groundwork to allow a preemptive nuclear strike by the United States. In their view, Reagan appeared to be throwing away the mutual assured destruction concept, which had been the basis of nuclear deterrence for decades. Given such a dramatic move, the Soviets had reason to fear that the whole foundation of mutual deterrence was beginning to crumble.

Soviet intelligence (KGB) estimates for the Politburo maintained that risks of an American attack were the greatest since the beginning of the

Cold War, and during 1981–1982 the Soviet Union initiated an elaborate human intelligence operation, codenamed RYaN. Its goal was to identify any activities suggesting the preparations for a Western Bloc preemptive missile attack. The Soviets knew it would be too late if their leadership was hit by a stealth decapitation strike, followed by a missile barrage. RYaN was a classic indications intelligence operation, dedicated to assessing a real Western Bloc threat in time to preempt it. It appears that Western intelligence did become aware of the "Warsaw Pact Early Warning Indictor Project," but only well after the fact, perhaps as late as 1985; the few released documents on the subject remain almost entirely redacted.

Even at this late date it is uncertain to what extent the seemingly provocative attitude of the early Reagan years was simply a reflection of Reagan's personal attitudes, a legacy of his political campaign or perhaps a much more complex psychological warfare effort, known to only a few very senior people around Reagan. A decade earlier Richard Nixon and Henry Kissinger had contrived the "madman" gambit, portraying Nixon as so frustrated by the Vietnam War that he might be willing to do virtually anything—including going nuclear—to preserve an American victory.[22] The assumption was that if Nixon appeared to be truly unstable, the North Vietnamese would be encouraged to negotiate a settlement. There remains speculation that President Reagan, or his advisors, might have once again turned to a version of the Nixon "madman" gambit.

The most confusing point is that a good deal of private material, from Reagan himself, appears to suggest a sincere and consistent personal agenda of disarmament. By 1983 Secretary of State George Schultz told his aides that Reagan was frustrated on that issue: "The President has noticed that no one pays any attention to him [on disarmament] in spite of the fact that he speaks of this idea publically and privately."[23] Was it possible that Reagan, whose long-term goal and eventual success were a dramatic reduction in nuclear weapons, was simply posturing, in an attempt to "scare" the Soviets into moving toward mutual disarmament?

A CIA historical study by Ben Fischer presents perhaps the most detailed analysis of the 1983 Soviet war scare and includes speculation and some indication of just such a top-secret American psychological warfare operation—one known only to a "small circle of White House and Pentagon aides."[24] Either there was indeed such an operation in action, or the Soviets did have ample reason to fear that the Reagan administration was preparing for a nuclear attack or attempting to provoke one. For example, we know from SAC commanders that during this period, there was a common practice of intermittently sending bomber formations over the North Pole and fighter bombers toward Soviet borders in both the west and east. During peak efforts such probes occurred several times a week.[25] Given that the Chrome Dome and SAC aerial alerts had ceased years before, the Soviets were being given clear evidence of a renewed American aggressiveness. Other sources describe complete America squadrons flying right up to Soviet airspace and "peeling off" only at the last minute, all the time under Soviet air defense tracking.

In addition there were totally unprecedented American Navy activities including combat exercises in the vicinity of some of the most vital Soviet Far Eastern bases. Nothing like that had ever happened before, and for the first time the Soviets observed American carrier battle groups operating close to some of their most sensitive military and industrial areas.[26] In one incident a number of American aircraft operating off the carriers *Midway* and *Enterprise* flew simulated bombing runs over a fortified Soviet island in the Kuril chain, part of the Soviet's Far Eastern defenses; some sixty aircraft participated in the flyovers.

That incursion reportedly so infuriated the Soviet leadership that several Soviet commanders were dismissed and Soviet general secretary Yuri Andropov himself issued an unprecedented order that unknown aircraft over Soviet territory were to be consider hostile and were to be shot down.[27] One consequence of that order was the downing of a Korean commercial airliner that strayed off course over the Kamchatka Peninsula. In another incident, possibly unknown to President Reagan, the American carrier *Enterprise*—operating in the Indian Ocean—came within strike range of the Soviet aircraft carrier *Kiev*. The American commander apparently decided it would be a useful opportunity to carry out a long-range attack exercise. Several aircraft were launched and actually conducted a mock attack on the Soviet carrier.[28]

The Soviets expressed their growing fears and concerns through a personal meeting between Yuri Andropov and newly appointed American envoy Averell Harriman, in June 1983. In welcoming Harriman, Andropov specifically stated that the Soviets were concerned about the constant politics raised during American election campaigns. It appeared to them that American presidential campaigns always raised issues of the Soviet threat, calls for more armaments and resulted in each new administration coming into place during a context of heightened "mistrust and enmity." Based on the remarks made during the election and very possibly remarks by Reagan himself, Andropov bluntly stated that the Soviets simply had no "confidence" in the true intentions of the Reagan administration.[29] Apparently Reagan's speeches had convinced the Soviet leadership that he simply refused to accept the legitimacy of the Soviet system, that his attitude was blocking any progress on the nuclear weapons talks begun in 1980 and that he was simply "dedicated to bringing down the [Soviet] system."[30]

Given such fears, the Soviets became further sensitized by a series of American and NATO exercises conducted in the fall of 1983—exercises held under the overall umbrella of "Autumn Forge 83." The large-scale exercise simulated a conventional blocking action against Soviet movements into Scandinavia. One element of the exercise involved a totally radio-silent deployment of Army units from the U.S. to Europe, conducted by some 170 Air Force transport shuttle flights. The forces were designated to block the Soviet move, but in the context of the exercise, the conventional effort failed and escalation to nuclear battlefield combat developed.

Specifically, the Able/Archer portion of the exercise appears to have reinforced Soviet speculation that the West was actually practicing for a surprise attack. That exercise was originally intended to involve the most senior American military commanders up to National Command Authority and simulated a transition from conventional warfare to limited nuclear exchanges. Strategic Air Command bombers and tankers were utilized in the Able/Archer exercise. The roles of the SAC aircraft appear to have been strictly conventional, used in flexible attacks against highly mobile Soviet formations and targets. Yet the SAC after-action report on the exercise noted that on several occasions radio transmissions relating to B-52 "strikes" were made; there was concern was that Soviet monitoring of the exercise could have interpreted such transmissions relating to the use of the SAC bombers for strategic nuclear attacks. Later, information from senior Soviet officials related that at least two fighter bases in East Germany and Poland had been moved to full alert during the American exercise—for the first time in the Cold War. Other units of the Soviet Fourth Air Army had moved to increased redness levels.

By December 1983, President Reagan was receiving backchannel information from representatives inside the Soviet Union that both the average Soviet citizen and its elite leadership were in fear of imminent war. The reports went so far as to warn of absolute paranoia at the highest levels of leadership and concern that the Soviet leadership was on the verge of irrational decision-making, virtually "obsessed with the fear of war."[31] By continuing and expanding the new weapons programs begun during the Carter administration, by its own immense surge in military spending and by announcing the Strategic Defense Initiative, the Reagan administration had also seriously raised the cost of competition in the military arena of the Cold War.

By continuing and expanding military exercises that clearly seemed to include the option of merging conventional and nuclear combat—as strongly advocated by Zbigniew Brzezinski during the Carter administration—the United States seemed to be giving every indication that it was positioning itself not only to counter but to reduce the strategic nuclear parity that the Soviets had spent so heavily to acquire. And all the while, in the background, the Strategic Air Command and the Navy were directly "pushing" the Soviet military—on the Air Force's part at a level not seen since the 1950s and in the Navy's case at a totally new level. Anecdotal reports suggest that the top Soviet generals felt increasingly cornered, privately stating that the only option might be a preemptive attack "before the imperialists gain superiority in every sphere."[32]

Given the breadth and aggressiveness of the Reagan administration's initial approach to the Soviets, not to mention Reagan's own personal remarks equating "evil" and the Soviet Union, it is rather surprising to find a number of insider comments suggesting that President Reagan was actually surprised and perhaps shocked to find that the Soviets actually feared an attack by the United States. When he was first given the news, including supporting commentary from British intelligence, the president and his senior staff seem to have felt the reports simply to be a Soviet ploy. After further inquiry and additional corroboration, Reagan asked his National Security Advisor, Robert McFarlane, "Do you suppose they can really believe that . . . I don't see how they could believe that . . . but it's something to think about."[33] Reagan's personal remarks tend to support the view that he may not have been fully aware of the impact his administration had on the Soviets. His personal diary entry of November 18 contains an entry on Soviet paranoia, noting that without appearing "soft" it might be necessary to tell them the United States had no intention of actually attacking them. Years later, in his memoirs, he noted that he had been surprised to find out that "people at the top of the Soviet hierarchy were genuinely afraid of America and Americans. Perhaps this shouldn't have surprised me, but it did."[34]

We seem to be left with two choices with regard to Reagan-era nuclear strategy. One option would be that of a highly risky yet ultimately successful psychological warfare gambit, perhaps not fully appreciated even by the president—a gambit that ultimately did result in the first major moves to mutual disarmament. The second alternative would be a series of unthinking and extremely high-risk actions that convinced the Soviets that their huge missile expenditures, their ongoing investment in a gigantic air defense system and a parallel effort to create a survivable command-and-control system were all about to be compromised.

The only thing that is certain is the end result; by 1983 some of the most senior Soviet leadership felt themselves to be facing a fearful choice. They would be forced to essentially write off the immense effort and expenditure that had given them strategic missile parity, including defense and command-and-control buildups far beyond those of United States. That would effectively leave them at the diplomatic and military mercy of the Reagan administration, and of an American president they felt was unpredictable and possibly irrational. In short they faced returning to a state of strategic weakness they had spent more than three decades overcoming. Their options were limited; they could preempt before they were totally left behind or they could delay in hopes that Reagan would show some sign of flexibility—fortunately, he did.

On December 17, 1983, President Reagan informed Secretary of State Schultz that he wished to make a major public speech on getting rid of nuclear weapons. He drafted a letter to Chairman Andropov, explicitly stating, "We do not seek to challenge the security of the Soviet Union and its people."[35] And in a speech on January 16, 1984—broadcast to Europe—Reagan totally surprised virtually all his listeners by focusing not on politics but on dialog with the Soviet Union, on "constructive cooperation," on "peaceful competition" and specifically on the elimination of all nuclear weapons.[36]

In retrospect it appears that President Reagan had not truly understood the level of Soviet fear of the United States in 1983, even in a state of nuclear parity, just as Premier Khrushchev had not understood the American fear of a Soviet preemptive strike, even with its position of massive strategic superiority in 1962. Indeed, much of the story of the Cold War appears to be one of fear factors, of emotional reaction rather than response action based on verifiable indications and warnings intelligence.

Given the ongoing levels of fear and emotion, it is also strange that there was an ongoing lack of National Command Authority participation in the nation's defensive plans and exercises. From a distance, it appears entirely too similar to the lack of involvement by the War Department and even President Roosevelt, before the Japanese surprise attacks that began World War II. It is one thing to know a nuclear attack might be coming; the American military constantly prepared for such a contingency. We will find that the same cannot be said for its senior civilian commanders.

Chapter 13

....

REALITY CHECK

I n the early years of the Cold War, defending against a Soviet surprise attack was predicated on America's ability to detect Soviet war
preparations, including concentration of forces and increasing readiness levels sufficient to support a first strike. One of the more classic
examples of that approach was reflected in an anecdotal remark by
General LeMay to a visiting member of a presidential advisory committee. LeMay told the analyst that SAC reconnaissance was constantly flying missions over Russia, and "If I see them amassing their planes for an
attack I'm going to knock the shit out of them before they take off the
ground."[1] No doubt there was a certain amount of hyperbole in the remark; however, U.S. planning did accept that if sufficient strategic intelligence of an imminent attack was available, SAC would be dispatched
to interdict it. Ultimately both the United States and the Soviet Union
became geared to "launch on warning"; by the late 1960s SAC began
to refer to the launch-on-warning option as the "Midnight Express."[2]

During the Cuban Missile Crisis, American intelligence had detected no evidence that the Soviet Union had elevated its own military
readiness condition.[3] That was viewed as encouraging; senior American
commanders felt the Soviets had been too frightened to exacerbate the
situation once they had been caught in their Cuban deception. In reality, American intelligence had actually missed certain Soviet moves to
an advanced alert level. Soviet military sources have since reported that

both land-based strategic missile forces and aviation forces elevated their readiness. The Soviet missiles were not fueled or raised to firing position but were loaded with nuclear warheads, deployed from their normal storage depots. In addition, aviation forces were removed from their normal training and maintenance status and assumed a runway alert status. Both status changes were extremely hard to monitor at a distance, and officially U.S. intelligence had taken the position that the Soviet bombers had not been placed on alert.[4]

Over time American intelligence missed other Soviet alerts. In 1968, a number of intermediate-range ballistic missile sites across the Eastern Bloc were moved to increased alert condition, just short of maximum readiness, in advance of the Soviet move into Czechoslovakia. That alert also included mating nuclear warheads to the missiles. And in 1973, when the United States raised its own alert levels during the Arab–Israeli conflict, American intelligence failed to detect that the Soviets had also increased alert levels of some of its strategic rocket forces.[5]

In 1982, increasingly fearful of a Western preemptive strike, the Soviets conducted a major military exercise. The exercise involved the launch of a number of both offensive and defensive missiles. Analysis of those launches revealed that the Soviets had significantly exceeded their known capabilities. Equally important, preparations for the exercises had been detected or reported—the Soviet actions became visible only as the missiles began to launch.[6] It now appears that American military intelligence was somewhat overconfident in its ability to monitor Soviet force status and the Soviets had responded to more American actions than realized at the time. Because the Soviets did not routinely maintain the sort of alert force that the United States did, low-profile response was necessary and seems to have escaped American analysts on a number of occasions.

In *The Logic of Accidental Nuclear War,* Bruce Blair provides detailed comparisons of the American and Soviet command-and-control structures. Blair notes that Soviet strategic weapons control was much more centralized and tightly controlled by the very top echelon of political/military Soviet command. While the United States planned for retaliation following a surprise attack, with a considerable level of pre-delegation for the release of nuclear weapons, the Soviets had little faith in pre-planned options.[7] Soviet achievement of strategic parity during the 1970s drove both nations to new levels of concern over command and control. The American concern was the increased ability of the Soviets to deal a massive nuclear missile attack on both SAC aircraft and even its hardened missile sites. Survivability of not just the force but of the command-and-control system became the first of two heated issues. The second was the challenge of maintaining continuity of civilian control during actual nuclear war fighting.

The American system had evolved to include an airborne SAC command post that could constantly provide communications to all its airfields and missile sites. The airborne command post was to maintain those links during and after an attack, staying in communication with the alert bomber force (which would be flushed into the air within fifteen minutes of warning) and with surviving missile command posts. In 1960, the first SAC Airborne National Command Post had gone on ground alert and proven that it could be airborne and on station in twelve minutes.

The airborne command post, designated "Looking Glass," was assigned to stay at thirty-thousand-feet altitude and in visual range of SAC headquarters. Its battle staff, including a designated Emergency Action Officer, was authorized to take command of SAC if communications were lost. In the event that a mushroom cloud was observed over SAC headquarters, the officer was authorized to issue the "go code" to flush the bomber force and move SAC to DEFCON 1 war alert status. The SAC airborne command aircraft were equipped for constant contact with the National Emergency Airborne Command Post (NEACP) designated "Nightwatch." The Nightwatch aircraft was at the disposal of the National Command Authority in Washington, stationed on fifteen-minute ground alert at Andrews Air Force Base. In addition to a complete communications staff, Nightwatch carried a military battle staff, trained to assist the president or his successors in maintaining operational control over both the military services and government agencies.

A single SAC airborne command center was sufficient for control; however, for ultimate survivability there had to be alternate aircraft as well as sufficient radio-relay aircraft to maintain the total communications network. Ultimately the system grew to include some twenty command-post aircraft and thirty-six airborne radio-relay stations.[8] Radio repeaters were also positioned along the attack routes into the Soviet Union and China, including the routes that extended down the coast of South America and on to Africa as well as the routes from California over Guam and the polar routes. Such defined corridors were required, especially over the continental United States, since SAC bombers launched during an attack would be flying through airspace that would have suddenly become a combat zone.

In the chaos of a nuclear attack, American interceptors as well as ground-to-air atomic missiles might well have engaged outgoing SAC aircraft by mistake. SAC did work out a system of radar identification beacons, known as "identification, friend or foe transponders" (IFF) to allow Air Defense Command to verify American aircraft. Due to congestion in certain geographic areas, it was also deemed necessary to establish "safe corridors" around air defense systems.[9] Both IFF and safe corridors remain in use today, yet once the Soviets established a large deployed missile force, there was some speculation that they might well identify safe corridors and in any surprise attack simply blanket the SAC deployment avenues with a series of hydrogen warhead explosions. Such a corridor attack would have presented major problems not only in maintaining communications with the aircraft, but blast and radiation damage could have threatened both the planes and crews early in their missions.

Given that SAC headquarters and the SAC commander would likely be destroyed early in any surprise attack, three separate systems were deployed to ensure SAC command-and-control survivability. The airborne alert command centers were the first backup, a series of rockets with transmitters programmed to broadcast attack codes were second, and the third option involved a series of very low-frequency "earth wave" transmitters and long trailing antennas to be deployed for low-frequency reception on the command-and-communications aircraft.[10] The Emergency Rocket Communications System would use three ballistic missile boosters to loft transmitters from Whiteman Air Force Base in Missouri, into trajectories that allowed them to broadcast for some thirty-seven minutes. A prerecorded emergency action message would have been broadcast through the course of the five-thousand-mile transmitter flight. The transmitters were to be launched over the Thule polar routes, over the route going across the Mediterranean and over Guam on the Asian route.[11]

SAC went to extremes in ensuring redundancy and alternate routing in all its communications from land lines to radio and teletype circuits. It would have been very difficult for even a surprise attack to totally negate SAC's ability to issue "go codes" and flush its alert aircraft, even if its Offutt headquarters was totally destroyed.[12] Its ability to exercise control as that force deployed globally was much more questionable. It did maintain a line of ground stations running in an arc from the Aleutian Islands in Alaska to Greenland (Green Pine sites). That provided some hope of ongoing radio communications until the planes began to proceed over the pole—at least if the Soviets did not attack the sites themselves or launch nuclear missiles specifically targeted to suppress radio communications in the far north. Beyond the range of the Green Pine sites, the bombers would have had to rely on their ultra-long-range single-side band radios and if a real attack had occurred, and multiple high-altitude bursts saturated the upper atmosphere, radio communications would have had to be considered problematic.

A separate system—and one with far less redundancy—was provided for communications with American nuclear missile submarines; orders to attack had to be passed down through Navy command at the Pentagon and on to the naval theater commanders (Commander in Chief Atlantic/CINCLANT at Norfolk, Virginia, and Commander in Chief Pacific/CINCPAC in Honolulu, Hawaii). From there, the orders would be relayed to the individual submarine commanders. The Navy theater commanders did operate their own alert airborne aircraft as alternate command centers—CINCLANT with five aircraft at Langley AFB in Virginia under the "Scope Light" program and CINCPAC with five aircraft out of Hickam Field in Hawaii under "Blue Eagle." However, the Navy aircraft were relatively small; with limited range and communications, there was concern that they would have great difficulty maintaining links to either remote missile submarines or to Washington.[13]

The channels for naval command and control were more extended than with SAC and involved a number of intermediate nodes, themselves exposed to attack. The shore radio stations were the last link to the submarines. There were some sixty of them worldwide, supplemented by radio relay from ships at sea. All were unprotected installations, exposed to any type of attack including local sabotage efforts. Worse yet, there were only a small number of very low-frequency stations, critical to transmitting to submerged submarines at levels below thirty feet, a depth allowing standard radio communications from buoys deployed just below the surface.[14] The Navy did make provision for alternative types of radio communications, but all were exposed to jamming as well as to the effects of electromagnetic pulse (EMP) interference.

In 1958, in one of the many experiments of the International Geophysical Year, two hydrogen warheads were detonated at high altitude over Johnston Island in the South Pacific. The first "shot"—"Teak"— was detonated at 252,000 feet, and the second—"Orange"—at 141,000 feet. At a height of 48 miles, the flash from Teak was observed in Hawaii, some 800 miles to the northeast. The purpose of the detonations was to create large bursts of highly ionized gas that could be used in determining the shape and extent of the newly discovered, charged upper-altitude particle belts. The belts, named the Van Allen belts for their discoverer, were revealed by instruments in the first artificial satellites launched in 1957 and early 1958. The atomic explosions contributed a great deal to the understanding of charged particle phenomena in the upper atmosphere, but they also produced an unanticipated magnetic storm that resulted in radio blackouts throughout the Central Pacific. Radios as far as 1,800 miles distant were put out of action for at least a full hour.[15]

As more was learned about EMP, it was assumed that any surprise attack would explode one or more large hydrogen weapons at high altitude over the target. A single high-altitude explosion at an altitude around sixty miles would have disrupted radio and possibly even land-line communications across virtually all of America's underground missile sites. Control centers were especially vulnerable, since the pulse would introduce damaging electrical currents, thousands of times over normal operating levels. The use of EMP as a weapon in surprise attacks could suppress radio communications over a very large area for many hours and very possibly damage communications equipment and even control units that had not been specifically designed and equipped to suppress magnetic bursts and surge currents.[16] Circuits and devices could be hardened against the worst EMP effects, but there remained a great number of questions about radio-based communications during and immediately following any attack involving multiple EMP bursts.

Given the many questions about survival of the command-and-control network in any surprise attack, the reality of the situation—and something kept very much secret—was that the United States' ability to launch both land- and sea-based missiles had been extended to individual missile-launch command centers and submarine commanders. Predelegation to unified and specified commanders had been credible during the manned bomber age, with radar detection of incoming strikes at long ranges and hours of warning. With the massive missile arsenals of the 1970s and 1980s, and with submarine-launched missiles possessing flying times of only minutes, the capability for retaliation following a surprise attack simply had to reside with local command—a fact largely hidden in the depths of congressional testimony from as early as 1960.[17]

Objectively it appears that the American nuclear command-and-control system was robust enough to launch the full SIOP, even during a surprise attack. In the worst case SAC's robust command system would have flushed its alert bombers and sent them on their way; it could also have carried out some number of missile launches. How well the Navy system would have performed with an immediate retaliatory attack is questionable; however, in a worst-case scenario the submarine force would have survived for a later strike or as a reserve force for continued exchanges.

Yet by the 1970s, the expectation that the top levels of the civilian chain of command would remain in control seems unrealistic, if not illusionary. The Ballistic Missile Early Warning System (BMEWS), involving huge radars in Alaska, Greenland and England, could track incoming Soviet ICBMs up to three thousand miles from America's borders, but even that translated to little more than fifteen minutes of flight time between detection and impact. At best the White House and

Pentagon National Military Command Center were within half an hour of an ICBM strike. New radars were being deployed that could detect low-trajectory submarine launches, but if the submarines were forward-positioned, there simply would have been no warning at all before warhead impact.[18]

By the 1980s the reality of the submarine threat had been acknowledged, and Nightwatch had actually been moved out of the Washington area, stationed on alert in the central United States, at Blytheville Air Force Base in Arkansas.[19] When the president traveled it was often deployed to airfields at a couple of hundred miles' distance, but clearly there was little hope that the aircraft would actually launch during a surprise attack with civilian National Command Authority figures on board. The secondary role for NEACP, assuming that it had failed to evacuate National Command Authority, was to somehow maintain communications, locate and pick up a "constitutionally designated successor" and move into radio communication range of the SAC Looking Glass airborne command post—which would allow civilian authority access to the surviving worldwide strategic communications system. The challenge with that mission was that even if Nightwatch had taken off, its initial location was quite well known and it would have been foolish to suppose that missiles—including at least one EMP burst—would not be targeted on it. The Soviet war planners definitely had strategies for such contingencies.[20]

Hindsight suggests that the United States would have successfully launched a massive retaliation against any surprise atomic attack. Controlling an ongoing nuclear exchange with hundreds of atomic and hydrogen warheads exploding was another matter entirely. Given the robustness of the entire system, especially the SAC communications network, at least minimal communications might have been maintained. Assuming continuity of communications was somehow maintained from combat units to National Command Authority, the civilian commanders would have faced an immense challenge, personally, and as command authority during a nuclear war.

One approach to assessing the human element under such conditions is to examine crisis-level events that provide us real-world insights into civilian command and control under stress. Our first exploration of such an event was the succession of Lyndon Johnson following the murder of John Kennedy in Dallas in 1963. Johnson's failure to assume an active role as military commander in chief, the performance of his military aides, the behavior of the secretary of defense and the Joint Chiefs at the Pentagon—many of the events of that day raise serious questions about National Command Authority effectiveness under stress circa 1963.

Given the extensive dialog and debate over the SIOP and nuclear war fighting in the 1970s and 1980s, it would seem reasonable to find some serious improvements in both communications and control in the years beyond 1963, at all levels of command. With the advent of the ICBM threat, the protocol for initiating National Command Authority and generating retaliation for a surprise attack was and remains very straightforward even in the 21st century, subject to an unwavering timeline.[21]

The North American Air and Aerospace Defense Command center is tasked with the responsibility of detection and warning. In the event of an apparent missile detection, duty staff at the detection centers have some fifteen seconds to forward a warning to NORAD, STRATCOM (the successor to SAC), and the NMCC at the Pentagon. Duty officers at those sites are to receive a warning no more than a minute after an actual missile detection; launches from forward-deployed submarines offer much less time. The North American Defense headquarters duty commander has no more than three minutes to evaluate and convey a threat-confidence level to a commander's telecommunications conference involving the National Military Command Center at the Pentagon, the Alternative Command Center at Fort Ritchie and STRATCOM headquarters.

At that point, a decision that the attack is real demands an expansion of the command conference, with the White House Situation Room advising the National Security Advisor to bring the president into the conference—to be joined by the principals or deputies of the Joint Chiefs, the secretary of defense, and the national security advisor.

The timeline of events has not changed in decades and assumes that well within ten minutes of the first indication of a surprise attack, National Command Authority will be in place and participate in evaluating the attack. The president and secretary of defense are expected to have full access to senior military staff offering both options and opinions. The best-case timeline then leaves some ten minutes for the president or secretary of defense to make the decision as to whether to retaliate. They must also determine and direct the appropriate SIOP option, some minutes prior to actual impact and detonation of warheads on the continental United States.[22] Even under ideal conditions the SIOP options would have to be selected with only ten minutes remaining prior to warhead impact. That best case represents missiles traveling from Russia, not from deployed submarines or short-range cruise missile attack. The implicit assumption is also that all parties resident in Washington have to reach their decision in the knowledge they will be dead within the following ten to fifteen minutes—nothing in the timeline allows for even an attempt at relocation.

If that timeline sounds brutal, it is most likely too generous. Defense analysts estimate that at least twenty-four Soviet submarine-launched missiles would be devoted to EMP bursts.[23] Even under the best assumptions, National Command Authority orders would begin to face heavy communications interference within ten to twenty minutes after attack detection. The detection and alert decision practices related to missile alerts are themselves straightforward and were routinely exercised. Test missile launches, new satellites, decay and reentry of boosters and various space debris—all have triggered "missile event conferences" requiring "immediate threat assessments." By the 1970s and 1980s such conferences were daily events, with multiple events on most days. Over the decades, there have been a number of extremely challenging incidents, and on occasion the threat conference alerting system has been initiated.

We noted earlier that atomic explosion detectors were installed near most American cities and many military facilities. The failure of a detector to register an atomic explosion in Tampa had helped resolve what appeared to be a missile launch out of Cuba in October 1962. In 1965, a massive power failure in the northeastern United States combined with circuitry errors to produce indications of atomic explosions. The Office of Emergency Planning moved to full alert; as far as can be told there was no NORAD or SAC response. A much more complex event occurred in 1968. A SAC B-52 on airborne overwatch of the

Thule base in Greenland caught on fire, the crew was forced to bail out and the pilotless bomber actually flew over Thule base before crashing seven miles offshore. The crash exploded the onboard fuel, and the nuclear weapon explosives (although not the weapon itself) detonated. In a worst-case scenario, if the aircraft had crashed into the base, taking its communications out, SAC would have faced two worst-case indicators that Thule had been attacked as the first step in a surprise strike. It was assumed that Thule would be the first point of attack; that fundamental assumption was the reason for the Thule airborne watch. If the bomber's atomic weapon had fully detonated, the presence of an atomic explosion indicator would have given virtual confirmation.

The Thule incident illustrated the complexity that circumstantial events bring to real-world decision-making. An incident in 1979 provides another illustration and shows that under stress, the military could be expected to respond to an emerging threat, whether or not civilian command could keep up. On November 9, 1979, the four key command centers including the National Military Command Center simultaneously observed detection warning displays indicating a growing number of incoming missiles. Acting against the proscribed timeline, within six minutes a warning was issued, interceptor aircraft were launched off strip alert, SAC command aircraft were flushed into the air and National Security Advisor Zbigniew Brzezinski was alerted.[24]

Brzezinski was fully aware that the president's decision time was between three and seven minutes, but he decided to wait for confirmation and targeting information before waking him. In the meantime, the Nightwatch aircraft was launched, with no national command official onboard. Within minutes Brzezinski received an update, advising that the number of missiles detected had grown dramatically and that a full-scale surprise attack was under way. He confirmed that SAC aircraft had launched but still did not immediately move to waken the president. According to Brzezinski, he was just about to do that when a third call arrived and he was informed that other detection systems had not confirmed a missile strike and that no attack was actually in progress.[25]

The 1979 incident had been caused by simulation test software mistakenly feeding data to the online threat displays. The exact cause of the malfunction was never determined. However, the incident demonstrates that the military response literally outpaced civilian command and control. The delay in even waking the president would appear to have used up virtually all his prescribed decision time, and no command conference involving actual National Command Authority was convened—Brzezinski held no such authority and it is unclear if the secretary of defense was even notified in real time. The malfunction had produced something quite close to the most probable surprise attack scenario, and the formal command-and-control protocol had failed at the highest civilian level. If it had been a real attack, National Command Authority would never have been involved in the SIOP decision at all.

In contrast, the military response and analysis of the detection data had allowed an effective determination that the attack was not real. At the military level, the basic detection and assessment protocols had worked in a timely fashion. Objectively it seems reasonable to say that in regard to bomber and missile threats, the detection and assessment system could work effectively under normal circumstances. How well it would have worked in the face of any complex, sophisticated surprise attack with a mix of weapons and tactics—including sabotage, pre-positioned explosives and even enemy Special Forces attacks—remains an open question.

Actual real-world surprise attacks provide the most realistic insights into the command-and-control system, especially those involving the full chain of command, including National Command Authority and the operation of civilian authority over the military. One such incident, involving the "fog of war," the realities of accurate intelligence analysis and "human factors" all the way up the chain of command, occurred during the summer of 1964, in the waters of the Gulf of Tonkin, off the shores of North Vietnam.

At the time, the United States was supporting the South Vietnamese in a series of covert warfare attacks on North Vietnam. The attacks had begun in 1962, and by early in 1964 the raids began to use U.S. Navy–provided Swift PT boats. By summer, the American Military Assistance Commander, General William Westmoreland, was shifting from commando attacks to shore bombardment from patrol boats being operated by the South Vietnamese.[26] The North Vietnamese responded by sending patrol vessels against raids. On the night of July 30, a group of four patrol boats chased South Vietnamese raiders some forty-five nautical miles. On their return north they passed within four miles of the U.S. destroyer *Maddox*, performing electronic intelligence in the Gulf of Tonkin.[27]

The naval ELINT and SIGINT patrols had been initiated independently of the covert operations, but research has determined that the American military mission commander in Saigon had specifically requested the patrols to collect information on targeted North Vietnamese coastal installations.[28] As the pace of the covert attacks quickened, the destroyer patrols moved inshore, from twenty miles out to only four miles off the North Vietnamese coast.[29] Ongoing signal interceptions revealed that the North Vietnamese were committed to repelling further attacks and the destroyer *Maddox* was being specifically monitored. North Vietnamese boats were being mustered near its patrol route; intelligence analysts warned that the *Maddox* was likely to be engaged if it continued its close-in shore patrols.

Based on that analysis, the National Security Administration sent warnings to all major commands responsible for operations in the area, including the American military assistance command in Saigon, Commander in Chief Pacific and Commander 7th Fleet. NSA did not send a warning to the destroyers themselves, assuming that normal command-and-control procedures would result in an appropriate warning and direction from the theater commands. In a pattern we will repeatedly observe, the strategic warning that the North Vietnamese were preparing to respond to the ongoing attacks was not initially issued to the *Maddox*.[30]

On August 2, as it proceeded on its SIGINT mission, Marine signals intelligence units intercepted radio traffic and orders indicating that the North Vietnamese thought the *Maddox* was supporting coastal boat raids and patrol boats were preparing to engage the destroyer. A Critic message was sent to all commands, and a tactical warning was sent to the *Maddox*. The October 2 attack on the *Maddox* was in no sense a surprise attack; signals intelligence provided a complete picture of the incident.[31] Ultimately three North Vietnamese patrol boats attacked the destroyer, causing no significant damage and themselves taking casualties and heavy damage from *Maddox* gunfire and attacks by Navy jets called to provide air support for the destroyer.

In response, Washington issued a warning and stated it would continue to assert the freedom of international waters. A second destroyer—the *Turner Joy*—was immediately sent to support the SIGINT patrols. The destroyer patrol commander advised his headquarters that it was clear the North Vietnamese considered themselves to be in a state of war and noted that both the *Maddox* and the *Turner Joy* had problems with detection and fire-control radars. Neither vessel was equipped to perform well against patrol boats at night; the commander requested cruiser support and constant air cover. A combat air patrol was initiated but further offshore from the destroyers, so as not to violate North Vietnamese airspace. As the destroyer patrols resumed, so did the covert attacks on the North Vietnamese. On the evening of August 3, three South Vietnamese boats attacked a military garrison and a radar site. Some 770 rounds of high explosives were fired during the attacks—all told some four separate attacks on North Vietnamese military targets had been made over five days.[32]

The following day, the destroyer patrol commander moved his ships well offshore to provide maneuvering room in case of attack. Both ships reported continuing technical problems with their radars, the *Maddox*'s air-search radar and the *Turner Joy*'s fire-control radars were both inoperative. From South Vietnam, the Marine SIGINT unit transmitted another Critic to the effect that some sort of military preparations were under way, implying that the destroyers were the likely target. There were no specific references in the signals; the assumption was that any activity would be targeting the destroyers. Anticipating a night attack, the destroyers began to report a variety of air and surface contacts. The carrier *Ticonderoga* dispatched a Navy jet to the scene; the pilot easily located both destroyers—quite visible by their wakes—but found no sign of any other vessels in the area. Navy Commander James Stockdale, in the air over the destroyers, was adamant: "I had the best seat in the house to watch that event and our destroyers were just shooting at phantom targets—there were no PT boats there . . . there was nothing there but black water and American firepower."[33]

In the dark and with a mix of chaotic and intermittent radar, sonar and visual observations, both American destroyers opened fire on perceived targets and reported themselves under attack. The incident evolved over some two hours, and within three hours the *Maddox* commander transmitted an after-action report advising that the *Maddox* had never positively identified an enemy vessel.

In the interim, the initial Critic warning of possible military action had arrived in Washington at 7:40 PM ET. At 9:25, with no further warnings, the secretary of defense had advised the president of a possible second attack in the making. At 10 PM a flash message reporting an attack was received, and within three hours President Lyndon Johnson had ordered a major retaliatory air attack against North Vietnam. The Maddox after-action report—which failed to confirm any enemy sighting—had arrived prior to that decision, along with word that the combat air patrol had also been unable to identify any attacking boats in the vicinity of either destroyer.[34]

At approximately the time the president's ordered was being issued, the admiral in command of the Pacific Fleet communicated that the earlier reports of enemy torpedoes in the water appeared doubtful. Freak weather, "over-eager" sonar observers and questionable visual observations were also noted. U.S. Admiral Grant Sharp recommended delaying any retaliation until his command had time to sort out the intelligence and fully confirm an attack. Additional SIGINT later seems to have persuaded Sharp that the attack was real; however, it is now clear that intelligence was mistranslated and misinterpreted. On the *Ticonderoga*, Commander Stockdale had already received his orders to launch retaliatory air strikes. He himself had no doubt about the overall situation: "We were about to launch a war under false pretenses, in the face of the on-scene military commander's advice to the contrary."[35]

Our focus in examining the attacks in the Gulf of Tonkin is not to evaluate the mistakes in intelligence analysis or the apparent rush to a major military decision by both the secretary of defense and President Johnson. For that we direct readers to the detailed signals analyst work of Robert Hanyok, a senior historian in the Center for Cryptologic History—as reported in the National Security Administration journal

Cryptologic—cited in our endnotes. Readers may also wish to refer to historian John Prados's study of the incident, in particular the sequence of remarks by senior Johnson administration officials.[36]

For our purposes the Gulf of Tonkin incident illustrates that in 1964, with a true worldwide military communications network in place, National Command Authority was capable of virtually real-time operational control over global military operations. It also confirms that signals intelligence had advanced to such a state that both strategic and tactical warnings could be generated on threats around the globe. But the Gulf of Tonkin incident also highlights an emerging problem: The wealth of intelligence being developed was beginning to create a false sense of certainty in real-time command and control, leading to premature decision-making. After action reports and additional information from the military personnel in the field were already arriving in Washington at the time, McNamara and Johnson were ordering major retaliation for an attack that had not actually occurred.

Worse yet, the most current studies strongly suggest that from that point on, intelligence data was classified or possibly even intentionally mishandled, to justify their decision. It would be decades until the full set of signals intelligence reports was released by the National Security Administration, and historians were able to demonstrate—with total certainty—that no second attack had actually occurred. In fact, the NSA documents show exactly the opposite: The signals intelligence was of such quality that it was possible to determine exactly what the North Vietnamese naval forces were doing—salvage operations for two patrol boats damaged in the previous night's attacks and a number of close-in coastal patrols. There was no indication of any approach to, much less engagement with, American vessels.[37] With the extensive SIGINT now available, a thorough analysis reveals no comparison at all between the North Vietnamese communications activity of August 2 when an engagement did occur, and August 4, when one did not.

Unfortunately, American ships were going to suffer very real surprise attacks during the 1960s, attacks that provide us with further insights into the real-world performance of both military command and control and National Command Authority. By 1967, the United States was fully engaged on the ground across Indochina, but the Soviets still remained the real strategic threat, and confrontations continued around the globe. To keep a closer eye on international events outside Southeast Asia, the NSA had begun to deploy a series of its own signals intelligence ships, primarily to Latin America and Africa. The NSA turned to modifying older cargo ships, which provided ample space for the extensive electronics required as well as large staffs of operators. The ships were also mounted with a large-dish antenna—towering some thirty-four feet above the deck—as well as some forty-four other antennas; they were described as looking like "porcupines," with a most distinctive appearance.[38]

In their first efforts, the ship *Oxford* was sent south along the coasts of South America, and the *Valdez* frequented African coastlines. Africa is a very large continent, too much for one ship, and the *Valdez* was soon joined by the *Liberty*—the *Valdez* on the east coast and the *Liberty* assigned to the west. By 1967, the *Valdez* needed a major bottom keeling to restore even her modest speeds, and she was brought back through the Suez Canal and the Mediterranean for a refit in the United States, leaving the *Liberty* as the sole intelligence vessel on African detail.

By the late spring of 1967, there were numerous indications that the Egyptians and Israelis might soon be in direct conflict again, this time with the Egyptians having been supplied with a considerable number of advanced Soviet weapons. The Joint Chiefs wanted intelligence, and the NSA's fleet of some ten intelligence vessels was spread around the world. Only the *Liberty* was in any position to proceed directly toward the potential conflict at the eastern end of the Mediterranean. It arrived on station after the fighting had already begun. With the Johnson administration desperate for real-time intelligence, the NSA had already deployed an Air Force C-130 signals intelligence aircraft, placing it in a figure-8 "racetrack" circuit off Israel and Egypt. The Navy had also dispatched its own four-engine intelligence aircraft; it flew missions out of Athens, Greece, where a large Air Force SIGINT facility was also tracking the fighting.[39]

It was at that point that the complexity of global multi-service command and communications began to reveal its weaknesses. While the

NSA section responsible for actually managing its various assets was aware of the *Liberty*'s movement straight into a combat zone, it appears to have been the only point of any initial concern. The ship was actually operated by the U.S. Navy, flying an American flag and declaring itself as American to passing ships. However, the *Liberty* had been tasked to missions controlled by a joint services group, the Joint Reconnaissance Center (JRC). The Joint Center, under extreme pressure for intelligence on warfare in the Middle East—and potential Soviet involvement—was definitely mission focused. Even when NSA protested about the danger of moving the *Liberty* into a danger zone, the JRC initially refused to modify its orders or slow its progress. NSA immediately lodged a formal complaint about the imminent hazard to the *Liberty*.[40] From that point on, serious problems with command and control—as well as related communications protocol—increasingly placed the *Liberty* at risk.

Following a series of strong protests from the Egyptians about American interference, the JRC did transmit an order to the *Liberty*, directing it to pull back from its assigned position some six miles off the coast to a full twenty miles. That order never made it to the *Liberty* due to a communications error at the Pentagon. In addition, the Navy was sending warnings to all its ships in the Mediterranean including the *Liberty*; however, they were being sent via a teletype circuit, which the *Liberty* was not monitoring. Within an hour of the first pullback message, another order was sent directing the *Liberty* to retreat one hundred miles off the coast. Given the level of perceived danger to the ship, the JRC placed a voice call to Navy command in Europe, advising that confirmation would arrive by standard message circuit. However, the Navy captain in charge refused to actually issue a warning and new orders to the *Liberty* before receiving the confirmation; that delayed the transmission of the warning by an hour. And at that point something all too familiar from our very first study of surprise attacks occurred: The communications center routed the *Liberty* warning through Hawaii, on the other side of the globe. That misrouting delayed the *Liberty*'s warning by more than sixteen hours; by that time the ship was under actual attack. Some five warning and alert messages had been sent to the *Liberty*; the ship had received none.[41] Even with advances in technology, errors in basic communications again resulted in the loss of American lives more than twenty years after Pearl Harbor.

The *Liberty* was aware that it was under surveillance; an aircraft had maneuvered around the ship early on the morning of the attack, and its own SIGINT operators had picked up transmissions from the plane.[42] The *Liberty* was flying the American flag, and with its extensive antennas and hull markings the ship was highly recognizable. Yet later that day, with no notice and no attempt to communicate with the *Liberty*, Israeli aircraft and boats attacked the ship over a period of close to a full hour. Afterward all parties to the attack—other than the captain and crew of the *Liberty*—officially portrayed the attack as a tragic mistake on the part of Israel. In reality, NSA intercepts held secret for decades reveal the Israelis had indeed observed the *Liberty*'s American flag and were very well aware that their ongoing attack was targeting and killing Americans on a United States ship.

The true facts of the attack were known in real time because one of the Navy signals intelligence aircraft operating out of Athens had monitored transmissions relating to the attack, including radio calls from the Israeli aircraft referencing an American flag on the target they were attacking.[43] However, the Navy aircraft was merely a collections tool; there were no analysts on board with access to other information—including the fact that an American vessel was indeed located right in the midst of the combat that was being monitored. Upon landing and learning of the attack on the *Liberty*, the NSA personnel on the aircraft concluded that they had monitored Israeli forces during the actual attack but that it was far too late to send a Critic message to Washington; protocol required that such alerts be sent within fifteen minutes of actual intercept.

The surprise attack on the *Liberty* was overwhelming and brutal. Israeli Mirage and Mystere jets attacked with rockets, napalm, cannon and machine guns. Ayah-class torpedo boats used machine guns and torpedoes. One torpedo penetrated the hull, leaving a forty-foot hole. The torpedo explosion immediately killed 25 NSA technicians in the signals intelligence area of the ship.[44] Following hours of repeated attacks, 34 of the *Liberty* personnel were killed and another 172 wounded—with many being disfigured for life by the napalm. The casualties were among the worst ever suffered by an American noncombatant Navy vessel and the greatest single loss ever to an American intelligence craft."[45]

While initially under attack, the *Liberty* itself had sent numerous requests for Navy assistance, and the 6th Fleet did receive those messages. No decision to respond was made for some fifty minutes—at that point the carriers *America* and *Saratoga* were each ordered to launch four armed attack aircraft to provide cover for the *Liberty*. The *Liberty* was sent a message: "Sending aircraft to cover you, surface vessels on the way."[46] The *Liberty* itself remained under ongoing air and sea attack. One of the carriers also responded by sending a Critic alert to NSA in Washington; some eleven minutes later both the National Military Command center and its European counterpart were alerted to the attack on the *Liberty*. In this case the communications system worked well, but the delay in response had dramatically reduced chances for providing any successful military response to the attack.

Some fifteen minutes after receipt of the Critic, President Johnson was advised of the attack on the *Liberty*. At the same time, Defense Secretary McNamara was also advised of the attack and began to seek information. It took some fifteen minutes for him to connect to Navy personnel who knew where the *Liberty* was and what it was doing. In his detailed study of the *Liberty* incident, James Bamford interviewed NSA personnel who told him that the next word they had received on the *Liberty* was that there was discussion of sinking the ship so as to avoid embarrassment for the Israeli government.[47] That information so enraged the NSA individuals involved that one immediately wrote a memorandum for the record and locked it away.

In the eastern Mediterranean, the *Liberty* was still under attack and sending radio calls pleading for help; the carrier aircraft were en route with orders to "destroy or drive off any attackers who are clearly making attacks on the *Liberty*."[48] At the same time, President Johnson was advised that the attackers were most definitely Israeli and not Soviet or Egyptian. At that point his main fear reportedly was that if the Soviets detected a formation of American aircraft entering the war zone, it might begin to launch attacks. A total news ban was ordered in place by the Pentagon. While the *Liberty* was still on fire, with numerous casualties and exposed to any further attacks, President Johnson ordered a recall of the aircraft sent to assist the *Liberty*. When the 6th Fleet commander protested to the secretary of defense, he was advised that President Johnson's primary concern was avoiding any embarrassment to the Israelis.[49]

For our purposes, the *Liberty* incident illustrates the advances in signals intelligence and in global communications that had come into place by the later part of the 1960s. The communications system worked well during peacetime; however, it was still subject to human error, such as the rigidness of the Navy captain who waited for written confirmation of a time-critical voice alert, the misrouting of a critical warning message for the *Liberty* and the lack of coordination on communications circuits that prevented a number of other warnings from reaching the ship. Beyond that, the response of the National Command Authority demonstrated the degree to which the military could indeed be superseded by an "operational president."

Among other issues, the surprise attack on the *Liberty* raises the question of whether or not advances in technology had created the "illusion" that with the intelligence sources available, and a global communications system, it was possible to provide centralized command and control for both conventional and nuclear warfare. As we have noted, the assumptions of the following two decades proceeded to the point where there was actually discussion of controlled nuclear exchanges. To this point our study of real-world attacks would seem to question that line of thinking. Examining yet another command-and-control crisis, the seizure of the American intelligence ship *Pueblo* by North Korea, provides further insight into that question.

NSA's work with electronic and signals collection vessels was increasingly successful, and, as we saw in the Gulf of Tonkin incident, theater military commanders such as General Westmoreland were increasingly eager to obtain tactical signals and electronic intelligence. We've also seen that the Navy itself was always more than eager for such intelligence, and eventually the Navy determined to field its own collections ships in addition to supporting the NSA on Joint Reconnaissance Service missions. To pursue the Navy mission, a number of relatively small trawlers were modified to serve as an addition to Navy planes and submarines already in use for intelligence collection. The trawlers were less conspicuous than the larger NSA ships such as the *Liberty* and could be operated under a cover of collecting oceanographic data that the Navy required for operations, in particular submarine operations.[50]

The first ship deployed in the effort was the *Banner*, dispatched to patrol offshore from Soviet facilities in Siberia. Over two years the *Banner* pursued its task, irritating the Soviets to no end and being "bumped, nearly rammed, placed under threat of cannon fire, and buzzed by both Soviet MiGs and helicopters."[51] Later it would be chased by and evade eleven Chinese boats off Shanghai during a mission in the East China Sea. To the Navy, all that harassment was an indication that the *Banner* was indeed conducting successful missions, and two more trawlers—the *Pueblo* and *Palm Beach*—were modified to perform similar missions. The trawlers were extremely small by Navy standards, but they were readily identifiable by their conspicuous radio antenna and aerials. Signals collected by the trawlers were evaluated by the Navy, but all data was also shared with the NSA for further analysis. Ultimately the Navy agreed to split missions with the trawlers, alternating between Navy and NSA tasking.

In late 1967, the Navy tasked the *Pueblo* with a mission focused on coastal operations near North Korea. Its task was to monitor North Korean military installations and naval activity, locate and profile coastal radars, intercept and monitor Soviet naval vessels and probe for any indications that the North Koreans were preparing for military action against the South. The security situation in South Korea caused increasing concern, as the North Koreans had become far more aggressive during 1967. They had begun covert operations teams into the south, trains were sabotaged and there were attempts to capture and kill both South Korean and American military near the demilitarized zone between the two countries. The escalation in incidents was dramatic, with some 360 during 1967 compared to 42 the previous year.

Given the worsening security situation and North Korean aggressiveness, the Navy appears to have dramatically underestimated the level of risk associated with the *Pueblo* mission. The North Koreans were notorious for ignoring the legal issues related to international waters; in 1965 their fighters had tried to shoot down a SAC reconnaissance RB-47 flying some eighty miles off the North Korean coast.[52] During multiple briefings in Hawaii and later in Japan, the captain of the *Pueblo* was assured of two things: His primary protection would be that of operating in international waters as a flagged American ship and the absolute guarantee of American retaliation in the event that he was attacked or seized.[53] The Navy also rejected multiple requests from the *Pueblo* captain to provide some means of rapidly scuttling his boat; he was informed that the required work would be too expensive.[54] That decision led to an intelligence disaster of mammoth proportions. In addition to a host of classified documents, the *Pueblo* sailed with a dozen code machines and a copy of the full electronic war plan for North Korea and Soviet coastal installations, listing all targeted military installations and associated frequencies and operational information.

The captain of the *Pueblo* was also informed that there were no available assets to provide quick-response military support to his mission. That would mean that rapid communications would be of supreme importance if he did come under some sort of attack. Historically communications in the Sea of Japan had always been problematic; the *Banner* had once taken twenty-four hours to establish a radio circuit. That sort of delay presented a major risk for any intelligence mission, especially one targeting the unpredictable North Koreans.[55] In the case of the *Pueblo*, when it was initially discovered and circled by North Korean boats, a situation report was sent to its command, but due to heavy traffic on the circuit assigned to the *Pueblo*—shared by numerous naval vessels—the message took fourteen hours to be passed and received.

The NSA did not share the Navy's apparent complacency in regard to the *Pueblo* mission. Given the lack of restraint and military aggressiveness of the North Koreans, the NSA advised the Navy and the Joint Reconnaissance Center that sending the *Pueblo* on a Korean mission had to be considered extremely risky. Because all such missions had to be approved by the Joint Chiefs and the national covert action committee, the NSA advisory should have been routinely forwarded to them—it was not. Instead it was routed only to the Navy, via CINCPAC. Confusion over the routing of the message resulted in its simply moving into a state of "limbo" for a full month. Once again, a warning advisory failed to get to its destination in time to affect the course of events. The *Pueblo* was dispatched on its mission, with orders to target both North Korean military facilities as well as Soviet naval units. The order specifically noted that the estimate of risk was "minimal."[56]

While the *Pueblo* was operating off the North Korean coast, the North dispatched a covert action team into South Korea with the intent of killing the South Korean president, the U.S. ambassador and other targets. Apparently the plan was to so destabilize the South that the North could move to take control of the country. American intelligence in Japan also began to receive indications of North Korean military activity far beyond levels normally experienced during the winter months. The covert attack was aborted and captives revealed the plans; the South Korean army mobilized and the North made ready for retaliation attacks.

The *Pueblo*, obviously an intelligence ship and under surveillance by the North, was not advised of such current events, given any change in mission directive or even moved further off the Korean coastline.[57] Messages regarding the situation in Korea were broadcast as part of general fleet broadcasts; it was assumed that the *Pueblo* would receive those, but its captain was focused on being monitored by the North Koreans. He was only scanning messages addressed to him, not reading piles of fleet traffic, much of which related to technical matters. No message about the attempted attack on the South Korean president was addressed to the *Pueblo*.

As its mission proceeded, the issue of American spy ships became a major topic of North Korean propaganda broadcasts, in both Korean and English. Numerous protests and warnings were made about the "hostile acts" of such vessels.[58] The warnings were even quoted in a Japanese newspaper. The threats were noted at Navy intelligence in Japan but discounted as simple propaganda. The U.S. admiral in charge considered the North Koreans unpredictable but felt there were no specific indicators that would call for a change in mission. Threats of action against the spy boats were not communicated to the commander of the *Pueblo*; he received no new orders.

In spite of confirmation that the *Pueblo* had been detected and was being monitored by the North Koreans, further communications were consistently frustrated. The ship itself had a relatively low-power transmitter, the assigned circuits were congested and at night it was virtually impossible to hold up a secure circuit to Japan. The ship could hear Japan, but Japan could not receive its message traffic. On its final day, the *Pueblo* did manage to send situation reports describing the arrival of North Vietnamese craft, but maintaining the circuit to Japan was a constant challenge.

Ultimately the North Koreans determined to seize the *Pueblo*, and the captain's first warning was the arrival of an armed submarine chaser. The *Pueblo* experienced repeated problems getting requests for help back to command, even after it began to receive fire and suffered casualties. As the actual firing began, the final option was a special high-frequency—Hi-Comm—clear-channel voice link to both Japan and Hawaii. The link was to be used only in emergency; it had been monitored for traffic but was off limits for outgoing use. Under attack, the *Pueblo* made a call on the Hi-Comm, requesting a change in frequency. It proved fruitless; the operator on the other end just kept repeating a new frequency setting over and over, and the *Pueblo* was unable to break in to report or request assistance.[59]

In an agonizing repeat of the *Liberty* incident, only fifty miles away an airborne electronics intelligence aircraft captured full details of the incident from North Korean military traffic. The intercepted broadcasts included their identification of the *Pueblo* as United States flagged and its obvious identity as a radio and radar intelligence ship.[60] The crew of the Air Force intelligence plane had no means of communicating directly with the *Pueblo*; in frustration they radioed Japan, warning that the *Pueblo* had moved into a trap. Still, no warning was sent from Navy command to the *Pueblo*.

The intercepted messages were relayed to Washington; they began to arrive at the Pentagon at 2:22 AM and the Situation Room at 2:44 AM respectively. At 3:04 AM the Pentagon received an intercept indicating that the North Korean sub chaser was demanding to escort the *Pueblo* into a North Korean port; that news did not make it to the White House

until 4:26 AM. Monitoring of the North Korean communications channels continued, and by 5:51 AM the Pentagon knew that the North Korean sub chaser was clearing away other vessels to begin firing on the
Pueblo. A full chronology of the intercepts, the *Pueblo*'s own messages
and the response by various points of command including the National
Command Authority is available; it demonstrates a total lack of preparedness for such an incident and an extended delay in the decision-
making process throughout the chain of command.[61]

The *Pueblo* scenario was all too familiar: warnings to surrender,
pleas for help from the *Pueblo* on those few occasions when it could
establish a circuit to command, shooting from the North Koreans, casualties, eventually a special plea to Hawaii on an emergency circuit
and finally seizure of the boat with a good deal of its intelligence assets
and equipment intact. Even during those times when the *Pueblo* could
establish communications, no senior officers came on the circuit—only
the teletype operator, with vague assurances that the Navy and Air
Force had both been informed. The only bases that could have sent
aircraft in time would have been in South Korea. The Air Force commander there had actually been aware of the *Pueblo* mission. Given the
worsening situation in the country, he had twice queried the Navy in regard to placing conventional armed aircraft on strip alert. His standard
alert aircraft were strategic alert fighter bombers with nuclear weapons.
On each query he received a response that the *Pueblo* mission carried a
minimum-risk status so no strip alert was justified.[62]

By the end of the 1960s, advanced technology had begun to produce a wealth of virtually real-time intelligence. The new worldwide
military networks had created a chain of command reaching from the
president to military units in the field, a chain of command when orders
could be issued around the world in minutes. The capability for command and control had evolved to the extent that by the 1970s, there
would be extensive discussion of actually being able to control atomic
exchanges. In retrospect, much of the confidence that spawned those
dialogs seems quite illusionary.

Communications hardly ever operated as effectively as assumed in
the plans, and when it did, human factors intervened to substantially

delay the transmission of warnings. Even when intelligence assets were in place to provide real-time information during attacks, that intelligence never made it to the targets of the attacks. And within the national command structure, decisions were never made in time to actually alter events during either conventional or surprise attacks. But perhaps that is too harsh a judgment—perhaps it was simply too much to expect the National Command Authority to be capable of responding quickly enough to deal with conventional surprise attacks overseas. Certainly the level of preparation for nuclear attacks must have been far greater, the response times much more in line with all the planning for response to a nuclear attack. To evaluate that point, we will turn our attention to National Command Authority preparations for true "bolt out of the blue" surprise attacks.

Chapter 14

....

PREPAREDNESS

xamining peacetime, conventional surprise attacks provided examples of the extent to which the human element can compromise communications, command and control. In the case of the *Liberty*, some five different warnings and command messages were sent to the ship, advising it of danger and actually ordering it first twenty miles and later one hundred miles back from its position. None of those messages made it to the ship, being sent via the wrong circuits or in one instance routed across the wrong ocean, with the message delayed some sixteen hours in transit. One critical voice warning was delayed for an hour, simply due to a demand by one of the officers involved in the communications for an observance of correct command "protocol."

Both human decisions and communications failures were responsible for the loss of the *Pueblo*. Even with threat conditions escalating dramatically, no warnings were communicated to the ship's captain and routine two-way communications were consistently poor or impossible. A last-resort emergency channel to Hawaii proved useless, apparently due to operator protocols. Finally, when under attack, and in limited communications with its Japan headquarters, no command officer came on the circuit to the ship, only the teletype operator.

Such incidents also illustrate the limitations of even amazingly good electronic intelligence collection. In 1962, a SAC ELINT aircraft off Cuba monitored the transition of Russian air defense systems moving from tracking to fire-control targeting—yet had no way to warn the U-2 pilot who was being targeted and who was shot down by the Russians. During both the *Liberty* and *Pueblo* attacks, American SIGINT aircraft monitored the attacker's communications with no way to directly alert the ships. In the instance of the *Pueblo*, warnings from the aircraft to Navy headquarters in Japan failed to be routed to the ship itself. Given the security surrounding the missions involved, and the compartmentalization of information, those failures are perhaps understandable. However, they reflect certain serious limitations of real-time intelligence collection in regard to command and control, even in peacetime.

In both the *Liberty* and *Pueblo* incidents, the chain of command fell far behind the actual attacks, reflecting the realities of command decision-making. Upon receiving the first call for assistance from the *Liberty*, Sixth Fleet issued no orders for some fifty minutes; only then were armed aircraft ordered to launch from the carriers *America* and *Saratoga*. One of the carriers sent a Critic message on its actions via the NSA and it took eleven minutes to arrive at the National Military Command Center. It took another fifteen minutes to advise President Johnson and an additional fifteen minutes for Defense Secretary McNamara to even receive basic information on the *Liberty* and its mission. Something like one and a half hours had elapsed beyond the first call for help received at Sixth Fleet command.

During the *Pueblo* incident, the Pentagon and White House Room were informed of the first clash with North Korean vessels at approximately 2:22–2:24 Washington, D.C., time. Information of the actual seizure of the ship arrived some fifteen minutes later, but that news was not passed to the White House for well over an hour. No effective command action was taken for more than three hours, when word was passed from the SIGINT aircraft that North Korean boats were being cleared away so that firing on the *Pueblo* could begin.[1] It appears that Navy theater commands responsible for both vessels had failed to prepare for attacks on either vessel, very possibly due to the fact that the ships were on special missions with convoluted chains of command and control. Irrespective of that, the incidents illustrate that both theater commands failed to be supported in a timely or effective fashion by the extended chain of National Command Authority.

Such incidents, occurring under peacetime conditions, with no intentional communications interference and with the chain of command itself not under attack, illustrate the delays in decision-making that can occur during even the most favorable national security incidents. In a true surprise attack, conditions would very likely be much more demanding. In the classic surprise attack scenario the president would be forced to react to a "bolt out of the blue" call at 2 AM—with an aide pounding on the bedroom door of the White House. At that time they would already be "on the clock"—fifteen minutes and counting. An alternative would find an aide pulling them off a podium or out of a school room during a public relations appearance in some American city. At best they would be told they needed to pick up the phone and assume command—mentally prepared to use their code word and issue a specific level of SIOP retaliation—immediately.

In the event that the president was not able to respond or "froze," it would be incumbent for the secretary of defense to be reached in the same elapsed time and issue the appropriate order. In neither case would there be more than approximately ten minutes to pass intelligence or respond to questions. If neither the president nor secretary of defense could be brought into the command process within ten minutes, the NMCC would have to contact the available successor to each and request his or her retaliation directions. In more contemporary times the national security trigger event might not be an incoming missile detection. It might well be a hijacked airliner within minutes of impact on the Pentagon—or the White House. It might be an EMP burst over the Sea of Japan, wiping out virtually all communications in the Western Pacific. It could be the loss of control over the Wall Street information systems that support global stock trading, with a worldwide panic and financial collapse possible within a matter of hours. Each incident could potentially demand American military or cyber-warfare response against a foreign state, or against non-state individuals or groups.

We will examine preparedness for the more complex contemporary threat environment in following chapters; historically we are able to turn to more detailed information on the actual state of national-security emergency readiness in regards to surprise atomic attacks. As we initially explored the attacks of 1941 to examine the basics of command and control, we will begin with an exploration of exactly how prepared those serving as National Command Authority were to respond to national security emergencies, specifically the worst-case situation requiring authorization of some version of the Single Integrated Operations Plan, within the fifteen-minute time frame needed to retaliate against nuclear attack.

Beginning in the early 1960s, as attack detection times spiraled down from days to hours at best, minutes in the worst case, the fundamental question was whether or not those in the line of National Command civilian succession understood the Single Integrated Operations Plan, its options (withholds) and the protocol required to initiate it. If they did not, or if they deferred on a decision until atomic weapons actually began to explode on American soil, the arrangements for predelegation would very likely have ensured a full-scale retaliation against as many Communist-Bloc targets as could be reached. It would be the height of naïveté to assume that the authorized senior American military commanders would accept the destruction of strategic military assets, major American population centers—as well as of their own commands and personnel—without ordering full atomic retaliation.

In an earlier chapter we noted the apparent lack of any preparation of Vice President Johnson with regard to the assumption of commander-in-chief duties and command responsibilities. The performance of the National Command Authority in the immediate minutes and hours following the shooting of President John Kennedy clearly left a great deal to be desired. There was a total failure to involve the new commander in chief in the national command process during his time at Parkland Hospital, waiting on the ground in Dallas on *Air Force One* and during the flight back to Washington. At no point was Johnson in secure voice communications with the NMCC or secretary of defense. We do have a transcript of voice communications to and from *Air Force One*, but there is no record of what messages may have been sent through its secure teletype link—the system available for National Command Authority orders. In fact there is no confirmation that such messages, including an elevated DEFCON condition, were transmitted to *Air Force*

One; if so Johnson was apparently not informed. Based on the voice communications transcript, following the death of the president *Air Force One* did not even perform a voice communications confirmation with the NMCC, the SAC communications network, Nightwatch or the alternate military command center.

The transcript reveals that early in the day on November 22, *Air Force One* was contacted by the SAC command post in Fort Worth, Texas, while in flight to Dallas. The contact was made via a communications "patch" at Andrews Air Force Base, the control center for all Special Air Mission (SAM) flights involving not only *Air Force One* but other VIP aircraft operated by that unit. Following the shooting in Dallas, and the death of the president, *Air Force One* remained in voice communication with the Situation Room at the White House and established a radio connection via patch to an aircraft carrying cabinet members to Japan. Beyond that the available tapes of *Air Force One* communications show only communications with an Air Force command post, apparently at Andrews AFB, during the flight back to Andrews AFB outside Washington. There is no indication of any calls to SAC command posts. There is also no indication of efforts by the NMCC or SAC command posts to contact *Air Force One*, even for basic communications checks.[2] For all intents and purposes, President Johnson did not assume a role in National Command Authority, and no effort was made to move him into that role.

The next indication of Johnson-era lack of SIOP familiarity emerged during the second Johnson administration, when a new secretary of defense determined that the existing "Furtherance" direction for actual implementation of the SIOP contained what was deemed to be exceptionally inflexible and "dangerous" language. The Kennedy administration had gone to great lengths to add at least some degree of flexibility to the SIOP. President Kennedy's main concern was that the targeting and war plans that his administration had inherited from the 1950s were essentially that of a total "spasm" retaliation to any type of atomic attack—even in the event of accidents or mistakes in detection and warning. SIOP-63 was developed with additional flexibility and improved "withholds" of both targeted nations and target groupings. Yet in 1968 Secretary of Defense Clark Clifford identified what were considered to be quite contrary instructions in the then-current Furtherance provided to designated military commanders. While that "Furtherance" has never been released to public review, the remarks about its issues seem to suggest that the actual operational instructions for a nuclear response issued to senior military command had been exceptionally broad. The guidance appears to have included instructions for full-scale SIOP nuclear retaliation in response to certain types of purely conventional attacks and to any use of nuclear weapons, even in small-scale tactical attacks or accidental detonation.

At some point the flexibility of the Kennedy SIOP seems to have been dramatically compromised by the actual wording of the Furtherance instructions, which governed military commanders' actual execution of the SIOP. It seems that those instructions would have been approved by both Secretary of Defense McNamara and the Joint Chiefs. Yet in 1968 Secretary of Defense Clark Clifford and the Chiefs appeared to be very surprised by the wording in the instructions and concurred in its immediate alteration. All we know for certain is that "Furtherance" execution directions then in existence were immediately canceled and new directions on SIOP execution were issued to senior unified and specified force commanders.[3] It appears that for some extended period, senior civilian command had not been aware of a key operational element of the nation's nuclear retaliation plan.

Beyond that particular "Furtherance" issue, more recent research indicates that periodic revisions to the SIOP targeting list had routinely expanded the SIOP itself. Researcher Janne Nolan found that those changes, listed in "revisions reports," required official approval by the secretaries of defense. Yet none of the revision reports were actually delivered to the secretaries or any civilian authority until the late 1980s.[4]

In general it seems that President Johnson, consumed by conventional warfare in Southeast Asia and a variety of other global incidents, paid relatively little attention to preparing for a bolt-out-of-the-blue nuclear attack. That also appears to be true for President Richard Nixon, whose administration was characterized largely by covert action against perceived Communist expansion. Perhaps reaching the plateau of mutual assured destruction had led to the conviction that surprise nuclear attack was simply beyond any sane consideration.

We do have a report that President Gerald Ford became personally involved with reviewing both the SIOP and its execution procedures. Ford took the time to actually visit SAC headquarters at Omaha, Nebraska, and meet with the joint targeting group. He took his CIA director, William Colby, along on the visit and was fully briefed not only on the SIOP but on its execution options. Up to that point, a general lack of civilian involvement with the targeting SIOP staff, combined with the fact that damage criteria for the SIOP itself were held only in Omaha, illustrates a notable lack of senior civilian command authority with the American plan of nuclear retaliation.

President Carter also spent some time reviewing the SIOP options; reportedly he was interested in dialing back the level of "overkill" that had developed and felt that reliance on the nuclear-submarine missile force provided an alternative to overreaction with the full range of forces in the war plan. Yet in the end no significant changes were implemented during his administration.[5] We also know of at least one nuclear attack exercise in which President Carter participated. The military aide to National Security Advisor Zbigniew Brzezinski organized a drill in the Situation Room, involving President Carter and all the parties that would be required on a surprise-attack conference call. The upshot of the exercise was that Carter "found the notebook that contained U.S. attack options hard to follow. . . . Carter told them to redesign the instructions and come back and try it again."[6] At that point the "bomb bag" release guidelines and SIOP nuclear release protocol had been in place for some fifteen years.

There seem to have been few instances in which presidents, much less vice presidents, secretaries of defense or elected civilians in the presidential line of succession, were involved in actual nuclear attack exercises, in the Situation Room or anywhere else. While the military continually exercised its detection and analysis functions, National Command Authority seems to have been left to its own devices and appears to have had limited understanding of and virtually no practice with crisis response protocols—including the raw mechanics of communications other than in the Situation Room. There is also no evidence of civilian leadership drills or exercises involving the National Airborne Emergency Command aircraft, the alternative command centers or in general with presidential military aides including the bomb bag officer. We have only one record of a president ever being onboard the Nightwatch aircraft. Nixon's political aide H.R. Haldeman recorded Richard Nixon using the Nightwatch plane for a flight back to Washington. Nixon was unfamiliar with the command aircraft, very impressed by its displays, communications and personnel. He found the plane "fascinating" and asked a number of questions, apparently taken aback by the routine battle staff discussion of nuclear capabilities, kill results and "millions of deaths."[7]

Details on the preparation of individuals on the civilian succession list for National Command Authority are almost totally lacking. Presidents through Reagan and Carter continued the pre-delegation arrangements for nuclear retaliation ("pre-authorized command authority") first put in place by President Eisenhower, but reportedly Jimmy Carter intentionally withheld National Command Authority identification codes from individuals in the presidential line of succession stipulated by the 1947 succession act. Presidents do not actually carry actual launch codes; those are retained within the military chain of command. National Command Authority civilians only carry cards with codes used to identify themselves to the military command. Aside from Carter, during his administration only the vice president and presumably the secretary of defense were issued identification.[8]

It would not be until 1981, and the assassination attempt on President Ronald Reagan, that we have enough detailed information to truly explore the human-factor elements of a National Command Authority emergency. That incident provides us with a very real evaluation of crisis preparedness at the highest civilian levels of government, with individuals operating under high stress, although considerably less than that of an actual surprise attack on the nation.

The work of *Washington Post* investigative reporter Del Quentin Wilber provides us with extensive insights gained from interviews with many of those involved with the Reagan shooting crisis, as well as document references. Wilber also provides a detailed chronology of key events, meetings, remarks and announcements during the period immediately following the attack on President Reagan. His book *Rawhide Down: The Near Assassination of Ronald Reagan,* is an invaluable source for evaluating the national security response that followed the Reagan shooting.

In contrast to Dallas, the Secret Service agents with Reagan were able to use their own communications network to inform their command post almost immediately following the shooting at 2:27 PM in the afternoon. The Secret Service command post at the White House began to monitor the president's status almost immediately, although due to the nature of Reagan's injuries it was some time before it was understood that he had actually been seriously wounded. The White House Situation Room also responded quickly, its presidential locator displaying "En Route to GW Hospital" within minutes of the shooting. Beyond that, much as in 1963, many major administration officials learned of the shooting of the president from media broadcasts, often alerted by aides rushing in with the news. Reagan's chief of staff James Baker was advised that Reagan was incapacitated, possibly having suffered a heart attack, after being checked into the hospital.

Secretary of State Al Haig was the first cabinet officer to contact Baker at the White House. Haig took the initiative to begin organizing a meeting of cabinet secretaries in the Situation Room and told Baker that he would contact Vice President George Bush. Bush was in Texas and had just completed a luncheon speech; his aircraft had departed Fort Worth at 2:45 PM. Bush was flying on board a Special Air Mission aircraft, referred to as *Air Force Two* but identical to the aircraft normally flown by the president as *Air Force One*. A few minutes into the flight the pilot was contacted by ground control and asked if he had a flight request change, diverting to Washington.[9]

The pilot replied he did not, puzzled by the call. Shortly afterward the pilot was informed that the aircraft had received a high-priority message. The Secret Service lead agent with Bush had received a brief voice message that an attempt to shoot President Reagan had occurred; two agents were down, but there was no sign of injury to the president.

A few minutes later, Haig's telephone call reached the vice president's plane. The voice connection was so poor that neither Haig nor Bush could understand each other. In 1981 the presidential aircraft apparently still had no secure voice capability. Within minutes, the secure teletype circuit brought a message from Haig to Bush that President Reagan had been seriously wounded and was in the hospital, pending the decision on whether or not to operate immediately.

As of approximately 2:55 PM, Al Haig seems to have been the first person to reach Vice President Bush in regard to the assassination attempt, approximately twenty minutes after the shooting. The vice president had not been contacted by the Situation Room, the National Military Command Center or the secretary of defense. If the attack on Reagan had been part of a decapitation strike by the Soviets, the critical fifteen-minute window would have passed with no apparent dialog between the secretary of defense—at that point the only civilian in the chain of command—and either the Joint Chiefs or Vice President Bush. Haig advised that Bush return to Washington immediately. The only other information received on Bush's plane was coming in via a fuzzy television news broadcast on a conference-room television.

By approximately 3:15 PM, Haig and Reagan's national security advisor Richard Allen had moved to the Situation Room. Several White House staff, the treasury secretary and the attorney general joined them, but Defense Secretary Caspar Weinberger was at the Pentagon; he arrived at the White House at around 3:30 PM. But Weinberger arrived without a military aide, and without a "bomb bag." Allen had requested a bag be brought to the Situation Room and obtained a National Command Authority (NCA) identification card (which he was not legally empowered to use). Functionally with President Reagan either unconscious or barely conscious, Vice President Bush had inherited National Command Authority and responsibility. As the situation evolved, it appears that the legal consideration of vice presidential "succession" to command had never been fully resolved. According to Weinberger, he considered that both he and the vice president constituted National Command Authority at that point. Of course Weinberger, as the only NCA official in the room, had his own NCA identity card—Reagan's card was at the hospital and Bush had his card on board *Air Force Two*, along with a military aide and a bomb bag.

Conceptually, Weinberger should have been in the NMCC, with the Joint Chiefs, connected to the Situation Room by phone or teleconference and in direct communications with Bush on board *Air Force Two*. Instead, he was in the Situation Room, in a meeting that by all appearances Secretary of State Haig was running—or more and more animatedly attempting to run. In the midst of that meeting, with its focus on Reagan's health and the statements and press releases that needed to be issued, Weinberger and Clark began to discuss the possibility of alerts to SAC and other military commands, something like an hour and a half after the attack on the president. In 1963 it had taken some forty-five minutes to issue a basic global military alert following President Kennedy's shooting. In 1981 more than an hour and a half after the attack on Reagan, it seems that not even a standby alert had been issued, nor had any readiness levels been elevated.

At that point, Haig, joined by the treasury secretary, began arguing against any increase in readiness. In what was becoming an emotional debate, with President Reagan unconscious and on the operating table, Weinberger remarked that it was necessary to at least consider an increase in DEFCON levels, only the most modest move though; he felt DEFCON 2 would be appropriate. Others, including Haig, were shocked as the secretary of defense seemed to misunderstand the DEFCON levels—DEFCON 2 was only one step short of the assumption of hostilities.[10]

The secretary of defense may have been briefly confused; however, matters became increasingly tense as Secretary of State Haig remarked that with Reagan unconscious: " . . . the helm is right here [literally in his chair at the Situation Room conference table] . . . and that means right here for now, in this chair, constitutionally, until the Vice President gets here."[11] Those around him were concerned that Haig did not appear to understand the legal line of succession or National Command Authority. At that point Weinberger represented the only officer of National Command Authority present; the legal successor to the full powers of the presidency was George Bush, and the next individual in the legal chain of presidential succession was the speaker of the house. As secretary of state, Haig held no legal position in either chain of command. And after decades of planning and millions of dollars spent on worldwide communications and networking, the vice president of the United States—even while in the air on *Air Force Two*—was apparently isolated not only from Washington but from the complete chain of American military command and control.

The fundamental confusion over issues of National Command Authority did not remain hidden from the public for long. In the partially controlled chaos of the situation, debate continued over what to tell the public and how to express it. The group in the Situation Room was still wrestling with those issues when Haig noticed that live television was carrying a dialog between the Deputy White House press secretary a number of reporters. The group had not briefed or prepared him to speak to the press, and he simply had no answers for many of the questions being thrown at him. In frustration, Haig rushed to the press area, encountering National Security Advisor Allen on the way. Allen and others tried to stop Haig, to get him to compose himself, but they were unable to do so and Haig took over the podium. Clearly tense, Haig began to take questions and triggered an explosion in the press room when he stated that the line of succession went from the president to the vice president to the secretary of state and that he—Haig—was in control of the government pending the arrival of the vice president.

Everyone within earshot knew that Haig was totally incorrect in terms of legal succession. It also appeared that Vice President Bush was totally out of touch even though he was on *Air Force Two* and in transit to Washington from Texas. The immediate result of Haig's taking the podium was a general impression that the secretary of state was either woefully ignorant of constitutional succession or not in full control of his faculties. That same question was being asked in the Situation Room, where the secretary of defense had just received word that Soviet submarines had been detected unusually close to the American East Coast. That shortened the flight time of their missiles; ten minutes to impact was the new projection. Weinberger ordered an increase in readiness for SAC, moving more crews to runway alert.

By that time Haig was back in the Situation Room and upset by the fact that he had just told the press that the U.S. had not increased its military alert, since the secretary of defense was doing just that. The two men continued to debate alert status and military response. Weinberger made it clear that he held command authority, having discussed that point with President Reagan's special cabinet-level advisor earlier—seemingly a point which the secretary of defense should have been clear on without consultation. At that point Haig appears to have challenged Weinberger once again on the issue of constitutionality, implying that such matters needed to be referred to Vice President Bush.[12]

Given that Vice President Bush was on a White House aircraft, supposedly equipped and staffed to support National Command Authority, the lack of any ongoing real-time communications between him and the Situation Room or the secretary of defense reflects poorly on the crisis preparations of all those involved, on the true capability of the command-and-control communications network, or very possibly on both. To some extent it appears that the vice president was being more or less ignored by everyone. *Air Force Two* had to land in Texas for refueling, but no fuel truck appeared. A Secret Service agent had to locate a fuel truck engaged with a commercial jet and requisition it for the vice president's plane. Bush did not actually depart Texas for Washington until some two hours after the shooting of President Reagan. Based on available material, other than the one unsuccessful telephone patch from Haig and the one secure teletype, the vice president had been left to his own devices and had made no move to insert himself into the crisis response or into his national command responsibility.

The stress and chaos of a real-world attack, not on the nation but on the commander in chief, is clearly illustrated in the activities of the senior members of the Reagan administration in the hours immediately following the attack on President Reagan. The incident occurred during a period of escalating international tension with the Soviets, frequent dialog about the strategic balance, increasingly assertive pressures on the Soviets and dialog on controlled nuclear engagement. Yet it appears that none of the senior Reagan administration figures had been specifically briefed on their appropriate crisis roles and authorities. It also appears that command-and-control procedures, as well as secure voice communications, were no better in 1981 than in 1963.

As the dialog in and around the Situation Room continued, it became evident that even the most practical question of what to do if the president became incapacitated had not become part of any established practice. Congress had dealt with the issue following the death of President Kennedy in 1963, passing legislation that spelled out the correct legal protocol. Yet in the intervening two decades, actual implementation in terms of documents and procedures seems to have been left to each new administration. Reagan administration legal counsel Fred Fielding had seen it as an issue and had begun drafting an "emergency briefing packet" on exactly what to do if President Reagan was killed or injured. The package was not complete, and the legal process was far too complex for a crisis environment. With Reagan unconscious and unable to transfer power himself, it required the vice president and the majority of the cabinet officers to sign documents transferring full presidential authority to the vice president.[13] In the event of any true surprise attack, either strategic or conventional, on Washington, D.C., that would have been totally unrealistic.

In short, after almost two decades, by March 1981 the exercise of American National Command Authority functioned no better under stress—and arguably more chaotically—than it had following the assassination of President Kennedy in November 1963. We previously explored the potential issues that might well have compromised much of the technical capability of the C3 (communications, command and control) system during any actual nuclear exchange, yet whatever their limitations, it appears that the human element was an even greater concern. The incidents we have examined to this point all took place during peacetime; there were no combat "degradations" to communications, and the tools and equipment were at their full capability. While the military constantly performed training, exercises and drills on crisis response, the civilian authorities simply had done nothing comparable. It appears that any formal preparation of those in the line of presidential succession was very limited, generally not extending beyond the president. Cabinet members, with the possible exception of the secretary of defense, received virtually no detailed training or drills. With constantly cycling administrations, what there is of "institutional memory" in Washington seems not to have come into play during actual crises.

The Soviet senior leadership appears to have paid much more attention to such matters, perhaps more fundamentally concerned about actual surprise attacks from the West. In that regard, the Soviets consistently prepared for a more flexible response; they had nothing equivalent to the American SIOP and were much less tied to a "spasm" retaliation.[14] The practical derivative of that strategic position was that the Soviets had to devote much more attention to keeping their top command structure alive and operational in control of all their military resources. Given the Soviet reliance on total central control, they were also driven to far more direct measures to maintain nuclear weapons control. In general it appears that the pre-delegation retaliation authority granted to the American military simply was not an option for the Soviets—who also put a good deal more effort into creating "feedback" systems to ensure that their central command had direct access to the status of their individual weapons, in particular their nuclear missiles.[15]

The Soviet plans for top command survival were similar to the American plans: alternate sites—but all in deep bunkers—with numerous hardened command posts and shelters throughout Russia. U.S. estimates placed the hardened Soviet leadership command facilities at somewhere between 1,500 and 2,000 sites. The United States had nothing comparable. The Soviets' practical preparations for evacuating senior leadership were also far more extensive. Buried train tunnels branched out from Moscow to a network of distant bunkers. Senior officials maintained radio telephone access at all times when traveling.

In one 1970s exercise, Soviet leadership members in several limos were alerted to an incoming American strike, and all used prepared routes to quickly relocate to a hardened bunker, from which they assumed full operational control of a retaliatory missile response.[16] The Soviets also maintained a fleet of airborne command posts. Those aircraft were not maintained on either airborne or strip alert as were the American command posts; the same was true for their communications relay aircraft. The general assumption seems to be that they would have been alerted during a rise in international tensions, with time to bring them to some state of readiness prior to any conflict. Like the United States, the Soviets appear to have worked two scenarios, the first being engagement after the evolution of an international crisis (a common assumption in the early American Net evaluations) and the second that of responding to an American surprise attack.

Overall it appears that the Soviet leadership was more practiced and perhaps more mentally prepared for an American nuclear attack, possibility as a result of the many years in which they had faced the fact of massive American nuclear superiority. In contrast, senior American civilian leadership may have understood the possibility of a Soviet surprise attack, but it seems never to have translated into an ongoing series of practical preparations. There was very limited training or briefing and very few exercises; the exercises that we know of were also quite limited. Without realistic exercises, and with the history of American superiority, the possibility of actual nuclear combat seems simply not to have been felt at a "gut level" by the individuals in top American leadership positions—it was just not personal enough. With limited exceptions, there was no true "ownership." In consequence, responding to a "bolt out of the blue" attack—as compared to dealing with ongoing domestic and international political challenges—was simply not a priority in the daily affairs of America's senior leadership.

Having said that, something extremely personal does appear to have happened with at least two of America's leaders. President Kennedy's personal involvement in the Cuban Missile Crisis has been previously discussed, as have his efforts to step back from atomic warfare and his moves toward tighter national command authority and the creation of a much more flexible SIOP. The second president to become personally and emotionally involved with atomic warfare was Ronald Reagan.

In 1982, following Reagan's recovery, his national security advisor Richard Allen resigned his position. Reagan turned to a longtime friend, William Clarke, to replace him. Clarke had no military experience and little international experience other than having served for a short time in 1981 as deputy secretary of state. However, he was a trusted Reagan friend, and in turn, he brought Thomas Reed to assist him in his new position. Reed had personal experience in nuclear weapons design and extensive experience in telecommunications, having worked at the Pentagon in modernizing nuclear command-and-control networks. He had served as secretary of the Air Force under President Gerald Ford and was extremely knowledgeable of the worldwide military communications system. David Hoffman, in his book *The Dead Hand*, details Reed's work and his involvement of President Reagan in what may have been a seminal event in Reagan's eventual decision to personally approach the Soviets in a push toward nuclear disarmament.

Reed quickly determined that the entire situation of command and control at the White House was, in simple terms, a mess. While President Carter had issued a directive calling for a steering committee and upgrades to communications, the military had been less than enthusiastic and nothing had come of the directive. According to Reed, "The system as I found it would have been headless within minutes of attack."[17] Reed began an urgent push to restore the system to some level of functionality and in the interim learned that a major military exercise was being planned for the National Military Command Center at the Pentagon. He decided it would be an excellent opportunity to get the president involved and managed to get the time to hold a briefing for Reagan and a few White House staff members: addressing how information would come in during a crisis, how to communicate and what the evacuation procedures were. Apparently it was the first such briefing for the president, who had already been in office for a year at the time.[18]

When the military exercise ("Ivy League") was held in March 1982, the White House was involved, although Reagan did not participate as commander in chief. Apparently Reagan either did not want to telegraph his actual reaction during a crisis or perhaps was not yet comfortable with his knowledge of the protocols. The exercise proceeded under the assumed time frames and reportedly impacts began to show so quickly—including nuclear weapons on Washington, D.C.—that Reagan was told the president was acting in command on the Nightwatch aircraft. In something less than half an hour, the displays showed the United States as "a sea of red dots" from atomic explosions. Reed watched Reagan closely; he was apparently stunned by seeing the nation essentially destroyed in less than a single hour.

The Situation Room exercise was followed by an evening meeting with advisors and Pentagon personnel. Reagan was given a more detailed overview of the SIOP and his precise role. He was also given an extended verbal description of the effect of the planned strike on the Soviet Union. According to Reed, "The SIOP briefing was as scary as the earlier presentation of the Soviet attack. . . ." Reed was not done with the president; at a third meeting with only him and National Security Advisor Clark, he personally rehearsed Reagan on SIOP options and the use of his authentication code in issuing orders for nuclear weapons use. When the session was complete, Reed's take was that "in Reagan's mind it was not over at all . . . it was something that really had happened to him. It focused his mind on the need for protection against those red dots."[19]

Reagan's attention was also captured by an ultra-realistic TV movie portraying an atomic attack on America, aired in 1983. *The Day After* focused on the horrific human impact of an atomic strike on American missile sites in Kansas as well as an associated bombing of Kansas City. A copy of the movie was sent to the White House, and Reagan's personal diary described his watching the tape and feeling the power of the movie, which left him "depressed" and convinced to do everything possible to prevent a nuclear war.[20]

In many ways Reagan's reaction sounds quite similar to President Kennedy's reaction to the Cuban Missile Crisis. Kennedy was moved to push for controls over the use of nuclear weapons and toward improving Soviet relations; his death ended his efforts in that direction. Reagan, himself well aware of his own mortality, became the first American president to personally and effectively propose mutual nuclear disarmament to the Soviets. Although certain of Reagan's earliest remarks and policies had truly frightened the Soviets, the events of 1982–1984 convinced him that something had to be done, and in taking counsel he consulted with General Andrew Goodpaster, who had served as staff secretary and defense liaison officer to President Dwight Eisenhower.[21]

Goodpaster detailed Eisenhower's very personal approach to such challenges, combining strength tempered by civility. Based on such counsel, Reagan began to seek a personal dialog with the Soviet leadership. In 1986 Reagan met with Soviet premier Mikhail Gorbachev in Iceland.

Gorbachev had privately turned to Nikita Khrushchev for advice, apparently receiving remarks similar to those Eisenhower had given Reagan. The meeting prompted a dramatic breakthrough in the arms reductions talks that had been in process since 1980. The end result was the 1987 nuclear weapons treaty. That agreement abolished all short- and intermediate-range missiles—including cancellation of the Pershing II, a missile greatly feared by the Soviets as a weapon capable of preemptive strikes on their leadership and command-and-control networks.

The Reagan/Gorbachev dialogs opened the way for further dramatic reductions in nuclear weapons. In 1991 President George H.W. Bush and Gorbachev reached an agreement for unilateral elimination of several classes of both atomic weapons and delivery systems. Bush ordered the removal of all nuclear weapons from Navy ships (other than submarines) and the elimination of tactical nuclear weapons in Europe. At that point the U.S. Army was taken out of the nuclear warfare scenario and the role of the Navy sharply limited, focused on the strategic role of its submarine force.[22]

By the end of 1991, in December, ongoing internal challenges led to the dissolution of the Soviet Union. It was the end of the Communist Soviet state, the beginning of an era of independent republics and for many the perceived end of the Cold War. In September 1991 President Bush ordered SAC to shut down all alert forces; in June 1992 he ordered SAC dissolved. In 1992 SAC was replaced by a new unified command, the Unified Strategic Command (STRATCOM), which held strategic nuclear responsibilities with a much smaller bomber and missile force. By 2010 STRATCOM controlled a nuclear force of 96 long-range bombers and 450 Minuteman III ICBMs. It also had access to fighter bombers that were nuclear capable, although none were normally maintained in a state of nuclear readiness. As of 2013, the U.S. Navy operated 14 Ohio strategic nuclear submarines estimated to be capable of launching 1,152 independently targetable nuclear warheads.

Major changes in continental air defense had already been in progress since 1979. At that point the SAGE system had begun to transition to the Joint Surveillance System, supplemented by airborne warning and control (AWACS) radar aircraft. The transition was completed in

1983, assigning the major role of surveillance radar operation to the Federal Aviation Administration (FAA). Military radar sites were either shut down or handed over to the FAA, which provided radar tracking information to NORAD control centers.[23] Major FAA radar centers maintained ground-to-air communications capabilities for coordination with military aircraft operated under the direction of NORAD.

In 1993 the commander in chief of the North American Aerospace Command gave regional air defense commanders authority to set their own fighter alert readiness levels; previously all fighters had been operated at twenty-four-hour alert status. The 1990s would see the end of dedicated Air Force interceptor squadrons, and routine air defense tasking would be assigned to Air National Guard squadrons. Reportedly there was considerable thinking at senior staff levels that an air defense mission was no longer required.[24] A dramatic reduction in the actual number of strip alert fighters began, with more and more air defense activity being transferred to Air National Guard units. Regional commands began to be consolidated, and the DEW Line radar network was shut down.[25] There continued to be strong pressure to further reduce air defense, with opponents suggesting only four bases were really needed, one in each corner of the continental United States. NORAD pushed back, and the compromise was a seven-base network. In 1990 there had been 200 interceptors on alert across the continental United States; by 1997 the alert fighters had decreased to 175—by the fall of 2001 there were only 20 alert interceptors stationed across some ten bases in the United States and Canada.

In 2001 George W. Bush announced that the United States would unilaterally lower its strategic force to under 2,000 warheads during the following decade; Russian premier Vladimir Putin responded with a similar reduction in the Russian nuclear stockpile. Between them, the two Bush presidencies had cut the American nuclear stockpile of some 22,000 weapons existing in 1991 by more than 75%.[26] Beyond the warhead reductions, over the years the SAC bomber force had literally faded away; in 1967 SAC had 219 bombers and 928 ICBMs on alert. Ten years earlier there had been no missiles but 1,769 bombers. In 1968 SAC had removed the nuclear weapons from all its airborne alert bombers.

At almost the same time, a new generation of Soviet nuclear subma-rine missiles (SS-N-6) placed the entire network of SAC bases, as well as its ground-alert command posts and the Nightwatch aircraft under thir-teen minutes' time from launch to impact. Pragmatically the entire con-cept of fifteen minutes' response time to a nuclear surprise attack had become truly unrealistic. Yet the overall national command timeline of fifteen minutes to detect, analyze and order retaliation had remained in place. It was all an illusion; any true Soviet surprise attack would have started with a decapitation strike. Only the scenario of escalating to a controlled level of nuclear exchange held the potential for true national command involvement.

After extensive study, nuclear strategy analyst Bruce Blair conclud-ed that controlled American nuclear retaliation was possible only in the event that some level of warning had allowed the "generation" of SAC ground-alert aircraft in advance of an actual Soviet strike. If that control was going to be civilian, it was highly questionable if fifteen minutes' warning from BMEWS would have been enough. That may explain why most nuclear exchange scenarios operated under the as-sumption that they would only grow out of a series of engagements that moved from conventional combat to limited nuclear exchanges. With-out that assumption, it would have been all too obvious that National Command Authority would no longer exist to control the SIOP retalia-tion. This may have become obvious to Nixon in the exercise when he was told the "president" was commanding from aboard Nightwatch. Blair sums up the fundamental problem—refusing to face up to the real-ity of command and control in a surprise attack—in a concise critique:

> The United States embarked on a fixed course and too
> few paused to review what had come to pass. Analysts
> retreated into the abstract and mechanistic world . . .
> where capabilities turned on the size and technical
> composition of the respective weapons deployments,
> even though that same view of the world had created
> a policy that left glaring deficiencies in the means by
> which those weapons would be managed in wartime

. . . for the next 15 years analysts anchored themselves to the conception of the strategic problem that treated nuclear weapons as instruments of prewar and intra-war diplomacy, a means by which to influence the opponent's decisions and that, in effect, denied the possibility of an attacker striking an opponent's command system.[27]

The analysts and strategists of the 1970s and 1980s devoted themselves to the challenge of using nuclear weapons—in a state of weapons parity between East and West—for international diplomacy, working under the assumption that they could control their use even if diplomacy failed and combat began. In retrospect all their dialog appears to have been fundamentally unrealistic, conducted under the illusion that nuclear warfare was controllable in some fashion—even after the probable exchange of hundreds if not thousands of atomic warheads.

In reality, Defense Secretary Robert McNamara's eventual 1983 view was far more realistic: "Nuclear weapons serve no military purpose whatsoever. They are totally useless . . . except to deter one's opponent from using them."[28] In retrospect, McNamara's ultimate conclusion on the value—and limits—of nuclear deterrence appears quite accurate. It also mirrors the seemingly ironic but imminently realistic motto of the Strategic Air Command: "Peace is our Profession."

For a time in the 1990s it appeared that the nuclear threat was over and the Cold War a matter of history. For more than some fifty-plus years of highly armed confrontation, the nation had remained inviolate. Military deterrence and ultimately mutual assured destruction had worked. The temptation to engage in limited use of nuclear warfare had been avoided, and Americans had not been attacked. With the end of the Cold War, a new illusion briefly emerged: the illusion of true national security. During the following decade that illusion would slowly fade and then totally disappear. And for the first time in generations, major American cities, including the nation's capital, would suffer actual surprise attack.

Chapter 15

....

OUT OF THE SHADOWS

A new threat to America emerged toward the end of the Cold War. It came from a totally different type of enemy, not an enemy nation or bloc of nations but stateless individuals who simply considered themselves to be at war with the United States for a variety of reasons. The one commonality among them was that they began to target Americans, internationally and ultimately, within the United States itself. Classic intelligence practices, particularly human intelligence, demonstrated little success against attacks that came seemingly at random. The initial response to this new threat was to treat each individual attack as a crime, to be investigated by law enforcement agencies, in particular the Federal Bureau of Investigation, and prosecuted in American or foreign courts. That approach was fundamentally legal in nature and focused on prosecution rather than on interdiction—the initiative remained totally with those planning and carrying out the attacks.

The attacks themselves almost all involved individuals from either the Middle East or North Africa, carried out by individuals motivated by the Palestinian/Israeli conflict. Airline hijackings began as early as the 1960s; in 1969 a TWA flight out of Rome was seized and flown to Syria. The Palestine Liberation Organization (PLO) and its affiliates engaged in an ongoing series of aircraft and even ocean-liner seizures; the frequency of incidents escalated into the 1980s. American citizens were targeted for special attention, hostage-taking and in several instances outright murder. The attacks were directed toward "soft" targets, targets involving civilians and offering little to no risk of military opposition. The objective was intimidation, blackmail and the generation of raw fear. The motive in the attacks was clearly political, and those involved were affiliated with various organized groups. The attacks were publicly treated as crimes, the attackers individually charged, prosecuted and jailed simply as criminals, not dealt with as "combatants," even if they and their groups considered themselves to be at war.[1]

From the American legal perspective, domestic intelligence and criminal counterterror activities were conducted in accordance with the Foreign Intelligence Surveillance Act (FISA) of 1977. That legislation had been passed in reaction to congressional investigations of the domestic activities of both the CIA and FBI, in particular illegal activities that had been conducted against Americans involved in civil rights and anti–Vietnam War activities. The act did allow intelligence surveillance (electronic monitoring and physical searches) of foreign groups and individuals inside the United States, but ongoing monitoring required the issuance of an order from a special FISA national security court within seventy-two hours of the beginning of the activity. Additional rules and directives were implemented within the FBI, with oversight by the Justice Department. Those directives were aimed at separating intelligence collection from actual criminal investigations and created a "wall" that restricted automatic circulation of foreign intelligence data to the criminal sections of the Bureau. Those procedures, intended to protect the legal rights of American citizens, proved to be acceptable with regard to the standard intelligence activities of foreign nations but eventually proved to be administratively challenging when dealing with the emerging radical Islamic terror network, much of which successfully operated under the cover of tourism, education and training, embedded within established immigrant communities within the United States.

The challenges of a legal/criminal approach to international terrorism became increasingly apparent as early as 1985, with the seizure of an Italian cruise ship, the *Achille Lauro*. During the hijacking an elderly, wheelchair-bound American was brutally murdered. The terrorists eventually landed the ship in Egypt, surrendering with the promise of safe passage out of that country. President Ronald Reagan was incensed by the murder and the Egyptian bargain. He ordered American military aircraft to intercept the Egyptian aircraft carrying the terrorists out of Egypt to Tunisia. The airliner was forced to land at a NATO base in Italy, producing a tense confrontation with Italian authorities and ultimately the surrender of the terrorists to the Italians. The four men were convicted in Italian courts; three eventually fled when released on parole or furlough. One of them later became active in training insurgents in Iraq, while another was suspected of aiding associations with a terrorist network in Spain.

The Reagan administration certainly did recognize the growing threat of global terrorism, and the fact that no single U.S. intelligence group totally focused on it. Based on the recommendations of an intelligence panel, in 1986 the CIA established an integrated analysis and operations unit, the Counterterrorism Center (CTC). Its goal was to identity and track terrorists globally and potentially to interdict attacks through the use of covert operations. As might be expected in any organization, the agencies' existing geographic divisions and their regional field offices initially viewed the new group as a potential competitor.

The internal reaction to the emergence of the CTC was "grudging" at first, but over time its growing resources of both people and money gained it at least a certain level of acceptance in the field.[2] The somewhat restrained acceptance of the CIA's CTC group may also have been related to the appointment of Dewey Clarridge as its first chief. Clarridge had been involved in the Reagan-era Nicaraguan contra activities, famed for originating the proposal to mine Nicaraguan harbors. That operation created an international furor that ended with the CIA's being ordered out of contra "lethal" activities by Congress. Despite that fiasco, President Reagan and CIA director William Casey reportedly admired Clarridge's aggressive style and felt it would be good for counterterrorism operations.

One of Clarridge's first personal initiatives was to pursue the establishment of special clandestine action teams, using foreign nationals, primarily Middle Eastern contract employees. Years of Palestinian terror attacks had created a core of potential recruits, especially in Lebanon and Israel. The teams were to be used for covert protection for the CIA's own clandestine officers operating in the Middle East. Beyond that a secondary duty was to have been totally deniable rendition of terror suspects. It would have been the first practice of the forced apprehension of suspects and their extrajudicial transfer to secret locations for intense interrogation. In concept it was a precursor to actual practices that would begin under the Clinton administration and dramatically accelerate under George W. Bush, following the attacks of 9/11. However, in 1986, Clarridge's concept of such a deniable action group worried a number of his fellow officers: "What? We're going to arm some foreigners, with their own hates and axes to grind, and send them to kidnap people they are hostile to, in a foreign country, beyond the control of any CIA officer?!"[3]

From a 1980s intelligence standpoint, matters were further complicated because certain nations engaged in and essentially subcontracted terror attacks based on their own regional political agendas. Libya, under Mu'ammar Gaddhafi's rule, became well known for support of Palestinian groups, in some instances using their activities as cover for terrorist acts by his own agents. Those activities, added to his own military incursions in neighboring nations such as Chad, ultimately led President Reagan to a direct military action against Libya in 1986. Air strikes against Libya were ostensibly intended to reduce Gaddhafi's ability to support terrorists but more specifically to personally intimidate Gaddhafi. The American attack appears to have had no permanent effect. Gaddhafi was later shown to have orchestrated further terror operations, including airline hijackings and the bombing of Pan American Flight 103 in December 1988. That aerial explosion killed 250 people aboard the aircraft. Attacks focused on commercial aircraft continued to be a common terrorist tactic. American intelligence continued to have considerable difficulty in establishing patterns in the terror attacks or in developing solid threat indicators for what appeared to be intermittent and seemingly random attacks.

In the early 1990s the CIA began to develop a variety of leads to what appeared to be a new type of non-state threat, based not only in the Palestinian conflict but expanding to include radical Islamic opposition to the presence of Western influence in the Arabian Gulf nations. The first solid indication that the radical Islamic threat was associated with an actual organization, one with international reach, was noted in the appearance of highly organized, trained and well-funded Arab units in the Bosnian fighting. The Arab fighters were veterans of the battles against the Soviets in Afghanistan, and their funding was eventually tracked to the Sudan, specifically to a series of charitable and veteran support organizations financed by conservative Saudis, the most visible being Osama bin Laden.[4]

As the 1990s progressed, American intelligence began dealing with an increasing number of terrorist attacks around the globe, including the first domestic attacks in the United States. Their problem was that it all appeared to be a "hodgepodge": During 1993, a Palestinian-Kuwaiti man organized a bombing attack on the World Trade Center; an apparent "lone wolf" from Baluchistan carried out an attack at CIA headquarters in Virginia; and an Egyptian cleric attempted to pull together a plot to bomb major landmarks in New York City, including the Lincoln Tunnel, the Holland Tunnel, the George Washington Bridge and an FBI office. But no organization or group had claimed credit for any attack or issued any threats to the United States.[5] At that point, the realization that many of the individuals were networking in their war against a common enemy—America—had not taken hold within the American law enforcement and intelligence communities. The existence of such a social and financial network began to emerge during the follow-up investigations to the World Trade Center bombing.

The mastermind of that attack, Khalid Sheikh Mohammed, had been educated in America, graduating with an engineering degree. Following graduation, he had not returned to his home in Kuwait, instead traveling to be with his brother in Pakistan. His brother Zahid had been doing charity work in Pakistan, raising money for causes ranging from mujahedeen arms purchases for the fight in Afghanistan to child welfare. In his work, he had become close to Abdullah Yusuf Azzam, a Palestinian refugee from the Israeli occupation of the West Bank in 1967. Formerly a PLO member, Azzam was a graduate in Islamic law and a longtime voice for jihad against Israel and its sponsor, the United States. Prior to moving to Pakistan, Azzam had held a teaching position in Saudi Arabia, becoming close to many Saudi officials and having Osama bin Laden as one of his students.[6]

As the fighting against the Soviets progressed, Azzam became even more personally involved, moving to the Pakistan–Afghanistan border and setting up the Office of Services, a clearinghouse for supporting Arab volunteers joining the fight in Afghanistan. His former student, bin Laden, followed him, bringing funding and a personal commitment to the Afghan crusade. Zahid, Azzam and bin Laden bonded during the Afghan jihad, and during 1988 a fourth individual entered their circle.

Khalid Sheikh Mohammed's nephew, Ramzi Yousef, flew to Pakistan during a summer break from electrical engineering at a university in Wales; while studying in Wales he had joined the Muslim Brotherhood. After graduation he returned to Pakistan, serving as a trainer for the mujahedeen. The four men had many things in common, but first among them was a fundamental religious belief in a call to war against Israel and the United States. That call was expressed succinctly by Ramzi Yousef: "All Muslims have a right to regard themselves in a state of war with the United States."[7]

It was and remains difficult for most Americans to comprehend that such individuals do not consider themselves to be terrorists: "We are not terrorists, we are jihadists and jihad is not terrorism."[8] The jihadi movement is one of individuals, individuals involved in extremely violent and brutal warfare but not the sort of warfare the nation had ever previously known. Both American intelligence and political leaders initially had considerable difficulty differentiating jihadi warfare from the Palestinian terror attacks of the previous two decades—or fully appreciating its dramatically expanded scope of operations.

The 1993 attack on the World Trade Center in New York provides an illustration of the global reach of the new anti-American terrorism and considerable insight into its mode of operations. The attack came to involve a number of disparate individuals, reflecting the extreme intelligence challenge such "networked" operations present. In September 1992, Ramzi Yousef flew Pakistani International Airlines out of

Peshawar, Pakistan, and deplaned in New York City.[9] He had no visa but claimed asylum; upon release by immigration he proceeded into the city and contacted Mahmud Abouhalima, a graduate of one of the mujahedeen training camps funded by Osama bin Laden. Abouhalima himself was already connected into a local and militant anti-Jewish network whose members had targeted the Jewish Defense League in attacks. Its leading figure, a radical cleric named Omar Abdel Rahman, had escaped house arrest in Egypt, charged with organizing an Islamist insurgency group in that country.

Rahman, known as "the blind sheikh," had made several visits to New York City following his escape from Egypt, becoming involved with a mosque that had been active in recruiting, processing and sending off recruits to Pakistan—for training as mujahedeen in the Afghan war against the Soviets. He obtained a visa for temporary residence in the United States and, with the unsolved murder of the mosque's leader, effectively took control of the center. One of his followers was charged with the murder of a Jewish Defense League figure in 1990. Apparently as a consequence, Rahman's visa was revoked, but he was neither charged with any crime nor deported. Under Rahman's control, members of the mosque became increasingly militant and began to prepare plans to conduct bombing attacks against Jewish sites in New York. The activities of radicals in the mosque had come to the attention of the FBI, who successfully infiltrated it both before and after the bombing. For reasons never fully explained, the FBI's informant inside the group was terminated a few months before the World Trade Center plot came into being, leaving the FBI with no intelligence during the period in which Rahman arrived and began networking with the group.

Following his arrival in New York City and contact with Rahman, Yousef persuaded the group to join in his own American mission, a mission developed by him and his uncle/mentor in Pakistan, Khalid Sheikh Mohammed. Yousef organized members of the mosque and others into a self-proclaimed Liberation (Palestine) Army.[10] During the next six months, the group—most likely using money supplied by Yousef through the jihadi funding channels in Pakistan—acquired some 1,200 pounds of explosive materials and timer fuses. When preparations were completed he procured a Ryder rental van; a bomb was assembled in the van and driven into the World Trade Center underground parking garage. The timer fuses successfully detonated the explosives, leaving six people dead, more than a thousand injured and significant damage to several lower floors and the underground parking area—but the towers did not fall. Yousef was shortly on his way back to the western border region of Pakistan via Pakistani International Airlines and a transfer through Karachi.

Follow-on investigation and reports on the first attack on the World Trade Center allow us to identify several operational elements that became standard practice in future radical jihadist terror attacks. First, Yousef used a variety of aliases both before and after the attack. He and another participant traveled separately from Pakistan, using forged and altered passports. Yousef's partner, Ahmad Ajaj, used an altered passport, which raised suspicions and upon examination bomb-making instructions and other material in his baggage, and he was arrested. Yousef himself claimed political asylum, was given a hearing date and was allowed to enter the United States. He successfully "played" the immigration system in a manner so as to allow himself to essentially disappear inside the country.[11] While in the United States Yousef made telephone calls to Khalid Sheikh Mohammed in Pakistan, receiving advice and directions. He was also sent a $660 wire transfer. However, at that point, American intelligence agencies were not at all attuned to either the social or financial networks that were evolving to support the expanding jihadi network. Eventually the transfer of even minor amounts of money would be seen as a key indicator in defining such networks, and the movements of known members became key to early detection of terror operations. Unfortunately, it would take years and the events of 2000 and 2001 to fully instill the importance of such intelligence indicators.

Initially, the CIA and FBI investigations of the 1993 World Trade Center attack concluded that the bombing had largely been a matter of circumstance, of participants simply meeting through coincidence and coming up with an attack plan. That assessment failed to consider the seminal impact of the Afghan jihad on global terrorism. In Afghanistan, and across the border in Pakistan, a decade-long struggle against the Soviets had produced a network of organizers and fighters, loosely coupled by both mutual goals and by their experiences with an extensive system of training centers, logistics specialists and layered financial resources. That social network was reaching out to any Muslim who viewed Israel—and by extension America—to be his or her enemy.

As of 1994, the extent to which official and private financing of the jihad in Afghanistan had created a deeply layered global logistics and financial network was seriously unappreciated. Later investigations would reveal that money passed for charitable causes could easily be filtered through many hands, without the donors themselves being aware of its ultimate destination or use. In some cases it was easy for radicals to infiltrate established charities; in other instances new "non-governmental organizations" could be created. In yet other instances it was simply enough to send fighters posing as students or even tourists and allow them to solicit fellow Muslims or countrymen for aid in housing, transportation or even the loan of laptop computers or cell phones. Over the better part of a decade, the radical jihadi network expanded throughout southwest Asia, across the Arabian Peninsula, stretched through North Africa and moved across the Western Pacific to North America. In its own way it was comparable and perhaps even more resistant to intelligence penetration than many of the best covert networks created by the Central Intelligence Agency during the Cold War.

Counterterrorism specialist Richard Clarke—head of the Clinton Administration National Security Council's Counterterrorism Security Group (CSG)—described the frustrations with truly understanding terrorist financing. Early on in its mission the CSG concluded that the FBI could not tell them anything about al-Qaeda they couldn't read in a newspaper and that "there are only a handful of guys at the CIA who know anything about how bad guys move money around the world—and none of them are part of the [CIA] Counterterrorism Center."[12] It did not take long for Clarke's group to conclude that it was not bin Laden's personal fortune that was the driving force behind the extended jihadi social network but rather "a vast, global fundraising machine," with both legal and illegal elements but with the most important source being "continuous fundraising efforts through Islamic charities and nongovernmental organizations [NGOs]."[13] One of the key elements was an ancient South Asian *hawala* "money exchange" system that used small business offices around the world to transfer money with virtually no paper trail.[14] The source of much of the money being floated to the al-Qaeda network was soon found to be religious donors in Saudi Arabia, using nongovernmental entities that were largely ignored and unpoliced by the Saudi government. Extended diplomatic entreaties to the Saudis produced promises of information and support but ultimately little practical assistance.[15]

The intelligence problem of operating against such a diffuse and evolving terror network, one that generated attacks seemingly at random, was a very fundamental one. Both strategic and tactical intelligence rely on the collection and analysis of "indications." It was one thing to identify bin Laden and his al-Qaeda organization ("the base" in Arabic) as a source/enabler of terror attacks. But to a large extent the technical and human resources that had been developed to support threat detection during the Cold War simply were not applicable against a threat that was fueled by decades of militant Palestinian struggle against Israel, combined with a new jihadi religious fervor of bin Laden's recruits. The jihadi political/religious complex was a totally new type of intelligence target; it was a loosely networked group of individuals, from a broad range of countries and backgrounds. They maintained no fixed bases of support, no standing military, no communications or transportation infrastructure and few visible assets of any sort. Instead they used purely public means of communications—satellite phones, cell phones, public phones and a variety of electronic meeting places and email contacts via the Internet.

The Islamic radicals used commercial transportation, bought their supplies where they were to be used and relied on a sophisticated financial and funding system as well as the even easier option of simply accessing aid from a variety of charitable and support organizations—ranging from support groups for mujahedeen to Saudi international charitable organizations.[16] As to the fighters themselves, they were continuously mobile, becoming visible only during the attacks themselves.

They operated from Pakistan to the Sudan, from Afghanistan down across the horn of Africa and into the east African nations. They ranged from the nations of North Africa across the Pacific to the islands of Malaysia and into the Philippines. This was a region largely ignored during the Cold War, one covered by minimal American technical intelligence assets and even less in the way of human intelligence resources.

As we noted early on, anticipating surprise attacks requires characterizing the target's normal state of readiness/military activity so that any variations can be noted and evaluated as indications of either an emerging threat—or an attack in progress. Strategic indicators are steps that the potential attacker must take "in preparation for hostilities."[17] In contrast, a tactical "indicator" is one that shows the enemy actually in motion toward a target. America had assembled immense Cold War detection networks to deliver tactical warnings, including belts of radar stations to scan for bombers and over-the-horizon radars and satellites to monitor missiles launches from deep inside Russia or from submarines. It had sophisticated high-altitude photographic aircraft and extensive networks for signals collection and sophisticated code breaking. U.S. Navy submarines had tapped underwater Soviet command-and-control cable systems, and signals-snooping satellites in low orbits could pick up even the most routine military communications. It had taken decades to put those extensive technical assets in place; few would initially be of any value against the emerging terror threats.

Of course efforts were made to use the very high-tech Cold War assets; several were directed specifically against bin Laden. Following his relocation to Afghanistan in 1996, advanced imaging satellites ("Crystal"), with mirrors similar to those of the Hubble Space Telescope, were focused on bin Laden's camp at Tarnak Farm in Afghanistan. NSA could "virtually walk the streets" in the camp, and it was hoped that detailed digital mapping would enable a kidnap mission by the CIA's limited Afghan indigenous assets.[18] But the photography was not quite good enough to reveal bin Laden himself, to confirm his absolute identity and location, and given his frequent movements, no operation ever came to fruition. It was the same at other locations: The CIA could obtain some level of tracking but never enough to ensure a kidnap effort or a cruise missile strike. Worse yet, the satellite photographs often showed bin Laden in the immediate vicinity of numerous women and children, or in buildings adjacent to hospitals or other similar sensitive facilities. Ultimately advanced technology would prove of value in the campaign against bin Laden and al-Qaeda, but it took time and much patience before technology became effectively integrated into new counterterror initiatives.

Following the World Trade Center attack of 1993, the individuals who had inspired and organized the bombing continued to operate effectively in the shadows of the new radical network for the remainder of the decade. Khalid Sheikh Mohammed and Ramzi Yousef both relocated from Pakistan to the Philippines in 1994. Their appearance in the Philippines was far from coincidental. In the late 1980s, bin Laden's brother-in-law Mohammed Khalifa had moved to the Philippines, setting up a series of financial fronts to be used by al-Qaeda. Khalifa had a long history with the Muslim Brotherhood in Lebanon and Pakistan; he had recruited mujahedeen for the war in Afghanistan. Upon arriving in the Philippines he set up some dozen businesses and charities, including the Islamic Wisdom Worldwide Mission (eventually identified as a channel for bin Laden money) and the International Relations and Information Center (the main money channel for a major new terror operation developed in the Philippines). Khalifa also became the first head of the Philippine branch of the International Islamic Relief Organization, ultimately designated by the United States as a terrorism funding channel in 2006.[19]

Khalid Mohammed had first traveled to the Philippines in 1991, to assist in training of militants as well as working with bin Laden's brother-in-law in laying the groundwork for networking with radical Muslim groups in both the Philippines and Malaysia.[20] When Mohammed traveled to the Philippines with Yousef in 1994, their immediate work involved assisting a group of Afghan veterans who had formed a group named Abu Sayyaf. Its goal was establishing an independent Muslim nation in the southern part of the Philippines. The two World Trade Center bombing organizers taught bomb-making classes for the local militants and were joined by Abdul Murad, a childhood friend of

Yousef's from Kuwait. While Yousef had been in Wales studying electrical engineering, Murad had been in the United States attending pilot training in Texas, upstate New York and North Carolina.

Murad received his commercial pilot's license in June 1992.[21] He joined Mohammed and Yousef in the Philippines, and the three men began to plan a sophisticated terror attack that was to have a global impact. Its goal was to simultaneously blow up a large number of airliners flying across the Pacific to destinations in the United States—the plot's codename was Bojinka. To accomplish their goal the men developed a sophisticated chemical bomb and tested it by planting it onboard an airliner bound for Tokyo. The bomb worked perfectly, killing one passenger, injuring ten others and blowing a hole in the aircraft. Despite seriously crippled steering systems, the plane managed to make an emergency landing.[22]

By early January 1995, the men had recruited local volunteers and were building bombs for a multi-airliner attack, scheduled toward the end of the month. The airliner bomb plot was intended to kill more than three thousand people. Yet the arrival of the plan's organizers and the emergence of a militant Muslim insurgency had not escaped the notice of Philippine intelligence and security services. Physical surveillance and telephone wiretaps began to reveal connections between the new arrivals and local insurgents. Ultimately a fire in Yousef's apartment resulted in a thorough property search, which revealed elements of the Bojinka plot. Differing reports describe the fire as either a result of the bomb preparation work or a police provocation allowing access to the building. As a result, Murad was captured and intensely interrogated, and word of the plan was communicated to the United States.

Among others, Richard Clarke received a message that police in the Philippines had taken New York bomber Ramzi Yousef into custody. They had immediately learned of the Bojinka plot and began a frantic effort to locate and recall the targeted aircraft. Some bombs were recovered on the ground, but some of the flights were still in the air on intermediate legs of their journey to the U.S. Clarke immediately contacted the FAA with a request to land the targeted aircraft but was told only the secretary of transportation could issue such an order. Clarke's next call was to National Security Advisor Tony Lake, who brought in White House Chief of Staff Frederico Peña. Peña acted immediately, saying, "If the Secretary has the authority, the President does too. Tell the airlines to ground them by order of the President."[23] Flights were turned around and landed, interim searches were made, and beginning the next day no passenger could carry a bottle of fluid on board—Yousef's group had concocted special fluid bombs, easily disguised as water, perfume or other liquids. Surprisingly the entire Bojinka incident, although well publicized in the American media—including Yousef's later remarks about flying planes into buildings—appears not to have made an impact on FAA airline security practices.

Philippine investigators reported that under interrogation Murad had described a second phase to the plot, including crashing hijacked airliners into major American targets including CIA headquarters.[24] Philippine security personnel later claimed that full information on the second phase of the plot was shared with the FBI, but no solid confirmation of that has been found in released documents or subsequent official investigations. Still, any intelligence group following the Bojinka plot in the news should have noted a new, highly significant "indicator"—Arab students attending U.S. flight schools, in particular students with questionable credentials or connections to suspected radical figures or organizations. As we will see in examining the attacks of 9/11, certain FBI agents and field officers clearly did understand the possible risks of foreign students' taking flight training in the U.S., especially those with suspicious histories or social connections. Yet due to administrative sensitivity to legal constraints, including fears of complaints over discrimination and "profiling," field office concerns achieved little or no traction at FBI headquarters prior to 9/11.

Yousef managed to escape the Philippines and returned to Pakistan; he was arrested there within months and taken to the United States for prosecution in the World Trade Center bombing. His uncle Khalid Sheikh Mohammed was more successful in his escape. Khalid Sheikh used numerous aliases, finally traveling to Qatar, where he was shielded by influential supporters including the interior minister, a member of the royal family. When Qatar came under pressure for his extradition in the bombing

plot, Mohammed once again managed to successfully flee, ultimately joining Osama bin Laden, who had relocated to Afghanistan in 1996. While
Sheikh himself was far from being a devout Muslim, his hatred for Israel
and America bonded him to bin Laden's radical jihadi agenda.

Despite speculation about an al-Qaeda network connection to the
Philippines and the Bojinka plot, the realization that bin Laden intended
to use al-Qaeda for militant attacks on a global scale was still not fully
appreciated—until his highly public declarations of war. In August 1996
bin Laden issued a personal thirty-page "Declaration of War against the
Americans Occupying the Land of the Two Holy Places." It was a call for
all Muslims to destroy Americans as their common enemy, "using fast-
moving forces that work under complete secrecy."[25] Bin Laden's declaration appears to have been fueled by the first Israeli air and artillery attacks
on Lebanon and its capital Beirut in some fourteen years. Beginning in
April of 1996 a major Israeli military operation designated "Grapes of
Wrath" was conducted in Lebanon. In an effort to stop terrorist shell-
ing of its northern border region, Israel flew more than 1,100 air strikes
and conducted a massive artillery bombardment over a sixteen-day period. During the artillery strikes, shells hit a United Nations compound in
Qana, Lebanon, killing 800 civilians and injuring another 116.

The 1996 bin Laden pronouncement initially seemed to focus the
potential threat on American facilities and Americans working in the
Arabian Gulf region. Bin Laden's personal fatwa (religious ruling) escalated the covert American intelligence effort against him, an effort
that had begun in the earliest years of the Clinton administration. In an
immediate response and with presidential authorization, CIA director
George Tenet directed the establishment of specialized sections within
the CIA's Counterterrorism Center. One of those groups, designated the
Alec Station, began its work with studies of the financial and charitable
networks that were being leveraged by Islamic militants of all stripes.
However, Alec Station soon became almost totally focused and, according to some, "obsessed" with Osama bin Laden. In addition to Alec
Station, another and much smaller CTC group focused on Islamic extremists. Such separation was deemed useful at the time but ultimately
resulted in compartmentalized information and a lack of vision of the

overall terror threat. As an example, Khalid Sheikh Mohammed (KSM) was handled in the Islamic Extremism unit, and according to the CIA it did not actually connect Khalid Sheikh's terror activities to the al-Qaeda network or to bin Laden until after the attacks of September 11, 2001.

To some extent a similar bin Laden obsession can be seen in the overall Clinton administration approach to radical Islamic terrorism. President Clinton pursued a covert strategy for combating al-Qaeda, but efforts became largely focused personally on bin Laden. Originally the perception was that al-Qaeda was essentially a regional threat, an enabler for militant Sunni Islamists seeking to replace existing Arabic regimes with conservative religious governments implementing strict Sharia law. At the time that seemed a reasonable view; initially bin Laden himself had made no threats against the United States or even against Americans overseas. He was extremely vocal in opposing the Western military presence in Saudi Arabia during the first Gulf War against Iraq; however, his protests were made directly to the Saudi rulers. His focus certainly seemed to be on the religious and political dynamics in the Arab states themselves, so much so that he was essentially displaced from Saudi Arabia in 1991—first to the Sudan, then later to Afghanistan by 1996. Due to the nature of al-Qaeda and the religious bonding of its followers, it proved virtually impossible to obtain human intelligence on its members, their activities, movements and plans. Initially so little was understood about the internal social networking of al-Qaeda that the World Trade Center bombing investigations totally failed to establish links between those involved, nor was any association identified between Khalid Sheikh Mohammed and either bin Laden or al-Qaeda.[26]

There is no doubt that counterterrorism became a major ongoing national priority during the Clinton administration. In February 1997, guidelines for the use of military force in a variety of situations, including military support for civilian authority within the United States, were established within the Department of Defense. Section 4.7.5 of DOD Directive 3025 specifically established rules of force related to the use of the American military against terrorism and specified that only the president can direct and authorize such action in regard to domestic terrorism. It also specifies concurrence of the secretary of defense and the secretary is required to approve any military action that may involve the use of lethal force. In general terms the legislation was an extension of the long-standing nuclear National Command Authority to military action against terrorism. Limitation of authority to the president and secretary of defense was consistent with the approval for SIOP execution during the Cold War.[27]

The Clinton administration further accelerated its terrorist focus during 1997, supporting increased activities and spending by both the CIA and NSC counterterror groups. At the level of National Security Council, the counterterror effort was largely driven by Richard Clarke, appointed chairman of the NSC's Counterterrorism Security Group. The CSG and Alec Station's efforts against bin Laden in Afghanistan have been widely documented and are beyond our focus here; readers are referred to Clarke's own book *Against All Enemies: Inside America's War on Terror* as well as Henry Crumpton's book *The Art of Intelligence: Lessons from a Life in the CIA's Clandestine Service*. Crumpton describes the CIA's efforts, both in the agencies' Counterterrorism Center and field operations against bin Laden inside Afghanistan.

From 1996 to early 1998, bin Laden maintained an exceptionally low profile, operating under Taliban protection in Afghanistan and establishing a courier-based communications network with fellow Muslim radicals and insurgents from Egypt to Kashmir in the north of India and on to Bangladesh to the northeast of India. In February 1998 a group of militant Islamists including radical figures from Egypt, Pakistan and Bangladesh joined bin Laden in a call for Muslims everywhere to attack America as the sponsor of the Jewish state of Israel. The call was in the form of a religious ruling calling for war against the United States. It concluded with instructions to Muslims everywhere to carry out attacks against America on a global basis: "The ruling to kill the Americans and their allies—civilians and military—is an individual duty for every Muslim who can do it in any country in which it is possible to do it. . . . [E]very Muslim who believes in God and wishes to be rewarded to comply with God's order to kill the Americans and plunder their money wherever and whenever they find it."[28]

The American response to what was clearly a far-ranging declaration of jihadi religious war focused largely on continuing the covert effort targeting bin Laden as an individual. The intelligence services were still wrestling with understanding the financial network supporting al-Qaeda and trying to obtain some geographic fix on its operations. President Clinton's 1998 "capture or kill order" on bin Laden was largely neutralized by the difficulties of operating in a hostile and denied area such as Afghanistan.

In retrospect what can only be called a CIA/Alec Station operations' fixation on bin Laden consumed energies and time that might better have been directed against the broader radical terror threat. Defining that threat, even building a minimal picture of the radical network, was proving immensely challenging. There was, however, at least one known window of opportunity. When bin Laden moved to the remote mountains of Afghanistan in 1996, one of his advisors in London had recommended a satellite phone as a solution to his isolation; the phone had been obtained using a University of Missouri student as an unknowing cut-out. The number of the phone turned up in notes and materials seized from militants in Egypt and Kenya, allowing the NSA to monitor bin Laden's satellite phone calls for the better part of two years.[29]

Reportedly nothing in the calls themselves revealed any specific plans or plots; it appeared that bin Laden was serving as an instigator and enabler rather than a tactical coordinator. That function was being left to his associates, many of whom were very "loosely coupled" to bin Laden through shared experiences in the mujahedeen campaign against the Soviets in Afghanistan. In turn, they were recruiting fighters from the global Muslim community ranging from North Africa across the Middle East and on to the Western Pacific.

The details of the NSA signals tracing on bin Laden's satellite phone are and will remain secret for decades; however, we do know of one particular number that did emerge from the calls—that of a residence in Yemen, associated with a former Afghan volunteer named Ahmed al-Hada. His efforts in fighting against the anti-Taliban Northern Alliance outside Kabul, Afghanistan, in 1996 had earned him considerable respect among the mujahedeen fighters and in various camps being sponsored by bin Laden. Apparently the respect extended to bin Laden himself. Upon his return to Yemen, al-Hada received an ongoing series of calls from bin Laden's satellite phone.

His residence became identified as a hub for message-passing to a variety of individuals who would come to participate in future terror plots and attacks. A great deal has been written about the "hub" in Yemen and the NSA's monitoring of calls to and from the residence. It is clear that the NSA collected information on the calls, sharing raw data and even transcripts over some periods of time and withholding details during others. Exactly how the NSA technically monitored the calls is murky, and there is some chance that much of the data may actually have been provided to the NSA through a sharing operation with British intelligence.

Recent leaks from former NSA employee Edward Snowden describe signals intelligence from a British base designated the "Overseas Processing Center," located on the northern coast of Oman. Reportedly the base has access to undersea communications cables passing through the Strait of Hormuz, into the Persian Gulf. Sites in Oman also conducted monitoring on radio and satellite communications into Yemen.[30] It is unknown how long the cable access has been in place, but certainly any sharing arrangement would explain a good deal about why the NSA initially appeared to be extremely protective—with both the CIA and FBI—concerning raw information from the "Yemen hub."

The actual transcripts of calls through the Yemen hub proved of limited use in providing operational intelligence, since the callers used a simple conversational code in their dialog. It was the telephone numbers themselves that proved especially valuable, allowing intelligence officers to build up a pattern of calls that could be used as a baseline for spotting new movements and potential developing plots. Still, that sort of collections and analysis process takes time, and al-Qaeda's first strike came within months of bin Laden's 1998 declaration of war.

In early August, 1998 truck bombs were used against American embassies in Nairobi, Kenya, and Dar es Salaam, Tanzania, in East Africa. In Nairobi, 200 people were killed and more than 4,000 injured. In Tanzania, 11 people were killed and 85 injured. Twelve

Americans were killed in the two bombings. The attackers included a Palestinian, a Yemeni, and men from East Africa, the Middle East, South Asia and even an individual from Comoros, a tiny island nation in the Indian Ocean. It was becoming obvious that the radical Islamic network and al-Qaeda recruiters could reach into any number of mosques, Arab student group gatherings or Afghan veteran networks around the globe.

Following the post-attack investigations it would be learned that Mohamed al-Owhali, a Saudi veteran of the Kabul fighting in Afghanistan and personal friend of al-Hada, had been recruited for the embassy attack in Kenya, traveled through Yemen and made at least one call back to his parents in Saudi Arabia. Following his stay with al-Hada in Yemen, he returned to Pakistan to make a martyrdom video and then traveled to Kenya to assist in preparation of the truck bomb to be used in the attack. He was a nervous terrorist, calling back from Kenya to Yemen at least three times, possibly for nothing more than reassurance from his friend al-Hada.

The expectation was that al-Owhali would be killed during the embassy attack, but he survived—with no arrangements to get out of the country. He made three calls back to Yemen in the following two days, and the NSA also tracked three calls from bin Laden's satellite phone into Yemen following the bombings. Bin Laden stopped using his satellite phone not long after that, but the calls became key evidence in tying the bombings to al-Qaeda and bin Laden. The NSA continued tracing calls through the Yemen hub, with one exception: Due to legal ramifications of the Foreign Intelligence Surveillance Act, the NSA was not tracing calls between the hub and the United States.

The NSA's decision reflected the legal concerns mentioned earlier and was consistent with the "wall" that had been put in place within the intelligence communities, separating general intelligence collection from intelligence developed for specific crimes being investigated and prosecuted by the Department of Justice and the FBI. Prior to the attacks on America in 2001, there was an overriding legal concern for the privacy of American citizens and the agencies involved in both domestic and foreign work. Both the NSA and FBI tended to be very cautious in their collections activities. That level of caution was perhaps most visible within the FBI. CIA clandestine officer Henry Crumpton witnessed it first hand and provides key insights. Crumpton was assigned as a CIA counterterrorism liaison to the FBI's office of International Terrorism Operations in the weeks following the embassy bombings in Africa.

Crumpton was immediately struck by the huge number of resources the Bureau assigned to the embassy bombing investigations. He was also struck by the fact that the FBI's work was totally focused on law enforcement; there was little to no evidence of any "forward-looking" intelligence collection or analysis. In fact, he noted that the FBI personnel simply could not understand why there was a legitimate need to share FBI-developed intelligence with other agencies; "sharing evidence as intelligence was anathema to them."[31]

Crumpton observed that the FBI field office in New York would not even share information with FBI headquarters, in order to ensure a successful prosecution within their own Department of Justice district. The bottom line was that a "deep systemic constraint" existed within the Bureau; evidence was not to be "tainted" by sharing it with anyone other than the Justice Department prosecutor's office handling a case.[32] And as we will find, the reverse view held as well: Intelligence that could not be tied to an actionable crime was held on the other side of the "wall," where there were far fewer resources and deep concerns about jeopardizing future investigations with speculative information. All of this speaks well to the Bureau's ability to respond but less to a reliance on it for defense against potential attacks.

Following the prompt and extensive FBI criminal investigation of the embassy bombings, the National Security Council informed President Clinton that the attacks had definitely been carried out by al-Qaeda–affiliated fighters, and the principals of the NSC were adamant that al-Qaeda must be attacked and destroyed. President Clinton directed a series of immediate overt and covert actions; his order was to "get rid of them once and for all."[33] However, President Clinton did not ask Congress for a declaration of war against al-Qaeda, nor did Congress proceed with such a declaration at its own initiative, that being a constitutional responsibility of Congress.

Instead, the National Security Council and the president took direct—albeit limited—military action and increased covert efforts in response to the embassy attacks.[34] From a historical perspective, military retaliation by the commander in chief had a long-standing precedent. During the late 1700s, several European nations as well as America experienced ongoing seizure of their commercial vessels by a variety of pirates operating out of ports in North Africa. When protests were registered, the response was unabashed and unambiguous. In March 1785, Thomas Jefferson and John Adams were bluntly told that the justification for the seizure of ships and enslavement of crews and passengers was a fundamentally religious act, albeit an extremely profitable one. Tripoli's ambassador to London told Jefferson that "it was written in the Koran, that all Nations who should not have acknowledged their authority were sinners, that it was their right and duty to make war upon whoever they could find and to make Slaves of all they could take as prisoners, and that every Mussulmen [Muslim] who should be slain in battle was sure to go to Paradise."[35]

President Jefferson, facing ongoing Barbary Coast piracy, which was having a significant impact on the growth of United States trade, approached Congress with regard to a declaration of war. In response Alexander Hamilton argued that America was already in a state of war, initiated by the pirate attacks. Hamilton maintained that the president, as commander in chief, needed no formal declaration of war in order to respond to enemy attacks and defend the country's interests. President Jefferson responded, immediately sending American naval units into action against the pirates.

In retrospect, the Clinton military retaliation against al-Qaeda demonstrated a woeful lack of appreciation for the true nature of "the base" as well of its operations. It began with cruise missile strikes on Afghanistan training camps and facilities in the Sudan. A diplomatic approach was also made to Pakistan for assistance in locating and eliminating bin Laden. In addition President Clinton issued an order applying economic sanctions against both al-Qaeda and the Taliban. That proved more than challenging for the agencies involved, which had no experience at all in combating the type of financial network that had evolved to support "the base." To a large extent, it was that funding network, rather than a constantly changing mix of both anti-Israeli, anti-American militants and true jihadi religious insurgents, that was enabling the new global terror attacks. Other than the limited military strikes and financial sanctions—and ongoing efforts of Alec Station to kidnap or kill bin Laden—that was largely the extent of the embassy-attack retaliatory effort. In the end, the initial Clinton administration spasm attack on al-Qaeda facilities produced no notable results, and the rest of the Clinton-era overseas offense against al-Qaeda proved largely a lesson in frustration for those involved. The failure was fundamentally one of concept: The United States was trying to fight "al-Qaeda" as if it were a single, unified entity.

Instead, the real battle was with a multi-headed threat, surprise attacks carried out by radicals with differing agendas and motivations: militant Palestinian supporters, mujahedeen veterans, jihadi radicals and eventually radical Islamic insurgents in nations throughout the Muslim world. Their common bond was simply seeing America and regimes that America supported as the enemy, including not just Israel but ultimately any Muslim state viewed as open to Western religion and culture. CIA clandestine and Counterterrorism Center officer Henry Crumpton expresses the initial failure and the fundamental problem succinctly: "I realized that war itself was changing and the U.S. government was not organized to understand the enemy and not prepared to fight in this new environment. Law enforcement alone was not the answer. Neither was covert action. Conventional military force alone would not work. Economic sanctions would have minimal impact. Diplomacy with AQ [al-Qaeda] was impossible."[36]

Within the United States itself, there was initially no coordinated effort to preempt foreign terror attacks. As far as the FBI was concerned, surveillance of radical Islamic groups or of potential al-Qaeda recruiting simply was not a priority at field-office level. The Bureau existed to investigate and aid in the prosecution of federal crimes, and at that point al-Qaeda was far back in the shadows—most agents had no idea what it was or where to look for it. Federal investigations required cause. NSC counterterror chief Richard Clarke was told that local U.S.

attorneys were focused on other concerns and for that matter they were working under Attorney General Guidelines that strictly prescribed the types of individuals that the FBI could even build files on. Those guidelines had not changed even after a decade of international terror attacks.[37] The reality of organized terror attacks still had not penetrated domestic agencies inside the United States.

Beyond that, the entire national security system seemed somewhat "conflicted." Senior government officials began to speak of being at war with al-Qaeda—in later years that would become the far more generic "war on terror"—when no legal or military state of war existed. Presidents from Clinton on refrained from asking for formal declarations of war, and Congress followed their lead. Under the United Nations Charter, nations can declare a state of war as a matter of self-defense. That justification has been used repeatedly in legally justifying foreign American military actions against terrorists, yet without a formal declaration of war. The ongoing issue became one of how self-defense translates to domestic action when the nation is not legally at war.

Extensive precedents did exist for the Federal Bureau of Investigation to take a proactive role in regard to the investigation of treason or subversive activities covered by federal legal code.[38] During much of the Cold War era, the Bureau was actively engaged in an ongoing and aggressive search for Communist agents, spies and even "fellow travelers." During declared wars, the Bureau made a priority of searching for spies, preventing sabotage and investigating possible treasonous activities by American citizens. Yet without the nation being in a declared state of war, the focus and priorities of the Bureau (as well as the Department of Justice) have largely depended upon the personal attitude and priorities held by successive FBI directors, and by the presidents under which they served. In his earliest years FBI director J. Edgar Hoover had personally driven his Bureau to focus considerable attention on the possibility of Communist subversion and sabotage; later he turned its domestic focus first to acts of both white and black racial violence and ultimately to Vietnam antiwar protests. With the Cold War over, FBI director Louis Freeh did not initially drive the Bureau with the same level of intensity often displayed by Hoover. It was only in the last years of the Clinton administration (1998–1999) that he moved to elevate the terror threat to the level of being a major FBI priority.

During 1999 there were increasing indications that al-Qaeda was planning something very serious for the end of the century—the millennium. Indications began to surface of a global campaign of coordinated terror attacks. This time those attacks would include strikes inside the United States. American intelligence agencies were still struggling with the basics in terms of being able to move against al-Qaeda globally. But as the months passed, there were ongoing warnings that al-Qaeda might be taking advantage of the experience it had already gained in working inside America's borders. Its first attack—the bombing of the World Trade Center—had been carried out without its influence being understood or even recognized. It had used the next six years to expand its network and to establish an infrastructure for attacks. Its coordinators and organizers had become familiar with the practices needed to insert operatives and move them around inside the country. The only question was whether they could convert that experience into an orchestrated series of domestic and global attacks as 1999 turned to 2000.

Chapter 16

....

SHADOW BOXING

eginning in 1995, the Clinton administration submitted and Congress approved a request doubling the budget for counter-terrorism—annual spending was to increase to $11.1 billion by 2000. The FBI's budget for counter-terrorism escalated some 570% over that same period, and the Bureau added a significant number of personnel to the effort. More than a hundred agents and analysts were working in the FBI's Counterterrorism Center when CIA officer Henry Crumpton was assigned there as the CIA liaison in 1999. Yet there had been no new enabling legislation in certain key areas such as adding additional FBI authority for terror-suspect wiretaps, making funding of terrorist groups a felony, easing access to suspects' travel records or accelerating deportation of individuals associated with terror fronts. And there was growing concern that, with some fifteen different agencies involved in the counter-terror effort, coordination and intelligence sharing were an ongoing problem.

In 1998 a special congressional appropriations subcommittee focused on the issue of interdepartmental coordination, taking testimony from a variety of law enforcement principals. Their remarks all sounded well informed and sincere. Justice Department chief Janet Reno spoke first for the FBI and its initiative to "prevent terrorist attacks before they occur," the need for foreign intelligence and in particular intelligence on "the movements of international terrorists." She also spoke of multi-agency threat assessment and the positioning of appropriate resources to develop those assessments.

However, most of the actual details mentioned in her remarks were in regard to FBI response to attacks. She described response preparedness exercises, field training in setting up response centers, the support of first responders and investigation of attacks. She also spoke extensively of FBI support for emergency responders—but much less about any details of interdiction plans and activities.[1] Reno made no appeals for new legislation comparable to what Clarke and the National Security Council's counter-terror group had independently identified as necessary for increasing federal effectiveness in counter-terror operations. The attorney general spoke at length about partnerships, about the need for equipment and new technology; she raised no issues in regard to operating with the limitations and "walls" that had come into place in response to the Foreign Surveillance Intelligence Act. Based on her testimony, senior FBI managers could certainly have assumed that they were acting appropriately within their legal boundaries and that Attorney General Reno was comfortable that those limits presented no significant obstacles to their counter-terror activities.

In speaking of interagency relationships, particulary in the collection of terror information, Reno described a largely one-way process, coming from the CIA through FBI liaison and then distributed to local field offices. FBI field offices would make the decisions on appropriate investigation and, as applicable, the provision of actual warnings to potential targets—which would presumably include commercial entities such as airlines or agencies such as the FAA. She made no specific remarks about the actual process for those warnings, an area that would become a major point of failure in preventing the attacks on America that would come within two years.[2]

Reno also noted that under the 1995 Clinton Presidential Decision Directive 39, the FBI and Federal Emergency Management Agency (FEMA) held the primary responsibilities for dealing with domestic counter-terrorism. The FBI had the lead in crisis management—although she described the FBI role as basically one of "law enforcement response." FEMA was to take the lead in "consequence management" following any such domestic incident.

One distinction that must be kept in mind in reviewing the roles of federal agencies in regard to terrorist attacks is the distinction between "security" and "defense." It is not uncommon to think of the Department of Justice/FBI as carrying the responsibility for defending against terror attacks. However, their role is actually that of "homeland security" rather than literal "defense." Overall defense of the nation from physical attack rests with the Department of Defense (DOD). Legally "homeland security" and "homeland defense" are not one and the same, and different organizations carry primary mission responsibility for each.

DOD leads the mission for the use of force in responding to actual attacks. DOD is authorized to conduct a "layered defense," being responsible for intelligence and military operations overseas that are intended to identify, deny access of and actually defeat attacks before they strike domestic targets.[3] While the FBI has the authority to identify and investigate conspiracies/plots to commit crimes, it walks a fine legal line in terms of when and how it can perform arrests to prevent an actual attack. The Department of Defense also walks a fine line in that it is legally allowed to respond to the DOJ or other federal agencies such as the FAA in regard to specific requests for military action; however, any such request must be approved by the president and authorized by the secretary of defense.[4] In that regard, gaining approval for American military action against terror attacks follows along the same strict National Command Authority protocol as did the authorization of SIOP authorization in response to a nuclear attack.

Related to the DOJ/FBI and its mission, it seems worth noting that Attorney General Reno spent considerable time detailing exercises and training, including guidelines for including the military—however, nearly all that dialog was related to responding to attacks. And in a rather obvious indication of turf battles, several congressional committee members made a point of asking her about possible NSC interference with the FBI. It seems clear that in his NSC counter-terrorism role, Clarke had pushed for more aggressive FBI action and certain parties had not taken that well. Following the attacks on America in 2001, the 9/11 Commission report noted—in politic language—that Reno had been concerned about turf issues from the beginning, demanding specific language to limit Clarke's role to providing "advice on budgets" and "coordinate the development of interagency guidelines."[5] The questions fed to Reno during the appropriations hearing raised the possibility that the NSC—and by implication Clarke—was overstepping its authority.[6] Reno responded quite positively (and politically) with regard to the NSC/CSG while at the same time politely reasserting the primacy of her departments.

There does seem to have been at least a limited amount of "pushing" between Clarke and Reno. In his first counter-terrorism meeting (as head of the new National Security Council Counter-Terrorism Security Group) with Janet Reno (head of the Department of Justice) and the FBI, Clarke was told that any information developed during a criminal investigation simply could not be shared with "civilians." The best he could aspire to was a verbal understanding—which Reno never committed to in writing—that if Justice or the FBI did get information on what might be terrorism involving a foreign group, they would share it with a "few senior NSC officials."[7] Clearly communications between the FBI and the NSC remained something of an issue, and it's hard to avoid the impression that Reno was protecting her department-level "turf." In light of the FBI's future failures, one might wish that the legislators in the hearing had asked more pointed questions about exactly what the issues were that had caused Clarke to push the FBI on operational matters of counter-terrorism.

FBI director Louis Freeh followed Reno before the subcommittee. Freeh did identify certain areas where legislation was desirable and would assist the Bureau's efforts. In contrast to Reno, Freeh specifically mentioned the areas previously identified by Clarke—the need for legislation adding to the FBI's ability to investigate areas of terrorist financing, the ability for multi-point wiretaps, the call-tracing registers and the availability of emergency, quick-response wiretap authorization. He pointed out that existing law made those tools available for serious criminal offenses but not terrorism.[8] He mentioned a few similar items and offered to provide a list to the subcommittee. Freeh's remarks suggest that as early as 1995 Clarke had been forthright and accurate in citing issues with FBI legal investigatory limits—and that those issues had not been addressed in the following three years.

The subcommittee remarks of Janet Reno are especially important in that they confirm that the Department of Justice and the FBI are officially designated as holding the operational responsibility to identity and thwart terrorist attacks inside the United States. The outstanding question prior to the 2001 attacks was whether the FBI was truly organized and managed to perform a proactive role in securing the nation against terror attacks. The question revolved around whether or not the DOJ/FBI headquarters and field personnel viewed terror-attack detection and disruption as a priority in their daily activities. One source for exploring that question is the Department of Justice's Five-Year Interagency Counter-Terrorism and Technology Crime Plan, finalized in September 1999.

That plan gives us valuable insight into where the DOJ and FBI were focusing their attention and resources. As a cross-check on that 1999 plan, we also have a review of the FBI's overall counter-terrorism program performed by the Department of Justice's inspector general, in September 2002. That document is particularly important, as it highlights areas of weakness existing even a full year following the attacks of 2001.

The goals of the 1999 DOJ/FBI five-year counter-terrorism plan reveal its focus and priorities.[9] Its major goals included the identification and acquisition of technologies for dealing with new forms of terror attacks involving weapons of mass destruction (atomic), biochemical attacks and cyber attacks on computer systems and networks. Protecting the national information structure was a particular priority. Information-system and infrastructure attacks were major topics discussed in the plan. A second major priority was the integration of crisis management and efforts to fully engage state and local law enforcement in crisis response.

A review of the overall plan reveals that it appears to lean heavily toward preparations for crisis and crisis response ("consequence management")—some nine pages of the plan address that topic, with attention toward communication and public safety following an attack.

Interagency alerting and public communications following an attack are also a primary focus, addressed in some twenty-four pages, with another ten pages devoted to response planning and preparedness exercises. The plan was also heavily weighted toward measures to deter or respond to new types of attacks, including chemical/biological, cyber warfare and weapons of mass destruction. Discussion of steps to be taken to address infrastructure vulnerabilities in the areas of computing, networking, telecommunications and financial transaction processing—including new technologies to deal with infrastructure and new weapons—cover some twenty-five pages.

Needed revisions to existing legal statutes, discussed by Clarke and Freeh with regard to preemption and interdiction of individual terrorists or attack teams, were noted—but only in the section related to deterring cyber warfare attacks on the nation's infrastructure. The concept of Red Team penetration testing, using skilled personnel to assess and conduct attacks as potential terrorists might, was acknowledged as critical in effective defensive planning. Yet in the 1999 plan it was mentioned only in regard to computer and network attacks.[10] And perhaps most importantly, only three pages in the plan appear to have been devoted specifically to interagency intelligence collection and communication. There was no specific discussion of any effort to enlarge or enhance the FBI's threat analysis capabilities.

There is no doubt that the Clinton administration considered al-Qaeda, and in particular bin Laden, a priority threat to America. Clinton's presidential capture-or-kill order on Osama bin Laden was the first known incidence of a presidential elimination directive to the CIA since the projects initiated against Patrice Lumumba and Fidel Castro during the Eisenhower administration, decades earlier. Clinton ordered specific attacks on al-Qaeda and bin Laden, ineffective as they proved. The CIA had created Alec Station, its first-ever unit targeted on intelligence collection against a single individual, and both the CIA and the NSC's counter-terrorism unit were involved in ongoing attempts to locate and neutralize bin Laden inside Afghanistan.

Given the attention of the Clinton administration effort to bin Laden and al-Qaeda, it is more than a little surprising not to find more emphasis or priority allocated to al-Qaeda in the DOJ/FBI 1999 counter-terrorism plan. While bin Laden's declaration of war is noted, al-Qaeda was simply lumped in with a host of other foreign terror threats. The DOJ/FBI plan contains nothing of the focus that we see in several of Clinton's directives or of the CIA's and NSC's efforts against bin Laden. The best that can be said is that the plan represented a form of institutional inertia within the Bureau, illustrating the fact that presidential administrations come and go but federal agencies have their own longer-term cultures and well-established patterns of behavior. We saw something similar to this in the failure of the Kennedy administration's effort to introduce flexibility into the American nuclear retaliation plan. Institutional inertia within both the military and civilian agencies is clearly a force not to be underestimated—even by American presidents.

As with all plans, the limitations of the 1999 DOJ/FBI plan are obvious only in retrospect. The planning document mentions only bombing attacks as prior examples of terrorism and makes no reference to airline hijackings at all, perhaps the most common terror activity over the previous three decades. This seems to be a true oversight given that the Bojinka plot, targeting multiple airliners destined for the United States and carrying more than three thousand passengers, was well known to the FBI. FBI agents had taken custody of two of the primary Bojinka participants, and Ramzi Yousef had been brought back to America by the FBI and successfully prosecuted for the New York World Trade Center bombing. In spite of that, the plan's focus on defending American infrastructure makes no mention of transportation infrastructure, neither commercial airline nor rail—both areas that expose large numbers of civilians to coordinated terror attacks.

The plan also failed to address any need for improvements in FBI field office/headquarters communications or in the analysis capabilities of FBI headquarters. No particular mention was made of making a priority of exchanging information with the CIA with regard to international terrorist movements and tracking. There were also no remarks about the creation of specific terrorist watch lists, databases or of any modifications to legal statutes that would enable improved surveillance and tracking of suspects. In general, the weakest areas of the 1999 DOJ/

FBI plan lie in its limited scope of threat assessment, its lack of attention to coordinated, real-time threat analysis, and the failure to address issues with internal practices relating to surveillance and disruption activities. In terms of detail and priorities, it certainly seems like a plan designed to respond to terror attacks, rather than a plan designed to aggressively identify and disrupt them.

That subjective impression of the DOJ/FBI plan seems to have some confirmation in the remarks of a Department of Justice inspector general's (IG) review of the FBI counterterrorism program, conducted during 2002.[11] The report's first area of comment was on the absence of a comprehensive, interdisciplinary written terror-threat assessment, still incomplete a year after the attacks of 9/11. Such an assessment was seen as key, since it should not only define the "nature, likelihood and severity of the terror threat" but it would specifically "identify intelligence gaps which needed to be addressed." In March of 2002, the FBI had prepared its first draft of a threat assessment, but the draft did not deal with an attack on the United States. It also failed to address numerous areas including capabilities, intent, potential targets and even the methods most likely to be used by terrorists.

Even following the attacks of 2001 the draft included no remarks on resource allocation issues, no identification of priority intelligence requirements and no recommendations on improvement in practices or process. The IG review also raised the issue, suggested by some FBI officials, that the Bureau "lacked the analytical capability or resources to complete such a broad threat assessment" and offered the opinion that FBI counter-terrorism managers had a tendency to rely on their own experience rather than a structured threat assessment. The threat assessment project had held such a low priority within the Bureau that it took the inspector general's office more than a month to even identity anyone familiar with it or with its first draft.

One encouraging point noted in the IG review was that the FBI had recognized its weakness in the area of analysis and, in May 2002, had established an Office of Intelligence, which had added twenty-five new analysts. In a less encouraging vein, the report noted—and attempted to politically respond to—criticism from the FBI's executive assistant director for counter-terrorism. He had responded to the IG review by stating that the FBI "knows the risks and threats of terrorism facing the United States." He believed that he was fully aware of the threats, both before and after September 11, 2001—based on the breadth of the FBI's counter-terrorism cases and his frequent discussions with FBI employees. He stated, for example, that he routinely met with the special agents in charge of the fifty-six field offices and assessed both threats and vulnerabilities. He also noted that he constantly received information from the intelligence community on counter-terror issues—adding that he did not believe a formal, written threat assessment would improve the FBI's ability to understand or address terrorist threats.[12]

Remarks from Crumpton and Clarke, both from outside the Bureau but each with his own firsthand experience with the FBI counter-terror efforts, give us a view of internal FBI communications that is not nearly as sanguine. In 1998, early in his assignment to the FBI's counter-terror effort, Crumpton had asked an FBI counter-terror analyst what he thought was a very basic question: "What is the status of the FBI investigation of AQ [al-Qaeda] in the U.S. homeland?" The analyst did not know; in fact, the analyst didn't know who might know and was not sure anybody did know. He didn't know because the headquarters analysis group had no insight into what the field officers were doing—but he would check. In a week he was back with Crumpton: "Five, I think we have five leads in the U.S. but I'm not sure."[13] In some respect that made sense; as of early 1999 al-Qaeda had committed no known crimes in the United States, and the FBI was traditionally geared to react to crimes.

Based on working with FBI personnel and managers, whom he personally liked, Crumpton made several key observations. First, while the CIA and FBI both valued sources, the FBI pursued them only where criminal investigations were concerned. Given that sources and suspects were sometimes one and the same, there was great concern in potentially contaminating future cases or prosecutions. FBI agents also did a good deal of oral rather than written communication, possibly to protect information from discovery during legal prosecutions. Investigation and arrests were emphasized and rewarded more than report writing and analysis. The field offices worked closely with their own judicial districts, often providing information to prosecutors that was not shared outside an investigation or prosecution in progress.

Perhaps most importantly, the Bureau had no functional, centralized information system. Each field office functioned independently, and in advance of a major crime/investigation, any analyst would have to travel to multiple field offices and spend days or weeks working with agents there—agents with their own, already full schedule.[14] The Bureau had been organized and was devoted to investigating and assisting in the prosecution of crimes; realistically Crumpton describes an organization very consistent with the majority of the 1999 DOJ/FBI counter-terror plan we just reviewed. The Bureau was obviously highly capable, and its field offices could be highly effective in counter-terrorism—if they were given the correct direction and priorities.

During 1999 Clarke and the CSG group began to make increased headway in focusing the FBI field offices toward the threat of domestic terrorism, but only because Clarke and his FBI counterpart had begun to gain the personal support and involvement of senior FBI officers in Washington. Those officers were in turn given some very specific new instructions, coming directly from FBI director Freeh and endorsed by President Clinton. What made the difference was really quite simple, clearly expressed in directions given to FBI field office managers by Clarke's FBI counterpart: "your bonus, your promotion, your city of assignment all depend on how well you do with this mission. . . . I mean it, I have Louis's [Louis Freeh, FBI director] backing . . . If you don't believe me, try me."[15] That sort of language creates an immense degree of focus, not to mention accountability. We've seen something of that sort before, decades earlier when General LeMay was building the "we are already at war" culture of SAC. Of course, the challenge is keeping that message in place long enough for it to be internalized. According to Clarke, counter-terrorism became an urgent mission for the FBI during the final months of 1999—but that focus would not necessarily survive the transition to the next presidential administration.

As 1999 progressed, the NSC and CIA counter-terrorism groups continued to encounter leads indicating that plans for new terror attacks were in progress. One common thread seemed to be timing that would coincide with the New Year and the millennium celebrations. There were also a number of indications that the State Department was going to face attacks at its embassies and other overseas facilities. The African bombings had demonstrated that al-Qaeda considered embassies to be priority targets, and there were some 180 State Department facilities globally, many designed with little physical security and others with little hope of adequate protection from the host nations.

Clarke went directly to Secretary of State Madeleine Albright, convincing her to authorize a massive, multi-agency security initiative for overseas sites. Teams were sent to assess each location from a terrorist perspective. It was the sort of assessment the Strategic Air Command had been famous for conducting on its own bases—although in the case of SAC, they also included actual penetration and sabotage drills conducted by special teams, to thoroughly test security preparedness. Clarke's teams couldn't go that far, but they did drastically improve security measures, and if facilities could not be secured or were in those countries that would not step up to provide adequate protection, the facilities were simply closed and traveler advisories issued. The Clinton State Department also managed to gain congressional approval for supplemental appropriations for embassy "hardening" and increased security.[16] The practical result was that were no further successful embassy attacks during the remainder of the Clinton administration. Still, after only a few months, the new priorities had begun to fade and there was no supplemental appropriation submitted with the State Department FY2000 budget.

As 1999 and the 20th century were both winding down, the concerns and warnings about al-Qaeda gelled into a verifiable and immediate threat. Jordanian intelligence had infiltrated a group of terrorists who were receiving aid from Afghan veterans in Pakistan. They learned that the cell was planning New Year's Eve attacks on a Western hotel in Jordan, Christian tourist sites and local airports. One of the participants was a cabdriver who had worked in New York but who had also been active in recruiting volunteers in Turkey, Syria and Jordan—then sending them to Afghanistan for training. Given al-Qaeda's preference for simultaneous attacks, there was grave concern that other locations, including some within the United States, would be targeted. Concerns were further heightened when monitoring of the Yemeni hub revealed that known and unknown al-Qaeda operatives were traveling to what appeared to be a major meeting in early January 2000 in Kuala Lumpur, Malaysia. The meeting might be a prelude to some action in Southeast Asia or cover for yet another millennium plot in progress.

In December 1999, Cofer Black, head of the CIA Counterterrorism Center, issued a "call to battle stations." Major disruption efforts (arrests, interrogations, overt surveillance) were conducted in eight countries overseas. CIA director George Tenet ordered all stations to use any means to disrupt al-Qaeda activities, and President Clinton signed a new directive authorizing action against bin Laden's leadership; the goal was capture, but lethal force was authorized.[17] A major warning was sent out to overseas embassies, military bases and some eighteen thousand police agencies in the United States. Personnel were warned to look for suspicious activity and to pull in suspects for questioning. In Washington State an alert customs officer noticed one individual who refused to make eye contact during routine screening. When requested to move out of line for further questioning, he bolted—his car was found to contain explosives and a map of Los Angeles International Airport. The "challenge" technique worked; the only question was whether or not the disruption efforts would work equally well.

Communicating the millennium terror alert was one thing; having it change people's daily behavior was another matter. That was only going to happen with intense pressure from the top, and according to Clarke, it was National Security Advisor Sandy Berger who obtained the required attention and backing of the NSC principals and the president himself. A political–military alert was prepared, and with pressure from cabinet- and director-level principals, the state of national readiness improved virtually overnight. In particular, the FBI threw thousands of agents out onto the street, pulling suspects in and using the "challenge" tactic to probe for leads and disrupt any operations in progress. Follow-up on the Washington State incident flushed out a totally unknown mujahedeen cell in Alberta, Canada. Leads from the Royal Canadian

Mounted Police pointed to cells in Boston and New York, and the FBI followed up with an arrest in Brooklyn. The Justice Department accelerated handling of Foreign Intelligence Service Act (FISA) requests for wiretaps targeting suspects under the Act.[18]

Daily cabinet principals meetings (not deputies or staff) kept the pressure on, asking questions that let the people in the field know they were being supported and monitored. As we first saw in our earliest chapters, command is one thing; command and control is another. When the War Department issued its warning to Hawaii and the Philippines in the fall of 1941, it assumed local commanders would fully carry out defensive measures and implement the same priorities held in Washington. That didn't happen. In 1999 it appears that there was sufficient high-level command follow-up to ensure that the warning was fully appreciated. Later it was learned that one planned attack, in Yemen, had proceeded to the point where the terrorists had loaded a boat with explosives, for a strike on *The Sullivans*, a U.S. Navy guided-missile destroyer. But in the end, there were no successful millennium attacks overseas or within the United States as 1999 turned to 2000.

For a few weeks the CIA's CTC and the NSC Counterterrorism Security Group had effectively worked with the FBI in a common counterterrorism push. It had worked, but the push had required the active personal involvement of the president, the national security advisor and key cabinet principals. Later it would become clear that its scope had actually been somewhat limited. There is little evidence that the 1999 millennium alert gained the attention of senior leadership at the FAA, at commercial airlines and other public transportation authorities and carriers.

Given the extensive history of aircraft hijackings by terrorists, as well as the highly public Bojinka airliner bombing plot, there had been some focus on mitigating threats to airliners. In 1998 new legislation created the Computer-Assisted Passenger Prescreening System (CAPPS) and authorized the FAA to maintain a watch of individuals known to pose, or suspected of posing, a risk of air piracy or terrorism or a threat to airline passenger safety.[19] The goal was to preemptively identify potential terrorists; however, its actual implementation in the CAPPS program was quite limited. The initial version of CAPPS functioned by having "watch list" name matches trigger an inspection of checked baggage. But the protocol called for no personal screening or interviews at boarding checkpoints. Because of its focus on baggage, it provided no opportunity for a "challenge" that might have worked to intimidate or reveal terrorists intent on actually seizing the aircraft.[20]

The year 2000 brought further bad news about the terror threat. A "lessons learned" review of the millennium effort, similar to standard military "after action" reviews, confirmed that a domestic terror threat did exist. There were al-Qaeda associates in the United States, and there were networks in place to shield and fund them. That was a conclusion that the FBI had previously rejected, claiming that there was no "indigenous threat" and that the number of radical Islamic sympathizers was small and under effective surveillance. The FBI's National Security Division had been focused on Chinese and Russian espionage, not terrorism. Its field offices had been focused primarily on drugs and organized crime. Clarke notes that it was those activities that brought persecutions and promotions; an obsession with terrorism had simply not been conducive to promotion within the Bureau.[21] The question of any change in ongoing FBI priorities would depend largely on the next presidential administration and the attitude of its senior leadership, in particular that of the next attorney general.

In hindsight, there were signs that the practices of the millennium alert had not been truly institutionalized. There were also indications that the foreign and domestic terror threat was ongoing. In October 2000, bin Laden and al-Qaeda successfully carried out an explosives boat attack against an American destroyer docked in Yemen, the USS *Cole*. Seventy American seamen were killed, another forty injured. Once again the attack was treated as a crime, with the FBI taking the lead in the investigation.

In the final months of the Clinton administration, the FBI did work with the CIA to trace the individuals involved. Apparently the CIA, acting with caution given the difference between an intelligence case and a legal case that the Department of Justice might choose to prosecute, produced a "preliminary report" attributing the attack to al-Qaeda. President Clinton later stated that he had expected a definitive assessment and if he had received it a major military response would have been in order.[22] In the face of conflicting claims as to why the report was not more strongly titled, it can only be said that once again any response to what al-Qaeda represented—essentially an act of war—was buffered by the American justice system responding to it legally, within the guidelines for responding to it as a criminal act.

As the Clinton administration came to an end, the most active counter-terror activity in progress was the creation of a comprehensive plan for engaging the global threat. It was produced by Clarke's NSC counter-terror group, entitled "Strategy for Eliminating the Threat from the Jihadist Networks of al Qida: Status and Prospects." It proposed operations to "roll back" al-Qaeda over a period of three to five years and specifically contained warnings about the presence of al-Qaeda operatives inside the United States. To what degree the plan would actually be implemented depended on the next administration and its decisions on how to respond to the ongoing terror threat—it would be a question of transition.

Senior CIA staff were very much of the opinion that the al-Qaeda threat was a true national-security-level priority. Two months before George W. Bush was elected, CIA officials had briefed him, specifically stating that "Americans would die in terrorist attacks inspired by bin Laden." The Commission on National Security also pushed to warn the new president, requesting a meeting before his inauguration; they received no invitation—before or after his inauguration. In his own personal transition meeting with Bush, President Clinton went into length on the al-Qaeda threat, later writing that Bush "listened to what I had to say without much comment, then changed the subject."[23] As Richard Clarke, one of the few individuals to work counter-terrorism in both the Clinton and George W. Bush administrations, puts it, "The incoming Bush administration leadership thought that he [Clinton] and his administration were obsessed with al-Qaeda." They simply could not understand why Clinton was so "worked up" about al-Qaeda that he would make it a major topic of his outgoing conversation with the new president.[24]

Although Clarke was retained within the Bush administration, one virtually immediate change was that his position, National Coordinator for Terrorism, was downgraded. He no longer attended meetings with the National Security Council principals, the cabinet-level officers.[25] Instead he met with their deputies and was only allowed to brief the president on subjects approved by the National Security Advisor, Condoleezza Rice. Rice made it very clear to Clarke, from her first days, that his access would be limited and that his priorities would need to match those of the new administration. Despite repeated requests, Clarke was never allowed to brief President Bush on al-Qaeda or radical Islamist terrorism. The only presidential briefing approved by Rice was on cyber terrorism—this despite Clarke's warnings of an imminent and potentially catastrophic al-Qaeda terror attack.[26] With the FBI holding no standing priority on al-Qaeda and Clarke essentially out of the picture in carrying warnings to the senior levels of government, alerting the president and obtaining an elevated counter-terrorism priority was left to CIA director Tenet, who had also come into the Bush administration from Clinton-era service.

In the meantime, the CIA's Alec Station was left with the responsibility of serving as the source of front-line warning of any emerging terror threat. Obtaining detailed intelligence on the radical jihadi threat continued to be a daunting task, if for no other reason than its network was constantly producing new sets of "fighters," in countries around the globe. However, if nothing else, by 2000 there was no doubt that a known network of individuals had been behind both the first attack on the New York World Trade Center and the Bojinka plan to blow up some dozen airliners destined for America. Those individuals had the motive and had demonstrated the capability to plan and carry out attacks targeting America and attacks on American soil. Their movements and the movement of anyone who could be connected to them had to be seen as primary indicators of any new plot.

At that point basic threat intelligence should have produced an "indications list" associated with those individuals; such a list drives intelligence collection, establishes collection priorities and serves as the trip wire for tactical warning. There are many types of indicators, but one of the most basic is a change in movements. Such observations may take months—or years—but when several indicators begin to go positive at the same time, an alert is justified.[27] For example, any sign that one or more individuals on record as being connected to individuals involved in the World Trade Center and Bojinka plots were intending to travel to the United States should have triggered a broad alert; specifically the CIA and Alec Station should have made sure that the FBI was apprised and that the NSC counter-terrorism unit was informed.[28]

A list of names had been provided by Philippines security officers who had seized materials from the Bojinka plotters—among them the personal phone directory for Ramzi Yousef, which included the name of his uncle in Pakistan, Zahid Sheikh Mohammed. Zahid Mohammed was the brother of World Trade Center bombing organizer Khalid Sheikh Mohammed (commonly referred to as simply KSM). According to a number of Philippines officers, they had also shared information with the FBI that there had been plans for further attacks inside the United States. In its post-9/11 investigation a joint congressional report did verify that both the FBI and CIA were informed that the plotters discussed crashing an aircraft into CIA headquarters, and an FBI memorandum on the first World Trade Center bombing records the plotters' plans for additional attacks inside the United States.[29]

As we noted in the preceding chapter, signals intelligence was being used against the al-Qaeda network whenever possible. But bin Laden, his senior personnel and associates were becoming increasingly security conscious, using innocuous verbal substitution codes. They also turned to public phones and borrowed cell phones and used public Internet sites whenever possible. Still, as of November 1999, the NSA was collecting information from a known al-Qaeda safe house in Yemen. That information demonstrated that a group of al-Qaeda associates were in motion and that a seemingly important meeting was to be in Kuala Lumpur, Malaysia. The NSA wrote up a report on the upcoming meeting and transmitted it to both the FBI and CIA. Given the international nature of the meeting, the CIA was charged with the lead in following-up on the meeting. And one of the names mentioned, Khalid al-Mihdhar was recognizable, traceable back to both the World Trade Center bombing and the Bojinka plot. The lead itself definitely looked serious; only three specific names had been turned up, but some eleven "young guys" were traveling—that kind of movement was very suggestive of an attack in development.[30] Perhaps the meeting was a cover or even a diversion related to one of the anticipated millennium attacks. The Malaysia meeting and the "young guy" travel were even included in a briefing to National Security Advisor Cofer Black during the NSC millennium principal team meetings.

Alec Station did make an effort to obtain information on two of the individuals as they departed for Malaysia from Pakistan and Yemen respectively. Due to a failure in the monitoring, one left Pakistan undetected. The individual flying out of Yemen was screened in customs, and his Saudi passport contained a multi-entry visa for travel to the United States, specifically to New York. The fact that a known al-Qaeda figure was traveling to a group meeting in Malaysia and that he appeared to be planning to go on to New York further suggested that something serious might be in the works. Alec Station asked Malaysian security officials to place him under surveillance and sent cables to a number of CIA stations that a potential threat needed to be monitored.

Surveillance on the Kuala Lumpur meeting revealed the young men to be acting suspiciously, taking precautions to make untraceable calls; the meeting place itself was by an individual with terrorist associations. But for some reason Alec Station, focused on its operations in trying to kidnap or kill bin Laden in Afghanistan, seems to have treated the meeting as somewhat routine, if anything as a precursor to planning for a new attack somewhere in Southeast Asia. Alec Station did not even request a full-name search on the original intercept from the NSA, and the NSA itself had not done a full search at the time of the intercept. Alec Station also failed to query the State Department personnel in Yemen. If they had, they would have learned that the visas for both Malaysia and New York had been issued on the same day, suggesting that the Kuala Lumpur meeting was directly tied to a developing operation targeting the United States.

Surveillance on the meeting did generate the information that three of the men were leaving Malaysia for Bangkok, Thailand. Alec Station sent a priority alert to Bangkok to monitor their arrival and activities, but no general watch alert was more widely distributed. But Bangkok was not supplied with known names of the travelers until after the plane had landed and its passengers dispersed. At that point CIA asked both Thai intelligence and the NSA to place names from the Malaysian meeting on international travel watch lists, but it was too late—and Alec Station made no further attempts to actively trace the men.[31] In February a routine follow-up query on the Malaysian meeting was sent to Kuala Lampur, which in turn queried Bangkok. A month elapsed before Bangkok advised that one of the men had been identified and had flown out of Thailand for the United States. Alec Station was notified in March 2000 that a known al-Qaeda terrorist was apparently inside the United States, yet Alec Station failed to advise the FBI and apparently took no action to elevate the issue within the CIA counter-terrorism group or with the CIA director's office. The individual, Khalid al-Mihdhar, flew into the U.S. (the CIA had not placed him on the TIPOFF list of suspected terrorists), spent some months inside the country, then returned to the Middle East, ultimately obtaining a visa to return to the U.S. once again in 2001.

The Malaysian meeting had initially been seen as so suggestive that it was tracked in daily briefings during the late 1999 millennium security push, but somehow during the transition to the new Bush administration, its import had simply faded away, with no questions asked and no follow-up made—until late in the spring of 2001. An al-Qaeda team was on the move, several of the men's whereabouts were totally unknown, and one other had been identified and was known to possess a passport with visa clearance for travel to the United States. Another had been verified as flying to the United States—but Alec Station failed to add the key names to the international travel watch list, which would have alerted U.S. Customs and a range of American law enforcement agencies to watch for arrivals in the United States. As early as January 2000, the first two members of the 9/11 "planes operation" arrived in Los Angeles, undetected, quickly disappearing into the general Saudi community of southern California.

The Kuala Lumpur incident illustrates the significant problems that existed within the inter-agency intelligence sharing system, regardless of the 1999 DOJ/FBI Counter Terror Plan and the testimony given by Attorney General Janet Reno. The CIA claimed the FBI had been advised, and the FBI adamantly claimed it had received no notification at all.[32] A post-9/11 congressional investigation supported the FBI's claim, and there is no sign that the CIA had confirmed FBI receipt of a significant alert indicating terrorist travel to the United States. The issue was never adequately resolved, and no CIA personnel were disciplined.

Warnings failure also occurred beyond the CIA. We will explore several instances in which FBI field officers generated key warnings about individuals with the potential to conduct domestic terror attacks, and FBI headquarters failed to seriously respond to them. And in 2001, in the final weeks before the 9/11 attacks, the FBI was advised by the CIA that a key al-Qaeda member from the Kuala Lumpur meeting had arrived and was at large within the United States. Even with that knowledge, the FBI's own intelligence work—which should have easily located him and exposed other 9/11 operatives—failed miserably. We will explore those intelligence failures in more detail in the following chapter, primarily because they reveal an endemic weakness in coping with domestic terror threats, a weakness that may or may not have been adequately resolved even after the 2001 attacks.

The story of the origins of the attacks on America that occurred during the first year of the George W. Bush presidency and the detailed stories of the men who carried them out have been covered at great length elsewhere. One of the most recent and comprehensive studies is contained in Anthony Summers and Robbyn Swan's 2011 book, *The Eleventh Day: The Full Story of 9/11*. For our purposes in exploring the broader subject of surprise attacks, we will turn our focus to two specific areas. The first will be a virtual litany of failure in basic intelligence practices, including the CIA's own eventual admission of a total "failure to produce any [word redacted but possibly "actionable"] coverage of Khalid Sheik Mohammad from 1997–2001."[33] That story is important for two reasons: It illustrates the dramatic decline in the practice of threat and warnings intelligence analysis that followed the end of the Cold War, and, more importantly, it reveals the fact that strategically the attacks of 9/11 were no surprise at all.

At this point, there is overwhelming evidence that the most senior levels of the Bush administration had been repeatedly warned of the al-Qaeda threat and of the imminent danger of a major terror attack. Numerous individuals, including Director Tenet from the CIA and Clarke from the NSC, had constantly carried warnings to President Bush, his national security advisor and members of his cabinet. But as strategic warnings specialist Cynthia Grabo writes, "[W]arning does not exist until it has been conveyed to the policymaker . . . and that he must know he has been warned."[34] Yet rather than accepting the warnings and initiating a proactive defense, the Bush administration simply allowed the "system" to deal with the threat, relying on its established priorities and practices. And as we have already illustrated at some length, that security system—led by the DOJ/FBI and FEMA—was largely tuned to respond to attacks, both in terms of emergency response and legal prosecution. It was not organized or focused to identify and disrupt terror threats. Making that happen would have required active personal involvement from the most senior levels, as had occurred at the end of 1999. As we will see, nothing similar occurred in 2001.

Chapter 17

....

INERTIA

In December 1941, the United States was attacked in Hawaii and the Philippines; thousands of military personal and civilians were killed and injured. Neither attack was strategically a surprise; indeed, the attacks in the Philippines were preceded by hours of notice that the United States was actually under attack by Japan. Following the victories of World War II, the United States entered into decades of "Cold War" with the Communist-Bloc nations. There were ongoing threats, warnings, alerts and confrontations. The conflict was not truly "cold," and American servicemen were lost throughout the Cold War. Yet the nation itself suffered no attack. A decade after the end of the Cold War, and some sixty years after the blows of 1941, in September 2001, two major cities in the United States were attacked and the nation suffered thousands of casualties.

Strategically the 2001 attacks were no more surprising than the Japanese strikes of 1941. In 1998 a global network of jihadi radicals had declared war on America and Americans. During the following three years they had carried out major, orchestrated attacks and would have killed thousands of Americans if the Philippines-based jihadi plot to simultaneously explode a series of airliners destined for the United States had not been aborted. The months before the attacks of 9/11 saw an escalating series of warnings—in July 2001 Osama bin Laden was videotaped making a declaration that it was time to hit America where it would hurt the most.

On September 11, 2001, Defense Secretary Donald Rumsfeld began the day with an early morning meeting with a congressional delegation at the Pentagon. In that meeting he spoke of terrorism, predicting that sometime within a matter of months, there would be an event "sufficiently shocking that it would remind people again how important it is to have a strong, healthy Defense Department . . . ."[1] We have no reason to feel that any specific incident or threat was on Rumsfeld's mind on the morning of September 11, 2001. However, in the years following the attacks, we have learned that warnings of an imminent terror attack on the United States were actively and widely communicated within the Bush administration. The administration received a steady stream of such warnings intelligence from both the NSC's Counter Terrorism Security Group and the director of the CIA. The director of the FBI had been carrying the same message to the new Bush administration, up to his sudden resignation in June 2001.

Concern over an imminent attack was so significant that on August 6, 2001, the CIA's Presidential Daily Briefing, submitted to and reviewed with George W. Bush, was titled "Bin Laden Determined to Strike in the U.S." That briefing noted that bin Laden himself was reported to have spoken of attacking Washington and noted that al-Qaeda "apparently maintains a support structure of personnel inside the United States who were capable of aiding in attacks." Perhaps most importantly, the briefing cited recent FBI information that indicated "patterns of suspicious activity in the country consistent with preparations for hijackings or other types of attacks." It also noted that recent information of surveillance on federal buildings in New York suggested that the city might be a priority target for an al-Qaeda surprise attack.[2] Based on the testimony of his principal advisors, President Bush gave no specific instructions to either National Security Advisor Condoleezza Rice or Attorney General John Ashcroft in response to the CIA's warning. When interviewed during follow-up inquiries into the attacks, neither the president, Rice nor Ashcroft could recall any instructions following the CIA briefing. There appear to have been no discussions of moving to an elevated alert level or of any new security measures. CIA director George Tenet told investigators that "no formal tasking" had resulted from the CIA efforts to get the White House to "pay more attention" to a threat the CIA considered "current and serious."[3] President Bush remained on vacation in Texas. He was still there at the end of August when the CIA was updated with information a local FBI field office had uncovered in Minnesota. That "DCI Update" noted an Islamic fundamentalist had traveled to the United States to learn to fly 747 aircraft; he had paid for his training in cash and wanted information on London-to-JFK airport flights. That was only the latest in a series of indications that aviation-related terror attacks were under development.

In November 1999, the FBI investigated what can now be interpreted as a reconnaissance effort for the "planes operation," which bin Laden and Khalid Sheikh Mohammed had launched only months earlier. Two young Saudi students flying on an America West flight from Phoenix to Washington, D.C., had acted most suspiciously, one covertly trying to enter the pilot's cabin. They had been reported to the FBI, interrogated and released. Further inquiry revealed that both were associated with Islamic extremists; one of the two men had received explosives and car bombing training in Afghanistan. One of the men's known associates was interviewed by the FBI and openly stated that he felt the United States was legitimate target; a poster of bin Laden was on display in his room. One of the man's friends had studied flying in the United States.

As 1999 proceeded, the FBI received reports that terrorists were planning to send men to the United States to study flying; however, "the purpose of this training was unknown." The FBI sources noted that the training was considered especially important and that "open-ended funding had been approved to ensure its success." The FBI counter-terrorism unit did order field investigations; however, later 9/11 inquiries would find no sign that that field offices actually carried out such investigations. No reports of anything of that nature were ever located.[4] During 2000 and early 2001 the al-Qaeda "planes operation" personnel traveled to the United States, established themselves and began preparations, including extended and well-funded aircraft pilot training at a number of American commercial aviation training centers.

The CIA's Alec Station was aware, during the period of the millennium alert, that some sort of new al-Qaeda operation, involving a number of young men, was in progress. It discovered that Khalid al-Mihdhar was among the group and that his Saudi visa contained multiple entry permissions for the United States. At that point Alec Station seems, by all available evidence, to have consciously made the decision not to inform the FBI or to put his name on a watch list for U.S. entry. The question as to why that decision was made has never been resolved—reportedly when an FBI liaison within Alec Station learned of the information and challenged why the FBI was not being informed, he was told that "this is not a matter for the FBI."[5]

There has been widespread speculation about the CIA's decision not to inform the FBI or add al-Mihdhar to the appropriate watch lists. Perhaps the simplest explanation was that al-Mihdhar was being monitored by the CIA in regard to developing terror activities, specifically two different plots against American naval vessels. Given Alec Station personnel remarks that the Kuala Lumpur meeting was thought to be associated with potential attacks in Southeast Asia, the station may have decided that it wanted to avoid any risk that the FBI would begin its own criminal intelligence operation against al-Mihdhar—quite possibly interrogating him if he showed up in the United States.[6] There is circumstantial evidence that al-Mihdhar may have been involved with both the abortive attack on the USS *The Sullivans* in January 2000 and the successful attack on the USS *Cole* later that same year.[7] He had gone to Yemen in advance of the attempted attack on *The Sullivans*, and he left the following day. When the USS *Cole* was attacked, he was back in Yemen and again left the next day.

Given the limited number of known operational al-Qaeda personnel, the CIA may have decided to "preserve" al-Mihdhar for their own intelligence collection rather than running the risk of his being taken out of action at a time when he was being considered active in ongoing plots. If he had indeed been of interest in the ship plots, it would not have been unusual for the CIA to withhold intelligence about him, bringing the FBI's attention to him only after the *Cole* attack. It would also be standard practice to obfuscate the matter, protecting source, methods and personnel. Interestingly, in the spring and summer of 2001, the same CIA officer who had withheld information from the FBI in early 2000 was reassigned to liaison duty with the FBI counterterror unit. At that point he became involved in actually bringing al-Mihdhar to the attention of the FBI and promoting its domestic investigation of him.

In the first three months of 2001, Richard Clarke continued to coordinate proposals for counter-terrorism actions. But his top priority was simply gaining an audience with the NSC principals committee, the cabinet-level officers whom he had routinely briefed and worked with during the Clinton administration. However, in accordance with new practices initiated by National Security Advisor Condoleezza Rice, Clarke was authorized to meet only with the Deputy Secretaries Committee. Rice informed him that only proposals endorsed by that full committee would move forward to the principals. The Deputies Committee did not even consider terrorism for the following three months, and when they did, Deputy Secretary of Defense Paul Wolfowitz simply could not understand why they were even spending time on a "little terrorist in Afghanistan . . . talking about this one man, bin Laden."[8]

Meanwhile, the only Bush administration terrorism initiative of 2001 occurred in May, completely independent of the counterterrorism groups of the CIA, NSC or even FBI. President Bush directed Vice President Dick Cheney to independently address the issue of terrorist attacks by heading a new task force; his order created the Office of National Preparedness within the Federal Emergency Management Agency. The announcement of Cheney's appointment focused on increasing FEMA's ability to respond to the consequences of any disaster, natural or otherwise. Reportedly Cheney's responsibility included the preparation of a new national terrorism response plan that was to be reviewed at NSC level; as of September 2001 Cheney's staff was only just beginning to be put in place to prepare that plan.[9] The FEMA director and 350 representatives from some forty-seven states did meet at a national conference on domestic preparedness in Montana beginning on September 8, 2001—the conference was intended to extend through September 12 but was dismissed early due to the attacks on America on September 11. Some attendees were flown home on special military flights. Vice President Cheney was not in attendance at the conference.[10]

The Cheney preparedness initiative is difficult to understand given the low priority being given to terrorism in the earliest months of the Bush administration. Following the 9/11 attacks, administration principals consistently affirmed that there had been no particular warning of a terrorist attack during the first months of 2001. That, combined with the lack of priority and access given to Clarke for discussions of terrorism at both the principals and deputies meetings, leaves it unclear as to what triggered the new vice presidential assignment. Without an answer to that question, we are left with the matter of record that President Bush's only pre-9/11 initiative in regard to counterterrorism dealt the consequences of a terror attack but with no corollary actions to increase security or disrupt or defend against such an attack.

In May 2001, Tom Wilshire, the Alec Station officer who had been involved with the al-Mihdhar issues in early 1999, moved from his position at Alec Station and into a role as CIA liaison to the FBI's International Terrorism Operations Section. One of his first activities was to review the cables from the Kuala Lumpur meeting with an Alec Station analyst. He then requested that an FBI liaison analyst review the entire meeting file. It would be three months before the FBI liaison, Margaret Gillespie, would complete that review and inform the FBI about al-Mihdhar, including the fact that he had now entered, exited and re-entered the United States for a second time.

Also in May 2001, the Phoenix FBI field office alerted FBI headquarters and the FBI counter-terrorism unit of what it saw as a developing effort by bin Laden and al-Qaeda to send "students" into the United States for aviation training. The Phoenix office advised that its records indicated that an "inordinate" number of individuals of "investigative interest" were becoming involved with aviation. The special agent in charge specifically suggested that checks be made of aviation schools around the country.

His reports to FBI headquarters laid out concerns in considerable detail, including mention of the two Saudis who had been investigated as early as 1999 in regard to entering an America West cockpit in flight. FBI headquarters appears to have given the Phoenix field office concerns no serious consideration. The reports received extremely limited circulation and were essentially set aside with the comment that there would be concerns of "racial profiling" if the issue were pursued. Yet only a week earlier all FBI offices had been issued a special counterterror alert and asked to "exercise extreme vigilance."[11]

There seems to be little doubt that, at least as far as Washington was concerned, there was no new "top down" FBI pressure on counterterrorism as a field office priority. The true operational priority for counterterrorism at DOJ/FBI headquarters is difficult to determine. That would become a point of major contention in the inquiries that followed 9/11. What we do know is that in June 2001, Louis Freeh, longtime FBI director, had abruptly resigned, giving no notice. Reportedly he and the new head of the Department of Justice, John Ashcroft, had not agreed on FBI priorities—with Ashcroft being primarily focused on the prosecution of violent crimes and drug offenses.[12] Individuals attending meetings with the two men related that Ashcroft had his priorities and was not particularly interested in hearing Freeh's terrorism concerns.[13]

The swearing-in of his replacement, Robert Mueller, was delayed several months due to Mueller's August surgery for prostate cancer. In the interim, Deputy Director Thomas Pickard served as acting director in the months leading up to the 9/11 attacks. Pickard's position was obviously temporary—he was close to retirement. His interim role apparently proved to be especially trying for him, for a variety of reasons.

From the beginning Pickard found himself constrained by Ashcroft's direction. He was ordered never to give a briefing on Capitol Hill or at the White House without Ashcroft's approval—or to release an FBI press statement without Department of Justice approval.[14] He also was not happy with the priorities of the Department of Justice under the new attorney general—with counterterrorism not making it onto the top ten list released under Ashcroft. Yet it was clearly going to be Ashcroft's priorities that drove the FBI during the months immediately before 9/11.

Pickard formally told the 9/11 Commission that he, too, had briefed Ashcroft on al-Qaeda threats but that the second time he had brought up the subject he was bluntly told that Ashcroft did not want to hear anything further about them. Pickard was adamant about his actual recollection of the exchange; he stated that Ashcroft had literally snapped at him, saying, "I don't want to hear about that anymore. . . . There is nothing I can do about that!" Upon being pressed to pass on a warning to his CIA counterpart, Ashcroft became even more adamant: "I don't want you to ever talk to me about al-Qaeda, about these threats. I don't want to hear about al-Qaeda anymore."[15]

In his own remarks and 9/11 Commission testimony Ashcroft was equally adamant that such an exchange had not occurred and terrorism was a top priority for him. His remarks aggressively shifted the blame for any FBI failings toward actions of the Clinton administration, stating that the FBI had been "isolated" and "handcuffed" by restrictions on information.[16] Ashcroft's own staff supported his position against Pickard's claims, while one of Pickard's staff, also attending the meeting with Ashcroft, confirmed that Pickard had personally challenged Ashcroft over his lack of priority for counterterrorism.[17]

As with much other testimony given to the 9/11 Commission, it is impossible to resolve the two men's conflicting remarks. However, Freeh's sudden resignation, and Ashcroft's later rejection of an increase in the FBI's counterterrorism budget, seems to be consistent with the conflict in priorities described by Pickard. In addition, the FBI's assistant director for counterterrorism stated to the 9/11 Commission that he felt the new Justice Department leadership "was not supportive" of a newly proposed strategy that would have made it more active in counterterrorism.[18]

Given such remarks from several of Ashcroft's senior subordinates at the FBI, it seems strange to find that when Ashcroft himself flew on vacation to Missouri in late July, he traveled on a chartered aircraft rather than flying commercial as was general practice. When asked by CBS News why the attorney general was not flying on a commercial airliner, the Justice Department responded that it was in response to a "threat assessment" and that he would be flying only on charter aircraft during the rest of his term.[19]

Perhaps the best overall assessment is that of the 9/11 Commission: "The domestic agencies never mobilized in response to the [terror attack] threat. They did not have direction and did not have a plan."[20]

Whatever the priority the attorney general held for counterterrorism, he was not pushing his own subordinates to more intense or broader action on the subject. That point seems clear from the behavior and remarks of his FBI directors. And as we have seen before, especially within the FBI, if no one at the top is pushing, it's all too easy for both headquarters and the field to pursue their traditional priorities.

It appears to have taken an actual public relations initiative by bin Laden to reinvigorate the discussion of terrorism, at least at some levels of the Washington hierarchy. In July 2001 bin Laden personally went so far as to state in a videotaped interview that it was time to hit both Israel and America "where it hurts them the most." The interview reached the CIA and Alec Station, where it was recalled that bin Laden had issued a similar warning before the African embassy bombings. The State Department issued a worldwide warning and the CIA was overwhelmed with "chatter" from sources around the globe about an upcoming "big event."

On July 10, CIA director Tenet was given a new strategic assessment by his senior staff. It included the fact that the known mastermind of the *Cole* attack had disappeared from Afghanistan and that other known operators were similarly disappearing around the globe. His staff told him that they believed a truly major attack would be launched within weeks. According to Tenet, one of the briefers, Rich Blee, stated with absolute conviction, "they're coming here." According to Tenet, only silence followed.[21] Tenet immediately requested a meeting with National Security Advisor Condoleezza Rice, taking senior staff including Blee with him. Richard Clarke joined the meeting at the White House. Rice was told in certain terms that there would be an attack within weeks or a few months at most.[22]

Reportedly the attack was characterized as being massive, with strikes overseas but possibly including actions within the United States. Perhaps the most surprising and accurate warning of an impending American attack came from a totally unexpected source. Author Anthony Summers writes of a warning passed by the Taliban inside Afghanistan.[23] The Taliban foreign minister used his contacts within Pakistan to arrange a private meeting with an American State Department counsel in western Pakistan. A second, and still unnamed, American was present. Apparently not all the members of the Taliban regime were happy with the radical Arab element that had deeply inserted itself into Afghan affairs and the Taliban administration.

The Taliban representative informed the Americans that fundamentalist sources in his country were talking about a "huge attack on the United States . . . killing thousands of Americans." Taliban leadership were concerned that their "guests" were about to do something that would result in a major military response against them. The meeting, at the end of July, warned of an "imminent attack" inside the United States. Their suggestion was that the United States should itself launch a military initiative to push the "foreigners" out of Afghanistan.[24]

It appears that the State Department representative simply took the Taliban warning as one more of many warnings, deeming that there was insufficient evidence to cry wolf once again. It was only shortly later that Richard Clarke and others informed the deputy cabinet members that a new covert American initiative in Afghanistan would be the only thing that might divert what was felt to be an imminent attack. A proposal was drawn up and submitted to President Bush; however, bureaucratic delays and the president's fall vacation found it still sitting there on September 11.

There seem to have been only two proactive responses to the July warnings. First, Richard Clarke called a special multi-agency counterterrorism meeting in the White House Situation Room; his intent was to increase awareness and stimulate some increased level of sensitivity. However, without the sort of high-level support he had received at the time of the millennium counterterror offensive, the most that was accomplished was the generation of a new series of security advisories, including one on hijackings by the FAA. And as events would prove, the Federal Aviation Administration was displaying an amazing lack of attention to measures for defending against terrorist actions.

The second result of the surge in warning "chatter" was that personnel at Alec Station took another look at the Kuala Lumpur meeting files. They quickly found that two of the men at the meeting were well known to the CIA and that both had carried visas with entry permissions for the

United States. The State Department was notified, but at that point the warning was almost two years old; by the time their names were entered on the TIPOFF screening list they had been in the country for more than a year and a half and the attacks of 9/11 were only eighteen days away.

In what can only be viewed as a fundamental weakness in domestic security, the TIPOFF airline boarding watch lists were used only in conjunction with international flights; there was no mechanism to monitor even identified terror suspects in regard to travel within the United States. The last-minute CIA watch list advisory had gone to the FBI, the INS, customs and the State Department but not to the FAA. Some nineteen terrorists had flown into and around the United States a total of thirty-three times, through ten different airports—and none of them had ever been seriously challenged. Al-Qaeda had managed to merge new recruits with no history into its network and had used considerable skill in connecting them with experienced members.[25] Equally important, they had taken advantage of and manipulated existing American customs procedures, effectively defeating both American intelligence and the immigration system.[26]

On August 21, FBI liaison Margaret Gillespie contacted an FBI headquarters colleague and analyst, Dina Corsi, and communicated information on al-Mihdhar, including the fact that he had now entered, exited and reentered the United States for a second time. Gillespie also requested that the CIA notify the FBI, INS, State Department and customs and place al-Mihdhar and a known associate who appeared to have been traveling with him on watch lists—which the CIA did. At that point, systemic failure set in. Known al-Qaeda terrorists were in the United States; the FBI had been advised but the men were not on watch lists for domestic travel. Corsi stipulated that the information from the CIA could only be treated as an intelligence lead—a misinterpretation of rules pertaining to the "wall" between intelligence and criminal investigations—and the lead was routed to a single, brand-new FBI intelligence analyst rather than to its much larger, and very experienced criminal division team.

The FBI analyst, on his very first assignment, was told by Corsi that the goal was simply to locate al-Mihdhar for a potential interview; he was given no special instructions and apparently was not advised of the seriousness of the search. Given the lack of any priority, the analyst spent the next five days on an apparently more important assignment, having to do with a hijacking. In the meantime, the State Department revoked al-Mihdhar's visa but inspectors were told not to detain him; what they were told to do is missing from the records.[27] When the analyst did begin his search, he apparently did not make use of some of the readily available databases used by the FBI, including ChoicePoint and in particular National Crime Information Center information. Whether or not this was due to his inexperience, or a belief that the "wall" between general intelligence and criminal investigation prevented his doing so, never became clear. As a result, he simply did not locate his target; later others would find that information on al-Mihdhar was readily available—a priority effort by an experienced analyst would have quickly located al-Mihdhar.

Events only weeks before the 9/11 attacks—at the height of the summer warnings and the time of the new CIA presidential warning briefing on al-Qaeda attacks—confirm the view that the FBI was simply not being pushed or supported in any proactive, priority counterterror defense. On August 15, 2001, an employee at the Air International Flight Academy in Minneapolis, Minnesota, had phoned the FBI, advising them of a very odd foreign student who had no light plane experience or training yet was spending a large amount of money on airliner training. He had paid $6,800 in cash, stating that he wanted simulator training on a flight from London to New York City. In his very first session he began asking numerous questions about the aircraft, including its fuel load and how much damage it would cause if it struck something. The FBI field office responded immediately, detaining him on a visa expiration issue and questioning him and a companion traveling on a Saudi passport. The companion openly commented on his fundamentalist beliefs and his approval of "martyrs" and stated that he himself was preparing to fight. Intelligence inquiries produced a response from the French that Zacarias Moussaoui, the "student" interested in flying routes into New York, had been in an al-Qaeda training camp in Afghanistan.

The Minneapolis office was totally convinced that the incident had potential terror attack implications and sent some seventy messages to FBI headquarters in Washington as well as asking for authority to conduct further investigations. However, FBI headquarters essentially blocked any further fieldwork, authorizing no search warrant and actually chiding the field office about not having anything solid enough to prove the suspect was a terrorist. After being rebuked, the special agent in charge of the office responded to headquarters by stating that he was trying to gain some visibility for the incident so that someday the suspect would not "take control of a plane and fly it into the World Trade Center."[28]

Given the Phoenix and Minneapolis field office examples, it is hard to avoid the impression that foreign terrorism simply was not a priority with FBI headquarters personnel. Richard Clarke has pointed out that it never really had been, most likely due to the Bureau's law enforcement history and established legal restraints. It was only a heavy push from the top, from FBI director Freeh and President Clinton, that allowed Clarke to push field office agents onto the streets in 1999 to interdict the millennium plots. Such support does not appear to have existed inside the Gorge W. Bush Administration in 2001.

In general it is difficult to avoid characterizing the attitude of FBI headquarters as one of "inertia" with regard to the foreign terror threat. Of course, inertia can also be a function of simply following your bosses' priorities. Clarke's experience with the FBI during the Clinton administration illustrated that it was only when it was made clear to the special agents in charge of the field offices that counterterrorism was going to be at the top of their appraisals and that their annual performance reviews would reflect their focus on the fact that their behavior changed. Minus that sort of incentive, it is easy to understand how their attention would have shifted back to standard law enforcement practices and the priorities of the new attorney general.

As it was, the terrorists operated inside the United States relatively openly, using their own names and in a very visible manner, including enrolling in and taking a wide variety of both light plane and commercial pilot training sessions. Some of them even rented private planes to fly training sessions on the Hudson River Corridor, which passes key sites in Manhattan, including the World Trade Center. Others, particularly the so-called "muscle men" who were designated to take over the aircraft, took one-on-one combat lessons. In Florida one of them had lessons from a trainer who had previously worked with the bodyguard of a Saudi prince. Several of the men took ongoing commercial flights across the United States to familiarize themselves with the types of aircraft they were targeting for their mission. And several of the men were stopped, sometimes more than once, for traffic violations; however, the checks on them showed nothing because certain of their known names were never entered into the American law enforcement system databases.

Still, if FBI headquarters was essentially sitting on the Minneapolis warning, the information did get to the director of the CIA. Only nineteen days before the attacks of 9/11, a DCI Update was generated, with the information that a suspected jihadi terrorist had traveled to the United States to learn to fly 747 airliners, that he paid for his expensive training in cash, that he specifically wanted training on London to New York's JFK Airport and that the FBI had picked him up on a visa violation. Tenet was out of the office at the time, but his deputy was briefed on or around August 21. The briefing was entitled "Islamic Extremist Learns to Fly."[29] Senior CIA officials received at least five updates on the Minneapolis situation; later inquiries revealed that no senior FBI officers ever received any similar briefings. It seems as if inertia was spreading.

Unfortunately, the attitude and performance of the Federal Aviation Administration demonstrated the group's own level of inertia. The lack of FAA response is especially difficult to understand since it was routinely copied on alerts and even advisories about new hijacking threats. As with the FBI, the FAA's lack of any new initiative appears to have come from its headquarters staff and its senior leadership.

In August 1999, its Civil Aviation Intelligence security office had identified several new hijacking scenarios, one being a "suicide hijacking operation." Its analysis was that such an option was a low probability, since it provided no chance for hostage trades for prisoners.[30] That assessment was very much a traditional one, reflecting decades of previous airliner seizures. If the security group had been directed to consult more broadly with other agencies, they might well have become updated on the newest trends in radical group–suicide operations. Then again, the agency did not seem to be consulting with itself internally either. According to the FAA's own reports, it was aware that "suicide was an increasingly common tactic among terrorists in the Middle East."[31]

It appears that the Civil Aviation Intelligence group was not the only area within the FAA that was not dealing with current realities. Following the midair bombing of Pan Am 103, the FAA had been directed to develop "measures to improve testing of security systems." In response the FAA had organized its own "Red Team," a penetration unit designed to covertly test airport and aircraft security. In 1997 another directive required that "Red Team type testing should also be increased by the FAA, and incorporated as a regular part of airport security action plans." Frequent, sophisticated attempts by these Red Teams to find ways to dodge security measures are an important part of finding weaknesses in the system and anticipating what sophisticated adversaries of our nation might attempt.[32] A former Red Team leader later testified to a government commission that his team did discover major vulnerabilities in aviation security and reported them through their chain of command. In addition to cargo and passenger screening problems, they specifically noted serious issues with the Computer-Assisted Passenger Prescreening System (CAPPS) and the Threat Image Projection System—as noted previously, several of the 9/11 hijackers were identified by CAPPS but implementation of security protocols was so restricted it prevented none of them from boarding.

Despite the fact that the FAA itself had issued some fifteen terrorist warnings prior to 9/11, the Red Team reports were seemingly ignored by FAA managers, including headquarters officials. The FAA whistleblower also stated that in 1998 he had personally submitted written reports on security issues through his chain of command directly to the FAA administrator, who simply did not respond at all. Eventually he received a reply from the secretary of transportation but observed no actual response to the points mentioned in his communication. The former Red Team leader stated his opinion that senior management simply did not wish to pursue the issue with commercial carriers or to disrupt their established operations.[33] While the FAA's own inspector general's office did not acknowledge all of the criticisms itemized by the former Red Team leader, it was forced to find "considerable merit" to many of his points, especially in regard to report handling and the actual performance of any "corrective actions."[34]

In terms of its actual operations and required security measures, the FAA seems not to have responded at all to the litany of alerts sent its way. The Chief of Civil Aviation security admitted to the 9/11 Commission that he had not even been aware that the State Department maintained the key TIPOFF terrorist watch list—containing some 61,000 suspects including two of the 9/11 plotters. The FAA had not taken advantage of the most critical screening tool available to it—apparently some managers were aware of it but felt it would be a burden to the commercial airline industry. There is no doubt that widespread implementation of TIPOFF screening, not only for international flights but potentially for domestic flights, would have been a significant effort. It would also have required proactive coordination with both the CIA and FBI. History demonstrates that such efforts are administratively painful; they just don't occur unless there is major top-down pressure. That pressure was not present in 2001, and as a result, the FAA's own official "no fly" watch list had a total of twenty names on September 11, 2001.[35] In terms of screening, the key first line of defense, the FAA had only its own extremely limited "no fly" list and its CAPPS baggage screening trigger list. It had made no effort to proactively incorporate new tools such as TIPOFF that were available.

It had also made no new efforts to engage with airlines to improve onboard aircraft security of any sort. There were no new procedures in regard to access control for the cockpit area. Although cockpit doors were lockable, flight attendants and crew members carried keys and could easily be forced to unlock the doors—as happened on 9/11. No "panic alarms" were in place that attendants could use to advise the cockpit crew of a hijacking in progress. And there was no crew training in defensive procedures; indeed, the same training was still in place that had been used for decades. Those guidelines advised all crew members to accede to the hijackers, not attempting to use any sort of force to oppose a hijacking attempt.

All that is not to say that any new practices short of armed "air marshals" could have stopped the 9/11 hijackings, but the lack of any visible precautions could only have encouraged the terrorist teams. Any change in protocol, the announcement of new measures or any change in established security practices during 2001 might have at least created some disruption or reformulation of their plans. Instead, they took repeated flights and observed exactly the same standard practices, on all airlines and all flights. Perhaps worse, even with what clearly was a vastly heighted fear of attacks and hijackings, there were no changes in boarding screening practices, no new training for airport staff or any new rules or regulations that would have increased "challenges" or reporting of suspect behavior.

On September 11, in Boston three Arab men had been selected as potentially suspect by the CAPPS airline registration system, their checked baggage was screened, and their carry-ons were examined. By the time they got to the gate, one of them was "sweating bullets . . . his forehead was drenched."[36] But the gate agent had no compelling reason to stop him or call for a personal interview, so he was allowed to board. In another instance, a check-in agent had found individuals—who later turned out to be hijackers—to be very suspicious, but "the only consequence was that their checked baggage was held off the plane until it was confirmed that they had boarded."[37] It is hugely frustrating to read of instances in which airline personnel noted suspicious behavior on the part of the actual 9/11 terrorists yet felt that they had no legal authority or FAA sanction to either challenge the men or report them to any type of security or law enforcement authority.

This will be discussed in more detail in the following chapter, but it must be remembered that with the end of the Cold War, the FAA had actually assumed a front-line role in American air defense. FAA control centers and controllers held the responsibility for monitoring all commercial and civil air traffic for indications of potential terrorist activity, including hijackings. When a hijacking was suspected, the determination was to be made by the FAA, who in turn alerted NORAD and requested military assistance as required.

Given that the air-defense surveillance radar system had largely been integrated with FAA radar centers, in certain instances FAA controllers were also expected to function in guiding the interceptors to suspect aircraft. That task was relatively routine as long as the aircraft's radar transponder was operating. If the transponders failed or were turned off, interception became much more challenging—something like the earlier "ground-controlled intercept," requiring considerable skill and practice—especially with targets engaging in low-level flight or other evasive maneuvers. It is unclear to what extent the FAA devoted any particular effort to training or exercising the majority of its controllers in that role, including the most basic notification and communication protocols. FAA communication and plane identification problems contributed significantly to the failure in engaging any of the hijack attacks of 9/11.[38]

The best that can be said is that the FAA, too, had not "mobilized"; there were no new directions and no new plans to deal with an imminent threat. And as with the DOJ/FBI there seems to have been no senior official demanding that it do anything differently. That was true at not only at the highest levels of the FAA but also at its own cabinet-level management. The Department of Transportation was the oversight agency for the FAA, the Coast Guard and other agencies that play a key role in homeland security. Yet Norman Mineta, the head of Transportation, testified that he had never been briefed, advised or attended any inter-agency meetings dealing with terrorism. The subject had never been brought up in any of the White House meetings he had attended. When asked whether or not he felt that indicated a failure, his only response was "we had no information of that nature at all."[39] In the broadest sense, the lack of new domestic counterterror initiatives reflected the lack of counterterrorism "engagement" in both agencies' parent organizations and their cabinet-level principals, Mineta at Transportation and Ashcroft at Justice.

In retrospect, perhaps the strangest aspect of the warnings and alerts of 2001 was that as the intensity grew, the highest levels of government seemed to have "distanced" themselves from taking any new actions. In fact, several of the most senior individuals, including cabinet-level officers, seemed to have moved into what amounted to a state bordering on resignation. At the CIA, its Counterterrorism Center director Cofer Black remarked that what they had always feared, a major attack against the U.S., was developing—however, no actionable intelligence was being produced. He is on record as stating, "We are going to be struck soon. . . . Many Americans are going to die and it could be in the U.S."[40]

In its 2004 report on the attacks of September 2001, the National Commission on Terrorist Attacks on the United States (the 9/11 Commission) noted that it had found several inconsistencies, contradictions and failures of memory related to specific remarks of cabinet members and senior White House staff, including President Bush himself. In addition, the Commission acknowledged that it had faced ongoing roadblocks in obtaining key internal documents such as the CIA's Presidential Daily Briefings. However, its final report formally concluded that "both President Bill Clinton and George Bush and their top advisers told us they got the picture—they understood bin Laden was a danger. . . . We do not believe that they realized how many people he might kill and how soon he might do it. . . . At some level that is hard to define we believe the threat had not yet become compelling."[41]

That statement might have been acceptable in 2004; it may also have been quite politic in the earliest years of the "war on terror." Readers interested in the political context of the 9/11 Commission's work are encouraged to read Philip Shenon's *The Commission: The Uncensored History of the 9/11 Commission* for a deeper appreciation of the political counterpoint to certain assessments of the Commission.[42] With information now available, the Commission simply does not appear to have made an accurate evaluation of the Bush administration response as compared to that of the Clinton administration.

At the beginning of his second term, Clinton had introduced his new national security team with remarks that terrorism was first among the challenges facing the nation.[43] Clinton's National Security Advisor Sandy Berger determined that Clarke should sit in principals committee meetings and that the CSG should provide reports directly to the principals rather than their deputies. During the last month of 1999, Berger had organized a daily "drumbeat" of high-level warnings concerning potential terror attacks. During December of that year he had organized almost daily meetings, involving all cabinet secretaries with security responsibilities as well as CIA director Tenet and FBI director Freeh. Berger demanded that they all shake the trees, pushing their direct reports and agencies for information and proactive action.[44] Indeed, the 9/11 Commission report notes that an outstanding example of the government effectively dealing with the terrorist threat occurred near the end of the Clinton administration when Berger and Clarke were given the leverage to essentially throw the full force of the federal government—including the FBI—against a general terrorist threat.

That threat was no more specific than the chatter that was building during July and August of 2001, yet the Commission report notes that in 1999 the information flow within the FBI was particularly "remarkable." Warnings and information were forced all the way down to domestic law enforcement channels and local police departments. Local airport managers, customs agents, border crossing personnel all got the word. And, perhaps most critically, "the effort engaged the frequent attention of high officials in the executive branch and in both Houses of Congress."[45] One can only imagine the response that would have been produced by a report titled "Islamic Extremist Learns to Fly" in 1999.

Objectively, based solely on the demonstrated actions of the Clinton administration and the support given by Berger and Clinton to both the CIA and NSC counterterrorism efforts, the Clinton administration did "get it" and acted accordingly. Its results were mixed, ineffective against bin Laden as an individual but more effective in interdicting and disrupting both the millennium plots and further attacks on American embassies overseas. The actions of the principals of the Bush administration reflect no similar priorities, enablement of subordinates or demands for broad counterterror action.

Even at the height of the chatter and warnings during July and August of 2001, National Security Advisor Condoleezza Rice never demonstrably elevated presidential and cabinet attention to a potential terror attack—or attempted to push security and intelligence agencies into action in the manner demonstrated by Berger. In January 2001, Clarke sent an elaborate counterterrorism proposal to Rice, urgently requesting a principals meeting. Rice made no response to the memorandum, and no principals meeting on al-Qaeda was held until almost eight months later, on September 4.[46] Beyond that, Clarke was never allowed to directly brief President Bush on al-Qaeda and the jihadi terror threat. Using the 9/11 Commission's own criteria, it is simply not possible to conclude that the Bush administration attention to a counter-terrorism had "engaged the frequent attention of high officials in the executive branch" prior to the attacks of September 11, 2001.

In examining the attacks on both Pearl Harbor and in the Philippines, we found failures at two distinct levels. The first failure was one of command expectations: The theater commanders simply did not respond to very specific warnings with the intensity and thoroughness that their headquarters had expected and assumed. The second set of failures involved a significant lack of coordination and information sharing between the units involved in the defense, the Navy, the Army Air Force, the local Army commands and the field units involved with attack detection. More generally, there were major disconnects between defense plans and the actual priorities and actions of the front-line units.

The attacks of 1941 were not strategic surprises. American intelligence was very much aware that the Japanese were positioning themselves for military strikes. At theater levels in both Hawaii and the Philippines, various units were informed and quite aware of the imminent Japanese threat. They repeatedly tried to offer feedback to their commanders that there were serious issues of security and defense that needed to be addressed. The commanders, with their own priorities, rebuffed or simply discounted those internal warnings. In the end several opportunities for final warning were either missed or consciously ignored. Ultimately, internal military reviews of the attacks specifically addressed the issue of command failure. Arguably, there were numerous issues—their headquarters had also failed in terms of its control responsibilities, but in the end no one could argue that the theater had been given warnings; they had been placed on war alert in the end, and from a military command perspective they were judged to "own" the failure.

In 2001 senior CIA and NSC personnel repeatedly carried warnings to the president, the national security advisor and cabinet members responsible for national security and domestic security. As the months passed, the warnings and the level of intelligence became increasingly strident, albeit not definitive. Later investigations would find no evidence that any of those senior individuals translated those warnings into new orders or "tasking." The CIA and the NSC's CSG group were consistently providing warnings and alerts, but those were going laterally to other agencies. Lateral alerts are treated as advice, not commands or orders—leaving each agency to pursue its own priorities, and subject to its own inertia.

The 9/11 Commission specifically raised questions of who had the final responsibility for managing the counterterrorism effort to ensure that all necessary measures were taken, to push back, to ask the tough questions, to essentially demand that the job was being done. The answer they received from the CIA's deputy director of operations was that it was "everyone's" job, but primarily the responsibility lay in the field: "The job of headquarters . . . was to support the field and do so without delay."[47] They received a similar response from the FBI, who placed the "primacy" of operations on the field. Those answers seem strikingly similar to the command attitude in 1941—the field command holds the responsibility; if they fail it is their failure and not that of headquarters. Decades earlier a congressional committee had found such an attitude unacceptable; the 9/11 Commission report section on hindsight and foresight is much more "politically correct," only speaking of failures in "operational and institutional management" and adding comments about ongoing "management challenges."[48]

It is unlikely that the military inquiry that reviewed the attack on Pearl Harbor would have been satisfied with a response that "everyone" was responsible for the defense of the island or of security for the military assets based there. Still, there is a distinction between military "command"—which demands ownership of failure—and "management." There are responsibilities of command, and there are penalties for failing those responsibilities. The same cannot necessarily be said for management.

Command-and-control failure in 2001 was much less complex than that of 1941 in the Pacific. Despite ongoing and escalating warnings, the National Command Authority simply issued no orders for new security or defensive measures. Warnings had been delivered, they had been said "often enough and loud enough," but the message resulted in no new directives and no new "tasking" other than to initiate a new crisis response initiative involving the vice president and the Federal Office of Emergency Management.

Issues of roles and responsibility are important but not our primary focus. They represent only part of the total story. As we saw in 1941, aside from command-and-control issues, there were specific points of failure in responding to the attacks. A great deal was learned from those failures, including the absolute value of reconnaissance and early warning. The attacks of 9/11 offer similar, if painful, lessons. To draw them it will first be necessary to study the actual attacks in as great a detail as possible.

Chapter 18

....

ATTACK

I n the aftermath of the attacks on September 11, 2001, many American citizens could not comprehend the fact that America had been unable to defend itself against a handful of radical religious terrorists. In the aftermath of the Soviet Union's collapse, the United States was generally perceived as being the single remaining global superpower. Its military was the largest in the world; it had been victorious in the Gulf War of the 1990s, and it had faced aircraft hijackings and terror attacks for well over three decades.

Yet four commercial airliners, on scheduled flight plans over the most populous cities of the nation, were seized and flown by virtual novice pilots directly into what had always been the two most recognized terror "target" cities in the nation—one of which had already been attacked by jihadi radicals in the first bombing of New York's World Trade Center in 1993. The four aircraft had flown through the nation's busiest and most controlled air corridor, and none of them were even approached, much less engaged, by a single element of the American military—it seemed almost unbelievable.

In the weeks and months that followed, the disbelief only grew. It emerged that one of the most trying decisions in those critical hours had been what to do if the hijacked aircraft were located. It seemed there had been no established rules for military engagement of aircraft seized as potential weapons carriers or as weapons themselves. National Security

Advisor Condoleezza Rice specifically testified to the 9/11 Commission that very few government or military officials had considered that hijacked planes might themselves be used as weapons. Rice's statement was continuously echoed, by the president, and even the commander of NORAD—even with all the intelligence linking terrorists with aircraft, absolutely no one had ever even contemplated commercial aircraft being used as weapons in attacks on American cities.

It is true that the continental air defense we have become familiar with in previous chapters no longer existed. The polar Distant Early Warning line had become obsolete in the 1980s. It was replaced by the North Warning System, composed of a mix of some forty-seven long- and short-range surveillance radars.[1] Very long-range radars and warning satellites provided surveillance of potential incoming ballistic missiles, but to a large extent long-range detection of aircraft or cruise missiles was largely abandoned following the collapse of the Soviet Union. International commercial flights were and are tracked over at least some portions of their routes by automatic interrogation of aircraft radar transponder beacons—originally developed for military use in identifying friend from foe (IFF).[2]

In 1982, a new air control concept was announced—the National Airspace System Plan. The plan included new radar systems for the FAA's Air Traffic Control, a military surveillance radar network (the Air Route Surveillance Radar System) and the fielding of more advanced aircraft radar transponders. The Air Route Surveillance Radar network operated primarily along the borders and coastal regions of the continental United States. The search radars in the Air Route network normally service a range of some two hundred miles and have a limited ability to determine aircraft altitude.

By 1983 NORAD sector air-defense control centers had become almost entirely dependent upon the Air Route Surveillance radar and FAA control centers for aircraft tracking information.[3] If the FAA encountered any aircraft incidents or emergencies requiring military assistance, it held the responsibility for calling NORAD. Major FAA radar centers maintained ground-to-air communications capabilities to control intercepts—most of which had to do with private aircraft.

NORAD currently operates three sector operations centers, equipped with battle control displays. The northern sector center is located at Peterson AFB in Colorado, collocated with NORAD's own headquarters. In 2001 the East Coast was divided into north and south, with the northeastern center (NEADS) being in Rome, New York, and a southern center in Florida. The two were consolidated into an eastern center in 2005, located at the Rome facility. The western center is at McChord Field in Washington. The regional control centers report to Continental Aerospace Command Region (CONR) in Panama City, Florida. CONR is collocated with the United States First Air Force, tasked with continental air defense operations. CONR and the regional centers hold the responsibility for air defense and provide operational military support for NORAD.

Compared to the Cold War era, the alert interceptor force available to NORAD had been reduced dramatically—to 200 in 1990, then again to 175 by 1997. In 1993, the Cold War–era twenty-four-hour alert had become a thing of the past; regional commanders were given the authority to set their own alert levels.[4] As of 2001 the entire alert interceptor force assigned to defend the United States consisted of fourteen aircraft, spread across only seven bases. None of those interceptors were operated by dedicated Air Force units; the nation's air defense had been delegated to eleven Air National Guard fighter wings in four geographic sectors.[5] In September 2001 only two bases on the East Coast had quick-response aircraft available, Otis Air National Guard Base in Massachusetts and Langley Air Force Base in southeastern Virginia. These aircraft were not maintained in the classic the Cold War–era "hot" strip alert. Even when the final order was given for the pilots to launch, it still required some five minutes to get the aircraft into the air.

Contrary to many of the media statements immediately following the 9/11 attacks, NORAD had been quite active in practicing for commercial airliner threats over a number of years. It would take time—years—for the details to emerge, but when an actual record of NORAD annual air defense exercises became available, it became apparent that NORAD was perhaps the only entity to have developed and exercised scenarios quite similar to what actually happened on 9/11. Aircraft hijackings were common scenarios in its annual command exercise, designated "Vigilant Guardian."

Vigilant Guardian 1999 had involved one NORAD Western Sector (WEADS) exercise in which an incoming commercial aircraft was determined to be executing a "suicide run" into downtown San Francisco. This was designated as a "Hijack Procedures/Shootdown" involving the basic "shoot or not shoot" question. Another Western Sector exercise involved the hijack of an airliner with the possibility of chemical weapons on board. NORAD tasking in the exercise was simply to arrange for shadowing of the aircraft—which was thought to be tracking toward Washington, D.C. In such an attack the plane would have crashed into its target to disseminate the chemical or biological weapons.[6]

Another 1999 NATO headquarters exercise (Amazon Condor 00-1) involved a hijacking with weapons of mass destruction on board an airliner tracking toward either Washington, D.C., or New York. The scenario held off shootdown until the last moment, when the crew overpowered the hijackers (a violation of all FAA crew guidance).[7] Previously, regional NORAD drills had included domestic aircraft hijackings in which passenger and crew hostages were killed. Another scenario, involving the suicide crash of a hijacked aircraft into the Pentagon, had been proposed, discussed and then rejected as being "unrealistic."[8]

One Vigilant Guardian 2000 exercise had included NORAD dealing with a scenario in which a stolen FedEx transport aircraft was flown by "suicidal" pilots and deliberately crashed into the United Nations high rise headquarters, only blocks from the World Trade Center towers in New York City. NORAD's Northeast Air Defense Sector control center (NEADS) had participated in that exercise.[9] The October 16, 2001, phase of that exercise involved following hijack checklists and exercising command and control and interagency coordination. A second phase, on October 24, involved coordination with jet fighters intercepting the stolen aircraft. It remains unclear what end game the exercise concluded.

In 2001, NORAD Southeast sector (SEADS) conducted exercise Amalgam Virgo, involving an aircraft suicide mission targeting SEADS control itself. The exercise was declared a ROE (Rules of Engagement) scenario involving a "martyr" and appears to have concluded with undefined military action. On September 6, 2001, a Vigilant Guardian exercise, involving NORAD headquarters, is described as involving the Commander in Chief NORAD in directing "shootdown" of a hijacked aircraft. Another Vigilant Guardian exercise of September 9, 2001, involved terrorists hijacking a commercial airliner and attempting to detonate explosives over New York City. In the exercise, the aircraft was "diverted" and blown up away from New York, with no survivors.[10]

Clearly there were individuals within NORAD who were giving thought to realistic scenarios in which terrorists carried out commercial aircraft attacks on the United States, focusing on obvious, high-profile targets such as New York City. They were conducting realistic simulations and exercises with both their sector control centers and their interceptor resources. Many of the NORAD exercises are described as involving—or possibly only simulating—threat teleconferences with the FAA and NMCC.

Yet many of the exercises were also out of sync with the actual security measures still being implemented by the FAA, including crew and pilot training and well as hijack protocols. One NORAD exercise—ending with the crew overpowering the hijackers—was in direct conflict with all the FAA instructions being given to commercial airline crew and pilots. Strangely, the 9/11 Commission Report seems to gloss over the dramatic degree of disconnect between NORAD and the FAA. Although its own documents include a list of NORAD exercises, provided to it very late in its inquiry, the report states only that FAA protocols "did not contemplate an intercept"—assuming that fighters would be vectored some five miles behind any suspect airliner and that their only role was to monitor the aircraft.[11] A superficial review of a number of the NORAD exercises seems to suggest that some level of FAA management had participated in scenarios where interceptors engaged and actually shot down commercial aircraft. Unfortunately, the exercises were apparently not investigated in any great detail and received very limited comment in the 9/11 report.

If FAA personnel or senior FAA and Department of Transportation managers were involved in the NORAD exercises, the scenarios involved appear to have totally escaped their attention. It also seems that the general FAA controller workforce was not involved with, briefed or trained on any of the more contemporary hijacking scenarios. There is no indication that any significant number of the FAA's controllers were generally involved in NORAD exercises, especially the more complex ones involving the crashing of aircraft into high-rises in New York City or the shooting down of airliners carrying chemical weapons or explosives. For that matter there is also no indication that senior Pentagon command and most specifically cabinet-level officers were involved in any of the exercises, even those legally requiring authorization from the president and secretary of defense.

It does appear that actions taken by the Joint Chiefs and the secretary of defense in 2001 appear to have complicated the military command response to hijack attacks and resulted in a level of uncertainty regarding authorization and rules of engagement similar to the confusion at play within the FBI over the interpretation off the intelligence "wall" related to investigating terror threats. In January 2000 the Joint Chiefs had issued directive CJCSI 3121.01A, Standing Rules of Engagement for U.S. Forces. Peacetime operations inside the jurisdiction of the United States were to be governed by use-of-force rules identified as enclosures H and I; unfortunately for our studies, those enclosures were not released along with the available copy of the directive.[12]

We do have anecdotal statements from NORAD personnel and pilots confirming that aircraft intercepts had been handled in a straightforward manner, using a graduated series of actions. First the interceptor would signal the suspect aircraft by rocking its wings or making a pass in front of it; if the aircraft ignored increasingly assertive moves in and around it, the interceptor could be ordered to fire in front of it to demonstrate the seriousness of the challenge. Depending on the possible threat posed by the aircraft, and its location, with command approval it might be physically attacked to force a landing.[13]

The standard practices used by the FAA to request military support for possible aircraft in trouble and for suspected hijackings had also been routine. FAA controllers notified their headquarters and requested military assistance from NORAD. Requests might be made concurrently to both NORAD headquarters and the controller's NORAD sector control center. From that point on, NORAD bore the responsibility for calling in available interceptors, and the FAA controller worked the intercept with NORAD sector control and on some occasions directly with the interceptor pilots. FAA documents record some sixty-seven such incidents—many of them quite routine and involving communications or transponder failures on board aircraft—requiring military support during the period between September 2000 and June 2001. The 9/11 Commission Report states that "the defense of U.S. airspace on 9/11 was not conducted in accordance with pre-existing training and protocols."[14] It does not mention that the protocol had been changed only three months before the attacks, that it appears to have been poorly communicated at best and that none of the operational personnel it affected appear have been trained or provided guidance in accordance with the brand-new protocol.

Well-established and simple protocols had changed—or were intended to—with a standing order issued by the Joint Chiefs of Staff on June 1, 2001.[15] The June 1, 2001, JCS directive stipulated that immediately, any request from the FAA for military assistance would have to be routed through several levels of notification, with approval only at the "highest levels of government." The directive also introduced the National Military Command Center into the operational process, complicating what had been a routine FAA/NORAD communication protocol for requesting military support and shadowing intercepts.

The new protocol appears to have added numerous approval levels to calls for time-critical incidents; it also redirected FAA notification of hijackings from NORAD to the National Military Command Center at the Pentagon. The NMCC is not an operational command; it holds three main missions: monitoring global events for the Joint Chiefs of Staff, organizing teleconferences to allow Pentagon staff to facilitate crisis response coordination, and transmitting directives for defense condition changes, alerts—and, if necessary, Emergency Action Messages related to strategic military action. In its crisis management role the NMCC moves though a structured process to establish a variety of conferences involving both personal participation and conference calls.[16] A basic conference is event driven, designated a "Significant Event

Conference"; as events proceed, the conference may be redesigned as a "threat" conference. The NMCC maintained protocols and calling lists for both Air Event and Air Threat conferences; the major difference between types and levels of conferences is simply who is on the participant list.

The verbiage in the JCS directive also seemed to suggest that "any" requests for military support had to be forwarded to and apparently approved by the secretary of defense. Clearly such a requirement would have been unworkable for the number of requests for assistance that the FAA had routinely generated in previous years. In any event, the directive added a level of command-level complication that virtually ensured a delay in response to any FAA declaration of a hijacking and request for military assistance—if the FAA went to the NMCC. The directive actually provided for no specific notification of NORAD at all, although it appears to suggest that the NMCC would normally call NORAD to respond to the request for assistance—if approved by the secretary of defense.

The 9/11 report notes how much difficulty the NMCC had in bringing FAA representatives into an "air threat conference" on 9/11. However, the report itself does not comment on or explore the issue that such conferences were not routine for the NMCC and that the FAA was not even listed as a participant for what was essentially a military coordination conference, not an operational/command activity. Specifically the FAA was not on the NMCC call list for either a Significant Event (SIED) or Air Threat Conference (ATC). On 9/11 the operator was asked to add the FAA Operations Center to the call but could not get through; eventually the FAA was connected but only though assistance of the White House switchboard. As of 9/11 the NMCC was also "not aware" of the FAA Control Center in Herndon, Virginia, or of the military liaison at the FAA Operations Center.[17]

Upon questioning the NMCC staff, the 9/11 Commission determined that there had been no Air Threat Conference initiated at the NMCC for at least the previous two years. There was no discussion or comment concerning whether or not the NMCC staff or FAA had exercised the new protocols specified by the June 1 Joint Chiefs Directive—the events of 9/11 suggest they had not.

Despite all of NORAD's exercises involving hijacked aircraft as weapons, it appears that no communications or command protocols were established to operationally implement the new June 1 directive for a military air threat response requiring approval by the "highest levels of government." There is no known evidence to show that it was ever actually practiced following its issue. Beyond that, our studies of false alarms and alerts during the Cold War reveal no instance in which adequate response times involving civilian command authority were actually achieved.

The new June 2001 JCS directive was distributed to all Bush administration principals including the Department of Transportation and the FAA. It was also distributed to the NMCC and Commander in Chief NORAD. What remains unclear is whether any of the agencies offered comment or response—and more importantly to what extent they communicated the new directive to their field operations and control centers. As we will see in our review of actual 9/11 events, none of the FAA controllers followed the new protocol. The National Military Command Center did not represent operational combat control over the air defense, nor did the NORAD representative on the Air Threat Conference. No specific orders were passed via the Air Threat Conference that was convened; it eventually did relay the shootdown order when it was communicated from the White House.

The FAA ran its own teleconference during the attack; however, FAA controllers appear to have received little or no FAA headquarters assistance or guidance other than an eventual order to ground all commercial and private aircraft. That lack of headquarters guidance continued long after the initial attacks. During the first twenty-four hours, FAA controllers with no military experience or training were left largely on their own to do tactical threat assessment and to make calls for military support. In his memoirs a veteran Air Force fighter pilot assigned to lead an air combat patrol over Atlanta on September 11 writes of an FAA air controller giving him "clearance to fire" if asked. The pilot thought the idea was ridiculous—unless he observed an "airliner roll over and dive for downtown," and even if he fired, what of the wreckage?[18]

Later the same pilot participated in an alert scramble placing him over Charlotte, North Carolina—with an FAA controller declaring a "free fire" zone for twenty miles around the Charlotte airport. The veteran quickly told the controller he just could not do that and directed other fighters in the area to disregard. As events proved, the unknown aircraft the controller was designating as probable targets were Special Operations Command helicopters out of Fort Bragg. Yet on 9/11, with no military training and with no experience in actually running ground-control interceptions, FAA controllers were effectively taking the lead in the air defense of the United States.

The fundamental issue of pre-delegation of authority for lethal action during an actual attack indicates the degree to which senior military and civilian command seems to have failed to prepare for the defense of the nation prior to the attacks of 9/11. Apparently senior managers or commanders had not translated several years of NORAD exercises into the command realities of surprise attack. Even in the earliest days of the Cold War there had been a pragmatic awareness of pre-delegation in the event of surprise attack. Pre-delegation for military action when under attack had been authorized throughout the Cold War. Yet on 9/11, even if the NORAD interceptors had been able to locate and engage the airliner flying toward the South Tower of the World Trade Center— and they were close—they would apparently have had no choice but to either hold back from engaging or to have made the decision on their own. Given the later remarks of some of the interceptor pilots involved, they might well have taken on the burden of that command decision, risking their own lives in attempts to force the airliners off course by crashing into their engines or tail sections.

All of which takes us to the actual events of September 11, 2001. In our effort to explore the response to those attacks, and in particular to evaluate the effectiveness of the nation's command-and-control system under its first actual attack since 1941, we will attempt to detail the most currently known chronology of that day. The story of what exactly happened with America's defense on 9/11 took some years to fully emerge. Even in its final report, the 9/11 Commission noted that several items of information given to it in initial testimony, particularly by senior Air

Force officers, were "incorrect."[19] In point of fact it took considerable time for a public understanding of just how much information had been withheld from the Commission by both Air Force and the FAA head-quarters personnel.[20] That information included actual time-stamped audiotapes of communications at both FAA and NORAD control centers. The tapes, once they were finally obtained and studied in detail, told a detailed story of both civilian and military field personnel coping with a desperate situation, with minimal information.

In the following chronology, we will focus on FAA and military activities, highlighting command-and-control issues, decisions and timing. One of the most relevant records of the day comes from tapes recorded at NORAD's northeastern control center (NEADS). One of the first members of the public to actually be allowed to listen to the tapes—made available only in 2006—was journalist Michael Bronner. Bronner's research and his article in *Vanity Fair* magazine provided the core information for the following chronology (all times listed are Eastern Daylight Time); it is supplemented with more recent information as noted in the text.[21]

8:37 AM—An air traffic controller at the FAA's Boston Center called NEADS and advised them of a hijacked aircraft heading toward New York. The controller requested a scramble of fighter aircraft for "help."

Given standing FAA protocol, any responding fighter would have only been expected to "shadow" the aircraft, at a distance of some five miles behind it.

NEADS immediately contacted the closest alert aircraft unit, at Otis Air National Guard Air Base on Cape Cod in Massachusetts. NEADS reported information from the FAA that there might be a hijacking in progress; Otis replied that it had heard the same information and had begun to work a response. The NEADS operations room commander ordered two Otis fighters to "battle stations," sending the alert pilots to their jets to strap in. Further orders were required to actually start the engines and get into the air, a process taking approximately five minutes. In the meantime, NEADS frantically tried to locate the hijacked plane. It had an airliner identification, but the best the FAA controllers could give them was that it was somewhere north of JFK Airport.

8:40 AM—NEADS was told the aircraft was some thirty-five miles out of JFK; that was all the information the FAA controller could give them other than that a hijack was in progress and threats had been made on board the aircraft. Normally FAA controllers follow flights using transponder information that gives aircraft identity and altitude. The hijackers had turned off the aircraft's transponder, leaving controllers to switch to direct radar displays—with no flight ID and limited altitude information. NEADS was dependent upon its Air Route Control Radar, with displays showing only "blips" of literally hundreds of planes in the dense northeastern air traffic corridor. There was no way to physically isolate the hijacked aircraft, especially once it dropped low enough to go entirely off radar.

8:45 AM—With no further location information coming from the FAA, the Otis operations commander determined he should at least get his fighters into the air; he ordered the alert aircraft to launch. The best he could do was simply to head them toward New York. In the interim, the NEADS battle commander was communicating with NORAD's continental combat control (CONR) at Tyndall AFB in Florida. He advised them that they were putting planes in the air and feverishly trying to locate the hijacked airliner.

8:45 AM—An FAA controller at Indianapolis Center noted lost radar contact with a flight out of Washington's Dulles Airport, flying transcontinental to Los Angeles. Indianapolis reported the alert to FAA headquarters, but neither the Indianapolis Center nor FAA headquarters notified NEADS or NORAD headquarters—or the NMCC for that matter.

8:46 AM—Terrorists flew the first hijacked airliner into the North Tower of the World Trade Center.

8:51 AM—FAA Boston Center advised NEADS that a plane had crashed into the World Trade Center. At that same moment, the two fighters launched from Otis—some thirteen minutes after the initial hijack call from the FAA. As they launched they still had no "target," but at their own initiative the pilots went supersonic, flying on afterburner toward New York.

NEADS immediately attempted to confirm the impact with the New

York FAA control center but found they had no information on the crash—and apparently had no alert of an incoming hijacked airliner.

8:52 AM—Following the report of the crash into the North Tower of the World Trade Center, the Otis jets were directed to the south of the city, off Long Island. Otis is some 150 air miles from New York City, and the fighters were some 70 miles south of the city when the second hijacked airliner was flown into the South Tower of the World Trade Center.

At that point the first round of confusion began to set in, over what aircraft were being hijacked and what their apparent destinations were. The nature of the overall threat truly remained unclear throughout the morning, with hijacked aircraft transponders being turned off (and a few of those on some of the three thousand aircraft in the air having problems or with their crews failing to respond immediately to check verification calls). The various FAA control centers were able to provide little in the way of specific location information to NORAD or NEADS.

The Air Route Control radar system proved of very limited value without supplemental transponder information. Warnings—such as that of an aircraft ultimately headed into Washington, D.C.—became available only at the very last minute, when short-range air traffic control radar was able to pick out aircraft acting suspiciously. Even the airlines proved to be of little help; it was several hours before the company operating the first aircraft to hit the World Trade Center would even confirm it was their plane.[22]

8:55 AM—President Bush arrived at an elementary school in Florida. He spoke briefly with Condoleezza Rice and others, receiving the news that a plane had crashed into the World Trade Center. He proceeded on into the school to continue with his planned student reading exercise.

The fact that both the president and the national security advisor initially felt the WTC crash to be an accident suggests the extent to which both were simply not thinking about terrorism. Given that the World Trade Center had been the target for the first terror strike on America, that recent intelligence had discussed suspicious terrorist surveillance of potential targets in New York, and that terror warnings were at an all-time high, even the crash of a small aircraft on a clear day with unlimited visibility into a New York landmark should have immediately triggered some thought of a terror attack.

9:00 AM—NMCC operations contacted the FAA for information on the New York crash, apparently prompted by CNN news coverage. A hijacking was discussed during the call, but there was no mention of air defense, nor did the NMCC proceed to notify the White House or communicate with the presidential party. For that matter, neither did NORAD, which should have been actively seeking National Command Authority directions on rules of engagement and lethal engagement authority.

9:03 AM—Terrorists flew the second hijacked airliner into the World Trade Center South Tower.

9:03–9:05 AM (approximate)—Richard Clarke convened a Counterterrorism Security Group crisis session in the White House Situation Room. He received permission from Vice President Cheney and Condoleezza Rice. Clarke has written that as his own crisis video conference moved forward, both Secretary of Defense Rumsfeld and CIA director Tenet were "on screen"; however, he makes no comment about either actually joining in the discussion.[23]

Despite Clarke's remarks, confusion exists on Rumsfeld's participation—the 9/11 Commission Report determined that he had been in a congressional breakfast and then moved into his daily intelligence briefing; he was in that briefing when advised after the second strike on the World Trade Center and continued in the briefing until the Pentagon itself was struck.[24]

The leadership present at Clarke's crisis team meeting qualified the meeting as a "principals meeting," normally chaired by the national security advisor; Rice was initially present but asked Clarke to run the meeting. She proceeded to join the vice president in the Presidential Emergency Operations Center (PEOC), a bunker under the East Wing of the White House. Although there is confusion on the timing, both she and Cheney appear to have arrived at the PEOC between 9:20 and 9:30 AM. Neither was in the Situation Room as Clarke's crisis teleconference began by 9:30. Rice and Cheney communicated with Clarke from the bunker, although Clarke notes ongoing problems keeping the line open to them.[25]

9:05 AM—President Bush was in a classroom listening to children reading. Assistant to the President Andrew Card entered the room and whispered, "A second plane hit the second tower. America is under attack."[26] Bush remained in the classroom until 9:15, finishing the reading session and a series of photographs. He then moved to a separate room where he watched television and spoke by phone to individuals including Vice President Cheney and FBI director Robert Mueller. Bush remained at the school for approximately twenty minutes.

It must be noted that the commander in chief, during his time on the ground before the departure of *Air Force One*, upon his return to the aircraft or while in flight, apparently made no direct contact with NORAD, with the NMCC, the secretary of defense or anyone in the actual chain of command relating to military operations. Only President Bush and Defense Secretary Rumsfeld were legally empowered to order military action against hijacked aircraft. Historical practice during a war situation would also have called for the president and *Air Force One* to rendezvous with the Nightwatch national airborne command post, providing the best communications and a trained battle staff to support his actions as commander in chief.[27] There is no evidence that option was considered, even during the later National Military Command Center conference call that discussed the president's movements and fighter cover for *Air Force One*.

9:07 AM—NEADS operations was aware there could be additional attacks in progress and requested that the FAA allow a combat air patrol over New York City. Instead, under FAA control, the fighters were put into a holding pattern offshore while the FAA began to clear private and commercial aircraft out of the skies over New York.

In addition, the battle commander at NEADS requested permission from NORAD combat control (CONR) to launch fighters from the second alert base in the northeast, at Langley AFB in southeastern Virginia. That request was refused, although NEADS was allowed to move two Langley alert fighters to "battle stations."

As of approximately 9:15 AM NEADS and NORAD battle command (CONR) in Florida appear to have been working the air threat virtually unassisted.

9:19 AM—Discussion continued at NEADS and with NORAD battle control on the subject of what to do if their fighters were able to intercept hijacked commercial airliners. It is clear that no orders had been received from NORAD headquarters or National Command Authority in regard to what to do if intercepts were made. The NEADS officers began their own discussions of what weapons to use and where to strike the threat aircraft.

9:28 AM—Clarke passed word to the White House bunker that someone needed to advise the president to stay away from Washington and most importantly that the military needed authorization to engage hijacked passenger aircraft, to shoot them down if necessary.[28] Clarke was familiar with that requirement from an attack exercise he had led in 1998.

9:21 AM—Boston control advised NEADS that a hijacked airliner appeared to be flying towards Washington, D.C. As it turned out the report was false and Boston appeared to have confused radar tracks, following one of the early New York City hijackings and thinking it had maintained its original track when it had simply dropped below radar coverage. By that point the individual FAA control centers were dealing with flight transponders that had been turned off, and suspect aircraft were immersed in the radar tracks from all the northeast corridor traffic.

In response to the "phantom hijack" warning, NEADS ordered Langley to scramble its "battle station fighters" and directed they be sent towards the Washington, D.C., area. The scramble orders actually issued to the pilots did not include specific target location and distance—a specific target was not known at the time. Rather than immediately heading toward Philadelphia/Washington, D.C., area, the pilots were routed out of local airspace by the FAA and moved to an offshore staging area, away from commercial air traffic.

9:25 AM—The FAA's Herndon Center, with orders from FAA administrator Jane Garvey, issued a national "ground stop" for all aircraft; the order was intended to freeze all FAA-controlled aircraft on runways and keep any new flights out of the air.

9:28 AM—Cleveland FAA control had begun to suspect another hijacking. Sounds of an apparent fight in the cockpit of an airliner were heard by the controller. Cleveland control communicated up the FAA chain of command, but this particular alert (which was all too real) was not reported directly to NEADS—nor did FAA Headquarters communicate it to NEADS, NORAD headquarters, the NMCC or anyone else.

9:30 AM—Three multi-agency teleconferences were in progress, one initiated by Clarke in the Situation Room, the two others involving Defense Department and FAA personnel respectively. The FAA conference had begun at approximately 9:20 AM. The NMCC monitored the FAA call, but participants later stated that it provided little information.

The 9/11 Commission Report concluded that neither the initial DOD nor the FAA conference, which involved no senior personnel, made any "meaningful" contribution to coordinating an air defense response to the hijackings.[29]

9:32 AM—NEADS control center officers were still discussing what they would do—or could do—given a successful intercept of any hijacked aircraft.

9:33 AM—An alert radar monitor at NEADS noted that the Langley interceptors were going the wrong way—a heated dialog ensued before the FAA controller was convinced to immediately direct the jets toward Baltimore. The Langley fighters were still some 150 miles away from the Washington area at the time the Pentagon was actually struck—by a totally different and very real hijacked airliner, not the "phantom hijack" which had initially triggered the Langley scramble.

The 177th Fighter Wing, stationed at Atlantic City International Airport, was not an alert air defense base; however, it did routinely launch aircraft each morning for practice bombing runs in the Pine Barrens of New Jersey. Something over an hour after the initial hijacks had begun and as a pattern of air attacks became clear, NEADS was authorized to order the 177th to prepare and launch fully armed F-16s.

By this time a conference between FAA centers had been established; NEADS joined the call, and it appears to be the first time NEADS was advised of a possible hijack of a flight out of Washington, D.C.

9:35 AM—FAA Boston Control advised NEADS of a suspect aircraft six miles southeast of the White House and moving away. They offered no other information, but NEADS immediately contacted to the

Langley fighters, ordering them supersonic. At that point the Langley interceptors were still 150 miles and some ten minutes away.

9:35 AM—An E-4 airborne command aircraft arrived over Washington, D.C., and was observed and filmed circling low over the White House.

Sightings of the E-4 became one of the ongoing mysteries of 9/11 as the Air Force and other government agencies officially denied such an aircraft was over Washington that day. Only in 2007 did government sources anonymously confirm the aircraft's identity and presence; its identity was known to the 9/11 Commission, which, according to one commissioner, had not deemed it significant enough to mention in the Commission's report.[30] A mystery does remain in regard to who ordered the aircraft over the nation's capital and why it was close enough—being normally stationed with STRATCOM in Offutt, Nebraska—to make it to Washington so quickly. The exact location of the four E-4 airborne command post aircraft on 9/11 is still unknown. One or more were likely participating in the STRATCOM Global Guardian exercise. It seems at least possible that an airborne command aircraft, involved in the Global Guardian exercise, was operating just off the East Coast from New York or Washington. We do know that an AWACS aerial early warning aircraft was flying off Florida's east coast as part the week's exercises. It was routed to the Washington area later that day.

9:35 AM—President Bush's motorcade left the Florida school en route to *Air Force One*.

9:37 AM—Terrorists crashed a hijacked airliner into the Pentagon.

Defense Secretary Rumsfeld had reportedly been monitoring the Situation Room crisis call up to the point of the crash; he then left his office to view the damage and personally assist but continued to play no active role in command and control. He had no further contact until joining the Clarke crisis conference call at around 10:30 ET. Rumsfeld refused advice to move to the alternate military command center, stayed at the Pentagon and sent his Deputy Paul Wolfowitz to the NMCC. A helicopter was dispatched to remove the speaker of the house from the Capitol.[31]

During the attack on the Pentagon, its communications systems went down due to system overload and the number of calls being placed. The overload and shut down were reminiscent of the failure of the Washington, D.C., telephone network on November 22, 1963— too many personal calls from too many people overriding operational communications. For a short time the only Pentagon communications reportedly available was via personal wireless devices.[32]

9:29–9:32 AM (approximate)—According to the 9/11 Commission Report, the NMCC convened a "significant event" conference at 9:29 AM, beginning with a recap of events including the two strikes on the World Trade Center, another probable hijacking and fighters scrambled out of Otis. A transcript of the NMCC Command Center conferences has been released and provides additional insight into crisis coordination.[33] The conference initially included Air Force HQ, NORAD HQ, and the Joint Chiefs' Chairman's Office, although neither the chief (traveling abroad) nor his deputy actually joined in the call during the period of the actual attacks.[34]

9:37–9:39 AM (approximate)—The NMCC commander convened an "air threat" call, but as the FAA was not on the list for air threat calls, it took some time to connect with an FAA representative. No FAA representative joined until 10:05 AM. The NMCC commander opened by stating that an air attack on America appeared to be in progress and asked NORAD for an assessment—NORAD was able to offer only limited information. A request was made for the secretary of defense to join the conference; he could not be located and did not join until approximately 10:30 AM.

The FAA representative who did join the "air threat" call had no familiarity with hijackings, no access to decision-makers and no current or relevant information. The 9/11 Commission Report states that at this point there was no sign of any meaningful communication or coordination between NORAD command and FAA operations leadership. The Department of Defense seems to have relied on the NMCC conference call for coordination but failed to obtain meaningful FAA participation.[35] The 9/11 Commission Report cites at least one participant as describing the concurrent NMCC and Situation Room crisis conferences as competing for attention and presenting contending "venues" for decision-making.[36]

9:40 AM—NEADS was advised of yet another possible hijack, south of Cleveland. The aircraft was located on radar, potentially tracking toward Chicago. NEADS had no alert aircraft even remotely in position for an intercept. NEADS commanders sent a request to Air National Guard bases in the area, but the only response was from a base in Selfridge, Michigan. They could provide only two unarmed fighters, already in the air returning from a training mission. Later the FAA confirmed the Cleveland report was a mistake, but for the next few hours NEADS continued to receive numbers of similar suspected hijacking reports.

9:42 AM—The FAA, with a directive from Transportation Secretary Mineta, issued an order directing all airborne planes to immediately land; it was the first step in clearing the skies in order to make hijacked aircraft more obvious to controllers.

9:42 AM—President Bush arrived at *Air Force One*; he was told of the Pentagon crash and talked briefly with Vice President Cheney prior to takeoff. He was advised not to return to Washington, and *Air Force One* was in the air by 9:54 AM—with no specific destination.

President Bush was unable to maintain even regular voice connections for any duration while *Air Force One* was in flight. Individuals monitoring the flight reported a series of constantly dropped phone patches. One of Bush's advisors, attempting to place a call, was told by the military operator, "Ma'am, I'm sorry, we can't reach *Air Force One*."[37] Communications seem to have been as bad if not worse than in 1981 when Vice President George H.W. Bush was largely out of reach during his flight back from Texas following the attempted assassination of President Ronald Reagan. On 9/11, it appears that the *Air Force One* secure voice circuits were virtually unusable for any effective ongoing command and control while the aircraft was in flight. The communications available on *Air Force One* reportedly made it impossible for the president to participate in any of the crisis management teleconferences in process.

9:49 AM—The NORAD commander ordered all "air sovereignty" aircraft armed and moved to "battle stations." He issued no specific Rules of Engagement or engagement guidance.

9:59 AM—A White House military aide joined the NMCC conference and requested fighter escort for *Air Force One* and a combat air patrol over Washington, D.C.

Apparently there were no standing orders for providing military air protection to *Air Force One* during presidential travel. If there had been, the alert fighters supporting the Southeast Air Defense Control would have been the first choice for standby presidential air support. Those fighters were on twenty-four-hour alert at both Homestead and Tyndall air bases in Florida, under command of First Air Force. They could have been airborne to provide cover for *Air Force One* even before it took to the air. Instead, while en route to the Strategic Command base at Barksdale, Louisiana, *Air Force One* was met by Air National Guard fighters from Texas. Regional FAA control advised *the Air Force One* pilot that there were "fast movers" at his 7 o'clock position; the pilot had received no other notification—the aircraft could well have been hostile.[38]

10:02 AM—Flight 93, suspected as a hijacking by a Cleveland Center FAA controller but never reported to NEADS or any other military authority, had been retaken from the terrorists by its passengers and was in pieces on the ground in Pennsylvania.

10:03 AM (**approximate**)—NSC staff member Paul Kurtz, in the Situation Room, made a note that the president had to be asked for "shootdown" authority. Yet another attempt to connect with the president on *Air Force One* failed, and it appears that a connection was made to Vice President Cheney in the deep White House bunker. Between 10:10 and 10:20, having been advised of a hijacked aircraft inbound to Washington, D.C., the vice president verbally issued a "shootdown" order.[39]

As of 10:03 AM the FAA was still not represented on the NMCC "air threat" teleconference.

10:07 AM—One of the Langley fighter pilots, having been moved into combat air patrol over Washington, called NEADS, advising that Baltimore FAA control reported an aircraft over the White House. NEADS commanders immediately ordered the fighters to intercept— under FAA controller guidance—in order to "divert" the aircraft. The NEADS operations commander then asked his battle control commander, "What else . . . intercept and what else?"

NEADS believed it had an intercept in progress over the White House and still had no command authority to engage what appeared to a clear and present threat. Something like an hour and a half had passed, and absolutely no one in the air defense chain of command above CONR had become operationally involved in command decisions regarding on ongoing terror attack. The only response NEADS received was that their request for rules of engagement would be passed up the chain of command.

10:10 AM (approximate)—NEADS began to receive word of another hijacked airliner. It was the airliner that Cleveland and FAA headquarters had never initially reported to anyone. By the time NEADS began to work the report, Flight 93 had already been flown into the ground during the struggle by the passengers to regain control.

At 10:10 the operations commander at NEADS had still received no authorization for engagement of any sort, much less lethal action. The tapes show that he was still being forced, under tremendous stress and pressure, to give "negative clearance to shoot" instructions.

NEADS continued to try to locate the reported aircraft in the vicinity of the White House. They were experiencing communications problems reaching the Langley fighters because the aircraft were flying at such low altitudes. NEADS began to suspect the target was really a helicopter. In the end the remaining suspect airline hijackings all proved to be false alarms, and the target near the White House was actually a report of the Langley jets on combat patrol. Because the FAA controller was unaware of the Langley fighters, they had been sent to intercept themselves.

10:15 AM (approximate)—A "shootdown" order from Vice President Cheney was relayed through the Situation Room and passed to the NMCC at the Pentagon by a White House staff lieutenant colonel. A note recovered by the 9/11 Commission recorded that as of 10:00– 10:18 the order had been issued by the vice president but needed to be confirmed with President Bush.[40] It was never determined how the order was passed on through the NORAD command chain. At the time it was issued the NORAD commander was out of communication, driving to NORAD headquarters. He stated that the order was in effect by the time he arrived.

10:15 AM—NEADS received word from the FAA's Washington Center that the hijacked airliner out of Cleveland was "down"; upon querying the FAA about where it had landed, they were told "He did— he did—he did not land."

10:31 AM—The vice presidential "shootdown" authorization had made its way to NORAD and on to NEADS. General Larry Arnold ordered a general broadcast on the NORAD alert system, stating that the vice president had cleared the Air Force to intercept tracks of interest and shoot them down if they did not respond.[41] Yet even with legal authorization, there were no instructions on specific rules of engagement up to and including lethal action.

10:35 AM—Defense Secretary Donald Rumsfeld joined the crisis call. Rumsfeld provided a forces update, stating that the Atlantic Fleet had departed Norfolk, Virginia, and was moving carriers toward New York. In recalling Rumsfeld's remarks, Clarke noted that no orders had been given for that move but thought that on 9/11 military initiative of any sort was a very good thing. At that point some 120 fighters were reported to be in the air over the United States.

Rumsfeld seems to have played little or no role at all in the crisis response; he had been absent from the conferences for the better part of an hour. In joining the call, he learned of the "shootdown" order for the first time—an order issued far too late to deal with any of the terror strikes but that legally should not have been either issued or implemented without his knowledge and approval.[42] The national Defense Condition level had not been raised and would not be until after two o'clock in the afternoon. Apparently Rumsfeld made no mention of DEFCON status while continuing to monitor the teleconference. It remains unclear exactly who ordered the advanced defense condition.[43]

A transcript reveals Vice President Cheney himself had little understanding of the procedure for issuing the lethal force order. Rumsfeld asked whom Cheney had given the order to—Cheney had passed it to the Situation Room via Richard Clarke, who was leading the crisis response meeting. Rumsfeld then asked if the order had been passed to the military. Cheney answered that it had and that fighters "had already taken a couple of aircraft out."[44] Clearly Cheney—functionally assuming the role of commander in chief—was uninformed on what was actually going on with the air defense and apparently had no personal contact with the NMCC, with NORAD or NEADS.

Later, Rumsfeld commented that Cheney technically had not been in the chain of command to issue such an order, which consisted of the president and himself.[45] Rumsfeld's remark may indeed have been technically correct; however, it appears that ongoing communications problems between the White House and *Air Force One* had essentially removed the president from any credible real-time command and control. Rumsfeld himself had been either out of touch or essentially inactive during the crisis during the entire morning. Under those circumstances, with the vice president acting in the chain of succession to the presidency, it can easily be argued that Cheney made the right decision in assuming authority for the order. It can also be argued that both Bush and Rumsfeld were remiss in not having issued an order authorizing at least some level of military force (such as disabling or physically diverting a hijacked aircraft with attacks on its engines or tail assembly) much earlier.

Both the NEADS and NORAD commanders have stated that they were so uncomfortable with the lack of instructions accompanying the vice presidential authorization that no "shootdown orders" were sent to the fighters. At the point Cheney told Rumsfeld that aircraft had been "taken out," the only orders actually in operational effect were to locate aircraft and report their tail identification numbers.[46]

10:53 AM—The NORAD commander transmitted an operational instruction ordering pilots to intercept suspect aircraft for identification, to divert them from metropolitan areas and to request clearance from him for further action—"most likely you will get clearance to shoot."[47]

In dialog with the 9/11 Commission, NORAD commander Eberhart remarked that he felt the shootdown orders were contingent on "hostile intent" and that interceptors would have to identify such intent before requesting permission to engage.[48] At that point three commercial aircraft had been crashed into buildings including the Pentagon. It seems difficult to understand how "hostile intent" could be determined prior to the aircraft actually lining up on final approach to its target—at which time diversion or shootdown would be difficult and possibly involve considerable destruction and casualties on the ground.

11:45 AM—*Air Force One* landed at the Strategic Command base at Barksdale, Louisiana. The Strategic Command had been heavily involved all week in a Global Guardian exercise, simulating a nuclear exchange and atomic war fighting with the Russian Federation. The exercises were being worked in tandem with NORAD's Vigilant Guardian, Air Combat Command's Crown Guardian and Space Command's Apollo Guardian—all annual exercises.

12:00 noon—President Bush arrived at Barksdale AFB headquarters. During his time at Barksdale he worked on and delivered a broadcast speech, devoted to hunting down and punishing the 9/11 attackers. There appears to be no record of Bush's direct participation in any command-level or crisis conferences while on the ground for almost two hours in the Barksdale facilities.

1:44 PM—The president departed on *Air Force One*, flying on to Strategic Command's Offutt headquarters in Omaha, Nebraska.

2:14 PM—DEFCON 3 went into effect as of 14:14 Zulu military time.[49] By the time DEFCON 3 was declared, Force Defense Condition Delta (terror attack threat) had already been in place for some unspecified time. Normally Delta condition applies only to localized areas or facilities, but on 9/11 it was issued globally for all U.S. military forces and installations.

During the remainder of the day NEADS and NORAD continued to respond to false reports of hijackings. NORAD and the Air Combat Command had established combat air patrols over major cities—bringing some three hundred fighters into place over the nation by the following morning.[50] By early afternoon an EW-3 Sentry AWACS (airborne early warning and control center aircraft) had flown from a training mission off the coast of Florida and was operating over Washington, D.C., providing military-quality radar surveillance for the northeastern metropolitan centers. The Sentry provided the capability of tracking aircraft at low altitudes up to 250 miles and aircraft at higher altitudes up to a 400-mile range.

It took years for a relatively detailed story of the command-and-control chronology of 9/11 to emerge. Many key documents, relating to Bush administration principals and the various organizations involved—including tapes and transcripts from the Air Force and FAA—were initially withheld, and some have yet to be released. In addition, several internal agency investigations are still being held as confidential, including any personnel actions that may have been taken in response to their findings.

Over the months and years following the 9/11, a series of organizational and operational changes were made in response to the attacks. We will proceed to explore those changes and the extent to which they were meaningful rather than merely changes in organization charts. It would be remiss to leave the attack itself without noting that no Federal Agency managers or deputy/principal cabinet-level officials were cited for mismanagement in regard to national security on 9/11. The 9/11 Commission Report carefully chose not to "point fingers." As far as is known, no senior military officers were subject to Boards of Inquiry or personnel action.

Chapter 19

....

POINTS OF FAILURE

The immediate explanations offered, in response to America's inability to defend itself against the attacks of 9/11, all echoed the theme indicated that the acts of terrorism had been a total surprise: There had been a failure of intelligence, a failure of warning. President Bush, National Security Advisor Rice and other Bush administration principals were adamant that they were aware of only a general terror threat but had received no specific warnings of an attack such as actually occurred—one often-heard response was that no one had ever thought of hijacked aircraft being used as weapons. The second most-heard explanation was that the nation's intelligence services were looking overseas, expecting a foreign attack; there was no warning of an impending domestic attack inside the continental United States.

We explored the realities of those responses in the preceding chapters. Now, with more than a decade's worth of data, a more detailed assessment is possible—offering the opportunity to identify a series of very specific "points of failure" relating to the attacks of 9/11. Identification of specific failures offers the baseline needed for moving forward in exploring whether or not the extensive attack response of the following years truly addressed the core weaknesses of American's defense against terror strikes. As with our studies of previous surprise attacks, the first area to examine is that of warnings intelligence.

One conclusion that can be drawn from all the attacks we have studied is that any realistic defense is developed from strategic threat/ warnings intelligence. At its most basic, that begins with an assessment from key intelligence groups with regard to the most probable pending threats to the nation. It was just that sort of strategic intelligence that led to the preparation of a very accurate forecast of the Japanese threat circa 1941. Based on warnings intelligence, a very specific defensive plan for Hawaii and Pearl Harbor was developed. The plan proved to be an extremely accurate projection of the attack that actually occurred on December 7, 1941. The success of the Japanese attacks was due to failures in plan execution rather than strategic warning or planning.

To some extent, the same can be said with regard to warnings intelligence and even defensive exercises conducted prior to the 2001 attacks. A variety of intelligence agencies had already defined an al-Qaeda terror threat. As early as 1996–1998 dialog and even simulations had anticipated suicide aerial attacks against major American targets. Richard Clarke wrote at length about preparations to protect the 1996 Atlanta Olympics from terror attacks. He organized a multi-agency task force for the effort, and one of the individuals he consulted was a retired Navy admiral—and former Navy SEAL—who was heading FAA security at the time. One of the threats discussed during the planning for the Olympics was a terror attack using a rented or stolen aircraft as a weapon against the games. The first suggestion the FAA security chief offered was to ban air traffic in the general area through a "Notice to Airmen."

Clarke's immediate response was that such a ban would not stop a terrorist from hijacking an aircraft and flying it into the Olympic venue in a suicide attack. In response to expressing that scenario, he was told that it was possible to request special radar monitoring but that the chance of the Air Force intercepting such a flight was slim. The larger and more fundamental problem was even more daunting. It was clearly defined by the FAA security chief: "But, of course, we could not even see them on radar if they shut down the transponder on the aircraft. You see, our radars are not defense radars. Our air traffic controllers rely on the aircraft sending out a signal to tell us its altitude."[1]

Next Clarke was told that shooting down a commercial aircraft was a violation of international law so that wasn't even an option if a hijacked airliner was a direct threat to the Olympics—or the city of Atlanta for that matter. In frustration, Clarke then asked the counter-terror team whose job it was to stop a hijacked airliner from flying into the Olympic Stadium. The only answer he received was from the FBI representative: "Don't let them hijack an airliner in the first place."[2]

Irrespective of certain public statements immediately following 9/11, the concept of using hijacked aircraft as weapons was not something that had never really occurred to anyone. In 1997, the highly popular action-adventure writer Tom Clancy opened his newest novel, *Executive Orders*, with a hijacked airliner being flown by a terrorist into the United States Capitol building during a Joint Session of Congress. The crash killed the president, virtually all of his cabinet and Congress as well as majority of the Supreme Court and Joint Chiefs of Staff in one stroke. In point of fact, Clancy's book had been so widely read that a great number of people immediately thought of his book even in the earliest hours of the 9/11 attacks. Clancy was interviewed on CNN that day—in regard to his apparent prediction of terrorists using hijacked airliners as weapons. While the concept was no surprise to him, he stated he would simply never have thought of simultaneous attacks.[3]

There was strategic warning of terror attacks against targets inside the continental United States, and both counterterrorism professionals and the American military had conducted simulations and exercises in line with private and commercial aviation attacks. In 1998 a White House counterterror exercise included a scenario in which terrorists loaded a Learjet with explosives and "took off on a suicide mission to Washington."[4] More significantly, in terms of actual interdiction of such an attack, NORAD actually exercised against the threat of hijacked airliners being used as weapons in a variety of ways—including being crashed into buildings. Such exercises were performed from 1998 to 2001, and according to the exercise summaries, FAA representatives had participated. While none of the exercises were an exact match for the attack of 9/11, several were quite similar and involved the necessity of shooting down commercial aircraft during an attack.

Point of Failure: Air Defense Exercises

NORAD exercised in defending against a wide variety of aerial terror attacks, some exceedingly similar in detail to those that occurred
on 9/11. It is difficult to imagine that such exercises did not surface
the same basic issues—loss of tracking due to transponder shutdown,
low-altitude evasive maneuvers and time-critical authority for military
action against a threatening aircraft. Those same concerns that Clarke
relates were discussed in 1996, during counterterror planning for the
Atlanta Olympics. In his session with the 9/11 Commission, NORAD
commander Ralph Eberhart commented on the general lack of interest
within the FAA of participating in NORAD exercises but provided no
details on the actual level of FAA participation or the individuals involved. He made no mention of any standing concerns relating to radar
tracking threatening aircraft, or of the lack of pre-designated rules for
engaging or shooting down commercial airliners.

Based on Eberhart's remarks, it appears that the NORAD exercises
had not sufficiently surfaced some very fundamental real-world issues.
He stated that all the attacks simulated by NORAD assumed that even
after being hijacked, the aircraft crew would be in control, that the
aircraft's transponders would be on and "squawking" and that there
would be a "substantial" period to pursue the rules of engagement with
National Command Authority.[5] The 9/11 Commission appears not to
have pursued questions of lessons learned from the NORAD exercises or of "after-action" assessments. However, based on the events of
2001, it appears that the exercises must not have fully tested real-world
elements of air defense coordination and command, coordination with
the FAA and involvement of the full chain of command up to National
Command Authority. The exercises also appear not to have surfaced
the need for pre-designated detailed Rules of Engagement and guidance
for military action against commercial aircraft.

During the first hours of the 9/11 attacks there seems to have been a
critical element missing from the air defense—beyond issues of inability
to track aircraft without live transponders. It constantly shows up in
the dialog at NEADS and in their communications with combat control

at CONR. They needed rules of engagement, and they needed instructions on what they could do in using force to engage passenger-carrying hijacked airliners. Either such rules (ROE) did not exist or had not been communicated to the front-line NORAD air defense. In his interview with the 9/11 Commission, NORAD commander Eberhart notes that he spent time after 9/11 developing new, formalized rules of engagement for such circumstances.[6]

Given all the exercises that NORAD and the FAA conducted over the previous three years, it seems that after-action debriefings should have made it quite clear what would be needed if hijackers did seize an aircraft and move to use it as a weapon—regardless of whether that be as a delivery system for chemicals or explosives or with the fueled aircraft as a single gigantic bomb. With the history of the NORAD preparations, it must have been frustrating for those involved in the exercises to hear a post-attack remark such as that from the deputy chairman of the Joint Chiefs of Staff, General Richard Myers: "You hate to admit it, but we hadn't thought about this."[7]

Point of Failure: Access Denial

In 1996 Richard Clarke had chaired a counterterror working-group discussion, with a team that included FBI and FAA advisors. The threat of aerial terror attacks proved to be one of the most challenging addressed by the team. Clarke asked whose job it was to prevent such attacks—and got no answer. After much head-shaking and in considerable frustration he asked the group what could be done; the only answer he received was from the FBI representative: "Don't let them hijack an airliner in the first place."[8] Clarke described no comment from the FAA representative, whose agency represented the final line of defense against a hijacking.

The FAA would appear to have had as much—or more—strategic warning of the aerial terror threat than any other government agency. The Clinton administration counterterror initiative paid particular attention to the FAA, with funding including more than $91 million for checked baggage screening and another $37 million for screening carry-on luggage. Monies for security research and vulnerability testing amounted to more than $25 million. The FAA security force was doubled, with funding of $18 million; canine search teams were funded to another $9 million. There were other monies for personnel additions as well as for passenger security database and terror profiling systems.[9]

In statements and remarks given to the 9/11 Commission, both FAA and Department of Transportation managers essentially gave a disclaimer—to the effect that in 2001 nobody at senior levels of the Bush administration had ever talked to them about a terror threat and terrorism had not been a subject in cabinet meetings. Norman Mineta, head of the Department of Transportation and the cabinet-level officer responsible for the activities of the FAA, testified to the 9/11 Commission that he had never been briefed or advised or attended any interagency meetings dealing with terrorism. He also stated that the subject of terrorism and terror attacks had never been brought up in any of the White House meetings he had attended. When asked whether or not he felt that indicated a failure, his only response was "We had no information of that nature at all."[10] Mineta also appears to have had no knowledge of the ongoing NORAD hijack exercises (apparently involving at least some personnel at the FAA) that had been going on for some three years. Certainly there is no evidence that the FAA itself was raising alarms in regard to tracking or interdicting hijacked airliners.

While several of Mineta's remarks about administration communications appear to be consistent with those of other principals, the 9/11 Commission's inquiry did confirm that there was general knowledge of an aviation terror threat within the FAA.[11] More specifically, the Commission noted that in 2001 the FAA itself provided warnings about terror threats. Between July 27 and September 11, the FAA had issued five new security directives to air carriers and an additional eight general warnings contained in FAA circulars. Several of those were in regard to overseas threats; one generically addressed the carry-on of disguised weapons.

In retrospect, with information circulating between multiple FBI field offices in regard to suspected terrorist aviation activities—including numbers of suspects taking flight training on commercial aircraft—tactical warnings of some sort of al-Qaeda "planes" operation seem to have been plentiful. During the spring and summer of 2001, FBI field offices reported on a flurry of young, foreign Arabian men involved in expensive commercial flight training; some of the men's associates openly expressed their support of martyrdom attacks to FBI agents. In a classic sense, a number of key warning "indicators" were being tripped. Yet either the FBI was not providing any related warnings to the FAA or the warnings were not being addressed.

The FAA/DOT response indicated they were not told about such things—the corollary being that they neither aggressively asked for information about recent changes in the nature of terror threats nor responded to information given to their Security Division. If nobody was pushing information onto them, they had the responsibility for keeping themselves, their procedures, practices and training current with contemporary intelligence. It was the FAA/DOT's responsibility to deny terrorists access to commercial aircraft, not only to the aircraft themselves but to the flight deck of those aircraft. Yet as of the fall of 2001 the FAA had initiated no new practices to screen terrorists during travel on domestic flights, to report suspects to law enforcement prior to boarding, to protect flight crews or to secure the flight deck. They had taken no initiative to explore known hijack issues—such as tracking aircraft with transponders turned off—with their military support, NORAD. Throughout 1941 Japanese observers in Hawaii reported on the American Navy's offshore air surveillance patrols. Those patrols maintained the same flight schedules and routes, even after the war alert was issued, right up to the time of the actual Japanese attacks. Over the course of two years of taking domestic flights around the United States, the jihadi terrorists had observed no new "disruptive" commercial airline security measures of any sort; the airline security screening and onboard practices remained the same.

If anyone truly "didn't get" terrorism, it appears to have been the DOT and FAA. In the previous chapter we have explored many of the details concerning exactly how they failed—even in the face of warnings by their own Red Teams. The question remains as to why FAA headquarters seems to have been so deeply mired in inertia. Certainly FAA personnel had observed the grounding of more than a dozen international flights out of Asia during the Bojinka incident; anyone with an interest in aviation security would have followed that story out of the Philippines, even if only in the newspapers. The terrorists' trial was held in New York City and the incident had been the subject of ongoing newspaper coverage as recently as 1996.[12] Media coverage alone should have triggered some ongoing interest and inquiries from the FAA to the CIA and FBI about an al-Qaeda focus on airliner attacks.

Nobody at FAA or DOT appears to have stepped up to mentally "owning" the responsibility for denying potential access to commercial aircraft. In 1941 the commanders in Hawaii and the Philippines constantly complained to the War Department about the lack of training, personnel and equipment. Those commanders knew they owned the defense of their commands. But as of 2001, there appear to be no signs that any senior FAA manager (other than individuals on their own Red Teams) barraged their bosses with terror defense issues—if so, they made no mention of that to the 9/11 Commission.

Point of Failure: Interdiction

In 1941, before today's extensive intelligence community existed, warnings about a probable and increasingly imminent Japanese attack came from within the American military itself—primarily from Navy signals intelligence—via radio tracking of Japanese fleet movements and reconnaissance (both aerial and submarine) by both Army and Navy assets. Observations of Japanese operational movements continued, and in November 1941 a primary indicator "tripped." Japanese forces were making efforts to conceal their locations while clearly engaged in movements toward known targets; intelligence analysts could only assume that some type of attack was in the making, and a special war alert was justified.

The War Department (Army) and the Navy Department expected the commanders assigned to the alerted areas to take command responsibility. That meant developing and carrying out the actions needed to detect and interdict anticipated Japanese attacks. There was no expectation that there would necessarily be any specific tactical warning (exactly when, where and with what weapons) prior to the earliest phases of the actual strikes. While the commanders of both the War and Navy departments reported directly to the president, there was also no expectation that the president was involved in actual preparation of a defense against the strategic threat. The commands had been warned; they owned the defense.

In the attacks of 9/11, the point can be made that the CIA failed to provide critical information to the FBI, information that would have provided very early indications that known al-Qaeda operatives were moving toward the United States. Yet by 2001, as an institution, the FBI had years of experience with terror attacks, domestically including the first bombing of the World Trade Center and internationally with the Bojinka airliner bombing plot and the attack on the USS *Cole*. Its files covered numbers of al-Qaeda operatives, many of whom would later be associated or participate in the "planes operation" of 9/11. It could have moved on its own initiative to aggressively "watch" for them, as conspiracy suspects—much in the fashion it had "watched" organized crime and drug networks for years.

Even without any special "watch" alert, the FBI had begun to receive indications of commercial aircraft-related terror activities as early as November 1999. Its Phoenix field office had reported on an apparent effort by two suspicious foreigners to collect detailed information on aircraft security measures, including flight-deck access security. Further inquiry revealed that both men were associated with Islamic extremists; one of the two men had received explosives and car bombing training in Afghanistan. One of the men's known associates was interviewed by the FBI and openly stated he felt the United States was a legitimate target; a poster of bin Laden was openly displayed in his room. Based on that incident alone, the Bureau had a solid lead that radical Islamists were inside the United States, very possibly in the early phases of developing an aircraft-related operation. Within months that indication was corroborated by additional reports that terrorists were planning to send men to the United States to study flying, even though the reports noted that the purpose of this training was "unknown." Beyond that the leads should have been given significant priority, since the Bureau sources had specifically described the aircraft training as highly important, supported by unlimited spending— "open-ended funding had been approved to ensure its success."[13]

Historically the FBI's lack of centralized information practices was a well-known problem, immediately obvious even to outsiders assigned to work FBI liaison. Yet in May 2001, when the Phoenix FBI field office reported to FBI headquarters and the FBI counterterrorism unit with regard to a developing effort by bin Laden and al-Qaeda to send "students" into the United States for aviation training, the field office included a reminder of the 1999 flight-deck access incident. The Phoenix office advised that its records indicated that an "inordinate" number of individuals of "investigative interest" were becoming involved with aviation—a trend that had actually been going on for more than two years since the 1999 report.

Regardless of any earlier delays by the CIA, on August 21, 2001, an FBI liaison to the CIA had advised FBI headquarters about multiple United States entries of a major al-Qaeda suspect. At that point the Bureau had firm notice that a number of radical Islamists were "operational" inside the United States. That knowledge alone was far more than was known at the beginning of the 1999 millennium alert. One of the standard guidelines in indications intelligence is that when the threat's "capability" is seen to significantly increase, it is time to generate warnings. In this instance the most fundamental warnings indicator had tripped—multiple terror suspects had moved from overseas into the United States. That alone would have justified a domestic security alert with the priority and urgency of the millennium effort of December 1999.

During that same period, only weeks before the 9/11 attacks, an FBI field office in Minneapolis advised headquarters of a very suspicious foreigner who wanted simulator training on a flight from London to New York City. The FBI field office responded immediately, detaining him on a visa expiration issue and questioning him and a companion traveling on a Saudi passport. The companion openly commented on his fundamentalist beliefs and his approval of "martyrs" and stated he himself was preparing to fight. Intelligence inquiries produced a response from the French that the "student" interested in flying routes into New York had been in an al-Qaeda training camp in Afghanistan.

Given the proactive work of certain of its field offices—as well as several weeks' warning that a known al-Qaeda figure had traveled to the United States, back overseas and then back inside the United States once again—as an organization the Bureau had considerable warnings intelligence that al-Qaeda was not only operating domestically but that its associates were very much involved with flight training, commercial aircraft and specifically interest in New York City. As an organization it had produced much of that intelligence internally, even without any major "push" from either FBI headquarters or the Department of Justice. In retrospect the point of FBI failure was clearly not in its field officers; it was most definitely at headquarters level.

The simple fact is that no effective defense assumes the absolute advantage of tactical warning against a standing threat; it has to be proactive and ongoing, exercised for months or even years. Changes in key indicators—such as the movement of combatants—simply allow warnings to be provided to those charged with the defense, as well as the nation's national security leadership. Perhaps the most pragmatic description of a classic defensive mindset can be taken from SAC's early commander, General Curtis LeMay. He believed a truly dedicated defense functions as though the war has already begun; it's just a matter of where and when the first or next attack occurs. If your forces are not constantly on alert and ready to defend against an attack, there is no way to defeat it. Such a defense has to be routinely and thoroughly exercised at all levels, from the operations personnel to the headquarters commands. That was a lesson LeMay and most of the World War II military leaders had learned from Pearl Harbor and equally from the Philippines.

In the last months of 1999, the United States had moved to initiate its first global-terror "war alert," based largely in warnings relating to imminent attacks in Jordan. That overseas threat was immediately generalized into both global and domestic counterterror initiatives, with National Security Advisor Sandy Berger bluntly addressing a cabinet principals meeting: "I spoke with the President and he wants you all to know [Attorney General Janet Reno, FBI director Louis Freeh and CIA director George Tenet] . . . this is it, nothing is more important, all assets. We stop this."[14]

Berger directed Clarke to develop a consolidated political-military plan for a millennium alert, alerting units, increasing security and rounding up suspects around the world. And in the United States itself, in today's vernacular, there was a surge in counterterrorism interdiction efforts, with thousands of FBI agents moving onto the streets pushing for leads on plots and asserting general disruption pressure against potential terror operations in progress.

In its restrained fashion, the 9/11 Commission noted that, based on information in hand, in 2001 the responsible national security agencies failed to be proactive and that "effective operations [interdiction] were not launched."[15] Domestically, only the FBI had the authority and legal permission to carry out the field-level operations that could have delayed or disrupted the attacks of 9/11. A footnote to the Commission Report points out that the most effective action to disrupt the attacks in the short term would have been for the FBI to issue a "Be On the Look Out" advisory (BOLO), possibly combined with a media campaign. Yet it goes on to state that that would have been done only if there was a concern of an immediate al-Qaeda terror attack and that "no one in the FBI—or any other agency—believed that to be true."[16] With the information we have detailed, that remark seems highly questionable. Such warnings most definitely were given, and as was demonstrated by later inquires, if a BOLO alert had been initiated or if experienced FBI analysts and investigators had been pushed to search against the data that was available in the weeks before the attacks, they would have located "planes operations" participants and very possibly could have disrupted the 9/11 plot.

Point of Failure: Ownership

Fundamentally the commander in chief "owns" the national security and the physical defense of the United States. That command ownership is reflected in the evolution of what has become the National Command Authority, limited to the president and the secretary of defense. Beyond that ownership, historically and operationally, defending the nation and its people against physical attack from foreign forces has routinely been the responsibility of the military. In the era of the World Wars, defense was a responsibility of the War Department; by the era of the Cold War it lay with the Department of Defense. Yet the state of war declared by al-Qaeda had not been interpreted as a foreign military threat—terror attacks were treated as violations of law, not acts of war. The terrorists were themselves legally viewed to be acting as criminals, not military combatants. The result was that overseas, the response to terror attacks fell to the State Department, addressed through international legal relations with the governments of foreign nations. Domestically, terror attacks were to be addressed as a law enforcement matter for the Department of Justice and the FBI.

Both federal agencies developed practices for responding to terror attacks, ranging from crisis management to legal investigation and prosecution. In contrast, the operational side of disrupting or otherwise interdicting actual attacks was far more complex, especially with regard to jihadi terror attacks inside the United States. The FBI was expected to receive intelligence from both CIA and NSA and to develop its own threat intelligence—within FISA guidelines and compartmentalized to support DOJ legal action where charges evident of conspiracy or intent were indicated.

The 9/11 Commission Report points out that the CIA's practice of indications analysis began to decline following the collapse of the Soviet Union; the CIA's counterterrorism group had not developed an equivalent level of expertise prior to 9/11. The report fails to highlight that similar skills had never existed within the FBI, other than as related to very specific task forces such as its Organized Crime Unit. In point of fact, with the FBI assigned as the first line of continental terror defense, a dramatic increase in predictive threat analysis should have been a focus for the Bureau. The Bureau also needed to organize its activities around detailed threat assessments—something it did not do and was not doing even a year after the 9/11 attacks. The Bureau was active in preparing for response to terror attacks, plus investigating and assisting to prosecute them. Yet it is hard to avoid the conclusion, not stated in the 9/11 Commission's Report, that there had been a serious failure of "ownership" of disruptive terror defense at the highest levels of the Department of Justice—as well as at FBI headquarters.

In 2001 the FBI failed to carry out proactive disruption activities, even with some four months' notice that al-Qaeda operatives were inside the United States and with some very clear information from its own field offices demonstrating a strong interest not just in learning about commercial aircraft but in piloting such aircraft. Attorney General Janet Reno assertively positioned the FBI in a lead role against terrorism, even pushing back against intrusion on FBI "turf." Legally and functionally the FBI/DOJ held ownership; Attorney General Reno had specifically noted the DOJ/FBI responsibility to "prevent terrorist attacks before they occur." The agencies had accepted and even claimed the mission, but based on the data now available it is highly questionable that at a headquarters level they were acting as if they "owned" the prevention aspect of that mission.

A Government Accountability Office (GAO) report on issues in combating terrorism, issued in 1999, notes that while the FBI had indeed conducted interagency "exercises" with a variety of other government agencies, they were virtually all scenarios involving response to terror attacks ("consequence management"). Exercises ranged from working on joint investigation of terror bombing with the ATF to "tabletop" exercises with FEMA on interagency and intergovernmental government issues (FEMA was hesitant to perform field exercises due to lack of resources). Relatively large-scale field exercises were conducted with the Department of Defense, again "consequence" focused. In 1997 the FBI and DOD carried out an exercise built around terrorist release of chemical agents in New York City. The FBI also worked "consequence" management exercises with the Department of Veterans Affairs.[17]

Reno claimed ownership for her agencies but appears to have established a form of ownership focused on responding to attacks, not disrupting or preempting them. From that perspective, her successors in the Bush administration were largely following the same set of practices and priorities.

The one group that does not appear at all in the GAO summary, the agency that seems to have been totally isolated from even FBI counterterror planning and consequence exercises, is the one organization that actually served as the last line of defense in any terror activity involving aircraft—the Federal Aviation Administration. It was up to the FAA, working with the FBI and local law enforcement, to perform "access denial." Yet the FAA is totally missing from the GAO report's summary of federal agencies working with the FBI to exercise and capture lessons from counterterrorism operations.[18]

It appears that the FAA had not embraced the ownership of counterterrorism, working neither proactively with the FBI nor with NORAD. That is particularly significant given that in terms of real-world operations, the FAA "owned" the continental airspace. The American military was not legally authorized to respond to a suspected aircraft hijacking without an FAA request, and even then the military aircraft were to be placed under a mix of NORAD combat control and FAA airspace control. Only in the event that the NORAD commander declared continental airspace under total military control were military combat controllers given airspace command priority. If that was not complicated enough during the stress of an actual attack, new orders from the Joint Chiefs in June 2001 had placed the National Military Command Center in an operational role for all FAA requests for military assistance—yet the NMCC appears never to have convened an air threat conference or an air threat exercise prior to 9/11, and there is no available evidence that the FAA briefed or attempted to exercise its controllers on the new protocol.

Point of Failure: Command and Control

Ownership, whether it be of interdiction, disruption, access denial or fully realistic drills and exercises, was a point of failure before the morning of September 11, 2001. But once the first hijacked aircraft struck the North Tower of the World Trade Center, issues of owning the defense against terror attacks moved to another level. At that point defense of the nation became a matter of command. Unfortunately, the facts indicate that however well those on the front lines performed—and they did exceptionally well given the constraints placed on them—the same cannot necessarily be said for the top levels of the chain of command. To be effective, a defense against any attack only works when the defenders either have the weapons they need ready to hand, or are very quickly supplied with them. The official record claimed the failure was simply a lack of situational intelligence. Specifically, NORAD Commander, General Ralph Eberhart, told the 9/11 Commission that if his people had been kept effectively informed by the FAA, they would have been able "to shoot down all three aircraft—all four aircraft."

Yet as we know from our exploration of the chronology of 9/11 events, such an outcome would have been literally and factually impossible.[19] No "shootdown" authorization had even been issued at the time of the last of the hijacked airliner strikes. Of equal concern is the fact that as late as March 2004, Eberhart told the 9/11 Commission that he had "no knowledge of the circumstances that initiated the scramble" of fighter jets from Langley AFB and had only recently come to know about the launch of the first interceptors that day—a statement that certainly reinforces the impression that he had either been misinformed in regard to his remarks about being able to successfully "shoot down" all four airliners or that NORAD staff had not done a through and accurate after-action study and/or timeline of events.[20]

It is difficult to judge Eberhart's firsthand knowledge of the day's events. We know that he did participate in the NMCC military threat conference, but there is no record of his personal, real-time communications with NEADS, CONR, First Air Force or any of the military units involved in front-line response. In his 9/11 Commission interview Eberhart described maintaining contact with the Pentagon during the crisis, in particular with General Richard Myers, Deputy Chairman of the Joint Chiefs. However, as noted in the chronology of events, Myers himself was not at the Pentagon; he had been in a meeting with Senator Max Cleland and appears not to have participated in the NMCC air threat conference until after all the airliner strikes were over.

On 9/11, as NORAD commander, Eberhart held the authority to assert continental military control in respect to the declaration of an air security emergency (SCATANA/Security Control of Air Traffic and Air Navigation Aids). Such a move would have placed NORAD in control of American airspace and the FAA controllers under the control of the military. Contrary to much of what had been written about 9/11, American airspace had actually been cleared of all commercial traffic and a total ground stop put in place previously—three times, in 1960, 1961 and 1962. Each year NORAD conducted major military exercises to test the American air defenses. During those defense exercises, conducted as Operation Skyshield, NORAD had closed and controlled the continental airspace, and some six thousand penetration and interception missions were flown by aircraft from the United States, Canada and the United Kingdom.

On 9/11 Eberhart initially deferred to the FAA in terms of continental airspace control, telling the 9/11 Commission that he felt the FAA controllers would be more effective in clearing commercial traffic.[21] That decision left FAA controllers independent of military authority, giving a secondary role to NEADS combat controllers. It was some two hours after the second hijacked airliner hit the South Tower that Eberhart ordered full military control of American airspace. With regard to the effort to clear airspace and avoid potential accidents, the decision made sense. However, it also resulted in issues such as the failure to establish immediate combat air patrols over New York and Washington, D.C. Military control priority might have also eliminated the NEADS/FAA controller disconnect that sent the Langley fighters out of commercial airspace rather than directly to the Washington/Baltimore area as ordered.

More importantly, the issue of "owning" the air defense repeatedly surfaced in the ongoing dialog about authorizations and ROE that occurred at NEADS, beginning as early as the initial launch of the Otis fighters toward New York City. NEADS and the CONR combat center in Florida consistently discussed what they should do if they managed to locate and intercept a hijacked aircraft. The tapes clearly demonstrate that they were frustrated by a lack of orders or directives as much as their inability to locate the airliners. They are recorded on tape discussing the issue as early as 9:17 AM. Yet based on the released transcript, NORAD command does not appear to have raised the issue of ROE during the "air threat" teleconference; apparently no calls were made to Air Force headquarters, no one sought out the Secretary of Defense for "shootdown" authority and direction, and neither the NMCC nor NORAD headquarters contacted the commander in chief. The issue seems to have been left to be raised by Clarke in the Situation Room, with actual authorization by Cheney in the White House bunker. That of course raises serious command-and-control issues. Subjectively it is difficult not to feel that the top levels of the chain of command failed the front-line NORAD personnel at NEADS and CONR for well over an hour—while the nation was clearly under air attack.

Even worse, at the point at which Cheney informed Secretary of Defense Rumsfeld that a "shootdown" order had been issued and interceptors were actually "downing" hijacked aircraft, the order had only just made its way down through NORAD to be broadcast to its control centers—including NEADS. And we now know that due to the lack of directions or conditions supplied with the authorization, NEADS did not immediately issue actual attack authority, nor did the NORAD commander. Only just before 11 AM did the NORAD commander issue an order to "divert" target aircraft, stating that if requested, "shootdown" clearance would "most likely" be given.

We noted in earlier chapters that the 9/11 Commission became so dissatisfied with the information that it was getting from the Air Force and the FAA—including the withholding of operations center tapes—they began to suspect they were actually being misled about the events of September 11, 2001. The Commission was especially concerned about the information they had received from senior NORAD officers. The head of the Commission, former New Jersey governor Thomas Kern, commented, "We to this day don't know why NORAD . . . told us what they told us. . . . It was just so far from the truth. . . . It's one of those loose ends that never got tied."[22]

The Commission's panel members were so frustrated that they held a secret meeting in the summer of 2004 as their work was ending. Members felt that they held emails and other evidence that would have met the rules of probable cause for violation of the law in certain testimony. Many members reportedly wanted to refer the matter to the Justice Department for criminal investigation, citing false statements given to the Commission as legal violations. In covering the story, *The Washington Post* noted that by that point there was considerable "tension" between the Bush administration and the 9/11 Commission. In the end the Commission compromised by the simple expedient of turning its allegations over to the inspectors general of the Departments of Defense and Transportation for their investigation.

When queried by *The Washington Post*, a Pentagon spokesman said that it was preparing a report on whether or not the statements given to the Commission were "knowingly false." The DOD report eventually took the same tack it had in May 2005, blaming any inconsistencies on Department of Defense record keeping. A Transportation Department spokesperson said that an internal report had been completed but that there would be no public comment on the inspector general's inquiry.

With regard to the defense of the United States on 9/11, the official government "after-action" assessment stands as represented by the statement of General Richard Myers, commander of NORAD until February 2000 and acting chief of the Joint Chiefs of Staff on 9/11. Myers offered prepared testimony on the events of 9/11; his statement declared that "lines of authority, communications and command were clear; and the Commander in Chief and Secretary of Defense conveyed clear guidance to the appropriate military commanders."[23]

It should be noted that General Myer's testimony was not based in real-time, first-hand knowledge of the operational military events of 9/11. Although the Joint Chief's Vice Chairman's Office (Myers)—represented by the Vice Chairman's Executive Officer—joined the NMCC "significant event/air threat" conference call from its inception, Myers himself was on Capitol Hill. He was meeting with Senator Max Cleland regarding upcoming hearings related to Myers's proposed appointment as the new chairman of the Joint Chiefs.[24] He remained in Cleland's office for some forty-five minutes after the second aircraft had been flown into the South Tower of the World Trade Center. It is true that the Joint Chiefs, not even its acting Chairman, have no command authority in real-time military operations, so Myers's personal presence was not mandatory. However, it is important to note that there is no record proving he was privy to the decision-making and activities we find in the tape of the NMCC conferences—and in certain instances his later statements appear to be in direct conflict with those taped events.

Still, the most fundamental problem with Myers's overall assessment of command and control is that a detailed study of the primary documents related to the military response on 9/11 (the NEADS and NMCC transcripts), as well as a detailed chronology of events of the day, simply do not support his assessment. The lines of authority were clear but were not followed in practice. The commander in chief's access and instructions were extremely limited during the initial hours, both by his own actions and by problems in communications from and to *Air Force One*. The Secretary of Defense, when present on command calls, was primarily an observer and was not consulted on many of the most fundamental decisions of the morning, including the "shootdown" directive. None of the senior commanders immediately exercised their responsibility in clarifying instructions and rules of engagement to support the "shootdown" authorization when it was given, largely with a nod of the head by the vice president.

The failure to recognize—or admit to—such basic facts is a point of failure in and of itself. More important than simply protecting individuals from criticism, it relates back to a much more basic issue that we have seen throughout our study of surprise attacks. While front-line organizations and commanders spend immense amounts of time planning, organizing and exercising their response to an attack, those exercises most often occur without the participation of the most senior commanders, and almost never with the active involvement of National Command Authority figures. Simply if bluntly stated, senior civilian leadership generally does not have combat or crisis response experience, spends little time rehearsing or otherwise practicing its command responsibilities, and when a crisis does occur, almost never carries out its responsibilities in accordance with the plan or in a timely fashion.

In addition, the senior civilian leadership—including not only the principals but those in line of succession—infrequently request, demand or spend sufficient time learning and practicing their crisis roles. We have seen exceptions, but only rarely. Beyond that, in the midst of a crisis, under stress, military aides seem to be loath to tell presidents, vice presidents and secretaries of defense what they should be doing, knowing full well that such advice, if taken badly, could end up being a "career-limiting move."

There is at least a partial solution to this quandary, one we saw develop early in the Cold War. It requires that rules of engagement and even retaliation be developed in detail, down to the specific elements of guidance for field commanders. Authorization is then given in the form of "pre-delegation" for those rules to be followed if the chain of command is not intact or disrupted by communications issues during an attack. We explored that practice in detail early in this work. As a former commander, President Eisenhower understood the situation well enough not only to authorize pre-delegation for defense but to personally prepare very specific instructions of guidance for those commanders given special authority.

Something of that nature should have been developed in the face of escalating terror threats and attacks from 1998 to 2001, especially given significant concerns about the use of chemical, radiation and other weapons of mass destructions in terror attacks. Clearly it was not— either that or the failure in command was even worse on 9/11 than is now evident. Of course, in retrospect it is possible to outline a variety of other preparedness measures that could have been taken. In the following chapter we will review post-9/11 security changes and explore contemporary security and preparedness issues.

Chapter 20

....

GOING FORWARD

The jihadi terror attacks of 9/11 resulted in deaths and injuries comparable to the Pacific attacks of 1941, almost entirely among civilians and first responders. In the aftermath of the attacks, the nation became involved in more than a decade of large-scale and immensely expensive military combat and nation building overseas, new legislation was immediately enacted to deal with terrorism at home, and major changes were made in the American security infrastructure. The changes were so broad and the ensuing decades of overseas combat so extensive that it's a challenge to isolate and evaluate those specific areas that relate to the "points of failure" we explored in the preceding chapter.

Despite all the dialog and assurances, there were only limited efforts made to fully characterize the ongoing jihadi terror threat or acknowledge what was effectively a state of global warfare against the United States. President Bush did not request a formal declaration of war against al-Qaeda or its associates—nor did Congress move to make such a declaration at its own initiative. Instead, Congress gave the president an Authorization for the Use of Military Force (AUMF), granting permission for him to take whatever military action he deemed to be appropriate to act specifically against those who had "committed, directed, authorized or aided in the 9/11 attacks."[1] The authorization cited the nation's right to self-defense and established a legal basis for preemptive action using either covert or overt force.

That authorization has continued in force through both the Bush and Obama presidencies and became the legal justification for ongoing military actions directed against not just those involved in the 9/11 attacks but a much broader range of individuals and groups associated with jihadi terrorism and insurgencies. The AUMF was also used to justify a series of domestic electronic surveillance activities conducted outside the oversight mandated by the Foreign Intelligence Surveillance Act of 1978. The ongoing legal reliance on the AUMF, with no further congressional action over some fifteen years, is reminiscent of the continued use of the Tonkin Gulf resolution to justify military action across Southeast Asia, far beyond its initial context.

President George W. Bush characterized the American response to the 9/11 attacks as "acts of war," and he routinely described America as being engaged in a broad series of domestic and military actions as parts of a "war on terror." Yet no declaration of war had been made by the U.S. Congress, and the language in the AUMF had actually been written to limit the actions of the president. In his assessment of the AUMF, written for Congress in 2007, national defense specialist Richard Grimmett noted that broad initial language in the initial AUMF drafts would have given the president open-ended authority to act against any nation, group or individuals considered to be potential aggressors or terrorists—with no limits on the duration of the authorization. That language was altered and the final document was specifically worded to authorize action only against those "directly involved in aiding or materially supporting the September 11, 2001, attacks on the United States."[2] Grimmett makes it clear that the AUMF, as passed by Congress, was not written to authorize military action "against terrorists generally."[3]

He also noted in his report to Congress that the Congressional Joint Resolution authorized military force against "organizations and persons" linked to the 9/11 attacks. Previous authorizations had permitted action against "unnamed nations" but never against organizations and persons. Given that Congress had not issued a declaration of war "against terrorists generally" but broadly against the "organizations and persons" associated with the 9/11 attacks, ongoing actions were conducted very much at the personal discretion of Presidents Bush and Obama. Many of the counterterror initiatives of the Bush administration were based in administration legal interpretations of its authority under the AUMF—such as exemptions from FISA—or by legal opinions produced by the staff of its attorney general. Terms such as "war on terror," "enemy combatant" and "acts of war" were often used to describe the Bush administration actions. In reality both Bush and Obama acted against the threat of terror attacks in much the same way previous presidents had acted against the threat of global Communism during the decades of the Cold War—at their own initiative, in their role as commander in chief, and in accordance with their responsibility for national security.

With regard to actual ownership, terror plots continued to be treated as illegal acts by individuals rather than acts of war. The FBI retained the lead role in domestic security, including the identification and disruption of potential terror attacks; the State Department retained its former responsibilities in regard to attacks overseas.

There were changes to the overall national security structure, largely in response to the 9/11 Commission's findings of failures in intelligence sharing and inadequate intelligence analysis.[4] The Office of National Intelligence was created to function as the principal advisor on intelligence matters to the president, the National Security Council and a new entity, the Homeland Security Council. Its director effectively became the chief advisor to both the president and the National Security Council. The Director of National Intelligence (DNI) also served on the cabinet-level principals committee and the deputy on the Deputies Committee of the cabinet. Ostensibly the objectivity of the DNI director provided additional balance to national threat assessments, and the director has the authority to demand intelligence sharing through policy directives as well as in setting the national priorities for intelligence collection.[5]

In addition, a new Department of Homeland Security (DHS) was created to provide centralized oversight over security activities and assigned to coordinate domestic counterterror activities across a broad range of federal, state and local law enforcement agencies. One notable organizational change did occur between the George W. Bush and Obama administrations. President Obama viewed homeland security as "indistinguishable" from national security and moved to create a single, integrated staff structure to deal with both under the National Security Council.[6] That move consolidated the independent foreign and domestic terror responsibilities of the Bush administration into a single staff structure reporting to the National Security Council. A new presidential directive on the consolidation of reporting also elevated the role of the national security advisor within the Obama administration, bringing it back to a level of functionality seen during the administration of Bill Clinton. In that role the national security advisor acts more as a "broker" on issues presented to the president, providing analysis of pros and cons, monitoring implementation and serving only the president as a constituency.[7] While President George W. Bush preferred to make the final decision on consensus proposals, Obama reportedly preferred to see options and analyses, crafting his own solution.

It remains difficult to assess the reorganization as a truly fundamental change; it appears similar to earlier organizational attempts to consolidate intelligence efforts of the various military services through the creation of the Defense Intelligence Agency (DIA) or the earliest efforts of the Truman administration to consolidate and centralize the analysis and reporting of foreign intelligence under the Central Intelligence Agency. It is tempting to make the observation that whenever communications or oversight issues arise within a given agency or among agencies, the most politically correct response is simply to add another layer of consolidation and oversight as a solution. Whether such actions are truly productive remains an open question. For a detailed study of that issue, readers are referred to a National Defense University Study of 2011 that provides a contemporary and highly insightful discussion of organization changes related to the National Security Policy process.[8]

Following 9/11 both covert and overt warfare against overseas terrorism fell directly under presidential authority and was conducted in an increasingly complex legal context, merging covert operations with overt action by military forces in a type of "gray warfare."[9] Under the Obama administration overseas military efforts against terrorism began to evolve from major military deployments and nation building toward a focus on military assistance programs. Specific military attacks against al-Qaeda and evolving efforts against the rise of the fanatically radical

ISIS movement became focused on military support for local groups or nations—aimed at preventing jihadi insurgencies from taking control of physical territories. In turn, the more radical jihadists began to focus on creating their own geographic domains, claiming territory and generating new fears of denied staging areas for terrorist plots.

In an effort to maintain our focus on the subject of surprise attacks, we will avoid America's foreign efforts against jihadi terrorism and focus specifically on post-9/11 changes made to address the 9/11 attacks.

Interdiction

As far back as the 1997, points were raised about limited areas of law that needed to be altered not only to allow the FBI more freedom in collecting real-time intelligence on suspected terrorists/networks but to share it more broadly within the Bureau. The need for limited changes of that nature had also been mentioned by FBI director Louis Freeh in his remarks on the 1999 FBI counterterror plan.

One of the first responses to the 9/11 attacks was a call from the Department of Justice for immediate legislative action support to expand its powers in counterterrorism investigations. That request was fulfilled with congressional passage of the Patriot Act.[10] If the nation had declared war or broadly addressed the new international terror threat, Congress might well have revisited and reworked the body of the National Security Act of 1947 as well as legislation relating to the CIA and NSA. That legislation and its related legal code had become dated both with the end of the Cold War and the emergence of the ongoing challenge of global jihadi attacks and insurgencies.[11]

Instead, the Patriot Act took a criminal approach to dealing with terrorism, classifying a number of activities as crimes and extending the punishments for terror-related crimes in general. Specifically Title VII of the act designated terrorism as a criminal activity. In addition the Patriot Act amended the National Security Act of 1947 to deal with intelligence issues related to terrorism.

The post-attack discussions of 9/11 intelligence failures highlighted limitations on the types of domestic surveillance allowed, its timeliness and the legal "wall" that was felt to impede the sharing of foreign intelligence. In point of fact, as we saw in previous chapters and as documented by the 9/11 Commission, most of the problems with the surveillance and intelligence "wall" had actually come from internal confusion and misunderstandings by FBI and DOJ employees.

The new Patriot Act addressed that issue, albeit a bit ambiguously. Title IX: Improved Intelligence of the Patriot Act specified that international terrorist activities fell under the scope of foreign intelligence under the National Security Act of 1947. It required the CIA director to work with the attorney general to ensure that electronic search and surveillance information collected by the CIA under FISA was disseminated for efficient and effective foreign intelligence purposes; however, no specific guidelines were described in regard to that dissemination.

The rather vague language related to CIA practices was followed by very specific language calling for the attorney general to inform the CIA director of any foreign intelligence obtained by the Department of Justice and to promptly advise the CIA of any FBI/DOJ intention to investigate a foreign intelligence source including any investigations "tipped off" by a member of the intelligence community. Whether or not this new wording resolved the "wall" issue is uncertain, but it did charter the attorney general and CIA director with doing so. If nothing else, it allowed the FBI to claim foreign intelligence sources as part of an investigation, forcing the CIA to immediately provide information related to those sources. If actually acted on accordingly by the CIA, at least some of the intelligence-sharing issues related to the 9/11 plot would have been resolved. Title IX also dramatically expanded the types and availability of orders for all aspects of surveillance, including electronic, computer and physical surveillance.

Title II of the Patriot Act specifically allowed the gathering of foreign intelligence from both U.S. and non-U.S. citizens. Most significantly, the Patriot Act allowed any United States district court judge to issue surveillance orders, extending the access to such orders considerably beyond that of the FISA courts. This point addressed the reality that American citizens had both wittingly and unwittingly enabled terror acts and likely would do so in the future.

That practice was not inconsistent with prior FBI activities, in which American citizens were singled out for surveillance in conjunction with special classes of crimes including sabotage, treason during wartime or organized crime activities and racial terrorism during peacetime. Still, there had been constant protest against such practices and similar objections developed as a result of the Patriot Act's authorization of broader surveillance against American citizens. The protests were magnified by the scope of surveillance—extending to computer files, voice mail, and Internet sessions—including a major expansion of what specific usage data could be demanded for both voice and data services. Both the scope and the quantity of data being collected for counterterrorism (as well as potentially for other foreign intelligence and federal criminal investigations) became major points of privacy contention. Those same concerns extended to the greatly expanded National Security Agency collections activities authorized by congressional legislation following the 9/11 attacks.

In 2001 the NSA began collecting "metadata" from telephone companies and international Internet services. The type of data does not include the actual content of the call or messaging but does characterize the communication—with information about the devices involved, the routing of the messaging, and account identity of the sender and receiver. It also provides certain geolocation information, especially for wireless device communications.[12] The metadata descriptive information can be used in computer searches based on location, account identity, user numbers and other transaction information used in processing both voice and data communications. The goal of such "bulk" metadata collections was to build massive databases that could be searched for leads and associates in the event that a terror suspect was identified.

Such a search could develop a picture of a suspect's extended social network, something key to the operations of jihadi operations. Metadata searches, combined with electronic and physical surveillance information, can also reveal individuals making use of anonymous accounts of various sorts. While multiple users can protect their identities through the use of a common anonymous account, when actively using the account the dates and locations of access are visible in the metadata.

Used in conjunction with physical surveillance on one or more suspects involved, their anonymous identities can be revealed or confirmed by matching account access to the surveillance.

Bulk data collections (sometimes referred to as "warrantless surveillance") became a special source of legal contention, even early on within the Bush administration. Although the FBI and intelligence agencies felt it to be useful, they could not produce hard data to show that its value justified the controversial practice. An FBI study of the first four years of the program determined that only 1.2% of new leads came from the program. In 2004 the Deputy Attorney General, James Comey, threatened to resign if the program was extended without changes. In the end, President Bush agreed to modifications and the program was reauthorized only under that agreement.[13]

Beyond NSA warrantless/bulk data activities, specific objection to the Patriot Act centered on a limited number of basic privacy issues.[14] One issue pertained to its vagueness in language as to what must be specified regarding suspicion or probable cause when requesting a court order. The act authorizes an order to be issued for "any tangible thing" including personal and business records relevant to a terrorism inquiry, with no further definition required. Another issue is the "roving John Doe wiretap," which permits a request for an order that does not name either the individual or the facility to be tapped. The use of national security letters (NSLs) is another major point of privacy contention as it allows communications, financial and credit records of anyone to be accessed, simply by declaring the individual "relevant" to a terrorism investigation. Tracking the national security letter program has been especially difficult in that the law initially authorized a "gag order" preventing the receipt of a request to be revealed, even to the individual named in the letter. The Patriot Act reauthorization of 2005 did allow receivers of a letter to disclose the matter when seeking legal counsel. In addition it charged the inspector general of the Deparment of Justice to monitor the program for effectiveness as well as for improper or illegal use of the letters. The first IG report, of 2007, itemized a number of FBI violations in its use and application of the law. IG reports for 2007, 2008 and 2010 are available for review.[15]

Without doubt it is the "bulk collection" aspect of both the Patriot Act and the activities of the National Security Administration that continue to receive the most attention. Criticism maintains that the new powers would not have been needed to uncover and prevent the 9/11 attacks and asserts that no examples or data have been provided that such powers have made any impact on follow-on counterterror operations. A 2014 study of some 225 terrorism cases inside the United States since 9/11 identified only one instance where telephone record metadata searches, by themselves, had been used to identify a suspect charged in a terror plot.[16] The group conducting the study, the New America Foundation, noted that in the majority of the cases, traditional sources, informants and law enforcement practices had provided the tips that started the terror investigations. The study was corroborated by a White House review group that also concluded that bulk data collection was not essential to preventing attacks.

Both studies pointed out that the real key to attack prevention, as we saw in the 9/11 attacks, is the sharing of information obtained from standard law enforcement and foreign intelligence practices. They also noted that FISA courts could be used to obtain the same leads that were extracted from the bulk metadata collection. While both points are undoubtedly true, they do fail to note that metadata searches are primarily used to develop pictures of extended social networks and that understanding such networks is fundamental to longer-term intelligence analysis.

From 2001 into 2014, the NSA itself served as the gatekeeper for metadata collection. During reassessment of the overall program, in January 2014, President Obama announced that access was going to be turned over to the FISA court system. In March 2014 the Foreign Intelligence Surveillance Court granted the U.S. government authority to continue the collection of telephone metadata in bulk form. Readers interested in a detailed discussion of the history of the NSA's metadata collection program—and the issues pertaining to it—are referred to a comprehensive work by James Bamford, *The Shadow Factory: The Ultra-Secret NSA from 9/11 to the Eavesdropping on America*.[17]

While serious questions exist in regard to the value of broad-based, warrantless data collection, the importance of social and financial networks as enablers of jihadi terrorism has been proven. On occasion that enablement may be totally unknown to the individuals and organizations involved. The ability of the terror networks to skim money from Muslim religious support and charitable organizations is well documented. Very complex computer analysis tools can spot changes in fund transfers, movements of money, movements of people and a host of other indicators invaluable to both analysis and warnings intelligence. In that view, the metadata is indeed not a law enforcement tool nor a resource for legal prosecution; it is strictly an intelligence tool. There is, however, at least one instance in which Internet metadata could prove useful as a suspect identification tool; we will discuss that during our examination of "radicalization" attacks.

In terms of overall assessment—and from the perspective of a proactive terror defense—the Patriot Act did remove certain legal barriers that might have prevented quick-reaction surveillance related to what was perceived as an immediate threat. It has been argued that the FISA courts were actually very responsive and timely, but clearly the ability to use local district courts and the much less demanding requirements for what must be in the request resolve any concerns about timeliness. The expanded scope of "wiretapping" also ensured that virtually any mode of communication was accessible at any time, clearly an advantage in counterterror operations.

While the Patriot Act granted the FBI and other law enforcement agencies virtually anything they could have asked for—and a great many things the FBI had never previously brought up as roadblocks—it remains extremely broad. For example, the Patriot Act grants the right to use "sneak and peak" warrants for any federal crime, including misdemeanors. The "sneak and peak" provision, while arguably intrusive, allows a real advantage in ferreting out true suspects who are themselves very suspicious about and sensitive to any type of ongoing surveillance. As with the "bulk collection" issues we noted above, that raises considerable concern about law enforcement overreach.

The FBI retained its lead position in terror attack interdiction following 9/11, and it received a great deal of additional legal empowerment. In addition to the new legal tools, in 2002 the FBI also incorporated a small but highly focused Foreign Terrorist Tracking Task Force, which formed immediately after the attacks to search for other terrorists who might be operating domestically. In support of that mission, the task force conducted an intense study of acknowledged intelligence-sharing failures. One eventual result of the studies was the creation of the Justice Department's National Security Analysis Center (NSAC, in turn, absorbed the original task force). NSAC is a relatively small agency, with an estimated 400 employees—300 of them analysts—and only a $150 million budget. Its strength is not in its size but in the scope of government, homeland security, intelligence, law enforcement, and commercial databases it is capable of accessing for "link and pattern analysis" of associations, movements, and transactions.[18] While the FBI remains NSAC's primary customer, the center also services the American military, and a number of other agencies maintain liaison staff with the NSAC.[19] One of the center's key missions is to use its data search tools proactively to reveal linkages that are not obvious and potentially may involve individuals in unknowing or even clandestine association with potential terrorists. One of the more recent projects at NSAC reportedly focused on screening individuals in the Syrian Free Army, as well as identifying potential terrorists for the Pentagon.[20] Still, as with any "proactive" intelligence work, NSAC's activities continue to raise a range of privacy concerns.

In addition to the obvious issue of intelligence sharing, another major problem of the pre-9/11 period was the lack of a truly aggressive "ownership" of the counterterror responsibility, at least among the highest management levels of the FBI/DOJ. It will likely be decades before we can fully determine to what extent that changed in the aftermath of 9/11. Based on the public data available, it seems that it did. At the time of this writing, the Bureau's public stance on counterterrorism and both its actual efforts and results appear to be far more consistent than what we found during the period of 1999–2001. Without a doubt, the number of ongoing terror plots and attempted attacks ensured that terror attacks remained a priority.

In December 2001 an attempt to blow up Flight 62 from Paris to Miami failed only because of a detonator problem with the explosive. The bomber was a British Muslim convert, radicalized at an extremist mosque outside London. After radicalization he traveled for training in Pakistan and Afghanistan, becoming an al-Qaeda member. During 2002, 2003 and 2004 plots to attack the Brooklyn Bridge, the New York Stock Exchange and the New York subway were thwarted. Attempted attacks continued into the Obama presidency. Airline passengers prevented the triggering of a bomb over Detroit in 2009, and other plots targeted the Sears Tower in Chicago and Times Square in New York. A plot to attack soldiers at Fort Dix, New Jersey, was broken up with arrests by the FBI. A paid FBI informant had been the key to exposing that effort.

It appears that, following the 9/11 attacks, the FBI did make terrorism a proactive Bureau priority—not just in the sense of investigating and prosecuting criminal acts of terror but as stated in the FBI's own new mission statement, "to identify and disrupt potential terror plots by individuals or terror cells."[21] Particularly important, in addition to moving agents from criminal programs to counterterror activities, the Bureau doubled its number of intelligence analysts and tripled its number of linguists, a critical resource in intelligence collection. The FBI also increased the number of FBI-led multi-agency Joint Terror Task Forces from 35 to 104 with personnel growing from 1,000 to 4,500. FBI headquarters also opened its own Joint Terror Task Force with members from some 41 agencies.

Perhaps most importantly, based on its own experience prior to the 9/11 attacks, in 2003 a Terrorist Screening Center was tasked with maintaining a single database of all terror suspects and associates. That database was used to produce a consolidated watch list—a tool notably missing circa 2001. Such metrics only tell part of the story, but clearly the Bureau's focus is much different than what we saw in 2001, with terrorism not even making the top ten list of Bureau priorities and counterterror funding being significantly cut. One of the most convincing indications of change is found in the Bureau's own description of its Directorate of Intelligence. FBI copy points discuss special agents, intelligence analysts, language specialists and support personnel working directly with FBI field offices, ensuring that intelligence is "embedded" within investigations and field office activities.

Beyond its own metrics and statements, there also seems to be solid evidence that the Bureau is being proactive in its counterterror activities. In 2010, a naturalized U.S. citizen from Somalia attempted to detonate an explosives-packed van at a Christmas-tree lighting ceremony in Portland, Oregon. He had been monitored for months in an FBI undercover operation; the bomb itself had been rendered inert before the attempt. The terrorist, a resident of Corvallis, Oregon, was convicted in federal court.[22] In 2012 the FBI interdicted a bombing attack on the Federal Reserve Bank of New York City; the attacker had come from Bangladesh to wage jihad inside the United States.[23] Also in 2012, a Virginia resident who had become radicalized via the Internet plotted to blow himself up at the entrance to the U.S. Capitol, if necessary fighting his way into position with a MAC-10 assault weapon. Instead, he was seized as he parked his car with vest and weapon in a parking garage near the Capitol.[24] He had been identified through undercover work by an FBI agent representing himself as an al-Qaeda agent.

Such incidents indicate an evolution of the purely domestic jihadi terror threat. The threat from single, self-radicalized individuals has been growing—especially with individuals who are either U.S. citizens or holders of legal entry credentials—and illustrates one of the greatest challenges to the FBI. From one perspective, the only way to interdict such threats is to identify and attempt contact with individuals of radical persuasion before they connect with true jihadi elements. Such "stings" are not at all unusual for the Bureau; they are used against everything from organized crime and drug dealing to gun running. But in the case of terror stings, a counterargument is that the individuals involved are prompted into more aggressive behavior and possibly would never have represented a serious threat if not encouraged by a sting operation.

That view leads to charges of entrapment and is supported by statements that the individuals lack the skill to be dangerous—if left to their own devices.[25] The response to that claim is simply that a dedicated jihadi can produce a considerable number of civilian casualties with nothing more than an illegally purchased assault rifle and a number of ammunition magazines—or homemade explosive devices such as those used in the Boston Marathon bombing of 2013. When it comes to ideological terrorism, a fanatic dedication to the cause and a willingess to accept martyrdom compose a threat in and of themselves.

With the increasing occurrence of "self-radicalized" individuals, fueled by jihadi Internet website visits and by electronic contact with overseas radicals—especially religious leaders—the argument for at least some level of targeted Internet surveillance has been strengthened. A metadata search that connects someone visiting a radical website to known terror suspects provides the sort of early warning of a developing terrorist that can be key to interdiction. It is also seen as a critical element in dealing with so-called "bounce back" threats, resulting from citizens traveling overseas to participate in combat with the most radical groups fighting in Syria, Iraq and other locations targeted by the new "caliphate" movement.

Apart from legal protests of entrapment, there is another risk for the FBI in working terror contacts via stings. Such operations most definitely expose the Bureau to "counter-stings" by their suspects. It is possible for any terrorist to present himself or herself as an informant, or to work on one plot with FBI undercover agents while actually preparing a far different attack. There are a number of instances of such counter-stings from the FBI's work with Klan informants in the South during the 1960s. It is very unlikely that we will learn how many contemporary counter-sting operations have occurred; certainly such information will be withheld for decades, and quite possibly it will never surface.

While the FBI remains as the first line of defense in detecting, disrupting or preempting terror attacks, the next change for defense against truly major terror attacks rests largely at the level of weapons access. Given that the terror groups and even singleton terrorists actually stage their attacks both to create maximum media attention and escalate public fears, mass transportation targets ranging from subway, rail and bus systems remain key targets. But the prime transportation target of choice has been, and remains, commercial airliners.

Access Denial

Jihadi terrorists most definitely have not ceased plotting airliner attacks; in the most recent bombing attempts noted above, airliner crew passengers alert to the threat intervened and physically prevented bomb detonations onboard the planes. Given the lessons of 9/11, terrorists are much less likely to actually seize aircraft, with both passengers and pilots understanding that successfully resisting them is literally do or die. That awareness and willingness to act have been critical to preventing several attempts and have little to do with actions of the FAA. What has emerged is a return to suicide attacks using various types of undetectable explosives, in particular liquid explosives similar to those developed for the Bojinka plot. One of the most ambitious contemporary plots, on the same level of magnitude as Bojinka, occurred in 2006.

Ten transatlantic airliners were targeted, flying routes from the United Kingdom to the U.S. and Canada.[26] At least twenty-four individuals were arrested in the plot, orchestrated by a British Muslim who had connected participants to al-Qaeda via contacts in Pakistan. A returnee from Pakistan was observed to be carrying suspicious luggage items, and a massive British police surveillance effort ultimately led to the arrests. The attacks were intended to be carried out using "carry-on liquids" to mix bombs on board the aircraft, then explode them with battery-driven detonators. Following arrest, seven of the individuals charged were found to have already prepared martyrdom videotapes to document their mission.

The security challenge of dealing with bombs assembled from individual components—many quite innocuous in and of themselves—on board the aircraft is a daunting one. Two new threats have appeared in recent years, the first being a trend toward suicide attacks in which individuals actually conceal explosives within their bodies.[27] Most recently, intelligence reports focused on the creation of new sorts of devices that would pass through standard scanning systems undetected. Such devices would be concealed in electronics devices and footwear. In July 2014, those reports produced a general alert for flights coming out of Europe to the United States. Supposedly terror groups based in

Yemen and Syria plan to use nationals who have been fighting with ISIS in Syria—and who carry Western passports—to carry the new bombs onto aircraft.

Defending against such tactics raised calls for even more sophisticated electronic scanning technology—but it also raises the point that human suicide volunteers can easily grow quite nervous as they move to the final stages of their mission. On numerous occasions car and truck bomb operators have panicked during a security challenge, exposing their plan. Observations training for screeners and security officers had become even more critical, as has the use of suspect name databases. The value of human-centered "threat awareness" in access denial was one of the main points of an airline industry review conducted on the tenth anniversary of 9/11.

In a white paper, the Airline Pilots Association (ALPA) maintained that detection of threat items was only part of the solution and that "trusted airline employees" must be used as the "eyes and ears" of the security system.[28] In its assessment, ALPA cited immediate security improvements from quick post-9/11 implementation of suggestions from joint industry/DOT rapid response teams. Those teams had conduced security reviews immediately after the attacks. ALPA also endorsed the transfer of security policies, passenger screening and other related functions from the FAA to the new Transportation Security Administration as a positive move, along with the growth in the Air Marshal Service and its operation by the TSA.

In terms of policy changes, beyond the expansion of the Air Marshal Service, legislation and training that placed armed flight crew in the cockpits of both commercial and cargo aircraft were seen as a significant deterrent. The white paper notes that literally thousands of volunteers served as Federal Flight Deck Security Officers. Flight-deck security was further enhanced not only by reinforced doors but by secondary barriers used whenever the main door needed to be opened during flight operations. Those barriers, on the passenger side, serve to "impede" access while the crew are at the door, giving them time to secure it and also making any effort to force entry immediately visible to both crew and passengers.

ALPA's strongest recommendations for further improvements were built around "threat-based" security, which focuses on individuals most likely to be true threats. Such an approach combines background, database-type screening with behavior pattern recognition and human-factors assessment. It sounds intuitively logical, but in addition to the training investment required, such an approach immediately runs up against a host of legal objections ranging from "profiling" to privacy and personal rights challenges. Given the history of lawsuits and profiling claims airlines have already faced, without additional federal legislation, it's difficult to see such tactics being generally adopted. Several of the early computer-list screening proposals were defeated on the grounds of profiling. To some extent the call for threat-based airline security is reminiscent of some of the earliest calls to pass legislation that would have expanded FBI surveillance powers prior to 9/11—an intuitive change, certainly, but one very difficult to effect given traditional American values and legal protections. In the balance between privacy and fear, the American public historically tends to demand its privacy—until some event dramatically raises the fear factor.

The removal of access denial from the FAA to the Transposition Security Administration certainly addressed the issue of prioritizing air travel security post-9/11. There is no doubt that security is to be priority one for the TSA; there is also some reason to believe that isolating security from airline regulation was a desirable action. An argument can be made that businesses with a critical eye toward the bottom line see security as an expense. Their views on how much security is "enough" may well differ from the views of associations like the ALPA and can have an influence on the federal agency that regulates them. Maintaining security responsibility with an independent agency conceivably reduces any conflicts of interest on the core issues. Regardless of intention and focus, there remains the issue of actual effectiveness. In that regard, the bad news is that in its most recent tests, undercover Homeland Security teams found that TSA screeners failed to detect both weapons and explosives in virtually every instance. The failure rate was estimated to be at least 95%, and indications were that poor maintenance and management of screening equipment was a major contributor to the failure.

The agency's own inspector general has recommended an extended series of actions to improve the equipment situation; however, it appears that regardless of its charter and focus, TSA may be failing in one of its most critical access-control functions.[29]

The screening issue is of great concern, but another less visible issue is the extent to which access security may be compromised by legal challenges. Both airlines and the TSA face an ongoing number of lawsuits over privacy issues, but the most significant to our focus on defense are those lawsuits that could conceivably allow future terrorists to further "game" the security system, using privacy claims and lawsuits as a tool. In discussing earlier attacks ranging from the first World Trade Center bombing to the 9/11 attacks, we noted that individuals in the terrorist network used knowledge of the customs and immigration system rules to work around certain standard practices and procedures, inserting themselves into the country illegally but relatively invisibly. There is no reason to believe that at some point either terrorists or "enablers" might play the legal card, especially in the guise of profiling complaints, to essentially dial down the security watch list system.

Before 9/11 FBI personnel actually handicapped their own abilities by misunderstanding certain DOJ legal guidelines and concerns over charges of profiling. The Patriot Act largely resolved those problems, whatever negative privacy impact it may have had. The question remains to what extent transportation security may be compromised by lawsuits and privacy concerns.

At of the time of this writing, one of the open TSA issues that applies equally to U.S. Customs is the extent to which watch lists might already have been undermined by legal or political considerations. One insight into that might—or might not—come out of inquiries made by a U.S. congressman from Iowa. The congressman's staff received copies of internal customs office emails expressing concern that they would not be able to block a certain individual from entering the country. The traveler was a member of the Muslim Brotherhood with "indirect ties" to Hezbollah, Hamas and the Palestinian Islamic Jihad.[30] The traveler had already sued DHS twice, and apparently as a result, he and certain other individuals of similar ilk had been designated as individuals not to be blocked in further travel into and out of the United States. The traveler's name had reportedly been removed from the suspect watch list in 2010.

The Iowa congressman took the matter up directly with the Secretary of the Department of Homeland Security. The Secretary's office did not respond directly, referring the matter to customs which in turn denied that there was any "hands-off list"—something rather different than simply removing individuals from the official watch list. The reply also contained general statements on customs protocols and practices. A follow-on "briefing" offered nothing further. The denial of a "hands-off" list fails to address the question as to whether legally aggressive individuals might simply be removed from existing lists and actually fuels the concern that legal and political sensitivities may once again be emerging as a security issue. That concern was heighted by a remark in the letter to the congressman that the individual involved in the query had indeed had his records removed and that then-DHS secretary Janet Napolitano been involved in the action.

Having reviewed the post-9/11 changes at the FBI and the FAA/TSA, we now turn to the last line of the homeland defense, the American military. While it is true that new practices and passenger awareness may have dramatically reduced the chances of hijacked airliners being used as weapons, terrorists still have the option of obtaining private planes. This can easily be done through rentals or even purchase of a variety of aircraft up to and including large corporate-class jets. Beyond that, private aircraft including small cargo planes could be seized or stolen on the ground. Worse yet, the advent of large drones, capable of carrying chemicals and even modest amounts of very high explosives, presents an entirely new challenge.

Engagement and Point Defense

Military defense of the United States remains a challenge and is continuously becoming more complex. Following the attacks of 9/11, the Department of Defense performed its own reorganization, consolidating command assignments. A single command (NORTHCOM) has the responsibility of defending the continental U.S. and associated areas. Hawaiian defense was assigned to U.S. Pacific Command. NORTH-COM was assigned both an active defensive mission and a military support mission in support of a variety of federal agencies, as well as the Department of Homeland Security. In 2004 Admiral Timothy Keating became the first Navy officer to command NORTHCOM. In light of the 9/11 attacks, it was also extremely significant that the admiral received a concurrent assignment as the commander of NORAD. Such a dual command arrangement is rather unique but clearly resolved ownership issues and could only improve responsiveness during any type of future attack on the continental United States.

Defending against terror attacks, whether airborne, seaborne or ground, requires extremely broad continental surveillance—space, air and maritime—by NORAD. That mission now includes monitoring of all ocean approaches for maritime terror attacks, with certain harbor facilities such as liquefied natural gas and petroleum storage facilities classified as mass-destruction class targets. Aerial terror defense remains one of the most challenging tasks for both NORAD and NORTHCOM, requiring an exceedingly quick response. In today's venue there is no distant early warning line, no thirty-minutes-to-impact warning, perhaps not even fifteen minutes to flush planes off strip alert as with SAC during the Cold War. If future terror attacks occur, they are going to resemble the attacks of 9/11 more so than the surprise attacks anticipated during the Cold War—possibly with even less warning time. There are a limited number of options for engaging such threats, all based in some combination of quick interception and point defense.

The first option, and one instituted as of the afternoon of September 11, is putting a combat air patrol in flight over known terrorist targets such as major metropolitan areas. That option is excessively expensive in terms of aircraft, personnel and support—however, it remains viable for strategic targets as well as special events that draw very large crowds and/or high-profile attendees. The air defense operation developed for that purpose went into effect on September 14, 2001, and continues today; it is designated "Operation Noble Eagle."[31] A joint operation between NORAD, National Guard units and Coast Guard units designates both fighters and helicopters to be available for "battle station" alert. The battle station aircraft are launched to divert suspect flights before they can penetrate areas considered to be national-level targets. In addition to the fixed national level-targets, there are also National Special Security Events (including presidential travel) and special events that may be designated for protection, such as the Super Bowl.

Noble Eagle missions routinely launch out of some sixteen bases, from Hawaii and Alaska to across the continental United States. The pilots receive special training and work with designated FAA controllers responsible for national-level target areas. Their alert aircraft are fully armed with both live missiles and cannon ammunition. Perhaps most importantly, rules of engagement have been fully codified and designated to "engagement authorities" at NORAD's regional control centers. While pilots cannot fire at their own initiative—unless themselves under attack—the engagement authorities can issue orders for tiered military action, using a fixed, and classified, set of guidelines.[32] Pre-delegation has returned to the American air defense.

FAA/military coordination has also been extensively reworked. Measures were taken to establish interior radar surveillance, and NORAD control centers now have access to both FAA and alternative radar scans at locations across the continent. In turn, the FAA developed a "domestic events network" (DEN), which allows real-time communications with NORAD. Any event that leads to a pilot's reporting an incident to his or her airlines or the FAA triggers a DEN condition and all parties are informed. The DEN incident becomes immediately visible to NORAD, and protocol requires that intercept assets are identified—from that point on the incident is monitored to either cancellation or interceptor scramble. The system provides both the FAA and NORAD with a level of situational awareness far beyond the capabilities available on 9/11.

Operation Noble Eagle averages more than a hundred full-fledged scrambles per year, but beyond that, it has returned American air defense to an era of true readiness exercises. Given that one of the most challenging contemporary air threats is the small, private aviation aircraft, Noble Eagle practices such engagements under the Falcon Virgo and Fertile Keynote programs. Civil Air Patrol pilots fly private aircraft in simulated threats, allowing the entire command-and-control process to be tested—ranging from detection, through alert assessment, intercept and inspection.[33] With the lessons of 9/11 still in mind, the exercises go well beyond innocently wandering aircraft. Some events specifically include simulated terrorist aircraft and the steps to respond to them, beginning with radio warnings, flights directly in front of the aircraft and the dropping of flares in its flight path. If that fails, NEADS assumes intercept control and escalates the exercise to the actual point of shootdown.[34]

As part of its overall mission, Noble Eagle, flying under control of the northeastern regional NORAD control center (NEADS), protects a parameter around Washington, D.C., extending approximately fifteen miles out from city center. In between that parameter and one final point defense system, the capital's airspace is guarded by the National Advanced Surface-to-Air Missile System (NASAMS).[35] The NASAMS consists of a "box" launcher containing several missiles and support detection (radar and electro-optical), control and communications equipment. The systems began to go into place in 2005; they are not concealed, and multiple sites are located in suburban areas and beside major roadways—within protective firing range of the capital.

The third and essentially final option is that of target "point defense." Point defense currently utilizes both guns and ground-to-air missiles of various types and is geared to respond to an extremely minimal warning. It is in use now, officially to protect the Washington, D.C., area, and unofficially at whatever points are deemed to be either especially critical or the subject of imminent threat. The preferred system—known as Avenger—is operated by the Army and is mobile, consisting of a mix of FM-92 missiles and 50-caliber machine guns, mounted on a Hummer vehicle.[36] Avenger can also be put into fixed emplacements and is installed at various locations around the nation's capital, including a site adjacent to the White House. In the future, systems such as Avenger will very likely be joined by field-mobile, laser-point defense systems with the response time needed to engage an emerging generation of commercially available low-cost drones.

Consumer-class drones present a seemingly low-level threat due to weight-carrying constraints, but with precise control they could conduct very effective symbolic attacks against the White House or even lethal attacks against individuals. In March of 2015, the operator of a hobbyist drone lost control over it when flying it from his apartment, and the drone was later recovered on the White House grounds, having gone undetected during its approach and landing. The following month, a drone containing a radioactive liquid was landed on the roof of the Japanese prime minister's residence.

Point defense laser systems—adaptations of systems such as those operationally deployed the U.S. Navy late in 2014—would be one solution for dealing with drones as well as with ultralight aircraft and gyrocopters such as the one flown onto the White House grounds in April 2015. Engaging such craft with missiles or rapid-firing guns carries a high risk of collateral damage inside metropolitan areas such as Washington, D.C. Drones or personal flying craft, operated by "self-radicalized" domestic terrorists, could be destroyed or disabled by relatively low-power laser weapons. Until such systems are deployed, given the rapid advances in size and sophistication of commercial drones, an alternative may simply be to equip trained Secret Service agents with 12-gauge shotguns.

Command and control, including engagement launch authority, for all types of surface-to air-missiles as well as the Noble Eagle interceptors and helicopters is under NORAD's National Capital Region (NCR) Integrated Defense Network. A mix of guns, missiles and interceptors has now returned to defend the nation's capital, in some ways reminiscent of the integrated defense systems discussed during our Cold War chapters.

Command, Control and Readiness

As we've seen through the decades, a key element in dealing with any surprise attack is "readiness." Readiness is generally defined in terms of the ability of a given unit—military or civilian—to accomplish its assigned mission. Training, supplies, equipment, logistics and even attitude (morale) all factor into readiness. Drills, exercises and simulations (including realistic "war games" in the military) are all measures of the readiness and capabilities of a given unit.

In evaluating the post-9/11 readiness of federal agencies, the internal reviews of agency inspectors general are a key resource. Exercises conducted by the Department of Justice, the Department of Homeland Security, the Federal Emergency Management Agency and the Federal Aviation Agency provide considerable insight into their priorities and the "realism" of their preparedness. One benchmark for evaluating the "reality" of readiness is the extent to which front-line agencies such as the FAA utilize and respond to the results of Red Team exercises—a critical tool for highlighting real-world risks and threats.

One of the major functions of Red Teaming—which involves highly experienced personnel functioning as both "adversaries" and "devil's advocates"—is to challenge the target organization's "norms," exposing weakness in basic organizational structure and culture. Red Team personnel are selected not only for their specialty knowledge but for their ability to "think outside the box" in regard to potential threats as well as to demonstrate a "penchant for critical analysis."[37] Red Teaming is felt to be one of the best tools to combat organizational inertia, if the organization truly pays attention to its lesson. When used effectively, it can also address one of the most potential sins of any defense—"complacency."[38] The risk is that if it's not used correctly, there is the danger of simply thinking something positive is occurring when indeed inertia continues to rule. That appears to have been the case with FAA Red Teams prior to 9/11 when Red Team findings essentially disappeared at headquarters level. Such a risk is a known point of failure in readiness efforts, described as being "captured by the bureaucracy."[39]

To be of real value, the Red Team work must extend not only to threat identification but all the way through the counterterror response. Given the legal limitations on the Department of Defense role within the United States, the use of force in response to terror attacks often involves local law enforcement. That reality has generated a growing demand for paramilitary, counterterror training at the state and local agencies, as well for a variety of law enforcement groups. The need for such training has led to the establishment of specialized firms that provide counterterror/simulation training and organize Red Team and counterforce exercises for public agencies as well as the military.[40]

Even before 9/11 the Department of Justice, in its lead role, had begun exercises focused on weapons of mass destruction—the exercises were conducted under the Top Officials (TOPOFF) program. TOPOFF included counterterrorism training and was intended to involve both planners and top officials from local and state governments as well as federal agencies. The exercises were supposed to be as authentic as possible with no participant forewarning as to location, date or time of attack, and decision-making is a major element in the simulations. Each exercise included an after-action assessment.

The TOPOFF exercises began prior to the 9/11 attacks, when a ten-day simulation in 2000 focused on chemical attacks in Denver, Colorado and Portsmouth, New Hampshire. In 2003, exercises simulating a dirty-bomb radiation attack were organized in Seattle, Washington, and a biological attack in Chicago, Illinois. More than 8,500 people participated in the exercise. TOPOFF 2005 exercises were held in Connecticut and New Jersey, with some 10,000 participants responding to simulated chemical and bioweapon attacks.

In 2009 the TOPOFF exercise program was renamed the Tier 1 National Level Exercise and integrated with existing FEMA programs.[41] The annual National Level Exercises are intended to concurrently test responses to a series of different national catastrophes and terror attacks. The 2009 exercises were focused on preventing follow-on attacks within the United States following a major international terror attack. President Obama participated in the 2009 exercises, working with a crisis staff from the White House Situation Room. In contrast to earlier exercises, the 2009 series was totally focused on "prevention and protection" rather than "contingency response." From 2009 on, the National Level Exercise programs alternated between protection and recovery. The exercise of 2010 dealt with a terror attack using a nuclear weapon, 2011 with a massive earthquake on the New Madrid fault line, 2012 with a large-scale cyber attack on the nation. President Obama again joined in the 2012 national exercise, providing further positive indication that such exercises are gaining National Command Authority attention.

The National Level Exercise program for 2014, "Capstone," contained several elements including a response exercise to a major earthquake and tsunami in Alaska ("Alaska Shield"), and Department of Defense support for the Alaska natural catastrophe responses ("Ardent Sentry 14"). Additional exercises included a nuclear weapons transport accident inside the continental United States ("NUWAIX"), recovery operations following a national catastrophe ("Silver Phoenix"), and alternate site continuity of government exercise for federal government agencies ("Eagle Horizon").[42]

This all sounds good, and certainly these sorts of field exercises are preferable to tabletop and simulation sessions. Yet as we saw in FBI exercises prior to 9/11, even with the best intentions, such exercises can lack certain vital elements compared to the more demanding field exercises and "war games" that the military practices. Military exercises are often designed to put some level of stress on the participants. Internal critiques of the more realistic military exercises are performed within the organization itself and can be educational. However, outstandingly poor performance can also be career limiting. Not all military exercises take that approach—military Red Team exercises are normally organization- and not personnel-focused—but in some of the more strategic commands, exercises and even inspections can have a career impact. If a Cold War–era Air Force SAC unit or a Navy (SSBN) ballistic missile submarine performed poorly during an alert exercise—even a security penetration test—the results could affect both reviews and promotion. Most recently, poor performance in tests and inspections conducted at U.S. Strategic Command (STRATCOM) missile launch sites seriously affected careers at multiple levels of command.

It is difficult to evaluate the full impact of DHS and FEMA exercises given the breadth of individuals and agencies involved. And simply because exercise after-action reviews occur, nothing really happens unless the individual agencies or participants meaningfully respond to what was learned. Independent assessments of the agencies and their exercises come from the Government Accounting Office (GAO) and the office of the Homeland Security (DHS) Inspector General. The DHS inspector general's evaluation of the DHS National Level TOPOFF 2011 exercise provided a detailed review of the function and organization of the overall TOPOFF program. It also noted that the exercise began with personal participation of both the DHS secretary and the FEMA administrator.

The 2011 exercise was notable, in that for the first time the exercise was totally designed to "break the system" and then recover it—previous exercises had only gone as far as breaking the system.[43] That advancement is especially important because it takes the exercise beyond the point of identifying where logistics and resources are not able to sustain the response and specifically identifies the fixes and changes required. Summary reports from the TOPOFF exercises are then submitted to the NSC staff for review and action proposals. The 2011 exercise appears to be the first in which virtually all corrective actions were completed even prior to the NSC summary being submitted.

The 2011 TOPOFF exercise assessment seems encouraging, but GAO reviews indicate that there is still need for significant improvement at DHS. One particular concern is that DHS continually has the highest employee turnover of any federal agency, even at the senior management levels of its various groups. It also has the lowest employee satisfaction rating. Many of its problems seem to stem from the fact it was an artificial melding of independent agencies and is subject to the congressional control of some ninety committees and an additional thirty oversight task forces. As recently as 2014, the GAO continued to list the Department of Homeland Security on its high-risk federal agency list—areas that would be classified as impacting readiness were among those cited as particularly poor. In addition, the GAO specifically critiqued the work of the DHS intelligence "fusion centers" in coordinating the sharing of information related to preventing terrorist attacks.[44] Given that that intelligence sharing was one of the primary reasons for creating the department, the fact that it is still having problems with that mission after more than a decade in operation seems a significant concern.

With regard to FEMA, while its exercise program itself appears to have improved considerably post-9/11, the downside is that its more recent exercises have not satisfactorily forced corrective action. In 2012 the DHS inspector general reported that fewer than 40% of the corrective actions identified in National Level Exercises had been completed within FEMA itself. The OIG report cited the lapse as being due to failures in program management and specifically referenced exercises in 2007 and 2009. The failure was specified as occurring within the Exercises Evaluation Program Steering Committee. Worse yet, the OIG report stated that FEMA had not "validated" corrective actions to ensure they had actually been performed and ensure that actions learned during the after-action sessions had been implemented. Both the OIG and the congressional oversight committee for FEMA questioned the long-term value of the exercises if the process for installing fixes could not be corrected.[45]

In terms of overall readiness, one specific area of exercise effectiveness stands out in our exploration of real-world attacks and national emergencies—that is the involvement and preparation of the senior levels of national command. While there are some indications that cabinet-level officers and even President Obama have participated in National Level Exercises, the challenge of realism and command ownership remains. We have reviewed multiple examples of principals and even National Command Authority figures who were at least superficially involved in Cold War–era national attack/crisis exercises—yet when required to perform under crisis-level stress, their performance was often less than satisfactory.

One problem is that the most senior civilian figures of command are either appointed or elected officials, and under stress they seem to revert to their comfort level—thinking first of public and political concerns rather than command and control. In November 1963, Lyndon Johnson, upon assuming the presidency, appears to have given little thought at all to his responsibilities as commander in chief. Johnson used all his time even while in flight on *Air Force One* to make social and political calls. He was even reported to have worried about "missiles flying" while himself not having made any personal contact with the NMCC, NORAD, SAC, the Joint Chiefs and only the most minimal contact with the national security advisor and secretary of defense. We found much the same lack of command involvement by Vice President George H.W. Bush following the attempted assassination of President Ronald Reagan. And most recently we reviewed command-and-control issues relating to President George W. Bush following 9/11, noting that even when he arrived at Barksdale AFB and had access to superior communications facilities, he spent his time writing and delivering a speech to the nation rather than immediately inserting himself in his role as commander in chief.

Clearly there is a challenge for civilians occupying top-level national defense and security positions. No contemporary president has had the experience of military command under combat conditions common to Presidents Truman or Kennedy. Perhaps it is even unrealistic to expect cabinet members, presidents, vice presidents and congressional leaders in the chain of succession to devote enough time to training and crisis exercises to develop an alternate command persona—but it remains a serious issue in national readiness. President George W. Bush encountered that risk a second time, following 9/11, in the national crisis created by Hurricane Katrina. The president responded in standard public relations fashion, viewing the damage from the air, then addressing the public with messages of support and encouragement. While doing that, he relied totally on FEMA chief Michael Brown to manage the details of the federal disaster response.

Brown himself, while having management and legal experience, had no personal background that would have prepared him for directing his agencies' crisis response. Afterward he made it clear that he was no "first responder." There was no indication that President Bush engaged in any detailed dialog with Brown on local and state requests or offered to insert presidential authority to speed the FEMA response. Following Bush's media flight over the afflicted area, he landed in Mobile, Alabama. There he addressed the press: "Again, my attitude is, if it's not going exactly right, we're going to make it go exactly right. If there's problems, we're going to address the problems. And that's what I've come down to assure people of . . . and, Brownie, you're doing a heck of a job."[46] Yet within days the entire Katrina relief effort had become a nightmare and Bush was accepting Brown's resignation.

The hurricane crisis continued to deepen, and it became clear that it was far beyond any readiness levels for which FEMA had ever prepared. Unfortunately, in the midst of it Brown himself sent a number of personal communications that raised serious questions as to how much owner-ship he was taking and to what extent he had personally invested himself into the crisis. Particularly galling was an email to the FEMA public rela-tions deputy director the morning of the hurricane: "Can I quit now, can I come home?" Days later he wrote a friend, "I'm trapped now, please rescue me."[47] Much later Brown would offer his own rebuttals, accusing Bush of "yielding to the poor judgment of staff aides who insisted upon photo opportunities that overrode common sense" and himself fighting a federal chain of command that slowed down the FEMA response. He also noted that President Bush was "sheltered from reality."[48]

There is a clear risk that presidents, as fundamentally political indi-viduals, can be trapped in their public relations persona and fail to iso-late themselves from the public in order to truly assume command au-thority. In those early days of the Katrina disaster President Bush could likely have eliminated some of the command chain problems Brown faced—but only if he had thrown himself into the role of assuming Na-tional Command Authority over FEMA itself, forcing out and dealing with issues that people in the bureaucracy might have preferred to keep isolated from outside oversight.

The Katrina crisis response is not for us to detail or assess here; however, it is very possible that some of Brown's observations from the event are relevant to our discussion of both "readiness" and "command." Clearly history has shown us that presidents' political concerns can lead to micromanagement and dangerous delays in military/security–related command decisions. Presidents Johnson and Nixon have both been heartily condemned for military micromanagement as well as letting policy and political concerns drive command decisions in Southeast Asia. During President Obama's first term, senior special operations commanders heartily praised the degree of independent decision-making they were being allowed in regard to largely clandestine and low-profile counterterrorism operations. Yet by 2014, Obama and his national security advisor Susan Rice were seriously criticized over delayed decision-making and micromanagement in the much more public and high-profile American military effort against ISIS. Reportedly Rice herself was taking a highly proactive role, with heavy involvement of the

National Security Council principals in meetings, and an "obsessive" attention to detail and reporting of operational activities.[49]

At approximately the same time in the fall of 2014, an international and national crisis relating to fears of an Ebola epidemic raised questions about FEMA's health emergency preparedness. Despite ongoing exercises relating to biochemical attacks and regional medical emergencies, FEMA appeared to have little visible role in responding to Ebola incidents across multiple states, leaving the matter largely to the Centers for Disease Control (CDC). Rather than turning to FEMA, with growing concerns about the lack of national response to a potential epidemic, President Obama was pressed to appoint an Ebola "czar." In doing so he chose an individual with no prior medical or even emergency response experience. The appointed "czar" was Ron Klein, a longtime Democratic Party political figure, previously serving as chief of staff to Vice Presidents Joe Biden and Al Gore. At the time of appointment Klein was employed as president and general counsel of an investment group. The White House justified the appointment based on Klein's management experience and his relationships to members of Congress and administration principals. As we noted in the Katrina disaster discussion, Michael Brown had earlier been appointed to a key emergency response position not on job-related experience but on the basis of his management and legal experience—and administration connections. At times it seems that neither the White House nor Washington, D.C., in general has a particularly good memory.

In summary, lessons were certainly learned from 9/11, and in the aftermath changes were made with regard to the nation's security as well as continental defense. Only time—and just possibly improved readiness exercises—will tell if those changes will win out over the institutional dangers of inertia and complacency. Yet even with far-ranging changes in the domestic defense, there remained a constant jihadi terror threat to Americans remaining overseas. In the next chapter we will examine one more surprise terror attack on Americans, finding lessons that had once been learned but that appear not to have made it into "institutional memory."

Chapter 21

DIPLOMATIC INSECURITY

The years immediately following the 2001 attacks on America were extremely demanding for the American military. That is not our story here, since virtually all the military action was offensive. Yet despite major conventional military action in Iraq and Afghanistan, there continued to be ongoing, if generally unsuccessful, terror attacks on the American homeland. Overseas there were a series of successful large-scale and extremely lethal terror attacks in Western Europe. At the time, all of these events—including the American move into Afghanistan to eject the Taliban, the full-scale invasion of Iraq and the eventual nation-building efforts in both countries—tended to meld together. Security and defense trends that might have received considerable attention in earlier years were often buried inside the larger events. One of those trends was the move toward privatizing elements of America's overseas diplomatic security—traditionally supported by American military personnel. The other was the routine operation of American diplomatic missions in the midst of either active combat or active insurgencies.

The United States State Department and its Foreign Service personnel have always been at greater risk overseas than the American public has appreciated. Historically such exposure was often related to the fact that at least some of an embassy or consulate's staff actively engage in intelligence collection as well as establishing political contacts aimed at furthering their nation's agenda inside the host country. We touched on overseas intelligence activities of both Japanese and American diplomats in our earliest chapters—ranging from obtaining information on weapons and military capabilities to monitoring force movements. In Hawaii, individuals associated with the Japanese diplomatic mission actually went so far as to prepare targeting maps to guide the air strike on Pearl Harbor.

The Soviets were extremely active in using diplomatic cover for pure spying and for making contacts with sympathetic ideological "fellow travelers" inside their host nations. Those contacts went as far as collecting information for sabotage efforts against American military targets.[1] In turn, American overseas diplomatic missions routinely obtained intelligence through their designated military attachés, and also housed covert CIA stations, with CIA personnel using either State Department or U.S. Agency for International Development (USAID) staff positions as covers for their work.

Diplomatic spying and political action was generally not life threatening; expulsion was often the major threat upon discovery. But beginning in the late 1960s and 1970s, with the rise in political terrorism, kidnapping for ransom and even murder became increasingly common. As early as 1969 the U.S. Ambassador to Brazil was kidnapped and the following year German, Swiss and Japanese consuls were kidnapped and released in prisoner exchanges. Diplomatic kidnapping in Latin America was not uncommon in the 1970s but it was in the Middle East where diplomats were in increasingly in danger. The American Ambassador and one of the diplomatic staff were kidnapped and ultimately killed in the Sudan in 1973. More American diplomatic staff were killed there in 1974, after being forcefully taken from the Saudi Arabian embassy. In 1977 the U.S. Ambassador to Lebanon and the American economic counselor were kidnapped and later killed. The threat of kidnapping and execution extended to other nations' staff as well; several Soviet diplomats were kidnapped and one was killed in Lebanon in 1985.

Such incidents had become so common by the mid-1980s that the State Department was forced to organize Foreign Emergency Support

Teams (FEST) to respond to overseas terror attacks. FEST teams are composed of individuals from multiple agencies and stand by on constant alert. However, there is no formal military component involved with FEST, and the teams are run by the Department of State. Operationally the FEST teams are managed by the State Department's counterterrorism coordination office. Their mission is assessment and coordination following an attack. Standard practice was to rely upon the host government to provide security—just as the host country was expected to provide physical protection and security for diplomatic facilities and personnel. Such arrangements were considered necessary to maintain the purely diplomatic function of the mission, but relying on host-country security has proved to be less and less viable in more recent decades.

Diplomatic risk can dramatically escalate during periods of host-nation internal political instability, as the Carter administration learned in 1981. Iran had been a decades-long ally, but with the overthrow of the Shah, any supporters of the old regime were suspect. With the seizure of the American embassy in Teheran, 52 Americans and the entire nation suffered during a 444-day hostage crisis, with the new Iranian government actively supporting the imprisonment of the Americans. On occasion the security of even active American allies has failed, not only for Americans in general but even for the American military. In 1996, American Air Force personnel stationed in Saudi Arabia and staying at a Saudi housing complex named Khobar Towers were attacked with a huge truck bomb. The attack killed 19 American military personnel and injured another 498.

The surprise attack inside Saudi Arabia, ostensibly a strong American ally with extensive security forces of its own, illustrates two of the major issues involved in defending Americans overseas, particularly in the Middle East and increasingly across Africa. First, threats and warnings are so common within the region that the "noise level" frequently obscures—or desensitizes response to—signs that might be taken more seriously if they were not so constant. In late 1995 a car bombing in the capital of Saudi Arabia killed five Americans, leading to an increased threat condition at Khobar Towers. Anonymous warnings followed, and U.S. security personnel inside the compound noted suspicious activities around perimeter fences—raising the second major issue. In Saudi Arabia and elsewhere, host countries absolutely forbid any military activity outside compounds; as to the case of the Khobar Towers, that meant that U.S. military security could do nothing to engage the potential threat, and according to reports, the Saudis themselves provided no increased security.

Radical jihadi terrorists smuggled in large quantities of explosives from Lebanon and prepared a huge bomb, placing some twenty thousand to thirty thousand pounds of TNT inside a sewage tanker truck. When challenged at the main compound entry checkpoint, they simply drove to a parking lot, serving a small mosque adjacent to the compound. The blast of the explosives was tremendous, felt some twenty miles away. Survivors of the attack were not hesitant to point out that violence and bombings had been increasing throughout the area all during the winter and early spring. In January an Air Force Office of Special Investigations report specifically warned about the dangers of vehicle bombs along the extended Khobar compound perimeter.[2] The perimeter was bordered on two sides by Saudi housing areas and on another by an open local park. Additional measures were taken inside the compound but given the long perimeter, only an active Saudi presence—including constant external patrols—would have presented an effective defense. As in other instances, concern for not offending the host country may have outweighed internal American military requests for additional security; certainly some of those who suffered from the attack felt that the Saudis should have been more strongly pressed.[3]

The reality is that there are many reasons to place State Department facilities in foreign nations, even quite unstable and insecure ones. In such instances the missions are viewed not in simple commercial terms or as support for American businesspeople or travelers. They are projections of American geopolitical strategy. If that were not true and if security were the primary concern, there should have been no significant diplomatic presence in Iraq following the ousting of Saddam Hussein, or in Afghanistan after the fall of the Taliban. Both nations were absolute security nightmares. Beyond that, other diplomatic missions continued throughout the region, from relatively stable and friendly nations such as Saudi Arabia, Jordan and Turkey to those with active insurgencies such as Pakistan, Yemen, Syria and Algeria; all suffered terror attacks and American casualties from 2004 through 2014.

Following 9/11 the State Department was not only facing a variety of escalating overseas security challenges but also the fundamental question of how it was going to continue to conduct its basic diplomatic missions. During the First World War the State Department created what was effectively its own "secret service"—the Secret Intelligence Bureau—focused not on physical security but on defending against sabotage, espionage and fraud as well as conducting counter-intelligence. Diplomatic Secret Intelligence primarily focused on protecting information.[4] The new force was staffed largely with former postal inspectors, individuals already familiar with the investigating fraud, theft and illegal transport. After the Second World War, agents were also assigned "escort" duties, not only for the American Secretary of State but for foreign heads of state visiting America. Such escort duties ultimately evolved into the contemporary Bureau of Diplomatic Security (DS), the security and law enforcing arm of the Department of State. Diplomatic Security personnel are responsible for duties ranging from protection services to threat analysis and counterterrorism work. Currently, the DS operates eight domestic field stations, bases for carrying out their core investigative mission, conducting criminal and counterterrorism inquiries and carrying out background investigations.[5]

Overseas the Diplomatic Security Bureau is responsible for some 275 foreign diplomatic missions, charged with both protective measures and field response to attacks and incidents. While we think of contemporary foreign threats as being largely regional, a review of the State Department's own record of attacks against its facilities and diplomatic personnel strongly refutes that perception—while illustrating the immense global task involved in State Department security.[6] In 2013 incidents outside the Middle East occurred in nations ranging from Brazil and the Philippines to Kosovo and Colombia. The list for 2012 had been even longer with facilities and personnel threatened in England, China, Indonesia, Mali, Peru, the Sudan, Libya, Tunisia and Colombia—plus attacks across the Middle East.

Historically, the State Department and the Diplomatic Security (Bureau of Diplomatic Security/DS) group relied on the American military, primarily uniformed U.S. Marines, to provide internal security within its facilities and compounds. It was the responsibility of host nations to provide general security including securing facility parameters and providing access control, using either local law enforcement or host military personnel. That model proved workable during much of the 20th century, but as radical nationalism and jihadi terrorism began to spread, reliance on host-nation security began to be increasingly questionable.

Security was especially difficult in areas with central governments under challenge and with "fluid" security forces (groups who might protect Americans one day and simply retire from the scene the next). And governments like those in the Sudan, Somalia, Yemen, Libya, Bangladesh and even Pakistan did not generally welcome or even tolerate America's uniformed military forces providing American diplomatic security. Even when central governments wanted American support, a visible American security presence served simply to incite violence from radical elements already generally opposed to those same governments.

The Diplomatic Security group moved to form its own paramilitary security staff, but in terms of daily protection operations in high-risk locations—especially in "combat zones" such as Iraq and Afghanistan— the decision was made to maintain a low profile and use commercial security contractors. In that regard, the State Department was actually following the greater trend toward the use of private security services. Using security companies to protect domestic American installations had already become routine practice. Increasingly government agencies had transferred security duties to private contractors such as Wackenhut Corporation, noted for its early work in protecting nuclear facilities and other national security installations. Wackenhut was founded in 1954 by four former FBI agents, including George Wackenhut. Initially operating under the name Special Agent Investigators Inc., the company renamed itself as simply Wackenhut. In 2002 it was acquired by a Danish security-business-holding company, Group 4 Falck. Wackenhut was to be one of the first security contractors hired by the State Department for overseas facilities security.

Prior to Afghanistan and Iraq, the State Department used private contractors in Jerusalem and in Bosnia, contracting with another well-known security company named DynCorp. In Afghanistan, one of the State Department's first challenges was to provide personal protection for the U.S.-backed leader of the post-Taliban government, Hamid Karzai. There was no reliable internal security force to protect him, and initially military personnel from the U.S. Navy's SEAL Team 6 were assigned for his security. However, during one attack on Karzai, the SEAL Team members responded according to their protocols, and in the resulting gunfire three Afghan citizens trying to protect Karzai had been killed. That and other incidents raised worries that even low-profile American military security was giving the appearance that Karzai was simply a figurehead for the United States. The State Department solution was to work Karzai's protection into its existing contracts. It turned to a subcontractor for DynCorp, a relative newcomer to security contracting named Blackwater. That contract evolved into a detail of some forty-six paramilitary personnel, a mix of former military and law enforcement officers. As nation building and security demands in Afghanistan continued, the small initial contract evolved into something over $43 million in work for Blackwater.[7]

Embassy security in Afghanistan had initially been provided by a force of Marines, but that unit was withdrawn as part of the troop drawdown following in the country in 2005. The State Department replaced them with contract personnel from Global Strategies of McLean, Virginia. That contract, worth $6 million a month, was awarded without bidding on the grounds that State had received too little notice for the normal contract process. Later its own inspector general found that the Defense Department had given a full six months' notice and cited the State Department for poor planning.[8] The initial high-cost contractor was replaced with ArmorGroup—the contract dropped to $2 million per month.

Reportedly, to justify the bid the contractor turned to lower-cost personnel, many of whom could not speak enough English to follow instructions. There were shortages of guards, shortages of armored vehicles, and over more than two years nine specific warnings were issued including a threat to terminate the contract. Despite the problems, the State Department stuck with ArmorGroup/Wackenhut, extending its contract for a year. In 2009 public reports of extreme personnel hazing and a media incident proved to be the final straw. Eight of the American embassy guards were fired by the State Department, resulting in a huge public relations scandal. The guards had been involved in a sensational and broadly covered sex scandal.[9] In 2010—during a period in which many smaller but similar security firms were also changing names due to image problems—Wackenhut's name was changed to G4S Secure Solutions. Currently the company employs some fifty thousand personnel, serving a multitude of customers in both the government and private sectors.

Although the details and timing are somewhat unclear, it appears that the State Department now operates under guidelines allowing its embassies in Iraq, Afghanistan and Pakistan to be exempted from lowest-bidder contracting—they rank as dangerous posts and, as such, bids are allowed to be taken under "best value," with price not being the only factor in the selection.

The decisions about which State Department foreign missions deserve special security proved extremely challenging. In any given year it is possible to tabulate multiple threats, incidents and attacks for missions in upward of a dozen countries around the globe. Since 1968 six American ambassadors have been killed in conjunction with their missions, beginning with John Mein in Guatemala and later deaths in the Sudan, Cyprus, Lebanon, Afghanistan and Libya. That sort of ongoing risk can easily be translated into a demand for dramatically increased security at a considerable number of diplomatic facilities. Taking that path is obvious, but a number of experienced diplomats were and remain concerned that the State Department has been politically forced into a practice of not just risk management but risk avoidance.

The State Department began constructing hardened and fortified facilities during the overall security push of 1998, locating them in areas away from crowded streets and more isolated from vehicle bombs. Unfortunately, more isolated buildings call for more perimeter security—a host-government responsibility—and larger contingents of interior security guards.[10] Experienced field diplomats remain concerned over the emergence of a "bunker mentality," with senior State Department managers more and more risk averse, leaning toward excessive security and actually undermining the effectiveness of the field missions.[11] The emergence of heavily fortified embassy facilities, the practice of diplomats traveling in armed convoys, breaks with decades of tradition and intimidates potential contacts who have no wish to enter a "compound" or have a convoy show up at their residence.[12]

Experienced diplomats are aware of the risks and the fact that they are required to balance risk with their mission, a fact that seems not to be fully appreciated by the American public. The reality is, in contemporary times, America's diplomats are at risk in a great many overseas assignments. Given that they conduct their activities in full public view, they are often as at risk as uniformed military—jihadi insurgents and terrorists view them as equal targets. At times it takes the full weight of the American military to extract diplomatic missions. In 1991, the American mission in Somalia was considered to be under sufficient threat for it to be totally evacuated. It required nine days to organize and conduct the rescue ("Eastern Exit"), but in the end a Marine Expeditionary Brigade, Navy SEALS, Air Force transport aircraft, a Navy amphibious assault ship and Navy amphibious transport ship went into service to successfully take out some 281 Americans.

All of which brings us to one of the most highly visible and politically controversial surprise attacks of recent history: the terrorist attack on the American Special Mission in Benghazi, Libya, in 2012. The story of the American political controversy over Benghazi is once again a subject far beyond our focus; however, it is important to examine the Benghazi attack in the context of threat intelligence, defensive measures and the command-and-control response to the attack itself.

Strangely, much of the political and media dialog about Benghazi has largely ignored several fundamental points that lie at the heart of the entire matter. One of those points is why the United States would run the risk of putting its diplomats into such a volatile and dangerous place as post-revolutionary Libya. By all assessments, there was a radical, well-armed and aggressive jihadi movement in the country, especially to its east in the Benghazi region. Beyond that, there was no national security establishment, the country was effectively controlled by a variety of militia groups each with its own agendas and quite "fluid" in terms of supporting a national government. Only a limited number of those groups and elements of the new Libyan government had any particular attachment to the United States.

The level of risk in Libya was undeniably high, but as we have seen, that situation has become almost routine in American diplomatic posts. In 1983 a suicide bombing killed sixty-three people in Lebanon, with seventeen American deaths including diplomatic and CIA staff as well as several soldiers. In more contemporary times, the risk situation in Libya seems comparable to that faced by diplomatic missions in Somalia, the Sudan, Tunisia or Yemen—all of which have seen ongoing attacks, several with American casualties.

The fact is that for decades America sent its diplomats into high-risk assignments. And American foreign policy, under both the George W. Bush and Barack Obama administrations, remains what in Cold War days was called "forward leaning." Having suffered from decades of foreign terror attacks, both administrations decided it best to continue to engage the threat overseas. That means supporting governments that actually face jihadi insurgencies in an attempt to obtain intelligence, to provide military assistance and to prevent the creation of denied access staging areas such as developed early on in the Sudan and later in Afghanistan. Cold War forward-leaning practices placed American diplomats in high-risk areas with active insurgencies and ongoing combat—in Laos, Vietnam, the Congo, Lebanon and across much of Latin America during the 1970s and 1980s. In the 21st century forward-leaning and preemptive efforts against radical jihadi insurgencies are taking them across the breadth of North Africa, through the Middle East and into the Western Pacific.

One point of significant contemporary difference is that in most instances, even if the regimes involved accept some level of American contact and support, they remain extremely nervous and essentially hold such contacts at arm's length. The answer to that problem in Iraq and Afghanistan was for the State Department to spend massive amounts of money on contract security. Yet foreign security scandals and civilian deaths at the hands of security contractors in both nations became widely publicized and produced immense amounts of ill will. In particular, incidents involving Blackwater received exceptional notice, even from the American military. Colonel Thomas X. Hammes (Ret.), then the U.S. Army head of reconstruction, minced no words about Blackwater: "They made enemies everywhere. I would ride around with the Iraqis in beat-up trucks, they were running me off the road. We were threatened and intimidated . . . [but] they were doing their job, exactly what they were paid to do and in the way they were paid to do it, and they were making enemies on every single pass in and out of town . . . it broke the first rule of insurgency . . . you don't make any more enemies."[13]

A 2007, a Blackwater firefight in Baghdad left seventeen Iraqi civilians dead and resulted in the company being banned from the country. Four of the security contractors were charged with violations of U.S. law.[14] In the wake of the international publicity about private security contractors in Iraq and Afghanistan, a number of the high-risk State Department missions faced the issue of nations refusing to allow such private companies into their countries. The new government of Libya specifically banned the entry of the private corporations that had provided security in Iraq and Afghanistan.

In the end, for Benghazi security, the State Department was forced to rely on the services of a small British security contractor, Blue Mountain, for general guard duties, providing personnel security with a handful of its own Diplomatic Security Bureau personnel. The role of the British contract employees and local militia members at the time of the 2012 attack remains extremely vague. Certainly none of them provided warnings, and they may have actually been intimidated to open the front gate to the facility—or left it unlocked as they fled.[15] Their daily activities are not detailed in any of the government reports, and no contract employees are mentioned as being among the mission evacuees. To confuse matters further, CBS News and *60 Minutes* were forced to retract a number of reports based on statements from a British contractor whose information was later determined to be inconsistent and questionable; a book relating his experiences was also pulled from publication.[16]

In assessing the attack in Benghazi it is important to note that the mission was designated as both "special" and "temporary"; the main facility functioned largely as a residence for a series of State Department personnel rotating in and out of Benghazi as diplomatic "principal officers." The American ambassador, John Christopher Stevens, did not routinely travel to Benghazi as his normal station was at the embassy in the capital of Tripoli—he had not been in Benghazi for the better part of year. The compound did contain offices but was not classified as a full-time State Department facility, officially notified to the host Libyan government—exempting it from certain of the department's own security standards.[17] Its treatment as a "special/temporary" facility also excluded it from a variety of department security oversight and review processes.

The story of the full American presence in Benghazi was—and remains—somewhat mysterious. While the Special Mission appears to have routinely been staffed by only a single diplomat, along with Diplomatic Security personnel, a much larger—full-time—American presence existed at the second American facility in Benghazi. Referred to as the mission "annex," that facility was actually a CIA operations base, located a mile and a half from the State Department compound, with its own special force of professional military security personnel. The overall staff of the annex/CIA base was apparently several times that of the rotating diplomatic staff at the mission compound, with estimates ranging from twenty to thirty persons. The CIA base staff included case officers, analysts, translators and other special staff as well as CIA Global Response Staff (GRS), military professionals who had entered the country under State Department diplomatic cover.[18]

The contrast between the two security groups was significant; between them the State Department Security officers had something like a dozen years of military service and the GRS staff had close to one hundred years, much of it with "elite" operations groups.[19] While ostensibly State Department employees, they were actually CIA security contractors.[20] One of the issues that emerged following the Benghazi attack was that Special Mission staff appear to have had a different understanding than the CIA Annex operators regarding the extent to which the CIA personnel would provide "quick reaction" military support for the diplomatic compound. The GSA operators were supporting covert CIA activities even though "officially" working under State Department employment cover. When the attack on the special mission began, the CIA-based commander's first preference appears to have been to call on a local militia group for quick military response, rather than to dispatch the GRS military personnel.

The CIA had been on the ground early in Benghazi, apparently collecting counterterrorism intelligence and initiating a program designed to interdict weapons such as man-portable anti-aircraft missiles being shipped out of Libya to jihadi groups in North Africa and the Middle East. As a diplomatic envoy to the Libyan insurgency, Stevens himself had worked out of Benghazi during the revolution, eventually moving from a hotel to the CIA Annex, for increased security. There is good reason to believe that Ambassador Stevens later used his Libyan/Benghazi contacts to assist the CIA staff in ongoing weapons interdiction efforts.[21] The CIA covert activities going on in Libya and in Benghazi were and are still very much a contemporary story of American forward-leaning against jihadi activities across North Africa and in Syria. But that is a story of its own; our first topic in exploring the Benghazi attack is that of warnings intelligence and what it tells us about the risks to other American overseas diplomatic missions in the future.

The State Department's official inquiry into the Benghazi attack noted, without details, that there had been a serious failure in communication among the headquarters "bureaus" responsible for security at the special mission. It also maintained that constant requests for additional security from the embassy in Tripoli and the mission in Benghazi had not received priority attention in Washington. One of the apparent problems was that the diplomatic mission was viewed as temporary, and its lack of permanent status argued against building up a local security force beyond that already assigned. Another major problem proved to be the reliance upon local Libyan militias for perimeter security and quick response duties. While the local militias had responded to mission incidents previously, at the time of the attack protests over salary and working hours had resulted in their ceasing to even accompany special mission personnel vehicles outside the facility.[22]

Initially the Benghazi community had been receptive to Americans, especially due to American and NATO support of their revolution, in which forces from the Benghazi region had been key. However the post-attack State Department inquiry acknowledged that security conditions there had seriously worsened throughout 2012, with increasing violence against foreign nationals. Its report lists twenty different Benghazi incidents that year. Only four involved the American diplomatic mission, but a June attack on a British diplomat's car convoy involved machine guns and rocket-propelled grenades. Two security personnel were killed in that attack, and the British closed their mission the following day.

One of the problems in projecting warnings for the Special Mission was that the ongoing political turmoil and repeated moderate violence in both Libya and Benghazi had increasingly become a fact of life, possibly desensitizing the diplomatic staff, including the ambassador.[23] It is striking that the post-attack inquiries describe Benghazi as essentially "lawless" at the time of the attacks. Although Ambassador Stevens had not been in Benghazi for almost a year he himself referred to the situation on the ground there as "dicey" and his own notes mentioned his being targeted on an Islamist "hit list."[24] Still, Ambassador Stevens made the decision to travel to Benghazi independently of Washington, and the details of his travel and activities were not "thoroughly shared" with the in-country embassy team.[25] Stevens's position as the leading Libyan policy figure and his personal experience and contacts gained from his presence in Benghazi during the revolution had resulted in the Ambassador being given an exceptional degree of autonomy.

Officially the State Department position is that the ambassador was in Benghazi to fill a timing gap in diplomatic presence due to personnel rotation, to appear at a school opening and to "reconnect with local contacts."[26] Stevens was to be in Benghazi for less than a week, and efforts were being made to keep the ambassador's presence and movements from being publicized (even though he was to participate in a local ribbon cutting event). That secrecy effort fell apart when the Benghazi City Council invited media to a private dinner with the ambassador. Given the general political instability in Libya and the increasing diplomatic challenges in the capital where the ambassador resided, there is considerable speculation that Stevens actually traveled to Benghazi to meet certain of his former contacts—including a major Libyan shipping company owner—in support of a covert CIA weapons control operation.

A majority report on the attacks, prepared by the House Armed Services Committee, noted that there was ample strategic warning of increasing volatility in eastern Libya, stressing that the level of risk to the mission had obviously been increasing.[27] Given the incidents cited in the Accountability Report from the State Department, in particular the recent withdrawal of the British mission, there is little doubt that risks had become elevated. That fact was known and reported from the American Embassy in Libya, which had generated ongoing requests for increased security for the entire Libyan mission. However, the intelligence cited in the Senate report—specifically calling out increased activity by al-Qaeda–associated groups—is centered in reports from the Defense Intelligence Agency, the Pentagon's Joint Staff, the AFRICOM command, and the CIA. The Senate report notes that Ambassador Stevens had access to the CIA reports as did the regional Department of State security officer; however, most of the warnings were coming from various military intelligence units and were not necessarily available to him.

A variety of memoranda and reports also make it clear that Stevens was quite aware of the worsening security situation and had made efforts to obtain increases in Benghazi security. The memoranda also show that security personnel had noted their concerns that the mission did not have the manpower, weapons, host-nation support or guard capabilities to defend against any organized attack.[28] A U.S. Senate Intelligence Committee inquiry report notes that in addition to confusion over who had approvals authority for such requests, an overriding factor very likely was that the Benghazi mission was considered temporary and was scheduled to be closed in December 2012. It is a matter of record that on two occasions in the weeks immediately before the attack, Stevens turned down offers from the Department of Defense to provide Benghazi security support via a special DOD team that had been operating in Tripoli; that team had previously provided security in Benghazi on at least a few occasions.

It is not discussed at any length within any of the available government studies but should be emphasized that the ambassador was running a very minimal diplomatic effort at the Special Mission. At the time of the attack all the personnel there were on temporary duty assignments, related to the ambassador's own visit. In contrast the CIA base at the Annex was well staffed, with its own resident Chief of Base. The State Department, Senate or House reports do not address the CIA operation in any detail other than noting the number of CIA security personnel stationed there and their performance during the attack on the mission and the Annex itself. They do, however, confirm a base security team of at least nine to ten dedicated, armed military operators.

When the ambassador arrived in Benghazi he was accompanied by two State Department security officers. An information/communications officer arrived a week earlier, apparently in support of the ambassador's visit. Beyond that, five additional Diplomatic Security Service personnel were there on short-term temporary duty assignments. A diplomatic officer had been there on a rotational assignment but completed his thirteen-day tour and left for Tripoli upon the ambassador's arrival. That left a total of seven Americans at the mission: the ambassador, a communications officer and five security officers. In addition, there were three armed members of a local militia, three Libyan national police officers, and five contract security employees hired by the British Blue Mountain company.

At approximately 9:43 PM local time on September 11, several dozen armed men "swarmed" through the main mission gate; some carried walkie-talkies, and reportedly others had AK-47s and a few rocket-propelled grenade launchers. The local security personnel immediately fled, relaying no warning and possibly leaving the gate unlocked as the attackers approached.[29] The ambassador and the information/communications officer were in the ambassador's residence as the attack began; one of the security officers retrieved his body armor and M-4 rifle and immediately joined them, leading them into the safe-room area of the residence. The officer gave his cell phone to the ambassador, who immediately began making calls for assistance. The Diplomatic Security personnel were equipped with standard body armor; their only weapons were side arms and M-4 semi-automatic rifles. Shotguns were also available inside the facility. Their armament was nothing compared to the machine guns, grenade launchers and other equipment provided to the CIA-base security operators. The quickness of the attack isolated the rest of the security personnel from the ambassador, and they barricaded themselves in another residence building. At no time during the next two hours did the DS personnel actually engage the attackers with weapons fire.[30]

By 10:00 PM the attackers began to set fires within the complex, beginning with the barracks assigned to the contract militia guards. The attackers moved at will through the compound, penetrating the exterior of the ambassador's residence and setting more fires. Smoke quickly spread throughout the residence including the safe-room area. The DS officer led the ambassador and the communications officer into a bathroom with a window exit. Opening the window brought even more smoke into the building, and the DS officer then crawled through the smoke, attempting to lead the two others into an adjacent bedroom with a window. The DS made it through the window, but the ambassador and communications officer became lost in the smoke, and even though the officer reentered several times to attempt a rescue, he was unable to find them, ultimately exiting through the window while virtually unconscious from the smoke.

By that time the initial attackers had temporarily withdrawn and the DS officers inside the compound moved to the Ambassador's residence, rescuing the officer suffering from smoke inhalation and continuing to try to recover the ambassador and communications officer from the burning building. They did manage to locate and extract the communications officer, already dead from smoke and heat; they were unable to locate the ambassador despite several efforts.

The CIA Annex had received an early call for help, and its staff could hear explosions from the direction of the compound. A six-person GRS response team immediately prepared to deploy to the mission but was held back by the CIA station chief. According to team members it appeared that he either wanted to rely on militia for quick reaction to the attack or was concerned about an imminent attack on the Annex. GRS team members estimated that they were held back for some twenty minutes—they were clearly frustrated, feeling they had lost the advantage of engaging before the attackers fully controlled the mission grounds.[31] A great deal of later political dialog centered on whether or not a "standdown" order had been issued; based on the team's remarks, the real issue was the delay in receiving the station chief's approval to move out.

The GRS operators departed for the Annex and made contact with a number of friendly militia members as they approached the Special Mission compound. Members of the team advanced toward both the rear and front compound gates; the team moving through the rear gate area received small arms and rocket-propelled grenade fire. They were able to advance against the counterattack, and ultimately the GRS team made contact with the Diplomatic Security personnel. The GRS operators anticipated further counterattacks and advised the Mission be evacuated. At approximately 11:10 PM local time the Mission security officers, following warnings from the GRS team, used an armored vehicle to evacuate. The Special Mission compound and the Annex team, with the body of the communication officer, began to receive both rifle fire and rocket-propelled grenade attacks. After departing under GRS cover fire, the Mission vehicle continued to receive rifle fire and grenade attacks. Nearly avoiding an ambush, the group made it to the Annex, arriving with flattened tires. They were followed by the GRS operators, using a different route and avoiding any further direct attacks. Before midnight, all Americans were inside the CIA base at the Annex and the GRS operators were preparing for anticipated attacks.

Several waves of such attacks occurred during the morning hours, all successfully turned back by the GRS team. It was only in the final hour, with relief on the way, that a brief (five rounds) but very skillful, and extremely well targeted mortar attack resulted in the deaths of two of the GRS operators who had been stationed on the roof of the main Annex complex building.[32]

In its findings the Senate Intelligence Committee maintained that the attacks in Benghazi could have been prevented, although it—like the other inquiries—acknowledged that there was actually no tactical warning of an imminent attack. Objectively that wording seems questionable; given the growing jihadi insurgency inside Libya, the only way to actually prevent an attack would have been for the U.S. military to go on the offensive against known groups, similar to what it had been doing and continued to do in Yemen.

However, military action as conducted in Yemen required a cooperative central government, something not found in Libya and hardly feasible from a diplomatic standpoint in 2012. Actually defeating the attack itself would have required an American perimeter guard force that could have engaged the attack outside the mission compound. Such a military presence was not a practice at any of the high-risk missions and would no doubt have been opposed in Libya as in any of those regions' host countries.

The third option would have been to deploy a significant, heavily armed paramilitary force inside the mission compound. That force would have had to be large enough to maintain a twenty-four-hour security presence and to have established machine gun and/or advanced personal weapons positions inside the compound. The alert force and weaponry would have to have been sufficient to immediately engage and turn back a surprise night attack by several dozen armed men. As it was, the attack occurred so quickly that the five security officers in the compound were not able to engage the attackers throughout the initial surge that set the fires that killed the ambassador. In fact, they were so quickly isolated that they did not fire on the attackers at all.

Adding another half dozen DS security personnel armed with no more than M-4 weapons and shotguns might have successfully engaged the attack before it swept through the entire compound—if enough of them had actually been armed and on watch at the entrance. The question of "preventing" the attack on the CIA Annex is another matter entirely and raises fundamental policy issues in regard to covert operations under the cover of State Department diplomatic missions.

The subject of covert CIA operations conducted from the Benghazi Annex was carefully avoided by all the official inquiries and virtually all the political controversy over the attacks. In the Senate Intelligence Committee report, testimony is noted in which the CIA Chief of Base stated that there were firm plans to co-locate the State Department mission and the CIA base in 2012. Although CIA intelligence and political action staff are sometimes embedded as a base within State Department missions, it would be unique to find a relatively large CIA covert operations station co-located with a State Department diplomatic facility.[33] The Chief of

Base also testified that his Annex location allowed extremely low-visibility activities, especially in regard to people coming and going—which had not been the case for the personnel at the Special Mission compound. In contrast, commentary from the GRS operators at the base suggests that the nature of the CIA Annex was well known and an adjacent residence was used as a staging area for the first waves of attacks on the CIA facility.

To what extent the activities of the CIA Base might have actually triggered the Benghazi attacks remains an open question. There are indications that the ambassador may himself have been involved in CIA efforts to interdict and control weapons sales and the attacks and on the mission compound certainly targeted the ambassador's residence.[34] While not addressed in detail in any of the government inquiries, media reports based on observations made from mission security camera footage suggested that the attackers were very well armed, not only with various types of fully automatic assault weapons but with rocket-propelled grenades. The attackers also appear to have a good idea of the mission complex layout and immediately began to use stored fuel to set fire to its buildings.[35] Additional information suggests that the attack was tactically well planned and that a series of observations and even cell-phone camera photographs of the mission complex had taken place the day of the attack.[36]

The mysteries of the Benghazi attack remain those associated with the CIA Annex and with the actual motives and activities of the attackers—including their possible influence by members of al-Qaeda known to be in Libya at the time. It seems we are unlikely to resolve those mysteries either through information found in the government inquiries or in statements now being offered by individuals actually involved in the attacks. As evidence of that, the initial remarks from Benghazi suspect Ahmed Abu Khatallah, taken into custody in the summer of 2014, provide an extremely "understated" version of the attack. He describes no more than twenty men being involved, the attack as being essentially unplanned and involving a retreat to his group's camp to prepare for a subsequent attack on the Annex.

While all of the government inquiries into the Benghazi attack addressed the issue of the American military response—including the overall command-and-control process—the most detailed information comes from the House Armed Services Committee's Majority Interim Report.[37] That report also gives us the fullest picture of what happened following the evacuation of the State Department Special Mission compound and in the attack on the CIA Annex. It seems only fair to note that while in a previous chapter we faulted the 9/11 Commission Report for being too "politically correct" on some points, the House Committee's Majority Report appears to lean strongly in the other direction, positioning many of its comments for political effect. We deal with that to the best of our ability, with the objective of balance in regard to an event that has become politically polarized.

Among all the point and counterpoint, it is clear that there were no specific plans in place to stage specifically equipped, quick-reaction forces in response to attacks on the diplomatic missions in Libya, or for that matter any of the high-risk missions in the region. Such rescue missions had not been profiled, planned or exercised. There were diplomatic missions that had military response personnel immediately on call, particularly in Yemen and Somalia, but that was due to the fact that special Joint Special Operations Task Forces had been actively conducting counterterrorism operations in those areas. The Yemen/Somalia region was under the mission oversight of Combined Joint Task Force–Horn of Africa, with its own military assets and active military assistance programs in countries such as Yemen and Kenya.

Since 2004 the Horn of Africa Task Force had maintained a regional military installation in Djibouti, supported by all the services and with airlift and Special Forces components on call. Following an attack on the American Embassy in Yemen in 2008, the Joint Special Operations Command had begun actively targeting insurgent camps, military assets and leadership. No operations of that nature were going on in Libya or anywhere in North Africa at the time of the Benghazi attack. Because no military operations were in progress, no armed drones were deployed within flying distance of Benghazi nor were strike aircraft such as C-130 gunships available. Those sorts of assets are normally found operating in conjunction with active Joint Special Operations Command units.

The Armed Services committee majority report maintains that the security situation in North Africa and specifically in Libya and Benghazi was treated differently than in Yemen, and that is certainly correct.[38] In Yemen the United States was actively involved in a cooperative arrangement with the Yemeni government to conduct military operations against a jihadi insurgency. No such relationship existed then or exists now in Libya. The constantly evolving central government in Libya remains very protective of its authority, many of its elements being strongly opposed to any foreign intervention.

The Armed Forces committee report concurs with all other sources that there was no specific warning of any imminent attack related to Benghazi; in fact, its Department of Defense testimony indicates that at the time of the attack there were active warnings against facilities in Afghanistan, Iraq, Pakistan, Egypt and the Sudan, but not Libya.[39] In another important comment, the DOD testimony noted that the Department of Defense exercises its own initiative to protect its overseas personnel, relying on its own intelligence and threat assessments. No special measures were being taken in regard to DOD personnel assigned to Libya.

In regard to command and control during the attacks, General Carter Ham, the head of AFRICOM, was meeting with President Obama at the time of the attack. AFRICOM is one of the six American global combat commands and is charged with all military activities across the African continent as well as adjacent island nations and waters; it became an independent command in 2008 and is headquartered in Germany.

Ham received notice that the Benghazi compound had been entered and that the whereabouts and safety of the ambassador were unclear. General Martin Dempsey, chief of the JCS, also received the same word and briefed the secretary of defense while the initial compound attack was still in progress. From that point on, all the senior military personnel joined and remained with the president for some fifteen to thirty minutes. In his role as commander in chief, President Obama ordered the military "to do anything that was needed to protect [American] lives in Benghazi."[40] The Secretary of Defense and JCS chief then moved to the National Military Command Center at the Pentagon and assumed command for ongoing force activities.[41] The president gave no specific directions for the response and set no conditions; his military staff stayed in touch with the NMCC but placed no executive restrictions or limitations on the response. Given our previous studies, National Command Authority response to the Benghazi attack actually came in a timely fashion and as close as or closer to accepted "protocol" than any other crisis or surprise attack that we have examined.[42]

Despite that, the American military response to the continuing attacks on the Americans in Benghazi was constrained by the lack of relevant combat assets. The only asset immediately available was a Department of Defense reconnaissance craft operated by the American AFRICOM command; it was diverted from an intelligence mission and arrived over Benghazi at the time the compound was being evacuated. The craft was a Predator video reconnaissance aircraft.[43] As with the 9/11 attack, the preparation of a relatively detailed Benghazi chronology is essential to our study of both command and military response. Unfortunately, we have no primary source in the form of tapes or transcripts; the following chronology of military activities is compiled from the best available official sources.

As of midnight local time, all American personnel from the Special Mission compound were in the CIA Annex. The secretary of defense had authorized the use of all available resources to protect American personnel in Benghazi.[44] The first military move was the deployment of Marine FAST teams stationed in Spain as well as a Special Operations combat team training in Europe and another Special Operations unit to be deployed from the United States.

The FAST teams were the ideal force to respond to the ongoing attacks. Their normal mission involves security for high-value naval installations as well as counterterrorism operations. The teams consist of some 500 Marines, equipped with state-of-the-art weapons and capable of short-notice contingency operations. FAST teams had conducted embassy reinforcements from Cairo to Yemen during the street demonstrations and fighting of the early Arab Spring of 2010–2011. Preparing the FAST teams for departure from Spain required some six hours, and actually getting a team into Benghazi would have required quick logistic work in regard to transportation and combat action to secure areas for their insertion. The

Libyan government accepted the entry of the FAST teams but requested that they enter only in civilian clothing to avoid further inciting local opposition. As it was, the attacks on the CIA Annex ended some seven and a half hours after the initial entry into the Special Mission compound.

The first Marine FAST team arrived in Libya after the CIA Annex had already been evacuated; it was diverted to provide embassy defense in Tripoli and arrived there at 8:56 AM on September 12. The Special Operations units deployed from the United States and Croatia arrived at their forward staging area some ten hours after all Americans had been evacuated from the Annex.

No armed aircraft were directed toward Libya during the ongoing attacks on the CIA Annex, because none were available. No armed drones or C-130 gunships were in the region, even in transit status. Combat assets of that type were all far to the east, from Afghanistan down through the Horn of Africa. Air Force F-15 armed combat aircraft were operating in the Horn of Africa region, stationed in Djibouti, but that was some two thousand miles from Benghazi.

There were Air Force F-16 aircraft in Italy, on training assignments, but none were armed or on combat alert. Organizing fighter strikes would have meant assembling crews, arming aircraft and organizing tanker support flights—all a matter of several hours' work. Beyond that, ground-attack aircraft would need to be equipped with countermeasure devices and supported by airborne intelligence, surveillance and reconnaissance platforms (ISR) to be effective in an unfamiliar urban operations area; they would require guidance from airborne radar-support aircraft to be effective in close-in ground support. In addition they needed either detailed GPS coordinates or combat air controllers on the ground. The commanders in charge of the relief mission did not see a combat air option as being viable in the time frame they were facing.

It should also be noted that even if military assets had been immediately available, planning and coordination of any ground action would have been handicapped by the fact that the AFRICOM command was at least initially unaware of the existence of the CIA Annex. That would have created considerable confusion in interpreting real-time information about conditions on the ground and in planning for troop insertion.[45] The available reports do note that eventually the second Predator routed over Benghazi monitored the evacuation from the Annex but make no mention of who was actually controlling the unmanned aircraft or how they came to know about the Annex. The reports remark that someone inside the Department of Defense appears to have known about the Annex, if not AFRICOM. Given that there were military personnel in Tripoli on special missions, reporting to the Combined Joint Task Force—Trans Sahara (composed of both military and CIA personnel), it is possible that group may have been working on weapons interdiction with CIA staff in the Annex. In any event, the lack of AFRICOM knowledge about the CIA Annex raises a separate question: to what extent covert CIA operations are disclosed to regional military commands and to what degree the information is compartmentalized.

The Armed Services Committee Majority Report makes no mention of American naval forces in its discussion of military air assets; however, available information indicates there were no viable Navy forces available. There were a number of minesweepers and patrol boats offshore in Libya, cleaning up following the revolution and the NATO intervention—and reportedly running interdiction for arms shipments into or out of the country. The closest Navy aircraft carriers were under way in the Arabian Gulf and Arabian Sea, more than three thousand nautical miles away.[46]

Independently of the military deployments, upon hearing of the attacks in Benghazi, six security personnel, including two American military under independent command—apparently that of the Joint Special Operations Command–Trans Sahara—left Tripoli on a chartered aircraft. The four military personnel in Tripoli wanted to move immediately to Benghazi but were ordered to remain in Tripoli in anticipation of possible attacks there; they supplemented the resident State Department security personnel, numbering only some five individuals.

The first sustained attack on the CIA Annex began just after midnight and continued until 1 PM. During the first attack on the Annex, it was struck by rifle fire and rifle-propelled grenades. The American security personnel actively returned fire and are thought to have hit and, according to the CIA chief of base, possibly killed some of the attackers. At approximately 1:15 AM, the chartered flight carrying security personnel from Tripoli landed in Benghazi. In trying to assess the situation, they were given information that the ambassador might have been wounded and transported to the Benghazi hospital. They spent the next three hours trying to verify that rumor, determine the level of security at the hospital and avoid being lured into a trap by attackers who had somehow recovered Ambassador Stevens's cell phone.

Actually the ambassador's body had been recovered by friendly Libyans and was at the Benghazi Medical Center. Ultimately the Tripoli team, accompanied by members of one of the "friendly" militias, departed for the Annex at approximately 4:30 AM. The Tripoli team arrived at the Annex around 5 AM, and within fifteen minutes the final brief but deadly attack, using extremely well placed mortar fire, began. Two GRS operators were killed by the mortar fire, and two others were seriously injured. The mortar attack was of limited duration, some eleven minutes, but it was extremely well executed. Its accuracy suggested that the attackers were well trained and experienced.[47]

By around 6 AM, a heavily armed, friendly militia unit arrived at the Annex and helped evacuate Americans to the airport. State Department personnel had made arrangements for the ambassador's body to be separately transported to the airport. At 7:30 AM a chartered jet took some evacuees, including all injured personnel, out of Benghazi. Upon arrival in Tripoli the seriously injured personnel were accompanied by the embassy nurse to the Tripoli hospital. The Libyan government provided a C-130 aircraft to transport the rest of the Americans, including the bodies of those killed. The C-130 arrived in Tripoli at 11:30 AM. Two U.S. Air Force transports, flying out of Germany and carrying medical support staff, evacuated Benghazi personnel later that same day. The evacuees, including those wounded, arrived back in Germany some twenty-four hours after the initial attacks on the Benghazi mission had begun.

In hindsight, most elements of the military action are reasonably clear, including the fact that far too much value had been placed on indigenous security forces and the ability of the host government to protect American facilities at a distance from the capital in Tripoli. In that regard, Benghazi is simply the most recent example of host-country security failure. The history of attacks on American facilities overseas demonstrates that such attacks occur consistently and that even when host-country personnel do bravely attempt to stop them—as did the security guards in the Kenyan embassy attack of 1998—terrorists are generally successful in attacking the facilities. It simply becomes a question of how far they manage to penetrate, what weapons they use and how many casualties are taken.

Benghazi is somewhat unique in that there were multiple American facilities and the attacks continued over several hours. But with foresight there are measures that can be taken in dealing with such attacks—assuming that the U.S. will continue to place its personnel into high-risk/high-threat locations. One measure involves placing American military capability inside mission compounds, sufficient to turn back armed intruders breaching the perimeter. That option also assumes there is a hardened area capable of withstanding at least RPG and mortar attack until American quick-reaction teams can engage the attack. The risk remains that attacking terrorists could utilize fire or large vehicle bombs to destroy even a hardened compound. Given the size of the Khobar Towers bomb, even a perimeter defense can be seen to have limits. In any event, American quick-response units pre-positioned close enough to the facilities to intervene within hours are an absolute necessity.

Such measures do appear to have been taken very seriously by both Congress and the Obama administration. By the end of 2014 some thirty-five American missions that were not previously defended by Marine Security Guard Detachments were scheduled to have them in place. Units already stationed at twenty-seven other high-risk/high-threat locations were to have the size of those military detachments increased. Congress passed legislation to support the effort; the Obama administration directed the Marines to accelerate their schedule beyond the congressional directive—to date the Marine Corps is on track to meet that order.[48]

Equally importantly, Marine FAST platoons have been pre-positioned at forward locations. In addition to shortening their response time through geographic proximity, special airlift elements have been directly attached to the FAST teams. A larger Marine air-ground task force was assembled for rapid deployment. According to government reports, the Marine quick-response units have already moved to forward jumpoff points some twenty-six times.[49] There is no doubt such an effort is necessary; the only question is whether budget constraints will allow it to continue in the face of sequestration and decreasing military budgets. The funding for new diplomatic security efforts of 1997–1998 proved to be short-lived. The quick-response forces are expensive, especially in an era of spending sequestration and military budget cuts. If they survive long term, it appears they will have to be sustained by reductions elsewhere in the Marine Corps.

Of course, all those efforts are directed at reducing the impact of surprise attacks, not preventing them. The only way to actually prevent them is to respond as the Clinton administration did in 1997–1998 by eliminating high-risk missions or actually evacuating missions under threat, as the George H.W. Bush administration had done in Somalia during 1991. In the summer of 2013, some twenty-one missions were temporarily closed in countries with major Muslim populations. A threat originating in the Arabian Peninsula was declared a national security emergency, and the principals committee of the NSC was put on alert.[50]

In the spring of 2014, both the Turkish and Saudi Arabian embassies were temporarily closed, and in May a serious effort was made to prepare for a possible evacuation of the Libyan Embassy in Tripoli. The Libyan Embassy had been one of the first to receive deployment of a Marine Security Guard unit, backed up by a pre-positioned Marine Corps Embassy Security Group (MCEST). Earlier in the spring of 2014 a Marine Corps Embassy Security Group had deployed to Kiev in the Ukraine. As part of the pre-positioning needed to support the Libyan mission, some eight vertical takeoff MV-22 Ospreys were assigned to a Naval Air Station in Sicily, some 320 miles from Tripoli. The craft can carry twenty-four armed Marines or a larger number of civilian evacuees. To support a Libyan effort, three K-130 Super Hercules tankers were deployed along with the Ospreys.[51] In the event that the evacuation or rescue was to take place under fire, Ospreys could be equipped as light gunships using ramp- and belly-mounted mini-gun turrets; under an absolute worst-case scenario F-16 fighter bombers out of Italy or AC-130 gunships would be added to the effort.

FAST teams remain on global alert in Spain, Bahrain and Japan. And in July 2014, the Tripoli embassy was indeed evacuated due to an increasingly chaotic situation in the Libyan capital, with active combat between competing militia groups. The evacuation conducted in a highly effective, low-profile fashion using a car convoy. Approximately 150 personnel, including 80 U.S. Marines, quietly drove across the Libyan border into Tunisia. Yet even that surprise move was accompanied by an aerial overwatch of armed drones and armed F-16 aircraft providing secondary support.

The State Department also took the "high threat" issue seriously; in early 2013 it established the Directorate of High Threat Posts. The position was created to improve coordination with the Department of Defense, in particular with the global combat commands.[52] Its mission was to work on pre-positioning and coordinating American military of support in each geographic region. It also acknowledged that temporary closing and reopening of high-risk facilities would be standard practice and tasked its director of security with planning for such events. Beyond that DS was charged with general American evacuation in the fact of high-threat situations. DS coordinated the evacuation of thousands of American citizens and U.S. government citizens from Egypt during its civil strife in 2013.

One of the more obvious lessons learned from decades of overseas surprise attacks on American facilities is that there is simply no reliable substitute for American-managed perimeter and point defense—and pre-positioned quick-reaction support. Providing point defense or quick response to overseas diplomatic missions—and even military ones such as Khobar Towers—is expensive and can be extremely challenging from a diplomatic perspective. Historically the temptation has been to accede to the sensitivities of the host countries. More recently there has been a shift in the other direction, resulting in a series of increasingly fortified diplomatic facilities—which become obvious targets—and with ever-increasing security forces. According to many diplomats, that solution can actually exacerbate the threat and certainly can undermine their mission. There is no simple answer to the problem, but what remains clear is that American personnel working against the interest of jihadi insurgencies in any location will become targets. In the radical jihadi view a state of war exists between it and America—actually between it and Western culture in general; it's just a question of when the next attack occurs.

Chapter 22

....

HINDSIGHT AND FORESIGHT

eventy-plus years of threats, warnings, actual surprise attacks and national security crises both overseas and at home. Certainly the ongoing threat of radical Islamic attacks has added a new challenge to American warnings intelligence and preparedness efforts; attacks may come from foreign sources, returning American citizens having participated in jihad overseas or domestically from radicalized individuals. They also present a constant hazard for American diplomatic missions and commercial interests operating overseas. Such new threats consumed the nation's attention during the first decade of the 21st century, and the prospect of such surprise attacks will continue for the foreseeable future. We dealt with the response to such threats in the preceding chapters, assessing and critiquing the measures taken to restructure the nation's intelligence and security forces to deal with these new categories of threats.

If that challenge were not sufficient, during the new century's second decade tensions and fears felt to have ended with the demise of the Soviet Union and the end of the Cold War have reemerged. Those tensions quickly accelerated to a level of East/West military posturing and strong language regarding the value of strategic nuclear weaponry. Once again attention has turned to nuclear-force structure, spending on new atomic weapons and delivery systems and the security of assured nuclear retaliation. In a matter of only two to three years, the possibility of a new arms race, and its consequent economic risks, has become a major contemporary concern.

Current events return us to one of the most fundamental issues of the Cold War–era decades: the debate on whether military/strategic deterrence truly works or is largely a myth used to fuel the military-industrial complex and global weapons sales. A closer and more pragmatic look at the history that we have reviewed suggests that there are really two aspects of "value" in regard to deterrence: One deals with its true effectiveness in a military sense, the other in its value as a political device.

A strong argument can be made that strategic military deterrence is a valid concept, but only against rational enemies and only within certain parameters. Strategic bombing was positioned as a deterrent against Japanese advance in the Pacific, yet its power had not truly been demonstrated, and the new American long-range heavy bombers were not available in sufficient force to make it credible to the Japanese. The heavy bombers were not even available in enough numbers to provide long-range reconnaissance for Hawaii. If anything, in 1941, the developing American strategic bombing force proved to be a stimulus to Japanese military action rather than a deterrent. Yet by 1948–1949, the highly visible deployment of SAC nuclear bombers did make a significant impression on Joseph Stalin, sufficient to hold the Red Army in place in Eastern Europe. It even appears to have convinced Stalin, after initial hesitancy, to support the North Korean invasion of the south as a diversion of American military strength, offering the possible bonus of seeing American nuclear stockpiles quickly depleted in warfare against China.

There is also reason to think that President Kennedy's graduated but highly visible conventional/atomic initiative (and the overwhelming American nuclear power) forced Premier Khrushchev to back away from an attempt to militarily isolate Berlin in 1961. In that case the very real deterrent of the American military, frequently showcased in media coverage of the Strategic Air Command and the Navy's new nuclear ballistic-missile submarines, was extremely credible. Equally importantly, it had been deployed in a fashion to survive any preemptive strike. Visibility, credibility and survivability are clearly all critical elements of effective strategic deterrence.

Yet nuclear weapons were and are clearly not effective at deterring many forms of conventional or clandestine warfare——as Robert McNamara put it, nuclear weapons prove useful simply in deterring potential enemy nations from using them. In that regard it should also be stated that as a true deterrent, the nuclear weapons must be available and deliverable in sufficient numbers to ensure overwhelming retaliation. A number of studies suggest that while the concept of controlled nuclear-war fighting was and remains unrealistic, assured retaliation and destruction of a nuclear attacker remain viable deterrents. Of course, such assessments apply only to rational enemies. To date, the primary nuclear powers have been both rational and pragmatic. Early in the Cold War, Secretary of State Dean Acheson observed that it was impossible to actually negotiate with the Russians but they were masters of the "calculus of forces." If you simply demonstrated that what they might want to do militarily would be more costly than any potential benefit, they would not proceed. Otherwise they would act on their own agenda and schedule. To this point China has also demonstrated a similar attention to military calculus and pragmatism. Whether or not other nuclear-armed nations will be as analytical in their use of tactical atomic cruise missiles remains an ongoing concern. For example, there is reason to believe that Pakistan may soon deploy more nuclear weapons than either the United Kingdom or France. Pakistan has made known that it would not hesitate to use such weapons in the face of major, conventional attack by India——while India has officially stated that if such weapons are used it will respond with a massive nuclear strike. Given the history of the rapid escalation of prior confrontations between the two nations and the fact that as 2014 ended, shots were exchanged and soldiers on both sides killed in disputed border areas, the military situation on the Indian subcontinent continues to present another major test for mutual deterrence.[1]

The development and constant updating of military forces of such size as to establish not only a level of nuclear but conventional-force superiority against any surprise attack are another matter entirely—with far more cost and political implication. President Dwight Eisenhower worried that constant striving for an effective level of overall military deterrence might simply be too expensive to maintain over a long period, leading to either national bankruptcy or dictatorship. Yet that worry failed to stop him from supporting major defense and weapons programs throughout his administrations, even with knowledge that the popularly perceived Soviet bomber and missile gaps didn't really exist. Eisenhower's preference would have been toward budgetary caution; however, in the end he was forced to acknowledge the political risk of not appearing to be strong on national security and support major new spending, which he would have much preferred to avoid.

In contrast the early 1960s confrontations over Berlin saw President Kennedy pushing America's European allies to build up their conventional forces, to ensure conventional rather than atomic deterrence of any Soviet military moves. Kennedy was frustrated in his efforts, with the allies preferring to rely on American nuclear deterrence in contrast to significantly increasing their own spending. As a consequence, the deployment of American nuclear weapons in Europe remained in place for decades, constrained with the end of the Cold War but most recently solidified by new concerns over the resumption of a variety of Russian Federation military activities. B-61 nuclear bombs are still deployed on NATO bases in Germany, Italy, Belgium, Turkey and the Netherlands, and as of 2015 the National Defense Authorization Act allocated $2.7 billion to modernize and extend the lifespan of those weapons.[2]

For national leaders and politicians, there is clearly a second area of "value" related to military deterrence and national security, value based in its use in domestic political maneuvers. The political reach of any modern-day military-industrial complex, leveraged though astute lobbying and political donations, is not to be underestimated. Neither is the temptation for politicians to leverage national security as the easiest route to popular political appeal. In contemporary affairs, this is most visible in the actions of President Vladimir Putin of the Russian Federation. In his successful campaign to return to the presidency, Putin focused heavily on the decline of the Russian military and pledged to implement the most significant surge in military spending since the end of the Cold War. In doing so he personally campaigned with and sought major political support from Russian military industries and their owner-operators. Putin's campaign message was all about Russian national security; it was imperative to defend Russia: "We must not tempt anyone with our weakness. . . . Regarding this issue, there cannot be enough patriotism."[3]

While focusing on defense and huge additions to the Russian military—four hundred new ICBMs, dozens of submarines and some six hundred new aircraft—his related remarks made it clear that Putin strongly appealed to the Russian nationalism and a perceived popular desire for asserting Russian geopolitical clout. Putin maintained that Russia had fallen so far behind the strategic power curve that competing political powers could essentially act at will without considering Russia's agenda. His remarks recall Khrushchev's Cold War angst over the lack of Soviet political leverage after essentially backing down from a confrontation with the Western Bloc over Berlin in 1961. Yet in terms of internal political value, Putin's focus also served to consolidate his personal span of control within the Russian government—as well as building his own popularity with the Russian public.

It took the Soviets a decade to overcome the strategic imbalance of 1961; Putin's stated goal was to rebuild Russian military power by 2020. During the Cold War, Soviet leaders were able to finance their successful surges for military parity through absolute control of the Soviet consumer economy. Initially Putin's effort appeared to have a greater chance of success, based on the Russian Federation's huge oil and natural gas sales as well as long-term projections of healthy prices for crude oil. Continuing unrest and warfare in Middle East were seen as limiting regional production, maintaining high oil/gas prices and spurring Russian economic growth.

Putin visibly demonstrated his nationalist agenda, heavily investing in the 2014 Olympics, followed by denied conventional military interventions in the Crimea and the Ukraine. In the Ukraine, he projected Russian influence using the threat of forty thousand very well equipped combat troops—the same level of troop deployment that Nikita Khrushchev had used in Cuba in 1962. In many respects, Putin's tactical maneuvering in Crimea and the Ukraine has also been eerily similar to that of the Soviet "masking" operations in its Cuban surge. Even the American protests sounded similar to those in 1962. At the end of August 2014, Samantha Power, the American U.N. ambassador, directly accused Russia of lying about its deployment of forces around and into Ukrainian territory. "It has manipulated. It has obfuscated. It has outright lied. So we have learned to measure Russia by its actions and not by its words," Power said, calling for "serious negotiations . . . . In the face of this threat, the cost of inaction is unacceptable."[4]

The Russian Special Forces deployed into Crimea, along the Ukrainian border and covertly into eastern Ukraine—GRU Spetsnaz and elite airborne VDV troops—were crack units, extremely well equipped and at weapons parity (or better in regard to certain equipment) with NATO forces. Putin's spending program proved sufficient to put a force into the field that was capable of covertly supporting local insurgencies to seize border territories. The incursions also demonstrated Russian potential for intimidating a number of newly independent republics on the Russian Federation's borders. In another echo of Soviet-era practices, Putin showed himself to be especially adept at using surrogate antigovernment insurgencies, in the style of Stalin's immediate post–World War II political gamesmanship throughout Eastern Europe.

By 2014 at least a portion of the Russian military was revitalized and being used in a classic tactical fashion, very much reminiscent of the Cold War era. From a domestic political perspective, the strategy of relying on an aggressive national security theme and constant calls to Russian nationalism and patriotism dramatically elevated Putin's domestic popularity. Russian polling showed that between October 2013 and August 2014, Putin's popularity increased by a minimum of 20%. In the same period skepticism with regard to the nation's direction had dropped by more than 20%.[5] In concert, the increased defense spending made Putin even more popular with the Russian military-industrial complex, elements of the new Russian oligarchy and the Russian Federation's military. Clearly there is political value in the high-profile pursuit of national security and military deterrence, even when no clear, strategic threat actually exists.

In that regard, the resurgence of contemporary Russian military spending has certain similarities to that of the United States during the Eisenhower era. During Eisenhower's time in office, the Soviet Union actually presented no viable strategic threat to the United States—a fact secretly confirmed by ongoing aerial and satellite reconnaissance—despite broad-based public fear. Yet even with the hard-won knowledge of the true Soviet nuclear capability, American military spending was virtually unrestrained. The Strategic Air Command grew its bomber force exponentially, even as the Air Force and Navy were both bringing hundreds of intercontinental ballistic missiles online. At the same time the SAGE air defense system was developed and deployed, with a cost beyond that of the World War II Manhattan nuclear project. Duplication was the order of the day; virtually every Air Force fighter and fighter/bomber aircraft had a Navy equivalent, and there were broad duplications of Air Force, Army and Navy missiles in every class. Beyond that, each service implicated atomic strike capabilities across all its weapons systems. National security, public fears and military supremacy were political factors President Eisenhower could not ignore.

In the second decade of the 21st century, the Russian Federation faced no strategic military threat from the United States. Its own satellite reconnaissance systems, the joint Russian/American Open Skies surveillance program and ongoing on-site inspection programs related to the START nuclear disarmament agreements provided that assurance— as did the well-documented decline in American military spending and drawdown of its conventional forces that began following President Obama's second election. Yet Putin's resurgent theme of a modernized Russian nuclear capability and a concurrent military armaments initiative became increasingly expensive, ambitious and far-reaching.

Putin's military initiative invested heavily in strategic weaponry. The Russian TOPOL-M ICBM has become one of the world's most feared nuclear weapons carriers. Since being introduced in 1997, well after the end of the Cold War, some 80 of the new missiles have been put into service, most in hardened silos but with up to a third being road mobile—joining an existing force of some 170 first-generation road-mobile missiles. The TOPOL-M carries a full suite of re-entry warhead decoys and has the capability for at least four independently targeted nuclear warheads, although they are "officially" deployed with only one eight-hundred-kiloton device. The TOPOL-M is road mobile and extremely difficult to locate, even with satellite imaging. Beyond that, the 2011 Start III nuclear weapons treaty with the United States contained no limitations on rail-deployed missiles and the Russians appear to have initiated a serious program of rail-mobile TOPOL-M launchers, traveling across Russia's vast railroad network.[6] As of 2014 the road-mobile ICBMs compose a significant percentage of Russia estimated 473 deployed strategic missiles, which are capable of carrying 1,700 nuclear warheads.[7]

Beyond the mobile nuclear missiles, Russia pushed ahead to deploy both a new generation of Borei-class ballistic missile submarines and in September 2014 successfully conducted the test launch of its next generation Bulava submarine-launched ICBM. The new submarines carry up to twelve missiles, each with the capability of launching eighteen nuclear warheads over a range of five thousand kilometers. As the *Moscow Times* put it, such new weapons systems demonstrate that "Russia remains a nuclear power to be reckoned with even as Moscow's relations with the West sour over the Ukraine."[8]

With the TOPOL ICBMs, the Russian Federation has road- and rail-mobile retaliatory nuclear power as well as an existing force of nuclear-submarine-carried ICBMs—7 operational strategic missile submarines with 112 missiles. Even without the next-generation submarine missile force, that ensures massive destruction to any attacker considering a first strike. Under the START treaties Russia maintains an equivalent deterrent to America's triad of airborne, silo- and nuclear-submarine-based weapons systems. In comparison, based on the New Start treaty rules, the United States retains and plans to operate 447 ICBMs, 14 strategic nuclear submarines with up to 240 deployed missiles and 87 nuclear-capable bombers.[9] As of September 2014 the U.S. maintained a ready arsenal of 1,642 nuclear warheads while Russia held 1,643.

Regardless of the strategic balance, and once again mirroring concerns of the early Reagan presidency, Russian military leaders are openly concerned about a potential American decapitation capability. That issue is being used to justify a major restructuring and update of a large segment of their defense complex. This time, in contrast to the deployment of long-range cruise missiles in Europe, the Russians are worried about the future American deployment of hypersonic missiles, able to travel at five times the speed of sound and strike with extreme accuracy. Although such weapons are still early in development—and clearly a major technical challenge given their actual test history to date—the Pentagon is focused on them as a key weapon in "global strike" plans, providing the ability of precision attack anywhere on the planet within a single hour. Such a capability once again raises the fear of a preemptive American command-and-control strike against the Russian military and political leadership. In response, it appears that the Russian leadership is seriously considering a major restructuring of the long-existing Russian commands, merging the existing air and space forces into a combined aerospace command similar to that of the United States.[10]

On the conventional side, the ambitious Russian rearmament program has not gone as speedily as originally planned. The push to rebuild the Russian defense complex initially involved considerable foreign spending. A number of early efforts involved purchases of military assets from European sources, ranging from helicopter carriers (France) to the construction of a huge army training center (Germany). In 2014, NATO responses—in the form of economic sanctions—to Russian military actions in the Crimea and Ukraine raised serious questions as to how Russia would be able to source military assets from Europe, at least for a time. Western sanctions were likely one factor in slowing the Russian drive; even its own Defense Ministry projected that as of 2014 it had achieved only 26% of the planned armament modernization.[11] The Russian military modernization has also begun to run into some core problems relating to its own industrial infrastructure, including a serious lack of design engineers, especially those with large digital systems experience.[12] In early 2014, the Indian government announced that it was canceling a huge, joint advanced fighter-development project with one of Russia's premier aircraft firms—due to a host of design and quality issues.

In addition, Russia has fundamental manpower problems. Putin's ten-year program called for a one-million-man military force by 2013;

independent estimates including the Audit Project of Russia projected that it actually reached somewhere between seven hundred and eight hundred thousand. The Russian Army is manned by a large percentage of conscripts, and some units are estimated as being manned only at 40%–60% levels. Russian manpower problems are exacerbated by a falling birth rate and the fact that approximately 50% of potential recruits were being disqualified due to health considerations.[13]

Despite such structural problems, by 2014 Putin's efforts had dramatically succeeded in reinvigorating Russian nationalism and placing him and the industrial oligarchs who supported him in a position of renewed power. It's a familiar scenario, one that we have seen over the decades and one that speaks to the political attractiveness of the national security "card" and the usefulness of blaming domestic problems on foreign powers. On December 4, 2014, in his annual state of the Russian Federation address, President Putin retained his focus on a resurgent nationalism in foreign affairs: "It is pointless trying to talk to Russia from a position of strength. . . . No one can gain military superiority over Russia!"[14] He also continued a push toward increased internal security, targeting "speculators" whom he blamed for undermining the nation's economy.

More significantly, in regard to our discussion of the concept and associated risks of deterrence, as of late 2014, Putin's constantly escalating demonstration of Russian military "virility" began to create both a risk of international military incidents as well as the political context for a dramatic increase in Western European and American military spending, even in the face of serious budget deficits, debt and credit problems. Russia broke with years of post–Cold War practice, visibly stepping up overseas flights of its bomber forces. Russian bombers were increasingly tracked off the California coast and around American bases in the Pacific, as well as down the American coastline to Russian surrogate nations in Latin America. In 2013 Russian Tu-22M Backfire bombers conducted what clearly were simulated bombing runs against an American Aegis missile cruiser in the Pacific and American installations in Japan (in a manner quite similar to Reagan-era American Navy "training" flights). Russian ferret flights off Alaska have once again become routine. In one instance a formation of four nuclear-capable Tu-95 bombers moved directly toward Alaskan airspace, prompting the launch of a pair of F-22A Raptor alert interceptors. Two of the Russian bombers turned back, while a second pair continued all the way down the west coast of North America, traveling to within fifty miles of the California coast.

Russian planes also began to repeatedly operate around the border airspace of several European nations and conducted obvious bombing exercises against Scandinavian nations. In the spring of 2013, a flight of two Russian Backfire heavy jet bombers, escorted by four Russian air superiority fighters, conducted what was clearly a simulated night attack on Sweden, flying from St. Petersburg to within forty miles of Swedish territorial waters.[15] In 2014, attention refocused on the United States, with Russian bombers entering American airspace some sixteen times in only ten days. Such flights appeared more threatening than previous single Tu-95 border flights because they increasingly consisted of "strike" packages of tankers, bombers and long-range fighter escorts. In September 2014 a package of six such aircraft were intercepted by American escort fighters off Alaska, while at the same time two Russian bombers were separately tracked by Canadian fighters over the Beaufort Sea off Canada's northwestern coast. By November 2014 the Russian military leadership announced that they would be sending routine bomber patrols not only around the American east and west coasts but also off its coast in the Gulf of Mexico—something never done by the Soviet Union even at the height of the Cold War.

Of particular concern, Russian aircraft and ships also began a much more aggressive response to American aircraft and submarines performing surveillance activities in response to Russian military actions in Crimea and the Ukraine. Such intercepts had been fairly routine in the past; however, Russian responses became much more dramatic, with pilots flying much closer to the American aircraft, in a considerably more risky fashion. Russian Army exercises appear to be taking the same confrontational path. In August 2014 more than a thousand Russian troops, with extensive hardware and support from five attack helicopters, began exercises in the Kuril Islands, on territory actually claimed by Japan.

Increasingly large-scale Russian penetration flights began in late October 2014. In four separate flights, six strategic bombers, four long-range fighters and a significant number of shorter-range attack jets and fighters (accompanied by aerial tankers) were sent out of Russian bases. The aircraft moved into the airspace adjacent to the borders of several NATO and non-member nations and were tracked by interceptors from Portugal, Turkey, the United Kingdom, Denmark, Finland and Sweden. The unannounced Russian deployment of more than nineteen military aircraft in concurrent probing flights inside a twenty-four-hour period would have been highly unusual even during the Cold War era. The Russian activity was also of concern since none of the aircraft had filed routine flight plans and none of them operated onboard radar identification/location transponders or established any radio contact with civilian authorities. In March 2014, a Scandinavian commercial airliner flying out of Copenhagen with 132 passengers "narrowly avoided" a collision with a Russian military aircraft that had turned off its transponder. Fortunately, the Scandinavian airline's pilots visually spotted the intruding Russian jet.

The March incident involved a single Russian aircraft, but by fall, the frequency of multiple and simultaneous Russian military flights gave every appearance of a well-orchestrated military exercise against much of Western Europe—and, most dangerously, none of the aircraft had flown with operating identification transponders.[16] Russian military activities accelerated through the end of the year, and by December 2014, NATO announced that its fighters had responded to large groups of Russian aircraft flying over the Baltic Sea, off the Norwegian coast as well as one long-range flight from the North Sea down the Portuguese coast. The flights included formations of four to six Russian bombers, supported by tankers.

In reality, such actions, while damaging to international relations, are peripheral to the state of true strategic deterrence. Flights of bombers—whether by the Russian air force in the 21st century or the Strategic Air Command in the previous century—do not define effective deterrence any more than did the secret existence of twenty thousand nuclear warheads. Deterrence lies in having sufficient force to withstand a surprise attack and conduct a retaliation that outweighs any conceivable gains by the attacking nation.

With that said, the current Russian tactical military posturing follows a pattern that does seem familiar. Similar American actions during the Reagan administration convinced the Soviets that the Americans were behaving irrationally and might have convinced themselves that they could initiate limited and controlled atomic warfare against the "evil empire" of the Soviet Union, including either preemptive nuclear strikes or combat with a mix of conventional and nuclear weapons. That fear led the Soviet leadership into a final, and unsustainable, military spending surge. It seems at least possible that initially Putin may have considered such a strategy—a new version of the "irrational leader" or "madman" strategy—against a financially constrained America. Alternatively, he may have continued and even escalated an assertive Russian military posture from purely domestic political/power concerns—possibly frustrated by growing Russian financial problems and later his limited successes in breaking up or neutralizing the Ukraine.

American and Western response to Putin's military initiatives was largely tactical—beginning with pre-positioning tanks, armored vehicles and sufficient associated equipment to support a Marine Expeditionary Brigade of some fourteen thousand to eighteen thousand personnel in Scandinavia. The Army also deployed tanks and heavy weapons to Europe, creating a presence not seen since the 1980s. In addition, the Obama administration deployed additional air units into Eastern Europe, increased joint training exercises and has begun to rotate strategic bombers overseas in a fashion not seen since the end of the Cold War. In early 2015, as Russian military involvement in eastern Ukraine escalated, and with similar initiatives apparently spreading, NATO responded by forming a brigade-sized four-thousand- to five-thousand-troop "spearhead" force for rapid deployment. Perhaps most significantly, it also moved to establish integrated "headquarters forces" in six eastern NATO countries: Estonia, Latvia, Lithuania, Poland, Romania and Bulgaria. Pre-positioning of artillery and tanks was under way by NATO nations, and several members, including both Poland and Germany, moved to rapidly build up their own armored forces.

America's conventional military moves reflected a turnaround in previous Obama administration directives to shift military attention—

and spending—away from Europe. While Russian action produced a significant conventional response both from NATO and the United States, there have been doubts that the administration would actually proceed with spending on the estimated $1 trillion that would be required over some thirty years to maintain and modernize American nuclear weapons as well the triad of air, missile and submarine delivery systems. President Obama and the American Congress also refrained (largely due to fiscal constraints) from any major American military spending surge; in fact, prior to the midterm elections of November 2014, both the president and Congress had supported legislation capping the American defense budget.

By 2015 that agreement came under increasing pressure, not from only from Putin's European gambits but from the escalating operational expenses associated with the new military campaigns against ISIS ("Daesh") across Iraq and Syria. In its first month of air and naval strikes the new operation cost $424 million. By late November 2014, the American air campaign ("Inherent Resolve") was costing some $8 million a day with more than $832 million spent since the beginning of the strikes in August.[17] The Obama administration faced the need for additional funding for expanded military action against Daesh at the same time Russian military probing was forcing increasing spending on European operations ranging from forward deployments and basing to more numerous training exercises with Eastern European nations and provision of military aid to the Ukraine.

It also faced the fact that Russian media statements and military exercises had reignited the political issue of strategic nuclear posture. Initially President Obama, like both Presidents George W. Bush and George H.W. Bush, had pushed for ongoing nuclear disarmament agreements and the reduction of nuclear arsenals. The 2010 the New Start atomic-weapons delivery-system reduction agreement was followed by American dialog on even further reductions in actual atomic bombs and warheads. However, by November 2014, the increasingly confrontational attitude of the Russian Federation created a climate in which U.S. Secretary of Defense Chuck Hagel announced a broad plan for investing in and improving the entire American nuclear deterrent force. The plan, announced as part of a new Defense Innovation Initiative, called for an annual 10% increase to the nuclear-force budget for five years, including both maintenance and modernization of nuclear warheads. In broader terms, Hagel compared the new American defense initiative to the major efforts undertaken in the 1950s and 1970s.[18]

With the Obama administration facing the national security issues of both Russian assertiveness and the international jihadi threat, in a political sense the other shoe dropped. Dramatic 2014 midterm Republican election gains in both houses of Congress brought a number of military-oriented Congressmen into key positions on defense appropriations committees. Immediately following the election, the incoming chairman of the Senate Armed Services Committee, John McCain, began talking to the press in regard to the initial dialogs among senior Republicans about a new national security agenda. Key items were providing arms to the Ukraine, accelerating military efforts against ISIS, confronting Chinese encroachments in the South China Sea and most importantly ending budget sequestration and military spending caps. In fact, McCain listed the ending of sequestration and increasing military spending as his number one priority.[19] There seemed to be every indication that both the Russian Federation and American military budgets were moving upward, at a time when both nations were exposed to serious financial risk.

Inside the Russian Federation, the political attraction of invoking the national security card became even more evident. The Putin government moved to prioritize military spending and implement domestic spending cuts—appealing to public "sacrifice" in support of the Russian struggle against "American domination."[20] In a classic appeal to the Russian public, during his 2014 year-end address he declared there was no need to fear the Russian military, as the nation was not a "warmonger." He then went on to compare Russia to its most well-known symbol—the bear:

> *What would happen if our most recognizable symbol . . . the bear who guards his Taiga (forest) stopped chasing pigs and sat still, maybe eating berries and*

honey . . . they [the wild pigs] won't leave him alone.
They are always trying to put him on a chain. They
will always try to put him on a chain and as soon as
he is put on this chain, they will pull out his teeth and
claws. In today's terms we are speaking about our nu-
clear deterrence. As soon as, God forbid, this is done,
the bear isn't needed anymore.[21]

Putin's strong words are strangely reminiscent of President Ronald Reagan's remarks about the threat of the Soviet "evil empire," which so deeply worried the Soviet leadership of the time. Yet then as now, such language holds a strong appeal to nationalism, perhaps especially in Russia, which has a long history of responding to threats through solidarity, regardless of any issues with its own government. Geopolitical analyst George Friedman points out that one of the Russian people's fundamental strengths is they can endure burdens that would break other nations. Friedman also emphasizes that the Russian people tend to support the government regardless of its competence (or domestic policies) when Russia feels threatened. After sampling current views in Moscow late in 2014, he warned that Putin's appeals to Russian nationalism might well work in spite of sanctions, lost revenues and overall economic distress.[22] As of early 2015 it was clear that appeals for just that type of patriotic support were escalating among the Russian leadership; in January Deputy Prime Minister Igor Shuvalov warned an international meeting that "the Russians will never give up their leader. We will tighten our belt, eat less food, suffer any privations, but if outsiders want to force changes on us, we will be united as never before."[23] Shuvalov went even further, threatening that further economic sanctions would bring the world to the "verge of war." Shuvalov's rhetoric was some of the most dramatic since the earliest years of the Cold War.

How the American Congress deals with its financial risk remains to be seen; it does have recourse to spending and budgetary options, even if its record in actually exercising them has been inconsistent. In contrast, at the end of 2014 Russia suddenly found itself facing an unforeseen financial crisis. Putin's plans for a major military investment rested largely in a growing Russian economy, driven primarily by substantial oil and gas revenues. That economic growth had appeared robust enough to offset the Western economic sanctions that had followed Russian military moves in Crimea and eastern Ukraine. What was not anticipated was that the effect of the sanctions would be drastically multiplied by falling oil prices—down more than 30% by the end of the year. The 2015 Russian budget had been constructed against $100-a-barrel oil price point—in reality the price of oil had gone below $80 during the fall of 2014 and by early 2015 was in the $50–60 range, with no imminent rebound apparent.

In September 2014 the Russian news agency forecast a 21% growth in military spending in 2015, yet by October the Russian finance minister was quoted as saying the country could not afford its planned defense program.[24] By December the finance minister, Anton Siluanov, estimated that his nation would be losing more than $140 million a year and projected that Russia would find itself in a significant recession during 2015. Yet once leadership ties itself to an agenda of national security and deterrence, it has always been difficult to back away. President Putin rebuilt his popularity on that platform, and as events proceeded, he seemed almost bound to it, using an increasing spectrum of weapons to assert Russian independence. In a dramatic move, on January 14, 2015, Russia cut natural gas shipments shipped through the Ukraine, essentially and without warning cutting off supplies to some six European nations with no warning at all. The Russian statement that it would redirect shipments via a pipeline not transiting the Ukraine expressed a lack of concern that no infrastructure existed to carry gas from that pipeline to the European nations. The move was made at a time when Russia faced huge debt refinancing problems, depleted currency reserves and an economy headed for deep recession—the only apparent motive being that a gas cutoff represented virtually the only leverage whereby Putin could assert Russia's power for international action.[25]

Given Putin's apparent Cold War mindset, the question is whether Russia's ongoing military posturing, combined with a fiercely independent foreign policy, will once again spur a military spending surge, both in the United States and Europe. The history we have explored demonstrates that such actions can create a cycle of armament escalation beyond any sense of sanity. We saw that with the totally unrestrained growth in nuclear warheads, from the two hundred needed to destroy an enemy nation to some twenty thousand—simply to maintain "parity" with the other side. One nation's buildup has repeatedly frightened others into other "mirroring," generating unnecessary and questionable levels of military growth and spending. And if early signs hold true, Putin's actions may have done just that once again. During the first decade of the 21st century, America's strategic defense spending had definitely seemed on a downward trend, yet in 2015, Russian behavior had begun to generate real traction for a round of new U.S. nuclear arms development, including not only a new generation of long-range "global strike" bombers but a "ground-based strategic deterrent," which would replace the decades-old Minuteman III ICBMs with a new generation of boosters. The irony might well be that a recovering United States economy, based largely on gas and oil independence, could be used to fund new American weapons systems while Russia finds itself hard-pressed to pay for Putin's military initiatives due to the dramatic fall in oil prices and a Russian economy in virtual depression.[26]

It's not simply the size of the opponent's nuclear or even conventional arsenal that determines the "tipping point" where spending significantly accelerates; it's the apparent aggressiveness with which military forces are displayed—the point at which one side "scares" the other. In the 1950s and 1960s America not only actively displayed the capabilities of the Strategic Air Command and its ICBM submarine force but it "forward-deployed" both, as it did with its IRBMs in Western Europe and Turkey. Beyond that, the SAC airborne alert force continually rotated back and forth to "fail-safe" points within striking distance of Russia. Such actions effectively projected American military strength, but the associated fear factors fueled the immense growth of the Soviet's own military/industrial complex.

Later, the early Reagan-era high-profile military activity—both air and naval—in Europe and in the Pacific again elevated Russian fears, pushing it into another surge of spending and even briefly considering a first strike against the United States. America effectively projected its military deterrence but on occasion did so strongly enough to trigger the Soviets into huge levels of military spending, ultimately undermining their entire economy. It remains unclear and a matter of historical debate as to whether the early Reagan military actions were actually part of an orchestrated strategy at some level within the Reagan White House. A similar question exists as to whether President Putin might have embarked on such a strategy; however, more recent events suggest that his actions were more likely a product of his own personal KGB and Cold War experiences.

Contemporary history suggests that military deterrence involves an emotional calculus involving both the defender and potential attacker, a far more subjective matter than the highly secret targeting computations of the American SIOP—which led to levels of overkill by both sides. In short, it is a calculus of fear. Fear of retaliation must override the temptation to attack. But such deterrence is a mixture of weapons calculus and communications; it is not truly a contest, and it works only with potential enemies who are rational enough to calculate risk/reward. In spite of the extensive and erudite writings on the subject, in hindsight deterrence is truly as simple as stated by a fictional character in Pat Frank's 1959 drama of surprise Soviet atomic attack: "The point is, if they think they can get away with it, then we have lost."[27]

It is also important to observe that "overkill" does not constitute true deterrence, nor does either provocation or mind games (maskirovka). In fact, probing and unannounced military operations in the vicinity of other nations' borders create a level of risk that is beyond true deterrence. At present, that risk appears to be growing, with Russia carrying out increased aerial probing, the U.S. responding with ongoing electronic reconnaissance flights and both the U.S. and its allies actively engaging in interceptions. Our study of formerly secret Cold War events has shown us how risky such flights and encounters can be, and in a world of near instantaneous communications and an international public with camera phones, texting and video postings, mistakes or accidents could far too easily turn into actual military confrontations.

While deterrence may be both the most historically discussed and newest contemporary issue in regard to surprise attacks, it is far from being the only area we have explored. Based in the events of seventy-plus years, there are also observations to be made in regard to the effectiveness of warnings intelligence, strategic versus tactical warning, the need for pre-delegation and pre-positioning, and human-factor issues of command and control. Certain of the following remarks will no doubt prove controversial, yet all of them are based in the historical reality of the actual surprise attacks and crises management that we have explored.

First, despite protests and disassembly after the fact, threat/warnings intelligence works. From World War II to contemporary times, there have been virtually no true "surprise" attacks, simply because first military intelligence and later a much broader national intelligence community have done a thorough job of identifying and characterizing strategic threats. The United States government has always been aware of its potential enemies and pending threats. None of the attacks we have reviewed, from Pearl Harbor to the Tonkin Gulf to the USS *Pueblo* and even the attacks of 9/11, have occurred without warnings intelligence and alerts from segments of the intelligence community—in fact, all were preceded by specific warnings and alerts. In a number of instances, political agendas, command decisions, communications problems or a combination of all three have prevented those warnings from being actually acted upon in a timely fashion, or at all. Warnings intelligence works—whether or not the warnings themselves work is a matter of many factors. Intelligence professional Cynthia Grabo expressed it most concisely; fundamentally, she argues, it's a matter of whether the intelligence community says it "often enough and loud enough" and whether or not the policy maker—or the military commander—actually accepts the warning.[28]

On the other hand, reliance upon tactical warning has proved illusionary. It is simply too difficult to parse the exact location of timing of attacks from the ongoing "noise." That has become even more of a truism as warnings and threat noise levels have dramatically increased in contemporary times. The real-world attacks that we have reviewed demonstrate that threats can clearly be identified but that actual attacks occur with limited tactical warning—regardless of improvements in detection systems. Pearl Harbor had fifteen to thirty minutes' warning of incoming Japanese strikes; throughout the later decades of the Cold War the United States had some fifteen to thirty minutes before the first wave of warhead explosions. On 9/11, the warnings for hijacked airliners came within fifteen minutes of the impacts in both New York and Washington, D.C. A defense based on reliance on tactical warning will simply fail; the unpleasant reality is that a realistic defense has to be constructed on the premise that an attack is imminent at all times and prepared to preemptively respond within some fifteen minutes of warning.

Such a defense is extremely challenging, it's expensive and it receives few plaudits—General LeMay won few hearts by making similar observations even at the height of the Cold War. Yet the reality of surprise attack supports his position. In 1941 in Hawaii, General Short operated his radar units for extremely limited hours, even while under war alert. During the follow-on inquiries, Short was forced to admit that even if he had the material for a fully equipped network of stations, he would have operated them in the same training mode as he had done.[29] In the Philippines, General MacArthur issued orders only for reconnaissance to enable a bombing strike against the major Japanese air bases on Formosa—hours after combat had already begun and while the Japanese air attack from Formosa was incoming. Yet General Short, Admiral Kimmel and General MacArthur had all clearly viewed themselves as heavily involved in preparing for war.

In contrast General LeMay viewed SAC as being at war, simply waiting to detect the first or next attack. With that in mind, LeMay requested and monitored a series of simulated attacks against SAC bases. He quickly learned that even when Air Defense Command was advised of the exercises, they proved unable to intercept and defeat low-level attacks.[30] As the ultimate pragmatist, LeMay learned from that experience and accepted the fact that SAC was essentially on its own; the public might be reassured by NORAD and the SAGE system, but SAC would either be in the air in fifteen minutes or die on the ground.

The harsh realities of surprise attacks lead to another very unpleasant observation—in such an attack, National Command Authority is an illusion. That is not to say that national command is not extremely desirable and effective during a military confrontation. President Kennedy demonstrated the ultimate value of civilian control during dangerous confrontations in both Berlin and Cuba. The lack of objective civilian command during the Cuban Missile Crisis could easily have proven disastrous. As a side note, the Cuban Missile Crisis also proved that tactical reconnaissance can be both extremely valuable and extremely dangerous. Locating some but not all of the Soviet IRBMs—and almost nothing of the Soviet tactical nuclear weaponry poised to launch against an American attack—created a totally unrealistic, favorable military assessment of large-scale military action against Cuba.

Yet the command challenge during a "crisis of confrontation" is not at all the same as that experienced under actual surprise attack—and we have seen no instance in which National Command Authority responded in a timely or effective manner during an attack alert, an actual attack or even national crises that could have been the precursor to a surprise attack.[31] The Carter era war alert, in which all national command centers concurrently reported a major incoming Soviet ICBM attack, illustrated that reality. Within six minutes a warning was issued; alert interceptors and aircraft were launched. Even with ongoing word of more missiles showing on radar, the president was not actually awakened, and the entire time frame allowed for civilian decision-making and authorization of nuclear retaliation passed—before word was received that the alert had been issued due to a technical failure and was a false alarm.

The experiences of Cold War–era war alarms, of attacks on American vessels overseas and of the 9/11 attacks all demonstrate that pre-delegation, standing rules of engagement and guidance for lethal action in both defense and retaliation are critical to effective defense during surprise attacks. That appears to be an exceptionally difficult lesson to institutionalize. President Eisenhower initiated air defense and nuclear retaliation pre-delegation practices as early as 1957, yet as we saw in examining the transcripts from NEADS and CONR, on 9/11 standing authority and guidance for pre-delegation against airborne terror attacks were simply not available. At present, such delegation appears to have been instituted and is reportedly exercised on a routine basis under Operation Noble Eagle. It is unclear to what extent it is in place to deal with ground or maritime terror attacks.

There are indications that the Obama administration may be supporting the application of pre-delegation in a broader range of venues, backing additions to the military's Standing Rules of Engagement. As an example, prior to 2010, initiation of an active defense against computer cyber-attack required approval of the National Security Council. Yet any broad-based computer attack has the potential to seriously affect an unpredictable range of the nation's communications, at least initially. If coupled with an attack on the nation's space communications assets, sections of the national chain of command could be broken. Accordingly, in 2013 a news release noted that new rules of engagement now authorize pre-delegation of defensive cyber warfare. According to the reports, work on the new policy had been in place since 2005 but had stalled in legal disputes and surfaced only in highly bureaucratic working papers. The initial drafts and redrafts were neither as broad nor as forceful as the nation's Cyber Command, the secretary of defense and the Obama administration desired. By 2013 a new set of guidelines, felt to be "forward-leaning," had gone into place.[32]

In our exploration of the post-9/11 changes, several contemporary defense trends do suggest that lessons have been learned and practices improved. Pre-delegation, pre-positioning of military assets and point defense of key terror targets moves toward installing realistic quick-reaction forces—both air and ground—and broader, more realistic attack-and-response exercises are all encouraging. Of course, they are all expensive, and we have seen how easy it is for such efforts to simply fade away in the face of budget concerns and political agendas. As in the past, it's likely that the first elements to weaken will be those related to the human factors of command and control, especially within the National Command Authority and among the principals of any new administration. There are simply too many demands on elected leaders, and unlike in the military, no rules and regulations force civilian commanders—especially those in the line of succession—to spend time learning and practicing realistic crisis command and control. Our explorations suggest that is a situation that should be corrected; perhaps there should even be legislation demanding that civilian authority know and demonstrate some level of competency regarding command and control during national crises. The incidents we have studied provide adequate examples of such a need.

Other human-factor issues associated with command and control are much more challenging, even for experienced and trained military commanders. One documented and well-known issue is that of "career caution." In our earlier chapters we saw it occur in Pearl Harbor. By 6:40 AM on the morning of December 7, 1941, the destroyer USS *Ward* had engaged a Japanese submarine and radioed sinking it with depth charges. Within some twenty minutes the *Ward* established sonar contact with yet another submarine, immediately attacking and confirming its sinking. At that point a series of telephone calls began going up the Navy ship chain of command, slowed by a number of busy signals. At the same time, calls were going up the air patrol side of the command chain, relating the sighting of a submarine by a Navy patrol aircraft.

Word of the submarine engagements did reach the Pacific Fleet commander, Admiral Kimmel. Yet there had been previous false reports of submarine encounters, and Kimmel determined to wait for confirmations and more information, deferring on any orders to issue an advanced alert while waiting on "further developments."[33] The first wave of Japanese torpedo bomber strikes began at approximately 7:51 AM. Admiral Kimmel had been caught in a decision-making quandary, having been ordered to conduct his defensive measures without raising international tensions or arousing public fears. His quandary, as we've now seen, was far from unique.

In April 1952, a variety of indicators, including the tracking of new Soviet heavy bombers into Siberia, triggered concerns over some sort of imminent attack. On April 16, a warning from Air Force Intelligence to Air Defense Command described "ominous" new Soviet activities. Almost immediately tactical warnings began to come in, suggesting inbound bomber formations coming over Alaska. The duty commander of the Air Defense Command initially hesitated, desperately calling for more information—but then a new report of unknown aircraft approaching Maine arrived. Given the appearance of separate attacks coming in over the two major polar routes—exactly as anticipated in Soviet attack scenarios—a nationwide Air Defense Readiness alert was ordered at 3:10 AM. The feared attack turned out to be a series of off-course and off-schedule commercial airliners. Reportedly the Pentagon Air Staff responded with a strong criticism of the alert, charging that the Air Defense commander had overreacted.

In later years, as SAC became more and more exposed not only to Soviet ICBMs but to even shorter flight times from submarine-launched missiles, its commanders faced a definite career-limiting decision quandary. Those commanders had the authority to launch the SAC ground alert bomber force to protect it, yet in doing so in anything less than a real attack, they would have been observed by Soviet satellites, protests would have been lodged, a political firestorm would no doubt have ensued and the commander's career could well have been permanently jeopardized. Veteran nuclear strategist Paul Bracken evaluated the problem at length, creating a command-decision matrix. It was a very simple matrix: If it were a real attack and the commander had launched his alert force, he would be a dead hero; if he held back, he would be cursed by any survivors. If the warning were a mistake and he launched, he would have ruined his career, facing possible court-martial. In that analysis, the only reward was for taking no action.[34]

Command caution is a quandary that continues in contemporary times. On 9/11, the vice president issued a directive for lethal force against hijacked airliners. The command was effectively communicated to NORAD. The vice president advised the secretary of defense that the command had been issued and that American interceptors were actively engaging hostile aircraft with lethal force. Yet after the fact, it was confirmed that the NORAD commander had not issued any general authorization of lethal engagement. Interceptors had to maintain communications, advise command and receive final clearance for action against aircraft deemed hostile. They needed to establish the threat, report it and only then receive guidance, likely including orders to engage. Yet that sequence of events might have proved challenging. The events of the day show that NORAD Northeast Control was having difficulty maintaining radio contact with certain of its interceptors that were conducting patrols at low altitude, in particular those operating over Washington, D.C. If another terror strike had occurred, with no lethal engagement attempted, there would no doubt have been military-career consequences.

Bracken's assessment of the SAC command-caution issue offered no resolution—he also observed the same quandary occurring during alerts inside the Soviet Union, with similar restraint among Soviet defense commanders. He refers to it as command "paralysis," noting that the same procedures that prevent accidents in peacetime could effectively neutralize defense and retaliation. Obviously there is no easy answer, no good answer—other than ensuring that authority to engage is realistically extended to those commanders who do find themselves obviously facing hostile action at points of attack, and hoping that they use their precious fifteen minutes to the best effect.

The United States has considered itself to be under the threat of surprise attack for the past seventy years. The nation's most recently elected presidents, George W. Bush and Barack Obama, have both repeatedly declared America to be in a national security emergency—as of this writing that state of emergency has been in effect for more than fourteen years. During that time, the threat of jihadi terror attacks has both continued and broadened globally. In addition, certain tensions and fears of the Cold War era have resurfaced, with confrontation and harsh dialog between Russia, European nations and the United States. Issues thought secondary (including nuclear deterrence, new generations of atomic-weapons systems and a possible new arms race) have resurfaced and now present themselves as primary.

If jihadi terror and a resurgent arms race were not enough cause for concern, in 2010 a computer attack on the central servers at NASDAQ dramatically surfaced a totally new type of national security threat. And in response yet another national security agency, the National Cybersecurity and Communications Integration Center (NCCIC), carried out the crisis response, utilizing agencies ranging from the FBI and NSA to Treasury, Defense and Homeland Security.

Initial threat assessment of the cyber attack concluded that computer attackers representing a foreign-nation state had gained access to the American Stock Exchange. The president was informed and the meeting reconvened at the White House. National Security Council representatives were briefed on the threat, which included the possibility that the attack could manipulate or destabilize the entire trading platform. Beyond that, there was concern that it might be only the first move in a coordinated attack against the overall national financial infrastructure.[35]

In the end the attack was defeated; however, a worst-case scenario could have actually shut down stock trading for hours, perhaps a day or more. The financial impact of such an attack would have had a major impact on the nation's economy. In the case of such an event, National Command Authority would have been challenged and the Situation Room would have become filled with NSC principals acting in crisis response mode, just as during many of the other incidents we have detailed here.

In *Surprise Attack* we have explored some seven decades of America's efforts to identify a continually evolving range of threats and prepare responses to them. In the end we find that regardless of the warnings, the plans, the exercises and preparedness drills, success or failure is subject to the human factors within the chain of communications, command and control. The weapons improve and diversify, the technology evolves, yet the human factor remains the dominant element in differentiating a successful defense from defeat and destruction. It's a brutal but essential lesson to learn.

NOTES

CHAPTER 1: WARNINGS

1. Qtd. in Gordon Prange, *At Dawn We Slept: The Untold Story of Pearl Harbor* (New York: McGraw-Hill, 1981), 45.
2. John Prados, *Combined Fleet Decoded: The Secret History of American Intelligence and the Japanese Navy in WWII* (New York: Random House, 1995), 87.
3. Gordon Prange with Donald Goldstein and Katherine Dillon, *Pearl Harbor: The Verdict of History* (New York: McGraw-Hill, 1986), 41.
4. Gordon Prange, *At Dawn We Slept: The Untold Story of Pearl Harbor,* 34.
5. Cynthia M. Grabo, *Anticipating Surprise: Analysis for Strategic Warning* (Lanham, MD: University Press of America, Inc., 2004), 3.
6. Gordon Prange, *At Dawn We Slept: The Untold Story of Pearl Harbor,* 289–293.
7. Ibid, 353.
8. Qtd. in ibid, 370.
9. Ibid, 406.
10. Ibid, 447–448.
11. Gordon Prange with Donald Goldstein and Katherine Dillon, *Pearl Harbor: The Verdict of History,* 136.
12. William Bartsch, *December 8, 1941: MacArthur's Pearl Harbor* (College Station, TX: Texas A&M UP, 2003), 237.
13. Ibid, 43, 104 and 175.
14. Gordon Prange with Donald Goldstein and Katherine Dillon, *Pearl Harbor: The Verdict of History,* 295–296.

CHAPTER 2: INTERDICT OR INTERCEPT

1. Gordon Prange, *At Dawn We Slept: The Untold Story of Pearl Harbor* (New York: McGraw-Hill, 1981), 62.
2. Ibid, 63.
3. Ibid, 124.
4. Ibid, 354.
5. Karl Larew, "December 7, 1941: The Day No One Bombed Panama." *Historian,* Summer 2004, Issue 66:2, 278–299.
6. Gordon Prange with Donald Goldstein and Katherine Dillon, *Pearl Harbor: The Verdict of History* (New York: McGraw-Hill, 1986), 353.
7. Ibid, 371–372.
8. Gordon Prange, *At Dawn We Slept: The Untold Story of Pearl Harbor,* 497.
9. Paul Bracken, *The Command and Control of Nuclear Forces* (New Haven, CT: Yale UP, 1983), 68–71.
10. William Bartsch, *December 8, 1941: MacArthur's Pearl Harbor* (College Station, TX: Texas A&M UP, 2003), 43, 104 and 175.
11. Ibid, 154.
12. William Bartsch, *Doomed at the Start: American Pursuit Pilots in the Philippines, 1941–1942* (College Station, TX: Texas A&M UP, 2003), 430.
13. William Bartsch, *December 8, 1941: MacArthur's Pearl Harbor,* 230.
14. William Bartsch, *Doomed at the Start: American Pursuit Pilots in the Philippines, 1941–1942,* 429–430.

15. William Bartsch, *December 8, 1941: MacArthur's Pearl Harbor*, 262–283.

CHAPTER 3: ERRORS OF COMMAND

1. Gordon Prange with Donald Goldstein and Katherine Dillon, *Pearl Harbor: The Verdict of History* (New York: McGraw-Hill, 1986), 93–94.
2. Ibid, 227.
3. Ibid, 253–256.
4. Qtd. in ibid, 256; see also Joint Congressional Committee, Nov. 15, 1945–July 1946, *Pearl Harbor Report*, Part 3, 1,050.
5. Ibid, 298–300 and 355.
6. Ibid, 365.
7. Ibid, 367–371.
8. Ibid, 129.
9. Qtd. in Alan Armstrong, *Preemptive Strike: The Secret Plan That Would Have Prevented the Attack on Pearl Harbor* (Guilford, CT: The Lyons Press, 2006), 149–150.
10. Ibid, 152.
11. William Bartsch, *December 8, 1941: MacArthur's Pearl Harbor* (College Station, TX: Texas A&M UP, 2012
12. William Bartsch, *Doomed at the Start: American Pursuit Pilots in the Philippines, 1941–1942* (College Station, TX: Texas A&M University Press, 1995).
13. Gordon Prange, *At Dawn We Slept: The Untold Story of Pearl Harbor* (New York: McGraw-Hill, 1981), 483–494.
14. Alan Armstrong, *Preemptive Strike: The Secret Plan That Would Have Prevented the Attack on Pearl Harbor*, 259–262.

CHAPTER 4: A NEW THREAT

1. John Correll, "The Poltava Debacle," *Air Force Magazine*, Mar. 2011, 64–68.
2. William Burrows, *By Any Means Necessary: America's Secret Air War in the Cold War* (New York: Farrar, Straus and Giroux, 2001), 45.
3. Dean Acheson, *Present at the Creation: My Years in the State Department* (New York: Norton and Norton Co., 1969), 85.
4. Qtd. in Joseph Persico, *Roosevelt's Centurions: FDR and the Commanders He Led to Victory in World War II* (New York: Random House, 2013), 462.
5. Qtd. in ibid, 496–498.
6. William Burrows, *By Any Means Necessary: America's Secret Air War in the Cold War*, 66.
7. Qtd. in Richard Rhodes, *Dark Sun: The Making of the Hydrogen Bomb* (New York: Simon and Schuster, 1995), 225. Rhodes notes that neither the U.S. government nor any of its presidents ever formally endorsed the preventive war concept but that the extreme convictions of military, and in particular Air Force leaders, led to decades of military planning and preparation for either surprise attacks of either interdiction or preemption against the Soviet Union.
8. Ibid, 23–24.
9. Qtd. in ibid, 150–151.
10. Qtd. in ibid, 234–235.
11. Qtd. in ibid, 621–622.
12. David Cinciotti, "The USAAF faces Yugoslavian Yak-3s," *The Aviationist*, Sept. 4, 2009.
13. Richard Rhodes, *Dark Sun: The Making of the Hydrogen Bomb*, 196.
14. Joel Carpenter, "Guided Missiles and UFOs—A Tangle of Fear: 1937–53." The Carpenter essays are essential reading in regard to the Ghost Rocket phenomenon. Carpenter's detailing of the Scandinavian reports is extensive, containing primary materials ranging from newspaper articles to photos and

government documents. In addition, the *Project 1947* website contains an extensive series of Scandinavian reports for this period, provided by Dr. Thomas Bullard. See www.project1947.com.

15. On June 23, 1946, Major James Hamill (U.S. Army Ordnance) was sent an urgent and confidential message for Wernher von Braun. The Pentagon (War Department) wanted "an immediate evaluation of the German rocket technicians left in the Soviet zone of occupied Germany and how long it might take such experts to perfect an intercontinental missile." Von Braun responded, "There is no doubt that the bulk of the most capable members of the Peenemünde group are in the United States now. There are, however, many very good former Peenemünde experts working for the Russians too . . . the two most capable of these men . . . are: Dipl. Ing. Helmut Grottrup . . . and Engineer Martin. These two men are, according to the best available information, in charge of the Russian project—new development projects (Grottrup) and A-4 manufacture in Nordhausen (Martin). As regards future developments such as A-9, A-10, and A-11 Grottrup is a very able and clever leader of a development group. Compared with the situation found by the German group in the U.S. he has the advantage of having almost complete test stands and a complete production plant, which can easily be set going with the available number of trained members of these plants."

16. Qtd. in Joel Carpenter, "Guided Missiles and UFOs: A Tangle of Fear —1937-53."

17. Captain Henri Smith-Hutton, "U.S.S. Little Rock crew member transcript," U.S. Little Rock Association, www.usslittlerock.org.

18. On July 9, 1946, Eric Reutersward had photographed an object from an air tower 50 miles west of Vasteras. Fragments from an impact had been reported collected at Njurunda. A copy of the photograph appears to show an object very similar to a German V-1 rocket, in a trajectory dive characteristic of that device.

19. Walter Dornberger, *V-2: The Nazi Rocket Weapon* (New York: Ballantine Books, 1954), 122–125; and Frederick Ordway and Mitchell Sharpe, *The Rocket Team* (New York: Ty Crowell Co., 1979), 181–182 and 201. High-frequency radio control had in fact been one of the major goals of German missile development. It was a major priority for increasing the accuracy of the V-2 rocket. Radio guide beams had been tested that allowed a lateral dispersion of approximately one and a half miles. Their goal was less than a thousand yards. One operational radio-beam–guided V-2 unit did become operational before the end of the war. Radio control was also in development for other guided weapons, including the rocket-propelled glide bombs. There appears to be far less detail available on success with those devices; however, we do know that the V-1 missile could be programmed to make a number of course changes during flight in order to confuse tracking stations and complicate countermeasures. Both the U.S. and the Russians tested flexible radio guidance systems in their derivative versions of the V-1.

20. David Clarke and Andy Roberts, *Out of the Shadows* (London: Piatkus Books, Little Brown Group, 2002), cited in 22 Aug. 1946 Group Captain Simpson memo; PRO Files.

21. Qtd. in ibid, document PRO FO371/56988.

22. SCR 615 technical specifications, www.ibiblio.org/hyperwar/USN/ref/Radar/Radar-7.html.

23. David Clarke and Andy Roberts, *Out of the Shadows,* "ORIGINATOR: AAF / DISTRIBUTION: ID, P&O, R&D." While this report contains a much more educated view of the technology than the Navy report, it is also clear that the authors are not current on the air launch and guidance capabilities of the enhanced V-1 devices possessed by both the Russians and Americans at this time.

24. Memo, Vandenberg to Truman, "Ghost Rockets over Scandinavia," Aug. 1, 1946, LeMay files, box 20, file 131.

25. The Central Intelligence Group came into place following the disbanding of the Office of Strategic Services (OSS) at the end of WWII. In June 1946, General Vandenberg became its chief, with a staff of some one hundred persons. Vandenberg had been serving as the Army Director of Intelligence. He grew the new CIG organization during 1946, being succeeded by Rear Admiral Roscoe Hillenkoetter for a few months in early 1947—before the CIG was superseded by the creation of the Central Intelligence Agency. The creation of the CIA was given special impetus by a Joint Chiefs report on the evaluation of the atomic bomb as a weapon. In its report the Chiefs stated that the "protection against the catastrophic consequences of an atomic bomb surprise attack will require an intelligence service with a far greater effectiveness than any such agency this country has ever had in peace or war. Such an agency, charged with the duty of constant, world-wide scrutiny to determine whether atomic weapons (or other weapons of mass destruction) are being manufactured or readied for use must be our first bulwark of national defense." "The Evaluation of the Atomic Bomb as a Military Weapon," The Final Report of the Joint Chiefs of Staff Evaluation Board for Operation Crossroads, June 30, 1947.

26. Jerome Clark, *The UFO Book* (Canton, MI: Visible Ink, 1998), 247.

27. Michael Swords and Robert Powell, *UFOs and the Government: A Historical Inquiry* (San Antonio: Anamolist Books, 2012), 22–23.

28. Richard Rhodes, *Dark Sun: The Making of the Hydrogen Bomb*, 280.

29. Qtd. in ibid, 281.

30. Ibid, 283–285. While the 509th atomic-capable bomb wing had been preserved and stationed at the Roswell air base, it had no atomic weapons at its disposal in 1946. All the components were in the vaults at Los Alamos, hundreds of miles away. There was no ongoing training in the actual assembly, handling and combat use of atomic ordnance. As we will discuss, even when bomb stockpiles began to be established, they were not placed in Roswell, nor were the weapons initially under the direct control or access of the Army Air Forces.

31. Ibid, 278 and 282.

32. Ibid, 295.

33. A full (and unsanitized) picture of the American military position has emerged only in recent years. A 1979 book on

the Strategic Air Command describes the Bikini tests as so successful that the third bomb did not need to be dropped (Norman Polmar, *Strategic Air Command—People, Aircraft and Missiles*, Anapolis, MD: Nautical and Aviation Publishing Company, 1979). Historian Richard Rhodes offers a totally different perspective in *Dark Sun*, including the fact that the primary target, the battleship *Nevada*, was left afloat and that the B-29's bomb sight was later determined to have been miscalibrated. Manhattan atomic project chief General Groves proposed to the Joint Chiefs that it would be best to save the single remaining weapon in inventory, and they agreed (*Dark Sun*, 261–263). Another book on the Strategic Air Command remarks that future historians will record that the supply of primitive nuclear weapons in the Marianas available following the atomic bombings of Hiroshima and Nagasaki "effectively destroyed in a single day every Japanese city with a population in excess of 30,000 people." Instead, history now records that there were no additional atomic bombs available at all at that time. Richard Hubler, *SAC—The Strategic Air Command*, (New York: Van Rees Press, 1958), 66.

34. Norman Polmar, *Strategic Air Command—People, Aircraft and Missiles* (Annapolis, MD: Nautical and Aviation Publishing Co., 1979), 9.

35. Richard Rhodes, *Dark Sun: The Making of the Hydrogen Bomb*, 261–262.

36. Richard Hubler, *SAC—The Strategic Air Command* (New York: Van Rees Press, 1958), 66.

CHAPTER 5: HOLLOW FORCE

1. Major General Curtis LeMay memorandum to Commanding General, Strategic Air Command, Subject: Mission of the 58th Bombardment Wing, June 13, 1946, www.secretsdeclassified.af.mil/shared/media/document/AFD-100504-057.pdf.

2. Richard Hubler, *SAC: The Strategic Air Command* (New York: Van Rees Press, 1958), 76.

3. Harry Borowski, *A Hollow Threat: Strategic Air Power and Containment Before Korea* (Westport, CT: Greenwood Press, 1982), 43.

4. Richard Hubler, *SAC: The Strategic Air Command*, 77–82.

5. Harry Borowski, *A Hollow Threat: Strategic Air Power and Containment Before Korea*, 100–101.

6. Richard Rhodes, *Dark Sun: The Making of the Hydrogen Bomb*, (New York: Simon and Schuster, 1995), 321.

7. Qtd. in Harry Borowski, *A Hollow Threat: Strategic Air Power and Containment Before Korea*, 165.

8. Qtd. in Richard Rhodes, *Dark Sun: The Making of the Hydrogen Bomb*, 340–341.

9. Qtd. in ibid, 341.

10. Qtd. in Walter J. Boyne, *Beyond the Wild Blue: A History of the U.S. Air Force 1947–1997* (New York: St. Martin's Press, 1997), 101–102.

11. Qtd. in Richard Rhodes, *Dark Sun: The Making of the Hydrogen Bomb*, 347.

12. L. Wainstein, C.D. Cremeans, J.K. Moriarty, and J. Ponturo, Study S-467, "The Evolution of U.S. Strategic Command and Control and Warning 1945–1972," June 1975, 77–83. www2.gwu.edu/~nsarchiv/nukevault/ebb403/docs/Doc%20 2%20-%20strategic%20command%20and%20control---%20 evolution%20of.pdf.

13. Ibid, 162–162.

14. William Burrows, *By Any Means Necessary* (New York: Farrar, Straus and Giroux, 2001), 93.

15. Ibid, 94.

16. Ibid, 94.

17. Ibid, 95.

18. Joel Carpenter, "Guided Missiles and UFOs: A Tangle of Fear—1937–53," Part Three, www.project1947.com/gr/grchron3.htm.

19. Jan Aldrich, "Early Top Secret UFO Document Discovered," www.project1947.com/fig/jtt.htm.

20. David Cinciotti, "Operation Falun: Swedish PBY vs. MiG 15S," *The Aviationist*, www.theaviationist.com/tag/operation-falun.

21. Col. Donald Hardy, U.S. Air Attaché, Stockholm, *Air Intelligence Information Report*, Dec. 30, 1948.

22. William Burrows, *By Any Means Necessary*, 95–97.

23. Ibid, 98–100. In July 1948, Air Force director general Charles Cabell issued a directive to Alaskan Air Command, reminding them that "frequent repetition of search lines is imperative . . . to get technical characteristics of the signals." Ferret crews were to locate early-warning and air defense installations and expose themselves to stimulate response, which would reveal not only Soviet defensive capabilities but changes in those capabilities.

24. Dr. David Clarke, "UFOs in History: Operation Charlie." An updated version of Dr. Clarke's work was published in 2004. It is available at www.project1947.com and also www.uk-ufo.org/condign/histcharlie.htm.

25. Ibid, www.uk-ufo.org/condign/histcharlie.htm.

26. NICAP online document collection, www.nicap.org/470710harmon_dir.htm.

27. Michael Hall and Wendy Connors, *Alfred Loedding and the Great Flying Saucer Wave of 1947*, Chapter 5; also NICAP files, www.nicap.org/reports/470804bethel_report.htm.

28. Ibid, 90.

29. Ibid, Chapter 5. References cited by Hall and Connors include "Project Blue Book Files," Roll No.1, Case 59, listed as Incidents, 26–27 in 1947-era documents; Loren Gross, *UFOs: A History 1947*, (London: Arcturus, 1990) 44–45, and "Project Blue Book Files," Roll No.2, Case 63, listed as Incident 41 in 1947-era documents as well as Michael D. Swords, "Project Sign and The Estimate of the Situation and Project Blue Book Files," Roll No.2, Case 60, listed as Incident 27a in 1947-era documents.

30. Joel Carpenter, "Guided Missiles and UFOs: A Tangle of Fear—1937–53," Part Three, www.project1947.com/gr/grchron3.htm.

31. *Searching the Skies: The Legacy of the United States Cold War Defense Radar Program*, United States Air Force Air Combat Command, June 1996, 11–14.

32. Joel Carpenter, "Paper Threat—The First Intercontinental Weapons System: Japanese Fu-Go Balloons," www.project1947.com/gfb/fugo.htm.

33. An air defense for this area had initially been established in 1945 as part of the response to the Japanese Fu-Go stratospheric balloon bombs.

34. Kenneth Schaffel, *The Emerging Shield: The Air Force and the Evolution of Continental Air Defense, 1945–1960* (University Press of the Pacific, 2004), 54–56.

35. Ibid, 57–58.

36. Ibid, 45–48.

37. Kenneth Schaffel, *The Emerging*

Shield: The Air Force and the Evolution of Continental Air Defense, 1945–1960, 68–69.

CHAPTER 6: UNCERTAINTIES AT HOME

1. Qtd. in Norman Graebner, *The National Security: Its Theory and Practice, 1945–1960* (New York: Oxford UP), 1986, 10.
2. Michael Swords and Robert Powell, *UFOs and the Government: A Historical Inquiry* (San Antonio, TX: Anomolist Books, 2012), 36.
3. Robert Kilmarx, *A History of Soviet Air Power* (New York: Praeger, 1962), 230.
4. William Burrows, *By Any Means Necessary: America's Secret Air War in the Cold War* (New York: Farrar, Straus and Giroux, 2001), 98.
5. Ibid, 100.
6. Ibid, 101.
7. An air defense for this area had initially been established in 1945 as part of the response to the Japanese Fu-Go stratospheric balloon bombs.
8. Kenneth Schaffel, *The Emerging Shield—The Air Force and the Evolution of Continental Air Defense 1945–1960* (University Press of the Pacific, 2004), 54–56.
9. Kenneth Schaffel, *The Emerging Shield —The Air Force and the Evolution of Continental Air Defense 1945–1960*, 78–80. Air Force intelligence believed that a Russian attack was imminent in the spring of 1948, and General Stratemeyer ordered an immediate implementation of an Alaskan air defense as well as a functional air defense for Seattle and the Hanford plant. These orders were issued on March 27 and were to be implemented by April 3, 1948. A crisis atmosphere existed in the spring of 1948 and was reflected in a Joint Chiefs meeting with Defense Secretary Forrestal. The Air Force commander in the Far East had reported strange incidents and excursions over Japan and was concerned about the outbreak of war within a few months. This followed the Communist coup in Czechoslovakia in February of 1948.
10. Ibid, 71–71. The "Lashup" first-generation Air Defense radars (AN/CPS5 sweep radar used in conjunction with an AN/TPS10 height finger), which would go into service in 1948–1949, had a normal range of only sixty miles (and a maximum approaching one hundred miles with a target at maximum altitude) and an altitude limitation of approximately twenty-five thousand. They were especially limited at low altitudes with a range of thirty-five miles with the target at one thousand feet and less if the target were lower. Follow-on radars such as the AN/CPS5 would come into use in the 1948–1951 period, but they would still be limited to a range of something like two hundred miles and an altitude of forty thousand feet—just enough to track the highest-performance WWII fighters such as the P-51 Mustang and F-82 Twin Mustang as well as the first operational American jet fighter, the F-84 Thunderjet. More importantly, they would have the necessary altitude capability to track the B-29 and the Russian Tu-4 ("Bull") derivative.
11. Ibid, 23 and 95.
12. Ibid, 126.
13. David Winkler, *Searching the Skies: The Legacy of the Cold War Radar Defense Program* (Air Force Combat Command, 1997) 14–17. Although

the Air Defense Command had been reactivated in March of 1946 under General Stratemeyer, it initially operated no radars and was directed to make its plans around the use of National Guard aircraft. By 1947 only two Air Defense search radar stations were operating—one at Arlington, Washington, and one at Half Moon Bay near San Francisco. It would not be until March 1948 that similar sites would be ordered set up for Los Alamos, Kirtland Air Force Base (which hosted the Sandia atomic weapons facility) and Roswell Air Force Base. www.pinetreeline.org/articles/re-sartj.html. There were WWII–era radar sets in operation at various facilities, normally either military airfields or civilian airports. There were also very specific types of radar sets in use at research-and-development sites such as White Sands (missile- and balloon-launch test facilities) and Muroc Air Base (high-speed jet and rocket aircraft testing). These were not dedicated "search" radars, as they were used for a very specific period in support of sched-uled tests and not operated in a general search mode or for an extended period. The Army 8th Air Force actually had to schedule access to the White Sands Radar (which was normally staffed by civilian Signal Corps Laboratory personnel) for radar countermeasures training in 1947, www.project1947. com/roswell/baindoc.htm.

14. Ibid, 77. In 1946, the Army Air Force's sole U.S.-based operational night-fighter unit had been temporarily deployed to McChord Field, Washington. In November of 1947 it was relocated to Hamilton Field, California. The unit consisted of thirteen P-161 night fight-ers, the only unit of its type at the time.

The Air Force's only daylight pursuit squadron with P-47 aircraft had been moved to Don Field in Maine. Neither unit had actually gone fully operational during 1946.

15. Ibid, 68–69. In June 1947, the AEC requested that the Secretary of War review military protection at key facilities. The review determined that no special protection was in place for any AEC facility as of the end of the review in July 1947.

16. Ted Bloecher, *Report on the UFO Wave of 1947* (manuscript, 1967), I–14. Note: Hamilton AFB would soon undergo expansion to serve as a major Air Defense Command fighter base during the 1950s.

17. Michael Hall and Wendy Connors, *Alfred Loedding & the Great Flying Saucer Wave of 1947*, (Albuquerque: Rose Press, 1998) Chapter 5.

18. Wolfgang Samuel, *American Raiders* (Jackson, MS: UP of Mississippi, 2004), 95–99.

19. Ibid, 401–411.

20. Lawrence Fawcett and Barry Green-wood, *The UFO Cover-Up* (Engle-wood Cliffs, NJ: Prentice-Hall, 1984), 147–148. It should be noted that Director Hoover annotated a memo relating to Schulgen's request with a remark that an object recovered in Louisiana by the Air Force had not been shared with the Bureau. The object in question was definitely deter-mined to have been a crude hoax. That incident is documented in Blue Book files for July 7, 1947.

21. Ibid, 151–156.

22. Ibid. 156–159.

23. Edward J. Ruppelt, *The Report on Unidentified Flying Objects* (Garden City, NY: Doubleday, 1956), 59.

24. "Analysis of Flying Object Incidents in the U.S." Project Blue Book Files, Roll No. 1, Case 59, listed as Incidents 26–27 in 1947–era documents; see also U.S. Air Intelligence Report No. 100-203-79, www.nicap.org/harmon.htm.

25. Jerome Clark, *The UFO Book* (Canton, MI: Visible Ink Press, 1997), 482–486. As of September 1947, when the intelligence collections order was issued, Air Force staff had been studying at best a few dozen incidents, the majority from military personnel and pilots. At that point, clearly their professional assessment was that there were obvious commonalities in the reports that defined a reasonably clear picture of the craft in question, certain physical characteristics as well as certain patterns of operation. In 1953, the Air Force contracted with Battelle Memorial Institute (as a task added to Project Stork, a classified study of Russian technical warfare capabilities) to perform a computer analysis of UFO sightings. The study and report were not completed until 1955 and involved some 3,201 incidents. The Battelle study (which involved statistical analysis) was presented along with Blue Book report No. 14 and concluded that it could find "no trends, patterns or correlations." There was no reference to the 1948 intelligence study and its enumeration of commonalities in the early reports. In view of the 1947 and 1949 Project Sign profiles, it seems reasonable to challenge the position that no trends, patterns or correlations can be made from sightings screened and designated as highly reliable.

26. Michael Swords and Robert Powell, *UFOs and the Government: A Historical Inquiry* (San Antonio, TX: Anomalist Books, 2012), 480–481.

27. Memorandum from Headquarters Berlin Command to Deputy Director of Intelligence, European Command, Subject: Horten Brothers (Flying Saucers), Dec. 16, 1947, www.project1947.com/fig/horten1.htm.

28. In some respects, McDonald's comment might seem somewhat controversial, since there had been a number of observations near the Muroc air development base and the White Sands rocket and missile test facility, as well as in the area of the giant Seattle and Los Angeles aircraft manufacturing complexes. Still, in terms of specific American strategic targets it is important to note that the Air Force considered those to be the Hanford works (the first plutonium reactor complex); the Oak Ridge, Tennessee, atomic facility; and the Los Alamos atomic weapon assembly plants; as well as a series of underground atomic weapons storage facilities just going into construction in 1947. The first of those facilities would become operational in 1948, in the Mazano Mountains outside Albuquerque, New Mexico (adjacent to Kirtland AFB), and in the tunnel system in Killeen, Texas (adjacent to Fort Hood). In 1947, no weapons were actually stored at Roswell AFB, the base for the only atomic-weapon-capable B-29 squadron.

29. Joel Carpenter, *The Midland Fireball: Dow Chemical's Early Involvement with UFOs*, www.project1947.com/articles/dow.htm.

30. Sign Oral History Project interview with Doyle Rees, Col. USAF retired Thomas Tulian (copyright © 1999 AFS/Dialogue Productions LLC, 2545 Pillsbury Ave.

S., Minneapolis, MN 55404.) Interview available at www.project1947.com/shg/sohp/dreesint.htm.

31. Joel Carpenter, *Guided Missiles and UFOs: A Tangle of Fear—1937–53.* Part Three. www.project1947.com/gr/grchron3.htm.

32. Kevin Randle, *Crash: When UFOs Fall From the Sky* (Wayne, NJ: New Page Books, 2010), 93. It should be noted that in 1960, Elroy John Center, formerly a research scientist at Battelle, privately commented that while at Battelle he had analyzed material from a fallen UFO. Some researchers have speculated that his remark related to material ("memory metal") from the much-discussed Roswell news reports, but it seems probable that Center was actually speaking of the Washington, D.C., material that was officially given to Battelle for study, especially since it has been shown that Center worked on that study in the mid-1950s.

33. Cynthia Grabo, *Anticipating Surprise: Analysis for Strategic Warning* (Lanham, MD: UP of America, 2004), 39–41.

34. Memorandum for Chief, Air Intelligence Division, Subject: Analysis of Flying Object Incidents in the U.S., Oct. 11, 1948, www.project1947.com/fig/memo4chf.htm.

35. Michael Swords, Project Sign study, www.nicap.org/papers/swords_Sign_EOTS.htm.

36. Richard Rhodes, *Dark Sun: The Making of the Hydrogen Bomb* (New York: Simon and Schuster, 1995), Appendix 14.

37. Weapon Storage Sites / Q Areas, www.globalsecurity.org/wmd/facility/q_area-intro.htm.

38. "Nuclear Weapons Production, Processes and History, Weapons Assembly During 1946–1949," Department of Energy. Weapons assembly was actually carried out at both Sandia Base and at the Burlington Ordnance Plant in Iowa. In 1949 Sandia's assembly function was transferred to Burlington, and in 1951 another assembly facility would come operational at the Pantex Plant outside Amarillo, Texas. www.em.doe.gov/pdfs/pubpdfs/linklegacy_011_030.pdf.

39. Robert Hastings, *UFOs and Nukes* (Bloomington, IN: Authorhouse, 2008), 47.

40. Ibid, pp. 34–35.

41. Jerome Clark, *The UFO Book*, 259.

42. Edward Ruppelt, *The Report on Unidentified Flying Objects*, 56–59.

43. Bruce Maccabee, "The White Sands Proof," http://brumac.8k.com/WhiteSandsProof/WhiteSandsProof.html.

CHAPTER 7: FEAR FACTORS

1. George Kennan, Deputy Chief of U.S. Moscow Mission, Moscow to Secretary of State George Marshall, Feb. 22, 1946.

2. Norman Graebner, *The National Security: Its Theory and Practice* (New York: Oxford UP, 1986), 26–27.

3. Ibid, 342–344.

4. Richard Rhodes, *Dark Sun: The Making of the Hydrogen Bomb* (New York: Simon and Schuster, 1995), 343.

5. Ibid, 355–356; see also Ethan Heilman, "A Review of William Borden's 'There Will Be No Time: A Revolution in Strategy,'" http://ethanheilman.tumblr.com/post/29405762446/there-will-be-no-time-a-review.

6. Qtd. in "The Evaluation of the Atomic Bomb as a Military Weapon," The Final Report of the Joint Chiefs of Staff Evaluation Board for Operation Crossroads, June 30, 1947, www.trumanlibrary.

org/whistlestop/study_collections/bomb/
large/documents/pdfs/81.pdf.

7. Archive of Nuclear Data, www.nrdc.
org/nuclear/nudb/datab7.asp.

8. General Richard Kenney to General
Hoyt Vandenberg, Apr. 29, 1950,
www2.gwu.edu/~nsarchiv/nukevault/
special/doc03d.pdf.

9. Qtd. in Raymond Garthoff, "Estimating Soviet Military Intentions and
Capabilities," Center for the Study
of Intelligence, Central Intelligence
Agency, www.cia.gov/library/center-
for-the-study-of-intelligence/csi-
publications/books-and-monographs/
watching-the-bear-essays-on-cias-anal-
ysis-of-the-soviet-union/article05.html.

10. Cynthia Grabow, *Anticipating Surprise: Analysis for Strategic Warning*
(Lanham, MD: UP of America, 2004),
59 and 83.

11. Dean Acheson, *Present at the Creation: My Years in the State Department* (New York: W.W. Norton and
Co., 1969), 447.

12. Ibid, 463.

13. Richard Hubler, *SAC: The Strategic
Air Command* (New York: Van Rees
Press), 1958, 101–103.

14. James V. Edmundson, "Six Churning and Four Burning Part III," 92nd
USAAF-USAF Memorial Association,
www.92ndma.org/92bw/sixchurn-
ingpt3.pdf.

15. Dean Acheson, *Present at the Creation: My Years in the State Department*, 420–421.

16. Richard Rhodes, *Dark Sun: The Making of the Hydrogen Bomb*, 433–435.

17. The Atomic Energy Commission Q
Areas were initially under the oversight
of the Armed Forces Special Weapons Project (AFSWP) and later the
Defense Atomic Support Agency and

Defense Nuclear Agency. The sites were
adjacent to military reservations with
autonomous facilities and had their
own military guards. The Sandia Corporation (Sandia Labs) handled management of the Q areas, itself moving
from Los Alamos into Sandia Base, a
separate facility near Kirtland Air Force
Base in Albuquerque. Initial Q Area
sites were at Clarksville Base (adjacent
to Fort Campbell and Campbell AFB
in Tennessee/Kentucky; operational in
1948), Manzano Base in the mountains
east of Albuquerque (construction
started 1946; operational in 1949),
and Killeen Base in Texas (adjacent to
Gray AFB and Fort Hood; construction
started in 1947; operational in 1948).

18. Qtd. in Oak Ridge UFO report com-
pilation; Oct. 15–17, 1950, National
Investigations Committee on Aerial
Phenomena, www.nicap.org/oakridge-
501015dir.htm; also "Object Sighted
Over Oak Ridge," FBI Report dated
Oct. 17, 1950, www.nicap.org/docs_
oakridge/fbi501013doc2.htm

19. William Moore, memo from Col. John
Meade, AC of S, G2, Oct. 25, 1950,
The Mystery of the Green Fireballs,
(Prescott, AZ: William Moore Publica-
tions and Research, 1983).

20. Dan Wilson and Fran Ridge, Oak
Ridge report inventory, Nov. 29 & 30,
1950, RADCAT files, www.nicap.org/
reports/501129oakridge_report.htm.

21. Richard Rhodes, *Dark Sun: The Making of the Hydrogen Bomb*, 444–445.

22. Ibid, 445.

23. William Burrows, *By Any Means
Necessary: America's Secret Air War
in the Cold War* (New York: Farrar,
Straus and Giroux, 2001), 113.

24. Ibid, 446.

25. Ibid, 448.

26. Harry S. Truman, *Memoirs of Harry S. Truman: Years of Trial and Hope 1946–1952*, (Garden City, NY: Doubleday, 1955–56), 405.

27. "Border Bridges Bombed: UN Raid on Yalu River," *Sydney Morning Herald*, Nov. 9, 1950, http://trove.nla.gov.au/ndp/del/article/18185273.

28. Curtis Peebles, *Shadow Flights: America's Secret Air War Against the Soviet Union* (Novato, CA: Presidio Press, 2002), 29.

29. The first Soviet B-29 copied aircraft had been completed in the spring of 1947 and first flew on May 19, 1947. Flight tests continued through 1949, and full-scale production of the aircraft, under the designation Tu-4, began in 1947 at two separate aircraft plants; a third plant was added in 1948. According to Russian sources, when production of the Tu-4 finally finished in 1952, a total of 847 bombers had been produced. Western estimates of the Tu-4 build were much higher, assuming up to 1,300 would be deployed by 1954. Immediately after serial production of the Tu-4 was initiated, work began to adapt the bomber to strike at American territory. Some airplanes were outfitted to carry nuclear bombs and were designated "Tu-4A." During re-equipment, the bomber was equipped with a thermostatically controlled heated bomb bay, a suspension unit for the bomb was developed and biological protection devices for the crew were supplied. Some Tu-4 bombers were equipped with aerial refueling devices, and very few were outfitted with additional fuel tanks located under the wings. They were deployed in 1952, though the majority of the Tu-4 were not re-equipped with air refueling. In 1948, work on the "Comet" missile project was initiated to equip a modified Tu-4 with two KS-1 air-to-surface missiles and a special guidance system. The first Tu-4K prototype was finished in 1951, with production testing in 1951 and 1952. Between July 1952 and January 1953 the bomber was tested and subsequently deployed with naval aviation.

30. Curtis Peebles, *Shadow Flights: America's Secret Air War Against the Soviet Union*, 30–38.

31. *Searching the Skies: The Legacy of the United States Cold War Defense Radar Program*, United States Air Combat Command, June 1977, 20–25.

32. Kenneth Schaffel, *The Emerging Shield: The Evolution of Continental Air Defense* (Washington, DC: Office of Air Force History, 1991), 158.

33. James V. Edmundson, "Six Churning and Four Burning Part III," 92nd USAAF-USAF Memorial Association, www.92ndma.org/92bw/sixchurningpt3.pdf.

34. Joel Carpenter and Francis Ridge, "UFOs and Alert Scare, April 1952," June 2002, www.nicap.org/ncp/nn-020628.htm.

35. Ibid, 153–154.

36. Ibid, 156.

37. Ibid, 193–197.

38. Michael Swords and Robert Powell, *UFOs and Government: A Historical Inquiry* (San Antonio, TX: Anomalist Press, 2012), 195.

CHAPTER 8: MIRROR IMAGING

1. "Warsaw Pact War Plan of 1964," Parallel History Project on Cooperative Security, ISN Center for Security Studies, Zurich, Switzerland, www.php.isn.ethz.ch/collections/colltopic.cfm?lng=en&id=16239&navinfo=15365.

2. B. Bruce-Biggs, *The Shield of Faith: The Hidden Struggle for Strategic Defense* (New York: Simon and Schuster Inc., 1988), 100–101.

3. Ibid, 101.

4. Raymond Garthoff, "Estimating Soviet Military Intentions and Capabilities," Chapter V, CIA's Analysis of the Soviet Union, 1947–1991, www.cia.gov/library/center-for-the-study-of-intelligence/csi-publications/books-and-monographs/watching-the-bear-essays-on-cias-analysis-of-the-soviet-union/article05.html.

5. Norman A. Graebner, *The National Security: Its Theory and Practice 1945–1960* (New York: Oxford UP, 1986), 45.

6. Philip Wylie, *Tomorrow!* (New York: Farrar and Rinehart, 1954), 169–174.

7. Qtd. in Ibid, 231–238.

8. Raymond Garthoff, "Estimating Soviet Military Intentions and Capabilities," Chapter V.

9. Steve Blank, "Balloon Wars," Jan. 28, 2010, http://steveblank.com/2010/01/28/balloon-wars.

10. B.D. Gildenberg, "The Cold War's Classified Skyhook Program: A Participant's Revelations," *Skeptical Inquirer*, Vol. 28.3, May–June 2004, www.csicop.org/si/show/cold_warrs-quos_classified_skyhook_program.

11. Curtis Peebles, *Dark Eagles: A History of the Top Secret U.S. Aircraft* (New York: Ballantine Books, 1995), 36–37; see also Curtis Peebles, *Shadow Flights: America's Secret Air War against the Soviet Union* (Novato, CA: Presidio Press, 2002), 113–123.

12. Curtis Peebles, *Shadow Flights: America's Secret Air War against the Soviet Union*, 50–53.

13. Ibid, 124–127.

14. Ibid, 149.

15. William Burrows, *By Any Means Necessary: America's Secret Air War in the Cold War* (New York: Farrar, Straus and Giroux, 2001), 353–356.

16. Richard Hubler, *SAC: The Strategic Air Command* (New York: Van Rees Press, 1958), 123 and 149.

17. Qtd. in *Louisville Courier Journal*, cited in Frank Feschino, *Shoot Them Down: The Flying Saucer Wars of 1952* (Lulu Enterprises, 2007) 3.

18. Edward Ruppelt, *The Report on Unidentified Flying Objects* (New York: Doubleday, 1956), 1–5.

19. Frank Feschino, *Shoot Them Down: The Flying Saucer Air Wars of 1952*, 332–335.

20. B. Bruce-Biggs, *The Shield of Faith: The Hidden Struggle For Strategic Defense*, 93.

21. Ibid, 91.

22. Mark Morgan and Mark Berhow, *Rings of Supersonic Steel: Air Defenses of the United States Army, 1950–1979* (San Pedro, CA: Fort MacArthur Press, 2002), 24–25.

23. Kent Redmond and Thomas Smith, *From Whirlwind to MITRE: The R&D Story of the SAGE Air Defense Computer* (Cambridge, MA: MIT Press, 2000), 11–13.

24. Ibid, 17–18.

25. David Winkler, *Searching the Skies: The Legacy of the United States Cold War Defense Radar Program* (United States Air Combat Command, June, 1997), 33.

26. Qtd. in Kent Redmond and Thomas Smith, *From Whirlwind to MITRE: The R&D Story of the SAGE Air Defense Computer,* 125.

27. Warren Trest, *Air Commando One: Heinie Aderholt and America's Secret Air Wars* (Washington, DC: Smithsonian Books, 2000), 58–59.

28. L. Douglas Keeney, *15 Minutes: General Curtis LeMay and the Countdown to Nuclear Annihilation* (New York: St. Martin's Press, 2011), 220.

29. Special National Intelligence Estimate, "Strength and Composition of the Soviet Long Range Bomber Force," United States Central Intelligence Agency, June 5, 1958, www.foia.cia.gov/sites/default/files/document_conversions/89801/DOC_0000267654.pdf.

30. Norman Polmar, *Strategic Air Command: People, Aircraft and Missiles* (Annapolis, MD: The Nautical and Aviation Publishing Co. of America, 1979), 54 and 85.

CHAPTER 9: TARGETING

1. Richard Rhodes, *Dark Sun: The Making of the Hydrogen Bomb* (New York: Simon and Schuster, 1995), 561.

2. Document 207, National Security Council Directive, Foreign Relations of the United States 1950–1955, The Intelligence Community 1950–1955, Office of the Historian, U.S. Department of State, https://history.state.gov/historical-documents/frus1950-55Intel/d207.

3. CJCS Net Evaluation, Nov. 1, 1956, Memorandum from Admiral Radford, The Joint Chiefs of Staff, www.dod.mil/pubs/foi/operation_and_plans/NuclearChemicalBiologicalMatters/999.pdf.

4. Discussion of the 387th meeting of the National Security Council, Nov. 20, 1958, also Memorandum for Mr. Allen Dulles, Director of Central Intelligence from N.F. Twining, Chairman NET Evaluations Subcommittee, Oct. 29, 1959, www2.gwu.edu/~nsarchiv/NSAEBB/NSAEBB130/SIOP-1.pdf, www.foia.cia.gov/sites/default/files/document_conversions/5829/CIA-RD-P80B01676R001100060006-0.pdf.

5. Richard Rhodes, *Dark Sun: The Making of the Hydrogen Bomb*, 560–562.

6. L. Wainstein, C.D. Cremeans, J.K. Moriarty, and J. Ponturo, Study S-467, "The Evolution of U.S. Strategic Command and Control and Warning 1945–1972," June 1975, 45–58 and 179–192, www2.gwu.edu/~nsarchiv/nukevault/ebb403/docs/Doc%202%20-%20strategic%20command%20and%20control---%20evolution%20of.pdf.

7. "History of the Joint Planning Staff : Background and Preparation of SIOP-62," History and Research Division, Headquarters Strategic Air Command, www2.gwu.edu/~nsarchiv/nukevault/ebb285/sidebar/SIOP-62_history.pdf.

8. Ibid, 10.

9. Ibid, 21.

10. Ibid, 24–25.

11. Richard Rhodes, *Dark Sun: The Making of the Hydrogen Bomb*, 562.

12. Ibid, 563.

13. History of the 100th Bomb Wing (Med) 1956–1966, www.100thbombwing reunion.org/history.html.

14. Matthew Brzezinski, *Red Moon Rising: Sputnik and the Rivalries That Ignited the Space Age* (London and New York: Bloomsbury Publishing, 2007), 26–28.

15. Ibid, 35–36.

16. Ibid, 40–43.

17. Ibid, 39.

18. John Chapman, *Atlas : The Story of a Missile*, (New York, Harper and Brothers, 1960), 128–130.

19. Matthew Brzezinski, *Red Moon Rising: Sputnik and the Rivalries That Ignited the Space Age*, 58.

20. Special National Intelligence Estimate Number 11-10-57, "The Soviet ICBM Program," Director Central

Intelligence, www.foia.cia.gov/sites/default/files/document_conversions/89801/DOC_0000267695.pdf.

21. Memorandum to holders of NIE 11-5-58, Central Intelligence Agency, Nov. 25, 1958, www.foia.cia.gov/sites/default/files/document_conversions/89801/DOC_0000267653.pdf.

22. Memorandum for the Secretary of State, Defense and Atomic Energy Convention, "Policy Regarding Use of Atomic Weapons," Executive Office of the President, May 17, 1957, www2.gwu.edu/~nsarchiv/news/pre-delegation2/pre2-1a.htm.

23. "Instructions for the Expenditure of Nuclear Weapons," www2.gwu.edu/~nsarchiv/NSAEBB/NSAEBB45/doc3.pdf.

24. Memorandum of Conference with the President, June 27, 1958, www2.gwu.edu/~nsarchiv/NSAEBB/NSAEBB45/doc1.pdf.

25. Letter from President Eisenhower to Secretary of Defense Gates, Nov. 2, 1959, www2.gwu.edu/~nsarchiv/NSAEBB/NSAEBB45/doc2.pdf.

26. Memorandum from JCSIG Offutt Air Force Base, Nebraska, to JCS Washington, D.C., "JSTPS Activity," Apr. 1961, www2.gwu.edu/~nsarchiv/NSAEBB/NSAEBB130/SIOP-1.pdf.

27. David Rosenberg, "The Origins of Overkill," (Cambridge, MA: MIT Press, 1983) 116; see also Fred M. Kaplan, *The Wizards of Armageddon* (Stanford, CA: Stanford University Press, 1991), 269.

28. Contemporary tactical flexibility occurs under the guidance of the Joint Strategic Capabilities Plan, overseen by the Joint Chiefs of Staff.

29. Letter from President Kennedy to Supreme Commander, Allied Powers Europe, Washington, D.C., Oct. 20, 1961, Berlin Crisis – Oct./Nov. 1961, Foreign Relations of the United States 1961–1963, Volume XIV, 521–523, www2.gwu.edu/~nsarchiv/nukevault/ebb310/10-20-61.pdf.

30. Ibid, 313–321, www2.gwu.edu/~nsarchiv/nukevault/ebb310/9-10-62.pdf.

31. Andreas Wenger, *Living with Peril: Eisenhower, Kennedy and Nuclear Weapons* (Lanham, England, and New York: Rowman and Littlefield Publishers Inc., 1997), 273.

32. "Salt II and the Growth of Mistrust," Conference 2, The Carter–Brezhnev Project, May 6–9, 1994, 27–32, www2.gwu.edu/~nsarchiv/nukevault/ebb285/doc03.PDF

33. Norman Polmar and John Gresham, *DEFCON-2: Standing on the Brink of Nuclear War During the Cuban Missile Crisis* (Hoboken, NJ: John Wiley and Sons, 2006), 17–19.

34. Matthew Brzezinski, *Red Moon Rising: Sputnik and the Rivalries that Ignited the Space Age,* 154–155.

35. Ibid, 269.

36. Qtd. in Norman Polmar and John Gresham, *DEFCON -2: Standing on the Brink of Nuclear War During the Cuban Missile Crisis,* 16.

37. Qtd. in Pat Frank, *Alas, Babylon* (New York: Bantam, 1959), 31–33.

38. Norman Polmar and John Gresham, *DEFCON-2: Standing on the Brink of Nuclear War During the Cuban Missile Crisis,* 21.

CHAPTER 10: CRISIS

1. Norman Polmar and John Gresham, *DEFCON-2: Standing on the Brink of Nuclear War During the Cuban Missile Crisis* (New York: John Wiley and Sons, 2006), 24–25.

2. Rebecca Grant, "Victor Alert," *Air Force Magazine*, Mar. 2011, 58–62.

3. Ibid, 61.

4. Rebecca Grant, "The Perils of Chrome Dome," *Air Force Magazine*, Aug. 2011, 54–57.

5. Michael Dobbs, *One Minute to Midnight: Kennedy, Khrushchev, and Castro on the Brink of Nuclear War* (New York: Vintage, 2009), 280.

6. Norman Polmar and John Gresham, *DEFCON-2: Standing on the Brink of Nuclear War During the Cuban Missile Crisis*, 256–258.

7. Nikita Khrushchev and Strobe Talbot, *Khrushchev Remembers* (New York: Little, Brown and Co., 1970), 494.

8. One of Kennedy's personal friends, Paul Fay, described bringing the president's attention to the book *Seven Days in May* and described Kennedy's reaction after reading it. Kennedy discussed the book's scenario with friends, expressing his own belief that it would be possible under certain conditions. The president might be allowed one show of questionable decisiveness that would create some "uneasiness." A second such incident would raise serious concern about youth and inexperience. "If it were to happen a third time, if there were a third Bay of Pigs, it could happen." Richard Reeves, *President Kennedy: Profile of Power* (New York: Simon and Schuster, 1994), 306; see also Paul B. Fay, Jr., *The Pleasure of His Company* (New York: Harper and Row, 1966).

9. Key resources for understanding Operation Anadyr and the full extent of Soviet military deployment in Cuba are *DEFCON-2* by Norman Polmar and John Gresham (2006) and *One Minute to Midnight* by Michael Dobbs (2008).

10. Ibid, 126–127.

11. Norman Polmar and John Gresham, *DEFCON-2: Standing on the Brink of Nuclear War During the Cuban Missile Crisis* (New York: John Wiley and Sons, 2008), 57–65.

12. Michael Dobbs, *One Minute to Midnight: Kennedy, Khrushchev, and Castro on the Brink of Nuclear War* (New York: Alfred A. Knopf, 2008), 15.

13. Norman Polmar and John Gresham, *DEFCON-2: Standing on the Brink of Nuclear War During the Cuban Missile Crisis*, 16.

14. Ibid, 98–99; see also Kaufman, Annex 2, "Cuba and the Strategic Threat," Oct. 25, 1962. http://nsarchive.gwu. edu/NSAEBB/NSAEBB397/.

15. Qtd. in Andreas Wenger, *Living with Peril: Eisenhower, Kennedy, and Nuclear Weapons* (New York: Oxford, Roman and Littlefield Publishers, Inc., 1997), 277.

16. Michael Dobbs, *One Minute to Midnight: Kennedy, Khrushchev, and Castro on the Brink of Nuclear War*, 4–5.

17. Qtd. in Andreas Wenger, *Living with Peril: Eisenhower, Kennedy, and Nuclear Weapons*, 285.

18. Roswell Gilpatric, Deputy Secretary of Defense, meeting notes, "10/15 [Sic] at White House," Top Secret, www2.gwu.edu/~nsarchiv/NSAEBB/ NSAEBB398/docs/doc%203b%20 10-15-62%20White%20House%20 RLG.pdf.

19. Michael Dobbs, *One Minute to Midnight: Kennedy, Khrushchev, and Castro on the Brink of Nuclear War*, 49.

20. Captain William D. Hauser USN, Duty Officers Journal, The Adjutant Generals Office, Oct. 23, 1962, www2.gwu.edu/~nsarchiv/NSAEBB/ NSAEBB398/docs/doc%2010C%20

10-23-621%20duty%20offices%20
rg%20330%20secdef%20CMC%20
files%20box%201%20cuba%20
381,%201962%20%2820%20Oct-
25%20Oct%2062O-2.pdf.

21. Thomas Blanton, William Burr and
Svetlana Savranskaya, "The Under-
water Cuban Missile Crisis: Soviet
Submarines and the Risk of Nuclear
War," National Security Archive
Briefing Book #399, Oct. 24, 2012,
www2.gwu.edu/~nsarchiv/NSAEBB/
NSAEBB399.

22. Gordon Calhoun, "Task Force Alpha
in the Bay of Pigs," *The Daybook*,
Vol. 9, Issue 14, www.history.navy.
mil/museums/hrnm/files/daybook/pdfs/
vol9issueone.pdf.

23. Michael Dobbs, *One Minute to
Midnight: Kennedy, Khrushchev, and
Castro on the Brink of Nuclear War*,
87–91.

24. Richard Rhodes, *Dark Sun: The Making of the Hydrogen Bomb* (New York:
Simon and Schuster, 1995), 573.

25. William Burr, "The Cuban Mis-
sile Crisis Day by Day: From the
Pentagon's 'Sensitive Records',"
National Security Archive Electronic
Briefing Book No. 398, Oct. 12, 2012,
www2.gwu.edu/~nsarchiv/NSAEBB/
NSAEBB398.

26. Richard Rhodes, *Dark Sun: The Making of the Hydrogen Bomb*, 573.

27. Alice George, *Awaiting Armageddon:
How Americans Faced the Cuban
Missile Crisis* (Chapel Hill, NC: The
University of North Carolina Press,
2003), 57.

28. Michael Dobbs, *One Minute to
Midnight: Kennedy, Khrushchev, and
Castro on the Brink of Nuclear War*,
320–322.

29. Maxwell Taylor, Chairman Joint
Chiefs of Staff, Memorandum for the
President, "Evaluation of the Effect
on U.S. Operational Plans of Soviet
Army Equipment Introduced into
Cuba," Nov. 2, 1962, www2.gwu.
edu/~nsarchiv/NSAEBB/NSAEBB397/
docs/doc%2022%2011-2-62%20
memo%20to%20JFK%20re%20inva-
sion%20plans.pdf.

30. Michael Dobbs, *One Minute to Midnight:
Kennedy, Khrushchev, and Castro on the
Brink of Nuclear War*, 111.

CHAPTER 11: CONTINUITY OF COMMAND

1. L. Wainstein, C.D. Cremeans, J.K.
Moriarty, and J. Ponturo, Study S-467,
"The Evolution of U.S. Strategic
Command and Control and Warning 1945–1972," June 1975, 30,
www2.gwu.edu/~nsarchiv/nukevault/
ebb403/docs/Doc%202%20-%20
strategic%20command%20and%20
control---%20evolution%20of.pdf.

2. H.R. McMaster, *Dereliction of Duty:
Lyndon Johnson, Robert McNamara,
the Joint Chiefs of Staff, and the Lies
That Led to Vietnam* (New York:
HarperCollins, 1998), 12–13.

3. L. Douglas Keeney, *15 Minutes: General Curtis LeMay and the Countdown
to Nuclear Annihilation* (New York:
St. Martin's Press, 2011), 179–180.

4. L. Wainstein, C.D. Cremeans, J.K.
Moriarty, and J. Ponturo, Study
S-467, "The Evolution of U.S. Strategic Command and Control and Warning 1945–1972," 113–114.

5. Ibid, 115.

6. Ibid, 118–119.

7. National Command Authority consists
of the president and secretary of
defense, together with their legally
authorized successors and alternates.

The Speaker of the House and then Speaker of the Senate are next in line of succession following the vice president.

8. Ibid, 238–248.

9. L. Wainstein, C.D. Cremeans, J.K. Moriarty, and J. Ponturo, Study S-467, "The Evolution of U.S. Strategic Command and Control and Warning 1945–1972," 232–234.

10. L. Douglas Keeney, *15 Minutes: General Curtis LeMay and the Countdown to Nuclear Annihilation*, 289.

11. "The Worldwide Military Command and Control System: A Historical Perspective 1960–1977," Historical Division Joint Secretariat, Joint Chiefs of Staff, Sept. 1980, 12, www.dod.mil/pubs/foi/joint_staff/jointStaff_joint Operations/WorldwideMilitary Command_ControlSystem.pdf.

12. Ibid, 19.

13. H.R. McMaster, *Dereliction of Duty: Lyndon Johnson, Robert McNamara, the Joint Chiefs of Staff, and the Lies That Led to Vietnam*, 6–7.

14. Ibid, 7–9.

15. Qtd. in Michael Dobbs, *One Minute to Midnight: Kennedy, Khrushchev, and Castro on the Brink of Nuclear War* (New York: Albert A. Knopf, 2008), 22.

16. Qtd. in ibid, 23.

17. Michael Bohn, *Nerve Center: Inside the White House Situation Room* (Washington, DC: Brassey's Inc., 2003), 30.

18. Ibid, 9.

19. I.M. Destler, Leslie Gelb and Anthony Lake, *Our Own Worst Enemy: The Unmaking of American Foreign Policy* (New York: Simon and Schuster, 1984).

20. Michael Bohn, *Nerve Center: Inside the White House Situation Room*, 44–45.

21. Jerry Miller, *Stockpile: The Story Behind 10,000 Strategic Nuclear Weapons* (Annapolis, MD: Naval Institute Press, 2010), 24–26.

22. John T. Correll, "How Rolling Thunder Began," *Air Force Magazine*, Mar. 2015, 71–72.

23. William Manchester, *The Death of a President: November 20–November 25, 1963* (New York: Harper and Row, 1967).

24. Ibid, 62.

25. Ibid, 176–178.

26. Ibid, 193.

27. Bromley Smith, "Changes in Defense Readiness Conditions as a Result of the Assassination of President," White House Memorandum, Dec. 4, 1963.

28. William Manchester, *The Death of A President: November 20–November 25, 1963*, 253.

29. Ibid, 370.

30. John F. Davies, personal research and communications with the author.

31. Ibid, 63.

32. Ibid, 261.

33. Ibid, 261 and 346.

34. Qtd. in David Talbot, *The Hidden History of the Kennedy Years* (New York: Simon and Schuster, 2008).

35. "Instructions for the Expenditure of Nuclear Weapons," www2.gwu.edu/~nsarchiv/NSAEBB/NSAEBB45/doc3.pdf.

36. Memorandum for Mr. Bromley Smith, White House, "Instructions for the Expenditure of Nuclear Weapons in Emergency Conditions (Code Name: Furtherance)," Office of the Secretary of Defense, Dec. 30, 1968, www2.gwu.edu/~nsarchiv/nukevault/ebb406/docs/Doc%20 9A%2012-30-68.pdf.

37. "Preparation of SIOP-63, History of the Joint Strategic Planning Staff, History and Research Division,"

Headquarters Strategic Air Command, Jan. 1964, www2.gwu.edu/~nsarchiv/nukevault/ebb236/SIOP-63.pdf.

38. "History of the Joint Strategic Planning Staff, Preparation of SIOP-64, History and Research Division," Headquarters Strategic Air Command, Aug. 1964, www.dod.mil/pubs/foi/joint_staff/joint-Staff_jointOperations/335.pdf.

39. Notes of the President's Meeting, Subject "Furtherance," Oct. 14, 1968, www2.gwu.edu/~nsarchiv/nukevault/ebb406/docs/Doc%205A%20Furtherance%20document%20Oct%201968.pdf.

40. JCS message, "Alternate Methods for Executing the SIOP and General War Plans," Oct. 18, 1968, www2.gwu.edu/~nsarchiv/nukevault/ebb406/docs/Doc%209B%2010-18-68.pdf.

41. Notes of the President's Meeting, Subject "Furtherance," remarks and proposal by Secretary of Defense Clark Clifford, Oct. 14, 1968, www2.gwu.edu/~nsarchiv/nukevault/ebb406/docs/Doc%205A%20Furtherance%20document%20Oct%201968.pdf.

CHAPTER 12: MIND GAMES, MASKIROVKA AND ATOMIC WAR FIGHTING

1. Foreign Relations of the United States 1950–1955, The Intelligence Community 1950–1955, Document 207, Directive on a Net Evaluation Subcommittee, US Department of State, Office of the Historian. Also: Report of the Net Capabilities Evaluation Subcommittee, Nov. 3, 1954; Reports of the Net Evaluation Subcommittee, National Security Archives, The Nuclear Vault, George Washington University, http://nsarchive.gwu.edu/nukevault/ebb480/docs/doc%201%201954%20report.pdf.

2. Qtd. in Richard Rhodes, *Dark Sun: The Making of the Hydrogen Bomb* (New York: Simon and Schuster, 1995), 562.

3. Qtd. in Andreas Wenger, *Living with Peril: Eisenhower, Kennedy, and Nuclear Weapons* (New York: Oxford, Rowman & Littlefield, 1997), 53.

4. Ibid, 68–69 and 82–83.

5. Richard Rhodes, *Dark Sun: The Making of the Hydrogen Bomb*, 562–563.

6. Andreas Wenger, *Living with Peril: Eisenhower, Kennedy, and Nuclear Weapons*, 147.

7. Qtd. in Richard Rhodes, *Dark Sun: The Making of the Hydrogen Bomb*, 565.

8. L. Wainstein, C.D. Cremeans, J.K. Moriarty, and J. Ponturo, Study S-467, "The Evolution of U.S. Strategic Command and Control and Warning 1945–1972," June 1975, 16-23, 30, www2.gwu.edu/~nsarchiv/nukevault/ebb403/docs/Doc%202%20-%20strategic%20command%20and%20control---%20evolution%20of.pdf.

9. "Table of Global Nuclear Weapons Stockpiles, 1945–2002," Archive of Nuclear Data, National Resources Defense Council, www.nrdc.org/nuclear/nudb/datab19.asp.

10. Ibid.

11. Kalev I. Sepp, *The Pentomic Puzzle*, Army History, The Professional Bulletin of Army History, Washington, D.C., 2001, www.history.army.mil/armyhistory/AH51newOCR.pdf.

12. Jerry Miller, *Stockpile: The Story Behind 10,000 Strategic Nuclear Weapons* (Annapolis, MD: Naval Institute Press, 2010), 6.

13. L. Douglas Keeney, *15 Minutes: General Curtis LeMay and the Countdown to Nuclear Annihilation* (New York: St Martin's Press, 2011), 248–249.

14. Ibid, 292.

15. Jerry Miller, *Stockpile: The Story Behind 10,000 Strategic Nuclear Weapons*, 30.

16. "President's Review of Defense Posture San Clemente July 28, 1970[,] Selected Comments, Top Secret," www2.gwu.edu/~nsarchiv/NSAEBB/NSAEBB173/SIOP-14.pdf.

17. William Burr, National Security Archive Electronic Briefing Room #173, Nov. 23, 2005, www2.gwu.edu/~nsarchiv/NSAEBB/NSAEBB173.

18. Walter Slocomb, U.S. National Strategy, Presidential Directive NSC-18, Aug. 30, 1977, www2.gwu.edu/~nsarchiv/nukevault/ebb390/docs/8-30-77%20PD%2018.pdf.

19. Strategic Forces Employment Policy, Special Coordination Committee Meeting, White House Situation Room, Apr. 27, 1979, www2.gwu.edu/~nsarchiv/nukevault/ebb390/docs/4-4-79%20SCC%20mtg.pdf.

20. Draft PD on Nuclear Targeting, Mar. 22, 1980, www2.gwu.edu/~nsarchiv/nukevault/ebb390/docs/3-22-80%20Odom%20memo.pdf.

21. "Targeting," memorandum from William Odom to Zbigniew Brzezinski, Aug. 5, 1980, www.jimmycarterlibrary.gov/documents/pddirectives/pd59.pdf.

22. Scott Sagan and Jeremy Suri, "The Madman Nuclear Alert: Secrecy, Safety and Signaling in October, 1969," *International Security*, Vol. 27, No. 4, 2003, 150–183, http://iis-db.stanford.edu/pubs/20277/sagan_is_spr03.pdf.

23. George Schultz, *Turmoil and Triumph: Diplomacy, Power and the Victory of the American Ideal* (New York: Scribner, 1993), 376.

24. Ben Fischer, "Threat Perception, Scare Tactic or False Alarm: The 1983 War Scare in U.S.–Soviet Relations," CIA Studies in Intelligence, www2.gwu.edu/~nsarchiv/NSAEBB/NSAEBB426/docs/3.The%201983%20War%20Scare%20in%20U.S.%20Soviet%20Relations-circa%201996.pdf.

25. Ibid, 65.

26. Ibid, 66.

27. Ibid, 68.

28. David Hoffman, *The Dead Hand: The Untold Story of The Cold War Arms Race and Its Dangerous Legacy* (New York: Anchor/Doubleday, 2010), 63.

29. Memorandum of Conversation, Meeting with CSU General Secretary Andropov, June 2, 1983, www2.gwu.edu/~nsarchiv/NSAEBB/NSAEBB426/docs/14.%20Memorandum%20of%20Conversation%20between%20Gen%20Sec%20Andropov%20and%20Averell%20Harriman-June%202,%201983.pdf.

30. David Hoffman, *The Dead Hand: The Untold Story of The Cold War Arms Race and Its Dangerous Legacy*, 93.

31. Memorandum for Robert McFarland from Jack Matlock, "American Academic on Soviet Policy," Dec. 13, 1983, www2.gwu.edu/~nsarchiv/NSAEBB/NSAEBB426/docs/19.American%20Academic%20on%20Soviet%20Policy-December%2013,%201983.pdf.

32. Ben Fischer, "Threat Perception, Scare Tactic or False Alarm: The 1983 War Scare in U.S.–Soviet Relations," CIA Studies in Intelligence, 71.

33. Qtd. in ibid, 69.

34. David Hoffman, *The Dead Hand: The Untold Story of The Cold War Arms Race and Its Dangerous Legacy*, 96.

35. President Ronald Reagan, "Address to the Nation and Other Countries on United States–Soviet Relations," Jan.

16, 1984, www.reagan.utexas.edu/
archives/speeches/1984/11684a.htm

36. Ibid, 96–97.

CHAPTER 13: REALITY CHECK

1. Richard Rhodes, *Dark Skies: The Making of the Hydrogen Bomb* (New York: Simon and Schuster, 1995), 568.

2. Bruce Blair, *The Logic of Accidental Nuclear War* (Washington, DC: The Brookings Institution, 1993), 185.

3. Ibid, 24.

4. Ibid, 24–25.

5. Ibid, 25.

6. Ibid, 180.

7. Ibid, 34–35.

8. L. Douglas Keeney, *15 Minutes: General Curtis LeMay and the Countdown to Nuclear Annihilation* (New York: St. Martin's Press, 2011), 241.

9. Ibid, 219–220.

10. Ibid, 200.

11. Ibid, 290.

12. SAC operated its global long-range radio network out of its command post at Offutt, with backup from Liberty Station, the Collins Radio development site at its headquarters in Cedar Rapids, Iowa. Collins Radio not only installed and maintained the radio equipment aboard most military and executive branch planes; they also operated the station known as Liberty at Cedar Rapids. In normal times Liberty simply served as a relay station for radio communications between the White House, the Pentagon, *Air Force One*, and other aircraft operated out of Andrews Air Force Base near Washington. Collins had a contract with the Air Force to serve as either the primary communications station or as a backup whenever *Air Force One*, the presidential aircraft, and other aircraft in the VIP fleet carried

cabinet members or high-ranking military officers. See Collins Radio Annual Report to Stockholders, 1963–64, also "Collins Radio—The First 50 Years." Research provided by William Kelley to the author.

13. Bruce Blair, *Strategic Command and Control: Redefining the Nuclear Threat* (Washington, DC, The Brookings Institution, 1983), 96.

14. Ibid, 98–99.

15. William Sullivan, *Assault on the Unknown: The International Geophysical Year* (New York: McGraw-Hill, 1961), 137–138.

16. Bruce Blair, *Strategic Command and Control: Redefining the Nuclear Threat*, 90–93.

17. Ibid, 101.

18. Ibid, 109.

19. Ibid, 227.

20. Ibid, 110.

21. Bruce Blair, *The Logic of Accidental Nuclear War*, 188–189.

22. Ibid, 190.

23. Ibid, 91.

24. Available information suggests that SAC strip alert command and control aircraft became airborne; it is unclear if some strip alert SAC bombers were also launched.

25. Robert M. Gates, *From the Shadows: The Ultimate Insider's Story of Five Presidents and How They Won the Cold War* (New York: Simon and Schuster, 1996), 114.

26. Pat Patterson, Lieutenant Commander, United States Navy, "The Truth About Tonkin," *Naval History Magazine*, Vol. 22, No. 1, Feb. 2008, www.usni.org/magazines/navalhistory/2008-02/truth-about-tonkin.

27. Robert Gillespie, *Black Ops Vietnam: The Operational History of MACV-*

SOG (Annapolis, MD: Naval Institute Press, 2011), 23.

28. Robert Hanyok, "Skunks, Bogies, Silent Hounds and Flying Fish: The Gulf of Tonkin Mystery 2–4 August 1964," *Cryptologic Quarterly*, National Security Administration, 5, www2.gwu.edu/~nsarchiv/NSAEBB/NSAEBB132/relea00012.pdf.

29. Robert Gillespie, *Black Ops Vietnam: The Operational History of MACV-SOG*, 24–25.

30. Robert Hanyok, "Skunks, Bogies, Silent Hounds and Flying Fish: The Gulf of Tonkin Mystery 2–4 August 1964," 13.

31. Ibid, 14.

32. Pat Patterson, Lieutenant Commander, United States Navy, "The Truth About Tonkin."

33. Qtd. in Jim and Sybil Stockdale, *In Love and War* (Annapolis, MD: Naval Institute Press, 1990), 5–8.

34. Robert Hanyok, "Skunks, Bogies, Silent Hounds and Flying Fish: The Gulf of Tonkin Mystery 2–4 August 1964," 25.

35. Qtd. in Jim and Sybil Stockdale, *In Love and War*, 25.

36. John Prados, "The Gulf of Tonkin Incident, 40 Years Later: Flawed Intelligence and the Decision for War in Vietnam," National Security Archive Electronic Briefing Book No. 132, Aug. 4, 2004, www2.gwu.edu/~nsarchiv/NSAEBB/NSAEBB132.

37. Robert Hanyok, "Skunks, Bogies, Silent Hounds and Flying Fish: The Gulf of Tonkin Mystery 2–4 August 1964," 3.

38. James Scott, *Attack on the Liberty: The Untold Story of Israel's Deadly 1967 Assault on a U.S. Spy Ship* (New York: Simon and Schuster, 2009), 15.

39. James Bamford, *Body of Secrets: Anatomy of the Ultra-Secret National Security Agency* (New York: Random House, 2002), 194–195.

40. Ibid, 197.

41. Ibid, 197–199.

42. James Scott, *Attack on the Liberty: The Untold Story of Israel's Deadly 1967 Assault on a U.S. Spy Ship*, 39.

43. Ibid, 212–213.

44. David Walsh, "Friendless Fire," The Naval Institute Proceedings, U.S. Naval Institute, 2003, www.military.com/NewContent/0,13190,NI_Friendless_0603,00.html.

45. Ibid.

46. James Scott, *Attack on the Liberty: The Untold Story of Israel's Deadly 1967 Assault on a U.S. Spy Ship*, 84.

47. James Bamford, *Body of Secrets: Anatomy of the Ultra-Secret National Security Agency*, 223.

48. James Scott, *Attack on the Liberty: The Untold Story of Israel's Deadly 1967 Assault on a U.S. Spy Ship*, 86.

49. A great deal of additional information has been documented in regard to the attack on the *Liberty* and President Johnson's role in it, including extensive efforts made to suppress actual NSA signals intelligence demonstrating Israeli knowledge of the *Liberty* as an American-flagged ship. Readers are referred to James Bamford's *Body of Secrets*, David Walsh's "Friendless Fire" article in the U.S. Naval Proceedings and James Scott's *Attack on the Liberty*. Scott's work contains the most current details on the incident.

50. The practice of using small, dedicated intelligence ships continues into the 21st century. As of 2015 the Air Force uses the USNS *Invincible*, a

ship belonging to the Military Sealift Command but equipped with a highly sophisticated dual X- and S-band radar (Gray Star), to monitor foreign nations' missile launches. The ship is designated as a "missile-range instrumentation ship" but is deployed overseas, most recently in the Persian Gulf. David Axe, "The U.S. Air Force has a Spy Ship—Yes, Ship—in the Persian Gulf," Dec. 30, 2014, www. medium.com/war-is-boring/the-u-s-air-force-has-a-spy-ship-yes-ship-in-the-persian-gulf-6ebb07cc6a33.

51. James Bamford, *Body of Secrets: Anatomy of the Ultra-Secret National Security Agency*, 241–242.

52. Ibid, 245–246.

53. Jack Cheevers, *Act of War: Lyndon Johnson, North Korea, and the Capture of the Spy Ship Pueblo* (New York: NAL Caliber, Penguin Group, 2013), 11 and 42–43.

54. Ibid, 13.

55. Ibid, 32.

56. James Bamford, *Body of Secrets: Anatomy of the Ultra-Secret National Security Agency*, 251.

57. Jack Cheevers, *Act of War: Lyndon Johnson, North Korea and the Capture of the Spy Ship Pueblo*, 58.

58. Trevor Armbrister, *A Matter of Accountability: The True Story of the Pueblo Affair* (Guilford, CT: Lyons Press, 2004), 27–28.

59. Ibid, 48.

60. Jack Cheevers, *Act of War: Lyndon Johnson, North Korea, and the Capture of the Spy Ship Pueblo*, 62.

61. Pueblo Crisis, "Presidential Decisions and Supplementary Chronology," Dec. 12, 1968, www2.gwu.edu/~nsarchiv/NSAEBB/NSAEBB453/docs/doc23.pdf.

62. Trevor Armbrister, *A Matter of Ac-*

countability: *The True Story of the Pueblo Affair*, 9.

CHAPTER 14: PREPAREDNESS

1. Pueblo Crisis, "Presidential Decisions and Supplementary Chronology," Dec. 12, 1968, www2.gwu.edu/~nsarchiv/NSAEBB/NSAEBB453/docs/doc23.pdf.

2. Combined Air Force One Radio Tapes Transcript (D7), LBJ Library/Clinton Transcript, JFK Countercoup, Nov. 4, 2013, http://countercoup.blogspot.com/2013/11/combined-air-force-one-radio-tapes.html.

3. President's Meeting, "Project Furtherance," remarks and proposal by Secretary of Defense Clark Clifford, Oct. 14, 1968, www2.gwu.edu/~nsarchiv/nukevault/ebb406/docs/Doc%205A%20Furtherance%20document%20Oct%201968.pdf.

4. Janne Nolan, *Guardians of the Arsenal* (New York: HarperCollins, 1991), 255.

5. Jerry Miller, *Stockpile: The Story of 10,000 Strategic Nuclear Weapons* (Annapolis, MD: Naval Institute Press, 2010), 31.

6. Michael Bohn, *Nerve Center: Inside the White House Situation Room*, (Washington DC: Brassey's Inc. 2003), 52.

7. www2.gwu.edu/~nsarchiv/NSAEBB/NSAEBB173/SIOP-5.pdf.

8. Bruce Blair, *Strategic Command and Control: Redefining the Nuclear Threat*, (Washington, DC: The Brookings Institution, 1963) 50.

9. Del Quentin Wilber, *Rawhide Down: The Near Assassination of President Ronald Reagan* (New York: Henry Holt and Co., 2011), 132.

10. Ibid, 161–162.

11. Ibid, 167.

12. Ibid, 176–177.

13. Ibid, 167–168.

14. Bruce Blair, *The Logic of Accidental Nuclear Warfare*, 60–62.

15. Ibid, 65–67.

16. Ibid, 133–135.

17. David Hoffman, *The Dead Hand: The Untold Story of the Cold War Arms Race and Its Dangerous Legacy* (New York: Anchor/Doubleday, 2009), 37–38.

18. Ibid, 38.

19. Qtd. in Ibid, 40–41.

20. Matthew Gault, "The TV Movie That Depressed Ronald Reagan," posted on *War Is Boring*, www.medium.com/war-is-boring/this-tv-movie-about-nuclear-war-depressed-ronald-reagan-fb4c25a50044.

21. Jerry Miller, *Stockpile: The Story of 10,000 Strategic Nuclear Weapons*, 32.

22. Ibid, 33.

23. Routine FAA surveillance is heavily based in active identification transponder systems carried by all commercial and military aircraft. Those transponders routinely transmit identity and location of the aircraft. Given that long-range radar surveillance is relatively limited, transponders are a key element in aircraft tracking—if they fail or are turned off, the FAA has to fall back on its network of active approach control radars located around major cities and airports. This also sets certain real limits on the expertise and abilities of FAA personnel to direct and control Air Force interceptors, especially in instances where aircraft may be intentionally flying at low altitudes or maneuvering so as to avoid radar detection.

24. Leslie Filson, *Air War over America* (Public Affairs Office, Headquarters 1st Air Force, Tyndall AFB, Florida, 2003).

25. *Guarding What You Value Most, North American Defense Command Celebrating 50 Years* (NORAD Headquarters, Peterson Air Force Base, Colorado, 2008), 23.

26. Jerry Miller, *Stockpile: The Story of 10,000 Strategic Nuclear Weapons*, 35.

27. Qtd. in Bruce Blair, *Strategic Command and Control: Redefining the Nuclear Threat*, 128.

28. "McNamara Calls on NATO to Renounce Nuclear Arms," *New York Times*, Sept. 15, 1983, www.nytimes.com/1983/09/15/world/mcnamara-calls-on-nato-to-renounce-nuclear-arms.html.

CHAPTER 15: OUT OF THE SHADOWS

1. Historically, as part of an officially declared state of war, members of the Armed Forces of a state designated as an enemy are referred to as enemy combatants. In civil war or insurgencies the more general term "party to the conflict" is used. See "Laws and Customs of War," Conventions of 1949, Article 3.

2. Harry Crumpton, *The Art of Intelligence: Lessons from a Life in the CIA's Clandestine Service* (New York: Penguin Press), 2012, 122–123.

3. Qtd. in Glen Carle, *The Interrogator: An Education* (New York: Nation Books, 2012), 36.

4. Richard Clarke, *Against All Enemies: Inside America's War on Terror* (New York: Free Press, 2004), 137–138.

5. Ibid, 133.

6. James Bamford, *A Pretext for War: 9/11, Iraq and the Abuse of America's Intelligence Agencies* (New York: Anchor Books, 2005), 97–98.

7. Qtd. in ibid, 99.

8. Pamela Constable, "U.S. jihadists say they weren't planning attacks," *Boston Globe*, Jan. 5, 2010, www.boston.com/news/world/asia/articles/2010/01/05/5_us_jihadists_say_they_werent_planning_attacks.

9. Yousef used a variety of aliases, including Dr. Paul Vijay, Dr. Adel Sabah, Muhammud Azan, Rashid Rashid, and Kamal Ibraham.

10. James Bamford, *A Pretext for War: 9/11, Iraq and the Abuse of America's Intelligence Agencies*, 100–101.

11. "Foreign Terrorists in America," 1998 Congressional Hearings—Intelligence and Security, Federation of American Scientists, Feb. 2, 1998.

12. Qtd. in Ibid, 190.

13. Qtd. in Ibid, 191.

14. Patrick Jost, "The Hawala Money Remittance System and Its Role in Money Laundering," United States Department of the Treasury, Financial Crimes Enforcement Network, www.treasury.gov/resource-center/terrorist-illicit-finance/documents/fincen-hawala-rpt.pdf.

15. Richard Clarke, *Against All Enemies: Inside America's War on Terror*, 195.

16. Ibid, 192.

17. Cynthia Grabo, *Anticipating Surprise: Analysis for Strategic Warning* (Lanham, MD: University Press of America, 2004), 3.

18. James Bamford, *A Pretext for War: 9/11, Iraq and the Abuse of America's Intelligence Agencies*, 209.

19. "The Bojinka Plot," *History Commons*, www.historycommons.org/timeline.jsp?timeline=complete_911_timeline&complete_911_timeline_alleged_al_qaeda_linked_attacks=bojinka.

20. Ibid.

21. James Bamford, *A Pretext for War: 9/11, Iraq and the Abuse of America's Intelligence Agencies*, 135–136.

22. Ibid, 136–137.

23. Qtd. in ibid, 93–94.

24. Ibid, 138.

25. "Bin Laden's Fatwa," *PBS Newshour*, Aug. 23, 1996, www.pbs.org/newshour/updates/military-july-dec96-fatwa_1996/.

26. Richard Clarke, *Against All Enemies: Inside America's War on Terror*, 147.

27. "Military Assistance to Civilian Authorities," Department of Defense, Directive 3025.15, Feb. 18, 1997, www.cdmha.org/toolkit/cdmha-rltk/PUBLICATIONS/dodd3025_15.pdf. This DOD regulation on the approval of legal force was inserted into new 2001 guidelines related to the provision of military force to the FAA in response to hijackings and would become critical to the command-and-control decision-making of the 9/11 attacks.

28. Qtd. in "Jihad against Jews and Crusaders," World Islamic Front Statement, Feb. 23, 1998, www.fas.org/irp/world/para/docs/980223-fatwa.htm.

29. James Bamford, *A Pretext for War: 9/11, Iraq and the Abuse of America's Intelligence Agencies*, 162–165.

30. Duncan Campbell, "Revealed, GHCQ's Beyond Top Secret Middle Eastern Internet Spy Base," *The Register*, June 3, 2014, www.theregister.co.uk/2014/06/03/revealed_beyond_top_secret_british_intelligence_middleeast_internet_spy_base/.

31. Henry Crumpton, *The Art of Intelligence: Lessons from a Life in the CIA's Clandestine Service*, 110.

32. Ibid, 110.

33. Richard Clarke, *Against All Enemies: Inside America's War on Terror*, 184.

34. Ibid. 184–190.

35. Qtd. in Christopher Hitchens, "Jefferson vs. the Muslim Pirates," *City Journal*, Spring 2007, www.city-journal.org/html/17_2_urbanities-thomas_jefferson.html.

36. Qtd. in Henry Crumpton, *The Art of Intelligence: Lessons from a Life in the CIA's Clandestine Service*, 111–112.

37. Ibid, 216.

38. U.S. Federal Code 2381 specifies that citizens who wage war against the nation or who give aid and comfort either inside the United States or elsewhere to those doing so are guilty of treason. Separate code covers the recruiting of others for such acts. In 1945 the Supreme Court ruled that acts of treason are required to be proven by two witnesses. The Court determined that two witnesses are not required to prove intent to commit treason or that an overt act is treasonable. The witnesses, eyewitnesses or federal agents, are only necessary to prove the act of treason actually occurred.

CHAPTER 16: SHADOW BOXING

1. "Counterterrorism: Evaluating the Five-Year Plan," Special Hearing, Subcommittee of the Committee on Appropriation, 3–8.

2. Ibid, 12–13.

3. Walter Sharp, Director Joint Staff, Homeland Defense, Joint Publication 3-27, United States Joint Chiefs of Staff, July 12, 2007, vii.

4. Ibid, 1–2.

5. Qtd. in *The 9/11 Commission Report: Final Report of the National Commission on Terrorist Attacks upon the United States* (New York: W.W. Norton and Co., 2004), 101.

6. "Counterterrorism: Evaluating the Five-Year Plan," 24.

7. Ibid, 91.

8. Ibid, 34–35.

9. Five-Year Interagency Counterterrorism and Technology Crime Plan, Attorney General of the United States, Sept. 1999, 1–2, www.justice.gov/oip/docs/crime-plan.pdf.

10. "Red Team" testing evolved out of early military defensive exercises in which special, highly trained individuals and teams were assigned as "aggressors" and given the challenge of penetrating security facilities. The teams were encouraged to be as creative as possible and to use the most sophisticated and aggressive practices that would be expected from enemy infiltration and sabotage teams. In many instances the job was risky, as they were going against heavily defended targets with no notice at all. The Strategic Air Command made extensive use of Red Teams in improving its defenses, and the Army used them to evaluate the defense of key military targets such as the Panama Canal. Red Teams are an extension of war gaming and other exercises used to analyze strengths and weaknesses; they add a critical element of reality.

11. "A Review of the Federal Bureau of Investigations Counterterrorism Program: Threat Assessment, Strategic Planning and Resource Management," Report No. 02-38, Office of the Inspector General, Sept. 2002, www.fas.org/irp/agency/doj/oig/fbi02sum.html.

12. Ibid, FBI comments.

13. Henry Crumpton, *The Art of Intelligence: Lessons from a Life in the CIA's Clandestine Service* (New York: Penguin Press, 2012), 112.

14. Ibid, 112–113.

15. Qtd. in Richard Clarke, *Against All Enemies: Inside America's War on Terror* (New York: Free Press, 2004), 219.

16. Ibid, 206–207.

17. *The 9/11 Commission Report: Final Report of the National Commission on Terrorist Attacks upon the United States*, 176.

18. In October 1978 ,Congress had passed the Foreign Intelligence Service Act, which specified procedures for electronic and physical surveillance and collection of intelligence on individuals suspected of acting as "agents of foreign powers." The act allowed intelligence collection activities on American citizens and permanent residents of the United States but only as granted by a special U.S. Federal Court. The FBI or the NSA submits requests for special surveillance warrants to be issued against suspected intelligence agents or, more recently, individuals acting in support of terrorist activities.

19. "Security of Checked Baggage on Flights Within the United States," Federal Aviation Administration, Department of Transportation, *Federal Register*, Aug. 19, 1999, www.epic.org/privacy/faa/faa_profile_regs.pdf

20. The evolution of the CAPPS system—along with the use of and objections to a completely separate "No Fly List" created and updated by the Federal Terrorist Screening Center following the attacks of 2001—illustrates the ongoing conflict between the desire for security and the demands of personal privacy. In 2003 the Transportation Security Administration proposed CAPPSII, an expanded system to be administered by the government rather than the airlines, which would screen all passengers, not just baggage, and would cover all airlines and all airports. Law enforcement would be contacted if the passenger showed up on an enhanced watch list or had outstanding federal or state warrants. The CAPPSII system received extensive opposition from the ACLU and other privacy protection groups. TSA canceled the CAPPSII effort in 2004, proposing another program named Secure Flight, which would have many similar features. Congress blocked implementation of Secure Flight until TSA could show that it passed certain levels of accuracy and privacy protection. That has not happened as of this writing; however, other screening measures such as the No Fly List, the Selectee List and the Terrorist Watchlist implemented following the 2001 attacks are still in place and federally mandated for commercial air carrier use.

21. Richard Clarke, *Against All Enemies: Inside America's War on Terror*, 215.

22. *The 9/11 Commission Report: Final Report of the National Commission on Terrorist Attacks upon the United States*, 195–196.

23. Qtd. in James Bamford, *A Pretext for War: 9/11, Iraq, and the Abuse of America's Intelligence Agencies*, 303–304.

24. Richard Clarke, *Against All Enemies: Inside America's War on Terror*, 225.

25. *The 9/11 Commission Report: Final Report of the National Commission on Terrorist Attacks upon the United States*, New York, 199–200.

26. Richard Clarke, *Against All Enemies: Inside America's War on Terror*, 225–226.

27. Cynthia Grabo, *Anticipating Surprise: Analysis for Strategic Warning* (Lanham, MD: University Press of America, 2004), 28–32.

28. As late as 2004 a former Deputy Director of Intelligence would protest that

it was never certain that bin Laden or his organization had a role in either the World Trade Center bombing or the Bojinka plot. Ongoing research has demonstrated a network affiliation to a virtual certainty, and pragmatically the lack of any solid connection to al-Qaeda in 1999 should have had nothing to do with setting an intelligence priority for individuals connected to the men known to have been involved in both plots. Anthony Summers and Robbyn Swan, *The Eleventh Day: The Full Story of 9/11 and Osama bin Laden* (New York: Ballantine Books, 2011), 228.

29. Anthony Summers and Robbyn Swan, *The Eleventh Day: The Full Story of 9/11 and Osama bin Laden*, 230–231.

30. James Bamford, *A Pretext for War: 9/11, Iraq, and the Abuse of America's Intelligence Agencies* (New York: Anchor Books, 2005), 221–222.

31. Richard Clarke, *Against All Enemies: Inside America's War on Terror*, 227–229. Clarke notes that Alec Station was found to be "chronically delinquent" in submitting suspect names to terror watch lists. As of January 2000, it was holding information on at least fifty-eight suspected terrorists, none of whose names had been submitted to the appropriate watch lists.

32. Ibid, 224–225.

33. Ibid, 235.

34. Qtd. in Cythia Grabo, *Anticipating Surprise: Analysis for Strategic Warning*, 14.

CHAPTER 17: INERTIA

1. Secretary of Defense Donald Rumsfeld, "Interview with Larry King," CNN, Dec. 6, 2001, News Transcript, U.S Department of Defense, www.

defense.gov/transcripts/transcript. aspx?transcriptid=2603.

2. Anthony Summers and Robbyn Swan, *The Eleventh Day: The Full Story of 9/11 and Osama bin Laden* (New York: Ballantine Books, 2011), 327–328.

3. Ibid, 331.

4. Anthony Summers and Robbyn Swan, *The Eleventh Day: The Full Story of 9/11 and Osama bin Laden*, 285–286.

5. Qtd. in Lawrence Wright, *The Looming Tower: Al-Qaeda's Road to 9/11* (London: Allen Lane, 2006), 311.

6. The CIA's own inspector general recommended holding a number of CIA officers accountable for failures, primarily in regard to the participants in the Kuala Lumpur meeting and the monitoring of individuals known to be connected to certain of them. Then CIA director Porter Goss was not pleased with that approach and had those recommendations removed from the report. The final report, only recommending that accountability boards be convened, was presented to Goss in June 2005. Goss responded with a decision that no boards would be held and no officers held responsible for intelligence failures related to the 9/11 attacks. On the face of it, this seems a significant failure in accountability; it would be less so if the officers involved were knowingly acting solely in the agencies' own interest over several months, something that the CIA would not want on any official record.

7. Brian Whittaker, "Piecing Together the Terrorist Jigsaw," *The Guardian*, London, Oct.15, 2001.

8. Qtd. in Anthony Summers and Robbyn Swan, *The Eleventh Day: The Full Story of 9/11 and Osama bin Laden*, 307–308.

9. "FEMA, Cheney to head new office; Office of National Preparedness: Group will assess and respond to terrorism," *Telegraph Herald*, Dubuque, Iowa, May 9, 2001.

10. "Cheney to Oversee National Effort for Responding to Domestic Attacks," www.historycommons.org/context.jsp?item=a050801cheneytaskforce#a050801cheneytaskforce.

11. Anthony Summers and Robbyn Swan, *The Eleventh Day: The Full Story of 9/11 and Osama bin Laden*, 317.

12. "Ashcroft Denies Taking Little Interest in Terrorism," CNN, Apr. 14, 2004, www.cnn.com/2004/ALLPOLITICS/04/13/911.commission.

13. *The 9/11 Commission Report: Final Report of the National Commission on Terrorist Attacks upon the United States*, 209.

14. Phillip Shenon, *The Commission: The Uncensored History of the 9/11 Investigation* (New York: Hachette Book Group USA, 2008), 246.

15. Qtd. in Anthony Summers and Robyn Swan, *The Eleventh Day: The Full Story of 9/11 and Osama bin Laden*, 317–318.

16. Phillip Shenon, *The Commission: The Uncensored History of the 9/11 Investigation*, 247–248.

17. Anthony Summers and Robbyn Swan, *The Eleventh Day: The Full Story of 9/11 and Osama bin Laden.*

18. Phillip Shenon, *The Commission: The Uncensored History of the 9/11 Investigation*, 318. It should be noted that Ashcroft has denied making such remarks; Pickard conformed his position on the accuracy of his statement in regard to Ashcroft's remarks to the 9/11 Commission, in both testimony and in a written letter. Certainly the general attitude attributed to Ashcroft by Pickard is consistent with characterizations by Richard Clarke and by the attitude evidenced by FBI headquarters in essentially stonewalling field office efforts to move assertively in regard to suspected al-Qaeda terrorists. The attorney general's attitude, as characterized by Pickard, would also be consistent with the rest of the Bush cabinet officers, as described by others associated with them, including Richard Clarke.

19. Anthony Summers and Robbyn Swan, *The Eleventh Day: The Full Story of 9/11 and Osama bin Laden*, 318.

20. Qtd. in Ibid, 536.

21. George Tenet, *At the Center of the Storm: My Years at the CIA* (New York: HarperCollins, 2007), 158.

22. Ibid, 150–155; see also Bob Woodward, *State of Denial* (London: Pocket Books, 2006), 49–52.

23. Anthony Summers and Robbyn Swan, *The Eleventh Day: The Full Story of 9/11 and Osama bin Laden*, 325–326.

24. Qtd. in Ibid, 325.

25. James Bamford, *A Pretext for War: 9/11, Iraq, and the Abuse of America's Intelligence Agencies*, (New York: Anchor Books, 2005) 244–245.

26. "A Case Study in Terrorist Travel," *The 9/11 Commission Report: Final Report of the National Commission on Terrorist Attacks upon the United States*, 177–178.

27. "9/11 and Terrorist Travel, Staff Report of the National Commission on Terrorist Attacks upon the United States," 31–44 and 43, www.9-11commission.gov/staff_statements/911_TerrTrav_Monograph.pdf.

28. Anthony Summers and Robbyn Swan,

The Eleventh Day: The Full Story of 9/11 and Osama bin Laden, 332–333.

29. "DCI Update Terrorist Threat Review," Central Intelligence Agency, Aug. 23, 2001.

30. *The 9/11 Commission Report: Final Report of the National Commission on Terrorist Attacks upon the United States,* 345.

31. Qtd. in James Bamford, *A Pretext for War: 9/11, Iraq, and the Abuse of America's Intelligence Agencies,* 16–17.

32. Statement of Bogdan Dzakovic to the National Commission on Terrorist Attacks on the United States, Second Public Hearing, May 22, 2003, http://govinfo.library.unt.edu/911/hearings/hearing2/witness_dzakovic.htm.

33. Ibid.

34. Qtd. in Letter to the U.S. Office of Special Counsel Regarding Alleged Aviation Security Violations, Office of the Inspector General, United States Department of Transportation, Mar. 18, 2003, www.oig.dot.gov/library-item/4560.

35. Philip Shenon, *The Uncensored History of the 9/11 Investigation,* 115.

36. Qtd. in Anthony Summers and Robbyn Swan, *The Eleventh Day: The Full Story of 9/11 and Osama bin Laden,* 13

37. "A Case Study in Terrorist Travel," *The 9/11 Commission Report: Final Report of the National Commission on Terrorist Attacks upon the United States,* 3.

38. The FAA's failure in this regard would be so significant that 9/11 commissioners would conclude that FAA management had obfuscated, misled and possibly even lied to them during their inquiry. James Klatell, "9/11 Commissioners Expose Obstructions," Associated Press, Aug. 5, 2006, www.

cbsnews.com/news/9-11-commission-ers-expose-obstructions.

39. Qtd. in Philip Shenon, *The Uncensored History of the 9/11 Investigation,* 116.

40. Qtd. in James Bamford, *A Pretext for War: 9/11, Iraq, and the Abuse of America's Intelligence Agencies,* 241.

41. Qtd. in *The 9/11 Commission Report: Final Report of the National Commission on Terrorist Attacks upon the United States,* 342–343.

42. Philip Shenon, *The Uncensored History of the 9/11 Investigation.*

43. *The 9/11 Commission Report: Final Report of the National Commission on Terrorist Attacks upon the United States,* 101.

44. Richard A. Clarke, *Against All Enemies,* 213.

45. Qtd. in Ibid, 358–359.

46. Ibid, 201.

47. Qtd. in Ibid, 355.

48. Qtd. in *The 9/11 Commission Report: Final Report of the National Commission on Terrorist Attacks upon the United States,* 353–357.

CHAPTER 18: ATTACK

1. The major long-range radar surveillance of the Pacific and Atlantic approaches had been based on very large Over the Horizon Radar installations. In 1983 the West Coast installation was taken off-line and placed into "warm storage"; the Atlantic installation followed it into "warm storage" the following year. Joel Bagloel, "North Warning System: Protecting America's Back Door," http://usmilitary.about.com/od/weapons/a/northwarning.htm.

2. Aircraft pilots may be requested to broadcast ("squawk") a given code to confirm their identity against their transponder response. Transponder

codes are assigned for air traffic control and military identification purposes. Contemporary transponders can also be used to broadcast certain emergency codes including a hijacking alert.

3. Routine FAA aircraft tracking is normally carried out by transmissions from identification transponder systems carried by all commercial and military aircraft. Those transponders routinely transmit identity and location of the aircraft. Transponders are a key element in aircraft tracking—if they fail or are turned off, the FAA has to fall back on its network of air route surveillance radars (maintained by the FAA and jointly accessed by both the FAA and NORAD air defense sector centers) and active short-range-approach control radars located around major cities and airports.

4. *Guarding What You Value Most: North American Aerospace Defense Command Celebrating 50 Years*, NORAD Headquarters, Peterson Air Force Base, Colorado, 2008, 23.

5. Leslie Filson, *Air War over America; Sept. 11 Alters Face of Air Defense Mission* (Darby, PA: Diane Publishing Co., 2004), 28–30.

6. Much has been made of the point that NORAD exercises involved overseas flights inbound to the U.S.; however, there is no reason to presume the elements of intercept would have been different—inbound flights would have gone off radar, dropped to low altitudes and shut down their transponders as close to their point of attack as possible. In addition, during at least one 1998 CSG exercise a Learjet was loaded with explosives by terrorists and flown in a suicide mission against Washington, D.C. *The 9/11 Com-*

mission Report: Final Report of the National Commission on Terrorist Attacks upon the United States, (New York: W.W. Norton and Co., 2004) 457, end note 98.

7. NORAD Exercises Hijack Summary, 9/11 Commission Report, www. scribd.com/doc/16411947/NORAD-Exercises-Hijack-Summary.

8. Steven Komarow and Tom Squitieri, "NORAD Had Drills of Jets as Weapons," *USA Today*, Apr. 18, 2004, www.usatoday.com/news/washington/2004-04-18-norad_x.htm.

9. William Arkin, *Code Names: Deciphering U.S. Military Plans, Code Names and Operations in a Post 9-11 World* (Hanover, NH: Steerforth, 2005), 545; see also Senate Committee on Armed Services, U.S. Congress, Aug. 17, 2004, www.gpo.gov/fdsys/pkg/CHRG-108shrg24495/html/CHRG-108shrg24495.htm.

10. Lynn Spencer, *Touching History: The Untold Story of the Drama That Unfolded in the Skies over America on 911,* (New York: Free Press, 2008), 3.

11. *The 9/11 Commission Report: Final Report of the National Commission on Terrorist Attacks upon the United States,* 18.

12. "Standing Rules of Engagement for US Forces," Chairman of the Joint Chiefs of Staff Instruction, CJCSI-3121.01A, Jan. 15, 2000, www.fas.org/man/dod-101/dod/docs/cjcs_sroe.pdf.

13. Glen Johnson, "Facing Terror Attack's Aftermath: Otis Fighter Jets Scrambled Too Late To Halt Attacks," *Boston Globe*, Sept. 15, 2001, www.emperors-clothes.com/9-11backups/bg915.htm.

14. Qtd. in *The 9/11 Commission Report: Final Report of the National Commission*

on *Terrorist Attacks upon the United States*, 31.

15. "Aircraft Piracy (Hijacking) and the Destruction of Derelict Airborne Objects," Chairman of the Joint Chiefs of Staff Instruction, CJCSI-3601-01A, June 1, 2001, www.emperors-clothes. com/9-11backups/3610_01a.pdf.

16. Orientation Tour of the National Military Command Center (NMCC) and the National Military Joint Intelligence Center (NMJIC), Memorandum for the Record, National Commission on Terrorist Attacks upon the United States, July 21, 2003, http://media.nara.gov/9-11/MFR/t-0148-911MFR-00756.pdf.

17. Ibid.

18. Qtd. in Dan Hampton, *Viper Pilot: A Memoir of Air Combat* (New York: William Morrow, 2012), 159.

19. *The 9/11 Commission Report: Final Report of the National Commission on Terrorist Attacks upon the United States*, 34.

20. Philip Shenon, *The Commission: The Uncensored History of the 9/11 Investigation* (New York: Twelve, 2008), 202–203.

21. Michael Bronner, "9/11 Live: The NORAD Tapes," *Vanity Fair*, Aug. 2006, www.vanityfair.com/politics/ features/2006/08/norad200608.

22. Ibid, 3.

23. Richard Clarke, *Against All Enemies: Inside America's War on Terror* (New York: Free Press, 2004), 3.

24. Qtd. in *The 9/11 Commission Report: Final Report of the National Commission on Terrorist Attacks upon the United States*, 37.

25. Clarke comments that things were a bit difficult in the PEOC as Mrs. Cheney kept turning down the volume on the crisis center video teleconference so she could hear CNN News and the vice president kept hanging up the open line to the Situation Room. In addition, communications with *Air Force One* were so bad that Cheney could not maintain even a clear voice call to President Bush for any period of time. Richard Clarke, *Against All Enemies: Inside America's War on Terror*, 18.

26. *The 9/11 Commission Report: Final Report of the National Commission on Terrorist Attacks upon the United States*, 30.

27. The exact location of the Nightwatch aircraft on 9/11 is still unknown. Given the nature of the Global Guardian exercise going on that week, involving a simulated Soviet nuclear attack and all the related command-and-control procedures, it is possible that either Nightwatch or a similar E-4 airborne command-post aircraft was participating in that exercise.

28. Richard Clarke, *Against All Enemies: Inside America's War on Terror*, 6–7.

29. *The 9/11 Commission Report: Final Report of the National Commission on Terrorist Attacks upon the United States*, 36.

30. David Edwards and Muriel Kane, "CNN: Mystery Aircraft Was Military 'Doomsday' Plane," *The Raw Story*, Sept. 13, 2007, www. rawstory.com//news/2007/CNN_investigates_secret_911_doomsday_ plane_0913.html. For photographs of the mystery aircraft over the White House and an early discussion of the mystery see Mark Gaffney, "Why Did the World's Most Sophisticated Electronics Warfare Airplane Circle over the White House on 9/11," www.journalof911studies.com/ volume/200704/911MysteryPlane.pdf.

31. Richard Clarke, *Against All Enemies: Inside America's War on Terror*, 9.

32. Adam Herbert with General Philip Breedlove, "Airmen on 9/11", *Air Force Magazine*, Sept. 2011, Vol. 84, No. 9, 55.

33. Sept. 11, 2001, Air Threat and DDO Conference Transcripts, U.S Department of Defense, www.dod.gov/pubs/foi/homeland_defense/september11/The_DoD_Transcript_Air_Threat_Conference_Call_September_11_2001.pdf.

34. James Bamford, *A Pretext for War: 9/11, Iraq and the Abuse of America's Intelligence Agencies* (New York: Anchor Books, 2005), 39.

35. *The 9/11 Commission Report: Final Report of the National Commission on Terrorist Attacks upon the United States*, 37–38.

36. Ibid, 36.

37. Qtd. in James Bamford, *A Pretext for War: 9/11, Iraq and the Abuse of America's Intelligence Agencies*, 83.

38. David Cinciotti, "Air Force One journey on September 11: no escort during the attacks, 11 fighters when the airspace was completely free of airliners," *The Aviationist*, Sept. 9, 2011, www.theaviationist.com/2011/09/09/af1.

39. Anthony Summers and Robbyn Swan, *The Eleventh Day: The Full Story of 9/11 and Osama bin Laden* (New York: Ballantine Books, 201), 140–141.

40. Ibid, 142.

41. *The 9/11 Commission Report: Final Report of the National Commission on Terrorist Attacks upon the United States*, 42.

42. Anthony Summers and Robbyn Swan, *The Eleventh Day: The Full Story of 9/11 and Osama bin Laden*, 138.

43. Richard Clarke, *Against All Enemies: Inside America's War on Terror*, 15.

44. Qtd. Anthony Summers and Robbyn Swan, *The Eleventh Day: The Full Story of 9/11 and Osama bin Laden*, 121.

45. Ibid, 139.

46. *The 9/11 Commission Report: Final Report of the National Commission on Terrorist Attacks upon the United States*, 43.

47. Qtd. in Anthony Summers and Robbyn Swan, *The Eleventh Day: The Full Story of 9/11 and Osama bin Laden*, 146.

48. North American Aerospace Command Field Visit Site Visit, Interview with CINC NORAD, Edward Eberhart, Memorandum for the Record 9/11 Commission, Mar. 1, 2004, http://media.nara.gov/9-11/MFR/t-0148-911MFR-00788.pdf.

49. Sept. 11, 2001, Air Threat and DDO Conference Transcripts, U.S Department of Defense, 40.

50. Michael Bronner, "9/11 Live: The NORAD Tapes," *Vanity Fair*, Aug. 2006, 8.

CHAPTER 19: POINTS OF FAILURE

1. Qtd. in Richard Clarke, *Against All Enemies: Inside America's War on Terror* (New York: Free Press, 2004), 106.

2. Qtd. in Ibid, 107.

3. "America Under Attack," CNN News, Sept. 11, 2001, http://transcripts.cnn.com/TRANSCRIPTS/0109/11/bn.74.html.

4. *The 9/11 Commission Report: Final Report of the National Commission on Terrorist Attacks upon the United States* (New York: W.W. Norton and Co., 2004), 457, endnote 98.

5. Ibid.

6. North American Aerospace Command Field Visit Site Visit, Interview with CINC NORAD, Ralph Eberhart, Memorandum for the Record 9/11 Commission, Mar. 1, 2004, http://

media.nara.gov/9-11/MFR/t-0148-
911MFR-00788.pdf.

7. Qtd. in James Bamford, *A Pretext for War: 9/11, Iraq, and The Abuse of America's Intelligence Agencies* (New York: Anchor Books, 2005), 39.

8. Qtd. in ibid, 107.

9. Ibid.

10. Qtd. in Philip Shenon, *The Uncensored History of the 9/11 Investigation* (New York: Twelve, 2008), 116.

11. The Aviation Security System and the 9/11 Attacks, National Commission on Terrorist Attacks on the United States, Staff Statement No. 3, http://news.findlaw.com/hdocs/docs/terrorism/911comm-ss3.pdf.

12. Brian Jenkins, "Terrorism trial begins in New York: 3 men accused of plotting to bomb U.S. planes," *New York Times*, May 13, 1996.

13. Qtd. in Anthony Summers and Robbyn Swan, *The Eleventh Day: The Full Story of 9/11 and Osama bin Laden* (New York: Ballantine Books, 2008), 285–286.

14. Qtd. in Richard Clarke, *Against All Enemies: Inside America's War on Terror*, 212.

15. Qtd. in Ibid, 353.

16. *The 9/11 Commission Report: Final Report of the National Commission on Terrorist Attacks upon the United States*, 457, endnote 85.

17. Combating Terrorism: Issues to be Resolved to Improve Counterterrorism Operations, NSIAD-99-135, Report to Congressional Requesters, U.S. Government of Accountability Office (GAO), May 1999, 14–17.

18. Ibid, 22.

19. Qtd. in National Commission on Terrorist Attacks upon the United States, Transcript of twelfth public hearing,

June 17, 2004, http://govinfo.library.unt.edu/911/archive/hearing12/9-11Commission_Hearing_2004-06-17.htm.

20. 9/11 Commission, Memorandum for the Record: Interview with CINCNORAD Eberhart, prepared by Geoffrey Brown, Mar. 1, 2004, http://media.nara.gov/9-11/MFR/t-0148-911MFR-00788.pdf; see also transcript: "9/11 Commission Hearings for June 17, 2004," *Washington Post*, June 17, 2004.

21. Ibid.

22. Qtd. in Dan Eggen, "9/11 Panel Suspected Deception by Pentagon," *The Washington Post*, Aug. 2, 2006, www.washingtonpost.com/wp-dyn/content/article/2006/08/01/AR2006080101300.html.

23. Qtd. in Anthony Summers and Robbyn Swan, *The Eleventh Day: The Full Story of 9/11 and Osama bin Laden*, 147.

24. James Bamford, *A Pretext for War: 9/11, Iraq, and The Abuse of America's Intelligence Agencies*, 39.

CHAPTER 20: GOING FORWARD

1. Richard F. Grimmett, "Authorization for the Use of Military Force in Response to the 9/11 Attacks (P.L. 107-40)," Legislative History, CRS Report to Congress, Jan. 16, 2007, www.fas.org/sgp/crs/natsec/RS22357.pdf.

2. Ibid, 2–3.

3. Ibid, 4.

4. Alan G. Whittaker, Shannon A. Brown, Frederick C. Smith, and Elizabeth McKune, "The National Security Policy Process: The National Security Council and Interagency System," National Defense University, Aug. 15, 2011, www.virginia.edu/cnsl/pdf/national-security-policy-process-2011.pdf.

5. Ibid, 58.

6. Cam Simpson, "Obama Revamps National Security Posts," *The Wall Street Journal,* May 27, 2009, http://online.wsj.com/news/articles/SB124338073162756375.

7. Alan G. Whittaker, Shannon A. Brown, Frederick C. Smith, and Elizabeth McKune, "The National Security Policy Process: The National Security Council and Interagency System," National Defense University, Aug. 15, 2011, 51.

8. Ibid.

9. Qtd. in Larry Hancock and Stuart Wexler, *Shadow Warfare: A History of America's Undeclared Wars* (Berkeley, CA: Counterpoint, 2014), Chapter 26: "Merging Covert and Conventional."

10. "The USA Patriot Act: Preserving Life and Liberty (Uniting and Strengthening America by Providing Appropriate Tools Required to Intercept and Obstruct Terrorism)," U.S. Department of Justice, www.justice.gov/archive/ll/highlights.htm.

11. In its most militant forms it is capable not only of terror attacks but of on local levels of essential genocidal activities. The actions of ISIS in Syria and Iraq are potentially dangerous as those of Pol Pot and the Communist Khmer Rouge were in Cambodia during the 1970s.

12. "A Guardian Guide to your Metadata," *The Guardian,* June 12, 2013, www.theguardian.com/technology/interactive/2013/jun/12/what-is-metadata-nsa-surveillance#meta=0000000.

13. Evan Perez, "Report shows U.S. officials struggled to assess usefulness of post-9/11 warrantless surveillance," CNN, Apr. 25, 2015, www.cnn.com/2015/04/25/politics/nsa-warrantless-surveillance-report/index.html.

14. "Reform the Patriot Act," American Civil Liberties Union, www.aclu.org/reform-patriot-act.

15. National Security Letters, Electronic Privacy Information Center, www.epic.org/privacy/nsl.

16. Ellen Nakashima, "NSA Phone Data Does Little to Prevent Terrorists Attacks, Group Says," *The Washington Post,* Jan. 12, 2014, www.washingtonpost.com/world/national-security/nsa-phone-record-collection-does-little-to-prevent-terrorist-attacks-group-says/2014/01/12/8aa860aa-77dd-11e3-8963-b4b654bcc9b2_story.html.

17. James Bamford, *The Shadow Factory: The Ultra-Secret NSA from 9/11 to the Eavesdropping on America* (New York: Doubleday, 2008).

18. Sultana Khan, "Foreign Terrorist Tracking Task Force Databases," Feb. 1, 2015, http://sultanakhan.kinja.com/foreign-terrorist-tracking-task-force-databases-1707175449.

19. Foreign Terrorist Tracking Task Force/National Security Analysis Center, Federal Bureau of Investigation, Aug. 11, 2008, www.epic.org/foia/fbi/pia/FTTTF-National-Security-Analysis-Center-PIA.PDF.

20. William M. Arkin, "This Shadow Government Agency Is Scarier Than the NSA, *Phase Zero,* June 1, 2015, http://phasezero.gawker.com/this-shadow-government-agency-is-scarier-than-the-nsa-1707179377.

21. Qtd. in "Ten Years After: The FBI Since 9/11," Counterterrorism, The Federal Bureau of Investigation, Aug. 2011, www.fbi.gov/about-us/ten-years-after-the-fbi-since-9-11/just-the-facts-1/counterterrorism.

22. "Oregon Resident Convicted in Plot

To Bomb Christmas Tree Lighting Ceremony," U.S. Department of Justice, Jan. 31, 2013, www.fbi.gov/portland/press-releases/2013/oregon-resident-convicted-in-plot-to-bomb-christmas-tree-lighting-ceremony.

23. "Al-Qaeda-Inspired Operative Sentenced to 30 Years in Prison for Attempting to Bomb Federal Reserve Bank in New York, Defendant Traveled to United States Intent on Committing Terrorist Attack; Attempted to Bomb New York's Financial District on Behalf of al-Qaeda," U.S. Attorney's Office, Aug. 9, 2013, www.fbi.gov/newyork/press-releases/2013/al-qaeda-inspired-operative-sentenced-to-30-years-in-prison-for-attempting-to-bomb-federal-reserve-bank-in-new-york.

24. "Stopping a Suicide Bomber—Jihadist Planned Attack on the U.S. Capital," Federal Bureau of Investigation, Jan. 1, 2014, www.fbi.gov/news/stories/2013/january/stopping-a-suicide-bomber/stopping-a-suicide-bomber.

25. Kevin Johnson, "FBI Terror Sting Tactics Questioned," *USA Today*, Dec. 16, 2010, www.usatoday.com/news/washington/2010-12-15-fbi-sting_N.htm?csp=digg.

26. John Ward Anderson and Karen DeYoung, "Plot To Bomb U.S.-Bound Jets Is Foiled," *The Washington Post,* Aug. 11, 2006, www.washingtonpost.com/wp-dyn/content/article/2006/08/10/AR2006081000152.html.

27. "Convergence: The Challenge of Aviation Safety," *Security Weekly*, STRATFOR Global Intelligence, Sept. 16, 2009, www.stratfor.com/weekly/20090916_convergence_challenge_aviation_security#axzz362EdFx00.

28. "Aviation Security Ten Years After the 9/11 Attacks," ALPA Issue Analysis, Airline Pilots Association International, 2011, www.alpa.org/portals/alpa/pressroom/inthecockpit/ALPAIssueAnalysis_10YearsAfter9-11Attacks.pdf.

29. Eric Bradner and Rene Marsh, "TSA Screeners Failed to Locate Explosives, Weapons," CNN, June 1, 2015, www.cnn.com/2015/06/01/politics/tsa-failed-undercover-airport-screening-tests/index.html.

30. "Why Does the Government Have a Hands-Off List for Certain Terrorist Supporters?" *WhoWhatWhy*, May 20, 2014, www.whowhatwhy.com/2014/05/20/why-does-the-government-have-a-hands-off-list-for-certain-terrorist-supporters.

31. Qtd. in John Tirpak, "Noble Eagle Flies On," *Air Force Magazine*, Nov. 2013, 53–56.

32. Ibid, 54

33. Ibid, 55.

34. Aaron Church, "Capital Defenders," *Air Force Magazine*, Dec. 2012, www.airforcemag.com/Magazine-Archive/Pages/2012/december%202012/1212defenders.aspx.

35. Tylor Rogoway, "America's Capital Is Guarded by Norwegian Surface-to-Air Missiles," *FOXTROTALPHA*, Apr. 3, 2014, http://foxtrotalpha.jalopnik.com/americas-capitol-is-guarded-by-norwegian-surface-to-ai-1556894733.

36. Ibid.

37. "The Role and Status of DOD Red Teaming Activities," Defense Science Board Task Force, Office of the Undersecretary of Defense for Acquisition, Technology and Logistics, Sept. 2003, www.fas.org/irp/agency/dod/dsb/redteam.pdf.

38. Ibid.

39. Qtd. in Ibid, 5.

40. Stephen Sloan and Robert Bunker,

Red Teams and Counterforce Training (Norman, OK: University of Oklahoma Press), 211.

41. "Operation TOPOFF/National Level Exercise Fast Facts," CNN Library, Oct. 30, 2013, www.cnn.com/2013/10/30/us/operation-topoff-national-level-exercise-fast-facts.

42. National Exercise Program (NEP), National Level Exercise–Capstone Exercise 2014, FEMA Fact Sheet, www.fema.gov/media-library-data/1391701556671-2204c5ec-1c30a48ddd0b783989206b68/nep.pdf.

43. National Level Exercise 2011: Federal Partner Participation, Inspector General's Office, Department of Homeland Security, October, 2011, 6–7, www.oig.dhs.gov/assets/Mgmt/OIG_12-01_Oct11.pdf.

44. Charles Clark, "Homeland Security Moves Closer to Getting Off GAO's High-Risk List," Government Executive, May 8, 2014, www.govexec.com/management/2014/05/homeland-security-moves-closer-getting-gaos-high-risk-list/84169.

45. "FEMA National Level Exercises Lessons Not Realized," Committee on Homeland Security, Sept. 12, 2012, http://chsdemocrats.house.gov/press/index.asp?ID=750.

46. Qtd. in "President Arrives in Alabama, Briefed on Hurricane Katrina," The White House, Sept. 2, 2005, http://georgewbush-whitehouse.archives.gov/news/releases/2005/09/20050902-2.html.

47. Qtd. in "'Can I Quit Now?' Katrina Chief Wrote as Storm Raged," CNN News, Nov. 4, 2005, www.cnn.com/2005/US/11/03/brown.fema.emails.

48. Qtd. in Stephen Lowman, "'Heck of a Job Brownie' spreads Katrina blame in a new book," Political Bookworm blog, June 14, 2011, www.washingtonpost.com/blogs/political-bookworm/post/heck-of-a-job-brownie-spreads-the-katrina-blame-in-new-book/2011/06/13/AGgFebUH_blog.html.

49. Josh Rogan and Eli Lake, "Military Hates Micromanagement of ISIS War," *The Daily Beast,* Oct. 21, 2014, www.thedailybeast.com/articles/2014/10/31/military-upset-with-white-house-micromanagement-of-isis-war.html.

CHAPTER 21: DIPLOMATIC INSECURITY

1. A Soviet asset inside the United States designated "Tumbleweed" traveled to Mexico City to meet with KGB officers attached to the Soviet Embassy in Mexico City. One of his Soviet contacts was suspected of coordinating Soviet clandestine operations for North America including both plans for sabotage and assassination in the event of war with the United States. CIA Memorandum from Assistant Deputy Director of Plans to Acting Chief of Division, Nov. 23, 1963.

2. Dan Hampton, *Viper Pilot: A Memoir of Air Combat* (New York: HarperCollins Publishers, 2012), 151.

3. Qtd. in Ibid, 152.

4. "Special Agents, Special Threats: Creating the Office of the Chief Special Agent, 1914–1933," History of the Bureau of Diplomatic Security of the United States Department of State, 6, www.state.gov/documents/organization/176705.pdf.

5. Diplomatic Security Service locations by Region, www.state.gov/m/ds/about/c8849.htm.

6. "Significant Attacks Against U.S. Diplomatic Facilities and Personnel:

1998–2013," Bureau of Diplomatic Security, U.S. Department of State, www.state.gov/documents/organization/225846.pdf.

7. Larry Hancock and Stuart Wexler, *Shadow Warfare: A History of America's Undeclared Wars* (Berkeley, CA: Counterpoint, 2014), 492–493.

8. Mary Beth Sheridan, "State Department Has Rocky History of Managing Guard Contracts," *The Washington Post*, Sept. 13, 2009, www.washingtonpost.com/wp-dyn/content/article/2009/09/12/AR2009091202719.html.

9. Richard Sisk, "US Embassy Fires Eight Guards Involved in Sexual Misconduct Scandal," *New York Daily News*, Sept. 4, 2009, www.nydailynews.com/news/world/embassy-fires-8-guards-involved-sexual-misconduct-scandal-article-1.401751.

10. Ibid.

11. James Risen, "After Benghazi Private Security Hovers as an Issue," *The New York Times*, Oct. 12, 2012, www.nytimes.com/2012/10/13/world/africa/private-security-hovers-as-issue-after-embassy-attack-in-benghazi-libya.html?pagewanted=all&_r=0.

12. Ibid.

13. Qtd. in Jeremy Scahill, *Blackwater: The Rise of the World's Most Powerful Mercenary Army* (New York: Nation Books, 2009), 71.

14. In 2009, Blackwater, acknowledging its image problems, changed its name to Xe. Later, in 2010, it was sold to outside investors and underwent a third name change, to Academi. As of this writing Academi remains active in security work of various types, including training for private citizens and government employees. It operates training facilities in California, North Carolina and Connecticut.

15. Mitchell Zuckoff with the Annex Security Team, *13 Hours: The Inside Account of What Really Happened in Benghazi*, 12 (New York: Hachette Book Group, 2014), 85.

16. "'60 Minutes' Issues Apology About Benghazi Report," CBS News, Nov. 8, 2013, www.cbsnews.com/news/60-minutes-issues-apology-about-benghazi-report.

17. Accountability Review Board for Benghazi, Board Report, United States Department of State, 30, www.state.gov/documents/organization/202446.pdf.

18. Mitchell Zuckoff with the Annex Security Team, *13 Hours: The Inside Account of What Really Happened in Benghazi*, 5 and 29–30.

19. Ibid, 48–49.

20. Adam Entous, Siobhan Gorman and Margaret Coker, "CIA Takes Heat for Role in Libya," Nov. 1, 2012, *The Wall Street Journal*, http://online.wsj.com/news/articles/SB10001424052970204712904578092853621061838.

21. Larry Hancock and Stuart Wexler, *Shadow Warfare: A History of America's Undeclared Wars*, 544–547.

22. Accountability Review Board for Benghazi, Board Report, United States Department of State, 4–7.

23. Ibid, 15–16.

24. Mitchell Zuckoff with the Annex Security Team, *13 Hours: The Inside Account of What Really Happened in Benghazi*, 66.

25. Accountability Review Board for Benghazi, Board Report, United States Department of State, 6.

26. Qtd. in Ibid, 18–19.

27. Ibid, 9.

28. Ibid, 14–17.

29. Mitchell Zuckoff with the Annex Security Team, *13 Hours: The Inside*

Account of What Really Happened in Benghazi, 83–85.

30. Review of the Terrorist Attacks on U.S. Facilities in Benghazi, Libya, U.S. Senate Select Committee on Intelligence, Jan. 15, 2014, 5–6, http://apps.washingtonpost.com/g/documents/world/senate-intelligence-committee-report-on-benghazi-attack/748.

31. Mitchell Zuckoff with the Annex Security Team, *13 Hours: The Inside Account of What Really Happened in Benghazi*, 93–101 and 109–111. While no official inquiries comment on the issue, the use of covert CIA military staff to respond to public attacks on diplomatic facilities produces a major command-and-control conflict. In this instance it appears that the sensitivity to deploying the GRS operators did result in a significantly delayed response to the attack.

32. Ibid, 258–268.

33. Review of the Terrorist Attacks on U.S. Facilities in Benghazi Libya, U.S. Senate Select Committee on Intelligence, 26.

34. Larry Hancock and Stuart Wexler, *Shadow Warfare: A History of America's Undeclared Wars*, "Epilogue—Benghazi," 541–548.

35. "U.S. Studying Benghazi Security Cam Videos," United Press International, Oct. 9, 2012, www.upi.com/Top_News/World-News/2012/10/09/US-studying-Benghazi-security-cam-videos/UPI-11181349764200.

36. Mitchell Zuckoff with the Annex Security Team, *13 Hours: The Inside Account of What Really Happened in Benghazi*, 72-73 and 83.

37. Majority Interim Report: Benghazi Investigation Update, House Armed Services Committee, Committee on Armed Services, Feb. 2014, http://armedservices.house.gov/index.cfm/files/serve?File_id=C4E16543-8F99-430C-BEBA-0045A6433426.

38. Ibid, 9–11.

39. Ibid, 11.

40. Secretary of Defense Leon Panetta, response to questions by Sen. Lindsey Graham, Congressional testimony, Senate Armed Forces Committee, Benghazi Consulate Attack, Feb. 7, 2013.

41. Ibid, 14.

42. The degree of misinformation pertaining to command and control of the Benghazi military response is extensive, much of it seemingly intentionally so. Given the nature of the Internet, much of false information is still circulating years after the event. Readers interested in the extent of that misinformation and an objective assessment of the facts are referred to the Snopes analysis of the "Benghazi Bungle," www.snopes.com/politics/military/benghazi.asp.

43. Ibid, 6. Normally a Predator mission would have been deployed in support of a Joint Special Operations Group mission or operated by AFRICOM in support of CIA intelligence collection. Given that the NATO involvement in Libya was long over and no combat missions would have been operational, the presence of the Predator on a nighttime mission over eastern Libya fuels speculation of a covert CIA arms interdiction mission in Libya.

44. One of the early media stories on Benghazi made much of the fact that the NSC Counterterrorism Security Group had not been convened to deal with the attack; others suggested that the State Department's Security Division had erred in trying to operate a response on its own. In reality, from the very first

news of the attacks, the U.S. military had been designated to organize and direct the American response, and the control was operating though national command authority from the president, through the Security of Defense and executed by AFRICOM, the military command with regional responsibility for Libya. In regard to the State Department, as we have discussed, its own damage-response FAST teams are dispatched to assist in recovery and investigations following attacks on State Department facilities; they are not defensive rapid-response units. Sharyl Attkisson, "Sources: Key Task Force Not Convened During Benghazi Consulate Attack," CBS News, Nov. 12, 2012, www.cbsnews.com/news/sources-key-task-force-not-convened-during-benghazi-consulate-attack.

45. Majority Interim Report: Benghazi Investigation Update, House Armed Services Committee, Committee on Armed Services, 17.

46. "Ship Positions September 11/12, 2012," Office of Naval Operations, United States Navy, www.judicialwatch.org/wp-content/uploads/2014/02/NavymapBenghazi.pdf.

47. Ibid, 8–9.

48. Kate Brannen, "Marines Beef Up Embassy Security, but at a Price," POLITICO, Nov. 26, 2013, www.politico.com/story/2013/11/marines-beef-up-embassy-security-benghazi-100359.html.

49. Majority Interim Report: Benghazi Investigation Update, House Armed Services Committee, Committee on Armed Services, 27.

50. David Jackson, "Obama Team Meets on Terrorism Threats," USA Today, Aug. 4, 2013, www.usatoday.com/story/theoval/2013/08/04/obama-monaco-rice-mcdonough-terrorist-threats/2616247/.

51. Tyler Rogoway, "How the Marines Could Evacuate the U.S. Embassy in Libya," FOXTROT ALPHA, May 23, 2014, http://foxtrotalpha.jalopnik.com/how-the-marines-could-evacuate-the-u-s-embassy-in-liby-1580532779.

52. "Confronting Danger," Year in Review 2013, Bureau of Diplomatic Security, United States Department of State, 10, www.state.gov/documents/organization/225841.pdf.

CHAPTER 22: HINDSIGHT AND FORESIGHT

1. Chris Biggers, "Pakistan could soon have more nukes than the UK or France," www.medium.com/war-is-boring/pakistan-could-soon-have-more-nukes-than-the-u-k-and-france-e23307efab84.

2. Eliott Carter, "Congress Could Blow Billions on Obsolete Tactical Nukes," War Is Boring, Dec. 14, 2014, www.medium.com/war-is-boring/congress-set-to-blow-billions-on-obsolete-tactical-nukes-cfd424a1e2bb.

3. Qtd. in Ira Iosebashvili, "Putin Pledges More Defense Spending," The Wall Street Journal, Feb. 20, 2012, http://online.wsj.com/news/articles/SB10001424052970203358704577234960796991408.

4. Qtd. in Victoria Butenko, Laura Smith-Spark and Diana Magnay, "U.S. officials say 1,000 Russian troops have entered Ukraine," CNN, Aug. 28, 2014, www.cnn.com/2014/08/28/world/europe/ukraine-crisis/index.html?hpt=hp_t2.

5. Sam Greene and Graeme Robertson, "Examining Putin's Popularity: Rallying round the Russian Flag," The

Washington Post, Sept. 9, 2014, www.washingtonpost.com/blogs/monkey-cage/wp/2014/09/09/explaining-putins-popularity-rallying-round-the-russian-flag.

6. Tyler Rogoway, "Russia's Fast and Elusive TOPOL-M Ballistic Missile is Scary as Hell," *FOXTROT ALPHA*, Aug. 9, 2014, http://foxtrotalpha.jalopnik.com/russias-fast-and-illusive-topol-m-ballistic-missile-is-1618672889.

7. "Current Status," Russian Strategic Nuclear Forces, www.russianforces.org/current.

8. Qtd. in Matthew Bodner, "Russia Proves Nuclear Muscle with Ballistic Missile Launch," *The Moscow Times*, Sept. 10, 2014, www.themoscowtimes.com/business/article/russian-submarine-successfully-tests-new-nuclear-missile/506780.html.

9. "U.S. Strategic Nuclear Forces under New START," Arms Control Association, July 2013, www.armscontrol.org/factsheets/USStratNukeForce-NewSTART; updated as of Jan. 2015 based on "Snapshot of the Strategic Bomber and Missile Force," *Air Force Times*, Jan. 6, 2015.

10. Robert Beckhusen, "Russia's Future Air Force Could Resemble—The US Air Force," Jan. 2, 2015, www.medium.com/war-is-boring/russias-future-air-force-could-resemble-the-u-s-air-force-1a65d3b302f6.

11. "U.S. Strategic Nuclear Forces under New START," Arms Control Association, July 2013.

12. "Putin's New Model Army: Russia's Military Modernization," *The Economist*, May 24, 2014, www.economist.com/news/europe/21602743-money-and-reform-have-given-russia-armed-forces-it-can-use-putins-new-model-army.

13. Walter Pincus, "Russia's Military is the Largest in the Region, but it isn't the same Force as in Soviet Times," *The Washington Post*, Mar. 10, 2014, www.washingtonpost.com/world/national-security/russias-military-is-the-largest-in-the-region-but-it-isnt-the-same-force-as-in-soviet-times/2014/03/10/b3b955b8-a48c-11e3-a5fa-55f0c77b-f39c_story.html.

14. Qtd. in Simon Shuster, "Putin's Rambling State of the Nation Speech Unnerves Russian Elites," *Time*, Dec. 4, 2014, www.time.com/3619369/vladimir-putin-russia-state-of-the-nation.

15. David Cinciotti, "Russian TU-22M Backfire Bombers Escorted by SU-47 Flankers Simulate Night Attack on Sweden," *The Aviationist*, Apr. 22, 2013, www.theaviationist.com/2013/04/22/backfire-sweden.

16. Jamie Crawford, "Unusual Flights Concern NATO," CNN World, Oct. 30, 2014, www.cnn.com/2014/10/29/world/russian-aircraft-european-airspace.

17. Robert Windham and Jim Miklaszewski, "Months of Bombing Make Small Impact on ISIS Military Capabilities," NBC News, Nov. 20, 2014, www.nbcnews.com/storyline/isis-terror/months-bombing-makes-small-impact-isis-military-capabilities-n252066.

18. Chuck Hagel, Secretary of Defense, Reagan National Defense Forum keynote speech, Nov. 15, 2014, www.defense.gov/speeches/speech.aspx?source=GovDelivery&speechid=1903.

19. Eli Lake, "Republican War Hawks Already Have a War Plan for Ukraine, ISIS and Obama," *The Daily Beast*, Nov. 5, 2014.

20. Neil MacFarquhar and Andrew E. Kramer, "With Russia on the Brink of Recession, Putin Faces a New Reality," *The New York Times*, Dec 2, 2014.

21. Qtd. in Richard Allen Greene and Susannah Cullinane, "Putin: If Russian Bear Sits Still His Teeth, Claws Will Be Pulled Out," CNN World, Dec. 18, 2014, www.cnn.com/2014/12/18/world/europe/russia-putin-media-conference/index.html.

22. George Friedman, "Viewing Russia from the Inside," STRATFOR Global Intelligence, Dec.16, 2014, www.stratfor.com/weekly/viewing-russia-inside#axzz3MMHwaVum.

23. Qtd. in Ambrose Evans-Pritchard, "Russians Would Rather Starve than Surrender Putin to the Western Aggressors," *The Telegraph*, Jan. 23, 2015, www.telegraph.co.uk/finance/economics/11365497/Kremlin-hard-liner-Russians-would-rather-starve-than-surrender-Putin-to-Western-aggressors.html.

24. Jesse Solomon, "Crashing Oil Prices Could Crush Vladimir Putin," CNN Money, Oct. 15, 2014, http://money.cnn.com/2014/10/15/investing/oil-price-fall-russia-hurt.

25. Paul Roderick Gregory, "Putin Cuts off Gas Supplies to Six European Countries without Warning," *Forbes*, Jan. 18, 2015, www.forbes.com/sites/paulroderickgregory/2015/01/18/putin-cuts-off-gas-supply-to-six-european-countries-without-warning.

26. James Drew, "America Has a Very Expensive Plan to Replace Very Old Nukes," *War Is Boring*, Jan. 26, 2015, www.medium.com/war-is-boring/america-has-a-very-expensive-plan-to-replace-very-old-nukes-2451520c257d.

27. Qtd. in Pat Frank, *Alas, Babylon* (New York: Bantam Books, 1959), 33.

28. Cynthia Grabo, *Anticipating Surprise: Analysis for Strategic Warning*, (New York: University Press of America, 2004), 14–15.

29. Ibid, 365.

30. Warren Trest, *Air Commando One: Heinie Aderholt and America's Secret Air Wars* (Washington, DC: Smithsonian Books, 2000), 58–59.

31. President Obama did respond in a timely fashion during the Benghazi attack, giving military command immediate, sufficient and clear authority for a response—which was ineffective for a number of reasons described in this work. However, Obama had the fortune to actually be in a meeting with the AFRICOM commander at the time the news reached Washington. All senior military staff were available and able to quickly assemble at the Pentagon—however, while representing a surprise attack, the Benghazi strike was not a national security threat, comparable to actual threats to or attacks on the continental United States.

32. Zachary Fryer-Briggs, "Slowed by Debate and Uncertainty, New Rules Green Light Response to Cyber Attacks," *DefenseNews*, May 27, 2013, www.defensenews.com/article/20130527/DEFREG02/305270014/Slowed-by-Debate-Uncertainty-New-Rules-Green-Light-Response-Cyber-Attacks.

33. Gordon Prange, *At Dawn We Slept: The Untold Story of Pearl Harbor* (New York: McGraw-Hill, 1981), 497.

34. Paul Bracken, *The Command and Control of Nuclear Forces* (New Haven, CT: Yale UP, 1983), 69–70.

35. Michael Riley, "How the Russian Hackers Stole the NASDAQ," *Bloomberg BusinessWeek*, July 17, 2014, www.businessweek.com/articles/2014-07-17/how-russian-hackers-stole-the-nasdaq.

INDEX